LIFE APPLICATION® BIBLE COMMENTARY

MARK

Bruce B. Barton, D. Min.
Mark Fackler, Ph.D.
Linda K. Taylor
David R. Veerman, M. Div.
Neil Wilson, M.A.R.

Series Editor: Grant Osborne, Ph.D.
Editor: Philip Comfort, Ph.D.

Tyndale House Publishers, Inc.
WHEATON, ILLINOIS

Contributing Editors: James C. Galvin, Ed.D. and Ronald A. Beers

Life Application is a registered trademark of Tyndale House Publishers, Inc.

Scripture quotations marked NIV are taken from the *Holy Bible,* New International Version®. Copyright © 1973, 1978, 1984 by International Bible Society. Used by permission of Zondervan Publishing House. All rights reserved. The "NIV" and "New International Version" trademarks are registered in the United States Patent and Trademark Office by International Bible Society. Use of either trademark requires permission of International Bible Society.

Scripture quotations marked NKJV are taken from The New King James Version. Copyright © 1979, 1980, 1982, Thomas Nelson Inc., Publishers.

Scripture quotations marked NRSV are taken from the New Revised Standard Version of the Bible, copyrighted, 1989 by the Division of Christian Education of the National Council of the Churches of Christ in the United States of America, and are used by permission. All rights reserved.

(No citation is given for Scripture text that is exactly the same wording in all three versions—NIV, NKJV, and NRSV.)

Library of Congress Cataloging-in-Publication Data

Mark / Bruce B. Barton . . . [et al.].

      p.   cm. — (Life application Bible commentary)

    Includes bibliographical references and index.

    ISBN 0-8423-3028-3

    1. Bible. N.T. Mark—Commentaries.   I. Barton, Bruce B.

II. Series.

BS2585.3.M35   1994

226.3′06—dc20   94-3689

Printed in the United States of America

00

8   7   6   5   4   3

CONTENTS

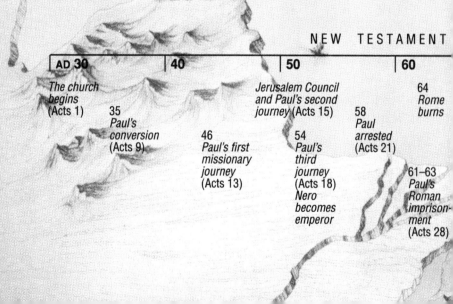

Gospels

MATTHEW:
MARK: between
LUKE:

ACTS:
Paul's Epistles
ROMANS: about 57
1 CORINTHIANS: about 55
2 CORINTHIANS: about 56–57
GALATIANS: about 49

EPHESIANS:
PHILIPPIANS:
COLOSSIANS:
1 THESSALONIANS: about 51
2 THESSALONIANS: about 51–52
1 TIMOTHY:
2 TIMOTHY:
TITUS:
PHILEMON:

General Epistles   JAMES: about 49

1 PETER:
2 PETER:

JUDE:

NEW   TESTAMENT

AD 30	40	50	60

The church begins (Acts 1)

35 Paul's conversion (Acts 9)

46 Paul's first missionary journey (Acts 13)

Jerusalem Council and Paul's second journey (Acts 15)

54 Paul's third journey (Acts 18) Nero becomes emperor

58 Paul arrested (Acts 21)

64 Rome burns

61–63 Paul's Roman imprisonment (Acts 28)

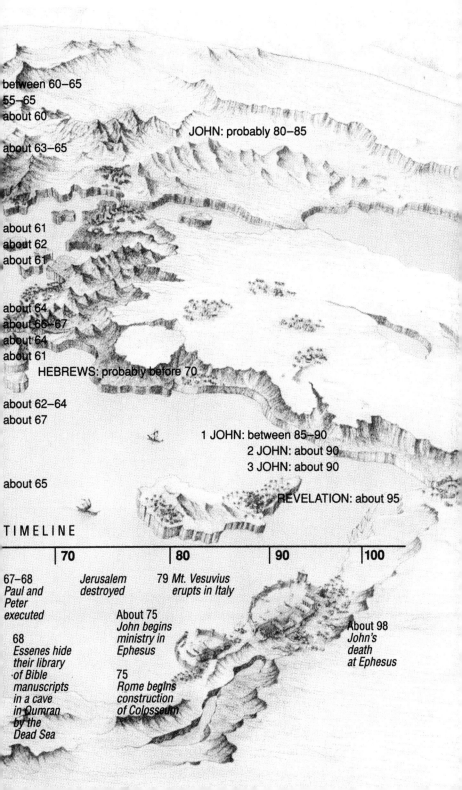

between 60–65
55–65
about 60

JOHN: probably 80–85

about 63–65

about 61
about 62
about 61

about 64
about 66–67
about 64
about 61

HEBREWS: probably before 70

about 62–64
about 67

1 JOHN: between 85–90
2 JOHN: about 90
3 JOHN: about 90

about 65

REVELATION: about 95

TIMELINE

70	80	90	100

67–68
Paul and Peter executed

Jerusalem destroyed

79 *Mt. Vesuvius erupts in Italy*

68
Essenes hide their library of Bible manuscripts in a cave in Qumran by the Dead Sea

About 75
John begins ministry in Ephesus

75
Rome begins construction of Colosseum

About 98
John's death at Ephesus

FOREWORD

The *Life Application Bible* Commentary series provides verse-by-verse explanation, background, and application for every verse in the New Testament. In addition, it gives personal help, teaching notes, and sermon ideas that will address needs, answer questions, and provide insight for applying God's Word to life today. The content is highlighted so that particular verses and phrases are easy to find.

Each volume contains three sections: introduction, commentary, and reference. The introduction includes an overview of the book, the book's historical context, a timeline, cultural background information, major themes, an overview map, and an explanation about the author and audience.

The commentary section includes running commentary on the Bible text with reference to several modern versions, especially the New International Version and the New Revised Standard Version, accompanied by life applications interspersed throughout. Additional elements include charts, diagrams, maps, and illustrations. There are also insightful quotes from church leaders and theologians such as John Calvin, Martin Luther, John Wesley, A. W. Tozer, and C. S. Lewis. These features are designed to help you quickly grasp the biblical information and be prepared to communicate it to others.

The reference section includes a bibliography of other resources and an index.

INTRODUCTION

ACTION—moving, doing, helping, getting going, making things happen. Some people think, some talk, but a few get involved; not content to observe from the sidelines, they get into the game—they get into life! This describes Mark and his father in the faith, Peter. And it's the picture of Jesus that Mark presents in this Gospel.

The Gospel of Mark is the shortest of the four records of Jesus' life, and it covers only three and a half years. On the first page, Mark jumps into the action, with John the Baptist's fiery preaching and the beginning of Jesus' public ministry. Then, moving swiftly through Jesus' baptism, temptation in the desert, and call of the disciples, Mark focuses his attention on Jesus' public ministry. He is interested in Christ's *works,* not just his *words.* In fact, Mark records eighteen of Jesus' miracles and only four of his parables.

Although Mark presents events in chronological order, he gives little or no historical linkage between the events. And to keep things moving and heighten the sense of action, Mark continually uses the phrase "straightway" (KJV) or "immediately." Readers feel, "Jesus is on the move; we'd better stay alert, or we'll miss something!"

Writing to a Roman audience, Mark does not have to recite Jesus' genealogy or refer to Old Testament prophecies that have been fulfilled. Gentiles don't need a Jewish history lesson; they need a clear picture of Christ. And the Romans believe in power and action. So Mark makes sure they have a no-nonsense, concise, action-packed summary. Mark pictures Jesus as powerful—giving sight to the blind, raising the dead, calming stormy seas, restoring deformed bodies. But he shows Jesus using this mighty power to help others, taking the form of a servant, not a king. Mark weaves the servant theme throughout his book and presents the servant Jesus as an example to follow: "and whoever wants to be first must be slave of all. For even the Son of Man did not come to be served, but to serve, and to give his life as a ransom for many" (10:44-45 NIV).

The Gospel of Mark is a short, action-packed account, bustling with life and focused on Christ's purpose. As you study Mark, be ready for fast-paced, nonstop action, be open for God's move into your life, and be challenged to move into your world to serve.

▌AUTHOR

Mark (John Mark): cousin of Barnabas (Colossians 4:10) and close friend of Peter (1 Peter 5:13)

The book of Mark names no one as author. Since the second century A.D., however, church leaders and scholars have accepted John Mark as the one who wrote this Gospel. (John is his Jewish name and Mark, *Marcus,* his Roman name.) The early church fathers unanimously accepted Mark's authorship. Papias (A.D. 110) makes the earliest statement to this effect:

■ *Mark, who was the interpreter of Peter, wrote down accurately all that he remembered, whether of sayings or doings of Christ, but not in order. For he was neither a hearer nor a companion of the Lord; but afterwards, as I have said, he accompanied Peter, who adapted his instruction as necessity required, not as though he were making a compilation of the Lord's oracles. So then Mark made no mistake when he wrote down thus some things as he remembered them, for he concentrated on this alone—not to omit anything that he had heard, nor to include any false statement among them. (Eusebius, Ecclesiastical History III, p. 39)*

Other church fathers, including Justin Martyr, Tertullian, Clement of Alexandria, Origen, and Eusebius, confirm this assessment of Mark as the author.

Mark was young, perhaps in his teens, at the time of Jesus' death and resurrection. Evidently his mother, Mary, was a well-to-do widow who had come to faith in Christ. Many surmise that Mary's house was the site of the Last Supper (14:12-26) and the home where the disciples gathered at Pentecost (Acts 2:1-4); some believe that Mark was the young man who ran away naked when Jesus was arrested in the Garden of Gethsemane (14:51-52). Regardless of the truth of these speculations, Scripture clearly states that fourteen years after the tumultuous events leading to the Crucifixion, in about A.D. 44, the church gathered at Mary's house to pray. King Herod had begun to persecute believers; he had executed James, the brother of John, and was holding Peter in prison. The church was praying for Peter's release. Luke explains that after Peter had been miraculously released from prison, "he went to the house of Mary the mother of John, also called Mark" (Acts 12:12 NIV). Mark was deeply involved in the drama of the Jerusalem church and was well-known to Peter and the other disciples.

In Colossians 4:10, Paul reveals that Mark is the cousin of Barnabas. Perhaps that is what motivated Barnabas and Paul to take Mark with them back to Antioch from Jerusalem (Acts 12:25). Soon thereafter, Barnabas and Paul were commissioned by the church in Antioch to begin their first missionary journey (Acts 13:1-3), and they included Mark as their helper (Acts 13:5). Early in the trip, however, at Perga, Mark abruptly left and returned to Jerusalem (Acts 13:13). Luke gives no reason for Mark's departure (perhaps he was homesick, fearful, or ill). Later, however, when Paul and Barnabas began to plan the second journey, Mark became the cause of a sharp disagreement between the two men. Barnabas wanted to include Mark again, but Paul was strongly opposed because Mark had "deserted" them on the previous trip. So Barnabas and Paul parted company. Barnabas sailed to Cyprus with Mark, while Paul chose Silas and traveled to Syria and Cilicia (Acts 15:36-41).

We know little else about John Mark. Evidently, he and Paul reconciled completely because later he joined Paul in Rome, during Paul's first imprisonment (A.D. 60–62) and was a comfort to him there (Colossians 4:10-11; Philemon 24). During Paul's second imprisonment and just before his death, he asked Timothy to bring Mark to Rome, "because he is helpful to me in my ministry" (2 Timothy 4:11 NIV). Mark must have matured emotionally and spiritually through the years and under the mentoring of cousin Barnabas.

Mark also enjoyed a very close relationship with Peter. In fact, Peter may have led Mark to Christ because he calls Mark "my son" (1 Peter 5:13). After Paul's release from prison in A.D. 62, Mark may have stayed in Rome (also called "Babylon"—1 Peter 5:13) to work closely with Peter. Mark probably left Rome in about A.D. 65 or 66, during Nero's intense persecution. Both Paul and Peter were executed by Nero in about A.D. 67 or 68. According to tradition, Mark died soon after.

John Mark provides a sterling example of how a young Christian can grow and mature. Perhaps basking in the attention of the spiritual giants Paul and Barnabas, and excited by the prospect of reaching the world with the gospel, he had sailed to Cyprus on the first missionary journey. A short time later, however, when the going got tough, Mark returned home. Whatever Mark's reason for leaving, Paul didn't approve; in fact, he wanted nothing to do with Mark after the incident. Yet fifteen years later, Mark was serving as a ministry companion to both Peter and Paul, and later he wrote the Gospel bearing his name. Little is known about Mark during those years, except that Barnabas took personal interest in him, encouraging Mark by continuing to work with him in ministry.

Do you know any "Marks"—young, Christian diamonds in the rough? What can you do to be their "Barnabas"?

DATE

Written in Rome between A.D. 55 and 70

Dating the Gospel of Mark with accuracy is virtually impossible because the text contains few clues. We can only surmise that Mark was written before A.D. 70 because there is no mention of the destruction of Jerusalem, which had been predicted by Jesus (13:1-23). (Jerusalem was destroyed by Roman armies under the leadership of Titus, after a siege of 143 days. During this battle, 600,000 Jews were killed and thousands more taken captive.) Irenaeus and other church fathers imply that Mark was written after the martyrdom of Peter and Paul, and the Anti-Marcionite Prologue (second century A.D.) states: "After the death of Peter himself, he wrote down this same gospel." If that statement is true, then Mark must have been written after A.D. 67. The only problem here is that many scholars consider Mark to be the first Gospel written and used as a source by Matthew and Luke. For that to happen, Mark had to have been written in approximately A.D. 55–60, prior to A.D. 60–65, the proposed time period for Matthew and Luke.

As mentioned earlier, Mark enjoyed a close working relationship with Peter (1 Peter 5:13) and probably received most of his information about Jesus from him. In fact, the book of Mark may be better termed, "the Gospel according to Peter." Some believe that Mark took notes from Peter's preaching so that many stories in this Gospel were probably presented verbally before they appeared in written form. Perhaps Mark worked with Peter on the Gospel in those earlier years together but then released it for wider distribution after Peter's death. Whatever the case, we know that Matthew, Mark, Luke, and John are accurate accounts of the life and message of Christ. Through the Holy Spirit, God used these men to bring his Word to the world.

Rome is identified as the place of writing because both Paul and Peter mention Mark as being there (Colossians 4:10; 1 Peter 5:13—"Babylon" probably refers to Rome).

All roads led to Rome, the capital of the vast and mighty Roman Empire. At that time, Rome was the largest city in the world, with a population of approximately one million. Wealthy and cosmopolitan, it was the diplomatic and trade center of the world, the epitome of power and influence. No wonder Paul and Peter were drawn to Rome—it was a strategic beachhead for the spread of the gospel.

We do not know who founded the church at Rome. It could not have been Peter because he ministered primarily to Jews and seems to have settled in Rome just after Paul's arrival in about A.D. 60. Also, it was not Paul, because in his letter to the Romans, he said as much (Romans 1:11-13; 15:23-24). Most likely, the church at Rome was begun by Jews who had traveled from Rome to Jerusalem for Pentecost in A.D. 30, had been converted through Peter's powerful sermon and the outpouring of the Holy Spirit (Acts 2:5-40), and then had taken their Christian faith with them back home to Rome. Soon those believers were joined by travelers like Priscilla and Aquila who had heard about Christ in other places.

Reading between the lines of the book of Romans, the church in Rome seems to have been strong, unified in worship and outreach, with no factions or divisions such as those that were plaguing other churches. Certainly the Roman church was strengthened even further through the ministry of Paul as he boldly taught for two years during his first imprisonment (Acts 28:16-31).

The political climate in Rome was volatile with a litany of palace intrigue, assassinations, and egocentric emperors. Nero, the fifth Roman emperor, began to reign in A.D. 54 at sixteen years of age. The first few years of his reign were peaceful. During that time, Paul had appealed to Caesar at his trial in Caesarea (Acts 25:10-11) and thus had been taken to Rome to make his appeal (A.D. 60). Even as a prisoner, Paul was allowed to debate with Jewish leaders (Acts 28:17-28) and to preach and teach about Christ to all who came to see him (Acts 28:30-31). Evidently, after these two years, Paul was released. Soon, however, the tolerance for Christians would take a terrible turn.

After marrying Poppaea in A.D. 62, Nero became brutal and ruthless, killing his own mother, his chief advisers Seneca and Burrus, and many of the nobility in order to seize their fortunes and solidify his power. Eventually, Nero's thirst for publicity in the arts and sports pushed him into excessive acts of decadence, including chariot races, combat between gladiators, and the gory spectacle of prisoners thrown to wild beasts. In A.D. 64, fire destroyed a large part of Rome. Nero probably ordered the fire himself to make room for a new palace, but he deflected blame by accusing the Christians. Thus began the terrible persecution of the church, with torture, executions, and Coliseum entertainment. Some followers of Christ were covered in animal skins and torn to pieces by dogs. Others were fastened to crosses and set on fire, serving as torches at night for the city.

During this reign of terror for Christians, Paul was taken prisoner again, apparently at Nicopolis, where he had intended to spend the winter (Titus 3:12). Transported to Rome, Paul was imprisoned in the Mamertine dungeon, in the center of Rome near the forum. There Paul wrote his final words. We know that Mark was not in Rome at this time because in 2 Timothy 4:11, Paul asked Timothy to bring Mark with him. If Timothy obliged, then Mark may have been in Rome when both Paul and Peter were martyred.

According to tradition, soon after writing 2 Timothy, Paul was executed by beheading on the Ostian Way outside Rome, shortly before Nero's own death, by suicide, in A.D. 68. Peter also was martyred at this time.

What would cause Mark to return to Rome where Christians were hunted and killed like animals? What would strengthen Mark to courageously face his own death at the hands of the Romans? What would motivate Mark to write the story of Jesus? He knew the Truth, and the Truth had set him free (John 8:32).

What keeps you from obeying God and living for Christ?

AUDIENCE

Roman Christians living in Rome

It is fairly certain that Mark directed his Gospel to Romans. One reason for this conclusion is that he took time to explain Jewish terms for his readers; for example, "He took her by the hand and said to her, *'Talitha koum!'* (which means, 'Little girl, I say to you, get up!')" (5:41 NIV). Mark also explained Jewish customs: For example, he wrote parenthetically that "the Pharisees and all the Jews do not eat unless they give their hands a ceremonial washing, holding to the tradition of the elders. When they come from the marketplace they do not eat unless they wash. And they observe many other traditions, such as the washing of cups, pitchers and kettles" (7:3-4 NIV). (See also 3:17; 7:11, 34; 14:12; 15:22, 34, 42.) Gentile readers would need such phrases and customs explained. There are other indications that Mark wrote to Gentiles in general and Romans in particular: He used several Latin words, some of which do not appear elsewhere in the New Testament. (This is evident in the original text of Mark

5:9; 12:15, 42; 15:16, 39.) He referred to the Old Testament less than the other Gospel writers; he did not use the word "law," which was mentioned often by Matthew, Luke, and John; he used the Roman way of telling time (6:48; 13:35). All of this evidence points to a Roman audience.

It also seems clear that Mark was writing primarily to Christians. He used distinctively Christian terms such as "baptize" (1:4) and "Holy Spirit" (1:8) without explaining them. And Mark seems to have assumed that his readers were familiar with Jesus' background, with John the Baptist, and with the major events of Jesus' life.

So who were these Roman Christians to whom Mark directed his Gospel? At first the church at Rome was Jewish, consisting of Jews who had come to believe in Jesus as their Messiah. But over the years, many Christians from all parts of the Roman Empire had migrated to Rome, some of them Paul's converts and many of them Gentiles. In addition, many citizens of Rome had come to faith in Christ through the ministry of other believers and Paul while he was in prison (see Acts 28:30-31; Philippians 4:21-22; Colossians 4:10-12; 2 Timothy 4:21). Eventually the church had a majority of Gentiles, with an influential Jewish minority.

Being a Christian in Rome meant being part of a distinct minority, religiously and socially. Rome was filled with gods, and the prevailing thought was that all the gods were real. Thus, Jews and Christians were viewed as atheists because they believed in only one God and denied the existence of all the pagan deities. Christians also came into direct conflict with basic Roman values. To Roman citizens, the highest allegiance was to the state, but for Christians, God took priority. Roman citizens were very class conscious, and non-Romans were seen as distinctly inferior. But Christians believed that "there is neither Jew nor Greek, slave nor free, male nor female, for you are all one in Christ Jesus" (Galatians 3:28 NIV). Believers also refused to participate in immoral activities (see Galatians 5:19-23). Christians stood out and eventually were singled out for terrible persecution. Mark wrote to men and women who could have felt overwhelmed by pressures and problems and needed a clear, fresh look at Christ.

In many ways, Roman culture resembles ours today. Certainly we live in an almost pagan society, filled with a wide variety of gods, both secular and religious, with true followers of Christ a distinct minority. In addition, ours is a Gentile church, with believers from all races, nationalities, and walks of life. So

Mark's Gospel translates easily to us today and provides a clear picture of Jesus.

OCCASION AND PURPOSE

To present a clear picture of Christ to Roman believers who were experiencing increased persecution

The exact occasion that spurred Mark to write this Gospel is unknown. Unlike many epistles written by Paul to counter heretical teachings or church divisions, Mark hints of no precipitating event or problem. It may have been that Mark simply felt led by the Holy Spirit to give Peter's eyewitness account of Christ, geared especially for the Roman people among whom they were ministering. Certainly the increasing pressure from the Roman government must have played a key role, because persecution can lead to doubts about the faith and discouragement. Believers needed assurance and hope. The Gospel of Mark gave them a close and personal look at Jesus, their Savior and Lord. They could be assured that the faith they were living and for which they were giving their lives was *true* and *reliable*. Jesus, the Son of God, had lived, served (1:1–13:37), suffered, and died for them (14:1–15:47). And he had risen from the grave (16:1-8)— their triumphant Savior was alive!

Today we enjoy the Bible, complete with Old and New Testaments. In fact, most Christians probably own several copies of the Scriptures. First-century believers did not have that privilege. The holy scrolls—ancient copies of the books of Moses, the prophets, and other Old Testament writers—were safely kept in the temple and in synagogues, and were cared for and guarded by rabbis. These scrolls were studied and memorized and read on the Sabbath. As for the New Testament, most of the books and letters were just being written and circulated among the churches. Thus Christians had to rely on the teachings and eyewitness accounts of the apostles and others who had known Jesus. Members of the church at Rome, especially Gentiles, desperately needed to learn about Christ and what it meant to follow him. Thus, inspired by the Holy Spirit, Mark provided an accurate account of Jesus and the twelve disciples.

Like most new believers, the Romans also needed to know the cultural, social, and personal implications of their faith. How should they live in a hostile environment, in a society with values totally at odds with their own? Mark's Gospel presented Jesus, the Servant, as their model to follow.

Centuries later, we live in a secular culture whose predominant values are far from Christian, and where under the banner of *pluralism,* government officials strain to remove every vestige of historic Christian faith from public life. While usually not as violent as Roman persecution, believers today still are pressured to forget Christ and are ridiculed for their faith. In a society replete with aberrant and heretical religious beliefs, cults, and idols, true followers of Christ have become an absolute minority. As in Rome, it would be easy to become discouraged, dismayed, and doubtful. As with the Romans, we need a fresh look at Jesus of Nazareth, the Messiah, our Lord.

As you read Mark, look at Jesus and see him for who he is— God in the flesh, the suffering Servant, your Savior and model for how to live.

▐ MESSAGE

Jesus Christ, Son of God; Jesus Christ, Servant; Discipleship; Miracles; Evangelism

Jesus Christ, Son of God (1:1, 9-11, 21-34; 2:1-12, 23-28; 3:7-12; 4:35-41; 5:1-20; 8:27-31; 9:1-13; 10:46-52; 11:1-19; 13:24-37; 14:32-42, 60-65; 16:1-8). Jesus was God in the flesh. When Jesus lived on earth, he clearly told his followers, the crowds, the religious leaders, and his accusers that he was the Son of God (see 14:60-65). And he demonstrated this truth by forgiving sins (see 2:5-12), controlling the forces of nature (see 4:35-41), and overcoming disease, demons, and death (see 5:1-43). In addition, Mark affirmed the divinity of Jesus by reporting the voice from heaven at Jesus' baptism: "You are my Son, whom I love; with you I am well pleased" (1:11 NIV), the Transfiguration (9:2-10), and the Resurrection (16:1-8). Truly Jesus was and is the Son of God.

Importance for Today. The truth that Jesus, the man, is also God means that Jesus has the authority to forgive sins and to change lives. In fact, he died in our place, paying the penalty for our sins. So we can trust in Christ for forgiveness and eternal life. It also means that he is Truth and our authority. Those who know Christ as Savior must obey him as Lord.

Christ was fully man, but he was much more—he was, and is, fully God. Do you know him as Savior? Do you follow him as Lord?

Jesus Christ, Servant (1:40-45; 3:1-12; 7:31-37; 8:22-26, 34-38; 9:33-50; 10:13-45; 12:38-44; 14:17-26, 32-50; 15:1-5, 12-47). Jesus fulfilled the Old Testament prophecies about the coming Messiah by coming to earth. He did not come as the conquering king that the people expected, but as a servant, keeping the fact that he was the Messiah a secret. Eventually Jesus would reign as King of kings and Lord of lords, but first he would reveal himself as the suffering Servant. Jesus served by telling people about God, healing them, and giving his life as the atoning sacrifice for their sins. Jesus suffered by being born into a poor family and by being tempted, questioned, rejected, falsely accused and convicted, beaten, hit, spat upon, tortured, mocked, and crucified. Giving his life and becoming sin on the cross was the ultimate act of suffering and service. Jesus taught and lived that "whoever wants to become great among you must be your servant, and whoever wants to be first must be slave of all. For even the Son of Man did not come to be served, but to serve, and to give his life as a ransom for many" (10:43-45 NIV).

Importance for Today. Those who claim Christ as Savior and Lord should follow his example by serving God and others. Real greatness in Christ's kingdom is shown by service and sacrifice. Instead of being motivated by ambition or love of power or position (as is true with most people), we should do God's work because we love him and his creation.

What does it mean for you to be a servant? What can you do to serve God today? To whom in your home, neighborhood, school, place of employment, or church can you give a "cup of water" in his name (9:41)?

Discipleship (1:16-20; 3:13-19; 6:7-13; 8:27–10:52; 13:1–14:52; 15:42–16:8). Through the eyes of one of Jesus' closest followers, Peter, Mark described the disciples' difficulty in understanding Jesus' true identity. They didn't understand Jesus' parables (see 4:13, 34; 7:18), his miracles (see 4:35-41; 6:45-52), his teaching on divorce (10:10-12), and his predictions of his approaching death and resurrection (8:32-33; 9:9-13, 32). In fact, in this Gospel they never did fully grasp who Jesus really was (see Peter's response to Jesus in 8:31-32) and why he had come to earth. Jesus knew that his disciples wouldn't truly understand his identity and mission until after the Resurrection, and he wanted to keep his true identity partially concealed until it would be revealed publicly after he had been raised from the dead. Yet he continued to teach the disciples about the cost of following him (8:34-38), about humility and kingdom living (9:33–10:31), and about the importance of serving others (10:35-45).

Importance for Today. We live many centuries after Christ and have the benefit of reading about his life, death, and resurrection. But do we truly understand his identity as God and man, as Sav-

ior and Lord? And do we realize the cost of being his disciple?
Following Jesus means dying to self, obeying him, and serving
others (8:34-35). What kind of disciple are you?

Miracles (1:29-34, 40-45; 2:1-12; 3:1-12; 4:35-41; 5:1-43; 6:30-56; 7:24-37; 8:1-10, 22-26; 9:17-29; 10:46-52; 16:1-8). Mark
records more of Jesus' miracles than sermons; in fact, every chap-
ter until his final ministry in Jerusalem (chapter 11) and subsequent capture, trial, and execution contains at least one miracle.
Mark's Roman readers could clearly see that Jesus was a man of
power and action, not just words. Jesus performed miracles out of
his compassion for people who were suffering (see 1:41-42), to
convince the people who he was (see 2:1-12), and to teach the
disciples his true identity as God (see 8:14-21).

Importance for Today. The more convinced we become that
Jesus is God, the more we will see his power and love. Christ's
mighty works show us that he is able to save anyone, regardless
of what he or she has done. His miracles of forgiveness bring
healing, wholeness, and new life to all who trust him. Nothing is
too big or too difficult for Christ to handle. We can give him all
our needs and tell him all our problems.

Are you struggling with doubts and fears? Trust Jesus. Are you
hurting or suffering? Tell Jesus. Do you need a miracle in your
life? Bring your request to Jesus.

Evangelism (1:2-8, 14-20, 38-39; 2:13-17; 3:13-19, 31-34; 4:1-34; 5:1-20; 6:1-13; 7:24-37; 9:33-41; 10:13-31; 12:28-34; 13:1-23, 32-36; 14:9). Jesus directed his public ministry to the Jews
first (1:21-28, 38-39), but he also went healing and preaching to
the non-Jewish world. Syrians (7:24-30) and other Gentiles (5:1-20; 7:31-37) were given the Good News. Jesus challenged his followers to take his message into all the world (6:7-13), preaching
the gospel of salvation.

Importance for Today. Jesus crossed national, racial, social,
and economic barriers to spread the gospel. His message of faith
and forgiveness is for the whole world, not just our church, neighborhood, community, or nation. We must reach beyond our own
people and needs to fulfill Christ's worldwide vision that people
everywhere might hear this great message and be forgiven of
their sins and receive eternal life.

Who do you know that needs to hear about Christ? What keeps
you from sharing the Good News with them? What can you do
today to begin to reach out beyond your circle of Christian
friends?

VITAL STATISTICS

Purpose: To present the person, work, and teachings of Jesus

Author: John Mark. He was not one of the 12 disciples but he accompanied Paul on his first missionary journey (Acts 13:13).

To whom written: The Christians in Rome, where he wrote the Gospel

Date written: Between A.D. 55 and 65

Setting: The Roman Empire under Tiberius Caesar. The Empire, with its common language and excellent transportation and communication systems, was ripe to hear Jesus' message, which spread quickly from nation to nation.

Key verse: "For even the Son of Man did not come to be served, but to serve, and to give his life as a ransom for many" (10:45 NIV).

Key people: Jesus, the 12 disciples, Pilate, the Jewish religious leaders

Key places: Capernaum, Nazareth, Caesarea Philippi, Jericho, Bethany, Mount of Olives, Jerusalem, Golgotha

Special features: Mark was probably the first Gospel written. The other Gospels quote all but 31 verses of Mark. Mark records more miracles than does any other Gospel.

OUTLINE OF MARK

A. BIRTH AND PREPARATION OF JESUS, THE SERVANT (1:1-13)

B. MESSAGE AND MINISTRY OF JESUS, THE SERVANT (1:14–13:37)

    1. Jesus' ministry in Galilee

    2. Jesus' ministry beyond Galilee

    3. Jesus' ministry in Jerusalem

C. DEATH AND RESURRECTION OF JESUS, THE SERVANT (14:1–16:20)

Of the four Gospels, Mark's narrative is the most chronological—that is, most of the stories are positioned in the order they actually occurred. Though the shortest of the four, the Gospel of Mark contains the most events; it is action-packed. Most of this action centers in Galilee, where Jesus began his ministry. Capernaum served as his base of operation (1:21; 2:1; 9:33), from which he would go out to cities like Bethsaida—where he healed a blind man (8:22ff); Gennesaret—where he performed many healings (6:53ff); Tyre and Sidon (to the far north)—where he healed many, drove out demons, and met the Syrophoenician woman (3:8; 7:24ff); and Caesarea Philippi—where Peter declared him to be the Messiah (8:27ff). After his ministry in Galilee and the surrounding regions, Jesus headed for Jerusalem (10:1). Before going there, Jesus told his disciples three times that he would be crucified there and then come back to life (8:31; 9:31; 10:33-34).

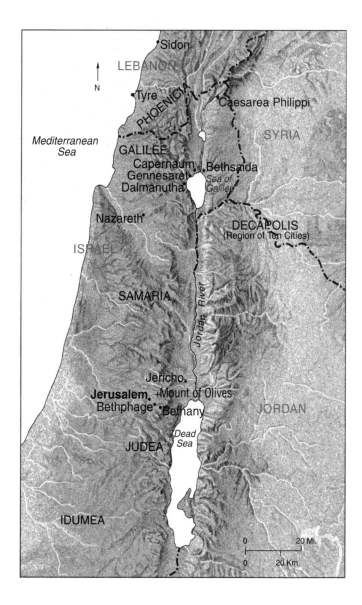

N

Sidon

LEBANON

Tyre

PHOENICIA

Caesarea Philippi

SYRIA

Mediterranean
Sea

GALILEE

Capernaum

Bethsaida

Gennesaret

Sea of
Galilee

Dalmanutha

Nazareth

ISRAEL

DECAPOLIS
(Region of Ten Cities)

SAMARIA

Jordan River

Jericho

Jerusalem

Mount of Olives

Bethphage

Bethany

JORDAN

JUDEA

Dead
Sea

IDUMEA

0   20 Mi.

0   20 Km.

Mark 1

The opening phrase in each of the Gospels lays a unique foundation for the structure of that book. Matthew began by placing Jesus in the history of God's chosen people. Luke provided a careful summary of the verbal accounts of Jesus' life that were being circulated among believers. John opened with a theological perspective, emphasizing Jesus as the only unique Word of God, come into his own creation. Mark uniquely introduced his account as "the gospel." Mark referred to the "gospel" (*euangelion,* good news, tidings) three times in his first chapter, while both Matthew and Luke waited until chapter 4 to introduce the term. John did not use the word "gospel." Mark knew exactly what he intended to write.

For Mark, the purpose of writing was to convey a crucial message, the life-changing Good News about Jesus Christ. Reading Mark's first words, we can sense his excitement. His account doesn't give background biographical information because he wanted his readers to see Jesus in action as quickly as possible. The power of Jesus' ministry and character alone would impact the reader.

With Mark's help, we can picture ourselves in the crowd as Jesus healed and taught, imagine ourselves as one of the disciples, and respond to his words of love and encouragement. And we can remember that Jesus came for us who live today as well as for those who lived two thousand years ago.

Before the curtain rises, already we can hear someone shouting. Words describing a desert place that needs to be changed come from a man who would be called wild-looking in any age. He lives in a geographical desert, and he preaches about a spiritual one. We meet John the Baptist as he sets the stage for Jesus' entrance.

1:1 The beginning of the gospel of Jesus Christ, the Son of God.^{NKJV} The first verse acts as both a title to the book and a summary of its contents. No mention is made of the author, generally

considered to be John Mark. Mark was
not one of the twelve disciples of Jesus
but probably knew Jesus personally.
The New Testament refers to Mark several times (sometimes as Mark [his

> Jesus is God brought
> into focus for human
> eyes. *Unknown*

Latin name], as John [his Hebrew name], or as John Mark):

- Upon his miraculous release from prison, Peter went to the house of Mary, the mother of John Mark (Acts 12:12).

- John Mark went with Barnabas and Paul from Antioch to Jeru-salem (Acts 12:25).

- Mark accompanied Paul and Barnabas partway on the first mis-sionary journey (Acts 13:5, 13).

- John Mark was the subject of a quarrel between Barnabas and Paul regarding whether he should accompany them on the sec-ond missionary journey (Acts 15:36-39).

- Paul sent greetings from Mark to the Colossians (Colossians 4:10).

- Paul asked Timothy to bring Mark along when Timothy paid a final visit to Paul in prison (2 Timothy 4:11).

- Paul sent greetings from Mark to Philemon (Philemon 1:24).

- Peter sent greetings from Mark to the believers (1 Peter 5:13).

(For further information about Mark, see the Author section in the Introduction.)

While we generally call this book the Gospel of Mark, the title correctly penned by Mark was *the gospel of Jesus Christ.* Mark's readers understood the word "gospel" to mean "good news," that is, the word *euangeliou* could refer to good news of any kind. But Mark gave this common word a spectacular meaning, for the news of Jesus Christ's life, death, and resurrection is the best news of all because it offers salvation and eternal life. The story of how God procured our salvation through Jesus Christ is indeed "gospel," good news; thus the word *euangeliou* came to refer to preaching about Jesus Christ. Paul later wrote to the same Roman audience, "For I am not ashamed of the gospel; it is the power of God for salvation to everyone who has faith" (Romans 1:16 NRSV). The Good News was breaking into human experience. This "gospel" consisted of two parts: (1) what Jesus preached—his message of redemption and (2) who Jesus is—his identity is the substance of his message.

Clearly, then, this was not the gospel of Mark, but the gospel

"of Jesus Christ." This expression, understood as an objective
genitive in Greek, means the gospel *concerning* Jesus Christ. As
a subjective genitive, it means "Jesus Christ's gospel"—the gospel he preached. The first name, "Jesus," was a common name in
Israel (Matthew 1:21; Luke 2:21) as the Old Testament form of
the name "Joshua" (meaning "Yahweh saves"), although the Jews
stopped using it after Christianity expanded. The second name,
"Christ," is from the Greek word *Christos* meaning "the Anointed
One" (the Hebrew equivalent is the word "Messiah"). Both
"Christ" and "Messiah" referred to one
divinely appointed and anointed by
God for a special mission. The
Anointed One, the Messiah, would ful-

> Mighty things from small
> beginnings grow. *John
> Dryden*

fill the Old Testament prophecies (see, for example, Genesis
49:10; Psalms 2; 110; Isaiah 9:1-7; 11:1-9; Zechariah 9:9-10).
Mark will explain Christ's mission as he recounts the Good News
in the story he is about to tell.

Mark gave no genealogy because he presented Jesus as the servant. A servant needs no pedigree, but demonstrates his validity
by the worth of the service he provides. Mark wrote this "gospel"
in the form of a fast-paced story, like a popular novel (often using
the words "immediately" or "straightway" as he changes from
one scene to the next). The book portrays Jesus as a man who
backed up his words with actions that proved he was the *Son of
God.* Because Mark wrote the Gospel for Christians in Rome,
where many gods were worshiped, he wanted his readers to know
that Jesus was the one true Son of God. He is coeternal with
God—and *is* himself God. He alone was fully man (Jesus), God's
anointed One (Christ), and fully divine (Son of God). Mark's
Gospel fully develops Jesus' claims to be the Christ and the Son
of God by showing how he was anointed by God's Spirit to carry
out the divine plan of salvation.

Without God's revelation, our finite minds cannot comprehend
the infinite. But because of what we know about Jesus (thanks to
writers like Mark), we can understand what God is like. Mark
gave the "punch line" of his Gospel in the very first verse, but
both Jesus' enemies and his disciples would not get it until Jesus'
resurrection. For us who read Mark today, the message is clear
that we must not ignore or reject Jesus Christ.

Mark called this book the *beginning* of the Good News.
Mark would tell the full story of Jesus Christ, from Jesus' forerunner (John the Baptist) to Jesus' ascension into heaven. Yet
this was only the beginning of the "gospel," for Luke would
recount its far-reaching effects in the book of Acts. And believ-

ers today are still writing the gospel—not to be finished until Jesus comes again.

WHY WOULD GOD HAVE A MISSION?
Any mission requires work, sweat, and cost. A difficult mission usually involves setbacks and sacrifice. Why would God go to the trouble?

Not because he had to. The Bible never pictures God as incomplete or frustrated, in need of something more.

Not because someone told him to. If God took orders from someone else, that someone else would be God.

Our only answer is that God had a mission because he wanted to. That's great good news. The Creator of the universe, the God who commands all things, is a lover above all. All the other attributes the Bible uses to describe God revolve like planets around this central and wonderful core: God is love!

That's why Jesus came.

1:2 It is written in Isaiah the prophet.^{NIV} Mark 1:2-3 is a composite quotation, taken first from Malachi and then from Isaiah. Malachi was a prophet to the Jews in Jerusalem who had returned to rebuild their beloved city after the exile. However, Malachi had to confront the Jews with their neglect of the temple and their false and profane worship. He wrote these words from God: "'See, I will send my messenger, who will prepare the way before me. Then suddenly the Lord you are seeking will come to his temple; the messenger of the covenant, whom you desire, will come,' says the LORD Almighty" (Malachi 3:1 NIV).

Isaiah was one of the greatest prophets of the Old Testament and one of the most quoted in the New. The second half of the book of Isaiah is devoted to the promise of salvation. Isaiah wrote about the coming of the Messiah and the man who would announce his coming, John the Baptist (Isaiah 40:3). Like Isaiah, John was a prophet who urged the people to confess their sins and live for God. Both prophets taught that the message of repentance is good news to those who listen and seek the healing forgiveness of God's love, but terrible news to those who refuse to listen and thus cut off their only hope.

Although quoting from two prophets (Isaiah and Malachi), Mark simply applied the words to Isaiah, the more popular of the two. The theme in both references is the focus on a "messenger" who would "prepare the way." With the help of the Holy Spirit, Mark understood the ministry of John the Baptist as fulfilling these promises.

MORE THAN JUST A STORY
Hundreds of years earlier, the prophet Isaiah had predicted that John the Baptist and Jesus would come. How did he know? God promised Isaiah that a Redeemer would come to Israel, and that a messenger calling in the wilderness would prepare the way for him. Isaiah's words comforted many people as they looked forward to the Messiah.

Knowing that God keeps his promises can comfort you, too. As you read the book of Mark, realize that it is more than just a story; it is part of God's Word. In it God is revealing to you his plans for human history.

"I will send my messenger ahead of you, who will prepare your way."ᴺᴵⱽ Under the guidance of the Holy Spirit, Mark applied the prophecy to John the Baptist's ministry. Mark slightly changed the wording of the prophecy to make his point; "prepare the way" in Malachi 3:1 became *prepare your way.* The speaker *(I)* is God; the *messenger* is John the Baptist; *your way* refers to Jesus' entrance into public ministry. This messenger was an envoy carrying a message. He came before Jesus—in birth by a few months, but in ministry by several years. His job was to make the way ready for Jesus. John the Baptist proclaimed the news of the impending arrival of the Messiah and called people to prepare themselves through repentance and make a public declaration of their repentance by being baptized.

1:3 "The voice of one crying in the wilderness: 'Prepare the way of the Lᴏʀᴅ; make His paths straight.'"ᴺᴷᴶⱽ This messenger considered himself a *voice crying* out to the people of Israel. The Greek word for "crying" is *boao,* meaning "to cry out with great feeling." Full of emotion, John the Baptist's message came directly from God; John was merely God's mouthpiece for the important message God sent to his people: *Prepare the way of the Lᴏʀᴅ.* How were they to do this?

The word "prepare" refers to making something ready (as in 1:2 above); the word "way" could also be translated "road." The picture could come from the Oriental custom of sending servants ahead of a king to level and clear the roads to make them passable for his journey. The people in Israel needed to prepare their minds—clear away the spiritual debris and straighten any "crooked" moral paths—in eager anticipation of their King and Messiah. The verbs are in the imperative, meaning that John spoke them as a military general would speak commands—to be obeyed immediately and without hesitation. Those who accepted John's status as a true prophet from God understood these words as God's words to them, humbled themselves, repented, received baptism, and opened the "way" for their Messiah to take hold of their lives. This verse comes from Isaiah 40:3 and was a theme verse of the early church and of the Qumran community (monastic-type Jews associated with the Dead Sea Scrolls). The early church gave the name "the Way" to their movement (see Acts 9:2).

John's call to *make His paths straight* meant much the same as "preparing the way." The "paths" are the way to people's hearts. For Jesus to be able to reach them, people should give up their selfish way of living, renounce their sins, seek God's forgiveness, and establish a relationship with the almighty God by believing and obeying his words as found in Scripture (Isaiah 1:18-20; 57:15). Again, the verb is in the imperative; John was issuing an impassioned command to his fellow Israelites (see also Luke 7:24-28).

PREPARING THE WAY
John the Baptist prepared the way for Jesus. People who do not know Jesus need to be prepared to meet him. We can prepare them by explaining their need for forgiveness, demonstrating Christ's teachings by our conduct, and telling them how Christ can give their lives meaning. We can "make His paths straight" by correcting misconceptions that might be hindering people from approaching Christ. Someone you know may be open to a relationship with Christ. What can you do to prepare the way for this person?

Why did this voice come from *the wilderness?* The word "wilderness," also translated "desert," refers more to a lonely, uninhabited place than to a sandy desert. John preached in the Judean wilderness, the lower Jordan River valley. Isaiah's use of the word "wilderness" alludes to the wilderness experience of the children of Israel on their exodus from Egypt to Canaan. The "wilderness" represents the place where God would once again act to rescue his people and bring them into fellowship with him.

John the Baptist's powerful, to-the-point preaching and his wilderness living made him a curiosity, separated him from the false piety of many of the religious leaders, and gave him an unmistakable resemblance to the ancient prophets. John chose to live in the wilderness for at least four reasons: (1) to get away from distractions so he could hear God's instructions; (2) to capture the undivided attention of the people; (3) to symbolize a sharp break with the hypocrisy of the religious leaders who preferred their luxurious homes and positions of authority over doing God's work; and (4) to fulfill Old Testament prophecies that said the Messiah's forerunner would be preaching "in the wilderness."

DO WE NEED A WILDERNESS?
Surrounded by comforts, computers, and friendly people, we might forget that we need God in our lives. Deprived of food, shelter, and cordial conversation, we might remember that without God, nothing makes much sense. Our most dramatic stories of people discovering God are set in difficult, sometimes tragic, circumstances—prisons, famines, plagues, earthquakes, hospitals, battles.

We experience a "wilderness" whenever we are lonely, tired, and hungry, and the universe seems not to care. There we wilt or grow strong, die or find new strength, come to despair or discover real faith. In the wilderness, life turns "bitter, brutish, and short"—or God breaks through to us.

1:4 And so John came.[NIV] Mark named this "messenger," this "one crying in the wilderness," John. There had not been a prophet in Israel for more than four hundred years. It was widely believed that when the Messiah came, prophecy would reappear (Joel 2:28-29; Malachi 3:1; 4:5). When John *came,* he burst onto the scene as though appearing on history's stage. The people were excited. He was obviously a great prophet, and they were sure that the eagerly awaited age of the Messiah had come. Indeed, it had, and God was ushering in a brand-new "covenant" and a new era in his dealings with humanity. Some people thought John himself was the Messiah. John spoke like the prophets of old, saying that the people must turn from their sin to avoid punishment and turn to God to experience his mercy and approval. This is a message for all times and places, but John spoke it with particular urgency—he was preparing the people for the coming Messiah.

In four words, Mark summed up the story that Luke would record in greater detail (see Luke 1:5-24, 39-45, 57-80). John was a miracle child, born to Zacharias (Zechariah, in some Bible versions) and Elizabeth. Elizabeth was unable to have children, and advanced age rendered them certain to remain childless. Zacharias held the position of a priest, and one day, while serving in the temple, the angel Gabriel appeared to him. The angel explained that Zacharias and Elizabeth would have a baby boy whom they should name John, adding: "He will turn many of the people of Israel to the Lord their God. With the spirit and

> John's appearance was an eschatological event of the first magnitude, and signified that the decisive turning point in the history of salvation was at hand. *William Lane*

power of Elijah he will go before him, to turn the hearts of parents to their children, and the disobedient to the wisdom of the righteous, to make ready a people prepared for the Lord" (Luke 1:16-17 NRSV).

John's mother, Elizabeth, was a cousin to Jesus' mother, Mary. Thus Jesus and John the Baptist were distant cousins. They probably knew each other, but John probably didn't know that Jesus was the Messiah until Jesus' baptism by John (see John 1:29-34).

Mark began his story with John the Baptist and did not even mention Jesus' birth. His reason stemmed from his target audience—the Christians in Rome. Important Roman officials of this day were always preceded by an announcer or herald. When the herald arrived in town, the people knew that someone of prominence would soon arrive and they would be called to assemble. Heralds also announced and gave the rules for the athletic games. Because Mark's audience was comprised of primarily Roman Christians, he began his book with John the Baptist, whose mission was to announce the coming of Jesus, the most important man who ever lived.

Baptizing in the desert region.^{NIV} John preached in the wilderness (or desert) in the area near the Jordan River, but he did more than that. He urged his listeners to take action—to be baptized. This verse is literally, "There arose John, the one who baptizes"— thus we have "John the Baptist."

Some scholars think that baptism by immersion (going down into the water) was a rite required by the Jews for Gentiles who wished to convert to Judaism. The ritual of immersion symbolized the death and burial of the old way of life; coming up out of the water symbolized the beginning of a new life. If so, then John took a known custom and gave it new meaning. While it was customary for Gentiles to be baptized in order to become Jews, John was demanding that *Jews* be baptized as a sign of repentance and in preparation for the Messiah. This was a radical departure from Jewish custom.

Other scholars think that John was emulating the Qumran practice of daily purification. But John's baptism was one-time immersion, and it was a visible sign that a person had decided to change his or her life, giving up a sinful and selfish way of living and turning to God. It was an outward sign of an inward change. The baptism did not "wash away" sins; instead, it was a public action signifying that a person had been cleansed of sin through repentance and had chosen a new way of life. After Christ's death and resurrection, baptism became an outward sign for identifying with Christ and his resurrection, and signifying entrance into the

Christian community. (See, for example, Romans 6:3-4; 1 Peter 3:21.)

And preaching a baptism of repentance for the forgiveness of sins.[NIV] The word translated "preaching" comes from the Greek word meaning "to be a herald, to proclaim." Mark pictured John the Baptist as a herald proclaiming news of the coming King, the Messiah. His preaching proclaimed that news, including the preparation of people's hearts through *a baptism of repentance.*

Repentance has two sides—turning away from sins and turning toward God. To be truly repentant, people must do both. Without apology or hesitation, John preached that the people could not say they believed and then live any way they wanted (see 3:7-8). They had to determine to rid their lives of any sins God pointed out and put their trust in him alone. They had to understand that they were sinners, that sin is wrong, and that they needed to change both their attitude and their conduct. When they did so, John would baptize them.

John baptized, but he only baptized people who humbly repented of their sins and sought *forgiveness of sins.* Baptism did not give forgiveness; baptism was a visible sign that the person had repented and received God's forgiveness for his or her sins. Matthew recorded that some of the Jewish religious leaders (Pharisees and Sadducees) came to be baptized and John angrily turned them away, for he knew there was no humble repentance in their hearts (Matthew 3:7-9).

ABOUT-FACE
Repentance means doing an about-face—a 180-degree turn—from the kind of self-centeredness that leads to wrong actions such as lying, cheating, stealing, gossiping, taking revenge, abusing, and indulging in sexual immorality. A person who repents stops rebelling and begins following God's way of living prescribed in his Word. The first step in turning to God is to admit your sin, as John urged. Then God will receive you and help you live the way he wants. Remember that only God can get rid of sin. He doesn't expect us to clean up our lives *before* we come to him.

1:5 And people from the whole Judean countryside and all the people of Jerusalem were going out to him.[NRSV] The verb form of "were going out" is in the imperfect tense, indicating continuous past action. From *Jerusalem* (the holy city of the Jews) and from *the whole Judean countryside,* a stream of people constantly flowed into the wilderness to hear John the Baptist

preach. Why did John attract so many people? He was the first
true prophet in four hundred years. He blasted both Herod and
the religious leaders, a daring act that fascinated the common
people. But John also had strong words for his audience—they
too were sinners and needed to repent. His message was powerful
and true. The people were expecting a prophet like Elijah (Malachi 4:5; Luke 1:17), and John seemed to be the one! John's popularity prepared the way for Jesus' even greater popularity (see
1:28, 33, 37, 45).

**And were baptized by him in the river Jordan, confessing
their sins.**NRSV This continuous flow of people who came to hear
John's preaching also *were baptized.* This verb is also in the
imperfect tense, indicating continuous past action. People constantly were coming; people constantly were being baptized. As
explained above, this baptism was a sign of repentance and forgiveness. To repent means "to turn," implying a change in behavior. It is turning from sin toward God.

For baptism by immersion, John needed water, and he used the
river Jordan. The Jordan River is about seventy miles long, its
main section stretching between the Sea of Galilee and the Dead
Sea. Jerusalem lies about twenty miles west of the Jordan. This
river was Israel's eastern border, and many significant events in
the nation's history took place there. It was by the Jordan River
that the Israelites renewed their covenant with God before entering the Promised Land (Joshua 1–2). Here John the Baptist calls
them to renew their covenant with God again, this time through
baptism.

The people "were going out," "were baptized," and were *confessing their sins.* The people had already repented of their sins
and thus had come to be baptized, but the Greek reveals that the
acts of baptism and confession occurred at the same time. Confession is more than simply acknowledging one's own sinfulness; it
is agreeing with God's verdict on sin and expressing the desire to
get rid of sin and live for God. Confessing means more than verbal response, affirmation, or praise; it means agreeing to change
to a life of obedience and service. In addition, the preposition *ek*
(out) reveals that this confession was not spoken quietly to John,
but was spoken loud enough for those waiting on the bank to hear.

What should we do about confessing sin today? For those who
believe in Christ, sins confessed to God are forgiven (1 John 1:9).
However, when accountability is needed, when change is difficult, when turning away from sin requires help, we need the support and involvement of others. We may confess to a friend, to

our prayer support group, to a minister, or even in some cases
before the church.

FREE ADMISSION
The purpose of John's preaching was to prepare people to
accept Jesus as God's Son. When John challenged the people
to confess sin individually, he signaled the start of a new way to
relate to God. Is change needed in your life before you can
hear and understand Jesus' message? You have to admit that
you need forgiveness before you can accept it. To prepare to
receive Christ, repent. Denounce the world's dead-end attrac-
tions, sinful temptations, and harmful attitudes.

**1:6 Now John was clothed with camel's hair and with a leather
belt around his waist, and he ate locusts and wild honey.**[NKJV]
John's clothes were not the latest style of his day. He was outfit-
ted for survival in the wilderness—like a desert monk. He
dressed much like the prophet Elijah (2 Kings 1:8) in order to distinguish himself from the religious leaders, whose flowing robes
reflected their great pride in their position (12:38-39). John's
striking appearance reinforced his striking message. Elijah too
had been considered a messenger preparing the way for God (see
Malachi 3:1).

His diet, *locusts and wild honey,* was common for survival in
the desert regions. Locusts were often roasted and were considered "clean" food for the Jews (Leviticus 11:22); wild honey
could be found in abundance, made by the wild bees who nested
in the clefts of rocks and in the trees of the valley.

LIFE WORDS
John the Baptist was markedly different from the typical religious leaders of his day. While many were greedy, selfish, and
preoccupied with winning the praise of the people, John was
concerned only with the praise of God. Having separated himself from the evil and hypocrisy of his day, John lived differently
from other people to show that his message was new. John not
only preached God's law, he *lived* it. Do you practice what you
preach? Could people discover what you believe by observing
the way you live?

**1:7 He proclaimed, "The one who is more powerful than I is com-
ing after me; I am not worthy to stoop down and untie the
thong of his sandals."**[NRSV] The word "proclaimed" again pictures
John's job as a forerunner heralding a coming king, who is identified as *the one who is more powerful* than John. The definite arti-

COMPARISON OF JOHN'S BAPTISM TO JESUS' BAPTISM

John	Jesus
Baptized with water	Would baptize with the Holy Spirit
Signified preparation for Christ's work	Would convey fulfillment of Christ's work
Person entered the water	The Holy Spirit enters the person to make him or her part of the body of Christ.
A ceremonial cleansing that could not save	The presence of the Holy Spirit is evidence of having received salvation.

cle is used in the Greek; John was not just heralding an important person, he was heralding the most important one. The Jews would have understood this to mean their Messiah.

Although John was the first genuine prophet in four hundred years, Jesus the Messiah would be infinitely greater than he. John was pointing out how insignificant he was compared to the one who was coming. In Oriental households, a lowly slave untied the sandals of guests and then washed their feet. John saw himself as even lower than that slave in comparison to the coming Messiah. John was not even worthy of doing the most menial tasks for him, like untying his sandals. The apostle John recorded these words of John the Baptist, "He must become greater; I must become less" (John 3:30 NIV). What John began, Jesus finished. What John prepared, Jesus fulfilled.

THE SERVANT
John lived above petty jealousy. Jesus was his distant cousin, someone he knew, yet John did not let this deter him from giving glory to Christ. How can we be sure that our lives will focus attention on Christ and not on ourselves? Remember Jesus' great love and humility. Though we are not even worthy to be *his* servants, he made himself a servant to all.

1:8 **"I baptize you with water, but he will baptize you with the Holy Spirit."**[NIV] John's baptism with *water* indicated immersion in the water of the Jordan River. John's baptism demonstrated repentance, humility, and willingness to turn from sin. This was the beginning of the spiritual process. John baptized people as a sign that they had asked God to forgive their sins and had decided to live as he wanted them to live. Baptism was an outward sign of commitment. To be effective, it had to be accompanied by an inward change of attitude leading to a changed life. John's baptism did not give salvation; it prepared a person to welcome the coming Messiah and receive *his* message and *his* baptism.

John's statement, *He will baptize you with the Holy Spirit,* revealed the identity of the "one" coming after John as the promised Messiah. The coming of the Spirit had been prophesied as part of the Messiah's arrival:

- I will pour out my Spirit on your offspring, and my blessing on your descendants. (Isaiah 44:3 NIV)

- The time is coming. . . . I will put my law in their minds and write it on their hearts. I will be their God, and they will be my people. . . . For I will forgive their wickedness and will remember their sins no more. (Jeremiah 31:31-34 NIV)

- I will give you a new heart and put a new spirit in you; I will remove from you your heart of stone and give you a heart of flesh. And I will put my Spirit in you and move you to follow my decrees and be careful to keep my laws. (Ezekiel 36:26-27 NIV)

- And afterward, I will pour out my Spirit on all people. Your sons and daughters will prophesy, your old men will dream dreams, your young men will see visions. Even on my servants, both men and women, I will pour out my Spirit in those days. (Joel 2:28-29 NIV)

The Old Testament promised a time when God would demonstrate his power among people and give special relationship and blessings to his people. This looked ahead to Pentecost (Acts 2), when the Holy Spirit would be sent by Jesus in the form of tongues of fire, empowering his followers to preach the gospel. All believers, those who would later come to Jesus Christ for salvation, would receive the Holy Spirit. When Jesus would baptize with the Holy Spirit, the entire person would be transformed by the Spirit's power. Jesus would offer both forgiveness of sin and the power to live for him. We need more than repentance to save us; we need the indwelling power of the Holy Spirit.

JOHN BAPTIZES JESUS / 1:9-11 / *17*

Mark had just described John the Baptist's baptism as a "baptism of repentance for the forgiveness of sins" (1:4). Then he proceeded, without explanation, to describe Jesus' baptism by John.

The double, audiovisual signs of the voice and dove from heaven affirmed Jesus' identity as the Son of God and accomplished Mark's objective—to show the uniqueness of Jesus' baptism. But the words of God the Father's declaration clearly signified who Jesus was. What Jesus was doing, including undergoing baptism by John, totally pleased God. Jesus was in no way "becoming" God's Son; instead, his true nature was being revealed. Jesus' baptism showed that he was identifying with sinful men and women without implying that he himself was a sinner. Mark further underscored his point by immediately adding the reference to Jesus' temptation—another example of Jesus identifying with sinners without committing sin.

1:9 At that time Jesus came from Nazareth in Galilee.^{NIV} The coming one was identified as *Jesus*. Although born in Bethlehem, Jesus moved to Nazareth when he was a young boy and grew up there (Matthew 2:22-23). Nazareth was a small town in Galilee, located about halfway between the Sea of Galilee and the Mediterranean Sea. The city was despised and avoided by many Jews because it had a reputation for independence. Nazareth was an unlikely hometown for so great a king as Jesus. Yet even Jesus' hometown demonstrated his humility and identification with ordinary people. Nazareth was a crossroads for trade routes, and Jesus had contact with people of other cultures. (See also John 1:46.) *Galilee* was the name of the northern region of Palestine; the other two regions were Samaria (central) and Judea (southern). *At that time* Jesus was probably about thirty years old (Luke 3:23). He traveled the long distance on foot (see map "Jesus Begins His Ministry"), along the dusty roads of Galilee and Samaria and into Judea, to meet John the Baptist and be baptized by him.

Baptized by John in the Jordan.^{NIV} If John's baptism was for repentance from sin, why was Jesus baptized? While even the greatest prophets (Isaiah, Jeremiah, Ezekiel) had to confess their sinfulness and need for repentance, Jesus didn't need to admit sin—he was sinless (John 8:46; 2 Corinthians 5:21; Hebrews 4:15; 1 John 3:5). Although Jesus didn't need forgiveness, he was baptized for the following reasons: (1) to confess sin on behalf of the nation, as Isaiah, Ezra, and Nehemiah had done (see Isaiah 6:5; Nehemiah 1:6; 9:1ff.; Ezra 9:2); (2) to fulfill all righteousness (Matthew 3:15) in order to accomplish God's mission and advance God's work in the world; (3) to inaugurate his public ministry to bring the message of salvation to all people; (4) to show support for John's ministry; (5) to identify with the penitent

people of God, thus with humanness and sin; (6) to give us an
example to follow. John's baptism for repentance was different
from Christian baptism in the church. Paul had John's followers
baptized again (see Acts 19:2-5). Jesus, the perfect man, didn't
need baptism for sin, but he accepted baptism in obedient service
to the Father, and God showed his approval. We need this same
attitude of humility, submission to God, and dedication to
servanthood.

**1:10 And just as he was coming up out of the water, he saw the
heavens torn apart and the Spirit descending like a dove on
him.**NRSV Apparently the action of the Spirit descending from
heaven like a dove was a sign for John that Jesus was the Messiah. John knew the Messiah was coming, but he did not know
when the Messiah would be revealed until this miraculous opening of the heavens (read John the Baptist's words in John
1:29-34).

The Bible does not tell us that anyone but Jesus saw *the heavens torn apart.* This event, and *the Spirit descending like a dove,*
revealed the Messiah to John. The "splitting" or "tearing open"
of the heavens presents God's intervention into humanity in the
human presence of God in Jesus Christ. It was as if the heavens
rolled back to reveal the invisible throne of God (Isaiah 63:19–
64:2).

The next sign, "the Spirit descending like a dove," was probably visible to all the people, for Luke recounts that "the Holy
Spirit descended upon him in bodily form like a dove" (Luke
3:22 NRSV). The descent of the Spirit, and the dove itself, represented to Israel God's mighty workings in the world. At creation,
"the Spirit of God was hovering over the waters" (Genesis 1:2
NIV). After the great Flood, the dove carried the news to Noah of
the receding waters (Genesis 8:8-12). The descending of the
Spirit signified God's workings in the world; the arrival of the
Messiah would have been marked by the descending of the
Spirit, in this case, in the form of a dove. Jesus himself would
read from the prophet Isaiah (Isaiah 61:1-2), "'The Spirit of the
Lord is on me, because he has anointed me to preach good news
to the poor. He has sent me to proclaim freedom for the prisoners
and recovery of sight for the blind, to release the oppressed, to
proclaim the year of the Lord's favor'" (Luke 4:18-19 NIV).

The dove is used as a symbol for the Holy Spirit. However, it
is not the bird itself that was important, but the descent of the
Spirit *as* a dove to emphasize the way the Holy Spirit related to
Jesus. The Spirit descending portrays a gentle, peaceful, but

active presence coming to indwell Jesus. In the same way, since Jesus has given us the Holy Spirit, he is available to us as well.

1:11 Then a voice came from heaven, "You are My beloved Son, in whom I am well pleased."^{NKJV} The Spirit descended like a dove on Jesus, and *a voice came from heaven* proclaiming the Father's approval of Jesus as his divine Son. That Jesus is God's divine Son is the foundation for all we read about Jesus in the Gospels. This "voice" came from the heavenly realm that had been briefly opened ("torn apart") in 1:10.

The voice said, *You are My beloved Son.* In Greek, the literal translation of this is "As for you, you are my Son, the beloved one." While all believers would eventually be called "sons of God" (or children of God), Jesus Christ has a different, unique relationship with God; he is the Messiah, and he is the one unique Son of God.

The phrase "in whom I am well pleased" means that the Father takes great delight, pleasure, and satisfaction in the Son. The verb in Greek is a constative aorist; that is, God's pleasure in the Son is constant. He has always taken pleasure in his Son.

Jesus did not *become* the Son or the Messiah at this baptism. Jesus already had his divinity from eternity past. The opened heavens, the dove, and the voice revealed to John the Baptist (and to us as readers of this incredible story) that Jesus was God's Son, come to earth as the promised Messiah to fulfill prophecy and bring salvation to those who believe.

The words spoken by the voice from heaven echoed two Old Testament passages. First, Psalm 2:7, "He said to me, 'You are my Son'" (NIV). Psalm 2 is a messianic psalm that describes the coronation of Christ, the eternal King. The rule of Christ described in the psalm will begin after his crucifixion and resurrection and will be fulfilled when he comes to set up his kingdom on earth. Second, Isaiah 42:1, "Here is my servant, whom I uphold, my chosen one in whom I delight" (NIV). Isaiah 42:1-17 describes the Servant-Messiah who would suffer and die as he served God and fulfilled his mission of atoning for sin on behalf of humanity. Thus, in the two phrases spoken, the voice from the throne of heaven described both Jesus' status as the Servant who would suffer and die, and as the King who will reign forever.

In this event, we see all three members of the Trinity together—God the Father, God the Son, and God the Holy Spirit. The doctrine of the Trinity means that God is three persons and yet one in essence. In this passage, all three persons of the Trinity are present and active. God the Father speaks; God the Son is baptized; God the Holy Spirit descends on Jesus. God is one, yet in three persons at the same time. This is one of God's incomprehensible mysteries. Other Bible references that speak of the Father, Son, and Holy Spirit are Matthew 28:19; Luke 1:35; John 15:26; 1 Corinthians 12:4-13; 2 Corinthians 13:14; Ephesians 2:18; 1 Thessalonians 1:2-5; and 1 Peter 1:2.

SIGNS AND SIGNALS
The dove and the voice from heaven were signs that Jesus was the Messiah. If faith were like science, we would not believe anything that did not have visible proof, and everything we did believe would require measurement and verification. But faith differs from science in that God cannot be measured and his way of doing business cannot be predicted by any theological calculus. Many people want something tangible, visual, and "real" before they believe. So Jesus did healings and other miracles, and God raised Jesus from the dead. Still people doubt.

   Will visible signs convince anyone? The "sign" that really brings us to faith is the power of God's message to answer the cry of the heart. To the confused, God offers a mind enlightened by faith. To the depressed, God offers a reason for joy. To the lonely, God offers eternal companionship. Don't look for a spectacular visible sign; instead, seek a cleansed and renewed life as evidence of his presence.

SATAN TEMPTS JESUS IN THE DESERT / 1:12-13 / *18*

This temptation by Satan shows us that though Jesus was human and subject to temptations such as we are, he was also divine because he overcame Satan and was ministered to by angels. Jesus' temptation was an important demonstration of his sinlessness. He faced temptation and did not give in. As his servants, we will also be prepared for discipleship by testing.

   As we study this most condensed account of Jesus' temptation (see the longer accounts in Matthew 4:1-11 and Luke 4:1-13), we can better understand our own temptations and how to overcome them. With Jesus in the wilderness were the Spirit, Satan, wild animals, and angels. The episode began with the Spirit's guidance. This shows that God's leading does not always guarantee safe circumstances. God's Spirit will lead us, as he led Jesus, into the places we need to go, even though they may be dangerous. As God's Spirit leads us, we can fully expect to be tempted by Satan and to be exposed to the wildness of the world with both its wonders and its dangers.

1:12 Immediately the Spirit drove Him into the wilderness.ᴺᴷᴶⱽ Mark

Jesus Begins His Ministry
When Jesus came from his home in Nazareth to begin his ministry, he first took two steps in preparation—baptism by John in the Jordan River, and temptation by Satan in the rough wilderness of Judea. After the temptation, Jesus returned to Galilee and later set up his home base in Capernaum.

used the word meaning "immediately" several times throughout his Gospel. The word keeps the narrative moving on a fast pace throughout the book, as it chronicles Jesus' travels throughout his three-year ministry on earth. The word could have the urgency of "right away" or "at once"; at times it meant "in due time," or even simply "when" or "then."

Jesus, empowered by *the Spirit,* takes the offensive against the enemy, Satan, by going into the lonely and desolate *wilderness* to fight temptation (see 1:13). The word for "drove" is very forceful in the Greek, conveying the meaning of "thrown out" or "cast out." (Mark used the same word to describe Jesus driving out demons, as in 1:34, 39.) Jesus was "thrust" into the wilderness—he was compelled to go there. This does not imply that Jesus was reluctant, but rather that he was intensely determined to go, in agreement with the

Spirit. As with Jesus' disciples, the Spirit may have in mind to test us in order to prepare us for greater service.

PERSONAL WILDERNESS
Jesus wasn't tempted inside the temple or at his baptism, but in the wilderness where he was tired, alone, and hungry, and thus most vulnerable. The devil often tempts us when we are vulnerable—when we are under physical or emotional stress (for example, lonely, tired, weighing big decisions, or faced with uncertainty). But he also likes to tempt us through our strengths, where we are most susceptible to pride. We must guard at all times against his attacks.

1:13 And he was in the desert forty days.[NIV] In the Old Testament, the *desert,* or wilderness, was a desolate and dangerous place where wild animals lived (see, for example, Isaiah 13:20-22; 34:8-15). Jesus remained alone there for *forty days;* Matthew and Luke add that Jesus fasted during that time (Matthew 4:2; Luke 4:2). The number forty brings to mind the forty days for rain in the great Flood (Genesis 7:17), the forty days Moses spent on Sinai (Exodus 24:18), the forty years of Israel's wandering in the wilderness (Deuteronomy 29:5), the forty days of Goliath's taunting of Israel prior to David's victory (1 Samuel 17:16), and the forty days of Elijah's time of fear in the wilderness (1 Kings 19:8).

Being tempted by Satan.NIV The Gospels of Matthew and Luke describe in more detail the temptation endured by Jesus. *Satan* is an angel who rebelled against God. He is real, not symbolic, and is constantly working against God and those who obey him. Satan tempted Eve in the Garden and persuaded her to sin; he tempted Jesus in the wilderness and did not persuade him to fall. The verb *being tempted* describes continuous action because Jesus was tempted constantly during the forty days. The word "tempted" means "to put to the test to see what good or evil, strengths or weaknesses, exist in a person." The Spirit compelled Jesus into the wilderness where God put Jesus to the test—not to see if Jesus was ready, but to *show* that he was ready for the mission to be accomplished. Satan, however, had other plans; he hoped to tempt Jesus to do evil and thereby thwart his mission.

PRESSURIZED
Jesus left the crowds and went into the wilderness where he was tempted by Satan. To be tempted is not a sin. Tempting others or giving in to temptation *is* sin. We should not hate or resent times of inner testing because through them God can strengthen our character and teach us valuable lessons. When you face Satan and must deal with his temptations and the turmoil he brings, remember Jesus. He used God's Word against Satan and won. You can do the same. A person has not shown true obedience if he or she has never had an opportunity to disobey. We read in Deuteronomy 8:2 that God led Israel into the wilderness to humble and test them. God wanted to see whether or not his people would really obey him. We too will be tested. Because we know that testing will come, we should be alert and ready for it. Remember, your convictions are only strong if they hold up under pressure!

Jesus' personal victory over Satan at the very outset of his ministry set the stage for his command over demons throughout his ministry, but it did not dissuade Satan from continuing to try to ruin Jesus' mission. For example, the religious leaders would tempt Jesus to prove his power by showing a sign from heaven (8:11) and to test his authority in deciding legal matters (10:2; 12:13-15); Peter would tempt him to stop talking about his death

(8:32-33); and ultimately, fear and horror would tempt Jesus to turn away from the cross (14:34-36).

He was with the wild animals, and angels attended him.^{NIV} As described above, the "desert" or "wilderness" was a dangerous and desolate place, inhabited by *wild animals.* The wilderness regions of Palestine had animals such as boars, jackals, wolves, foxes, leopards, and hyenas. Mark is the only Gospel writer to mention this, pointing out the hostile nature of the wilderness where Jesus spent forty days being tempted. Perhaps Satan tempted him with fear and with the desire to get back to civilization during those forty days. It is interesting to note that Adam and Eve fell to Satan's temptations in a beautiful garden where all their needs were met and all the animals were tame; Jesus was tempted by Satan and did *not* fall as he went without food and the basic necessities and was surrounded by wild animals. John Milton's epic poem *Paradise Regained* popularized the theme that Jesus' victory over Satan in the wilderness reversed the tragic consequences of Adam and Eve's fall and thereby prepared the way for paradise to be regained.

That *angels attended him* in no way lessens the intensity of the temptations that Jesus faced. The angels may have given Jesus food and drink because the Greek word *diekonoun,* usually translated "ministering," can also mean "serving food" (see 1 Kings 19:5-7 where angels ministered to Elijah). But it is more likely that the angels' ministry was spiritual in nature—attending to Jesus' spiritual needs. The verb indicates continuous action. As Satan's temptations lasted continuously during the forty days, so did the ministrations of the angels.

Angels are continuously present. Hebrews 1:14 defines "angels" as messengers for God and ministers to people. They show compassion for human beings. Passages such as Matthew 18:10, Luke 15:10, Acts 12:14-15, and Revelation 19:10 support the idea of guardian angels. As agents of God, they bring special help to believers (Acts 5:19-21; 12:7-10).

Angels, like these who waited on Jesus, have a significant role as God's messengers. These spiritual beings were involved in Jesus' life on earth by (1) announcing Jesus' birth to Mary, (2) reassuring Joseph, (3) naming Jesus, (4) announcing Jesus' birth to the shepherds, (5) protecting Jesus by sending his family to Egypt, and (6) ministering to Jesus in Gethsemane.

From Jesus' temptation we can learn that following our Lord could bring dangerous and intense spiritual battles. It warns us that we won't always feel good; there will be times of deprivation, loneliness, and hostility. It also shows that our spiritual victories may not always be visible to the watching world. Above all, it shows that we must use the power of God to face temptation, and not try to withstand it in our own strength.

JESUS PREACHES IN GALILEE / 1:14-15 / *30*

Up to this point, Mark has succeeded in sketching the character of Jesus as the fulfillment of Old Testament prophecy, the one who could identify with sinful humans without succumbing to sin himself, and the heaven-declared Son of God. Approximately one year elapsed between 1:13 and 1:14, which begins a new section. In this section Mark focuses on Jesus choosing his disciples.

This section also tells how Herod removed John the Baptist from ministry while Jesus' public ministry was beginning (see John 3:30). Mark then includes a summary of Jesus' message. Jesus echoed John's call for repentance and added the challenge that each person must believe the Good News. From the beginning, Jesus did not allow himself to be only a topic for debate or even admiration. He expected those who approached him to believe or to reject him. He never allowed the middle ground of indecision.

1:14 Now after John was put in prison.NKJV Mark mentioned the arrest of John the Baptist as merely a signal for the ministry of Jesus into Galilee, his home region. Luke explained that John was arrested because he publicly rebuked King Herod for taking his brother's wife. John's public protests greatly angered Herod, so he put John in prison, presumably to silence him.

> Fractures well cur'd make us more strong. *George Herbert*

The family of Herods were renowned for their cruelty and evil; it was Herod the Great who ordered the murder of the babies in Bethlehem (Matthew 2:16). The Herod who imprisoned John was Herod Antipas; his wife was Herodias, Herod Antipas's niece and formerly his brother's wife. The imprisonment of John the Baptist was only one evil act in a family filled with incest, deceit, and murder.

Jesus came to Galilee.NKJV Jesus moved from Nazareth, his hometown, to Capernaum, about twenty miles farther north. Capernaum became Jesus' home base during his ministry in the northernmost region of Palestine, *Galilee.* Jesus probably moved (1) to get away from intense opposition in Nazareth, (2) to have an impact on the greatest number of people (Capernaum was a busy city, and Jesus' message could reach more people and spread more quickly), and (3) to utilize extra resources and support for his ministry. Jesus' move fulfilled the prophecy of Isaiah

9:1-2, which states that the Messiah will be a light to the land of
Zebulun and Naphtali, the region of Galilee where Capernaum
was located. Zebulun and Naphtali were two of the original
twelve tribes of Israel.

PRISON MINISTRY
We must remember to bring the Good News of God's kingdom
to prisoners like John the Baptist. Being caged, denied the benefit of work and the comfort of family and friends, and always
under guard must make a person feel like an animal. Prisons
are filled with people who are filled with guilt.
   So Jesus taught that prisoners need the Good News; they
need relief and restoration. People put in prison because their
opinions challenge secular authority (as with John the Baptist)
need hope and vindication. All prisoners need to feel like
human beings again, important to God, capable of work,
needed by someone. As a Christian, you can share God's
Good News with prisoners and be an angel of mercy. Through
your words, faith can climb prison walls and set prisoners free.

Proclaiming the good news of God.^{NIV} What is *the good news of
God?* These first words spoken by Jesus in Mark give the core of
his teaching: the long-awaited Messiah had come to break the
power of sin and begin God's personal reign on earth. This was
indeed good news from God because most of the people who heard
this message were oppressed, poor, and without hope. Jesus' words
were good news because they offered freedom, justice, and hope.
Though at first the listeners thought he referred to political freedom
and civil justice, true disciples would learn after his crucifixion that
the freedom was from sin, the mercy was from God and not people,
and the hope was for new life with him.

**1:15 And saying, "The time is fulfilled, and the kingdom of God has
come near."**^{NRSV} Jews of Jesus' day understood exactly what Jesus
meant when he proclaimed *the time is fulfilled.* The Greek word
used for time, *kairos,* refers to a particular time period with its
beginning marked by an extremely important event. This placed
Jesus' coming in the center of God's plan for revelation and
redemption. The Old Testament prophets often spoke of the future
kingdom, ruled by a descendant of King David, that would be established on earth and exist for eternity. Thus when Jesus spoke of
the "time" and the presence of *the kingdom of God,* the Jews understood him to mean that the Messiah had come to "fulfill" or inaugurate his long-awaited kingdom. Jesus reassured them that God was
in sovereign control. He had begun to act in a new and decisive

way. The most critical time had come. The door to God's great future had been flung open.

Of course, this caused great excitement among the people. The problem arose, however, in the misunderstanding of the nature of this kingdom. The kingdom of God began when God entered history as a human being. But the kingdom of God will not be fully realized until all evil in the world has been judged and removed. Christ came

> Have we felt our sins, and forsaken them? Have we taken hold of Christ, and believed? We may reach heaven without learning or riches or health or worldly greatness. But we will never reach heaven if we die unrepentant and unbelieving. *J. C. Ryle*

to earth first as a suffering Servant; he will come again as King and Judge to rule victoriously over all the earth. The kingdom he inaugurated on earth would not overthrow Roman oppression and bring universal peace immediately. The kingdom of God that began quietly in Palestine was God's rule in people's hearts. The everlasting kingdom would not begin for many years (it has not yet begun), yet the kingdom was as *near* as people's willingness to make Jesus king over their lives. As Jesus said, "The kingdom of God is within you" (Luke 17:21 NIV). The everlasting kingdom may still be many years away for us, yet it is as near as accepting Jesus' sacrifice for salvation.

"Repent, and believe in the good news."^{NRSV} Jesus began his ministry with the very word people had heard John the Baptist say: *Repent.* The message is the same today. Becoming a follower of Christ means turning away from our self-centeredness and "self" control and turning our lives over to Christ's direction and control. As mentioned in 1:4, repentance has two sides—turning away from sin and believing *in the good news.* The Good News, the gospel, means that Jesus, the promised Messiah, has come to usher in a new age of God's dealings with his people.

GREAT NEWS
Jesus preached the gospel—the Good News—to anyone who wanted to hear it and to many who didn't. The gospel is that the kingdom of God has come, that God is with us, and that he cares for us. Christ can heal us, not just of physical sickness, but of spiritual sickness as well. There's no sin or problem too great or too small for him to handle. Jesus' words were good news because they fulfilled the promise of freedom, hope, peace of mind, and eternal life with God. He can handle your problems too.

Verse 15 provides a summary of Jesus' gospel message and gives us one of the most important expressions of the gospel in the New Testament. The first half details what God has done for us: He has fulfilled the time and brought near the kingdom of God. The second half details what we must do to participate: repent and believe.

FOUR FISHERMEN FOLLOW JESUS / 1:16-20 / 33

Jesus did not approach Simon and Andrew as strangers. We know from the Gospel of John (1:35-49) that they had had previous contact.

Jesus confronted these men with a challenge beyond the one he presented in his public preaching. He called the crowds to repentance and belief. He invited Simon and the others to follow him. They had already repented and believed. Now they were being called into discipleship.

The Lord used their previous vocation as a metaphor of their new calling. The former fishermen would now be fishers of men. God finds a way to make good use of every past experience we have to help us serve him.

1:16 **And as He walked by the Sea of Galilee.**^NKJV The Sea of Galilee is, in reality, a large lake—650 feet below sea level, 150 feet deep, and surrounded by hills. Fishing was the main industry for the approximately thirty towns that surrounded the Sea of Galilee during Jesus' day. The word "by" means alongside. Jesus was walking on the beach. He knew the fishermen for whom he was searching would be in this location.

He saw Simon and Andrew his brother casting a net into the sea; for they were fishermen.^NKJV Fishing with nets was the most common method. A circular net (ten to fifteen feet in diameter) was cast into the sea. Then it was drawn up, and the catch was hoisted into the boat. Their method was like gathering and harvesting. Fishermen on the Sea of Galilee were strong and busy men.

The first pair of men Jesus called to follow him were brothers, *Simon and Andrew.* This was not the first time Simon and Andrew had met Jesus. Andrew had been a disciple of John the Baptist who, when introduced to "the Lamb of God," turned and followed Jesus (John 1:35-40). Andrew then brought his brother Simon to Jesus. When Jesus met Simon he said, "'You are Simon son of John. You will be called Cephas' (which, when translated, is Peter)" (John 1:42 NIV). These men understood and believed

who Jesus was. Jesus arrived on the shore that day to change
their lives forever.

BUSY PEOPLE
People chosen by God for a special mission are never just sitting around, daydreaming, waiting, doing nothing—then suddenly, the CALL! No. Instead, when Jesus selected disciples to
train as evangelists, teachers, and missionaries, he looked to
hard workers and tradesmen—men in business, men up early,
men who were not just talkers, but movers.

People today who are busy at work should be grateful for the
energy and intelligence to compete for employment, and for the
skill required to achieve results. Such gifts are from God. Such
busy people should also be listening, in prayer and meditation,
for the call from the Lord that starts something new, a mission
suited to their talents, to aid in bringing God's kingdom nearer
to others.

**1:17 Then Jesus said to them, "Follow Me, and I will make you
become fishers of men."**^{NKJV} Jesus told Simon (Peter) and
Andrew to leave their fishing business and *follow* him. "Follow"
is a major term to signify discipleship in Mark's Gospel. It means
to accept Jesus as authority, to pursue his calling, to model after
his example, to join his group.

- In 2:14, Jesus told Levi, "Follow me."

- In 8:34, Jesus told the disciples to take up their crosses and "follow me."

- In 10:21, Jesus told the rich young man to sell all he had and
"come, follow me."

- In John 21:19, just before Jesus' ascension, Jesus told Peter to
"Follow me" even in death.
(See also 1 Peter 2:21 and 2 Thessalonians 3:9.)

In this verse, Jesus was asking these men to become his disciples
and then begin fishing for people to also follow Jesus.

In the Old Testament, God is the fisher of men, harvesting
them for judgment (Jeremiah 16:16; Ezekiel 29:4-5; 38:4; Amos
4:2; Habakkuk 1:14-17). The urgency for the gathering of souls is
that judgment is coming, so they were to bring people in while
there was still time. These disciples were adept at catching fish,
but they would need special training before they would become
able to fish for people's souls. Fishing for people would be harder
and more dangerous. Jesus was calling them away from their productive trades to be productive spiritually by helping others

believe the Good News and carry on Jesus' work after he was
gone. These men already knew Jesus, so when Jesus called them,
they were willing to follow him. *I will make* portrays Jesus as the
creative agent; our task is to follow him.

FISHING FOR PEOPLE
Jesus called the disciples to fish for souls with the same energy
they had previously used to fish for food. The gospel would be
like a net, pulling people into its grasp, transforming their lives.
Many people would be lifted from dark waters into the light of
day.
   How can God use you to be his fisher of men? How can you
train new converts to find new seas and cast new nets where
waters have never been fished before? The gospel makes missionaries of all God's people.

1:18 They immediately left their nets and followed Him.NKJV After
their previous meeting with Jesus, Simon Peter and Andrew had
returned to fishing. But when Jesus
called them to follow him as disciples,
they immediately left their nets. The
judgment was coming; they had to
respond at once. Their lives had
changed; their allegiance was now to

> Every great person has
> first learned how to obey,
> whom to obey, and when
> to obey. *William A. Ward*

their teacher. One pair left their occupation, the others their father
(1:20). Mark taught radical discipleship; a person must leave all
behind to follow Jesus.

LEAVE IT AND FOLLOW
What can we learn from the disciples' response to Jesus' call?
■ What does Christ expect you to leave behind to follow him?
■ What sacrifice of personal achievement, wealth, or position
  does Christ ask you to make?
■ What prevents you from following Jesus immediately and
  wholeheartedly?
■ What must you do to eliminate these hindrances from your
  life?

**1:19 As he went a little farther, he saw James son of Zebedee and
his brother John, who were in their boat mending the
nets.**NRSV Not far down the beach was another pair of brothers,
James and *John,* Simon Peter's partners (Luke 5:10). These men
were sitting in their moored boat *mending the nets.* The weight of
a good catch of fish and the constant strain on the nets certainly
meant that the fishermen had to spend a lot of time keeping their

nets repaired and in good shape. Holes had to be mended in preparation for the next night's fishing.

John had met Jesus previously. In his Gospel, John records his own and Andrew's discipleship with John the Baptist and then their turning to follow Jesus (John 1:35-39). We have no record of James previously meeting Jesus, but he probably knew about Jesus from his brother. In any case, James and John were also ready for Jesus' call.

IMMEDIATELY
James and his brother, John, along with Peter and Andrew, were the first disciples that Jesus called to work with him. Jesus' call motivated these men to get up and leave their jobs—immediately. They didn't make excuses about why it wasn't a good time. They left at once and followed. Jesus calls each of us to follow him. When Jesus asks us to serve him, we must be like the disciples and do it at once.

1:20 Immediately he called them; and they left their father Zebedee in the boat with the hired men, and followed him.^{NRSV} Both sets of brothers *immediately* left behind the lives they had known and embarked on an incredible adventure. Surely the impression Jesus made upon them must have been great, and the certainty of their call must have been strong for them to follow without hesitation. James and John left their father in the boat. Zebedee must have been a very understanding father; perhaps he too believed and would have gone along himself in younger days.

UNDERSTANDING PARENTS
Let's not forget that Zebedee's life was changed too. He had to say good-bye to his sons, trusted partners in the business, loyal workers, daily companions. What had he been working for, poor old Zebedee, if not to make his sons more prosperous in business than he had been? But Jesus changed all that.

Parents of children who sense a call to missions should not balk if the family business takes second place to God's business. Parents who have encouraged their offspring from early childhood to pray and follow Christ should not cry foul when son or daughter puts all of life on the altar of service.

Zebedee adjusted, we hope, and prayed daily for his sons. Parents today may heave a sigh, wonder about practicalities, and worry about a child's financial security. But then in faith, pray, support, and give those children anew to God.

![bar] **JESUS TEACHES WITH GREAT AUTHORITY /
1:21-28 / 34**

Earlier in chapter 1, Satan attacked Jesus in the wilderness. Then Mark directed our attention to Jesus' counterattack. He carried the spiritual warfare into the domain of Satan, to those controlled by evil spirits. As will be the case repeatedly, the battle took place in a synagogue on the Sabbath. Perhaps this shows that Satan can be active even in our houses of worship.

Mark draws our attention to the conclusion drawn by the eyewitnesses to what Jesus did that day in Capernaum. The people were struck by his authority. Not only were they amazed by his application of the Scriptures to their own lives, but they were equally amazed by how he fearlessly confronted demonic power.

Our familiarity with the words of Jesus should never lull us into thinking that they have lost power over the centuries. Jesus remains as powerful today as ever, but we must carefully listen and follow all he says to us.

1:21 They went to Capernaum.NIV Capernaum, located on the northwestern shore of the Sea of Galilee, was the largest of the many fishing towns surrounding the lake. Jesus had recently moved to Capernaum from Nazareth (Matthew 4:12-13). Capernaum was a thriving town with great wealth as well as great sin and decadence. Because it was the headquarters for many Roman troops, heathen influences from all over the Roman Empire were pervasive. This was a needy place for Jesus to challenge both Jews and non-Jews with the gospel of God's kingdom.

And when the Sabbath came, Jesus went into the synagogue and began to teach.NIV The temple in Jerusalem was too far for many Jews to travel for regular worship, so many towns had synagogues serving both as places of worship and as schools. Beginning in the days of Ezra, about 450 B.C., a group of ten Jewish families could start a synagogue. There, during the week, Jewish boys were taught the Old Testament law and Jewish religion (girls could not attend). Each Saturday, the Sabbath, the Jewish men would gather to hear prayers, the Scriptures read, and an interpretation from a scribe. Because there was no permanent rabbi or teacher, it was cus-

> In the presence of Jesus men are disturbed, and this disturbance is the precise act of fishing to which Jesus had called the four fishermen.
> *William Lawe*

tomary for the synagogue leader to ask visiting teachers to speak. This is why Jesus often spoke in the synagogues in the towns he visited.

1:22 They were astounded at his teaching, for he taught them as one having authority, and not as the scribes.[NRSV] The Greek word translated "astounded" is a strong word; it could also be translated "astonished" or "amazed." The people were completely amazed by Jesus' teaching. The Jewish teachers (the *scribes*) often quoted from well-known rabbis to give their words more authority. But Jesus didn't have that need. Because Jesus was the Son of God, he knew exactly what the Scriptures said and meant. He was the ultimate *authority*. The people had never heard such teaching. He created the urgency and alarm that a real prophet would cause, not the discussion and arguments of scribal tradition. He confronted the people with the claims of God on their lives.

ASTOUNDING AUTHORITY
Jesus' authority extended to every area of spiritual life and concern. He had
- authority in his teaching (1:22, 27)
- authority over demons (1:25; 5:6-7)
- authority to forgive sins (2:10)
- authority over the temple and its administration (11:28-32)
- authority to continue through the disciples the attack against demonic power (3:15; 6:7)

Have you given him authority over your life?

The "scribes" (called "teachers of the law" or "lawyers" in some Bible versions) were the legal specialists in Jesus' day. They interpreted the law but were especially concerned about the "halakah" or "rules" for life that came to be as binding as God's written law in the Torah. The scribes were the forerunners of the office of rabbi. Their self-assured authority, in fact, became a stumbling block for them, for they denied Jesus' authority to reinterpret the law, and they rejected Jesus as the Messiah because he did not agree with nor obey all of their traditions.

1:23-24 Just then a man in their synagogue who was possessed by an evil spirit.[NIV] Jesus' teaching, his powerful authority, and the astonishment of the people *just then* prompted an outburst by a man *who was possessed by an evil spirit.* Evil (unclean) spirits, or demons, are ruled by Satan. They work to tempt people to sin. They were not created by Satan, because God is the Creator of all. Rather, the evil spirits and demons are fallen

angels who joined Satan in his rebellion and thus became per-
verted and evil. The Greek is literally "in a spirit, an unclean
one." The evil spirit had entered the man's body, had taken up
residence, and now controlled him. Though not all disease
comes from Satan, sometimes demons can cause a person to
become mute, deaf, blind, or insane. But in every case where
demons confronted Jesus, they lost their power. Thus God limits what evil spirits can do; they can do nothing without his permission. During Jesus' life on earth, demons were allowed to
be very active to demonstrate once and for all Christ's power
and authority over them.

AWESOME NEW MESSAGE
If your mind ever wanders during a Sunday sermon, if you ever
think, *Hmm, I've heard this before,* remember the reaction of
these listeners to one who spoke with such authority and conviction about such unprecedented matters that the only reaction was "I am stunned, shocked, and amazed!" There was no
boredom that day in the synagogue. People were on the edge
of their seats. That's where listeners and worshipers should be
every time Jesus' message is preached.

    If you've started to take the message for granted, move up in
your seat, as if to say, "Did I hear that right? God . . . loves . . .
me? Amazing!"

**Cried out, "What do you want with us, Jesus of Nazareth?
Have you come to destroy us? I know who you are—the
Holy One of God!"**[NIV] This cry from the possessed man was
the voice of the demon—a horrible sound. The evil spirit knew
two facts—that Jesus had indeed come to *destroy* them (and
their power) and that Jesus was *the Holy One of God.* The
demon (indeed all the demons, for the demon used the word
"us") knew Jesus was the Messiah. While the people in the
synagogue were astounded at Jesus' teaching and wondered
who this man could be, the demon knew. At this time, people
believed that to know a person's precise hidden name was to
be able to gain control over the person. Thus the demon's first
attempt against Jesus was to state his name in public. The
demons knew that Jesus' coming marked the beginning of the
end of their power, but they tried every way they knew to
break him. Their master, Satan, had tried and failed—the
demons would try and fail as well. By including this event in
his Gospel, Mark was establishing Jesus' credentials, showing
that even the spiritual underworld recognized Jesus as the Messiah.

DEMONS
A man possessed by a demon was in the synagogue where Jesus was teaching. This man made his way into the place of worship and verbally abused Jesus. It is naive to think that we will be sheltered from evil in the church. Satan is happy to invade our presence wherever and whenever he can. But Jesus' authority is much greater than Satan's; where Jesus is present, demons cannot stay for long. The demons recognized Jesus' credentials and authority. The submission that the demons showed here and in 5:1-10 would have registered with the Romans (Mark's primary audience), who knew and feared the gods of the underworld (Hades).

Compare this view of the demons' encounter with Christ to the false views presented in the fictional media today. Movies show demons as enlarging in power when confronted by the power of Christ and true faith. In reality, demons diminish when they are thus confronted. In movies, demons ridicule and ignore true faith and the authority of Christ. In reality, they have no choice but to succumb.

1:25 But Jesus rebuked him, saying, "Be silent, and come out of him!"^{NRSV} The Greek word translated "rebuke" means to reprove or shame. Jesus judged the demon and then expelled him. He didn't use incantations or magic words; he simply and sternly commanded him to *be silent*—a strong word in the Greek that could mean "to muzzle." The word is used elsewhere for muzzling an ox (for example, 1 Corinthians 9:9 and 1 Timothy 5:18). Mark also used the word in Jesus' command when stilling the storm (4:39). A modern alternative would be "Shut up!"—a colloquial translation that also gives Jesus' attitude toward Satan. The demon was like a boxer, dancing and jabbing to find a weakness; Jesus was the champion who knocked him out with one punch: "Be silent!"

Why did Jesus tell the demon to be silent? Mark portrays Jesus as silencing the demon almost with a tone of insisting on secrecy (see also 1:34). He also commanded some of those he healed not to publicize their healing (see 1:44; 5:43). He even ordered the disciples to keep insights about his true nature and glory to themselves (see 8:27-30; 9:2-9). Two explanations may help us understand why Jesus asked this:

1. Jesus wanted to contain the enthusiasm for a political messiah. He did not wish to be the people's king in the way they desired, nor did he want to be a military leader.

2. To confess Jesus' deity without a proper understanding of his crucifixion is partial and invalid. He did not want people to wildly proclaim him to be God's Son unless they understood the

meaning of his death for them on the cross. This would explain why even his disciples lacked understanding until his resurrection.

EVEN THE DEMONS BELIEVE
Some people want to think that knowing *about* Jesus, or believing in his divinity, is enough for salvation. Here we see that even the demons knew about Jesus and believed in his divinity. As James would later write, "You believe that God is one; you do well. Even the demons believe—and shudder" (James 2:19 NRSV). The knowledge terrified the demons, for it sealed their final doom. But it need not terrify us for we have been offered the gift of salvation in Jesus Christ. Don't stop at the facts—turn to the *person,* Christ, to save you.

To silence the demon was not enough, for Jesus wanted to free the man possessed by the demon. So Jesus next commanded, *Come out of him!* again demonstrating his power and authority over Satan and his demons.

1:26 The evil spirit shook the man violently and came out of him with a shriek.^{NIV} Without any recourse except to submit to a higher authority, the evil spirit *came out* of the man. But first, to show its anger and protest, the evil spirit *shook the man violently.* This could have been a severe spasm or a blow that thrust the man to the ground. With a final shriek, the demon left. The true purpose of demon possession is revealed by this behavior. Demons have a deep-seated desire to do violence and to destroy all who are made in the image of God.

Many psychologists dismiss all accounts of demon possession as a primitive way to describe mental illness. Although throughout history mental illness has often been wrongly diagnosed as demon possession, clearly a hostile outside force controlled the man described here. Mark emphasized Jesus' conflict with evil powers to show his superiority over them, so he recorded many stories about Jesus driving out evil spirits. Jesus didn't have to conduct an elaborate exorcism ritual. His word was enough to send out the demons. Jesus' power over demons reveals his absolute power over Satan, even in a world that seems to be in Satan's control. Satan is presently under God's authority; when God chooses to command, Satan must obey. Satan's workings are only within God's prescribed limits; he can do no more evil than God allows. In the end, Satan and all his demons will be tormented in the lake of fire forever (Revelation 20:10).

WHY EVIL AT ALL?
If God is all-powerful and loves everyone, why is evil not eradicated immediately? The question has puzzled philosophers and theologians for centuries. The Bible's answer is not in the form of tightly wound logic, but in a story. From Genesis to Revelation, the story reveals God's redemption of our sin, his victory over evil through Christ, and the ultimate eradication of evil in God's heavenly kingdom. Sometimes it happens immediately, as it did for this man possessed by an evil spirit. But for most of us, we have to wait for final deliverance until we go to meet him when we die or when Christ returns. When we struggle with tribulations and sorrow now, we must remember that Christ is with us and he has overcome the world.

1:27 The people were all so amazed that they asked each other, "What is this? A new teaching—and with authority! He even gives orders to evil spirits and they obey him."NIV The word "amazed" in the Greek *(ethambethesan)* carries with it a note of fear or alarm. The people were astonished at Jesus' teaching and authority (1:22). Jesus' display of his authority in the showdown with a demon caused a certain terror in the people at what they had witnessed. With a simple and stern command, the evil spirit obeyed and the possessed man was set free.

The people called Jesus' teaching *new;* compared to the dry sermons they usually heard from their scribes, his teaching challenged them. Jesus taught with authority; he spoke to the powerful underworld with authority. Surely this man was someone to watch closely.

1:28 At once his fame began to spread throughout the surrounding region of Galilee.NRSV The people who left the gathering in the large synagogue in Capernaum had witnessed an authoritative and captivating new teacher with unheard-of power. The news spread *at once* across the region of Galilee. Jesus' growing popularity becomes a major theme in chapter 1 (see 1:33, 37, 45). This popularity among the common folk stands in glaring contrast to the religious leaders' opposition expressed in 2:1–3:6.

JESUS HEALS PETER'S MOTHER-IN-LAW AND MANY OTHERS / 1:29-34 / **35**

By this point in chapter 1, even a casual reader can see Mark's jumps in narration expressed by words like "at once," "without delay," "immediately," or "straightway." Most of these translate Mark's repeated use of *euthus* (immediately). The expression heightens the sense of rapid development and excitement in the event being described.

After ending his clash with the demons in the synagogue, Jesus immediately confronted the power of disease. He healed Peter's mother-in-law of a fever. By the time evening arrived, there was a "traffic jam" of the sick and demon possessed, crowding to Jesus for attention. Almost as an afterthought, Mark noted that Jesus was commanding the demons not to identify him. His goal was not to draw attention to himself, but to meet the real needs of others.

1:29 As soon as they left the synagogue, they went with James and John to the home of Simon and Andrew.[NIV] As the crowd hurriedly dispersed from the synagogue or continued talking among themselves, Jesus and the four disciples left for their own lodgings. They arrived at Simon Peter's home, where he lived with his wife (mentioned in 1 Corinthians 9:5), his mother-in-law, and his brother Andrew. Jesus and the disciples probably stayed in Peter's home during their visits to Capernaum (2:1; 3:20; 9:33; 10:10)

1:30 Simon's mother-in-law was in bed with a fever, and they told Jesus about her.[NIV] Simon Peter's wife's mother *was in bed,* meaning she was lying down; the Greek word *katakeimai* could be translated "to lie prostrate." The Greek word for *fever* in the noun form is also the word for fire; thus, she was burning with a severe fever. Luke (the doctor) wrote in his Gospel that she "was suffering from a high fever" (Luke 4:38 NIV).

This short passage reveals many details and carefully includes names (1:29). This is the first of many instances throughout this Gospel implying that Simon Peter may have been Mark's primary source.

It is interesting that Mark records that *they told Jesus.* These three words give us confidence to come to Jesus with our needs and problems. Often we look everywhere else before turning to God. We look for experts and remedies for everything from psychological ailments to financial shortfalls. But God's Word teaches us to tell Jesus. All of our problem-solving strategies need to begin with prayer.

1:31 He came and took her by the hand and lifted her up. Then the fever left her, and she began to serve them.[NRSV] Without speaking a word, Jesus went to the mother-in-law's bedside, *took her by the hand,* and *lifted her up* to her feet. Jesus' touch on the woman's hand brought instant and complete healing, as if she had never been ill. In fact, she went about serving the meal as she had probably planned.

Each Gospel writer had a slightly different perspective as he wrote; thus the comparable stories in the Gospels often highlight different details. In Matthew, Jesus touched the woman's hand. In Mark, he helped her up. In Luke, he spoke to the fever, and it left her. The accounts do not conflict. Each writer chose to emphasize different details of the story in order to emphasize a certain characteristic of Jesus. Mark showed Jesus' victory over Satan (1:12-13), his authority over demons (1:23-26), and his authority even over human illness (1:30-31).

Peter's mother-in-law was healed to serve. Jesus desires that all his disciples be enabled to serve. Yet often we face difficult circumstances with no relief in sight. Peter had obeyed Jesus and left all to follow him; still he had sickness in his family. But Jesus loves us to the end, and he leaves no work half-finished. The fever left Peter's mother-in-law, and she was completely restored by Christ's power so that she could serve. Christ gives renewing grace that strengthens us to serve, enables us to persevere, and encourages us to overcome our doubts.

JUST WAIT
Peter's mother-in-law gives a beautiful example to follow. Her response to Jesus' touch was to wait on Jesus and his disciples—immediately. Has God ever helped you through a dangerous or difficult situation? If so, you should ask yourself, How can I express my gratitude to him? God has promised us all the rewards of his kingdom; we should look for ways to serve him and his followers now.

1:32 At evening, when the sun had set, they brought to Him all who were sick and those who were demon-possessed.[NKJV] The people came to Jesus on Saturday *evening* after sunset. The day had been the Sabbath (1:21), their day of worship and rest, lasting from sunset Friday to sunset Saturday. Jewish law prohibited traveling and carrying burdens on the Sabbath, so they waited until sunset (they needed to first see three stars to know the sun had set). After the sun went down, Sabbath was over, and the people searched for Jesus.

News had spread quickly that the demon-possessed man in the synagogue had been freed from the demon, and the people *brought to [Jesus] all who were sick and those who were demon-possessed.* The Greek word for "brought" is *phero,* meaning "to carry a burden or to move by carrying." Many of the ill people were literally carried to Peter's home so Jesus could heal them. The verb is in the imperfect tense, signifying continuous action. A steady stream of sick and demon-possessed people were carried to Jesus.

1:33 And the whole city was gathered around the door. NRSV With a touch of hyperbole, Mark described the scene in front of Peter's house. The crowd must have been immense so that it appeared that *the whole city* had gathered there. The people who brought the sick, the sick themselves (perhaps on stretchers), and the people who brought the demon possessed settled themselves in front of Peter's house and awaited the touch of the divine healer. The Greek for "gathered" *(episunegmene)* literally means "to go with others and settle down together in a group." This was no unruly mob; the people had come on a mission and were there to stay until their mission was accomplished.

MERELY WATCHING
During this time when Jesus healed the people, there were three kinds of people present: (1) those who needed help; (2) those who brought their friends, neighbors, and loved ones; and (3) those who merely watched. Naturally people would be curious, but many who were attracted by rumors and miracles stopped short of embracing Jesus' spiritual mission and also ignored Jesus' claim on their lives. Don't get caught merely watching the action. Consider what Jesus wants *you* to do.

1:34 And Jesus healed many who had various diseases. NIV Jesus patiently *healed* all the sick people (the word *many* is a Hebrew idiom for "all who were brought," see also Matthew 8:16). Jesus' touch took away Peter's mother-in-law's fever because it could heal any disease. No disease took Jesus by surprise, and no disease was beyond his ability to heal. He healed them all. And as with Peter's mother-in-law, the healings were complete—as though the people had never been sick.

He also drove out many demons, but he would not let the demons speak because they knew who he was. NIV Jesus' authority over the demons continued to be revealed as he *drove out many demons* from the demon-possessed people brought to him. Again, Jesus simply had to command the demon to come out, and it obeyed. However, this time Jesus did not even allow the demons to speak *because they knew who he was* (as the demon-possessed man in the synagogue had proclaimed Jesus as "the Holy One of God," 1:24).

Why did Jesus not allow the demons to speak? (1) By silencing them, Jesus demonstrated his authority and power over them. (2) Jesus wanted the people to believe he was the Messiah because of what he said and did, not because of the demons' words. (3) Jesus wanted to reveal his identity as the Messiah according to his timetable, not according to Satan's timetable. Satan's purposes would be served if the people followed Jesus for what they could get out of him, not because he was the Son of God who could truly set them free from sin's guilt and power. Perhaps some would have preferred Jesus to be merely a healer and miracle worker. The demons called Jesus "the Holy One of God" (1:24) because they knew he was the Christ. But Jesus was going to show himself to be the suffering Servant before he became the great King. It is a recurring theme in Mark's Gospel for Jesus to conceal his true identity. To reveal himself as the Messiah and King too soon would stir up the crowds with the wrong expectations of what he had come to do.

KNOW YOUR AUDIENCE
Jesus prohibited the demons from identifying who he was. In 1:44 he also told those who were healed not to say anything. Jesus knew the waves his message would cause. He knew the anger, the resentment, the misunderstanding that could accompany "blurting out" the gospel. Jesus loved all the listeners, but he wanted them to hear at the right time, at the best place, and with eager hearts. Some people want to blurt out everything they know without a thought to time, place, or the condition of their listener. Take care to know your audience, to listen before speaking, to find words that meet your listeners' heart needs.

JESUS PREACHES THROUGHOUT GALILEE / 1:35-39 / *36*

Jesus had just spent a Sabbath in feverish activity. He had done practically everything except rest. Early in the morning of the next day, he set aside a time of prayer by himself. He spent time in prayer and in silence. Even though he was interrupted, Jesus maintained his intimate fellowship with his Father. By the time the disciples found him, he was ready to face the next challenge.

We must follow Christ's example by carving out time for worship and prayer. Those who help and serve on Sunday especially need to set aside time with God to restore their strength. Our ability to serve will be hindered if we neglect times of spiritual replenishment.

**1:35 In the morning, while it was still very dark, he got up and went
out to a deserted place, and there he prayed.**^{NRSV} Before the sun
came up (*the morning, while it was still very dark* refers to the last
watch of the night, between 3:00 A.M.
and 6:00 A.M.), Jesus *went out to a*
deserted place, the same kind of place
where he had met Satan's temptations
(1:12-13). In that deserted place, alone

> He prayeth best who
> loveth best. *Samuel*
> *Coleridge*

and prior to any other activities, Jesus *prayed.* During his ministry
on earth, Jesus was in constant prayer with the Father. Mark
recorded three of these times of prayer: (1) after the successful ministry in Capernaum with the healing of many sick and demon-possessed people; (2) after the miracle of feeding more than five
thousand people (6:46); (3) in Gethsemane, just prior to his arrest,
trial, and crucifixion (14:32-42).

THE VITAL LINK
Jesus took time to pray. Jesus prayed when he was baptized
(Luke 3:21), when he dealt with the crowds (Luke 5:16), and
when he was transfigured (Luke 9:29). Before choosing the
twelve disciples, Jesus spent the night praying to God (Luke
6:12). When people wanted to make him king, he prayed (Matthew 14:23 and John 6:15). He also prayed for individuals
(Luke 22:32; see also Luke 9:18; 11:1).
  Finding time to pray is not easy, but prayer is the vital link between us and God. If we attempt to live with little or no prayer
in our lives, we may find our grace, strength, and peace dimin-
ished. We need the mind of Christ to serve him. We cannot rely
merely on spontaneous prayer, but must set aside time for prolonged and deeper communication with God. Like Jesus, we
must break away from others to talk with God, even if we have
to get up very early in the morning to do it!

What did Jesus pray about? In Mark 14:35-36, Jesus prayed
for strength from God to fulfill his mission as planned. After his
great successes with the crowds in Capernaum and on the mountainside, his prayers may have focused on fulfilling his mission
as Suffering Servant, when it seemed (at least humanly) more
strategic to be a conquering king. Popularity was a temptation in
itself, for it threatened to turn Jesus away from his mission ("why
I have come," 1:38 NIV). Jesus had a mission to fulfill—and
death on the cross was the key, for only Jesus' death could accomplish salvation. Jesus, in his humanity, may have continued to
face the temptation to turn away from the difficult path and take
the easier one. He constantly needed strength from God. Going

into the wilderness, alone with the Father, helped Jesus focus on his task and gain strength for what that task entailed.

1:36-37 Simon and his companions went to look for him, and when they found him, they exclaimed: "Everyone is looking for you!"^{NIV} Apparently the people in Capernaum continued to arrive at Simon Peter's house the next morning hoping to hear more of Jesus' teaching and see him perform more miracles. When Jesus didn't appear, perhaps people began to knock at Simon Peter's door. When the disciples went to arouse

> A praying master, like Jesus, can have no prayerless servants. *J. C. Ryle*

Jesus, they discovered that he was gone. They were surprised that Jesus would not follow up on his great success from the previous day's ministry in Capernaum, but instead disappeared before anyone awoke. So they *went to look for him* and bring him back. But Jesus had a mission to fulfill and a very limited time to accomplish it. Their words, *Everyone is looking for you,* anticipate the even greater popularity that awaited Jesus when he extended his ministry beyond Capernaum (see 1:45).

REDESIGN

Were the disciples impatient that Jesus prayed in solitude while there was so much ministry to be done? How would you have responded if you had been the one to find Jesus in prayer? It's easy to be so caught up with ministry that we neglect times of solitude, individual worship, and prayer. Perhaps you need to redesign your schedule to find time for earnest prayer.

- Seek the Lord before your busy schedule takes over your thoughts.
- Withdraw from noise and demands so you can focus on God.
- Take Jesus' attitude of regular communion with the Father.
- Reflect on the priorities Jesus had for his life.
- Determine to pray on a more regular basis, not just in times of crisis.

1:38 Jesus replied, "Let us go somewhere else—to the nearby villages—so I can preach there also. That is why I have come."^{NIV} Not only was Jesus not going to capitalize on his great popularity in Capernaum, he was not even going back into the city. Instead, he was leaving on an extended trip throughout the region, beginning with *the nearby villages.* Many people needed to hear Jesus *preach* the Good News of the kingdom of God (1:14-15), as Jesus explained, *"That is why I have come."* Jesus could have simply meant that leaving on a preaching mission was why he had "come" out of Capernaum; or he could have meant that preaching the kingdom of God was why he had "come" to earth. In either case, Jesus would not be deterred from his mission to preach the Good News to as many people as possible. His primary mission was to bring people to a place of decision to have faith in God, not merely to remove their pain. Nevertheless, as Jesus preached, he also healed many people and cast out many demons, as he had in Capernaum.

1:39 And he went throughout Galilee, proclaiming the message in their synagogues and casting out demons.NRSV Jesus and the disciples left the early morning bustle of Capernaum behind and began a preaching and healing tour *throughout Galilee.* The Romans had divided the land of Israel into three separate regions: Galilee, Samaria, and Judea. Galilee was the northernmost region, an area about sixty miles long and thirty miles wide. Jesus did much of his ministry in this area, an ideal place for him to teach because there were over 250 towns concentrated there, with many *synagogues* where Jesus could proclaim his *message,* the Good News. Many of the towns were marketing villages that served the rich agricultural community. The Jewish historian Josephus notes that even the small towns had about fifteen thousand people. Though they were the size of towns, they had the cultural dynamics of villages. Jesus' action of *casting out demons* verified his authority and power and showed compassion to those who had been possessed and, by Jesus' word, had been set free.

JESUS HEALS A MAN WITH LEPROSY / 1:40-45 / **38**

Once the news was out that Jesus could heal diseases, people with serious needs converged from every direction. Mark wrote of Jesus healing a leprous man to show both Jesus' compassion as well as the complications that invaded Christ's ministry.

Perhaps the greatest handicap God accepted in coming to earth was to limit himself to space and time. He was a single individual with divine power in a sea of human needs. Even those he helped, like this man cured of leprosy, hampered Jesus by insisting on telling everyone of Jesus' miraculous power. By so doing, he drew attention to the sensational and miraculous aspect of Jesus' ministry and away from the need for repentance and faith that leads to a life of service.

1:40 A man with leprosy came to him and begged him on his knees, "If you are willing, you can make me clean."NIV *Leprosy* was a terrifying disease because of the social rejection and the devastating impact it had on its victims. And it was incurable. In

Jesus' day, the Greek word for leprosy was used for a variety of similar diseases; some forms were contagious, disfiguring, and/or deadly; some were as innocuous as ringworm. In keeping with the law in Leviticus 13 and 14, Jewish leaders declared people with leprosy (lepers) unclean. This meant that lepers were unfit to participate in any religious or social activity. Because the law said that contact with any unclean

> The chief of sinners may yet be brought near to God by the blood and Spirit of Christ. People are not lost because they are too bad to be saved, but because they will not come to Christ so that he may save them. *J. C. Ryle*

person made that person unclean too, some people even threw rocks at lepers to keep them at a safe distance. Even the mention of the name of this disabling disease terrified people because they were afraid of catching it. Lepers lived together in colonies outside their community. Most would remain there until they died. Sometimes, however, leprosy would go away. Then the person could return to the priest and ask to be declared "clean" before returning to the community.

That this man with leprosy *came to* Jesus reveals the man's great courage; his begging on his knees reveals his desperation and his humility; his words to Jesus reveal his faith. The priest would declare him clean, but only Jesus could make him clean. *"If you are willing"* reveals the man's faith in Jesus' authority in this matter of healing; Jesus' ability was never in question. What this man wanted was to be made *clean,* a huge request. The man wanted to become a person again, to be reunited with his family and community. He knew Jesus could do it. The question was, would he?

A DEADLY DISEASE
Like leprosy, sin is deadly—and we all have it. Only Christ's healing touch can miraculously take away our sins and restore us to real living. But first, just like the leper, we must realize our inability to cure ourselves and ask for Christ's saving help.

1:41 Filled with compassion, Jesus reached out his hand and touched the man.[NIV] Jesus' love and power go hand in hand. Mark revealed Jesus' heart of compassion. While all people shunned lepers, Jesus *reached out his hand and touched* this man covered with a dreaded, contagious disease. The fact that Jesus' touch precedes his pronouncement of healing indicates that Jesus disregarded the Jewish law not to touch a leper (Leviticus 5:3;

13:1-46; Numbers 5:2). This shows Jesus' compassion and his authority over the law.

"I am willing," he said. "Be clean!"NIV Whether lepers had been cleansed prior to this in Jesus' ministry is unrecorded; certainly none were cured in Capernaum, for they would not have been allowed into the town among the crowds. Jesus was probably walking between towns when this man approached him. Mark recorded Jesus healing of various sicknesses and the casting out of demons; here he recorded Jesus compassionately healing a man with a humanly incurable disease. Jesus showed himself both willing and able to meet this man's most basic need. With the words *Be clean!* the leprosy immediately disappeared. The words were simple but effective, revealing Jesus' divine authority over sickness.

1:42 Immediately the leprosy left him, and he was made clean.NRSV We are not told the stage of this man's leprosy—he may already have lost portions of his body to the disease. But when Jesus spoke, the man's health was restored completely. The disease did not go into a type of "remission"—it was gone. The man's becoming *clean* meant he had his life back. He could return to his community, to his family, and to worshiping in the synagogue.

TRUE VALUE
The real value of a person is inside, not outside. Although a person's body may be diseased or deformed, the person inside is no less valuable to God. No person is too disgusting for God's touch. In a sense, we are all people with leprosy because we have all been deformed by the ugliness of sin. But God, by sending his Son, Jesus, has touched us, giving us the opportunity to be healed. When you feel repulsed by someone, stop and remember how God feels about that person—and about you.

1:43-44 Jesus sent him away at once with a strong warning: "See that you don't tell this to anyone."NIV One of the key points in Mark's Gospel is that nothing could deter Jesus from his mission, nor from the urgency of it. Jesus' ministry was to preach the Good News of the kingdom of God—not just to heal people. Jesus always had compassion and did miracles to help those in need, not in order to become wealthy or famous. Thus this man, who probably met him along the road between towns, asked for and received healing. But Jesus *sent him away.* The Greek word for "sent away" literally means "to throw out." Jesus was concerned that the man go immediately and fulfill the law.

"Go, show yourself to the priest and offer the sacrifices that Moses commanded for your cleansing, as a testimony to them."NIV When a leper was cured, he or she had to go to a priest to be examined. Then the leper was to give a thank offering at the temple. Jesus adhered to these laws by sending the man to the priest, thereby demonstrating Jesus' complete regard for God's law. Jesus wanted this man to give his story firsthand to the priest to prove that his leprosy was completely gone so that he could be restored to his family and community. This would be done *as a testimony to them.*

There is debate as to the identification of "them." Some think "them" refers to the priests, not the people who witnessed the healing. People who take this view argue that when the man presented himself to the priest, the priest would have to declare that the man was healed, and the sacrifice would be living proof. Thus, if the priest declared that the healing had taken place but refused to accept the person and power of Christ who had done it, the priest would be self-condemned by the evidence. The word "testimony" is used in 6:11 and 13:9 in this negative sense and implies that the evidence would testify against them on Judgment Day.

On the other hand, there has been no mention yet of priests or of Jesus' challenge to them, so it seems more likely that Jesus intended the testimony to be a positive one to the people. Jesus' meaning would be, "Don't you proclaim it, but let the priest's pronouncement witness for me and for the healing." It would testify to everyone that the man had recovered, that Jesus did not condemn the law, and, most important, that the one who heals lepers had come.

Jesus also gave the man *a strong warning: "See that you don't tell this to anyone."* The warning was an earnest and forceful admonition—words Jesus commanded the man to obey. But why would Jesus ask this man not to tell anyone about his healing? Wouldn't this have been great advertising for Jesus, bringing more people to hear his message? While we might think so, Jesus knew better (John 2:24-25). Jesus' mission, as stated above, was to preach the Good News of the kingdom of God. If crowds descended on him to see miracles accomplished or to benefit from his power, they would not be coming with the heart attitude needed to hear and respond to the gospel. Jesus did not want to be a miracle worker in a sideshow; he wanted to be the Savior of their souls.

1:45 Instead he went out and began to talk freely, spreading the news.NIV The man disobeyed Jesus' strong warning. Perhaps the man thought he was helping Jesus' ministry; perhaps he just couldn't help himself. In any case, he talked freely and constantly (the Greek verb is in the present tense, speaking of continuous talking and spreading the news of his healing). His disobedience to Jesus' command, even if from good motives, hindered Jesus' work because the publicity Jesus received severely hampered his ministry in the synagogue. Mark doesn't say, but the man also might have disobeyed Jesus' command to go to the priest to be declared clean. This would have flamed the jealousy many religious leaders already felt toward Jesus, who seemed to be working against them by his authoritative preaching and growing popularity.

As a result, Jesus could no longer enter a town openly but stayed outside in lonely places.[NIV] Jesus had planned to go into towns throughout Galilee and preach in the synagogues. But his notoriety as a healer made this impossible. Mark recorded that Jesus couldn't enter any town openly—probably crowds of people pressed on him, all seeking special favors. There was no openness to Jesus' message under such conditions. So Jesus *stayed outside in lonely places,* that is, in the wilderness.

Yet the people still came to him from everywhere.[NIV] But the wilderness did not hinder people in need of healing or desiring to see this healer. They "came" (the Greek verb is imperfect, meaning they kept on coming) *from everywhere.*

Mark 2

Chapter 1 draws the battle lines between Jesus and the power of Satan. Chapter 2 introduces a new factor in the conflict: resistance to Jesus by the religious establishment (see 2:1–3:6). The religious leaders, accustomed to giving lip service to the idea of a coming Messiah, found that Jesus threatened their power and prestige. Jesus challenged their authority, questioned their teachings, and trampled on their way of doing business. Mark illustrated their reactions and rejection of Christ with five clashes that form chapter 2 and the beginning of chapter 3.

Jesus could have easily focused on just healing and feeding people. There were plenty of diseases to heal and mouths to feed. But Jesus made it clear that healing and feeding were means, not the ends, of his ministry on earth. He chose a paralyzed man to make his point. Presented with an obvious physical need, Jesus responded by forgiving the man's sins. The religious leaders regarded Jesus' claim as blasphemy because Jesus was assuming the role of God in forgiving sins.

Before they could publicly challenge him, Jesus made a second claim: he would heal the paralyzed man instantly. When the invalid leaped to his feet, the people were amazed. They were stunned by what they had seen but missed what they had heard. The Pharisees were quiet for the moment but certainly far from silenced.

Now, as then, those who approach Jesus with the demand that he fit their preconceived notions will be disappointed. He did not come to be our ally, but our Lord. What we believe must be conformed to his will, for he will never conform to our beliefs.

2:1 A few days later, when Jesus again entered Capernaum, the people heard that he had come home.^{NIV} The phrase "a few days" hardly seems like enough time for Jesus to have completed a tour "throughout Galilee" (1:39). The Greek *di' hemeron* is literally "after days," suggesting any length of time. It makes more sense to assume that after a significant amount of time elapsed, Jesus returned to Capernaum; then, a few days later, *the people* *heard that he had come home.* The people crowded to hear Jesus, but did not change their hearts (Matthew 11:23-24).

Capernaum became Jesus' base of operations while he was in Galilee; thus, Mark referred to this as Jesus' *home* (see 1:14). *Again* refers to his previous visit recorded in 1:21. This home may have been the home he set up there with his mother, Mary, or it may have been Simon Peter's house, where Jesus had stayed on his previous visit to the

> Never were people so favored as the people of Capernaum, and never did people appear to become so hard. Let us beware of walking in their steps. We ought often to use the prayer of the Litany: "From hardness of heart, good Lord, deliver us." J. C. Ryle

city and where he had preached and healed many (1:29-34).

2:2 So many gathered around that there was no longer room for them, not even in front of the door; and he was speaking the word to them.NRSV Mark recorded later in his Gospel that wherever Jesus went, he could not keep his presence a secret (7:24). Such was the case on his return to Capernaum. This time, while Mark did not describe the crowd as "the whole city" (1:33), he explained that *so many* came that they filled the house and spilled out the front door. However, this crowd was different from the crowd he had left behind (1:37-38), for the people were listening as Jesus *was speaking the word to them.* Jesus was not going through the crowd healing sick people; he was speaking, and the people had come to hear his message. Perhaps his abrupt departure from the city at the height of popularity had served to separate the curiosity seekers from those who truly sought the truth.

The Greek word for "speaking" is *laleo* (the word for "preaching" is *kerusso*). In Capernaum that day, Jesus was speaking in a conversational tone to the listeners. The Greek words separate the tone of Jesus' messages—at times he "preached" (proclaiming the Good News); at times he "spoke" (teaching, explaining, conversing). The verb is in the imperfect tense, showing continuous action. Jesus was preaching when the following event occurred.

What Jesus spoke about was *the word*—also called the Good News, or the gospel. The basic message remained the same: The long-awaited Messiah had come to break the power of sin and begin God's personal reign on earth. The miracles Jesus performed served as a sign to Jesus' identity, as well as revealed his compassion and love for the people he had come to save.

2:3 Then some people came, bringing to him a paralyzed man, carried by four of them.NRSV A small group of people also heard that Jesus had returned (2:1). Excited that the man who had healed so many people was back in town (1:34), they determined not to miss him, for they had a friend who needed Jesus' help. Four of these people were *bringing* (that is, carrying) *a paralyzed man.* He was lying on a mat (2:4), and they carried him on this mat to Jesus' home.

This man was fortunate in two ways. He had four friends or relatives to bring him, and he had an affliction that caused him to recognize his need. All of us need Jesus, but many people are "doing quite well by themselves, thank you," so they don't bother to come to him. Maybe our first step should be to find those who recognize their need.

 LATE ARRIVALS
Why did the friends of the paralyzed man wait so long to bring him? Were they working late? involved with family? lazy? Did they wonder if the new teacher was for real? Whatever their reasons, they came and found answers.

Today many people hesitate to bring their needs to Jesus, probably for similar reasons. We do not like to show weakness; we resist depending on others; we protect ourselves from hope aroused and then disappointment.

Jesus' compassion observes no schedule. He will see your need and hear your heart whenever you approach him. Crowded rooms mean nothing to him. But why wait? The Healer is eager to touch you and make you whole.

2:4 Since they could not get him to Jesus because of the crowd, they made an opening in the roof above Jesus and, after digging through it, lowered the mat the paralyzed man was lying on.^{NIV} The crowd had filled the house and the doorway (2:2), so the group *could not get him to Jesus because of the crowd.* The house was so full and the crowd wedged in so tightly that the people could not even move aside to allow this group and the man lying on the mat to pass through in order to get close to Jesus.

But these friends would not be deterred. Determined to get their friend to Jesus, *they made an opening in the roof above Jesus.* They could not get in the front door so they had to find a creative alternative. Hopefully we show as much creativity and perseverance in trying to bring our friends and loved ones to Jesus. In Bible times, houses were built of stone and had outside stairways that led onto flat roofs. Roofs were made with joists covered with a mixture of mortar, tar, ashes, and sand. Thus they had to "dig" through the roof. In addition, some homes had stone slabs underneath the mortar mixture—this was probably the case here, for Luke records that they "lowered him on his mat through the tiles" (Luke 5:19 NIV). These people carried their friend up the stairs to the roof where they dug apart the mortar mixture and pried up as many tiles as necessary. Then they attached ropes to each corner of the pallet and carefully lowered the paralyzed man in front of Jesus.

CROWDING OUT THE NEEDY
The crowd that had gathered made it impossible to bring the paralyzed man close to Jesus. In successful churches or in our busy Christian lives, we can be oblivious to needy people on the outside who want to see Jesus. In some churches, a needy person must forge ahead through crowds of strangers who give no hint of Christian warmth or joy. The people already present can become so preoccupied with their own relationships and agendas that they may not even see those trying to get in.

That should never happen. Where Jesus is present, let the faces of the faithful reflect his love, and let their hands extend to greet all people as friends.

2:5 When Jesus saw their faith, He said to the paralytic, "Son, your sins are forgiven you."^{NKJV} We might expect a popular preacher in the middle of speaking to an expectant crowd to be annoyed at this intrusion. Obviously several minutes were spent as the crowd observed these men who stubbornly refused to give up hope of having their friend healed. Besides, Jesus had already done much healing in Capernaum; he wanted the people to listen to his message. But *Jesus saw their faith* acted out in their determination. If they could but get their friend within Jesus' touch, they knew their friend would be restored.

Jesus and the crowd watched as the hole in the roof became larger, as the ropes were gathered and tied to the mat, and as the men steadied themselves to lower the paralyzed man to Jesus.

Among the first words Jesus said to the paralyzed man were *Son, your sins are forgiven you.* "Son" (Greek *teknon*) was simply a term of affection, used even with adults. Mark's focus in telling this story was not so much on the physical healing as on the spiritual healing given to this man. Several verses in the Old Testament reveal that sickness and death are the consequence of man's sinful condition (see for example Psalms 41:3-4; 103:2-3; and James 5:13-18 for the New Testament parallel). So God works forgiveness and healing together. That does not mean that we can measure a person's spiritual health by looking at his or her physical health. But all sickness and death are the result of evil and sin. This man was paralyzed because of sin in the world and in every human heart—that was the root cause. He also was aware of his own sinfulness. Jesus, perceiving this, spoke first to that condition. The man needed spiritual healing so Jesus forgave his sins. Then Jesus healed the man. We must be careful not to concentrate on God's power to heal physical sickness more than on his power to forgive and heal spiritual sickness in the form of sin. Jesus saw that even more than physical health, this man needed spiritual health. Spiritual health comes only from Jesus' healing touch.

Don't miss the power in the word "forgiven," for the forgiveness given to the paralytic is the same forgiveness offered to all who believe. The Greek word *aphientai,* translated "forgiven," is laden with meaning. It means to leave or let go, to give up a debt, to send away from oneself. When we say we have forgiven a person, we mean that we have renewed our relationship despite the wrong that the person did. But we cannot erase or change the act itself. But the Greek word *aphiemi* goes far beyond our human forgiveness, for it includes the "putting away" of sin in two ways: (1) The law and justice are satisfied, for Jesus paid the penalty our sins deserved—thus they can no longer be held against us; and (2) the guilt caused by our sin is removed and replaced with Christ's righteousness. We are so forgiven that, in God's eyes, it is as if we had never sinned. If Jesus had done this and nothing more, the man should have been satisfied. If Jesus had healed his body and not dealt with his sinful condition, the man would have been ultimately worse.

FAITH-FULL FRIENDS
It wasn't the paralytic's faith that impressed Jesus, but the faith of his friends. Jesus responded to their faith and healed the man. For better or worse, our faith affects others. We cannot make another person a Christian, but we can do much through our words, actions, and love to give him or her a chance to respond. Look for opportunities to bring your friends to the living Christ.

2:6-7 **Now some teachers of the law were sitting there, thinking to themselves, "Why does this fellow talk like that? He's blaspheming! Who can forgive sins but God alone?"**[NIV] These *teachers of the law* (also called scribes) were the legal specialists in Jesus' day. Jesus' teaching and his popularity had led to special investigation by the powerful leaders of the Jewish faith. These teachers had been dispatched from Jerusalem to Capernaum (Luke 5:17) and had made their way into the crowd that filled this house. Jealous of Jesus' popularity and power, these men hoped to find something to criticize or even condemn in Jesus' teaching. When they heard Jesus tell the paralyzed man that his sins were forgiven, they were shocked. For Jesus to claim to forgive sins was considered blasphemy, defined as claiming to be God or to do what only God can do. In Jewish law, blasphemy was punishable by death (Leviticus 24:16). The religious leaders were correct in their statement that only God can forgive sins (Exodus 34:6-7; Psalm 103:3; Isaiah 43:25; Daniel 9:9); the priests merely declared people ritually clean. They also rightly understood that Jesus was claiming to be God. But in labeling Jesus' claim to forgive sins as blasphemous, the religious leaders showed they did not understand that Jesus was *God*. Jesus had God's power and authority to heal bodies and forgive sins. Forgiveness of sins was a sign that the messianic age had come (Isaiah 40:2; Joel 2:32; Micah 7:18-19; Zechariah 13:1). Unfortunately, it did not occur to these Jewish leaders that perhaps this man was their Messiah.

STAND UP, DON'T SIT DOWN
The Pharisees were in a perfect position, sitting where they could observe and criticize. Pharisees were famous for giving criticism (and not so great at working toward spiritually strong solutions). Some sitting Christians follow their example.

Is the music at church too fast or too loud? Is the heat set too high or the sermon too low? Do people aggravate us by their simple habits or personal mannerisms, made wretched in weekly repetition? Does the church always seem to need more money?

The best form of criticism is healthy activism, the kind that gets involved to work with fellow believers toward real progress on common goals—sharing the gospel, helping the needy, building strong and caring disciples of Jesus Christ. But it's much easier to sit and criticize.

2:8 Immediately Jesus knew in his spirit that this was what they were thinking in their hearts, and he said to them, "Why are you thinking these things?"NIV God is all-knowing, and Jesus was God. He had access to all the information; he knew every person's thoughts. Hebrews 4:13 says, "Nothing in all creation is hidden from God's sight. Everything is uncovered and laid bare before the eyes of him to whom we must give account" (NIV). When Jesus became human, he restrained the full use of his powers, yet he could still see each person's heart and mind.

The teachers' *thinking in their hearts* probably focused on the slight ambiguity in Jesus' statement. Had he or had he not claimed to be God? He said the man's sins were forgiven; he may have been claiming the prophetic right of speaking for God, but this didn't necessarily mean that he claimed *to be* God. If they wanted to trap Jesus, the leaders couldn't do so on the basis of this statement because it just wasn't solid enough as evidence.

But nothing got past Jesus, for he *knew in his spirit that this was what they were thinking in their hearts.* Jesus may have read their minds, or he may have read the questions in the expressions on their faces. In any case, their hostility and anger at Jesus' words could not be hidden. Certainly this did not escape the rest of Jesus' audience. Would the teachers of the law respond, or did they, too, believe this man to be the Messiah? Jesus knew the teachers' dilemma and offered to prove his authority.

2:9 "Which is easier: to say to the paralytic, 'Your sins are forgiven,' or to say, 'Get up, take your mat and walk'?"[NIV] The teachers of the law knew about Jesus' ability to heal, and they probably had expected Jesus to immediately heal the paralyzed man. Instead, Jesus forgave the man's sins. To the teachers, this sounded like blasphemy, and it also sounded like an easy out. Anyone can just *say* someone's sins are forgiven, but it would take someone with great power and authority to heal a paralyzed person. Jesus asked them the question that they were asking themselves. He wanted to show that he had the power to forgive sins by showing that he had the power to make a paralytic take up his mat and walk. (In Greek, "start walking and keep on walking" indicates a complete and permanent cure).

GOD'S POWER
The more science discovers about the bigness of the universe and the smallness of the atom, the more God's amazing power becomes evident. The more social scientists probe the complexity of the human person, the more they reveal the awesomeness of God's own character, of which we bear an image. The more Jesus preached, healed people of illness, and forgave sins, the more we see God's compassion. God's power goes beyond our imagination.

That power comes to Christians today through the Holy Spirit. Every church needs more of it, and the more we receive, the more there is to give. Someday, maybe soon, God will break through in power so visible that people who do not believe will be ashamed. We must appropriate that power through prayer and employ it to make the gospel well known, to disciple believers in the faith, and to care for people in God's name. The Bible promises that Jesus, who came once as a man to win our salvation, will come again . . . in power!

2:10-11 **"But that you may know that the Son of Man has authority on earth to forgive sins. . . ."**[NIV] The awkwardness of the wording of these two verses has caused scholars to ponder the words of 2:10. The break in the middle of verse 10 (indicated by ellipses in NIV) and the "he said" break up Jesus' statements. Also, scholars have wondered about Jesus' use of the term "Son of Man" (an Old Testament name for the Messiah) at this early point in his ministry. This was his favorite designation for himself (alluding to Daniel 7:13; see also 2:28), but he used it most often after Peter's confession of faith (recorded in 8:29) and then usually when speaking to his disciples (see 8:31, 38; 9:9, 12, 31; 10:33, 45; 13:26; 14:21, 41, 62). The most likely explanation is that Mark placed this statement (certainly one Jesus could and would have made—even if not in this incident) to explain to his readers his reason for including this story—*that [we] may know that the Son of Man has authority on earth to forgive sins.*

The Greek word for "know" is *oida,* speaking of knowledge beyond a shadow of a doubt. By recording this incident, Mark hoped to prove to his audience beyond any doubt that Jesus was the Messiah. The "power" ascribed to Jesus is *exousia,* that is, delegated authority. The Son of Man has the delegated authority of God the Father to forgive sins. The teachers asked, "Who can forgive sins but God alone?" and the answer is, "No human except one delegated that authority by God himself. And the Son of Man has that authority." However, people cannot "see" sins forgiven; they can see physical healing. Therefore, Jesus turned to the paralytic, still lying on the mat in front of him.

AUTHORITY
God alone has the prerogative to forgive sins, so you can imagine the stir when Jesus assumed that authority . . . and he wasn't bashful about it. His actions communicated, "I'm in charge. Don't be so surprised."

When we share the story of God's love with people today, we introduce them to the only one who can forgive sins, the only one authorized to remove the barrier between us and God. Thousands of people today are certified to perform surgeries, to argue cases at law, and to referee basketball games. Only one is authorized to forgive sins.

When your conscience attacks you, when your doubts undermine your faith, when your problems overwhelm you, recognize Jesus' authority to heal and to forgive.

He said to the paralytic, "I tell you, get up, take your mat and go home."[NIV] With a commanding tone showing that Jesus

KEY CHARACTERISTICS OF CHRIST IN THE GOSPELS

Characteristic	References
Jesus is the Son of God	Matthew 16:15-16; Mark 1:1; Luke 22:70-71
Jesus is God who became human	John 1:1-2, 14; 20:28
Jesus is the Christ, the Messiah	Matthew 26:63-64; Mark 14:61-62; Luke 9:20; John 4:25-26
Jesus came to help sinners	Luke 5:32; Matthew 9:13
Jesus has power to forgive sins	Mark 2:5,9-12; Luke 24:46-47
Jesus has authority over death	Matthew 28:5-6; Mark 5:22-24, 35-42; Luke 24:5-6; John 11:1-44
Jesus has power to give eternal life	John 10:28; 17:2
Jesus healed the sick	Matthew 8:5-13; Mark 1:32-34; Luke 5:12-15; John 9:1-7
Jesus taught with authority	Matthew 7:29; Mark 1:21-22
Jesus was compassionate	Matthew 9:36; Mark 1:41; 8:2
Jesus experienced sorrow	Matthew 26:38; John 11:35
Jesus never disobeyed God	Matthew 3:15; John 8:46

expected to be obeyed immediately, Jesus told the paralytic to *get up,* that is, stand up on your previously useless legs; *take your mat* with arms that may also have been previously useless; and *go home.* The final words emphasize separation. As Jesus had sent away the leper (1:43), he sent away the paralytic. Jesus did not want the healed man to hang around as an advertisement of his power, thus drawing undue attention to it. Jesus' mission was to preach the gospel. His great power served to reveal his authority. Thus Jesus sent the man back to his home with a new life, for Jesus had forgiven his sins.

2:12 **Immediately he arose, took up the bed, and went out in the presence of them all, so that all were amazed and glorified God, saying, "We never saw anything like this!"**[NKJV] The man did not doubt Jesus' words; when Jesus told him to get up, he did so *immediately* because his healing was instantaneous. He obeyed Jesus' words to take his mat and go home (2:11). This he did *in the presence of them all*—including Jesus' critics. It was done in full view with plenty of witnesses. Mark also noted for us that true disciples immediately obey and follow through on Christ's words.

The healing unmistakably showed Jesus' power and authority.

The teachers of the law who questioned Jesus' ability to forgive sins (2:6-7) saw the formerly paralyzed man get up and walk. Jesus' question in 2:9 forced their answer: Jesus had the power to make the paralyzed man walk; thus he also had the authority to forgive his sins.

Jesus "astounded" the people with his teaching (1:22), "amazed" them when he cast the demon out of a man (1:27), and "amazed" them when he healed the paralytic. The amazement recorded here is picked up in Mark's use of a different Greek word for each verb, expressing the intensity of the amazement. The word means "to stand out of" and pictures the people wild with wonder. Their attention was so focused that they noticed nothing else. The people in Capernaum had already seen numerous healings by Jesus on his previous visit. But the crowd's amazement is expressed in Mark's words, they *glorified God,* and in Matthew's record, "they praised God, who had given such authority to men" (Matthew 9:8 NIV). While the religious leaders questioned and debated, the people recognized God's power and realized that Jesus had been given authority by God. His popularity was increasing daily.

JESUS EATS WITH SINNERS AT MATTHEW'S HOUSE / 2:13-17 / **40**

The next clash between Jesus and the religious leaders revolved around the company he kept. Not only had Jesus not separated himself from distasteful characters, he sought them out. Jesus wasn't accused of accepting sinners as his friends; he was charged with befriending sinners.

What a mystifying man Jesus was! He called Matthew to follow him, then visited Matthew in his own home! Jesus met Matthew in Matthew's "world" in order to explain why he had come into our world. The Pharisees who were watching believed that Jesus couldn't possibly affiliate with the "world" without being sullied by the contact. Jesus responded by saying that precisely the opposite was true; contact with him could change the world. In order to accomplish his mission, he knew he had to *be* with those he came to rescue and heal.

Just as Jesus entered the world to save sinners, he still enters sinful human lives to rescue those he loves. If we're sinners, we're on his home visitation list.

2:13 **Jesus went out again beside the sea; the whole crowd gathered around him, and he taught them.**NRSV Jesus left Capernaum and went back *beside the sea* (that is, the Sea of Galilee). A crowd of people *gathered* (the imperfect tense in Greek, meaning "they kept on gathering" or "they kept coming to him"), and Jesus *taught* (again in the imperfect tense, meaning "he kept on teaching" them). While Jesus often spoke in synagogues or homes, he also taught groups of people on hillsides (Matthew 5:1) or on the shore of the Sea of Galilee. The hillsides and sloping shoreline of the Sea of Galilee provided a convenient place for large crowds to gather, sit comfortably, and listen to the teacher standing at the foot of the hill, on the shore, or sometimes on a boat moored in the water (as in Luke 5:3). While the crowds followed, Jesus always taught.

TEACHING TIPS
How did Jesus teach? Did he lecture or prefer dialogue? Did he pronounce truth in categorical terms, or paint pictures of truth like an artist working on a canvas?

Surely Jesus used stories to teach (the Bible calls them parables), and he also used places to best advantage: seashores, hillsides, synagogues. He wasn't afraid to teach concepts that would only be understood much later (concerning his death and resurrection, for example), and he kept his focus. We have no record that he lectured on questions such as What language did Adam and Eve speak? or Where did Cain's wife come from? We have every reason to believe (based on the Bible's record) that Jesus treated his listeners as intelligent, responsible human beings.

Parents who use these teaching methods with children are apt to get a more attentive audience, as are pastors with congregations and Sunday school expositors with their freshly washed cherubs. Teaching is hard work. Following Jesus' example will not make it easy, just more successful.

2:14 As he walked along, he saw Levi son of Alphaeus sitting at the tax collector's booth.[NIV] *Levi* (also called Matthew, and later the author of the Gospel of Matthew) was a Jew who worked for the Romans (specifically for Herod Antipas) as the area's tax collector. He collected taxes from the citizens as well as from merchants passing through town. (Capernaum was a customs post on the caravan route between Damascus to the northeast and the Mediterranean Sea to the west.) Tax collectors were expected to take a commission on the taxes they collected, but most of them overcharged and kept the profits. Thus, tax collectors were hated by most Jews because of their reputation for cheating and because of their support of Rome. A Jew who accepted such an office was excommunicated from the synagogue and shamed his family and friends. Thus a Jewish tax collector was looked down

upon for valuing money over reputation, respectability, purity before God,
and concern for his own people, who
had to pay extremely high taxes to the
imperial power.

> I believe though I do not comprehend, and I hold by faith what I cannot grasp with the mind.
> *Bernard of Clairvaux*

The *tax collector's booth* was an elevated platform or bench. Everyone
knew who Levi was, and anyone passing through the city who
had to pay taxes could find him easily. Levi's tollbooth taxed
commercial goods being transported from the sea to land routes.
Obviously this was not the first time Jesus saw Levi, for Jesus
walked these shores many times. Apparently Jesus observed in
Levi what he could use in his ministry. For example, Levi's attention to detail and careful record-keeping skills can be seen in the
way he wrote the first Gospel. Certainly Levi had seen Jesus
before and, with the crowds, probably had been amazed at this
incredible man.

**"Follow me," Jesus told him, and Levi got up and followed
him.**[NIV] Mark's words emphasize the brevity of Jesus' call and
Levi's radical obedience. The man with leprosy in 1:40-43,
despised by the people, was touched and healed by Jesus. Levi
also was despised by his countrymen, not for a physical disease,
but for his occupation. Jesus also "touched" and "healed" Levi,
rearranging his priorities and choosing him to be one of his disciples.

Jesus' words, "Follow me," are in the imperative mood, meaning this was a command, not an invitation. The Greek word is
akolouthei; Mark used the same word in 1:18 when he wrote that
Simon and Andrew "left their nets and followed Him" (NKJV).
The word is in the present tense, signifying the commencement
and continuation of that action. Jesus called Levi to follow—that
is, to walk the same road. Levi recognized that Jesus wasn't inviting him; Jesus was calling him. So Levi *got up and followed.*

Levi's radical obedience is amazing for the change it would
effect in his life. Already ostracized by family and friends, following Jesus probably made no difference in this regard. But Levi
was probably very wealthy—tax collecting was a lucrative occupation. When Levi walked away from his booth, he snubbed
Rome, Herod Antipas, and a certain lifetime of great wealth. Levi
had been an outcast; now he was *wanted* as a member of a group.
But he would have to learn to live in poverty.

**2:15 And as he sat at dinner in Levi's house, many tax collectors
and sinners were also sitting with Jesus and his disciples—for**

there were many who followed him.^{NRSV} Levi responded as
Jesus would want all his followers to do; he followed his Lord immediately, and he called his friends together to meet him too.
Levi left a lucrative tax-collecting business to follow Jesus. Then
he held a *dinner* for his fellow tax collectors and other notorious
sinners so they also could meet Jesus. Levi, who left behind a
material fortune in order to gain a spiritual fortune, was proud to
be associated with Jesus.

In Levi's house there gathered a crowd that Jesus could not
reach in the synagogues. The tax collectors had been excommunicated. The term "sinners" referred to the common people who
were not learned in the law and did not abide by the rigid standards of the Pharisees. The Pharisees regarded these people as
wicked and opposed to the will of God because they did not
observe the rituals for purity, which enabled them to eat with
others. In any case, Jesus had attracted a following among these
people, for Mark recorded that *there were many who followed
him.* These people gathered at Levi's house, where they knew
they had a welcome, and they too sat with Jesus and his disciples
at dinner and listened to the message this marvelous teacher had
for them.

RESEMBLING LEVI
As a tax collector, Levi enjoyed a small portion of authority and
a relatively large portion of wealth. Levi had lots of friends, all
like him. We can imagine that his children anticipated a privileged education, and that his own prospects for advancement
were good. Any of us would have liked the advantages enjoyed
by Levi.

When Jesus called him, Levi's world changed dramatically.
His life would be marked forever by the events of that day. He
immediately left his work, his financial dreams, and his well-
padded position to follow Jesus. Jesus made demands on
Levi's life, and Levi responded positively.

Jesus also makes demands in our lives. What has Jesus
asked you to change? If he were to visit with you, what would
he ask you to leave behind to follow him?

**2:16 When the teachers of the law who were Pharisees saw him
eating with the "sinners" and tax collectors, they asked his
disciples: "Why does he eat with tax collectors and 'sin-
ners'?"**^{NIV} The *teachers of the law* (also called "scribes") were
the legal specialists of the time. They interpreted the law, but
were especially concerned about the "rules" for life that came to
be as binding as God's written law in the Torah. Many scribes

PROMINENT JEWISH RELIGIOUS AND POLITICAL GROUPS

Name and Selected References	Description	Agreement with Jesus	Disagreement with Jesus
PHARISEES Matthew 5:20 Matthew 23:1-36 Luke 6:2 Luke 7:36-47	Strict group of religious Jews who advocated minute obedience to the Jewish law and traditions. Very influential in the synagogues.	Respected the law; believed in the resurrection of the dead; were committed to obeying God's will.	Rejected Jesus' claim to be Messiah because he did not follow all their traditions and because he associated with notoriously wicked people.
SADDUCEES Matthew 3:7 Matthew 16:11-12 Mark 12:18	Wealthy, upper-class Jewish priestly party. Rejected the authority of the Bible beyond the five books of Moses. Profited from business in the temple. They, along with the Pharisees, were one of the two major parties of the Jewish council.	Showed great respect for the five books of Moses, as well as the sanctity of the temple.	Denied the resurrection of the dead; thought the temple could also be used as a place to transact business.
TEACHERS OF THE LAW (SCRIBES) Matthew 7:29 Mark 2:6 Mark 2:16	Professional interpreters of the law—who especially emphasized the traditions. Many teachers of the law were Pharisees.	Respected the law; were committed to obeying God.	Denied Jesus' authority to reinterpret the law; rejected Jesus as Messiah because he did not obey all of their traditions.
HERODIANS Matthew 22:16 Mark 3:6 Mark 12:13	A Jewish political party of King Herod's supporters.	Unknown. In the Gospels they tried to trap Jesus with questions and plotted to kill him.	Afraid of Jesus causing political instability; saw Jesus as a threat to their political future at a time when they were trying to regain from Rome some of their lost political power.
ZEALOTS Luke 6:15 Acts 1:13	A fiercely dedicated group of Jewish patriots determined to end Roman rule in Israel.	Were concerned about the future of Israel; believed in the Messiah but did not recognize Jesus as the One sent by God.	Believed that the Messiah must be a political leader who would deliver Israel from Roman occupation.
ESSENES none	Jewish monastic group practicing ritual purity and personal holiness.	Emphasized justice, honesty, commitment.	Believed ceremonial rituals made them righteous.

were also *Pharisees*—a strict religious group of Jews who also advocated minute obedience to the Jewish laws and traditions. Their job was to teach the Scriptures and the Law and to protect them against anyone's willful defiance. They saw themselves as righteous and everyone else as sinners.

Then along came this man, Jesus, who was popular, taught with great authority from the Scriptures, claimed to speak for God himself, and yet ignored their laws and seemed to condone sin by keeping company with sinners. They watched Jesus, followed his every move, and their anger continued to boil as he flouted their man-made rules, which they often elevated above the laws of God (see, for example, 7:8-13)!

The Pharisees, so strict in their observance of their laws as they attempted to retain their "purity," refused to eat with common people because the sins of the commoners might make them ceremonially impure. So when Jesus sat down to a meal with these *"sinners" and tax collectors,* the Pharisees were quite surprised. Here was a man who seemed to have the entire law at his fingertips, who taught with great authority, yet who stooped to the level of the poor, unlearned, common people (even sinners!). Thus the Pharisees pulled his disciples aside and asked why Jesus did this.

2:17 When Jesus heard it, He said to them, "Those who are well have no need of a physician, but those who are sick. I did not come to call the righteous, but sinners, to repentance."^{NKJV}
The question apparently made its way to Jesus' ears, and Jesus had an answer for the self-righteous, influential religious leaders. The first part of Jesus' answer was from a common proverb on the healthy and the sick. People who are well don't seek out a physician; the physician's waiting room is filled with people who are sick. They recognize their need and come to the one who can make them well. The physician, in turn, spends his time helping the sick get well.

> If you find someone who does not have the joy of faith but is weak of faith and seeks comfort, do not reject him but comfort him in the promised grace of Christ . . . firm, certain, eternal.
> *Johann Arndt*

Jesus carried the proverb a step further and explained his messianic mission. "No," he was saying to his detractors, "I do not spend time with such people because I am a glutton and a sinner at heart—far from it. I am here because these are the people who realize their need and welcome me." Jesus did not come to *call the righteous* (used ironically—those, like these Pharisees, who *thought* they were righteous) to repentance, for the self-

righteous did not recognize their sinfulness. But these *sinners*
saw their need. This was Jesus' audience. Jesus, the Great Physician, healed people of physical illnesses, but he knew that all
people are spiritually sick and in need of salvation. Luke
recorded Jesus' words about his mission as, "For the Son of Man
came to seek out and to save the lost" (Luke 19:10 NRSV).

GOOD ENOUGH?
The Pharisees wrapped their sin in respectability. They made
themselves appear good by publicly doing good works and
pointing at the sins of others. Jesus chose to spend time, not
with these proud, self-righteous religious leaders, but with
people who sensed their own sin and knew that they were not
good enough for God. In order to come to God, we must
repent; in order to renounce our sin, we must recognize it for
what it is.

RELIGIOUS LEADERS ASK JESUS ABOUT FASTING / 2:18-22 / 41

The Pharisees had almost constant skirmishes with Jesus. While
this exchange probably did not happen at Matthew's party, the
holy freedom exercised by Jesus and the restrictive views of the
religious leaders create an effective literary contrast.

At every turn, Jesus challenged the Pharisees' way of looking
at life. They lived by appearance; he challenged motives. They
constructed elaborate behavior patterns to indicate their holiness;
Jesus taught that good actions done for the wrong reasons have
no moral or spiritual effect.

In response to their questions about fasting, Jesus turned the
discussion from proper behavior to the reasons for fasting. Jesus
made it clear that fasting was not a self-justifying action. It was
right in its proper place, but there was also a proper place for
feasting and joy. To further underscore this truth, Jesus added two
other analogies (clothing repair and wineskin care). A worn item
of clothing cannot be repaired with a new piece of cloth that
shrinks when washed. A well-stretched wineskin filled with new
wine will expand and burst when the wine ferments. So also the
new spiritual age brought by Christ would burst the confines of
the old system.

2:18 Now John's disciples and the Pharisees were fasting.^{NIV} *John's*
disciples refers to the remaining disciples of John the Baptist.
These men and *the Pharisees* were fasting—that is, they were

going without food in order to spend time in prayer repenting and humbling themselves before God. The Old Testament law set aside only one day a year as a required day of fasting for all Jews—the Day of Atonement (Leviticus 16:29). The Pharisees, however, fasted on Mondays and Thursdays (see Luke 18:12) as an act of piety, and most likely promoted this among the people.

The tense of the verb indicates that the feast at Levi's house happened at the very time that these people were fasting, apparently on one of the weekly fasting days. John the Baptist was in prison, and these disciples erroneously sided with the Pharisees on this issue, fasting when they should have been feasting with Jesus. Naturally this caused a question: **Some people came and asked Jesus, "How is it that John's disciples and the disciples of the Pharisees are fasting, but yours are not?"**NIV

2:19 Jesus said to them, "The wedding guests cannot fast while the bridegroom is with them, can they? As long as they have the bridegroom with them, they cannot fast."NRSV The Pharisees fasted as a show of piety; the disciples of John the Baptist fasted as a sign of mourning for sin and to prepare for the Messiah's coming. But, like Jesus' disciples, they did not need to fast because the Messiah was with them! To be with Jesus the bridegroom is as joyous as a wedding feast. Wedding guests do not mourn or fast; a wedding is a time of celebration and feasting. Likewise, Jesus' coming was a sign of celebration, not mourning and fasting. Jesus did not condemn fasting—he himself fasted (Luke 4:2). He emphasized that fasting must be done at the right time for the right reasons.

2:20 "But the time will come when the bridegroom will be taken from them, and on that day they will fast."NIV In the Bible, people were expected to fast in times of disaster and as a sign of their humility and repentance. Fasting represented mourning. During that time, the people approached God with humility and sorrow for sin. Fasting focused their attention on God and demonstrated their change of heart and their true devotion (see, for example, Judges 20:26; 1 Kings 21:27; Ezra 8:21; Joel 1:14; Jonah 3:5). While Jesus walked the earth, his presence was a cause for celebration—the Messiah had come! The people did not need to mourn, they needed to rejoice.

But Jesus knew that soon he *(the bridegroom)* would be *taken from them.* The Greek word translated "taken from" is *aparthe*; a similar verb is used in the Septuagint version of Isaiah 53:8, a verse prophesying the Messiah's violent death. *That day* refers to the day of Jesus' crucifixion. On *that day,* Jesus' disciples would

indeed fast and mourn. John 16:20 says, "You will weep and
mourn while the world rejoices. You will grieve, but your grief
will turn to joy" (NIV). The disciples would grieve for their crucified Master, and the world (the mass of people opposed to Jesus)
would rejoice. But the disciples' grief would not last long; their
sorrow would turn to joy when they saw their risen Lord.

FASTING
Jesus did not condemn fasting. He himself fasted for forty days
(Matthew 4:2). Fasting—going without food in order to spend
time in prayer—is both worthwhile and difficult. It gives us time
to pray that we would otherwise use to eat and talk with others.
It teaches self-discipline and reminds us that we can do with a
lot less food. Jesus wants us to discipline ourselves quietly and
sincerely, not for show. Hunger reinforces our need for dependence on God, and some feel it clears the mind to seek God's
will. Whether or not we choose to go with less food or no food
for short periods of time, we all need to find ways to devote ourselves to prayer.

2:21 **"No one sews a piece of unshrunk cloth on an old garment; or
else the new piece pulls away from the old, and the tear is
made worse."**^{NKJV} Jesus' arrival on earth ushered in a new time, a
new covenant between God and people. The new covenant called
for a new way of expressing personal faith. The newness of the
gospel and its relationship to people could not be combined with
the religion of Judaism any more than a piece of *unshrunk cloth*
should be used as a patch on a worn-out garment. When the garment is washed, the patch will shrink, pull away from the old garment, and leave a bigger hole than before.

The gospel offered grace; Judaism offered law and rule keeping. The Christian church was never meant to be a sect of Judaism; rather, Christianity is the fulfillment of Judaism. The Jews,
patiently waiting for their Messiah, should have recognized Jesus
as the Messiah and should have believed the Good News. The
apostle John wrote, "The law was given through Moses, but
grace and truth came through Jesus Christ" (John 1:17 NKJV).
Both law and grace express God's nature—Moses' law emphasized God's law and justice; Jesus Christ came to express God's
mercy, love, and forgiveness. Moses could only give the law;
Christ came to fulfill the law perfectly (Matthew 5:17). The law
reveals the nature and will of God; Jesus Christ reveals the nature
and will of God. But while the law could only point out sin and
condemn us, Jesus Christ gave his life to bring us forgiveness of
sin and salvation. The parables of the cloth and the wineskins

(2:22) apply to more than just fasting or to the Pharisees; they speak of Jesus' entire mission and the new era he inaugurated by his entrance into human history.

A FRESH START
Jesus did not come to patch up the old religious system of Judaism with its rules and traditions. His purpose was to fulfill it and start something new, though it had been prophesied for centuries. Jesus Christ, God's Son, came to earth to offer all people forgiveness of sins and reconciliation with God. The gospel did not fit into the old rigid legalistic system of religion. It needed a fresh start. The message will always remain "new" because it must be accepted and applied in every generation. When we follow Christ, we must be prepared for new ways to live, new ways to look at people, and new ways to serve.

2:22 **"And no one puts new wine into old wineskins; or else the new wine bursts the wineskins, the wine is spilled, and the wineskins are ruined. But new wine must be put into new wineskins."**^{NKJV} In Bible times, wine was not kept in glass bottles, but in goatskins sewn around the edges to form watertight bags called *wineskins.* New wine expanded as it fermented, stretching its wineskin. After the wine had aged, the *old wineskin* (that had gotten brittle with age and couldn't stretch anymore) would burst if more new wine was poured into it. *New wine,* therefore, was always put into *new wineskins.*

Like old wineskins, the Pharisees and indeed the entire religious system of Judaism were too rigid to accept Jesus, who could not be contained in their traditions or rules. They were the self-appointed guardians of the "old garments" and the "old wineskins." Christianity required new approaches and new structures. Our church programs and ministries should not be so structured that they have no room for a fresh touch of the Spirit, a new method, or a new idea. We, too, must be careful that our heart does not become so rigid that it prevents us from accepting the new way of thinking that Christ brings. We need to keep our heart pliable so we can accept Jesus' life-changing message.

THE DISCIPLES PICK WHEAT ON THE SABBATH / 2:23-28 / **45**

Jewish life in Jesus' day revolved around the Sabbath. Elaborate laws had been designed so that everyone knew exactly how to "keep the Sabbath." It was difficult for Jews to get any rest on the seventh day because they were so busy making sure they didn't do any "work." The fourth clash between Jesus and the power of Satan recorded by Mark occurred on a Sabbath. Jesus and his disciples took a Sabbath afternoon stroll, pausing for a grain snack in a farmer's field along the way. On any other day, this would have been acceptable (Deuteronomy 23:25). But on the Sabbath, said the religious teachers, this kind of snacking was unlawful because it required you to *pick* the grain off the stock and was, therefore, work. Although not working themselves, the Pharisees were clearly on the job, confronting Jesus with his disciples' behavior. They must have expected to put Jesus on the defensive. Instead, he refuted both their accusation and their whole interpretation of the Sabbath.

The way Jesus kept the Sabbath irritated his critics to the point of fury. To us, their reaction seems overstated. We must remember that the religious leaders, by imposing a bewildering system of Sabbath laws, had in fact made themselves lords of the Sabbath and thus lords over the people. They made the seventh day dreaded rather than enjoyed.

By claiming the title of Lord of the Sabbath, Jesus was stating his own divinity. But this claim was also an affront to the position of the religious leaders. His remaking the Sabbath into a day of refreshment, worship, and healing pried open the tight-fisted control the Pharisees held on the people. No wonder Jesus' approach to the Sabbath led his enemies to plot his death.

2:23 One Sabbath Jesus was going through the grainfields, and as his disciples walked along, they began to pick some heads of grain.NIV Mark prepares us for a conflict with the opening words, *one Sabbath.* Jesus, determined not to be confined to the Pharisees' petty rules, always seemed to be doing something against those rules on the Sabbath. Mark continued to highlight the growing animosity of the religious leaders against Jesus.

2:24 The Pharisees said to him, "Look, why are they doing what is unlawful on the Sabbath?"NIV The Pharisees had established thirty-nine categories of actions forbidden on the Sabbath, based on interpretations of God's law and on Jewish custom. Harvesting was one of those forbidden actions; traveling any distance was another. By walking along and picking some heads of grain to rub in their hands to eat, the disciples were technically harvesting, according to the religious leaders. Jesus and the disciples were picking grain because they were hungry (as recorded in Matthew 12:1), not because they wanted to harvest the grain for a profit. The disciples, who were not farmers, were not doing their daily work on the Sabbath. Nei-

ther were they stealing grain, for God's law allowed for this
kind of sharing among his people (see Deuteronomy 23:25).
Thus, though they may have been violating the Pharisees' rules,
they were not breaking any divine law. The Pharisees, however,
could not (and did not want to) see beyond their law's technicalities. The disciples, not being learned in all the details of the
law, seemed all the more ignorant to these self-righteous leaders, thus making it less possible for Jesus to be any sort of valuable teacher and leader.

**2:25-26 And he said to them, "Have you never read what David did
when he and his companions were hungry and in need of
food? He entered the house of God,
when Abiathar was high priest, and
ate the bread of the Presence, which
it is not lawful for any but the
priests to eat, and he gave some to
his companions."**NRSV This story is
recorded in 1 Samuel 21:1-6. Each
week twelve consecrated loaves of
bread, representing the twelve tribes
of Israel, were placed on a table in the
house of God, here meaning the tabernacle. This bread was
called the *bread of the Presence* (or shewbread). After its use in
the temple, it was to be eaten only by priests. On one occasion,
when fleeing from Saul, David and his men were given this consecrated bread to eat by Abiathar, the high priest. (First Samuel
21:1 mentions Ahimelech as the high priest. Abiathar was Ahimelech's son and successor. Jesus obviously knew that Ahimelech was the high priest. Jesus was using a rabbinical method of
referring to a section of Scripture. In this section, Abiathar was
a more prominent name. Abiathar may have been in training at
the time and also involved in the incident.) The priest understood that the men's need was more important than ceremonial
regulations. The loaves given to David were the old loaves that
had just been replaced with fresh ones. Although the priests
were the only ones allowed to eat this bread, God did not punish David because his need for food was more important than
the priestly regulations.

The Pharisees knew the Scriptures thoroughly, yet Jesus' question, *"Have you never read"* reveals their ignorance of the true
meaning of the Scriptures that they claimed to know so well. Yes,
they had read this story many times, but they had obviously not
discerned or applied its meaning. Jesus justified his disciples'
action on the grounds that they were hungry and that their need

> Do all the good you can,
> By all the means you can,
> In all the ways you can,
> In all the places you can,
> At all the times you can,
> To all the people you can
> As long as ever. . .
> . . . you can! *John Wesley*

superseded the technicalities of ceremonial law. When Jesus compared himself and his disciples to David and his men, Jesus was saying, in effect, "If you condemn me, you must also condemn David." Jesus was not condoning disobedience to God's laws. Instead, he was emphasizing discernment and compassion in enforcing the ceremonial laws, something the self-righteous Pharisees did not comprehend. People's needs are more important than technicalities.

 HOW TO READ
Sometimes we read for information only, sometimes for pleasure, and sometimes for understanding. Reading the Bible for information only is to use it like a telephone book or encyclopedia. Becoming an expert in Bible trivia is a novelty, but it doesn't change anything for the better. Reading the Bible for pleasure only is to use it like a comic book—diversion, titillation, escape. Eventually you must put it down and get back to real life. Reading the Bible for understanding (which always includes information and may well include pleasure) means you are engaged with it, responsive to it, accountable for what you learn, open to new directions. This reading strengthens faith.

2:27 And He said to them, "The Sabbath was made for man, and not man for the Sabbath."NKJV The Pharisees, having added all kinds of restrictions for the Sabbath, had completely forgotten God's purpose in creating the Sabbath. God mercifully provided the Sabbath as a day of rest for his people—a day to set aside the normal duties of the workweek and spend time resting and worshiping (Genesis 2:1-3). But the Pharisees had only succeeded in making the Sabbath an impossible burden. While the Ten Commandments do prohibit work on the Sabbath (Exodus 20:8-11), "work" can be construed in many ways. One person's "work" is another person's leisure. Some work is necessary for worship; for example, the priests were allowed to work by performing sacrifices and conducting worship services. This "work" was serving and worshiping God. The prohibition of work is the letter of the law. Jesus always emphasized the intent of the law, the meaning behind the letter. The Pharisees had lost the spirit of the law and were rigidly demanding that the letter (and their interpretation of it) be obeyed. Jesus made clear that the Sabbath was created for people by their merciful God, providing them a day of rest. God did not create people in order to place impossible restrictions and burdens on their lives.

WITH EYES OF LOVE
We do not know what motives the Pharisees had for pursuing such legalistic interpretations of the law. Were they selfish men who wanted to control others with tight regulations? Were they archconservatives who wanted to maintain religious practice the way it had been done for centuries? Were they driven to protect the high honor of God and the purity of their traditions? We don't know, but it is clear that they had forgotten God's love and compassion.

Christians today must be careful not to impose harsher restrictions on the gospel than the Bible requires. We must not add rules, programs, or policies that make following Christ a burden for people. Be sure that God's love and grace come through in all your dealings with people.

2:28 "Therefore the Son of Man is also Lord of the Sabbath."NKJV
Whether Jesus actually said these words, or whether this is another editorial phrase added by Mark (as in the previous use of "Son of Man" in 2:10-11) is a question debated by scholars. In any case, Mark made the point Jesus would and could have made. Who created the Sabbath? God did. *Therefore,* because Jesus, the *Son of Man,* is God's Son, given authority and power by God himself, then he *is also Lord of the Sabbath.*

When Jesus said he was Lord of the Sabbath, he claimed to be greater than the law and above the law. To the Pharisees, this was heresy. They did not realize that Jesus, the divine Son of God, had created the Sabbath. The Creator is always greater than the creation; thus Jesus had the authority to overrule their traditions and regulations.

The "new wine" of the gospel, representing the entrance of the Messiah into history, could not be contained in the old traditions of the Pharisees any more than the new wine could be placed in old wineskins (2:21-22). The new kingdom brought an entirely new relationship between God and people, an attitude of joy and fulfillment, not burdensome restrictions. The ceremonial Sabbath rules simply did not apply when held against the needs of people. Christ brought something entirely new, and he had the power to decide when the rules could be overturned. The first incident recorded in chapter 3 illustrates Jesus' point further.

Mark 3

JESUS HEALS A MAN'S HAND ON THE SABBATH / 3:1-6 / 46

This episode completes a set of five escalating confrontations between Jesus and the religious leaders. Together they summarize the points of tension leading to Jesus' rejection. Jesus committed the following "indiscretions":

- He spoke as though he were God because he forgave sins (2:1-12).

- He consorted with known sinners (2:13-17).

- He dared to question long-standing traditions like required fasting (2:18-22).

- He refused to call picking grain on the Sabbath an act of work (2:23-28).

The Pharisees were watching Jesus' actions on the Sabbath, anticipating that he might do something that would allow them to condemn him. Jesus thwarted their plan by involving them in the decision to heal the man. Their anger drove the Pharisees to break the Sabbath by plotting Jesus' murder. They committed the very sin they wanted to pin on him.

> We still build our sanctuaries, and set up our standards, and institute our arrangements, and say to the sinning ones; If you will come to us, we will help you! The way of the Lord is to go and sit where they sit, without patronage and without contempt. . . . I am afraid, however, that the Church is not often criticized on these lines. *G. Campbell Morgan*

3:1 Again he entered the synagogue, and a man was there who had a withered hand.NRSV As was his regular custom (noted by the word "again"), Jesus went to the synagogue on the Sabbath (see 3:2). The definite article "the" is not present in the Greek, so this could be any synagogue in Galilee, although it was most likely in Capernaum (1:21). As Jesus entered, he saw a man *who had a withered hand.* He may have been born with this defect or acquired it by an accident or disease. In any case, the hand was

useless. Luke adds the detail that it was the man's right hand
(Luke 6:6).

**3:2 Some of them were looking for a reason to accuse Jesus, so
they watched him closely to see if he would heal him on the
Sabbath.**[NIV] *Some of them* refers to the Pharisees (3:6). These
men were following Jesus everywhere, *looking for a reason to
accuse* him (see 2:6-7, 16, 24). In this particular situation, they
watched Jesus' encounter with the man who had a withered hand.
As they followed Jesus, the Pharisees made sure to stay aloof
from the crowd. They were there, but they were separate. They
were spying on Jesus with the intention of finding some fault in
his actions that would discredit his claim as the Messiah.

WATCH HIM FALL
The religious leaders were scrutinizing Jesus' every action, hoping to trap him. They wanted to get rid of him. Many churches
today have lots of people ready to take up the job of accusing
their pastor. While no pastor should assume the authority of
Christ, we must be careful not to criticize unfairly. Pet peeves,
personal preferences, or desires for a certain style of pastor
should not cause us to reject a pastor. Don't take part in conversations that are merely gossip or faultfinding. Avoid problem
gathering where faults are recorded and respect is forgotten.

Jesus' reputation for healing (even on the Sabbath, see 1:21-
26) preceded him, but would he dare heal on the Sabbath with the
Pharisees watching? God's law prohibited work on the seventh
day of the week (Exodus 31:14-17); thus, the religious leaders
allowed no healing to be done on the Sabbath unless the person's
life was in danger. Healing, they argued, was practicing medicine, and a person could not practice his or her profession on the
Sabbath.

The Pharisees did not see a man in need; they saw only an
opportunity to accuse Jesus as a Sabbath-breaker. It was more
important for them to protect their laws than to free a person
from suffering. The man's condition was not life threatening; he
could have waited until the next day to be healed—Jesus could
have told the man to see him the next day for healing. But Jesus,
as Lord of the Sabbath, had the authority to overrule the Pharisees' traditions and regulations.

God's law for the Sabbath was never meant to keep people in
bondage. When Jesus saw a need, he filled it, no matter what day
it was. Healing the man not only revealed Jesus' authority over
the Sabbath but showed that in the new kingdom, every day is

holy, that salvation and healing can come to anyone on any day. The Sabbath, while an important day given to God's people as a day of rest and worship, was also a day to be merciful and kind to those in need. And that is exactly what Jesus intended to show the Pharisees when he spoke to the man.

In Matthew's account, the Pharisees directly asked Jesus whether or not it was lawful to heal on the Sabbath. Jesus answered, "Suppose one of you has only one sheep and it falls into a pit on the sabbath; will you not lay hold of it and lift it out? How much more valuable is a human being than a sheep! So it is lawful to do good on the sabbath" (Matthew 12:11-12 NRSV).

WHO'S WATCHING?
Famous people have always had to endure the watching eye of the crowd. News media and rumor mills plague their lives. People were constantly reporting on Jesus' religious opinions and observing his moral behavior. They were looking for a way to trip him up and discredit him. Not every Christian is famous or under the scrutiny of the news media, but people are watching to see if we really believe what we say we do. People are watching, and curious watchers become eager listeners. Living faith will draw a crowd. Witness to God's truth and power by your robust living (worshiping God and serving people) and humble, clear speech (sharing the message, the Good News).

3:3 He said to the man who had the withered hand, "Come forward."NRSV Jesus didn't avoid a confrontation with his adversaries; instead, he made a public display of this healing. Jesus needed to make the important point that he would not be bound by the Pharisees' burdensome laws and that, as God, he would perform an act of kindness and healing, even on the Sabbath. So Jesus commanded the man with the withered hand to *"Come forward"* to the center of the crowd so everyone could see him and his deformity. The Pharisees would not miss anything of what Jesus was about to do.

3:4 Then He said to them, "Is it lawful on the Sabbath to do good or to do evil, to save life or to kill?" But they kept silent.NKJV Actually, the Pharisees could have given an answer because they knew that it was lawful to heal on the Sabbath if someone's disease was life threatening. In this case, the man's disease wasn't endangering his life; so it is remarkable that the Pharisees remained silent.

To Jesus it didn't matter that this man's life was not threatened by the condition of his hand; it didn't matter that he could have waited until the next day to perform this healing legally. If Jesus had waited until another day, he would have been submitting to the Pharisees' authority, showing that their petty rules were equal to God's law. If he healed the man on the Sabbath, the Pharisees could claim that because Jesus broke their rules, his power was not from God. But Jesus revealed clearly that their rules were ridiculous and petty. God is a God of people, not of rules. The best time to reach out to someone is when he or she needs help.

DIVINE HEALING
Every religion has a way to try to make sick people well. Some use potions, dances, and magical offerings; others deny sickness altogether and declare everyone healthy (albeit with different levels of awareness).
　　Jesus healed with a simple word. Nothing fancy or dramatic. No fireworks; no elaborate emotional preparation; no hype. Christians should not despise medical science because all knowledge is a gift of God. But when we pray for healing, the only requirement is faith that God will command the body's chemistry according to his will. God's power does not need a grandiose stage set. Beware the healer who comes to town with publicity agents. If you're sick, get to the healer who merely gives a word. He is Jesus.

So Jesus asked a rhetorical question: *"Is it lawful on the Sabbath to do good or to do evil, to save life or to kill?"* But the Pharisees *kept silent,* for to answer would have left them without an accusation to pin on Jesus. Their own laws allowed people to do good and to save life on the Sabbath—the farmer who could rescue his only lamb from a pit on the Sabbath knew that. How absurd, then, to refuse to allow a person to do good to another person on the Sabbath. The Pharisees, by their silence, showed that they were refusing to debate with Jesus. They saw only the legal obligations; Jesus looked from his perspective of authority and morality. They were on different ground and refused to budge. The verb "kept silent" is imperfect, meaning that they kept on being quiet. In other words, Jesus asked his question and then allowed for an embarrassingly long silence on their part.

3:5 **He looked around at them in anger and, deeply distressed at their stubborn hearts, said to the man, "Stretch out your hand."**[NIV] The religious leaders, the guardians of the Jewish faith, the keepers of the law, the teachers of the people—these men with *their stubborn hearts* were so spiritually and morally blind and hardened that they could not see who Jesus really was, and they could not even acknowledge a man's need and rejoice in his healing. No wonder Jesus was angry and distressed. Jesus looked at the stubborn Pharisees with anger (divine justice) and distress or grief (divine love).

RELIGIOUS RULES
Christian faith involves rules that are meant to be governed by love. That makes love the highest rule, but it also moves Christians toward personal sacrifice, discipline, and responsibility—scarce resources in today's world.
   Does love govern the rules you follow? Ask yourself:
   1. Does the rule serve God's purposes?
   2. Does the rule reveal God's character—mercy, justice, and compassion?
   3. Does the rule help people get into God's family, or keep people out?
   4. Does the rule have strong biblical roots?
   Good rules pass all four tests.

"Stubborn hearts" is also translated "hard-hearted" or "hardness of heart." The Pharisees exhibited this, and it greatly angered and grieved Jesus; many Jews were hard-hearted in their refusal to believe in Jesus (John 12:37-40); and even his disciples at times revealed hard hearts in their lack of understanding (6:52; 16:14). Hard-heartedness generally refers to a callous and uncaring attitude. To the Jews, it meant a stubborn refusal to submit to God's will, a persistent resistance to his call. Hard-heartedness can be dangerous, for it is rooted in pride and can lead a person away from God. It is the very opposite of servanthood. This explains Jesus' anger and grief at the hard-heartedness of these religious leaders.

But the Pharisees' stubbornness didn't matter. Jesus planned to make his point and to kindly heal this man. So Jesus told the man to stretch out his hand.

He stretched it out, and his hand was completely restored.[NIV] In response to Jesus' command and with all eyes focused on him, the man stretched his hand out in front of him. The moment he did so, *his hand was completely restored*; that is, it became like it had been before. As with the leper (1:42) and the paralytic (2:11-12), Jesus gave this man his life back. He could work again, and he no longer had to face the embarrassment of his deformity.

No particular action of Jesus is recorded; he told the man to move and with that movement, healing arrived. Jesus did nothing that could be called "work," but the Pharisees would not be swayed from their purpose. Jesus had embarrassed them. He had overruled their authority (Luke 6:11) and had exposed their evil

attitudes in front of the entire crowd in the synagogue, showing
that the Pharisees were more loyal to their religious system than
to God. That was enough to cause them to get on with their mission of destruction.

CONSTRUCTIVE SOLUTIONS
Jesus was angry about the Pharisees' uncaring attitudes.
Anger itself is not wrong. It depends on what makes us angry
and what we do with our anger. Too often we express our anger
in selfish and harmful ways. By contrast, Jesus expressed his
anger by correcting a problem—healing the man's hand. Use
your anger to find constructive solutions rather than to tear
people down.

**3:6 Then the Pharisees went out and immediately plotted with
the Herodians against Him, how they might destroy Him.**NKJV
The *Pharisees* were outraged. Jesus had openly confronted their
authority and placed himself above them. Their curiosity about
Jesus turned to hatred because he had challenged and exposed
their proud attitudes and dishonorable motives. In their fury, the
only option they saw was to *destroy Him.* Ironically, the Pharisees had accused Jesus of breaking their law about healing on the
Sabbath, yet they themselves were planning to kill him. Their
hatred, combined with their zeal for the law, drove them to plot
murder—an act that was clearly against the law. Among the Gospel writers, Mark is the only one to point out that the leaders
began to plot Jesus' murder shortly after his ministry began.

In an unlikely alliance, the Pharisees *plotted with the Herodians.* The Herodians were a Jewish political party that hoped to restore Herod the Great's line to the throne. Thus their support of
Rome's leadership over Palestine brought them into direct conflict with the Jewish religious leaders. The Pharisees and Herodians had little in common—until Jesus posed a threat to them
both. Jesus threatened the Pharisees' authority over the people;
Jesus threatened the Herodians' political ambitions because his
talk of a "kingdom" caused them to think that this popular and
powerful man was planning to set himself up as a ruler. This
would jeopardize their authority derived from Herod's power. To
get rid of Jesus, the Pharisees needed the support of people with
some influence with the secular leaders. Thus the Pharisees and
Herodians, normally enemies, joined forces to discuss how to get
rid of Jesus.

Jesus demands a response from people. Either he is who he
said he is, or he is a fraud. The Pharisees chose the latter. They

were jealous of his popularity, his
miracles, and the authority in his teaching and actions. They valued their status
in the community and their opportunity
for personal gain so much that they lost
sight of their goal as religious leaders—

> "The irony: Mercy itself gets trampled by a mob seeking Mercy." *Kenneth Pike*

to point people toward God. Of all people, the Pharisees should
have recognized the Messiah, but they refused to acknowledge
him because they were not willing to give up their treasured position and power. When Jesus exposed their attitudes, he became
their enemy instead of their Messiah, and they began looking for
ways to destroy him.

LARGE CROWDS FOLLOW JESUS / 3:7-12 / 47

In contrast to the rejection of Jesus by certain religious leaders,
Mark described the attraction and adoration of Christ by the
crowds. The atmosphere was riotous, and Jesus took practical pre-
cautions by having a boat standing by to use if a strategic withdrawal was needed. Mark's details provide us a picture of the
context of Jesus' ministry. People were coming from literally
every direction (from Tyre and Sidon in the north; from Judea,
Jerusalem, and Idumea in the far south; from across the Jordan in
the east).

From this whirlwind of activity, Mark highlighted a number of
smaller interactions between Jesus and those around him. The
character of Jesus emerges under the constant scrutiny and
demand of the crowds. Jesus was rarely alone. Mark 1:35 may
indicate a conscious habit of early-morning solitude, but it cannot
have been an easy discipline to maintain. Jesus was in demand.

**3:7 Jesus withdrew with his disciples to the lake, and a large
crowd from Galilee followed.**NIV Up to this point, Jesus had
been aggressively confronting the Phari-
sees' hypocrisy. Then he decided to
withdraw from the synagogue before a
major confrontation developed because
it was not time for him to die. Jesus had
many lessons still to teach his disciples
and the people. So he *withdrew with his
disciples to the lake* (that is, to the Sea
of Galilee), but *a large crowd from Galilee followed.* As in 2:13, Mark recorded
that Jesus withdrew to the seaside after
a conflict with the religious leaders. It

> Our Father, sometimes Thou dost seem so far away, as if Thou art a God in hiding, as if Thou art determined to elude all who seek Thee. Yet we know that Thou art far more willing to be found than we are to seek. *Peter Marshall*

is as if he wanted to be as physically separated from them as he was morally and spiritually. The leaders hated Jesus so much that they began their plot to kill him. But Jesus was still immensely popular with the people, for when he went away, they followed. The actual twelve disciples had not yet been called, but those closest to Jesus were marked as following him. They had separated themselves from the religious establishment and were sharing in the glow of Jesus' popularity.

STRATEGIC WITHDRAWAL
Mark records several instances where Jesus set aside his work in order to spend time teaching the disciples, to pray, to escape his enemies, or simply to rest. For example:

- 1:12—Jesus went into the wilderness alone to be tempted by Satan.
- 2:13—Jesus went out to the seaside after the Pharisees considered him guilty of blasphemy because he claimed to forgive sins.
- 3:7—Jesus went out to the seaside after confronting the Pharisees regarding his healing on the Sabbath.
- 3:13—Jesus went up on the mountain and called to him those who would be his twelve disciples.
- 6:31—Jesus took his disciples away for a time of rest.
- 6:46—Jesus went up on a mountainside to pray.
- 7:24—Jesus and the disciples left Galilee and went into the pagan territory of Tyre after confronting the religious leaders with their hypocrisy.
- 9:2—Jesus took Peter, James, and John onto a high mountain to see his transfiguration.
- 14:32, 35—Jesus went apart from his disciples to pray in the Garden of Gethsemane.

Jesus withdrew to replenish his relationship with God the Father through prayer, and to build strong bonds with selected followers through long talks away from normal distractions.

Do you want to be a strong disciple today? It will require time, openness to a deepening relationship, and growing ties with God's people. Do you want to develop Christian disciples today? Jesus' methods work best.

3:8 **When they heard all he was doing, many people came to him from Judea, Jerusalem, Idumea, and the regions across the Jordan and around Tyre and Sidon.**[NIV] While Jesus was drawing fire from the religious leaders, he was gaining great popularity among the people—they came literally from all directions. News of Jesus had spread far beyond Galilee. *When they heard all he was doing,* people came from *Judea* (the southernmost region of Israel), *Jerusalem* (the key city of Israel, in Judea), *Idumea* (the region south of Judea), *regions across the Jordan* (which probably refers to Perea and Decapolis that lay east of the Jordan River), and *around Tyre and Sidon* (pagan cities to the far north on the coast of the Mediterranean Sea). The people came for various reasons with various motives. Some were simply curious, some sought healing, some wanted evidence to use against him, and others truly wanted to know if Jesus was the Messiah. Most of them could only dimly guess at the real meaning of what was happening among them.

MERELY CURIOUS?
The crowds were curious. Jesus had a reputation. Curiosity can indicate a desire to know more fully, or it can be merely inquisitiveness, a desire to know something strange or novel. The church contains many people who have come for a variety of reasons. Curiosity can be a way to distance ourselves from the demands of Christ. Are you fully committed to him, or merely curious?

3:9 Because of the crowd he told his disciples to have a small boat ready for him, to keep the people from crowding him.^{NIV} Only Mark recorded this detail, suggesting that this was an eyewitness report from one of the disciples whom Jesus asked (possibly Peter). This *small boat* was about the size of a rowboat. As Jesus walked along the shoreline with the crowds following, the little boat was rowed along close to the shore so it would always be ready in case the people crowded Jesus right into the water. The reason for Jesus' precaution is explained in the next verse.

3:10 For he had healed many, so that those with diseases were pushing forward to touch him.^{NIV} Jesus' reputation for healing had spread everywhere (see 3:8), and many people *with diseases* came from great distances just to touch Jesus and be healed. Picture people in the throng *pushing forward* and shoving each other out of the way, reaching out at Jesus, attempting to touch him. They were so desperate to be healed that such rudeness made no difference.

3:11-12 Whenever the unclean spirits saw him, they fell down before him and shouted, "You are the Son of God!"^{NRSV} Mark described a second encounter between Jesus and *unclean* (or evil) *spirits* (see also 1:23-24). Also called demons, these spirits are probably fallen angels who joined Satan in his rebellion. They are ruled by Satan, and at times, they enter a person's body, take up residence, and control him or her. Jesus cast out many demons from people during his time on earth, revealing his power and authority over them. The demons recognized who Jesus was, and whenever a possessed person saw Jesus, he or she *fell down before him,* not in worship, but to shout to everyone, *"You are the Son of God."* The demons recognized Jesus and feared him (see James 2:19). They knew his power, and they were aware that he had the authority to cast them out of their lodgings (inside a person) and even to send them away permanently (see 5:9-10). Jesus didn't want or need the demons to endorse him. His true identity would be revealed at the right time, at his resurrection. Thus, he spoke sternly to the demons and **gave them strict orders not to tell who he was**[NIV] (see also note 1:25).

Ironically, the demons recognized who Jesus was; the people didn't. Jesus warned the evil (unclean) spirits not to reveal his identity because he did not want them to reinforce a popular misconception. The huge crowds were looking for a political and military leader who would free them from Rome's control, and they thought that the Messiah predicted by the Old Testament prophets would be this kind of man. Jesus wanted to teach the people about the kind of Messiah he really was, because he was far different from what they expected. Christ's kingdom is spiritual. It begins, not with the overthrow of governments, but with the overthrow of sin in people's hearts.

TURN, TURN
The evil (unclean) spirits knew that Jesus was the Son of God, but they had no intention of following him. Many people followed Jesus but didn't understand his true purpose for coming. Some people came for miracles, some came to hear his teaching, but they didn't understand the way of the cross. Knowing about Jesus, or even believing that he is God's Son, does not guarantee salvation. You must also follow and obey him (see also James 2:17).

JESUS SELECTS THE TWELVE DISCIPLES / 3:13-19 / **48**

Earlier in this Gospel, Jesus invited several persons to follow him (1:16-19; 2:14). Soon hundreds and thousands of others also tracked Jesus' steps. Some were curious, some critical, and some were committed. From among all of them Jesus chose twelve.

Whatever Jesus' specific reasons for choosing each disciple, as a group they were hot-tempered, weak-faithed, and generally oblivious to much of what was going on around them. One became a traitor, and all of them abandoned Jesus in the heat of crisis. The apostles proved the truth of Jesus' words, "You did not choose me, but I chose you and appointed you to go and bear fruit—fruit that will last" (John 15:16 NIV).

> If ever there should be a monastery without a troublesome and bad-tempered member, it would be necessary to find one and pay him his weight in gold because of the great profit that results from this trial, when good use is made of it. *Bernard of Clairvaux*

Jesus chose the Twelve with the intention of building into them and bringing out of them his own character. The apostles were not Jesus' only planted field, but they were a public test plot. They did not apply for their roles, nor did they submit references. There were others who proved to be effective disciples even though they were not part of the Twelve: for example, the band of faithful women who accompanied Jesus and oversaw many of the practical needs of the inner circle (Luke 8:1-3); Joseph and Matthias were also two of an identifiable group who were with Jesus from the start of his ministry until the time of his resurrection (Acts 1:21-26).

The better we know the disciples, the more we come to see that God might actually choose us too. Grace does not make humanness a disqualifying characteristic. As disappointing as the disciples may have been, they leave room for us to hope. When we are aware of our unworthiness to merit God's mercy and love, we are in the best position to experience what he can do for us.

WHAT DOES IT MEAN TO HEAR THE CALL OF GOD?
First, God calls you to faith in Jesus. You will know this call by the growing desire in your heart to settle the matter of peace with God speedily. Respond to him—answer with a grateful, "Yes, Lord, I need you!"

Second, God calls you to service in Jesus' name. Wherever you are (and sometimes you need to move), whatever you're doing (and sometimes you need to upgrade your skills), God has a place of service for you. Jesus calls you and he wants you. Answer this call thoughtfully, seriously, in consultation with Christian advisers, "Yes, Lord, I love you and will follow you!"

3:13 He went up the mountain and called to him those whom he wanted, and they came to him.NRSV Jesus left the shore of the Sea of Galilee and *went up the mountain* (probably referring to the hill country of Galilee instead of to one particular mountain). Luke records that Jesus "spent the night in prayer to God" (Luke 6:12 NRSV) before calling *those whom he wanted*—that is, the twelve disciples. Jesus did not take volunteers; he chose and called those he wanted. Jesus "wanted" these men; so he *called* them, *and they came.* They did not hesitate to obey.

3:14 And he appointed twelve, whom he also named apostles, to be with him, and to be sent out to proclaim the message.NRSV Jesus had many disciples (learners), but he *appointed twelve, whom he also named apostles* (messengers). The apostles were Jesus' inner circle. He gave them special training, and he sent them out with his own authority. From the hundreds of people who followed Jesus from place to place, he especially selected these twelve to *be with him.* The Greek verb means that these men remained with him as his constant and closest companions. Many people followed and listened to Jesus, but these twelve received the most intense training. We see the impact of these men throughout the rest of the New Testament, for they started the Christian church. The phrase "whom he also named apostles" does not appear in some Greek manuscripts. In the Gospels these twelve men are usually called the disciples or the Twelve; in the book of Acts they are called apostles.

> Father, make of me a crisis man. Bring those I contact to decision. Let me not be a milepost on a single road; make me a fork, that men must turn one way or another on facing Christ in me. *Jim Elliot*

The choice of twelve men is highly symbolic. The number twelve corresponds to the twelve tribes of Israel (Matthew 19:28), showing the continuity between the old religious system and the new one based on Jesus' message. Jesus looked upon this as the gathering of the true people of God. These men were the righteous remnant who would carry on the work the twelve tribes were chosen to do—to build the community of God.

Jesus did not choose these twelve to be his disciples because of their faith—it often faltered. He didn't choose them because of their talent and ability—no one stood out with unusual ability. The disciples represented a wide range of backgrounds and life experiences, but apparently they may have had no more leadership potential than those who were not chosen. The one characteristic they all shared was their willingness to obey Jesus.

The apostles remained with Jesus for training so that Jesus could then send them out as his ambassadors or representatives *to proclaim the message.* Unlike the students of the rabbis, who merely learned and memorized facts, the disciples were being trained to carry out a mission. Their message was the good news of the gospel; they were to proclaim that message publicly and with the authority given to them by Christ himself.

After Jesus' ascension, the disciples were filled with the Holy

Spirit and empowered to carry out special roles in the growth of the early church. We should not disqualify ourselves from service to Christ because we do not have impressive credentials. Being a good disciple is simply a matter of following Jesus with a willing heart.

DISCIPLES FIRST
Jesus appointed the Twelve to be with him, and then he sent them out with his authority to proclaim the Good News. Many people want the authority of a Peter or John without first going through the school of discipleship. These twelve needed instruction, coaching, practice, and above all, time to mature. We must be willing to spend time learning from the Master before we go forward to do his public work.

3:15 And to have authority to cast out demons.^{NRSV} Not only did the disciples go out trained in the message of the gospel, they also had Jesus' *authority* over the forces of evil. Jesus empowered his disciples *to cast out demons.* This power was given to the disciples by Jesus; it was delegated authority. The disciples could speak the word, and God's power would cast out the demons. Why was this important? Because Jesus was extending his mission through them. Every demon was confronted one-on-one. Jesus needed to multiply his presence and authority to the Galilean villages.

3:16 Simon, to whom He gave the name Peter.^{NKJV} Mark listed these disciples by name or family name ("son of"). It is interesting to note the almost complete silence of the Gospels and the Epistles as to the future work of the vast majority of these twelve men. We know some about Peter, James, and John in the book of Acts; we know from 3:19 that Judas would betray Jesus. Otherwise, the Bible is silent about many of the disciples' activities. The Gospels and Epistles stressed the ministry of the twelve men together and its significance. The number was so important that when Judas Iscariot killed himself, another man was chosen to replace him (see Acts 1:15-26).

The first name recorded was *Simon,* to whom Jesus *gave the name Peter* (see John 1:42). Jesus "surnamed" him Peter, meaning that he gave him a name in addition to the one he already had—he did not change Simon's name. Sometimes Peter is referred to as Cephas. "Peter" is the Greek equivalent of the Aramaic *Cephas*—a word meaning "stone" or "rock." Peter had been a fisherman (1:16). He became one of three in Jesus' core group among the disciples. He also confessed that Jesus was the Messiah (8:29). Although Peter would deny ever knowing Jesus, he would eventually become a leader in the Jerusalem church, write two letters that appear in the Bible (1 and 2 Peter), and be crucified for his faith.

3:17 **James son of Zebedee and his brother John (to them he gave the name Boanerges, which means Sons of Thunder).**NIV James and John had also been fishermen (1:19). James would become the first martyr for the Christian faith (Acts 12:2). John would write the Gospel of John, the letters of 1, 2, and 3 John, and the book of Revelation. They may have been related to Jesus (distant cousins); thus, at one point they requested special places in Christ's kingdom (10:35, 37).

These brothers were given the name (or were surnamed, as with Peter above) *Boanerges,* an idiom interpreted to mean, *Sons of Thunder.* Scripture gives glimpses of these men, revealing that they were somewhat short-tempered and judgmental; for example, they wanted to call fire down from heaven on an inhospitable Samaritan village (Luke 9:52-56). Thus Jesus gave them an appropriate name.

3:18 **Andrew.** Andrew was Peter's brother and also a fisherman (1:16). Andrew had been a disciple of John the Baptist and had accepted John the Baptist's testimony that Jesus was "the Lamb of God." He left John to follow Jesus, and then brought his brother Simon Peter to Jesus (John 1:35-42). Andrew and John were Jesus' first disciples (John 1:35-37); they were the first to live with Jesus and share the good news with others.

Philip. Philip was the fourth to meet Jesus. John wrote, "The next day Jesus decided to leave for Galilee. Finding Philip, he said to him, 'Follow me'" (John 1:43 NIV). Philip then brought Nathanael (also called Bartholomew) as recorded in John 1:45. Philip probably knew Andrew and Peter because they were from the same town, Bethsaida (John 1:44).

Bartholomew. Bartholomew is thought to be the same person as Nathanael. In the list of disciples here and in Matthew, Philip and Bartholomew are listed together (Matthew 10:3; Mark 3:18); in John's Gospel, Philip and Nathanael are paired up (John 1:45). Thus, it stands to reason that since Bartholomew is not mentioned in John, and Nathanael is not mentioned in the other Gospels, then Nathanael and Bartholomew must be the same person. Bartholomew was an honest man; indeed, Jesus' first words to him were, "Here is a true Israelite, in whom there is nothing false" (John 1:47 NIV). Bartholomew at first rejected Jesus because Jesus was from Nazareth. But upon meeting Jesus, his attitude changed and he exclaimed, "Rabbi, you are the Son of God! You are the King of Israel!" (John 1:49 NRSV).

Matthew. Matthew was also known as Levi. He had been a tax collector (Mark 2:14). He had been a despised outcast because of his dishonest career, but he abandoned that corrupt (though lucrative) way of life to follow Jesus. He would later write the Gospel of Matthew.

Thomas. We often remember this disciple as "doubting Thomas" because he doubted Jesus' resurrection (John 20:24-25). But he also loved the Lord and was a man of great courage. When Jesus determined to return to Judea and enemy territory, Thomas said to the disciples, "Let us also go, that we may die with him" (John 11:16 NIV). Thomas was tough and committed, even if he tended to be pessimistic. Thus, when the other disciples said that Jesus was alive, Thomas didn't believe them. However, when Thomas saw and touched the living Christ, doubting Thomas became believing Thomas.

James son of Alphaeus. This disciple is designated as *son of Alphaeus* to differentiate him from James the son of Zebedee (and brother of John) in 3:17. He is also called "James the younger" (15:40). To add to the confusion, Matthew is called "son of Alphaeus" in 2:14, but James and Matthew were probably not related.

Thaddaeus. Thaddaeus is also called "Judas son of James" (see Luke 6:16; Acts 1:13).

Simon the Zealot.[NIV] Some versions of Scripture call this disciple Simon the Canaanite. Simon was probably not a member of the party of Zealots, for that political party did not appear until A.D. 68. Most likely the word "Zealot" used here indicates zeal for God's honor and not extreme nationalism; it was an affectionate nickname.

ORDINARY PEOPLE
Jesus chose "ordinary" men with a mixture of backgrounds and personalities to be his disciples. Today, God calls "ordinary" people together to build his church, teach salvation's message, and serve others out of love. Alone we may feel unqualified to serve Christ effectively, but together we make up a group strong enough to serve God in any way. Ask for patience to accept the diversity of people in your church, and build on the variety of strengths represented in your group.

3:19 Judas Iscariot, who betrayed him.^{NRSV} The name "Iscariot" is
probably a compound word meaning "the man from Kerioth."
Thus, Judas's hometown was Kerioth in southern Judea (see
Joshua 15:25), making him the only one of the Twelve who was
not from Galilee. It was Judas, son of Simon Iscariot (John 6:71),
who betrayed Jesus to his enemies and then committed suicide
(Luke 22:47-48; Matthew 27:3-5).

Mark presents a paradoxical picture of the disciples. They
doubted and they failed, yet they were used to build the church.
Some died for him, one betrayed him. The message is, what kind
of disciple will you be?

GOD'S TEAM
Anything but perfect, the twelve disciples were different people
called together for a common purpose. We could say that these
men were blue collar and white collar, strongly muscular and
desk-jockey thin, passionate and contemplative, transparently
simple and cunningly sophisticated, wealthy and dirt-poor.
From this disparate group came a message that changed the
world.
　　Will you help that change continue? Whatever your strengths
and no matter what your weaknesses, there's a place for you.
On God's team, no two people part their hair the same way.
Through cooperation, acceptance, and love, human differences
contribute to effective witness.

RELIGIOUS LEADERS ACCUSE JESUS OF BEING UNDER SATAN'S POWER / 3:20-30 / **74**

Mark never allowed his readers to get far from the fact that Jesus'
ministry was constantly being opposed. He balanced Jesus'
choice of disciples with the evolving group of opposition, including Jesus' own family, who was prepared to call him deranged.
The religious leadership chose to add the accusation of demon
possession. Jesus handled his family's doubts with compassion
(3:31-35). He neutralized his enemies' charge with a devastating
counterattack. How, he asked them, could he possibly be serving
Satan when his presence and his actions were causing such devastating damage to Satan's kingdom? Further, he pointed out that
their failure to recognize the Spirit, under whose influence he
was actually operating, indicated that they were dangerously
close to committing the unforgivable sin. By identifying the Holy
Spirit as Satan in Jesus' life, the religious leaders were committing unspeakable blasphemy.

Mark's placement of this incident at this point in the narrative

creates problems for scholars. We are not always sure when the
Gospel writers were recording chronological events and when
they were choosing incidents to illustrate themes in Jesus' ministry. When unique events show up in different settings among the
Gospel accounts, questions arise about when these events actually occurred. Some possibilities for alleviating these problems
include the following:

- Similar accounts in two or more Gospels do not have to refer to
  the same event. Given the number of miracles Jesus did and the
  different occasions when he spoke, we would expect many
  repeated situations and sayings (for example, the two feedings
  of the multitudes recorded in Matthew 14 and 15, and Mark 6
  and 8 tell of both, while Luke 9 and John 6 refer to only one;
  the two cleansings of the temple recorded in John 2 and Matthew 21; two extended "sermons" recorded in Matthew 5–7
  and Luke 6; two accounts of the Lord's Prayer recorded in Matthew 6 and Luke 11).

- Similar accounts in somewhat different time contexts may refer
  to the same events. Notice, for example, the sequence of incidents in Matthew 12 and Mark 3: Jesus heals on the Sabbath
  (in both accounts); large crowds follow (both, but Matthew
  adds an Old Testament reference and fulfillment); Jesus
  chooses the Twelve (Mark only); religious leaders accuse Jesus
  of being influenced by Satan (both, but Mark introduces Jesus'
  family in the details); religious leaders demand another miracle
  from Jesus (Matthew only); Jesus defines his true family
  (both). The parallel sequence indicates that both writers were
  dealing with the same series of events. They placed the series
  in a slightly different place in their Gospel accounts, in harmony with their overall outline. Each added details that may
  have been original to the events or that the events caused them
  to remember. It is not difficult to conclude that mentioning the
  huge crowds caused Mark to point out that in such a context
  Jesus chose the Twelve who would be his disciples. More
  likely, Matthew chose not to mention Jesus' appointment of the
  disciples because it was not a detail crucial to his outline.

While chronology is crucial in modern history writing, it was
not as critical to ancient historians. They did not write day-to-day
chronicles. Often they took a topical approach. The evangelists
were free to put events slightly out of sequence to emphasize the
message. But though the Gospel writers may not have been
bound to chronology, they were not careless with it either. When
we cannot discern the places where their order is topical and

where it is chronological, it may be safest to say that while *we* might get confused, *they* were not. Since they were doing the writing, humility demands that we submit to their order. To require the Gospel writers to submit to our stylistic or organizational rules fails to appreciate what they accomplished.

With respect to appreciating their style, it should be noted that Mark used a literary technique known as "sandwiching," wherein he inserted the Beelzebub incident in between the two sections that deal with Jesus' family coming to get him. When Mark does this, the two are meant to interpret one another. Jesus is called "crazy" by his family and "demon possessed" by the religious leaders. Both completely reject him and demean him.

3:20 Then Jesus entered a house, and again a crowd gathered, so that he and his disciples were not even able to eat.[NIV] The house Jesus entered was most likely in Capernaum and may have, once again, been Peter's house. The text suggests that after Jesus had spent some time on the mountain, probably training and teaching his newly appointed disciples, he returned to a house in the city. As had happened twice previously when Jesus entered a house in Capernaum, *a crowd gathered* (see 1:33; 2:1-2). Again, the demand of the people in the crowd made it impossible for Jesus and the disciples to have any quiet, to spend time in training, or even to eat (6:31).

TAKE TIME OUT
It's easy to get caught up in ministry and neglect proper care of ourselves. Jesus and his disciples were so busy that they didn't have time to eat. Perhaps other needs were set aside while Jesus was fulfilling his mission. Jesus knew he had a short time left on earth, so he was intensely busy. Some Christian workers approach life as though they, too, have only a few years to live. Their needs for eating, sleeping, and exercise give way to their ministry priorities. Jesus wants us to work and serve him, but not to treat our bodies as if we were living our last day on earth. As stewards of the resources God has given you, find the balance between work and rest so you can maintain your energy level and be useful for Christ your whole life.

3:21 When his family heard about this, they went to take charge of him, for they said, "He is out of his mind."[NIV] With the crowds pressing in on him, Jesus didn't even take time to eat. Thinking he had gone "over the edge" as a religious fanatic, his family came to him. John recorded that Jesus' brothers did not believe in him (John 7:5), although some later did believe (Acts 1:14). In fact, Jesus' brother James became one of the leaders in the church in Jerusalem and the writer of the book of James. Mary believed that her son was special, but she didn't understand his ministry either. Perhaps she thought the situation was getting out of hand, and she needed to protect her son from himself, from the demands of his ministry, or even from the relentless crowds. With an attitude of some irritation, Jesus' family decided he had truly gone out of his mind with this "Messiah stuff" and that they needed to *take charge of him.*

Jesus' family was concerned for him, but they missed the point of his ministry. Even those who were closest to Jesus were slow to understand who he was and what he had come to do. The story brings to mind another like it: Mary and Joseph's concern when they lost track of the then twelve-year-old Jesus in Jerusalem (Luke 2:41-52). Like any parents, they frantically searched for their son. They finally found him in the temple speaking with the teachers. Jesus' words to them could have been repeated here (indeed, perhaps Mary herself remembered them): "Why did you seek Me? Did you not know that I must be about My Father's business?" (Luke 2:49 NKJV).

ALL IN THE FAMILY
The family may be the most difficult place to be a witness for Jesus. To be the first or only believing Christian may go against the grain. Our faith may come across as criticism of the way others have conducted their lives. Our zeal may be misunderstood. We may be accused of being a hypocrite because other areas of our lives still fall short of Christ's ideals. Uncommitted people may view our commitment to the Bible as unreasonable bigotry.

Family members require the most patience. They see us at our worst when our guard is down. Remember that Christ's family rejected and ridiculed him. Jesus knows what you face by trying to be a witness for him in your own family. Stay true to your faith, and don't respond negatively to the attacks that may come. Over time, your love for them will have a positive effect.

3:22 And the teachers of the law who came down from Jerusalem said, "He is possessed by Beelzebub! By the prince of demons he is driving out demons."[NIV] Apparently another delegation had come from Jerusalem. These *teachers of the law* (or scribes) probably had been summoned by the Pharisees and Herodians who were already in league to destroy Jesus (3:6). The scribes and Pharisees could not deny the reality of Jesus' miracles and supernatural power—he had indeed been *driving out demons.* But they refused to believe that his power was from God because then they would have had to accept him as the Messiah. Their pride would not let them do that. So in an attempt to destroy Jesus' popularity among the people, the scribes accused him of having power from Satan.

Beelzebub occurs only in the New Testament (in Matthew 10:25; 12:24; and Luke 11:15) and not in other Jewish literature. In Greek, the term is *beelzeboul.* The Vulgate and Syriac versions tried to clarify the term by changing it to *beelzebub,* the god of Ekron (see 2 Kings 1:2-3, 6, 16). The religious authorities may have invented the term by combining two Hebrew words: *ba'al* ("lord," Hosea 2:16) stood for the local Caananite fertility god; and *zebul* ("exalted dwelling," 1 Kings 8:13). Everyone would have understood this term as referring to Satan, the *prince* (or leader) *of demons.*

ACCUSATIONS
These teachers of the law brought a nonsensical accusation against Jesus (Jesus would show its absurdity in his response). They tried to say that Jesus was driving out demons by the power of the prince of demons—in other words, that Jesus' power came from Satan, not God. They wanted the people to believe that Jesus himself was possessed (see 3:30). This would disprove his claim as the Messiah and place him instead in league with the devil.

The more effective we are in our Christian lives, the more extreme will be the attacks of the enemy. Satan may attack us through extreme accusations from other "religious" people, or dissensions and factions caused by "loyal" friends. Even the most ridiculous accusation will convince some when it's cleverly packaged to sound sincere and concerned. Stand firm for the truth even when clever attacks come from religious insiders.

3:23 And he called them to him, and spoke to them in parables, "How can Satan cast out Satan?"^{NRSV} Jesus, never afraid of a confrontation, *called* the teachers of the law to come closer so he could talk to them. He would refute their nonsense *in parables,* that is, short stories. A simple example from life would reveal the absurdity of their charge that Jesus was in league with Satan. Jesus first addressed the bottom line of their second accusation—that he was driving out demons by Satan's power—by simply asking, *"How can Satan cast out Satan?"* The Greek word for "how" means "how is this possible?" By the question, Jesus implied that it is impossible for Satan to cast out himself (or his own followers, demons). Why would Satan work against himself?

3:24 "If a kingdom is divided against itself, that kingdom cannot stand."NKJV Following the obvious conclusion of the accusation—that Satan was driving himself out of people—Jesus indicates that would then mean there was civil war in the kingdom of evil. No king would throw his own soldiers out of his kingdom; neither would Satan throw his soldiers out of his kingdom. His kingdom would then be *divided against itself*. Such a kingdom *cannot stand*.

3:25 "And if a house is divided against itself, that house cannot stand."NKJV People in a home, divided about their goals, working against one another, cannot long remain a home. Thus, like a kingdom, a house divided against itself also cannot stand.

3:26 "And if Satan opposes himself and is divided, he cannot stand; his end has come."NIV The answer to Jesus' question in 3:23, "How can Satan cast out Satan?" is that he doesn't and would not, for to do so would mean the end of his power. Satan's casting his own demons out of people would be civil war, and that would mean that his end had come. Obviously Satan is still very powerful and active; thus, his end had not come—not in Jesus' day, nor in ours. So Satan is not opposing himself, nor is he divided. The teachers' charge that Jesus was driving out demons by Satan's power was obviously false. But Jesus wasn't finished.

3:27 "In fact, no one can enter a strong man's house and carry off his possessions unless he first ties up the strong man. Then he can rob his house."NIV This picture reflects a situation in the ancient world where wealthy people's homes were virtual fortresses, and their servants could form a small army. Jesus pictured Satan as the wealthy man and his demons as his servants and possessions. Jesus called Satan *a strong man* in this parable. His *house* is the realm of evil where there is sickness, demon possession, and death. It also refers to a possessed individual in whom Satan's demons live. Satan's *possessions* are the demons—those beings through whom Satan carries out his work in the world. The only way those possessions could be carried off would be for someone to first tie up the strong man—the only way for the demons to be cast out is for someone to first limit Satan's power. Jesus' advent into the world did just that (1 John 3:8).

Although God permits Satan to work in our world, God is in control. Jesus, as God, has "tied up" Satan; Jesus is able to drive out demons and end their terrible work in people's lives. As such, every exorcism was a binding of Satan; one day Satan will be bound forever (Revelation 20:10). Jesus was not in league with Satan, as the teachers of the law tried to claim; rather, he had overpowered Satan by refusing his temptations and by constantly freeing people held in Satan's grasp—either through demon possession or through the power of sin.

Jesus was not the first to exorcise demons—although his constant success, the ease with which he did it, and the reactions of the demons did make Jesus' exorcisms notable. The Bible records that others performed exorcisms (9:38; Acts 19:13-14). Some Jewish leaders also did so. Matthew's and Luke's accounts of this exchange include that Jesus asked the question, "If I drive out demons by Beelzebub, by whom do your people drive them out? So then, they will be your judges" (Matthew 12:27 NIV; see also Luke 11:19). In other words, Jesus was saying, "If it takes Satan's power to drive out demons, then those of your own group who are driving out demons must also be demon possessed."

BINDING SATAN
Throughout Scripture, God is pictured as in control and overcoming the attempts of Satan to increase his influence.

- It is likely that when Satan was ejected from heaven (Isaiah 14:12-15), the rebelling angels (who became demons) were also ejected from heaven. They were able to influence the hearts and minds of people, but they could not control God's people without God's permission (Job 1:12; 2:6). Other rebellious angels have been bound until the last day of judgment (Jude 6).
- Satan's power was broken with the coming of Christ as demonstrated by Jesus withstanding Satan in the Temptation (Luke 4:1-13).
- Satan still functions as "god of this age (world)" (2 Corinthians 4:4), and he tries to exercise his lost lordship. But we can overcome Satan by identifying and uniting with Christ who holds the power to bind Satan (Romans 6:12-13; Ephesians 2:1-3; 3:10-12; 6:10-18; Colossians 2:15, 20).
- The final "binding" will occur first in the bottomless pit and then in the lake of fire (Revelation 20:10).

We need to recognize Satan's power but not fear him. Jesus has bound Satan. We are free so long as we follow Jesus and remain true to his Word.

3:28 **"Truly I tell you, people will be forgiven for their sins and whatever blasphemies they utter."**[NRSV] *Truly I tell you* (also translated, "Verily I say unto you" in KJV, "I tell you the truth" NIV, and "Assuredly, I say to you" NKJV) is a recurring phrase used only by Jesus prior to a solemn warning or pronouncement. It is like the Old Testament's "Thus saith the Lord." The words are divinely self-authenticating and guarantee the truth and importance of what Jesus would say next. No longer was Jesus reasoning with his accusers; he was giving them a solemn warning. Jesus had just been accused of being in league with Satan and had soundly refuted those charges. Here he had a few words for these so-called teachers of the law, the Jewish leaders.

First he made the incredible promise that *people will be forgiven for their sins and whatever blasphemies they utter.* Too often people miss this promise and worry about the warning in the next verse. But the fact is, those who believe in Jesus will be forgiven of all sins (evil acts, wrong actions, good actions not done, evil thoughts, evil motives, etc.) and of all blasphemies (evil words said against God). When there is confession and repentance, no sin is beyond God's forgiveness.

- Acts 13:39—Those who trust in Christ are freed from guilt and declared righteous.

- Isaiah 1:18—No matter how bad or deep your sinfulness, God can make you clean.

- 1 John 1:9—If you confess, God will forgive.

- Psalm 103:3; Ephesians 1:7; Colossians 1:14; 1 John 2:12—Jesus' death covered all your sins.

GOODNESS GRACIOUS

God is remarkably gracious. No offense blocks his forgiving love—no curse, no skepticism, no flat-out denial, no slander or angry outcry. When we confess our sins and turn away from them, they are all forgiven because we have put our trust in Jesus. Not many people would forget a rumormonger who spoils a family's reputation with malicious gossip—but God does. Not many people would forgive a recurring cruelty, a lasting scar, a persistent hurt, a screaming adversary—but God does.

We would all be quite hopeless if God kept track of offenses. God forgives without imposing penalties on us. Jesus paid for all our sins.

When you ask God to be forgiven, you are asking for what God loves to do best. Rest in that life-changing promise: By the Cross of Jesus you are gladly and fully forgiven.

3:29 **"But whoever blasphemes against the Holy Spirit can never have forgiveness, but is guilty of an eternal sin."**NRSV There is one sin that cannot be forgiven—blasphemy against the Holy Spirit. Blasphemy against the Holy Spirit refers not so much to a single action or word as to an attitude. Those who defiantly deny

Jesus' power and persistently refuse to believe that he is the Messiah are blaspheming the Holy Spirit. Matthew's Gospel states it this way, "Anyone who speaks a word against the Son of Man will be forgiven, but anyone who speaks against the Holy Spirit will not be forgiven, either in this age or in the age to come" (Matthew 12:32 NIV). Jesus was not talking about rejecting him, but of rejecting the power behind him.

Jesus' words were addressed directly to these teachers of the law. They had blasphemed the Spirit by attributing the power by which Christ did miracles to Satan instead of to the Holy Spirit. This is the unforgivable sin—the deliberate refusal to acknowledge God's power in Christ. It indicates an irreversible hardness of heart. Deliberate, ongoing rejection of the work of the Holy Spirit is blasphemy because it is rejecting God himself. The religious leaders accused Jesus of blasphemy (see also 14:63-64), but ironically they were the guilty ones when they looked Jesus in the face and accused him of being possessed by Satan.

> The sin against the Holy Ghost is ever attended with these two symptoms—an absence of all contrition, and of all desire of forgiveness. Now, if thou canst truly say that thy sins are a burden to thee, that thou dost desire forgiveness and wouldst give anything to attain it, be of good comfort; thou hast not yet, and by God's grace never shall commit that unpardonable offense. *J. C. Ryle*

Sometimes believers worry that they have accidently committed this unforgivable sin. But only those who have turned their back on God and rejected all faith have any need to worry. Jesus said they can't be forgiven—not because their sin is worse than any other, but because they will never ask for forgiveness. Whoever rejects the prompting of the Holy Spirit removes himself or herself from the only force that can lead him or her to repentance and restoration to God. Those who have seen the light and prefer the darkness are blaspheming the Holy Spirit. Their stubborn refusal to believe can only lead to a hardness of heart that cannot be penetrated; thus, forgiveness never will be possible because it never will be sought. It is *an eternal sin* because the consequences last for eternity (see also 1 John 5:16).

3:30 He said this because they were saying, "He has an evil spirit."NIV Mark added the note that Jesus made the solemn warning recorded in 3:28-29 because *they* (that is, the teachers of the law, 3:22) had said that Jesus was demon possessed *(has an evil spirit)*. The teachers had not said that Jesus was Satan, but that his power was from Satan. But his power came from the Holy

Spirit. While Jesus did not accuse the teachers of committing the unforgivable sin, his warning shows that they were very close to doing so when they attributed to Satan the Holy Spirit's power of exorcising demons.

JESUS DESCRIBES HIS TRUE FAMILY / 3:31-35 / 76

Mark displayed his storytelling skill by introducing Jesus' family. By bringing them up again (see 3:21), Mark smoothed the transition from one scene to another. It also heightened tension. At least some in Jesus' family thought he was suffering delusions, and they were on the way to straighten him out or take him under their control.

Jesus turned his rejection by his family into a compassionate invitation to recognize his true nature. They came to claim him as their family member; he challenged them to be members of God's true family. The conflict between Jesus and his family continues in our lives. Do we avoid Jesus' claim on us as the powerful Lord by reducing him to friendship status? Jesus is our friend and brother, but he is also our Lord. By treating him as any less, we may be neutralizing his rightful ownership of our thoughts and actions.

3:31 Then his mother and his brothers came; and standing outside, they sent to him and called him.NRSV This verse continues from 3:20-21 when Jesus' family arrived to take him home because he was "out of his mind." Jesus' mother was Mary (Luke 1:30-31), and his brothers were probably the other children Mary and Joseph had after Jesus (see also 6:3). Some Christians believe the ancient tradition that Jesus was Mary's only child. If this is true, the "brothers" were possibly cousins (cousins were often called brothers in those days). Some have offered yet another suggestion: When Joseph married Mary, he was a widower, and these were his children by his first marriage. Most likely, however, these were Jesus' half brothers, Mary and Joseph's other children (see 6:3-4), because Jesus' father was not Joseph, but God.

Apparently Mary had gathered her family, and they went to find Jesus. Mary hoped to use her personal relationship with Jesus to influence him. She saw her son in a busy ministry that was taking its toll on him, to the point that he had no time to eat (3:20). Perhaps she hoped to get him to come home; maybe she brought the brothers along to drag Jesus away from the crowd if necessary. When she tried to use her personal relationship with Jesus in hopes of dealing with him, she received a respectful but certain rebuke. In her attempts to spare or restrain Jesus from the crowds, Mary was clearly in the wrong. She had forgotten Jesus' words from Luke 2:49, "Didn't you know I had to be in my Father's house?" (NIV). In any case, they arrived at the house but could not get in. So they stood outside and sent their message in to Jesus.

STANDING OUTSIDE
Jesus' family was standing outside calling Jesus away from his work. They believed they were helping, not hindering. They did not realize how they were blocking Jesus' mission. None of us would consciously block Jesus' efforts, yet we become thoughtless of him when we pursue only our own interests and needs:
- We desire interesting and uplifting companions. He wants to include the unfortunate, disabled, and sick.
- We desire to get to know those who will help us get ahead. He loves the poor, the disenfranchised, the foreigner.
- We desire to get to know those we enjoy on a more intimate basis. He intends to reach all the people of the world, the millions who as yet still have not heard.
- We desire the comfort of family and selected friends. He desires everyone to be in his family.

3:32 **A crowd was sitting around him, and they told him, "Your mother and brothers are outside looking for you."**NIV Jesus sat in the house with the people *sitting around him,* listening to his teaching. The message from Jesus' family was relayed to Jesus. Obviously Jesus' family thought that their relationship with him precluded all others and that he would immediately answer their request.

3:33 **But He answered them, saying, "Who is My mother, or My brothers?"**NKJV Instead of immediately going outside to see what his family members wanted, Jesus looked at the crowd and asked an odd question, *"Who is My mother, or My brothers?"* Jesus knew why his family had come, and he wasn't about to be dragged home because they thought he'd gone crazy. So he used their visit as a lesson in discipleship. A relationship with Jesus is not limited to those in his immediate family. Jesus opened this relationship to all people. His question could be rendered, "Who are the types of people who can have a family relationship with me?"

3:34 **Then he looked at those seated in a circle around him and said, "Here are my mother and my brothers!"**NIV Jesus looked at those seated around him (not the entire crowd, but probably his disciples who were seated closest to him) and answered his own question. The types of people who can have a relationship with him are those who listen, learn, believe, and follow. In these words, Jesus explained that in his spiritual family, the relationships are ultimately more important and longer lasting than those formed in his physical family.

Jesus was not denying his responsibility to his earthly family. On the contrary, he was criticizing the religious leaders for not following the Old Testament command to honor their parents (Matthew 15:1-9). He provided for his mother's security as he hung on the cross (John 19:25-27). His mother and brothers were present in the upper room at Pentecost (Acts 1:14). Instead, Jesus was pointing out that spiritual relationships are as binding as physical ones, and he was paving the way for a new community of believers to be formed as Jesus' spiritual family. This family would be characterized by love; the members should desire to be together, work together, and share one another's burdens.

FAMILY
Not everyone has a brother or sister; not everyone enjoys the opportunity of having loving parents. But God's family has no orphans; an "only child" in Jesus' family doesn't exist. The church is God's family for us.

As important as kinfolk relations are, especially in Christian homes, Jesus establishes a prior relation. The Bible calls God our Father, and Jesus our brother and Savior. We have a true family in Christ, and the circle is still open. To become a Christian means we have many new family relations outside our bloodline, but quite inside the deep, wide, and beautiful circle of God's love. Welcome to the family!

3:35 "Whoever does the will of God is my brother and sister and mother."[NRSV] The key to discipleship in Mark's Gospel is radical obedience to God's will. While Jesus looked upon his disciples seated around him as members of his family, he broadened the scope to include *whoever does the will of God.* Knowledge is not enough—the religious leaders had that and still missed salvation. Following is not enough—the crowd did that and still missed salvation. Instead it is hearing God's Word and putting it into practice (Luke 8:21; James 2:24). When we do this, we come into an intimate relationship with our Savior. We are not saved into facts or rules or a system of worship or a cult of followers, we are saved into a family. We are not saved and made to change our lives; we are saved and then have our lives transformed.

FAMILY TIES
Jesus' true family are those who hear *and* obey his words.
Hearing without obeying is not enough. As Jesus loved his
mother (see John 19:25-27), so he loves us. Christ offers us an
intimate family relationship with him. God's family is accepting
and doesn't exclude anyone. Although Jesus cared for his
mother and brothers, he also cared for all those who loved him.
Jesus did not show partiality; he allowed everyone the privilege
of obeying God and becoming part of his family. In our increas-
ingly computerized, impersonal world, warm relationships
among members of God's family take on major importance.
The church can give the loving, personalized care that people
find nowhere else.

Mark 4

In the first three chapters, Mark recorded the quick pace of Jesus'
ministry. The crowds seemed to be running to keep up. The examples of Jesus' teaching were brief and punctuated with action.
Jesus' life demonstrated the truth that actions speak more loudly
than words.

Mark turned his attention to the content of Jesus' teaching.
The last chapters rapidly moved from one powerful encounter
to another. This chapter includes a series of parables. As was
his pattern, Mark anticipated this shift in the narrative by mentioning Jesus' use of parables in 3:23 and by including two
short examples in 2:19-22. The vitality of Jesus' actions and
teaching drew many different people with varied motives.
Jesus' parables entertained the many who were merely curious; more important, the parables enlightened the few who
genuinely sought to know God.

Parables are earthy stories with profound spiritual applications.
The parable of the sower, seed, and soils certainly provides a
clear example. This parable describes how the human heart
responds to the truth. We must respond to Jesus as good soil by
being receptive and obedient to his Word.

4:1 Again Jesus began to teach by the lake.[NIV] Jesus was *by the
lake* (that is, on the shore of the Sea of Galilee) teaching *again,*
as Mark also recorded in 2:13 and 3:7.

**The crowd that gathered around him was so large that he
got into a boat and sat in it out on the lake, while all the
people were along the shore at the water's edge.**[NIV] Jesus
already had chosen the twelve disciples who would be his closest companions and the recipients of his teaching and training
(3:13-19; 4:10). While he spent time alone with them, he also
had a ministry to all people. Jesus did not hide away with just
his disciples for the remainder of his time on earth; instead, the

disciples accompanied him throughout his ministry and learned from his example.

So Jesus was again teaching by the Sea of Galilee, and as always, a large crowd had gathered. The wording indicates that this was the biggest crowd that had gathered thus far. In fact, it was so large that instead of asking the disciples to have a boat ready in case he needed it (3:9), he went ahead and *got into a boat* anchored a little way off shore. The boat was surrounded by water; it was not moored to a dock. As noted in 3:9, the boat kept in readiness was probably a rowboat *(ploiarion),* while the boat in this verse, from which Jesus spoke, was probably a larger fishing vessel *(ploion).* From that position, Jesus taught the people who were standing or sitting *along the shore at the water's edge.*

> Here is a parable's uniqueness: It is about the only way of obtaining objective assent to truth from one who is personally involved. Judgment is passed before the judge realizes that he is the accused. *Joe Bayly*

4:2-3 He began to teach them many things in parables.[NRSV] Jesus used many illustrations, or *parables,* when teaching the crowds. Parables are short stories that use familiar scenes and everyday objects and relationships to explain spiritual truths. A parable compares something familiar to something unfamiliar. It compels listeners to discover truth, while at the same time concealing the truth from those too lazy or too stubborn to see it. Jesus' insights were hidden from those who refused to seek the truth and from those who would not come back and inquire. To those who were honestly searching, the truth became clear. Jesus spoke the parable to the entire crowd (4:1) but reserved the explanation of the parable for his disciples and other true followers (4:10). We must be careful not to read too much into parables, forcing them to say what they don't mean. All parables have one meaning unless otherwise specified by Jesus.

> There is enough light for those who only desire to see and enough obscurity for those who desire the contrary. *Blaise Pascal*

Mark explained that Jesus taught the people *many things* in parables; Mark has chosen only a few of these parables to record in his Gospel. Indeed, not all of Jesus' parables could have been recorded. This is reflected in what John said at the end of his Gospel: "There are also many other things that Jesus did; if every one of them were written down, I suppose that the world itself could not contain the books that would be written" (John 21:25 NRSV).

LISTEN UP!
The first responsibility of a Christian is to be a great listener. No awards are ever given for this kind of service, but nothing worth an award can be accomplished if our ears are not tuned to God's Word. That Word, the Old and New Testaments, is clear enough if we want to learn and obscure enough if we want to tune out. Listening has two requirements: time and concentration. Give these to God at the start of each day.

And in his teaching said: "Listen! A farmer went out to sow his seed."NIV Jesus, speaking from the deck of a ship anchored out in the water, called for the crowd's attention with the word *"Listen!"* The word was not spoken in harsh command, but as a kind summons. This crowd, many of them more interested in touching Jesus for healing or in seeing miracles, needed to settle down and "listen" to Jesus' teaching because he had an important message for them. Jesus closed this parable with the words, "He who has ears to hear, let him hear!" (4:9). All might listen, but only a few would really hear and understand what Jesus was saying through his parable.

This parable, the first "kingdom parable" recorded in Mark's Gospel, gave a familiar picture to Jesus' audience—a farmer sowing seed, with the resulting increase dependent on the condition of the soil. In ancient Israel, seed was sown by hand. As the *farmer* walked across the field, he would throw handfuls of seed onto the ground from a large bag slung across his shoulders. The plants did not grow in neat rows, as is accomplished by today's machine planting. No matter how skillful, no farmer could keep some of his seed from falling by the wayside, from being scattered among rocks and thorns, or from being carried off by the wind. So the farmer would throw the seed liberally, and enough would fall on good ground to ensure the harvest.

4:4 **"And it happened, as he sowed, that some seed fell by the wayside; and the birds of the air came and devoured it."**NKJV Why would a farmer allow precious seed to land on the *wayside* (path or road), on rocks (4:5), or among thorns (4:7)? In the first century, fields would be planted on both sides of a road to use all the available land. The farmer was not irresponsibly scattering seeds at random. He was using the acceptable method of hand-seeding a large field—tossing it by handfuls as he walked through the field. His goal was to get as much seed as possible to take root in good soil, but there was inevitable waste as some fell or was blown into less productive areas. That some of the seed produced no crop was not the fault of the farmer or of the seed. The yield depended on the condition of the soil where the seed fell.

Some of the seeds fell "by the wayside" (on the road). The hard and compacted soil of the road made it impossible for the seed to penetrate. So it sat on top, as tempting morsels for *the birds of the air* that *came and devoured* the seeds. In 4:15 we learn that the phrase "birds of the air" represents Satan.

GOOD SOIL
The farmer's expectation was for the seed to fall on good soil in which it could grow. He wasn't concerned about the statistic that each seed only had a one in four chance of survival. He just hoped for a good crop. As witnesses for Christ, we must sow his Word liberally, praying for good soil as we go.

4:5-6 "Some fell on rocky places, where it did not have much soil. It sprang up quickly, because the soil was shallow."NIV Some of that same seed (the seed was all the same—it was the soil that differed) *fell on rocky places.* Unlike the wayside, the rocky places had some soil to accept the seed, but not much. The seed *sprang up quickly* in the shallow soil. The rocky soil refers to places with a layer of limestone or other rock several inches under the soil. It trapped the moisture so that the plant grew quickly, but the sun took the moisture out so rapidly that the young plants withered.

"And when the sun rose, it was scorched; and since it had no root, it withered away."NRSV But the shallow soil meant little root for the seed and little moisture to nourish it. Thus, *when the sun rose, it was scorched* and it *withered away.*

4:7 "And some seed fell among thorns; and the thorns grew up and choked it, and it yielded no crop."NKJV Some of the farmer's seed *fell among thorns.* The farmer probably would not intentionally scatter the seed into an area filled with thorns and briers; this probably refers to the seed falling among seeds or roots of thorns that cultivation had not destroyed. Thorns rob the sprouts of nutrition, water, light, and space. Thus, when *the thorns grew up,* the good seed was choked out and could not grow to maturity and yield a crop.

4:8 "Still other seed fell on good soil. It came up, grew and produced a crop, multiplying thirty, sixty, or even a hundred times."NIV However, some of the seed landed in plowed and readied soil. This seed had the depth of soil, space, and moisture to grow and produce a crop. This seed multiplied and yielded thirty, sixty, or even up to a hundred times the amount of seed sown. A farmer would be happy indeed to see his crop multiply even ten times—thirty, sixty, or a hundred would be an incredible yield, for it would mean even more to plant and harvest in the coming year. Jesus pointed out that listening makes fertile soil. If we bear fruit, it is proof that we have listened. If others bear fruit, it shows that the seed we have planted has taken root in their heart.

SOW 'N' SOWS
This parable should encourage spiritual "sowers"—those who teach, preach, and lead others. The farmer sowed good seed, but not all the seed sprouted, and even the plants that grew had varying yields. Don't be discouraged if you do not always see results as you faithfully teach the Word. Conversion results cannot be forced to follow a mathematical formula (for example, a four-to-one ratio of seeds planted to seeds sprouted). Rather, it is a miracle of God's Holy Spirit as he uses your words to lead others to him. Productivity is in God's hands. Trust him and do your work.

4:9 And He said to them, "He who has ears to hear, let him hear!"NKJV Jesus' audience must have wondered at these strange words. Didn't they all have ears, and hadn't they all heard? But Jesus wasn't talking about the act of simply hearing his words. He was speaking of a deeper kind of listening with the mind and heart that is necessary in order to gain spiritual understanding. Some people in the crowd were only curious about Jesus, a few were looking for evidence to use against him, and others truly wanted to learn and grow. Jesus' words were for the honest seekers. Those who honestly seek God's will have spiritual hearing.

Jesus was indeed a strange teacher, different from any these people had ever heard (see 1:22). He did not bask in his huge following, for he knew too well the fickleness of the human heart (see John 2:24-25). Thus, Jesus purposely spoke in parables to weed out false followers from among the true ones. His words, like the farmer's seed, fell on various types of hearts. Those who truly heard and understood would become his followers. Those not ready for Jesus would not understand his words, would lose interest, and finally would either fade away or become his avowed enemies (as did most of the religious leaders).

In addition, it is easy for us to hear Jesus' words on others' behalf. We hear what Jesus says, and may even understand a deeper meaning, but we are quick to apply the message to some-

one else's need. When we hear Jesus' words, we should apply
them to our lives, not to someone else's.

OPEN YOUR EARS!
The hearing Jesus wants from us is not the kind we use to
listen to background radio music or when someone starts to
recount a long story we've already heard. To hear Jesus' words
is to believe them, to use them immediately in decisions and
attitudes, and to base life on them—our recreation and work,
family plans and money matters, schooling and voting, praying
and singing. To hear Jesus' words is to make Jesus our true
Lord. What is Jesus saying to you?

JESUS EXPLAINS THE PARABLE OF THE FOUR SOILS / 4:10-25 / **78**

The parable of the soils was one of many Jesus used to create
questions in the minds of his followers. Later, in a smaller group,
Jesus explained why he used parables and what they meant.

Although Jesus pointed out that the parables kept some people in
ignorance, he willingly explained their meaning to the disciples. Any
hearer who continued to be ignorant or confused did so because he
or she refused to learn. Those who failed to understand the parables
were not ready to obey the truth they taught. Modern readers who
are content with merely "hearing and seeing" will not "perceive or
understand." Therefore, they also will not turn from their sins to be
forgiven. As we read each parable, we should ask, "How is this story
about me?" and "What do I need to do about it?"

Explained according to its immediate historical context, the
"hard soil" may have referred to the leaders, the "rocky soil" and
"thorns" to the crowds, and the "good soil" to the disciples. Of
course, the parable has significance and application beyond the
time of Jesus' ministry; as such, the "hard soil," "rocky soil,"
"thorny soil," and "good soil" refer to the conditions of people's
hearts with respect to their reception of Jesus' message.

4:10 **When he was alone, those who were around him along with
the twelve asked him about the parables.**NRSV The change of
scene recorded here may not be chronological; in other words,
Jesus' explanation of the parable may not have followed immediately after he told it. Mark placed the explanation here to complete his narrative about the parable. In any case, when Jesus got
away from the crowd and was alone with his true followers (the
twelve disciples and the larger group of believers from whom the

Twelve had been chosen), a more intimate question-and-answer period followed. Perhaps these close followers did not want to reveal their ignorance about Jesus' words in front of the entire crowd. So as soon as they were alone with Jesus, his followers *asked him about the parables* in general and particularly in this instance about the parable of the four soils.

4:11 **And He said to them, "To you it has been given to know the mystery of the kingdom of God."**^{NKJV} Jesus revealed that there are only two choices about himself, resulting in two groups of people. Those who are "inside" have accepted the salvation Jesus offers; thus, to them *it has been given to know the mystery of the kingdom of God.*

The *you* to whom Jesus spoke was the group of his true followers, including the twelve disciples and others who believed in Jesus. They had been given a special gift by God, for only they—among the crowds around Jesus—knew *the mystery of the kingdom of God.* God had given this knowledge to these disciples as a permanent possession. They understood, though only partially, the "mystery" that God's kingdom had arrived among them in the person of Jesus.

The word "mystery" *(musterion)* to Greek readers signified a secret revealed to initiates. In the Greek translation of the Old Testament passage Daniel 2:18-19, the Aramaic word *raz* was translated as *musterion.* This Aramaic word refers to divine truths hidden from people until God's divinely appointed time. The apostle Paul would later write to the believers in Ephesus (and us as believers) that God "made known to us the mystery of his will according to his good pleasure, which he purposed in Christ, to be put into effect when the times will have reached their fulfillment" (Ephesians 1:9-10 NIV). Paul also used this Greek word to describe something that once was hidden or obscure but would be revealed in God's timing (see, for example, 1 Corinthians 2:7; 15:51; Ephesians 5:32; 1 Timothy 3:16).

 WHO'S READY?
Some people do not understand God's truth because they are not ready for it. God reveals truth to people who will act on it, who will make it visible in their lives. When you talk with people about God, be aware that they will not understand if they are not ready. Be patient, taking every chance to tell them more of the truth about God and praying that the Holy Spirit will open their mind and heart to receive the truth and act on it.

The kingdom of God was a mystery to the prophets of the Old Testament because, though they wrote about it, they did not understand it (as Paul explained in Romans 16:25-26). The believers who knew Jesus personally received spiritual insight that illuminated the mystery so that it was no longer a mystery to them.

"But to those who are outside, all things come in parables."[NKJV] Jesus was aware of the unbelief and outright hostility of many of his listeners. *Those who are outside* have not yet accepted the message of salvation and may never do so. Thus, for them *all things come in parables.*

Those "outside" (the religious leaders and the vast majority of the crowd) would never "solve" the mystery, for they would not come to God for the answer. Choosing not to believe in Jesus as their Messiah, they would not be able to understand the kingdom. Jesus would do no explaining or clear speaking to these people; he would answer questions about his parables with other parables. These outsiders had already rejected Jesus; no amount of explaining or talking would make any difference. The soil of their heart was hard; the seed of the word would not grow; the parables would be nothing more than strange stories to them. Jesus was not hiding truth from sincere seekers, because those who were receptive to spiritual truth understood the illustrations. To the "wayside, thornpatch, or rocky soil" people, the parables were only stories without meaning. The parables allowed Jesus to give spiritual food to those who hungered for it; but for the others, Isaiah's prophecy would explain their situation.

4:12 **"So that, 'they may be ever seeing but never perceiving, and ever hearing but never understanding; otherwise they might turn and be forgiven!'"**[NIV] God told Isaiah that people would hear without understanding and see without perceiving (Isaiah 6:9); that same kind of reaction was witnessed by Jesus. The parable of the sower was an accurate picture of the people's reaction to all of Jesus' parables.

HEAR AND OBEY
The parables explained many truths about the kingdom (4:2) to those who, with God's help, heard and understood. But for the Pharisees and the unbelieving crowd, the parables would remain vague and unclear, a penalty for their self-imposed blindness. This does not mean that all the people would be excluded forever from God's kingdom. Rather, it means that the mystery of the kingdom would remain hidden as long as they stubbornly rejected the truth. Stubborn refusal to believe eventually leads to inability to believe. We must be willing to both hear and obey. What area in your life does God want you to change? How are you going to obey God in this area?

The words *so that* could indicate either purpose or result. Jesus' parables would remain unclear to those outside for the purpose of keeping them from perceiving and understanding; or the parables resulted in the people being unable to perceive or understand. Some scholars have chosen the second option because, to them, it seems too harsh of Jesus to actually use the parables to purposely keep people from believing. The Greek wording in Matthew appears to say that Jesus used parables "because" the people were already blind. However, the words still clearly say that the parables "intend" to be a means of God's judgment on unbelievers. Compare this to God's dealing with hard-hearted Pharaoh in Exodus 7–12. God gave Pharaoh many opportunities to heed Moses' warnings. But finally God seemed to say, "All right, Pharaoh, have it your way," and the Bible says, "The LORD hardened Pharaoh's heart" (Exodus 9:12 NIV). Did God intentionally harden Pharaoh's heart and overrule his free will? No, he simply confirmed that Pharaoh had freely chosen a life of resisting God (see also Romans 9:14-18).

By quoting from the prophet Isaiah, Jesus was explaining to this inner group of followers that the crowd resembled the Israelites about whom Isaiah had written. God had told Isaiah that the people would listen but not learn from his message because their hearts had hardened beyond repentance. Yet God still sent Isaiah with the message because, even though the nation itself would not repent and would reap judgment, some individuals *would* listen. Jesus came to the Israelites hundreds of years after Isaiah, but the scenario was the same. Most would not repent because their hearts were hardened; but a few would listen, turn from their sins, and believe. The deafness to the message did not mean the message was false or that the messenger was somehow at fault. It is not for us to understand why some believe and some do not; instead, we are simply to continue to trust in God and proclaim his message.

Neither Isaiah's nor Jesus' audiences were denied the opportunity to *turn and be forgiven.* Instead, the point was clearly made that refusing to listen would mean inability to perceive and understand anything Jesus had to say. The Pharisees had already accused Jesus of being in league with Satan (3:22). Such an accusation revealed their stubborn blindness and their refusal to believe. Jesus used these words from Isaiah to refer directly back to the Pharisees' accusation. The verbs are singular, meaning that they would not be forgiven of their sin of blasphemy. No matter how much they saw of Jesus' miracles or heard of his teaching, they never would be able to understand because they had deliberately chosen not to. God does not override human will.

IT'S THE TRUTH
In the Bible, discovering truth always requires faith. The absence of faith puts us outside the reach of God's truth. God's Word never sounds like a scientific experiment, where the rule is test and retest until you're sure nothing else works. God's Word always sounds like a loving father saying, "Believe this, and follow this way!" When we trust and then obey God's Word, we come to know how true it is. Do what God says because you know his way is best. God can be trusted.

4:13 Then Jesus said to them, "Don't you understand this parable? How then will you understand any parable?"NIV Understanding the parable of the sower shows us how all the parables work. That is why this has been called "the parable of parables." People cannot see without the illumination of the Holy Spirit. To "understand" is like formerly blind eyes being made to see. By nature, humans are spiritually blind. But the spiritual insight given by the Holy Spirit illumines the parables and indeed all of God's Word so that believers can truly "perceive" and "understand" what God has to say (4:9). Jesus was speaking to those to whom the "mystery" had been revealed (4:11); thus, they shouldn't have needed any explanation at all. Neither Matthew nor Luke records these words of Jesus; the tone of rebuke fits in with Mark's portrayal of the disciples. Their failure to understand the parable is in keeping with that emphasis.

4:14 "The farmer sows the word."NIV The farmer was Jesus (see Matthew 13:37) and—by extension—anyone after him who would teach and preach *the word*. The seed that is sown is the Word of God (4:3). Jesus was telling the parable and exemplifying it; as he spoke of the farmer sowing the word, he was doing so among the crowd of followers. Jesus was revealing his mission while teaching the disciples about theirs.

THE HARDENED PATH
A pathway was a hardened surface trampled down and compacted by heavy traffic. It characterizes the hardened or unprepared heart. Nothing sinks in. These people pay no attention to sermons they hear. Even more probable, they are totally insensitive to any messages about God or spiritual truth. Jesus explained why others may be unresponsive: They are hardened. But we must keep our heart prepared and open to receive his will.

4:15 "Some people are like seed along the path, where the word is sown. As soon as they hear it, Satan comes and takes away the

word that was sown in them."ᴺᴵⱽ The parable revealed people's
varying responses to the gospel message. The attitude or condition of their hearts would govern their response.

The word makes no impression on some people. *As soon as
they hear it,* Satan (like the birds of the air, 4:4) takes it away. Perhaps the person feels no need in his or her heart, no desire for
anything other than this life, no guilt of sin or need of forgiveness. Satan has no trouble with these people. But he uses other
tactics on other types of people.

DROWNING IN SHALLOWS
Some new followers get excited about Jesus. They may attend
a concert, festival, or special meeting. They are temporarily
very enthusiastic, and they feel great happiness and joy. But it
may be merely an emotional response. At that point, their faith
is shallow, vulnerable, and unstable. Their faith hasn't taken
root in their minds, attitudes, or behavior. When conflicts come,
they get burned up. This explains why some professing followers fall away. It also reminds mature Christians to support new
believers, to re-explain the way of salvation, to get them into
Bible study, to include them in groups that will pray for them
and guide them through their conflicts. Evangelism is not
enough if it stops short of making disciples. Evangelism
requires follow-through care. Every new convert should be
anchored in Christ. We should never take for granted that a
confession of faith means actual conversion. We must help
new faith to persevere and mature.

4:16-17 **"Others, like seed sown on rocky places, hear the word and at
once receive it with joy."**ᴺᴵⱽ The *seed sown on rocky places* had
some soil to accept the seed, but not much. It "sprang up quickly"
in the shallow soil (4:5). These people joyfully receive the good
news of the gospel because of the promises offered. They grow a
bit and initially show some promise of growth.

**"But since they have no root, they last only a short time.
When trouble or persecution comes because of the word, they
quickly fall away."**ᴺᴵⱽ These people understand some of the
basics but do not allow God's truth to work its way into their
souls and make a difference in their lives—*they have no root* and
thus *last only a short time.* When trouble comes (the scorching
heat, 4:6), they decide not to believe the gospel or its promises
and thus fall away. Jews who accepted Jesus as Savior were
excommunicated from the synagogue and often disowned by
their families (see John 9:22-23). Satan can always use sorrow,
trouble, and persecution to draw people away from God. Ironi-

TODAY'S THORNS

We must welcome God's Word exclusively so nothing stifles or distracts us. We must weed out or avoid the thorn patches. As James wrote, "Do not merely listen to the word, and so deceive yourselves. Do what it says" (James 1:22 NIV).

The Thorn	*The Problem*	*The Solution*
Worries of this life. Society says, "Take care of yourself; no one else will."	Fear of persecution for being identified with Christ can neutralize people who are worried that they will be ridiculed. Daily concerns, schedules, and pressures can snuff out our time and energy to grow. Worry consumes our thoughts, disrupts our productivity, and reduces our trust in God.	James 1:12, "Blessed is anyone who endures temptation" (NRSV). Philippians 4:6, "Don't worry about anything; instead, pray about everything; tell God your needs, and don't forget to thank him for his answers" (TLB). Matthew 6:31, "Therefore do not worry" (NRSV).
Deceitfulness of wealth. Society says, "Wealth brings security, power, and happiness."	Wealth can take God's place in our lives. It can become an idol—the focus of our activities and devotion. It tempts us to deny our dependence on God, taking our eyes off eternal values. Wealth leads to pride.	Jeremiah 9:23, "Do not let the wealthy boast in their wealth" (NRSV). Luke 12:34, "For where your treasure is, there your heart will be also" (NIV). 1 Timothy 6:6, "Now godliness with contentment is great gain" (NKJV). 1 Timothy 6:10, "For the love of money is a root of all kinds of evil" (NKJV).
Desires for other things. Society says, "Indulge yourself; try it all; get all you can."	Indulging our desires leads to all kinds of problems. It weakens our will power, stifles our spiritual growth, and leads to companions who will pull us down.	Romans 13:14, "Rather, clothe yourselves with the Lord Jesus Christ, and do not think about how to gratify the desires of the sinful nature" (NIV). 1 Corinthians 15:33, "Do not be misled: 'Bad company corrupts good character'" (NIV). 1 Peter 1:13-14, "Prepare your minds for action; be self-controlled; set your hope fully on the grace to be given you when Jesus Christ is revealed. As obedient children, do not conform to the evil desires you had when you lived in ignorance" (NIV).

cally, those who let the message take root in good soil find that
sorrow, trouble, and persecution bring them closer to God.

4:18-19 **"Still others, like seed sown among thorns, hear the word;
but the worries of this life, the deceitfulness of wealth and the
desires for other things come in and choke the word, making
it unfruitful."**NIV This is Satan's most subversive tactic of all.
These people hear and accept the word and allow it to take root
in their hearts, giving hope of a harvest. But *thorns* grow up and
choke out the growing seed. Thorns rob nutrition, water, light,
and space from newly sprouting seeds. Distractions and conflicts
rob new believers of time to reflect on and digest God's Word in
order to grow from it, as well as robbing guidance and support
from interaction with other Christians. Jesus described the thorns:

- *worries of this life*

- *deceitfulness of wealth*

- *desires for other things*

Worldly worries (no matter how important or how minor), the
false sense of security brought on by (or merely promised by)
prosperity, and the desire for material things (including anything
that serves to distract a person) plagued first-century disciples as
they do us today. Daily routines overcrowd and materialistic pur-
suits distract believers, *making it* (that is, God's Word) *unfruitful*
in their lives.

SEED AND SOIL
"Wayside" people, like many of the religious leaders, refuse to
believe God's message. "Rocky soil" people, like many in the
crowds who followed Jesus, believe his message but never get
around to doing anything about it. "Thorn patch" people, overcome by worries and the lure of materialism, leave no room in
their lives for God. "Good soil" people, in contrast to all the
other groups, follow Jesus no matter what the cost. They listen,
obey, and follow through on what he says. Which type of soil
are you? What do you need to do to become good soil?

4:20 **"Others, like seed sown on good soil, hear the word, accept
it, and produce a crop—thirty, sixty or even a hundred
times what was sown."**NIV But other people are like the *good
soil*—they *hear the Word* and *accept it*. These are the true disciples—those who have accepted Jesus, believed his words, and
allowed him to make a difference in their lives.

Notice that the seed bears seed. In other words, those who

preach the Word yield others who preach the Word to others who preach the word and so on. These believers *produce a crop.* Paul understood this principle when he wrote to Timothy, "What you have heard from me through many witnesses entrust to faithful people who will be able to teach others as well" (2 Timothy 2:2 NRSV). There are varying yields, but that should never affect the farmer's desire to sow or the disciple's desire to spread the Good News.

Jesus' parable answered the question of why there were so many opinions about Jesus. In Jesus' day, people ranged from belief to hatred and all shades in between. The same is true today. The answer, said Jesus, lies not in the message, for that is always the same. Neither is the problem caused by the preacher or teacher if he or she sows the message appropriately. The answer is that the message falls on hearts that are in varied degrees of readiness. The message will not be accepted in the same way by all who hear it. Even the prophet Ezekiel had been told, "Whether they hear or refuse to hear . . . they shall know that there has been a prophet among them. . . . You shall speak my words to them, whether they hear or refuse to hear" (Ezekiel 2:5, 7 NRSV).

OPEN OR CLOSED
The four soils represent four different ways people respond to God's message. While Jesus was talking about four different kinds of hearts and each's readiness to receive the gospel, his words could also apply to us in two other ways: (1) different times or phases in our lives; (2) how we willingly receive God's message in some areas of our lives and resist it in others.

For example, you may be open to God about your future, but closed concerning how you spend your money. You may respond like good soil to God's demand for worship, but be like rocky soil with regard to helping people in need. Strive to be like good soil in every area of your life at all times.

4:21 He said to them, "Do you bring in a lamp to put it under a bowl or a bed? Instead, don't you put it on its stand?"NIV The parables in 4:21-25 occur also in Luke 8:16-18 and in several places in Matthew. While these may have been addressed to the disciples, more likely Jesus was speaking to the multitude, including the disciples.

In ancient Israel, a *lamp* was a lighted wick in a clay bowl that was full of oil. The lamp was not lit and then put *under a bowl or a bed,* that is, under a closed place where its light could not be seen. Instead, the lamp was lit and put on its stand in order to illuminate the room. The disciples may have wondered why Jesus seemed to be deliberately hiding the truth of the gospel through parables. Perhaps they thought that if the Word was going to fall on hard hearts, then why should they sow it so liberally? Shouldn't they just limit their teaching to those who were ready and eager to listen? But Jesus' words answered their question (whether spoken in private or considered in their mind in public). "No," explained Jesus, "I am not deliberately trying to hide the truth from people. That would be like lighting a lamp and then putting it under a bowl. Why then light the lamp at all? If I am hiding the truth, there is no reason for me to teach." The purpose of the parables is not to conceal the truth, but to reveal it; the parables explain in everyday terms truths that human minds cannot grasp. Thus the parables do not obscure, they clarify—but only to those who are willing to listen and believe.

The disciples may have been beginning to understand the mission to which Jesus had called them. Like the farmer in the parable, theirs would be the job of sowing the seed of the gospel in a largely hostile world. The light of the truth about Jesus had illuminated them, and it was their ministry to shine that light to a sin-darkened world. Their witness for Christ would be public, not hidden. The benefits of knowing Jesus and receiving salvation were not to be kept to themselves, but passed on to others. Christ's message is intended for all people. We should not hide our Christianity from the watching world.

BASKET CASES
Many Christians today are hidden from sight, reluctant to be identified as Christians. Such a Christian is like a brand-new light that never leaves the carton it came in. If a lamp doesn't help people see, it isn't worth much. Does your life show other people how to find God and how to live for him? If not, ask what "baskets" have hidden your light. Complacency, resentment, embarrassment, stubbornness of heart, or disobedience could keep you from shining.

4:22 "For there is nothing hidden which will not be revealed, nor has anything been kept secret but that it should come to light."ᴺᴷᴶⱽ Jesus continued his explanation for his use of parables. Although the truth may be *hidden* or *kept secret* for a while, it will not remain so. One day the truth will be *revealed* and *come to light.* Jesus was speaking of the days of his ministry as the time of using parables, concealing the truth, and being rejected by many. The time of revelation and coming to light could refer either to Jesus' resurrection and ascension (when his followers would fully understand Jesus' words) or the Second Coming. Jesus' followers did not understand everything about Jesus at that time, but all their questions would be answered one day.

NO SECRETS
What Jesus told his disciples privately, we must share with others. God's truth requires a clear and helpful explanation to the world. As light fills a room, God's Word drives out spiritual darkness. Disciples must participate in revealing God's truth to the world through witness in word (such as preaching and singing) and deed (helping hungry people). We dare not hide something as important as God's truth in a closet. How vocal and active is your witness? Maybe it's time to bring it out of hiding.

4:23 "If anyone has ears to hear, let him hear."NKJV This saying, which repeats 4:9, often concluded Jesus' important statements. As explained in 4:9 above, Jesus spoke of a deeper kind of listening: hearing not with the ears, but with the mind and heart. Only then could the hearers gain spiritual understanding from his parables. The honest seekers would understand the parables (see James 1:22).

4:24 And he said to them, "Pay attention to what you hear; the measure you give will be the measure you get, and still more will be given you."NRSV Because the parables are so important in what they teach, Jesus warned the people to *pay attention* to his words. We must treasure the words of Jesus. Those who heard, understood, and then shared with others would be given even more understanding to pass along. Believers are responsible to use well their God-given understanding, insight, and opportunities to share the gospel. Whether they have little or much, that is not nearly as important as what is done with what they have. It is the *measure* with which they give that determines what more will be given. Even then, *still more will be given* because a person's openness and perception of the kingdom message will bring great rewards. Ultimately, believers will receive eternal blessings in heaven.

4:25 "For to those who have, more will be given; and from those who have nothing, even what they have will be taken away."NRSV The people who listen and understand are *those who have.* To them God will give more understanding and blessings. They will continue to grow because they let God's Word make a difference in their lives. This is a principle of growth in physical, mental, and spiritual life. For example, a muscle, when exercised, will grow stronger, but an unused muscle will grow weak and flabby. If a muscle is not growing stronger, it is growing weaker; it cannot stay the same. Like the unused muscle, those who do not listen nor understand *(those who have nothing)* will lose whatever they had. Jesus' words here may have been directed to the Jews who had no understanding of Jesus and would lose even what they had—that is, their privileged status as God's people. Or Jesus might have meant that when people reject him, their hardness of heart drives away or renders useless even the little understanding they had. Eventually, any opportunity to share in God's kingdom will be taken away completely. To understand Jesus' message, people must listen and respond. Those who listen casually, for whatever reason, will miss the point.

TURN ON THE LIGHT
The light of Jesus' truth is revealed to us, not hidden. But we may not be able to see or to use all of that truth right now. Only as we put God's teachings into practice will we understand and see more of the truth. The truth is clear, but our ability to understand is imperfect. As we obey, we will sharpen our vision and increase our understanding (see James 1:22-25). Be patient; eventually you will see the truth.

JESUS TELLS THE PARABLE OF THE GROWING SEED / 4:26-29 / **79**

Many of Jesus' parables sprouted from similes. He focused on what people knew or saw and then pointed to a similarity between that and a characteristic of the kingdom of God. The way Jesus made use of his surroundings demonstrates that all of creation is filled with lessons and pointers. This parable teaches us that spiritual growth cannot be measured by a stopwatch. The kingdom of God may be planted in us in an instant, but its growth becomes apparent only with the passing of time and the practice of faithfulness.

4:26-27 **He also said, "This is what the kingdom of God is like. A man scatters seed on the ground. Night and day, whether he sleeps or gets up, the seed sprouts and grows, though he does not know how."**NIV This parable about the kingdom of God, recorded only by Mark, reveals that spiritual growth is a continual, gradual process that is finally consummated in a harvest of spiritual maturity. We can begin to understand the process of spiritual growth by comparing it to the slow but certain growth of a plant. The man *scatters seed.* Obviously, there would be no crop if the seed were not planted. However, after the planting, the man goes about his other responsibilities *night and day* and does not think about the seed. During that time, the seed is germinating, sprouting, and growing. The man *does not know how* this happens; but he can depend on the process and is certain of the growth of his crop.

> It is one thing to go through a crisis grandly, but a different thing to go through every day glorifying God when there is no witness, no limelight, and no one paying the remotest attention to you. *Oswald Chambers*

Even though the farmer does not understand the actual process of growth (and even modern scientists still cannot completely fathom the mystery of growth), his ignorance does not stop it from happening. He may not understand how growth happens, but he knows that the seed will grow. In the same way, the kingdom of God begins in a person's life with a seed of understanding that takes root in the good soil of a ready heart. That seed sprouts and grows into strong faith. But *how* that happens is God's responsibility. While God uses his followers to plant the seeds, he gives the growth. As Paul wrote to the Corinthians, "I planted the seed, Apollos watered it, but God made it grow" (1 Corinthians 3:6 NIV).

The disciples, wondering about the difficult mission ahead of them, were being told by Jesus that they need not worry about how the kingdom would grow. That part was up to God alone. Their job was to sow the seed. With his coming to earth, Jesus sowed the kingdom of God, and God would bring that harvest to fruition.

SEE HOW IT GROWS
Because the seed of spiritual life grows by the power of the Holy Spirit, we do not need to badger, dictate, cajole, or force people (even little people) to believe. In fact, we cannot. Belief requires voluntary acceptance. Anything that looks like a threat or a bribe spoils true belief. Anyone who truly believes is drawn by God himself. We may plant the seed of faith by our witness; God alone makes it germinate, sprout, and blossom. We need to faithfully minister to others and trust God for the growth.

4:28 **"For the earth yields crops by itself: first the blade, then the head, after that the full grain in the head."**^{NKJV} Jesus was still explaining "what the kingdom of God is like" (4:26). The farmer sows the seed and expects a crop, without understanding *how* that happens. The stress in this verse is on the words *by itself.* The process of growth, *the blade, then the head, after that the full grain,* is a mystery to us and happens without any intervention on our part. We can sow the seed, but the growth happens "by itself" (of course, meaning "with God's help," for God planned his creation to work just that way, see Genesis 1:11-13).

In the same manner, how God's kingdom grows in people's hearts is a mystery to us and happens without any intervention on our part. We sow the seed and allow God to let it grow. Notice, too, that the growth is slow and deliberate, like the growth of a plant. The plant doesn't shoot out of the ground overnight. The seed slowly germinates and grows almost imperceptibly—but it grows. Jesus was explaining that the kingdom would grow both in people's hearts and by adding people to it. The growth would be slow but certain. It would face obstacles but would continue to grow nonetheless. Our job is to faithfully sow the seed, trust God, and wait and look for signs of life.

GOD'S MYSTERIOUS WAYS
God's mysterious power as shown by the seed's growth cycle can be compared to how the gospel works in the hearts of believers and how the Holy Spirit works through each of us. This would have been a great encouragement for Mark's readers, who may have compared their small ministry with the power and position of Jerusalem or Rome and become discouraged. But the Holy Spirit works day and night. Sometimes growth is imperceptible. We must stay faithful to God and to his work because his power is working even if we can't always see the results.

4:29 **"But when the grain ripens, immediately he puts in the sickle, because the harvest has come."**NKJV The farmer lets the seed grow in the fields and goes about his other work (4:26-27), but *when the grain ripens,* he has work to do *because the harvest has come.* The farmer takes his *sickle* (a curved blade mounted in a short handle) and cuts the grain to harvest it into his barns. "Puts in the sickle" could mean "sending out reapers" who would cut and harvest the grain.

Likewise, the time will come when God will intervene decisively into the world's affairs. This verse has a tone of warning, echoing Joel 3:13, "Swing the sickle, for the harvest is ripe" (NIV). Joel prophesied about God's coming and the final judgment of the world. While some see Jesus' words as referring to evangelism, and others to spiritual growth in individual believers, it seems most likely that this pictures the mysterious coming of God's kingdom. Jesus came and sowed the seed, as did his followers after him. The Word takes root and grows in individuals, and the church grows throughout the ages. Then, at a time only God knows, he will re-enter the world, harvest the "crop," and separate the "grain" from the "weeds" (Matthew 13:24-30). The weeds (unbelievers) will receive judgment for sin; the good grain (believers) will be ushered into God's eternal kingdom.

LOOKING FORWARD
God promises that his harvest will be magnificent and prolific—the best fruit ever grown. Our witness may be weak and our efforts may seem to influence so few, but the Word of God is a powerful growth agent. We should keep our eyes on the great harvest to come and not let bad soil or weeds discourage us from faithful service and witness.

JESUS TELLS THE PARABLE OF THE MUSTARD SEED / 4:30-34 / 81

Mark concluded this sampling of Jesus' parables with a second lesson about the kingdom of God. He began the chapter with the parable of the four soils, which illustrates the variety of responses to the gospel. The two following parables focus on what happens when the truth finds a receptive heart.

The parable of the growing seed illustrates the growth rate of the kingdom of God. The parable of the mustard seed illustrates the surprising size of the growth from such a small beginning. In a world that often confuses size with value, the kingdom of God presents a contradiction. How can something so insignificant turn out to be so important?

4:30 He also said, "With what can we compare the kingdom of God, or what parable will we use for it?"NRSV As if repeating from 4:26, Jesus prepared again to explain the kingdom of God in a parable. While the parable of the seed planted describes the mystery of the growth of the kingdom, the parable of the mustard seed describes the extent of the growth. No one parable could completely describe God's kingdom in all its aspects, so Jesus employed several of them. The crowds, and even some of the disciples at this point, were expecting a political leader who would free Israel from Rome. The only "kingdom" they could picture was an earthly one (consider the special favor James and John requested in 10:35-37). So Jesus attempted to clarify the kingdom even further for them.

4:31 "It is like a mustard seed, which is the smallest seed you plant in the ground."[NIV] In this parable, Jesus stressed that his kingdom would have a small beginning—indeed, it began with Jesus alone and, upon his ascension, was left in the care of twelve apostles and a few hundred other followers. Jesus compared this beginning to the *mustard seed,* which was the smallest seed a farmer used. Though the mustard seed is not the smallest seed in all of creation, it was the smallest known seed at that time. Some have tried to use the fact that the mustard seed is *not* the smallest seed as an argument against the accuracy of the Bible. Jesus was not making a scientific statement. He was showing the relative size of a large plant growing from a small seed. The mustard seed was so small that it would take almost twenty thousand seeds to make one ounce. Perhaps this was encouraging for those disciples and early Roman Christians who were being persecuted by Rome or Jerusalem or who may have been comparing their small and paltry operation with the size and power of the Roman Empire.

Jesus stressed the future greatness of the kingdom, which at that time seemed insignificant. He also showed that the kingdom had small beginnings but would grow and produce great results.

4:32 "Yet when it is sown it grows up and becomes the greatest of all shrubs, and puts forth large branches, so that the birds of the air can make nests in its shade."[NRSV] From this very tiny seed would grow a large shrub—the largest shrub among all the herbs that the farmer would plant in his garden. A mustard shrub could grow ten to twelve feet in just a few weeks. Jesus' point was that just as a tiny seed can grow into the *greatest of all shrubs,* so God's kingdom can begin with a few people who truly believe and grow into such greatness that, upon Christ's second coming, it will overpower the entire earth and rule supremely forever.

Jesus' mention of *birds of the air* was probably meant to add color to his parable or to describe the size of this shrub, but probably did not have any allegorical meaning. However, some commentators say that the birds represent the Gentiles becoming part of God's kingdom (see prophecies such as Ezekiel 17:22-24; 31:6).

For the disciples, and for us, this parable meant that size or relative power does not indicate final results. The disciples needed to understand that while their mission might at times seem unattainable, God's kingdom *would* take root and grow across the world and through the years. This would be no political coup; the kingdom would grow slowly but surely in people's hearts, making a difference in people's lives and preparing them for life to come in God's eternal kingdom.

NO SMALL FAITH
Jesus used this parable to explain that although Christianity had very small beginnings, it would grow into a worldwide community of believers. When you feel alone in your stand for Christ, realize that God is building a worldwide kingdom. Don't be intimidated if your efforts seem small. Neither should you take credit for a prolific harvest. God has faithful followers in every part of the world. Your faith, no matter how small, can join with the faith of others to accomplish much for him.

4:33 With many similar parables Jesus spoke the word to them, as much as they could understand.[NIV] Mark made clear that he did not record all of Jesus' parables—there were probably too many to record. So he explained that Jesus spoke the *word* (that is, God's message) to *them* (the crowds, including the disciples). In addition, this master teacher taught *as much as they could understand.* Jesus adapted his methods to his audience's ability and desire to understand. He didn't speak in parables to confuse people, but to challenge sincere seekers to discover the meaning of his words. Jesus knew that some of the "seed" he sowed would fall on good soil—i.e., people to whom God had given the ability to hear and believe.

4:34 He did not speak to them except in parables, but he explained everything in private to his disciples.[NRSV] The crowds, in general, greatly misunderstood Jesus. If they *did* believe he was the promised Messiah, they thought he had come to free them from Roman oppression. The "kingdom" they wanted was an earthly kingdom of their own, free from Rome's grasp. Jesus' parables helped to separate the curious bystanders from the honest seekers, so when he spoke to the crowds, *he did not speak to them except in parables.* As explained in 4:2-3, Jesus spoke in parables to the crowds (see also 4:1), but *explained everything in private to his disciples* (see also 4:10). The disciples here are specifically the Twelve. Jesus "explained" (that is, he kept on explaining—the imperfect tense in Greek) "everything." Nothing went unexplained or unanswered. Jesus did not hide anything from his disciples. He wanted them to know and understand the truth about himself, his mission, and his teachings.

ALONE WITH JESUS
Even though the Word of God, like the seed, has awesome harvest-producing potential, it requires personal explanation, teaching, and application. Jesus took his disciples alone, away from the crowd, to explain his teachings. We cannot expect today's listeners to understand everything about the life and teaching of Christ from what they hear in sermons and Sunday Bible readings. There must be classes and small groups to teach, discuss, and apply the magnificent words of Christ to each person. What can your church do to teach the life of Christ so that it takes root in each person's life?

JESUS CALMS THE STORM / 4:35-41 / **87**

In this section, Mark shifted back to the action style so characteristic of his Gospel. He has described the intense encounters between Jesus and various groups (religious leaders, crowds, his own family), then given us a series of teaching parables. Next he recalled a series of miracles to demonstrate Jesus' power over the natural elements, the spiritual realm, and the human body. He presented a strong case for Jesus' startling uniqueness and divine nature.

Mark's details of Jesus' calming the storm are absent in the accounts of Matthew and Luke. These details indicate that Mark used Peter as a source. He gives intimate facts that only an eyewitness would have known.

Believers today profess trust in Jesus' power over the storms of life, but many fall short of demonstrating that trust when the storms arrive. Beneath a Christian veneer, there often lives a practical atheist. Saying we believe that Jesus can help us takes on a whole new meaning when we actually depend on him for help.

4:35 On that day, when evening had come, he said to them, "Let us go across to the other side."[NRSV] Jesus' *day* could have begun with the accusation of being in league with Satan (3:20-30). If so, he had dealt with the religious leaders, then with his family who had come to take him home by force (3:31-34). He had also told parables from the deck of a fishing boat anchored near the shore of the Sea of Galilee. So *when evening had come,* Jesus suggested that they *go across to the other side*—that is, to the east side of the lake (see 5:1 and map). If Jesus had gone back on shore, the crowds would have continued to hound him; his only escape and rest was to stay in the boat and simply sail away. The twelve disciples, his inner circle of followers, had been in the boat during Jesus' teaching. The boat probably belonged to one of the fishermen among the group, most likely to Peter. For Peter to set sail in the evening was not unusual because he was used to fishing at night (see John 21:3). Fishing was best then; storms usually came in the afternoon.

Thus, when Jesus finished speaking, the disciples pulled up the anchor and set sail. Jesus' ministry was never without purpose. He was crossing the sea in order to enter a new area of ministry. Along the way, the disciples would be taught an unforgettable lesson about his power.

ON THE MOVE
Jesus was always going somewhere, leaving some place and going to another. Not restlessly, but steadily he made his journey from town to wilderness to river valley and finally the big city. He knew his home was always heaven, but he had much to do on earth.

In fulfilling God's purpose in Christian ministry or in the careers and roles God leads us to do, we must not confuse restless activity with fruitful service. We may feel as though we're wayfaring pilgrims or nomads on the move, but Christ must always be our guide, and his Word our compass. As you do your activities and carry out your busy schedule, act as though Jesus is next to you.

4:36 Leaving the crowd behind, they took him along, just as he was, in the boat. There were also other boats with him.[NIV] A few people in the crowd probably expected Jesus to come ashore to offer more healing or teaching. But Jesus, human as he was, needed rest. So he left the crowd behind when the boat set sail. Jesus went with the disciples *just as he was.*

The detail that *there were also other boats* is recorded only in Mark and signifies an eyewitness account—perhaps from Peter who sailed the boat and had to watch out for these other boats as they made their way out into the lake. (Josephus, an ancient historian, wrote that there were usually more than three hundred fishing boats on the Sea of Galilee at one time.) The other boats accompanying Jesus may have been filled with persistent followers. The tiny detail gives us a picture of God's grace—many people on these other boats were also saved when Jesus stilled the storm.

4:37 A furious squall came up, and the waves broke over the boat, so that it was nearly swamped.[NIV] The Sea of Galilee is an unusual body of water. It is relatively small (thirteen miles long, seven miles wide); but it is 150 feet deep, and the shoreline is 680 feet below sea level. Because the Sea of Galilee is below sea level and is surrounded by mountains, it is susceptible to sudden storms. Winds sweeping across the land come up and over the mountains, creating downdrafts over the lake. Combined with a thunderstorm that appears suddenly over the surrounding mountains, the water stirs into violent twenty-foot waves. The disciples had not foolishly set out in a storm. In fact, they usually didn't encounter storms at night and did not see this one coming. Even though several of these men were expert fishermen and knew how to handle a boat,

> For proof of the truth that following God's guidance brings trouble, look at the life of the Lord Jesus himself. No human life has ever been so completely guided by God, and no human being has ever qualified so comprehensively for the description "a man of sorrows." *J. I. Packer*

they had been caught without warning by this *furious squall.* Their peril was real as they battled huge waves that *nearly swamped* their vessel.

MORE STORMS THAN CALM
Problems occur in every area of life. The disciples needed rest, but they encountered a terrible storm. The Christian life may have more stormy weather than calm seas and may present life-threatening challenges. It is not just smooth sailing and triumphant living. As Christ's followers, we must be prepared for the storms that will surely come. We must not surrender to the stress, but remain resilient, solve our problems, and recover from setbacks. With faith in Christ, we can pray, trust, and move ahead. When a squall approaches, we can praise God and lean into the wind.

4:38 Jesus was in the stern, sleeping on a cushion.[NIV] While this was happening, Jesus *was in the stern* (or back) of the ship; he had fallen asleep on a *cushion.* He probably had lain down on the low bench in the stern, where the steersman would sit, and had fallen asleep on the leather cushion. How Jesus could sleep during this storm indicates his complete exhaustion and reveals his human nature. That the noise, the violent rocking of the boat, and the cold spray of the water didn't awaken him gives us a glimpse of the physical drain on Jesus throughout his earthly ministry.

The disciples woke him and said to him, "Teacher, don't you care if we drown?"[NIV] The disciples had embarked on this journey at Jesus' request after a long day. They were probably tired too, but they had set sail anyway. Then, of all things, a storm blew in—and not just any storm, but a "furious squall" that was threatening to sink the boat and drown them. Worst of all, Jesus was sleeping through it! Didn't he realize that they all were going to drown? So they *woke him* and asked with a tone of rebuke, *"Teacher, don't you care if we drown?"* Their words were more of a criticism than a call for help. How easy it is for us to complain and criticize God for not coming to our aid, rather than making our request and then trusting him to answer. These words of the disciples occur only in Mark and prepare the way for the theme of the disciples' failure to understand Jesus. We may tend to voice similar complaints to God when we feel he doesn't care. Instead of accusing God, we should let our requests be made known to him (Philippians 4:6) and ask for his wisdom (James 1:5).

Although the disciples had witnessed many miracles, they panicked in this storm. Added to that, they revealed that they completely misunderstood their teacher. They had seen Jesus perform great miracles of compassion, but they dared to ask if he cared about them at all. Their question was rude; their misunderstanding was deep. They reacted with fear and anger at their situation. They knew Jesus could perform miracles; what they did not know was that he could control the forces of nature.

THE POWER
There is often a stormy area of our human nature where we feel God can't or won't work. When we truly understand who God is, however, we will realize that he controls both the storms of nature and the storms of the troubled heart. How do you react to danger and stress? Jesus' power that calmed this storm can also help you deal with the problems you face. Jesus is willing to help if you only ask him. Never discount his power, even in terrible trials.

4:39 Then He arose and rebuked the wind, and said to the sea, "Peace, be still!" And the wind ceased and there was a great calm.[NKJV] Jesus, abruptly awakened from a deep sleep, arose and without speaking to the disciples spoke instead to the elements. Standing in the stern of the rocking ship, Jesus *rebuked the wind, and said to the sea, "Peace, be still!"* The Greek words are the same as Jesus used when he told the demons to be silent (see 1:25). It means "Be calm and remain calm."

Anyone who has been in a frightening storm at sea, watching walls of water toss the ship, can understand what an incredible sight it was to have the sea suddenly become calm. What a relief as well. The forces of nature, when unleashed—whether in the form of a tornado, hurricane, earthquake, or waves of water on a rough sea—can be terrifying because we are completely at their mercy. The disciples' were shocked at the power of their teacher to speak and control the ocean waves. But they should not have been surprised. The storm was out of control, their fears were out of control, but Jesus was never out of control. He has power over all the forces of nature, and he listens to the appeals of those who love him.

4:40 He said to them, "Why are you afraid? Have you still no faith?"^{NRSV} The disciples had seen Jesus do incredible miracles, but they hadn't taken their knowledge of his power and carried it to its logical conclusion. Sure, he could heal the sick, but when it came to ocean waves, he'd better have a bucket ready for bailing water. Their rude words to him, "Don't you care if we drown?" (4:38 NIV) brought Jesus' appropriate response as he turned to them from his position in the stern of the ship on a now calm sea. *"Why are you afraid? Have you still no faith?"* They wanted him to do something; he wanted them to trust him! The Greek word for "afraid" *(deiloi)* means "cowardly fear." The disciples were acting like cowards when they should have acted with faith in their teacher. Despite all that the disciples had seen and heard thus far, and despite their belief in Jesus as the Messiah, they still had not grasped that Jesus was himself God, given God's power and authority over all of creation.

PANIC ATTACK
The disciples panicked because the storm threatened to destroy them all, and Jesus seemed unaware and unconcerned. Theirs was a physical storm, but storms come in other forms. Think about the storms in your life—the situations that cause you great anxiety. The disciples lived with Jesus, but they underestimated him. They did not see that his power applied to their very own situation. Jesus has been with his people for twenty centuries, and yet we, like the disciples, underestimate his power to handle crises in our lives. The disciples did not yet know enough about Jesus. We cannot make the same excuse. Whatever your difficulty, you have two options: You can worry and assume that Jesus no longer cares, or you can resist fear and put your trust in him. When you feel like panicking, confess your need for God, and then trust him to care for you.

4:41 And they were filled with great awe and said to one another, "Who then is this, that even the wind and the sea obey him?"^{NRSV} The realization of Jesus' incredible power terrified the disciples, for they realized that they were standing in the presence of God himself. This was not the "cowardly fear" of 4:40;

the Greek word used here is *phobeo*—it conveys the awe and reverence they felt in the presence of divine power. They may have remembered the words of the psalmist, "O LORD God Almighty, who is like you? . . . You rule over the surging sea; when its waves mount up, you still them" (Psalm 89:8-9 NIV; see also Psalms 104:5-7; 106:9; 107:29).

But the disciples still didn't understand, as betrayed by their question. They asked, "Since *even the wind and sea obey* this man, *who then is* he?" They should have known because this miracle clearly displayed the truth of Jesus' divine identity. Being with the human, compassionate Jesus was fine; being with the powerful and supernatural Son of God was terrifying.

When Mark recorded this event, persecution against Christians had begun. Thus the story had become an analogy of the persecution and trials of the early church. The disciples were surrounded by a sea that threatened to sink them; the church was surrounded by enemies who threatened to destroy it (first the Jews who tried to undermine the Christian faith, then the Roman Empire and its eventual widespread persecution of Christians). Having Jesus with us in the boat does not mean we will not encounter storms. Our peace and faith come with the knowledge that Jesus has power over all storms, whatever their source or strength. He can quiet them if he chooses. Often the early Christians hoped for Jesus to quiet the storm of persecution, but he did not. So they were forced to rely, instead, on their faith in the power of their Savior and the eternal rest promised to them.

When we become Christians, we enter a cosmic struggle because Satan hates people to believe in Jesus. Satan's limited power is launched against believers individually and the church in general, hoping to sink us to the depths of the sea. But we have the ultimate power on our side, and the final victory is assured. Jesus should not be a mystery to us, causing us to fearfully ask, "Who then is this?" He should be our Savior, to whom we turn with all our needs and fears, knowing that he *does* care and will help.

STORMY WEATHER
When caught in the storms of life, it is easy to think that God has lost control and that we are at the mercy of the winds of fate. In reality, God is sovereign. He controls the history of the world as well as our personal destinies. Just as Jesus calmed the waves, he can calm whatever storms you may face.

Mark 5

Though we may emphasize the love for the world that God expressed through Christ, we sometimes fail to apply it to individual people. That Jesus permitted the demons to enter the large herd of pigs strikes us as odd, and we might be surprised by Jesus' disregard for personal property. Jesus' action, however, demonstrated the value of the man possessed by the demons. The demons, not Jesus, incited the pigs in their suicidal stampede.

By any standard, the value Jesus places on each one of us cannot be measured. He did not hesitate to present his own life in exchange for our salvation. The story about the herd of pigs dramatically contrasts the purposes of God and the purposes of Satan for people. To Jesus, the crazed man was worth saving. To Satan, he was a soul targeted for destruction. Upon entering the pigs, the demons immediately revealed the destructive objective of their master. They accomplished in the pigs what they had been doing in the man.

5:1 They came to the other side of the sea, to the country of the Gerasenes.NRSV As Jesus had planned (see 4:35), he and the disciples arrived on *the other side* of the Sea of Galilee (see map). Since *the country of the Gerasenes* was located southeast of the Sea of Galilee, Jesus and the disciples had sailed south and east to come to this Gentile region. The precise location is uncertain because this country (or region) is sometimes written as "Gerasenes," "Gergesenes," or "Gadarenes" in various manuscripts. However, some scholars cite evidence that favors "country of the Gerasenes," probably referring to a small town called Gersa (modern-day Kersa or Kours). Others prefer "Gadarenes," citing the town of Gadara, one of the most important cities of the region. Gadara was a member of the Decapolis, or Ten Cities (see 5:20). These ten cities with independent governments were largely inhabited by Gentiles, which would explain the herd of pigs (5:11). The Jews did not raise pigs because, according to Jewish law, pigs were unclean and thus unfit to eat.

Whatever the exact location of their landing, the point is that Jesus had planned to go there. This was Gentile territory, revealing a new direction for his ministry.

5:2 When Jesus got out of the boat, a man with an evil spirit came from the tombs to meet him.NIV Matthew's account of this story refers to two demon-possessed men (Matthew 8:28), while Mark and Luke refer only to one. Apparently Mark and Luke mention only the man who did the talking, or the man who was the most severe case (the one with a legion of demons, 5:9). Mark's account is more graphic than the others, emphasizing what the demon had done to the man.

Healing A Demon-possessed Man

From Capernaum, Jesus and his disciples crossed the Sea of Galilee. A storm blew up unexpectedly, but Jesus calmed it. Landing in the region of the Gerasenes, Jesus sent demons out of a man and into a herd of pigs that plunged over the steep bank into the lake.

After they landed and *Jesus got out of the boat,* they saw a horrible sight. *A man with an evil spirit came from the tombs.* Most people have difficulty picturing the awful sight of this man, *with an evil spirit,* bloody (5:5), out of control, and apparently strong and frightening (5:4). The disciples, having just been through a terrifying storm at sea (4:37), were certainly terrified again by the sight of this man (most likely two men, as recorded in Matthew) who approached them as they got out of the boat. They had encountered demon possession before (1:23-27), and Jesus had given them authority to cast out demons (3:15). But this man looked especially dangerous. Mark stressed the man's pitiful and hopeless condition, as detailed in the eyewitness description given in the following verses.

Having an "evil" or unclean spirit means being demon possessed. Although we cannot be sure why demon possession occurs, we know that evil spirits can use the human body to distort and destroy a person's relationship with God. The evil spirit (or in this case, spirits, 5:9) had entered the man's body and were controlling him. Demons always try to destroy or distort God's image. This man cut himself with stones (5:5) and lived in *the tombs.* In those days it was common for cemeteries to have many tombs carved into the hillside, making cavelike mausoleums. These tombs often had enough room to store several ossuaries, with space left over for a visitor. Thus, there was enough room for a person to actually live in such tombs.

According to Jewish ceremonial laws, the man whom Jesus encountered was unclean in three ways: He was a Gentile (non-Jew), he was demon possessed, and he lived in "the tombs." But Jesus helped him anyway. We should not turn our back on people who are "unclean" or repulsive to us, or who violate our moral standards and religious beliefs. Instead, we must realize that every human being is a unique creation of God needing to be touched by his love.

The demon-possessed man *came . . . to meet* Jesus. The man may have rushed out to see who was coming ashore, or perhaps even to apply for mercy. We simply do not know. Mark stresses the confrontation between the demons and Jesus, and in 5:6-7 portrays the defensive nature of the demons' behavior.

OCCULT DANGERS
Demons exist and are active even today. They are dangerous, powerful, and destructive. While it is important to recognize their evil activity so that we can stay away from demons, we should avoid any curiosity about or involvement with demonic forces or the occult (Deuteronomy 18:10-12). Today people are still fascinated by horoscopes, fortune-telling, witchcraft, and bizarre cults. But Satan is no less dangerous today than he was in Jesus' time. Dabbling in the occult can open a person up to the influence of demons. Instead, we should resist the devil and his influences, and he will flee from us (James 4:7).

5:3 He lived among the tombs; and no one could restrain him any more, even with a chain.^NRSV This demon-possessed man's condition was clearly hopeless without Christ. He no longer had contact with society, but *lived among the tombs.* This could refer to a type of graveyard—an area in the low hills that surrounded the Sea of Galilee with caves hewn into the rock. The caves served as tombs for the dead. Such graveyards were often in remote areas. People with hopeless conditions, such as this man, could find shelter in the caves.

The man had also been through the basic "treatment" given to people considered to be insane or demon possessed. People had tried to restrain his violent acts by chaining him up, but the evil power of the demons within gave him almost superhuman strength. Mark brought out the severity of the man's situation. *No one could restrain him* or stop him, not even with iron chains (5:4). No one was strong enough.

5:4 **For he had often been chained hand and foot, but he tore the chains apart and broke the irons on his feet. No one was strong enough to subdue him.**^{NIV} To protect him from hurting himself and others, the man had been *chained hand and foot.* The verb indicates a job completed and done well. He had been thoroughly chained, with chains around his wrists and irons (fetters) on his ankles. But he *tore the chains apart* and *broke the irons,* indicating power not his own, but derived from the demons that held him. In fact, this man was so strong that no one could *subdue* (or overpower) him. The word for "subdue" *(damazo)* is used for taming a wild animal. This man probably seemed more like an animal than a human being. The fact that no one was strong enough to restrain him sets the scene for Jesus, the one who had God's power and authority.

5:5 **And always, night and day, he was in the mountains and in the tombs, crying out and cutting himself with stones.**^{NKJV} Sent away from civilization off in *the mountains and in the tombs,* the man's violence turned in on himself. His *crying out* was more of a shrieking scream—the voices of the demons (see also 1:26). The *cutting* of his skin with sharp stones refers to gashing and hacking at his body, leaving him bloody and covered with scars. This may have been either an attempt at suicide or a primitive form of demon worship common in ancient times (see 1 Kings 18:28). These horrible actions occurred *always, night and day* without stop. He was indeed a frightening creature.

SATAN'S EVIL INTENT
In *The Screwtape Letters,* C. S. Lewis writes of other kinds of demons that obscure our view of hell and make us pretend that all is well. At least this pathetic man from the country of the Gerasenes portrayed Satan's true intent; his behavior showed that evil is horrible and that Satan is fearful and destructive. Through his condition we realize
- *Satan's hatred of us.* When sent to the pigs, the demons destroyed the entire herd. Satan's purpose is to destroy. He would love to destroy each of us.
- *Satan's power.* The man was possessed with many powerful demons. When we ignore the power of Christ, Satan has free rein.
- *Satan's cruelty.* Satan didn't bring the man greater power and sophistication so he could live a wilder lifestyle as is so often portrayed. Instead, he caused the man to try to kill himself.

5:6 **When he saw Jesus from a distance, he ran and fell on his knees in front of him.**^{NIV} The man ran to Jesus from a distance, displaying the range of the demons' power. The man did not run to escape Jesus, but ran to confront Jesus and scare him away as he would do to anyone else who ventured into his territory.

When he came close to Jesus, the man fell on his knees, not in worship, but in grudging submission to Jesus' superior power. The demons immediately recognized Jesus and his authority. They knew who Jesus was and what his great power could do to them (see James 2:19).

5:7 **He shouted at the top of his voice, "What do you want with me, Jesus, Son of the Most High God? Swear to God that you won't torture me!"**^{NIV} These words of the demon were in response to Jesus' demand that the demons depart (see 5:8). The demon was on the defensive. Though aware of who Jesus was and of his power over it, the demon still attempted to defend itself by using a shrieking voice and by calling Jesus by his divine name. The loud voice shows the demon's fierce and violent nature.

The demon's first question, *"What do you want with me?"* is a request that Jesus leave them alone. The demon that possessed the man in the synagogue had cried out with the same question, "What do you want with us?" (1:24). A more literal translation would be, "What to you and to me?" or "What do we have in common?" In other words, the demon asked Jesus to leave them alone, for they had nothing to do with each other. Such a question and statement show the demons' ultimate rebellion. Jesus and the demons were as far separated as anything could be. Jesus' purpose was to heal and give life; the demons', to kill and destroy. But Jesus would not leave this man in such a condition.

Why did Jesus allow the demon to talk at all? According to 5:8, Jesus said, "Come out," but the demon talked back rather than obey. Some scholars believe this was done to set the scene for Jesus' revelation of overwhelming power over the demons. Jesus had spoken first to one demon. It did not leave the man because there were multiple demons inside him. Then the demon tried to control Jesus with an aggressive defense and then with bargaining.

Like the demon who had possessed the man in Capernaum (1:24), this demon tried using Jesus' divine name to control him. (See also 3:11, where demons identified Jesus as "the Son of God.") At this time, people believed that to know an adversary's full name was to be able to gain control over the person. The demon in the synagogue had called Jesus "the Holy One of God," but this demon referred to him as *Jesus, Son of the Most High God*. This is the highest title used for Jesus in Mark's Gospel and denotes that the demons recognized Jesus as God's divine Son. The words "Most High God" appear in the Old Testament, and often were used by Gentiles when speaking of the superiority of Israel's God over any idol. (See Melchizedek's words in Genesis 14:18-24; Balaam's words in Numbers 24:16; Isaiah speaking of a heathen king—sometimes interpreted as Satan—in Isaiah 14:14; Nebuchadnezzar in Daniel 3:26 and 4:2.) How amazing that people in Jesus' day were so blind, while the demons were so clear about who Jesus was.

Then the demon had the audacity to ask for Jesus' mercy! The statement *"Swear to God"* comes from the verb *horkizo,* meaning to put under oath. Ironically, the demon appealed to God as it requested that Jesus promise not to *torture* it. The word for "torture" is graphic and correct. The Bible says that at the end of the world, the devil and his demons will be thrown into the lake of fire (Revelation 20:10). Matthew recorded the demon's question as, "Have you come here to torture us before the appointed time?" (Matthew 8:29 NIV). The demon's question revealed that the demons knew their ultimate fate. The demons hoped that Jesus would not send them to their fate early.

STILL REBELLIOUS
The demon screamed to Jesus, "What do you want with me?" It was a shriek of fear, defense, and rebellion against God. No one today would like to admit to being demon possessed or bear the appearance of this man from Gadara, but most of our society, like the demon, is screaming at God, the church, and Christian values, "Get out of my life!" When a person rejects Jesus Christ and his authority, he is putting himself on the side of the demons and heading in the same direction. Every person must ask: Will I choose freedom, autonomy, and self-will leading to destruction, or will I choose Christ's loving leadership over my life, giving me forgiveness from sin, cleansing, and healing?

5:8 For Jesus had said to him, "Come out of this man, you evil spirit!"[NIV] Jesus' first command was to one evil spirit. When that one did not obey, Jesus commanded the demon to give him its name. The demon's answer revealed that there were many demons.

HIS COMMAND
Matthew reported that Jesus used only a simple command, "Go" (Matthew 8:31-32). By either Mark's account or Matthew's, God's power was evident. Jesus needed nothing more than a quick word to expel the mighty demons, and they immediately went. Jesus needed no three-ring circus to demonstrate authority. Whose power is greater? On whose side do you want to live? By a word God took charge, with dramatic results, and his transcendent power produced a completely transformed life. Don't ignore his plan for your eternal life. Don't rebel against his authority over you.

5:9 Then He asked him, "What is your name?"NKJV The demons attempted but failed in using Jesus' name in 5:7. Jesus gained mastery over the demon by finding out its name. The demon's self-disclosure meant it had to submit to Jesus.

And he answered, saying, "My name is Legion; for we are many."NKJV The evil spirit said its name was *Legion.* A legion was the largest unit of the Roman army; it consisted of three thousand to six thousand soldiers. Territories occupied by the Romans had become very familiar with the Roman legions. This man was possessed by not one, but *many* demons. There may have been a legion of demons, or this name may be a reference to the *telos,* a force numbering 2,048 men (thus accounting for the loss of two thousand swine, see 5:13). Either way, Mark was showing Jesus' power and victory over a fearsome array of demonic powers.

5:10 And he begged Jesus again and again not to send them out of the area.NIV Mark often highlighted the supernatural struggle between Jesus and Satan. The demons' goal was to control the humans they inhabited; Jesus' goal was to give people freedom from sin and Satan's control. The demons knew they had no power over Jesus; so when they saw Jesus, they *begged again and again* not to be sent *out of the area,* or into the abyss (see Luke 8:31). They wanted to stay in their home area where they could torment people. Luke 8:31 says the demons begged Jesus to spare them from the abyss, which is also mentioned in Revelation 9:1 and 20:1-3 as the place of confinement for Satan and his messengers (sometimes called the "bottomless pit.") The demons, of course, knew all about this place of confinement and didn't want to go there. Mark was pointing out that the demons wanted to be with people (in the area) and begged not to be sent into lonely exile where they could not torment people.

The demons undoubtedly knew that Jesus planned to free their prisoner—the human who was their abode. Their concern at this point was *where* he would send them. They knew where they did *not* want to go, and they knew Jesus had the power to send them to that place. So, they begged Jesus not to send them there.

Why didn't Jesus just destroy these demons—or send them away? Because the time for such work had not yet come. Jesus healed many people of the destructive effects of demon possession, but he did not yet destroy demons. In this situation, Jesus wanted to show Satan's destructive power and intent over the two thousand pigs. The same question could be asked today—why doesn't Jesus stop all the evil in the world? His time for that has not yet come. But it will come. The book of Revelation portrays the future victory of Jesus over Satan, his demons, and all evil.

5:11 A large herd of pigs was feeding on the nearby hillside.ᴺᴵⱽ According to Old Testament law (Leviticus 11:7), pigs were "unclean" animals. This meant that they could not be eaten or even touched by a Jew. This incident took place southeast of the Sea of Galilee in the region of the Gerasenes (5:1), a Gentile area. This explains how a herd of pigs could be involved. Pigs were used by Romans for the sacrifices their religions required. Romans also ate pigs. A normal herd of pigs would be 150 to 300 head. So this herd was unusually large.

5:12 So all the demons begged Him, saying, "Send us to the swine, that we may enter them."ᴺᴷᴶⱽ One demon had spoken for all the demons in 5:10; here *all the demons* chimed in, begging Jesus not to send them away, but to send them *to the swine.* The demons knew they had to submit to Jesus' power and authority, and they knew that he could seal their fate by returning them to the abyss or sending them far away. Notice that they did not ask to be sent into the city; they knew Jesus would not allow them to inhabit other people. But on the hillside were enough physical animal hosts for all these demons to inhabit. Pigs were unclean animals, and therefore, they could provide a fitting habitation for the demons, whom Mark characteristically calls "unclean spirits."

But why did the demons ask to enter the swine? Several possible answers have been suggested, but the Bible simply does not tell us. Perhaps the demons thought they could return to the tombs and caves later. Evidently they did not want to be without a physical body to torment. So they would rather destroy the pigs than be idle. Their action seems to portray their ultimate destructive intent.

DRIVING OUT DEMONS
We usually associate exorcism with small rooms, hushed tones, and special procedures. Actually, wherever the gospel is preached (or lived, spoken, written, and demonstrated), demons flee and God's kingdom advances. The Word of God always pushes against the darkness of evil. Today, Christians can cause demons to scatter with a testimony, a gift in God's name, a helping hand, or a word spoken in faith. Your spiritual gifts used at church, home, and work put God's enemies into retreat. Join Christ in driving out demons.

5:13 He gave them permission.[NIV] In every case where demons confronted Jesus, they were stripped of their power. God limits what evil spirits can do; these demons could do nothing without Jesus' permission. During Jesus' life on earth, demons were allowed to be very active to demonstrate once and for all his power and authority over them. Jesus did not command the demons to go into the swine; he *gave them permission* to do what they requested.

"Gave them permission" has theological thrust. Satan has no final authority but can do only what God "permits" for the short time he is allowed to be "god of this world" (2 Corinthians 4:4 NRSV). In Revelation 6 and 13, the four horsemen and the beast "were given" temporary authority, a divine passive that suggests the sovereign God permitted them to do evil for a time.

Perhaps Jesus let the demons destroy the pigs to demonstrate his own superiority over a very powerful yet destructive force. He could have sent the demons away, but he did not, because the time for judgment had not yet come. In the end, the devil and all his angels will be sent into eternal fire (Matthew 25:41). While Jesus granted the demons' request to enter the swine and destroy the herd, Jesus stopped their destructive work in people, and particularly the man they had possessed.

Jesus also taught a lesson by giving the demons permission to enter the pigs. He showed his disciples, the townspeople, and even us who read these words today the absolute goal of Satan and his demons. They desire total and complete destruction of their hosts.

And the evil spirits came out and went into the pigs. The herd, about two thousand in number, rushed down the steep bank into the lake and were drowned.[NIV] The sight must have been amazing. A rather peaceful herd of pigs feeding on the hillside suddenly became a stampeding horde that ran straight to its own destruction. One after another, the pigs kept running into the lake and drowning.

The demons' action proves their destructive intent—if they could not destroy the men, they would destroy the pigs. Jesus' action, in contrast to the demons', shows the value he places on each human life. Some people might have difficulty with the fact that all the pigs died, but Jesus considered the man to be more important than the pigs.

GREAT VALUE
This event challenges our own system of values. We can see this best illustrated through the eyes of another culture. A Bible translator working in an isolated society came to this very passage in translating the New Testament into a previously unwritten language. This language had words for "one," "two," and "many," but there were no words for large numbers since they were unnecessary. So the task of accurately conveying the number "two thousand" seemed insurmountable.

A rather lengthy discussion between the translator and his informant followed. As the tribesman grasped the size of the herd, he expressed great amazement. Puzzled, the translator asked him to explain his astonishment. The Indian responded with a question of his own: "Did Jesus really exchange such a large number of pigs for the life of one man?" Receiving the translator's affirming nod, he went on, "Among our people, when someone desires the death of another, the price for buying that person's life is one pig." Now it was the translator's turn to be astonished. What great value Jesus places on each of us!

5:14 Those tending the pigs ran off and reported this in the town and countryside, and the people went out to see what had happened.NIV When Jesus performed this miracle, he again gained immediate publicity. *Those tending the pigs,* astonished at what had happened, *ran off* and told the amazing story. The *town* mentioned was one of the towns in 5:20. Apparently more than one swineherd had been tending the pigs; they scattered in fear, some into the town and some to the *countryside* (literally, to the farms). Their story seemed unbelievable: Two thousand pigs floating on the edge of the lake would certainly be a sight, so those who heard the story *went out to see what had happened.* Among these would have been the owner of the herd who, doubtless, was not pleased at the loss of the livestock.

5:15 Then they came to Jesus, and saw the one who had been demon-possessed and had the legion, sitting and clothed and in his right mind. And they were afraid.NKJV What were Jesus and the disciples doing while the swineherds were spreading the story and the people were gathering to see for themselves? Probably attending to the man, newly set free from thousands of demons, dressing him and caring for his wounds.

Then looking up, Jesus and the disciples saw a crowd gathering above on the hillside. The crowd saw the pigs in the water, they saw Jesus and the disciples on the shore, and they *saw the one who had been demon-possessed . . . sitting and clothed and in his right mind.* The man was sitting, not running about uncontrollably; he was clothed, not naked and bleeding; he was in his right mind, not shrieking wildly. Jesus had restored this man's humanity; he was sane and self-controlled. Thus Mark accurately contrasted the rule of Satan and the rule of Jesus.

The people might have responded in several ways. They may have been overjoyed to see Jesus on their own shore—many people hunted Jesus down and longed to be with him. This popular preacher and miracle worker was available to them. They also may have responded with joy that the demon-possessed man had been healed and would no longer bother them. They may have just been thrilled to have seen a healing of such magnitude with their own eyes. However, Mark used one word for the people's response: *afraid.*

What were they afraid of? Perhaps such supernatural power as Jesus had displayed frightened them. Perhaps they thought Jesus would be bad for their economy (losing two thousand pigs in one day certainly cost someone). Perhaps they didn't want Jesus to change their status quo. In any case, their fear caused them to make a terrible mistake (5:17).

AFRAID OF JESUS?
Too often Jesus is pictured as a person so warm and gentle that no one would fear him. Yet at those moments when Jesus directly confronted the forces of evil in a contest of will and power, he may have struck a most intense and fearsome image. In his control of a volatile situation, he could have appeared intimidating. At that moment, Jesus appeared awesome and invincible.

Christians who enjoy Jesus' personal warmth should not forget that he is God and all-powerful. Don't underestimate Jesus' power as merely that of a teacher or philosopher. He is almighty God; he has come to restore us to our right mind.

5:16 Those who had seen it told the people what had happened to the demon-possessed man—and told about the pigs as well.NIV
The crowd moved down the steep slope and onto the shore. All the while, *those who had seen it* told the story again; now the

people could see the man and the pigs for themselves. "Those who had seen it" could have been the Twelve who had come with Jesus, the swineherds, or even those who had come along from the boats (4:36). Mark emphasized the eyewitness nature of those telling the story to confirm its reliability.

JESUS, PLEASE LEAVE!
The demons destroyed the pigs, which hurt the finances of those tending the pigs, but can pigs and money compare with a human life? A man had been freed from the devil's power, but the people thought only about their livestock. People have always tended to value financial gain above needy people. Throughout history, wars have been fought to protect economic interests. Much injustice and oppression, both at home and abroad, is the direct result of some individual's or company's urge to get rich. People are continually being sacrificed to the god of money. Don't think more highly of "pigs" than of people. Are you more concerned about property and programs than men and women? Human beings are created in God's image and have eternal value. How foolish and yet how easy it is to value possessions, investments, and even animals above human life. Would you rather have Jesus leave you than finish his work in you?

5:17 Then they began to plead with Him to depart from their region.^{NKJV} Why did the people ask Jesus to leave? Unlike their own heathen gods, Jesus could not be contained, controlled, or appeased. They feared Jesus' supernatural power, a power that they had never before witnessed. And they were upset about losing a herd of swine more than they were glad about the deliverance of the demon-possessed man. They would rather give up Jesus than lose their source of income and security. So *they began to plead with Him* to go away. Unfortunately for them, Jesus did as they asked. And there is no biblical record that he ever returned. Sometimes the worst possible thing that can happen is for Jesus to answer one of our requests.

5:18 As Jesus was getting into the boat, the man who had been demon-possessed begged to go with him.^{NIV} The people asked Jesus to leave their region, so Jesus and the disciples got back into the boat. The miracle of healing was lost on the crowd; instead, they saw only the destruction of the pigs. The only one who truly understood what had transpired was the formerly possessed man himself. Having been freed, he *begged to go with* Jesus. The man's request meant that he wanted to be one of Jesus' followers, with Jesus as a constant and close companion. We don't know if this man was a Jew or Gentile. We don't know his motive in asking to stay with Jesus. He may have wanted to be with Jesus out of adoration; he may have been afraid of being shunned by his people for indirectly causing the death of the pigs; or he may have been afraid the demons might return if Jesus went away. In any case, he asked to go with Jesus, but Jesus had other plans for him.

GADARA, A.D. 31
Rabbi, begone! Thy powers
Bring loss to us and ours.
Our ways are not as Thine.
Thou lovest men, we—swine.
Oh, get you hence, Omnipotence,
And take this fool of Thine!
His soul? What care we for his soul?
What good to us that Thou hast made him whole,
Since we have lost our swine.
And Christ went sadly.
He had wrought for them a sign
Of Love, and Hope, and Tenderness divine;
They wanted—swine.
Christ stands without your door and gently knocks;
But if your gold, or swine, the entrance blocks,
He forces no man's hold—he will depart,
And leave you to the treasures of your heart.
—John Oxenham

5:19 Jesus did not let him, but said, "Go home to your family and tell them how much the Lord has done for you, and how he has had mercy on you."[NIV] As Jesus had done when he healed the leper (1:40-42) and the paralytic (2:11-12), Jesus gave this formerly demon-possessed man his life back. We do not know how long the man had been possessed, but after being healed he could *go home,* something he could not do before. Certainly his family would rejoice to see him returned to sanity. When they inevitably would ask him what happened, the man was to *tell them how much the Lord has done* and about the Lord's *mercy* on a wretched and hopeless demon-possessed man who, left alone, would have eventually destroyed himself. These words probably calmed any fears the man may have had about the demons returning. This man, like the others, was permanently cured.

> May it never be said of us that we are saints everywhere else but wicked by our own fireside, talkers about religion elsewhere but worldly and ungodly at home! J. C. Ryle

Often Jesus asked those he healed to be quiet about the healing (1:43-45; 5:43), but he urged this man to *go . . . and tell* what the Lord had done for him. Why the difference? This man was returning to his home in a Gentile region. Jesus knew the man would be an effective witness to those who remembered his previous condition and could attest to the miraculous healing. Through him, Jesus could expand his ministry into this Gentile area. Jesus would not remain in the region, but he did not leave himself without witness. This man would be an incredible witness—for he knew that none other than *the Lord,* the God of Israel, the one true God, had healed him. In this pagan region of Decapolis came one healed man with an incredible story to tell.

This is the beginning of the "universal mission" theme in Mark's Gospel. Here Jesus prepared the way for the movement of the gospel to the Gentiles after Pentecost. This is illustrated in 5:20 where "all the people [meaning the Gentiles] were amazed" at Jesus' power.

GO AND TELL

The man quite naturally wanted more contact with this wonderful, powerful person who had saved his life so dramatically. But instead, Jesus asked him to tell his story to others. And he did. Without training or background, without the capacity to explain Old Testament prophecies or to expound on theories of the Trinity, this man simply told his story. From his heart and his life, he spoke. It was the man's way of saying thanks. He was truly a "missionary" before the word was invented.

We all have stories of faith: God's goodness to us, God's saving power in our lives. We should tell others our stories— people on the bus, brothers and sisters, hardware clerks, nurses at the clinic, next-door neighbors. This is the work of a missionary: telling what God has done, right here, today, wherever we are. When God touches your life, don't be afraid to share the wonderful events with your family and friends. Not everyone can travel as a missionary. Jesus knows the right position for each of us. Sometimes kindness at home and unselfish service means more than becoming a full-time Christian worker.

5:20 And he went away and began to proclaim in the Decapolis how much Jesus had done for him; and everyone was amazed.NRSV Although the man was healed and able to travel with Jesus, Jesus sent the man on a mission. And the man wasted no time. He *went away and began to proclaim in the Decapolis how much Jesus had done for him.* "Decapolis," or the Ten Cities, was a region located southeast of the Sea of Galilee. Ten cit-

ies, each with its own independent government, formed an alliance for protection and for increased trade
opportunities. These cities had been settled several centuries earlier by Greek
traders and immigrants. Jews were a
minority in the area. Many people from
the Decapolis followed Jesus (Matthew
4:25).

> What God chooses, He
> cleanses.
> What God cleanses, He
> molds.
> What God molds, He fills.
> What God fills, He uses.
> *J. Sidlow Baxter*

The man knew that "the Lord" had shown great mercy to him
(5:19), that Jesus had freed him from the demons, and that the
Lord and Jesus were one and the same. Though not versed in
Scripture or trained in preaching and teaching, the man realized
that he had looked into the face of the one true God and had
received divine mercy. His heartfelt response was to go and tell
others about Jesus. This man's behavior contrasts both with the
townspeople, who had experienced amazement and fear but still
had not been converted, and with the disciples, who still lacked
understanding and total conviction. This former madman may
have been known throughout the region. So when he returned to
that same region, his testimony had results—*everyone* who saw
and heard him *was amazed.*

GET EXCITED
This man had been demon possessed, but he became a living
example of Jesus' power. He wanted to go with Jesus, but
Jesus told him to go home and share his story with his friends.
If you have experienced Jesus' power, you too are a living
example. Are you, like this man, enthusiastic about sharing the
Good News with those around you? Just as we would tell
others about a doctor who cured a physical disease, we should
tell about Christ who forgives our sin.

JESUS HEALS A BLEEDING WOMAN AND RESTORES A GIRL TO LIFE / 5:21-43 / **89**

Mark often wove together events in Jesus' life. Jesus was told
about Jairus's daughter; on the way to see the ailing child, he met
a suffering woman. While he was dealing with her crisis, the message arrived that the sick girl had died.

The account rings with lifelikeness. We are familiar with the
jumble of urgency, delays, obstacles, and disappointments in life.
Mark demonstrates that Jesus knew the same experiences.

In an earlier passage (3:20-35), Mark introduced Jesus' family, digressed to a confrontation between Jesus and religious leaders over the source of his power, then resumed the account of Jesus' family. Recording events in this manner brings cohesiveness to the story and prevents the account from becoming one episode after another. This structure can be described both as an effective storytelling technique and also as an accurate reflection of the way life happens. Noting how Jesus handled interruptions helps us as much as seeing how he handled crises. We also have to juggle many facets of life.

The conclusion of this episode reintroduces Jesus' efforts to control his publicity. His compassion motivated him to constant action, but God's plan required that Jesus resist the pull of growing public acclamation.

Jesus was not worried about purity laws, but willingly touched a corpse and was touched by a woman with a flow of blood, both of which would render him unclean. Compassion outweighed legalism.

5:21 When Jesus had crossed again in the boat to the other side, a great crowd gathered around him; and he was by the sea.NRSV Jesus recrossed the Sea of Galilee *to the other side,* meaning that he went back to the eastern shore, probably landing back at Capernaum (4:35). As always, *a great crowd gathered around him* (see also 1:33; 2:2; 3:7, 20; 4:1). The contrast with Jesus just having been asked to leave the Decapolis region is unmistakable. Unfortunately, although he was popular with the people in Capernaum, they really were no more receptive to his message than were the people in Decapolis.

5:22-23 Then one of the synagogue rulers, named Jairus, came there.NIV The *synagogue* was the local center of worship (see the explanation on 1:21), and Jairus was a lay person elected as *one of the synagogue rulers* (a synagogue could have more than one ruler, see Acts 13:15). The synagogue rulers were responsible for supervising worship services, caring for the scrolls, running the weekly school, keeping the congregation faithful to the Law, distributing alms, and administering the care of the building. There was no permanent rabbi or teacher, so the synagogue rulers often would ask visiting teachers to teach.

Seeing Jesus, he fell at his feet and pleaded earnestly with him, "My little daughter is dying. Please come and put your hands on her so that she will be healed and live."NIV As a synagogue ruler, Jairus held a position of high esteem in the town. Many synagogue rulers had close ties to the Pharisees; therefore, it is likely that some synagogue rulers had been pressured not to support Jesus. But neither position nor pressure could stop Jairus from coming to the one man who could help his very sick daughter. For Jairus to fall at Jesus' feet and plead for Jesus to come heal his daughter was a significant and daring act of respect and worship.

Jairus's *daughter* was dying. (Luke adds that this was his only daughter—see Luke 8:42; and Mark adds later that she was twelve years old—see 5:42.) We do not know the nature of her sickness; apparently nothing had helped her, and she would soon die. But Jairus remembered someone who could help—someone whose touch had healed many people in Capernaum (1:33-34). When Jairus heard that Jesus had returned to Capernaum, he was among the crowd on the seashore (5:21). Pushing through, he made his way to Jesus. He was on a mission—nothing could stop this father's love. His request was simple yet full of faith. He asked for Jesus' touch on his daughter, knowing that if Jesus were to come, his daughter would *be healed and live.* Laying on hands for healing of disease was common then, but this girl's condition was extremely serious. Jairus didn't even dare try to bring her to Jesus; instead, he needed to bring Jesus to her. But there wasn't much time.

5:24 So Jesus went with him. A large crowd followed and pressed around him.[NIV] In Greek, the first sentence means "Jesus went off with him promptly." Jesus apparently heard the urgency in Jairus's voice and saw the strain of worry on his face, so filled with compassion, *Jesus went with him.* Jesus could have simply spoken a word to heal the girl. (Jesus did that for a centurion who asked that Jesus speak the word and heal his servant—see Luke 7:7.) This apparently had not occurred to Jairus; his faith was limited to Jesus' touch and to healing a sick daughter (he thought that if she died, it would be too late). Jesus worked within Jairus's request. So Jesus, Jairus, the disciples, and *a large crowd* made their way to Jairus's home. So many people thronged through the streets that they *pressed around* Jesus.

> Proximity to Christ does not necessarily imply appropriation. *F. B. Meyer*

5:25 Now there was a woman who had been suffering from hemorrhages for twelve years.[NRSV] In the crowd that pressed on Jesus was another person in need of divine help. A woman *had been suffering* (the Greek word means "to suffer pain") *from hemorrhages* (that is, bleeding; this may have been a menstrual or uterine disorder) for *twelve years.* The nature of her illness caused additional suffering. The bleeding caused the woman to be in a constant condition of ritual uncleanness (see Leviticus 15:25-33). She could not worship in the synagogue, and she could not have normal social relationships, for anyone who came into contact with her would also become unclean. Thus, the woman was treated almost as severely as a leper.

WEAK FAITH, STRONG FAITH
Was Jairus a midget in faith? He could have asked Jesus for merely a word instead of a house call; he could have shown less worry and urgency; he could have claimed the miracle before it was done. A midget in faith? He was a father, desperate and heartsick, out of breath pursuing a last attempt to reverse his daughter's slide into death. And Jesus followed him home.

Jesus responds to faith. Whether our prayers are midget or giant-sized, Jesus pays attention to faith; he wants to build it and affirm it, always. He loves faith.

We should stop trying to measure our faith and start using it. Jesus meets all of us on the road where weak faith, desperate and worried, becomes trusting and confident, where midgets grow into giants.

5:26 She had suffered a great deal under the care of many doctors and had spent all she had, yet instead of getting better she grew worse.[NIV] The Greek word for "suffered" in this verse is the same as in verse 25 above—this woman had suffered in pain even while *under the care of many doctors.* She had become destitute in trying to get a cure, having *spent all she had* on treatment. Mark added this detail (omitted in Matthew) to show that human endeavors had availed her nothing. She only continued to get worse, and there was no hope for alleviating her suffering until she heard about Jesus.

5:27-28 She had heard about Jesus, and came up behind him in the crowd and touched his cloak, for she said, "If I but touch his clothes, I will be made well."[NRSV] In the crowd that met Jesus on the shore that day, two people had come to seek him out—Jairus, in need of healing for his dying daughter, and this unnamed woman in need of healing for her own incurable disease. Both came in faith, knowing that Jesus could take care of their particular problem. Jairus had already petitioned Jesus, and Jesus was on his way. This woman *had heard about* Jesus' miracle-working power (apparently for the first time) and had come to Capernaum to find him (tradition says she was from Caesarea Philippi). On that day of Jesus' return, she worked her way through the crowd and *came up behind* Jesus. She knew

she only had to *touch his clothes,* and she would be healed. The
decision to touch Jesus' garment was due to the popular belief
that the clothes of a holy man imparted spiritual and healing
power (see 6:56; Acts 19:11-12). She may have feared that
Jesus would not touch her if he knew her condition (she may
have thought that Jesus would not risk becoming "unclean" in
order to heal her). Or she may have feared that if her disease
became known to the crowd, the people who had touched her
would be angry at having become unclean unknowingly. The
woman knew she could be healed, but she tried to do it as unob-
trusively as possible. She thought that she would just get healed
and go away.

DEMORALIZED, YET DETERMINED
Lots of life's battles nick us at the edges. Not strong enough to
kill us, they pester and provoke us, wear us down, use our
money, sap our vigor, cloud our joy. This woman had known
many such demoralizing days. Yet she came. What a move!
Despite years of weakness, she had not given up hope. Believing Jesus could help, she left her sickbed, joined the crowd,
and found her answer. She reached out in faith and was healed.
    We must never cave in to pestering problems. No problem
need keep us from God. He is always ready to help. Personally
coming to Jesus is the real secret of peace and healing. We
must connect with him.

**5:29 Immediately her hemorrhage stopped; and she felt in her
body that she was healed of her disease.**[NRSV] The moment the
woman touched Jesus' garment, *she was healed.* The disease that
had weakened her body for years suddenly disappeared. She felt
the difference and knew not only that the pain had stopped, but
that she was also completely healed of the disease. What a
moment of incredible joy this must have been for this woman!

UNCHANGEABLE
God changed a situation that had been a problem for years.
Like the leper and the demon-possessed man, this chronically
ill woman was considered unclean. For twelve years, she too
had been one of the "unclean" and had not been able to lead a
normal life. But Jesus changed that and restored her. Sometimes we are tempted to give up on people or situations that
have not changed for many years. God can change what
seems unchangeable, giving new purpose and hope. Keep
praying.

5:30 **Immediately aware that power had gone forth from him, Jesus turned about in the crowd and said, "Who touched my clothes?"**^{NRSV} The healing had been immediate upon the woman's touch (5:29); Jesus' knowledge of the healing was also immediate. As the woman felt the healing of her body, Jesus felt the supernatural *power* that performed healings go out of him. Someone had touched him in order to be healed, that person's faith had allowed the healing to take place, and Jesus perceived what had happened. Jesus' question, *"Who touched my clothes?"* had a definite purpose. Whether Jesus already knew who touched him or not is inconsequential. What mattered was that Jesus wanted to establish a relationship with this woman. She had hoped to go away undetected. Jesus, having healed her physically, wanted to heal her spiritually as well. He wanted the person to step forward and "own up" to having received healing.

In the meantime, Jairus must have been exasperated; he was already in a hurry due to the severe illness of his daughter. No doubt the slow movement of the crowd was frustrating him. Then, of all things, Jesus stopped to ask a seemingly silly question. Little did Jairus know that through all these events, he would be learning a valuable lesson about Jesus' power.

5:31 **And his disciples said to him, "You see the crowd pressing in on you; how can you say, 'Who touched me?'"**^{NRSV} The crowd pressed in on Jesus as he and the disciples were making their way through town. Then suddenly Jesus stopped and asked, *"Who touched me?"* The disciples were surprised by Jesus' question, so their reply seems almost rude. In effect they said, "How can you ask such a ridiculous question? Lots of people are touching you!" They did not understand that Jesus meant a different kind of touch—not the inadvertent touch of a pressing crowd, but the purposeful touch of someone who desired to be healed.

THE HEALING TOUCH
It was virtually impossible to get close to Jesus, but one woman fought her way desperately through the crowd in order to touch him. As soon as she did, she was healed. What a difference there is between the crowds that are curious about Jesus and the few who reach out and touch him! Today, many people are vaguely familiar with Jesus, but nothing in their lives is changed or bettered by this passing acquaintance. It is only faith that releases God's healing power. Move beyond curiosity. Reach out to Christ in faith, knowing that his mercy will bring healing to your body, soul, and spirit.

5:32 But Jesus kept looking around to see who had done it.^{NIV} Why
was Jesus so persistent in knowing the identity of this person?
Could it be that he wanted that person to identify himself or herself? Jesus waited and *kept looking around to see who had done
it.* Jesus looked around—the healed person could not have gone
far, for Jesus had stopped immediately upon being touched. He
knew that person was there. In the Greek, the article and partici-
ple are feminine in gender, indicating that Jesus was looking for a
woman. The gender could simply have been Mark's choice, writing afterward and knowing the identity of the person. Or it could
mean that Jesus somehow knew a woman had touched him—
from the slight and cautious touch, Jesus might have perceived
both her unclean condition and her desire to remain unnoticed.
But Jesus would not allow that. In his piercing gaze at the few
people nearest him in the crowd was the unspoken demand that
the person come forward. The crowd didn't understand what was
happening, the disciples thought Jesus was being unreasonable,
and Jairus was probably fuming. But one person *did* understand
what Jesus meant by the question, "Who touched me?" and she
knew she had no choice but to answer.

**5:33 But the woman, knowing what had happened to her, came in
fear and trembling, fell down before him, and told him the
whole truth.**^{NRSV} The woman *told him the whole truth*—that she
had been afflicted with a dreadful disease, that she had been
unclean and had come jostling through the crowd, that she had
dared to touch him (a man) and did so in her unclean state, that
she had hoped to remain undetected, and that she had been
healed. To top it off, she had to say all of that in front of a crowd.
No wonder the woman *came in fear and trembling.* She knew
what had happened to her. No human being had been able to heal
her; Jesus did what no human could do. But Jesus would not let
that be the end of the story; he wanted to deal with her soul. Jesus
wanted to teach the woman that his cloak did not contain magical
properties, but that her faith in him had caused the healing.

Jesus may also have wanted to teach the crowd a lesson.
According to Jewish law, a man who touched a menstruating
woman became ceremonially unclean (Leviticus 15:19-28). This
was true whether her bleeding was normal or, as in this woman's
case, the result of illness. To protect themselves from such defilement, Jewish men carefully avoided touching, speaking to, or
even looking at women. By contrast, Jesus proclaimed to hundreds of people that this "unclean" woman had touched him—
and then he healed her. In Jesus' mind, this suffering woman was

not to be overlooked. As God's creation, she deserved attention and respect.

5:34 He said to her, "Daughter, your faith has healed you. Go in peace and be freed from your suffering."NIV Far from being angry, Jesus spoke to the woman in gentle words, calling her *daughter,* revealing a father-child relationship. She came for healing and received it. But she also received a relationship and peace with God himself because of her faith. Jesus explained that it was not his clothing that had healed her; rather, her faith in reaching out to the one person who could heal her had allowed that healing to take place. She not only had faith, but she had placed her faith in the right person. This woman is one of the "little people" in Mark's Gospel because she exemplified true faith, while the disciples floundered. Genuine faith involves action. In fact, faith that isn't put into action is not faith at all (see James 2:14-26). This woman's faith had caused her, not to demand healing, but to know that with a simple touch, she would be healed. Her faith would put many Christians to shame.

The words "Go in peace" are more literally "Go into peace." With this healing, Jesus gave this woman her life. He opened a door and held it for her. Jesus wished her peace of both body and soul—renewed health for the body and eternal salvation for the soul. With the words "be freed from your suffering," the woman knew that her cure was permanent.

The disciples, no doubt, received a profound lesson in the value of planting seeds in even the most unlikely places. The crowd, while seeming to be nothing more than a hindrance on the way, held one pocket of "good soil" in whom Jesus planted a seed. Jairus, meanwhile, could think of nothing but his daughter; then, what he feared most, happened.

5:35 While Jesus was still speaking, some men came from the house of Jairus, the synagogue ruler. "Your daughter is dead," they said. "Why bother the teacher any more?"NIV The time taken by Jesus to seek out and speak to the woman was too long for the sick little girl at Jairus's house. During the delay, she died. The message was delivered to Jairus, undoubtedly calling him to come home; the opportunity for healing had passed, so *the teacher* would no longer be needed.

5:36 Ignoring what they said, Jesus told the synagogue ruler, "Don't be afraid; just believe."NIV The message of his daughter's death came to Jairus while Jesus was speaking to the woman who had been healed (5:35). Jesus overhead the message. (Jairus was probably standing near Jesus, for he had been in the process

of leading Jesus to his house when the healing incident occurred.)
To the crowd, it meant that Jesus was too late. But the very
"impossibility" of death was only an opportunity for Jesus. Death
did not make Jesus too late; instead, it meant that Jesus would do
an even mightier miracle. Jairus must have looked in despair at
Jesus, but Jesus made no indication of changing his plans. He
turned in the direction of Jairus's house and told Jairus, *"Don't be
afraid; just believe"* (see also 4:40; 6:6; 10:52; 11:22-25). Jairus
had come to Jesus in faith that Jesus could heal his daughter.
Jesus told Jairus to "keep on believing" with that same faith, even
in the face of death. Jairus must have wondered what Jesus was
going to do.

HOPELESS AND HELPLESS
When Jairus heard the news from home, it must have cut to his
heart: "Your daughter is dead." Jairus believed that Jesus could
heal, but this seemed to be the end of hope for him. Yet Jesus
ignored the unbelief of those around him and said, "Don't be
afraid; just believe." When you feel hopeless and afraid, when
others claim that "nothing can be done," remember that Jesus
is the source of all hope and promise. You may have to disregard the unbelief of others and hold firmly to Jesus.

**5:37 And He permitted no one to follow Him except Peter,
James, and John the brother of James.**NKJV No doubt the curious crowd had every intention of staying with Jesus, having
observed the healing of the diseased woman and hearing the
words of the men from Jairus's house. What would Jesus do
next? But Jesus wasn't interested in what might become a public event, a show. Sensitive to Jairus's pain, Jesus *permitted no
one to follow.* He planned to raise this little girl from the dead—
a sign to his disciples of his true mission, of his power, and as a
harbinger of his own resurrection. So he left the crowd and
nine of his disciples behind, followed Jairus, and took along
Peter, James, and John the brother of James. These three men
became Jesus' inner circle—his closest followers, the only ones
to see this miracle, observe the Transfiguration (9:2), and know
of Jesus' agony in Gethsemane (14:33). They would observe
his miracle and thus fulfill Deuteronomy 19:15, which required
two or three witnesses.

**5:38 When they came to the house of the leader of the synagogue,
he saw a commotion, people weeping and wailing loudly.**NRSV
The five men finally reached Jairus's house, and the *commotion*
of loud *weeping and wailing* filled the air. Such cries were cus-

tomary at a person's death; lack of weeping and wailing was the ultimate disgrace and disrespect. Some people, usually women, made mourning a profession and were paid by the dead person's family to weep over the body. Jairus, the leader of the synagogue, was an important person in the town. Thus, at the death of his only daughter, the town demonstrated their great love and respect for Jairus and his family by their weeping and wailing.

5:39 When He came in, He said to them, "Why make this commotion and weep? The child is not dead, but sleeping."[NKJV] Jesus entered Jairus's house where the tumult of weeping and wailing made a great *commotion.* The sound must have been dreadful, especially to the ears of Jesus, who knew that he was going to raise the child from the dead. He spoke words of encouragement, only to be met with derision (see 5:40). His words, *the child is not dead, but sleeping* probably made Jesus appear rather stupid—certainly anyone could tell death from sleep. Neither was she just in a coma from which Jesus would awaken her as some have proposed. The girl was indeed dead, and everyone from the family to the paid mourners knew it. Jesus knew it too, but his words tested the faith of the crowd and revealed to Jairus the hope beyond all hope of what Jesus was about to do. She was dead, but Jesus would bring her back to life, as if awakening her from sleep. Jesus used the image of sleep to indicate that the girl's condition was temporary and that she would be restored. Luke commented that when Jesus lifted her up, her spirit returned to her (Luke 8:55).

ONLY ASLEEP!
Jesus redefined death by calling it sleep. A lifeless body will live again, he claimed. The dead will wake up. Wait and see! While we mourn the loss of people we love, separation is not forever. Jesus shows us a wonderful hope: heaven, reunion, *shalom.* Trust the promise. Tell everyone about it.

5:40 But they laughed at him. After he put them all out, he took the child's father and mother and the disciples who were with him, and went in where the child was.[NIV] Jesus' words sounded ridiculous to the faithless crowd. They did not stop to wonder, they did not consider for a moment what Jesus might mean; they simply *laughed at him* in derisive, jeering tones. The mourners, weeping and wailing one moment, laughed in derision the next. Their laughter became their judgment—they would not witness the miracle, for Jesus *put them all out* of the room. The Greek

THE TOUCH OF JESUS

What kind of people did Jesus associate with? Whom did he consider important enough to touch? Here we see many of the
people Jesus came to know. Some reached out to him; he
reached out to them all. Regardless of how great or unknown, rich
or poor, young or old, sinner or saint—Jesus cares equally for
each one. No person is beyond the loving touch of Jesus.

Jesus talked with . . .	*Reference*
A despised tax collector	Matthew 9:9
An insane hermit	Mark 5:1-20
The Roman governor	Mark 15:1-15
A prominent religious leader	John 3:1-21
A homemaker	Luke 10:38-42
An expert in the law	Matthew 22:35
A criminal	Luke 23:40-43
A synagogue ruler	Mark 5:22
Fishermen	Matthew 4:18-20
A poor widow	Luke 7:11-17
A Roman centurion	Matthew 8:5-13
A group of children	Mark 10:13-16
A prophet	Matthew 3
An adulterous woman	John 8:1-11
The Jewish council	Luke 22:66-71
A sick woman	Mark 5:25-34
A rich man	Mark 10:17-23
A blind beggar	Mark 10:46-52
Jewish political leaders	Mark 12:13-34
A group of women	Luke 8:2-3
The high priest	Matthew 26:62-68
An outcast with leprosy	Luke 17:11-19
A royal official	John 4:46-53
A young girl	Mark 5:41-42
A traitor	John 13:1-3, 27
A helpless and paralyzed man	Mark 2:1-12
A woman from a foreign land	Mark 7:25-30
A doubting follower	John 20:24-29
An enemy who hated him	Acts 9:1-9
A Samaritan woman	John 4:1-26

word is *ekballo,* meaning "to throw out." Jesus took charge in Jairus's house and used force to get rid of the jeering mourners. He
had nothing further to say to them, and he had no use for their
mourning or their scoffing.

Then Jesus *took the child's father and mother* and the three disciples who had come (5:37) and *went in where the child was,* in
an inner part of the house. The grieving parents and the wondering disciples went with him. Jesus had come to earth to conquer
sin and death, and in this dramatic but quiet miracle, he would

show his disciples that power. And two bereaved parents would receive back their beloved daughter.

LAUGHING LAST

Jesus tolerated the crowd's abuse in order to teach an important lesson about maintaining hope and trust in him. Today, most of the world laughs at Christ's claims, which seem ridiculous to them. Who laughs at you for your faith? What beliefs cause the watching world to deride you? If you are true to your faith, you will clash with others' beliefs. When you are belittled for expressing faith in Jesus and hope for eternal life, remember that unbelievers don't see from God's perspective. Take heart! Remember that what God thinks about you is more important than what the crowd thinks. For a clear statement about life after death, see 1 Thessalonians 4:13-18.

5:41 He took her by the hand and said to her, *"Talitha koum!"* (which means, "Little girl, I say to you, get up!").NIV Jesus did no incantations and spoke no magic words. He simply went to the girl's bedside and *took her by the hand.* The fact that Jesus touched the girl's hand would have amazed the proper synagogue leader and the disciples. Touching a dead body meant to become unclean. But Jesus had already dealt with a demon-possessed man and a woman with an incurable issue of blood and had touched and healed them. Touching the dead girl confirmed once again that to Jesus, compassion was more important than the letter of the law.

Then Jesus spoke a simple command. *Talitha koum* is Aramaic, one of the languages of Palestine. Most Galileans spoke not only Aramaic, but probably Greek and Hebrew too. Mark alone recorded the original words, then translated them for his Greek-speaking readers. Mark showed a tendency to retain the Aramaic (see for example, 3:17; 7:11; 7:34; 14:36) and probably used it in this story to give great emphasis on the reality of the miracle. Again, this was probably Peter's eyewitness account. The words "I say to you" emphasize Jesus' complete control over the situation and his power over death.

5:42 Immediately the girl stood up and walked around (she was twelve years old). At this they were completely astonished.NIV Jesus took the girl's hand in his, issued a command, and the dead child awoke as if from sleep, *immediately* standing up and walking around. Just as the healings Jesus performed were always complete, so the rising of this young girl from the dead was complete. She didn't come back to life in the sick state in which she

left; she came back well, whole, and able to walk around. *At this,*
the three disciples and the girl's parents *were completely*
astonished. The Greek words mean that they were out of their
minds with amazement. One day all those who scoff at Christ's
claims will be astonished at him.

This was not the first time the disciples had witnessed the raising of a dead person. Luke 7:11-15 records Jesus raising a boy
near the village of Nain. Yet, even in this instance, the disciples
were amazed. When the girl came back to life, perhaps the disciples may have wondered (as they did after Jesus calmed the
storm), "Who then is this, that the dead can be brought back to
life?" Jesus would raise yet another person—his friend Lazarus
(dead and buried for four days—recorded in John 11). Then
finally, most dramatic of all, Jesus himself would arise from the
grave and spend time with the disciples before returning to his
Father. Jesus had authority and power over humanity's greatest
enemy—death.

**5:43 He strictly ordered them that no one should know this, and
told them to give her something to eat.**NRSV Jesus then gave two
further commands. First, he *ordered them* (that is, the parents and
the three disciples) *that no one should know* the details of what
had occurred. Obviously the girl was not to be hidden for the
remainder of her life; people would know she had recovered.
But, as Jesus' mother, Mary, had done, the parents were charged
to keep these matters to themselves and think about them (see
Luke 2:19). The facts would reveal the truth. Those in the unbelieving crowd would have to decide for themselves—no one
would try to convince them. In fact, no one would even tell them
what had happened.

Jesus told them to be quiet because he was concerned for his
ministry. Jesus did not want to be known as just a miracle
worker; he wanted people to listen to his words that would heal
their broken spiritual lives. Jesus' mission was to preach the good
news of the kingdom of God. If crowds descended on him to see
dead people raised, they would not be coming with the heart
attitude needed to hear and respond to the gospel (see also 1:43-
45). The disciples would talk about them and understand Jesus'
miracles after his resurrection—then they could write them down
for all of us to read and marvel as well.

Second, Jesus *told them to give her something to eat.* This is an
incredible picture of Jesus' compassion and his understanding of
human needs. The girl would be hungry and should be fed. This
command also revealed to the parents and disciples that the girl
was completely restored—she was well enough to eat.

Jesus' last word to Jairus was a directive for positive action: Feed the hungry girl. On other occasions, Jesus himself produced food for hungry people, but not here. Her parents had work to do in the aftermath of a miracle. Every miracle generates new responsibilities. God creates work for us whenever prayers are answered, whenever people are healed. We must follow through on the miracles God has done.

Mark 6

Following a section where great faith in Jesus is exhibited (5:21-43), Mark records a story where there is great unbelief (6:1-6). Not only his own family, but Jesus' entire hometown, wondered what was wrong with their "son." Earlier (3:20-35), Jesus' mother and siblings had gone to Capernaum, seeking to rescue their family member from his delusions. Here Jesus came home on his own. But rather than offering welcome and expressing community pride, Jesus' townfolk were offended by his presence and his teaching. Familiarity bred contempt.

The people of Nazareth came to the unfortunate conclusion that their preconceptions of Jesus were all they needed to know about him. Even their amazement at the authority and truth of his teaching turned to ridicule. They refused to believe the obvious. As a result, their rejection limited his ministry.

Preaching In Galilee
After returning to his hometown, Nazareth, from Capernaum, Jesus preached in the villages of Galilee and sent his disciples out to preach as well. After meeting back in Capernaum, they left by boat to rest, only to be met by the crowds who followed the boat along the shore.

6:1 Jesus left there and went to his hometown, accompanied by his disciples.ᴺᴵⱽ After the previous incidents in Capernaum, where Jesus healed the bleeding woman and brought a dead girl back to life, Jesus *left there and went to his hometown*; that is, he returned to Nazareth (1:9, 24). Nazareth was about twenty miles southwest of Capernaum. Mark mentioned that Jesus was accompanied by his disciples (a detail

Matthew omitted), setting the stage for the sending out of the twelve disciples, recorded in 6:7.

Jesus had been born in Bethlehem, but he was raised in Nazareth (Matthew 2:19-23; Luke 2:39-40). This was not the first time he had spoken and taught in Nazareth; Luke 4:14-30 states that Jesus went to Nazareth, "where he had been brought up [and] went to the synagogue on the sabbath day" to read and teach (Luke 4:16 NRSV). The response at that time was less than positive—in fact, the people had tried to kill him, but Jesus had walked away unharmed. Thus, this trip to Nazareth, recorded in Mark, is significant. The people of Nazareth were about to receive a second chance to believe; unfortunately, they again refused. Their rejection of Jesus was certainly a learning experience for the disciples, who would soon be sent out on their own (in pairs) to preach the Good News.

6:2 **And when the Sabbath had come, He began to teach in the synagogue.**NKJV Jesus' forums for speaking included homes (2:2), the seashore (4:1), and the local synagogues (1:21, 39; 3:1). Synagogue services were conducted by lay people under the leadership of one or more synagogue "rulers" or leaders. For example, Jairus, the man whose daughter Jesus brought back to life, was a synagogue ruler (see 5:22). It was common for a visiting rabbi to be asked to speak in the local synagogue. Jesus, a well-known and popular speaker, had no trouble gaining an opportunity *to teach in the synagogue* on the Sabbath.

The synagogue was the center of the town, controlling civic and social as well as religious life. The synagogue was not like a church today—it was not an empty building except on Sabbath days when only the devoted would come. Instead, everyone seemed to come to the synagogue, for this was the focal point of ancient Jewish life. This was really a key place for Jesus to meet the people—much like the city gate of the Old Testament.

Many who heard him were amazed. "Where did this man get these things?" they asked. "What's this wisdom that has been given him, that he even does miracles!"NIV As often happened when Jesus spoke, *many who heard him were amazed* (see also 1:22; 7:37; 10:26; 11:18). The Greek verb for "amazed" in all these verses is *ekplesso,* which literally means "to strike out of one's senses." The people were so amazed it was as if they had been struck with a blow, stunned. They were flabbergasted.

What was the source of their amazement? It focused on *this man* and where he, in particular, had gotten *these things* (referring to the *wisdom* of his teaching and the *miracles* he performed). They knew his miracles were supernatural, but they wondered about their source (the options were either God or Satan—see 3:22) and how Jesus could do them. These miracles were probably those they had heard about, for Mark recounted later that "he could not do any miracles there" because of their unbelief (6:5 NIV).

6:3 "Is not this the carpenter, the son of Mary and brother of James and Joses and Judas and Simon, and are not his sisters here with us?" And they took offense at him.NRSV Jesus was teaching effectively and wisely, but the people of his hometown saw him as only *the carpenter* whose family they also knew well. "He's no better than we are—he's just a common laborer," they said. The Greek word can mean "a stoneworker or carpenter." In Matthew 13:55, Jesus is called "the carpenter's son." Jesus was almost thirty years old before he began his public teaching ministry. For the years prior to that, he had been at home, learning the trade of carpentry from his father and probably helping to support himself and the family after Joseph's death.

> We never ought to despise others because they are poor. It is disgraceful to be a gambler, or a drunkard, or covetous, or a liar; but it is no disgrace to work with our own hands and earn our own bread by our own labor. The thought of the carpenter's shop at Nazareth should cast down the high thoughts of all who make an idol of riches. It cannot be dishonorable to occupy the same position as the Son of God and Saviour of the world. *J. C. Ryle*

When the townspeople called him the *son of Mary,* it may have been a derogatory remark. While it may have been true that Joseph was already dead, in any normal situation Jesus would still have been called "son of Joseph." But Jesus was conceived prior to Joseph and Mary's wedding (while they were engaged, Matthew 1:18), and perhaps the townspeople saw Jesus as not even being Joseph's son. Such was the stigma Mary continued to carry, even when Jesus was almost thirty years old. Apparently people saw Mary as less than honorable. Mary's obedience to God in carrying his blessed Son had changed the course of her life (Luke 1:26-38).

The listing of the brothers (probably some of whom had come earlier to try to take Jesus by force in 3:21, 31) indicates that the people knew the family well—the mother, the brothers, the sisters. Apparently they were all ordinary people and Jesus had experienced an ordinary childhood. Thus for Jesus to claim to be someone special (especially with what they considered his less than honorable beginnings) caused them to take *offense* at his words, meaning they stumbled over them and could not accept them. They were offended that others could be impressed by Jesus and follow him. Their rejection was complete and absolute; he was one of their peers, and their preconceived notions about who he was made it impossible for them to accept his message. Jesus had come to them as a prophet, but they saw only a hometown boy.

Jesus' brother *James* later became a believer, a leader in the Jerusalem church (Acts 15:13; Galatians 2:9), and the author of the book of James. *Judas* may have been Jude, author of the book of Jude. Nothing else is known of the other brothers and sisters.

HE'S ONE OF US
"He can't be any good; he's one of us!" The people of Nazareth knew Jesus' family background so well that they could not accept his divine authority. Today, many people look at the failures of churches (hypocrisy, narrow rule keeping, stinginess) and decadent leaders (overcome with sexual passions and enagaged in power plays) and conclude that spirituality and leadership are fiction. We need to weigh reality carefully but not allow human weakness in the church or its leaders to muddle the bright clarity of the gospel. Do we tend to reject leaders who emerge among us? We must be careful not to reject the leadership of someone else because we depreciate our own capacity for it. Allow God to do through someone else what he may not have chosen to do through you.

6:4 But Jesus said to them, "A prophet is not without honor except in his own country, among his own relatives, and in his own house."^{NKJV} Jesus used a common proverb found in rabbinic literature. It is significant that Jesus applied the word *prophet* to himself, thus specifically claiming to be a prophet. The word refers not to one who foretells future events (although that may be part of a prophet's ministry), but to one who speaks God's message. Jesus was not the first prophet to be rejected in his own country. Jeremiah experienced rejection in his hometown, even by members of his own family (Jeremiah 12:5-6). Jesus also experienced rejection by *relatives* and members *in his own house.* His family thought he had gone crazy (3:21), and most of them didn't believe until after his resurrection (John 7:5; Acts 1:14).

COST OF DISCIPLESHIP
Jesus said that a prophet is never honored in his hometown.
But that doesn't make his or her work any less important. A person doesn't need to be respected or honored to be useful to
God. If friends, neighbors, or family don't respect your Christian
work, don't let their rejection keep you from serving God. Often
Christian service is defamed merely because it brings people to
God—confronts people with sin and urges faith. Such rejection
is the cost of discipleship. Don't be discouraged by it. God
stands with you; God will keep you strong.

**6:5 He could not do any miracles there, except lay his hands on a
few sick people and heal them.**[NIV] That Jesus *could not do any
miracles* in Nazareth does not mean a restriction on his power.
Rather, Jesus could have done greater miracles in Nazareth, but
he chose not to because of the people's unbelief. In this Gospel,
Mark emphasized the power and presence of God revealed only
to those with faith. Jesus' mighty works were meant to further the
kingdom of God, not to try to convince a group of stubborn
people who had already thoroughly rejected him. To do miracles
would be of no value because the people did not accept his message or believe that he was from God. Therefore, Jesus looked
elsewhere, seeking those who would respond to his miracles and
message. This shows the limitation of simply being a model of
faith for others to observe. Jesus was the perfect model, yet
others rejected him. We need to verbally proclaim the gospel and,
at times, move on to other people and towns.

MIRACLES LIMITED
As a general principle, power follows faith! On some occasions,
Jesus did wondrous work in the face of unbelief (Paul's conversion, the Gadarene demoniac). Most of the time, however,
Jesus works in response or in cooperation with faith. Thus, it
was not impossible for Jesus to do miracles in Nazareth; Jesus
can do all things. But he wanted the person's faith to be part of
the process: "According to your faith will it be done to you" (Matthew 9:29 NIV).
   In the Bible, unbelief is regarded as a mind-set, a stubborn
refusal to believe, a moral rebellion, not merely a logical conclusion of evaluating evidence. So the Nazarenes had a moral
problem, not an intellectual one. They were hardened in their
attitudes. We must ask: Does my lack of faith prevent Jesus
from working in my life, my family, and my church?

Apparently even in Nazareth, *a few sick people,* humbled by their need, did come to Jesus for healing. And Jesus, always compassionate, healed them. These few came in faith and received what they desired. It is sad that so few of those who knew Jesus well would take him at his word and believe. The contrast between the humble carpenter and the supernatural prophet was too great for them to comprehend. So they chose unbelief, a choice that amazed Jesus (6:6).

6:6 And he was amazed at their unbelief.^{NRSV} This statement gives a subtle picture of Jesus' humanity. As the divine Son of God, Jesus would not be amazed at anything. But as a human being, Jesus went to Nazareth (this second time, see 6:1) probably hoping for a warmer reception than the first time. He had been rejected by the people in Decapolis (5:17), but the *unbelief* and rejection of his friends and family—people he grew up with, knew, and loved—*amazed* him. The word for "amazed" is the same word Mark used in 5:20, 12:17, and 15:5 to describe people's reactions to Jesus' miracles. The miracles "amazed" the people of Capernaum and Jerusalem; in turn, the stubborn unbelief of the people of Nazareth "amazed" Jesus. This certainly provided a key lesson for the disciples, who would themselves experience rejection as they began their ministries. Jesus left Nazareth this second time, and there is no record that he ever returned. Most people feel that they may have unlimited opportunities to believe, but often there is no second chance.

EYES OF FAITH
Jesus did few miracles in his hometown because of the people's unbelief. Unbelief blinds us to the truth and robs us of hope. These people missed the Messiah. How does your faith measure up? If you can't see God's work, perhaps it is because of unbelief. Believe, ask God for a mighty work in your life, and expect him to act. Look with the eyes of faith.

Then Jesus went around teaching from village to village.^{NIV} So Jesus left his hometown and *went around teaching from village to village.* The Greek offers a picture of his itinerary, "He went round about the villages in a circle." Jesus visited all the villages in the environs of Nazareth, going deliberately in a circular pattern. This sentence gives us a transition from Jesus' leaving Nazareth to Jesus' preparing his disciples to continue his itinerant ministry. The sentence also serves as a summary, much like 1:14 and 1:39.

JESUS SENDS OUT THE TWELVE DISCIPLES / 6:7-13 / **93**

When Jesus gave his disciples their first commission, he included directions about conduct and about content. As to their conduct, he sent them in pairs and instructed them to travel light, to appreciate hospitality without abusing it, and to leave if not received or believed. As to the content of their message, they were to follow the pattern that he had already established. It included preaching repentance, announcing the kingdom of God, healing the sick, and releasing those under demonic bondage. From Jesus' instructions to the disciples, we can learn that our conduct should not hinder our ability to communicate the gospel content.

Mark placed accounts about rejection both before (6:1-6) and after (6:14-29) his commissioning of his disciples (6:7-13). Mark thereby shows us that the mission will involve persecution. He further emphasized persecution by placing Jesus' review of the mission with his disciples (6:30) after the death of John the Baptist.

Even while Jesus was still with the disciples, he helped them to discover what it would be like to function without him. Mark already mentioned two other mission circuits that Jesus traveled (1:14, 39), indicating that at least some of the disciples had experience in itinerant ministry. For these Galilean towns, the disciples' visit may have provided another opportunity for exposure to the gospel.

6:7 Calling the Twelve to him, he sent them out two by two and gave them authority over evil spirits.[NIV] The disciples *(the Twelve)* had been trained in both the teaching they should give and the reception they could expect. It was time for them to do their "student teaching." Jesus could only travel so far and do so much. This sending out of six groups of disciples geographically multiplied his efforts (Jesus would later send out seventy-two others, also in pairs, see Luke 10:1-2). Jesus gave his disciples responsibility and authority to act as his representatives in both teaching and power. This was in keeping with the Jewish concept of *shaliach,* which means that someone's representative was seen as the very presence of that person. The Jews would understand the teaching and ministry of these disciples to be as if Jesus himself had come to them. This was why they had been chosen (Mark 3:14-15). That Jesus sent them out in pairs *(two by two)* was also common in Judaism, in keeping with the demand for two witnesses (Deuteronomy 17:6).

Jesus *sent them out* to witness. He did not issue an invitation to come to a meeting. Our churches should do more to go out to those needing to hear. For us to do so would require us to sacrifice the comfort and security that we have in church.

Mark mentioned only the *authority over evil spirits,* while Matthew included the ability to cure disease and sickness (Matthew 10:1). Mark focused on the disciples' power over the demonic realm in keeping with his constant emphasis on the cosmic conflict between God and Satan. Mark did mention that, upon their return, the disciples reported casting out demons and healing the sick (6:13). This authority and power authenticated their message. Jesus gave the disciples this authority; they did not have it on their own.

NO SOLOS
The disciples were sent out in pairs. Individually they could have reached more areas of the country, but this was not Christ's plan. The advantages in going out by twos are:
- They could strengthen and encourage each other.
- They could provide comfort in rejection.
- They could give each other discernment, and fewer mistakes would be made.
- They could stir each other to action as a counter to idleness or indifference.

Our strength comes from God, but he meets many of our needs through our teamwork with others. As you serve Christ, don't try to go it alone.

6:8-9 **These were his instructions: "Take nothing for the journey except a staff—no bread, no bag, no money in your belts. Wear sandals but not an extra tunic."**[NIV] While these instructions seem at first to be contrary to normal travel plans, they simply reveal the urgency of the task and its temporary nature. The disciples were sent out and then expected to return to Jesus with a full report. This was a training mission, and they were to leave immediately and travel light, taking along only minimal supplies. They were to depend on God and on the people to whom they were sent (6:10). Most people leaving on a journey would carry *a staff* for help in walking, *bread* to eat and strengthen them along the way, a *bag* (such as a wallet) to carry coins or other needs, *money* for food and lodging, *sandals* to protect their feet, and an *extra tunic* for added warmth at night. But Jesus allowed only the minimum: a staff and sandals. They were not even allowed to carry a bag because it was common for beggars to use such bags to solicit money. The disciples were not to be beggars, but were to live off the support of those who welcomed their message.

Mark recorded that the disciples were instructed to take nothing with them *except* staffs, while the accounts in Matthew and Luke, say that Jesus told them *not* to take staffs. One explanation for this difference is that Matthew and Luke were referring to a club used for protection, whereas Mark was talking about a shepherd's crook used for walking. Another explanation is that in Matthew and Luke, Jesus was forbidding them to acquire an *additional* staff or sandals, but instead to use what they already had. In any case, the point in all three accounts is the same: The disciples were to leave at once, without extensive preparation, trusting in God's care rather than in their own resources. Jesus' instructions pertained only to this particular mission. Indeed, just after Jesus and the disciples ate the Last Supper, "Jesus asked them, 'When I sent you without purse, bag or sandals, did you lack anything?' 'Nothing,' they answered. He said to them, 'But now if you have a purse, take it, and also a bag; and if you don't have a sword, sell your cloak and buy one'" (Luke 22:35-36 NIV). Different times and situations would call for different measures.

TRAVELING LIGHT
Modern missionaries would be missing the point to copy these instructions literally and mechanically. But Jesus' principles are valid for all time: (1) In your ministry, focus on God's spiritual power, not on worldly goods and frills. (2) Go further and do more than your current supplies allow. (3) Worry less, trust more. (4) Keep your lifestyle simple and efficient. (5) When your mission is over, the only achievements worth talking about will be stories of faith tested, enlarged, and affirmed.

6:10 **"Wherever you enter a house, stay there until you leave the place."**NSRV That a pair of disciples would *enter a house* meant that they had found a "worthy person" (Matthew 10:11)—a believer—and would either request or be invited to lodge in that person's home. Then Jesus commanded that they *stay there* until they left the city to move on. They were not to offend their hosts by looking for "better" lodging in a home that was more comfortable or socially prominent. To remain in one home would not be a burden for the home owner because the disciples' stay in each community would be short.

In a nutshell, Jesus instructed the disciples to depend on others while they went from town to town preaching the gospel. Their purpose was to blanket Judea with Jesus' message, and by traveling light they could move quickly. Their dependence on others had other good effects: (1) It clearly showed that the Messiah had not come to offer wealth to his followers; (2) it forced the disciples to rely on God's power and not on their own provision; and (3) it involved the villagers and made them more eager to hear the message. Staying in homes was an excellent approach for the disciples' short-term mission; it was not intended, however, to be a permanent way of life for them. Yet the faith and simplicity that this way of life portrayed would serve them well in the future.

TAKE CARE
Jesus said that those who minister are to be cared for. The disciples could expect food and shelter in return for the spiritual service they provided. Who ministers to you? Make sure you take care of the pastors, missionaries, and teachers who serve God by serving you (see 1 Corinthians 9:9-10; 1 Timothy 5:17). Invite someone over for a simple meal; write a note of thanks and encouragement; give such gifts as food, time, service, or money. Think about what you can do this week to show appreciation and support for someone who ministers to you.

6:11 **"If any place will not welcome you and they refuse to hear you, as you leave, shake off the dust that is on your feet as a testimony against them."**NRSV The disciples should also expect rejection, such as Jesus had faced in Decapolis (5:17) and in Nazareth (6:3). So Jesus further instructed that *if any place* did not *welcome* them (that is, take them in and offer hospitality) and refused even to *hear* them, then they should *shake off the dust* on their feet as they left.

Shaking off dust that accumulated on one's sandals showed extreme contempt for an area and its people, as well as the determination not to have any further involvement with them. Pious Jews shook dust from their feet after passing through Gentile cities or territory to show their separation from Gentile influences and practices. When the disciples shook the dust from their feet after leaving a *Jewish* town, it would be a vivid sign that they wished to remain separate from people who had rejected Jesus and his message and say that the Jews in that place had acted like "Gentiles" or pagans.

Shaking off the dust of a place, Jesus said, would be *a testimony against them* (see also 1:44). Its implications were clear and had eternal consequences. The act showed the people that the disciples had discharged their duty, had nothing further to say, and would leave the people to answer to God. By this statement, Jesus made it clear that the listeners were responsible for what they did with the gospel. The disciples were not to blame if the message was rejected, as long as they had faithfully and carefully presented it. Likewise, we are not responsible when others reject Christ's message of salvation, but we do have the responsibility to share the gospel clearly and faithfully.

DON'T GET DUSTED
The gesture of shaking the dust from one's sandals showed the people that the responsibility for their rejection was on their head. We must be careful in evangelism not to use threats, scare tactics, or manipulation. Yet we must communicate the urgency of coming to faith. While there are opportune moments that should not be scorned, we should stress the mercy of God as well as his judgment.

6:12 So they went out and preached that people should repent.^{NKJV} The disciples went out as Jesus' representatives, continuing his message. Jesus proclaimed "the good news of God, and saying, '. . . repent, and believe" (1:14-15 NRSV). So the disciples *preached that people should repent.* Mark used the Greek verb *kerusso,* meaning to make a public announcement of such authority and importance that it demanded to be heeded. Such was the important message the disciples carried. To "repent" means to turn, implying a change in behavior. It is turning from sin toward God. The disciples not only brought the message of the gospel; they called for action in the form of repentance and belief. The gospel can only be life changing if people allow it to change their lives. The change, for sinful humans, can begin only with repentance.

WHOSE TERMS?
People resist admitting blame, appearing humble, asking forgiveness. We'd rather be confident, capable, and "on top." But faith starts with this old-fashioned, humbling exercise called repentance. It recognizes that God is in charge and we are in need. It accepts Jesus' sacrifice, not as our right, but as his undeserved gift to us. On God's terms, not ours, we begin our journey of faith. As we go, we remind ourselves that grace, not pride or personal power, keeps the journey fresh and vital. Come humbly to God.

6:13 And they cast out many demons, and anointed with oil many who were sick, and healed them.^{NKJV} Jesus gave his disciples authority to cast out demons (3:15), as well as the power to heal the sick. Casting out demons extended Jesus' personal ministry, which was to confront Satan's power and destroy it. As the disciples went throughout Galilee, they would be announcing the arrival of the kingdom of God through their preaching and healing. If they had only preached, people might have thought the kingdom was only spiritual. On the other hand, if the disciples had only been given the power to cast out demons and heal the sick, without preaching, people might not have realized the spiritual importance of their mission. Most of their listeners expected the arrival of God's kingdom and the Messiah to bring wealth and power to their nation; they preferred material benefits to spiritual discernment. But the truth about Jesus is that he is both God and man, both spiritual and physical; and the salvation that he offers is both for the soul and the body. Any group or teaching that emphasizes soul at the expense of body, or body at the expense of soul, is in danger of distorting Jesus' Good News.

Of all the Gospel writers, Mark alone included the words *anointed with oil* in writing of the disciples' healing ministry. This "oil" was olive oil, used often at that time as treatment (both internally and externally) for many illnesses. Medicines were few in those days, and olive oil had proven to have exceptional qualities. The "anointing with oil" done by the disciples is explained further in James 5:14, where James instructed, "Is any one of you sick? He should call the elders of the church to pray over him and anoint him with oil in the name of the Lord" (NIV). For all its medicinal uses, the oil did not accomplish the healings; rather, it was the spiritual anointing and *praying* of the disciples on behalf of the sick person. However, God could use the medicine to heal *many who were sick.*

SEEING A DOCTOR
Should Christians resort to professional intervention to get well, or merely pray? The answer, of course, is both. God invites us to trust him at all times and in all conditions. We should confidently pray about getting well. God has also blessed the world with human intelligence, some of which is devoted to healing sickness. By all means use it. People who believe that prayer alone is more faithful must also believe, against all biblical evidence, that human intelligence is outside of God's will and purpose. Never spurn a good gift from God. *Carpe diem*: Seize the day. *Carpe Deum*: Seize God completely.

HEROD KILLS JOHN THE BAPTIST / 6:14-29 / **95**

Most of the narrative of Jesus' ministry has been told under the cloud of John's imprisonment. It was mentioned in 1:14 when Jesus began his public ministry. As such, 6:17-29 is a flashback.

As told in the previous section, Jesus sent out his disciples to carry out ministry on their own. Their mission may have been short in duration, but it was a great success. This development provided Mark with a place to tell how John the Baptist died.

People were trying to explain Jesus' success. They were not ready to acknowledge him as the Son of God, but they were willing to call him a new prophet or an old prophet like Elijah returned from the past. Some, like King Herod, were convinced that Jesus must be John the Baptist come back to life. Apparently, Herod was suffering pangs of guilt after ordering John's murder. He had gone along with his wife Herodias's scheme to take revenge on the irritating preacher by ordering him to be beheaded.

Told side by side, the success of the apostolic mission and the result of John's mission present a sobering lesson to those who obey God's calling: Sometimes discipleship means death. John, Jesus, and almost every one of the disciples backed up the truth of their ministry with their lives.

6:14 King Herod heard about this, for Jesus' name had become well known.^{NIV} The narrative about the disciples' preaching tour of Galilee continues at 6:30, having been interrupted with several verses telling the story of John the Baptist's death. The expanded ministry of the gospel by the disciples brought Jesus, who *had become well known,* to the attention of *King Herod,* ruler over the territories of Galilee and Perea. In 4 B.C. Herod had been named tetrarch—one of four rulers over the four districts of Palestine. He was the son of Herod the Great, who had ordered the killing of the babies in Bethlehem (Matthew 2:16). Also known as Herod Antipas, he heard Jesus' case before Jesus' crucifixion (Luke 23:6-12). The history of the Herod family is filled with lies, murder, treachery, and adultery. They were evil. Herod Antipas was known for his insensitivity and debauchery. Though he was popular with his Roman superiors, his unbridled political ambitions eventually led to his exile in A.D. 39 by the Roman emperor Caligula, who removed him on the basis of charges by his nephew (Herod Agrippa I) who ruled Galilee after Herod Antipas. While Herod Antipas was not officially a "king," Mark used the title for his Roman audience. The Romans applied the title to all eastern rulers. Some scholars think that Mark used the title to reflect Herod's self-importance and vanity.

John the Baptist was last mentioned in 1:14; John had been arrested just prior to Jesus beginning his public ministry. The arrest marked the end of John's public ministry. He was imprisoned for some time prior to his death (see Matthew 11:2-6). At this point, the reader is to understand that John the Baptist had died at Herod's hands. (Mark will record the story in detail.)

Some were saying, "John the Baptist has been raised from the dead, and that is why miraculous powers are at work in him."NIV The people, still trying to figure out where Jesus' miraculous powers came from (like those in Nazareth, 6:2), had three main explanations. First, perhaps he was *John the Baptist* who had been *raised from the dead.* Oddly enough, John had done no miracles; he had simply preached and prepared the way for Jesus. Apparently the people were willing to believe that John had died and had arisen and thus was in touch with unseen powers enabling him to perform miracles. However, they could not see Jesus for who he was (the Messiah) and his miracles for what they were (heavenly evidence of God's kingdom).

The *some* who *were saying* that this was a risen John the Baptist included King Herod, who said with certainty, "This is John, whom I beheaded; he has been raised from the dead!" (6:16 NKJV). While Herod had succeeded in silencing John, he had not succeeded in silencing his own guilty conscience. When news of Jesus reached the palace, Herod thought that John had come back to trouble him some more. Thus began Herod's great interest in Jesus and his long-standing desire to see him perform a miracle (Luke 23:8).

6:15 But others said, "It is Elijah." And others said, "It is a prophet, like one of the prophets of old."NRSV Second, *others* who were familiar with the Old Testament thought Jesus was Elijah, the great prophet who did not die but was taken to heaven in a chariot of fire (2 Kings 2:1-11). They applied the prophecy of Elijah's return in Malachi 4:5 to Jesus. But they should have applied the prophecy to John, then they would have realized Jesus' identity. Later Jesus explained to his disciples that John had fulfilled Malachi's prophecy (Mark 9:13).

Third, still others believed that Jesus was *a prophet, like one of the prophets of old,* someone in the tradition of Moses, Isaiah, or Jeremiah. While John the Baptist had been widely regarded as a prophet (and the first prophet to the nation in over four hundred years), the people refused to hear what John had to say about the one who would follow him (1:7-8) and instead regarded this "one" as just another prophet. Obviously, they didn't even listen to those they regarded as prophets—a problem Israel had throughout its history.

It was so difficult for the people to accept Jesus as the Son of God that they tried to come up with other solutions—most of which sound quite unbelievable to us. Very few found the correct answer, as Peter did (Luke 9:20). Many people today still cannot accept Jesus as the fully human yet fully divine Son of God, and they look for alternate explanations—a great prophet, a radical political leader, a self-deceived rabble-rouser. None of these explanations can account for Jesus' miracles or, especially, for his glorious resurrection; so these realities have to be rationalized. In the end, the attempts to explain away Jesus are far more difficult to believe than the truth.

MAKE UP YOUR MIND
Herod, along with many others, wondered about Jesus' true identity. Unable to accept Jesus' claim to be God's Son, they made up their own explanations for his power and authority. Today people still have to make up their minds about Jesus. Some think that if they can name what he is—prophet, teacher, good man—they can weaken the power of his claim on their lives. But what they *think* does not change who Jesus *is*. What do you think about Jesus? Make him your Lord.

6:16 But when Herod heard, he said, "This is John, whom I beheaded; he has been raised from the dead!"[NKJV] Herod's guilty conscience screamed the most obvious answer. Upon hearing about Jesus, Herod was certain that John, whom he had beheaded, had been *raised from the dead*. The readers had the first explanation of what happened to John. He had died, they knew from 6:14; but here they read that he had died by beheading. Mark hinted of Herod's incredible guilt over having ordered the beheading in recording Herod's words, "whom I beheaded" (these words actually appear at the beginning of the sentence, in an emphatic position). The "I" is also emphatic. Herod was placing the guilt of John's gruesome death on himself.

Some of Mark's readers might still wonder how that could have come about; Mark will fill in the details in a flashback sequence in the following verses.

6:17 For Herod himself had given orders to have John arrested, and he had him bound and put in prison. He did this because of Herodias, his brother Philip's wife, whom he had married.[NIV] Herod's personal guilt was well placed, for he had ordered John to be arrested. Again the readers might ask, "Why? What could John have possibly done to cause him to be arrested?" While Mark's Roman readers would have pondered that question, modern-day readers would be even more perplexed. But we must understand law and order in ancient days.

Kings had absolute sway; if the king wanted someone arrested, the arrest was carried out by the king's guards—no questions asked. Herod, empowered by Rome over the region of Galilee, simply had given the *orders* and John had been *arrested . . . bound and put in prison.* The Jewish historian Josephus pinpointed this prison as Machaerus, a fortress (combination palace and prison) near the barren northeastern shore of the Dead Sea in the region of Moab.

Why was John treated so harshly? Herod had to put John away *because of Herodias, his brother Philip's wife, whom he had married.* Apparently Mark's Roman readers knew enough about the Herod family to need no further information. But we would do well to try to grasp exactly what Mark meant by this sentence. *Philip* was Herod's half brother and another of Palestine's four rulers. His territories were Iturea and Traconitis, northeast of the Sea of Galilee (Luke 3:1). *Herodias* was the daughter of Aristobulus, another half brother. Thus Herodias was a half niece to both Philip and Herod (and they, in turn, were her half uncles). Herodias married her half uncle Philip and then divorced him to marry another half uncle, Herod. (Herod, meanwhile, had divorced his first wife.) Thus, in marrying, Herodias and Herod had committed adultery, as well as a type of incest. John the Baptist condemned Herod and Herodias for living immorally (6:18). Rebuking a tyrannical Roman official who could imprison and execute him was extremely dangerous, yet that is what John did.

SPEAKING OUT
Christians today face a world of moral compromise. Secular power sets standards that correspond to majority vote. But Christian standards begin with God's Word. To be faithful to God's Word, we must stand up against what is morally wrong. Responsible Christians must choose their battles. To fight every injustice, all the time, is the life of comic-book heroes, not human beings.

Start with prayers for wisdom, then prayers for courage. Once your battle is chosen, speak and act as a faithful follower of the living God. Witness with strength; move mountains by faith; overcome in love. Show the compromised world a little of John's stubbornness and fortitude.

6:18 **For John had been telling Herod, "It is not lawful for you to have your brother's wife."**[NRSV] John's denunciation of the marriage of Galilee's leader had been public as well as private. John had explained the obvious to Herod: It was against the law for Herod to be married to his brother's (that is, half brother's) wife (not to mention that she was also his half niece). Leviticus 18:16 and 20:21 describe the laws that Herod was breaking. Herod was Jewish, and whether or not he cared about the Jewish law, he *did* care about a revolt against him by the Jews.

> Be radical. Dare to be different. Dare to be Christian. Go to the world. Accept Jesus Christ, and live for him. I dare you to do it. *Charles Colson*

John's public denunciation of the incest and adultery of Herod and Herodias was too much for them to bear, especially Herodias, whose anger turned to hatred.

6:19-20 And Herodias had a grudge against him, and wanted to kill him. But she could not, for Herod feared John, knowing that he was a righteous and holy man, and he protected him.NRSV Herodias held a *grudge against him.* The phrase, in the imperfect tense, indicates that she never let up for one moment, but was waiting for her opportunity for revenge. So great was this grudge that she *wanted to kill him.* But Herod *feared John* with a superstitious kind of fear. He knew that John was a *righteous and holy man* (not the kind of man one should murder, he thought, for that could have terrible consequences). So he protected John from Herodias's murderous intentions by locking him in prison. Perhaps he hoped that stopping John's public speaking would end the problem and quiet Herodias. For the time being, Herodias *could not* have John killed—she had the desire but not the power. But she bided her time. Apparently Herodias was used to getting her way.

THE GRUESOME TWOSOME
Herodias nursed a grudge. Her trouble started with a private sin. For love, power, or politics, she married Herod. John confronted both of them and rebuked them with the truth about their sin. The truth pricked Herod's conscience and led him to inquire more of John. Herodias let her pride and anger turn to hatred, bitterness, and murder. She let a desire master her life and keep her far from God. A single desire or sin left unchecked and unrepented can harden our heart and separate us from God. Don't let grudges build up. Don't harden your heart against God's conviction of sin in your life.

When Herod heard John, he was greatly puzzled; yet he liked to listen to him.NIV Herod had little backbone. While he greatly respected John the Baptist as a holy and righteous man and *liked to listen to him,* he also kept John imprisoned for the sake of his evil wife and his incestuous and adulterous marriage. Herod was an evil man, so when he listened to John, *he was greatly puzzled.*

Some Bible versions might read "he did many things" instead of "he was greatly puzzled." The Greek phrases are very close: "He was greatly puzzled" is *polla eporei,* while "he did many things" is *polla epoiei.* "He was greatly puzzled" is the preferred translation.

6:21 Finally the opportune time came. On his birthday Herod gave a banquet for his high officials and military commanders and the leading men of Galilee.[NIV] That Herod had imprisoned John the Baptist was not enough for the angry Herodias. She continued to nurse her grudge against John for speaking publicly about her sins, biding her time until she would get her way and have John killed. Then on Herod Antipas's birthday, *the opportune time came.* Whenever we harbor guilt and hatred in our heart, Satan is busy creating opportunities for greater evil to happen. Herod *gave a banquet* for many notable men from governmental, military, and civil strata in Galilee. These were the "movers and shakers" of life in Herod's region. He hoped to entertain them, impress them, and win their respect and admiration by this elaborate party. Herodias, however, had another agenda in mind.

> Not that it is wrong in itself to give a good party, but such is the propensity of the human mind to wantonness that when the reins are loosed men easily go astray. *John Calvin*

6:22 When the daughter of Herodias came in and danced, she pleased Herod and his dinner guests.[NIV] Herodias's daughter (by her marriage with Philip, 6:17) provided the bait Herodias would use to get her way with Herod. *The daughter* was Salome, a young woman in her middle teens (*korasion* translated "girl" would refer to a girl of marriageable age). Herodias sent Salome into the banquet hall to dance for Herod and his roomful of male (and probably drunken) dinner guests. The dance she performed displayed the loose morals both of herself and her mother, for it was meant to be shocking, provocative, and sensual. Few women of respectable position would perform in such a way, but Herodias knew that Salome's dance would gain raucous approval from the all-male audience. Such approval would then cause her arrogant husband to offer a reward to the young woman.

PARTY ON?
What started out as a dinner party ended up in a murderous
tragedy. In today's tolerant society, it would be tough for a
preacher to get much of a hearing by condemning parties. Yet
a party atmosphere can create a hazardous environment for
Christian morals. Most parties where drinking is present seem
innocent enough, giving an atmosphere for people to relax and
get away from pressure and responsibilities. But when people
give up their moral standards and passions are enflamed, sin
quickly takes over. Stay away from parties where things can get
out of control.

**The king said to the girl, "Ask me for anything you want, and
I'll give it to you."**[NIV] When Salome ended her dance, the king
brought her to his side. He offered her *anything* she wanted.
Herod continued to flaunt his power, desiring in this promise to
show his ability to provide anything the girl might ask.

**6:23 And he promised her with an oath, "Whatever you ask I will
give you, up to half my kingdom."**[NIV] Herod couldn't leave his
promise to stand on its own—perhaps his word wasn't good
enough for that. In any case, he felt it necessary to add *an oath* to
show that he was really serious. Then he added that this reward
for Salome could be *up to half [his] kingdom.* Herod and all his
notables in the banquet hall knew that Herod had no kingdom to
give. Herod's power came from Rome as well as from the kingdom over which he ruled. Herod used a saying that revealed the
scope of his offer but was not meant to be taken literally (see, for
example, 1 Kings 13:8). But Salome understood that she could
ask practically anything and receive it.

POWERFUL WORDS
As a ruler under Roman authority, Herod had no kingdom to
give. The offer of half his kingdom was Herod's way to say that
he would give Herodias's daughter almost anything she
wanted. When Herodias asked for John's head, Herod would
have been greatly embarrassed in front of his guests if he had
denied her request. Words are powerful. Because they can
lead to great sin, we should use them with great care.

**6:24 So she went out and said to her mother, "What shall I ask?"
And she said, "The head of John the Baptist!"**[NKJV] Any young
woman might be prepared with a thousand possible suggestions
to an offer such as Herod's, but Salome left the banquet hall to
confer with her mother. Herodias must have told Salome to win

the reward and then to return to her before making her request. Salome's words, *"What shall I ask?"* could also be translated, "What shall I ask for myself?" She was not prepared for her mother to take the reward, but she obviously had no choice.

Salome's mother took no time to think about the offer; she already knew what she wanted. She responded triumphantly with the gruesome request, *"The head of John the Baptist!"* Herodias did not want only John's death, she wanted his head "on a platter" (6:25). Herodias wanted John killed and the gruesome proof

RASH VOWS

Ecclesiastes 5:2 says: "Never be rash with your mouth, nor let your heart be quick to utter a word before God." (NRSV). Scripture records the vows of many men and women. Some of these vows proved to be rash and unwise, and others, though extreme, were kept to the letter by those who made them. Let us learn from the examples in God's Word not to make rash vows.

Person	Vow	Result	Reference
Jephthah	To offer to the Lord whoever came out to meet him after battle (it turned out to be his daughter)	He lost his daughter.	Judges 11:30-31
Hannah	To give her son back to God, if God would give her a son	When Samuel was born, she dedicated him to God.	1 Samuel 1:9-11
Saul	To kill anyone who ate before evening (Jonathan, his son, had not heard the command and broke it)	Saul would have killed Jonathan if soldiers had not intervened.	1 Samuel 14:24
Micaiah	To say only what God told him to say	He was put in prison.	1 Kings 22:14
Job	To never speak wickedness or deceit	His fortunes were restored.	Job 27:2-4
Herod Antipas	To give Herodias's daughter anything she requested	Herod was forced to order John the Baptist's death.	Mark 6:22-23

of his death in the prison brought to the palace in Galilee. Herodias would have her way; Herod had no way out. John's death was sealed.

6:25 At once the girl hurried in to the king with the request: "I want you to give me right now the head of John the Baptist on a platter."NIV Salome *hurried* back to the banquet hall. There was no time to waste; neither Herodias nor Salome wanted the king to sober up or change his mind. Salome, apparently unashamed of the horrid request, delivered it to Herod as her own: *"I want you to give me . . . the head of John the Baptist on a platter."* The proof of John's death was to be delivered to her at the palace, and she wanted it *right now.* The request had to be carried out immediately—with no time for Herod to figure a way out of granting her request.

6:26 The king was deeply grieved; yet out of regard for his oaths and for the guests, he did not want to refuse her.NRSV When Salome grandly gave her request to Herod in the hearing of all the important officials, Herod suddenly realized what he had done— and he probably knew he had been trapped by the wife he so much adored. Mark wrote that he *was deeply grieved*—for his own stupidity, for having put himself in this position in front of all the people he wanted to impress, and for needing to order the execution of the holy man whom he both respected and feared (6:20). Herod had made a promise and had sealed it with an oath (6:23). Such words were considered irrevocable. To back out on the promise would show his important guests that Herod was not a man of his word or that he was afraid of this "unimportant" prisoner in a dungeon. So, out of regard for his oaths and for his reputation in front of the guests, Herod decided to show his power and authority by immediately fulfilling the girl's request. He certainly had the power to *refuse her,* but unfortunately, he did not have the courage.

TOO EMBARRASSING
Herod did not want to kill John the Baptist, but he gave the order so that he wouldn't be embarrassed in front of his guests. How easy it is to give in to the crowd and to let ourselves be pressured into doing wrong. Don't get in a situation where it will be too embarrassing to do what is right. Determine to do what is right, no matter how embarrassing or painful it may be.

6:27-28 So he immediately sent an executioner with orders to bring John's head. The man went, beheaded John in the prison, and brought back his head on a platter. He presented it to the girl, and she gave it to her mother.NIV Herod, who was probably

REAL LEADERSHIP
Mark gives us some of the best insights into Jesus' character.

Herod as a leader	Jesus as a leader
Selfish	Compassionate
Murderer	Healer
Immoral	Just and good
Political opportunist	Servant
Ruler over small territory	King over all creation

in his palace in Tiberias, fulfilled Salome's request to the letter. He *immediately* sent someone off to Machaerus (see explanation on 6:17) by the Dead Sea to behead John the Baptist. The *executioner* he sent was probably one of Herod's own bodyguards. While some time elapsed considering the trip to Machaerus and back (the guests would have been long gone by the time the man returned), it all took place as quickly as possible. The man went, beheaded John, brought the grisly trophy back to the girl, and she took it to her mother. Herodias had satisfied her lust for revenge.

Herod fulfilled his oath and saved face before his guests. But he had been shown up by his wife and was left with great fear over what he had done in killing a holy man. Herod's guilt could not be assuaged. Thus, when Jesus came upon the scene, he thought that John had come back to life (6:16).

NO HAPPY ENDING
John's death serves as reality therapy for Christians who believe the "health and wealth" gospel. Not every Christian lives to see the full realization of his or her faith in this life. The writer of Hebrews explained it this way: "They did not receive the things promised; they only saw them and welcomed them from a distance" (Hebrews 11:13 NIV). True discipleship may mean we'll not live to see the consolation of our faith and earthly ministry. But God's Word promises

- "I consider that our present sufferings are not worth comparing with the glory that will be revealed in us" (Romans 8:18 NIV).
- "For our light and momentary troubles are achieving for us an eternal glory that far outweighs them all" (2 Corinthians 4:17 NIV).

Don't expect every circumstance to be happy and pleasurable. God wants us to obey faithfully no matter what the outcome.

6:29 When his disciples heard of it, they came and took away his corpse and laid it in a tomb.^{NKJV} John the Baptist apparently still had disciples, even though many had left him to follow Jesus (which John was content for them to do, see John 1:35-37). When *his disciples* heard that John had been beheaded, *they came and took away his corpse and laid it in a tomb.* They wanted to give their leader an honorable burial instead of having his body disposed of by the guards in the prison. Matthew added that after burying the body, "they went and told Jesus" (Matthew 14:12 NRSV). Many of John's followers may have then chosen to follow Jesus. Some, however, had remained a separate group that persisted even into the days of the early church (Acts 19:1-5) and on into the second century.

JESUS FEEDS FIVE THOUSAND / 6:30-44 / **96**

The biographers of Jesus regarded the miraculous supply of food for a large crowd as a key event. Apart from the resurrection of Christ, it is the only miracle recounted in all four Gospels. In Matthew and Mark, this miracle follows the account of Herod's tragic feast where John the Baptist was killed. The placement of the event creates a stark contrast between Herod's deadly orgy and the miraculous feast that Jesus provided for the multitude.

Mark then brought the reader back to the immediate events in his story by recording the return of the disciples, who were very excited about their accomplishments. Their arrival swelled the crowds even more and brought conditions to the point of chaos. Jesus responded by leading the Twelve on a retreat. Their only refuge turned out to be a short boat trip, for the crowd realized their destination and rushed on foot to meet them there. Confronted with such overwhelming needs, Jesus was moved with compassion to meet them.

Like each of Jesus' miracles, the feeding of the five thousand demonstrated his control over creation, and it shows that God will provide when we are in need. Jesus was not transforming rocks into food, but multiplying bread and fish. He was doing instantly what he does constantly throughout nature. He was not breaking the "laws of nature," but was demonstrating that he was in control of these "laws." Christ's power to feed a multitude, walk on water, and heal diseases all point to his identity as Lord of creation.

6:30 The apostles gathered around Jesus, and told him all that they had done and taught.^{NRSV} The word "apostle" means "one sent" as a messenger, authorized agent, or missionary. The word became an accepted title for Jesus' twelve disciples after his death and resurrection (Acts 1:25-26; Ephesians 2:20). Mark deliberately used the word because the disciples had completed their teaching mission (6:7-13) and thus were official "sent ones."

The pairs returned (apparently at a prearranged time) to Capernaum and *gathered around Jesus,* giving him their reports of *all that they had done and taught.* This marked the first time the disciples had gone out on their own, so quite naturally, they were full of excitement upon their return—telling stories, sharing together the thrill of preaching the message and doing miracles in God's power. This had been their training mission, their "student teaching," and Jesus listened to their stories and answered their questions.

Perhaps it would be a great corrective for our furtive and sometimes foolish activities if we adopted the same practice of reporting our work to the Lord in prayer. We could ask him to sort out the wheat from the chaff, the important from the trivial. By so doing, we could seek his guidance for future activity.

6:31 And He said to them, "Come aside by yourselves to a deserted place and rest a while." For there were many coming and going, and they did not even have time to eat.[NKJV] Capernaum had never proven to be a place where Jesus and his disciples could find solitude. Indeed, so many people were *coming and going* that Jesus and the disciples *did not even have time to eat.* Jesus knew that his disciples were weary from their trip, so he kindly suggested that they all go away *to a deserted place and rest a while.* The disciples needed to be away from crowds and busy distractions in order to rest and regain their strength. Doing God's work is very important, but Jesus recognized that to do it effectively we need periodic rest and renewal. Jesus and his disciples, however, did not always find it easy to get the rest they needed. But they certainly wouldn't find it in Capernaum.

GETTING AWAY
Jesus told the disciples to take a break. He knew their weaknesses. There is only so much a person can do physically and spiritually; then the body needs rest and the soul needs refreshment. As if it were a new discovery, sports physiologists and motivational experts now preach the wisdom of hard work, then adequate rest. People who hope to accomplish big goals need this healthy rhythm for success and stamina.

Rest allows time for reflection, meditation, conversation, reading, and prayer. In all your work, take a little time to dream. Walk in the woods. Stare at the stars. Count your blessings. Sing a prayer of praise where only God can hear.

6:32 So they went away by themselves in a boat to a solitary place.NIV Jesus and the disciples got into a boat (probably the same boat that had transported them already on the Sea of Galilee, see 4:1, 35-36; 5:21) and *went away by themselves . . . to a solitary place.* The disciples apparently knew of a good location where they thought they could get away from the crowds. Luke tells us that they "withdrew privately to a city called Bethsaida" (Luke 9:10 NRSV), probably landing at a solitary harbor apart from the city, or else they went on foot into the hills to find the "solitary place" where they could rest.

6:33 Now many saw them going and recognized them, and they hurried there on foot from all the towns and arrived ahead of them.NRSV Popularity and recognition have their own pitfalls. The disciples, now almost as well known as Jesus after their preaching mission, were seen and recognized along with Jesus, and the crowds would not let them get away. Instead, those who *saw them going and recognized them* as Jesus and the disciples—now known for teaching and doing miracles—ran on foot from all the towns between Capernaum and Bethsaida. The news spread as more and more people joined the crowd that made its way to where Jesus and the disciples would land. Men, women, and children *hurried* along, walking so quickly that they actually *arrived ahead of* the disciples' boat. Either the people somehow heard where the boat was headed, or perhaps the boat sailed not quite out of sight along the horizon so that the people could follow it.

6:34 As he went ashore, he saw a great crowd; and he had compassion for them, because they were like sheep without a shepherd; and he began to teach them many things.NRSV As they drew near to shore, no doubt the disciples realized that their time alone on the boat was all the rest time they would have. A *great crowd* waited on the shore, some having walked for miles in order to be there when Jesus and the disciples arrived. This would provide another lesson for the disciples. Far from feeling impatience and frustration toward these needy people, Jesus *had compassion for them.*

The people had found Jesus to be an irresistable person. His teaching astounded them, he was far more interesting than the rabbis they were used to hearing, his miracles amazed them, and his obvious compassion for them warmed their hearts. When Jesus saw this crowd that had traveled many miles on foot, he felt compassion, for he knew these people were as pitiful as *sheep without a shepherd.* Sheep are easily scattered and lost; without a shepherd they are in grave danger. The people needed a true

Shepherd who could teach them what they needed to know and keep them from straying from God.

Several Old Testament passages tie together the "wilderness" (where Jesus would be teaching these people) and the "sheep without a shepherd" themes. In Numbers 27, the nation of Israel was in the wilderness. Soon Moses would die, so he prayed that God would choose a leader to take his place "so the LORD's people will not be like sheep without a shepherd" (Numbers 27:17 NIV). David wrote in Psalm 23, "The LORD is my shepherd. . . . He makes me to lie down in green pastures; he leads me beside the still waters" (Psalm 23:1-2 NKJV). Ezekiel 34 promised the coming of one, like David, who would "tend them and be their shepherd . . . that they may live in the desert and sleep in the forests in safety" (Ezekiel 34:23, 25 NIV). God has often described his people as sheep in need of the tender nurture and loving guidance of a shepherd. Sheep are completely dependent on the shepherd for provision, guidance, and protection. The crowds were like lost sheep needing their Good Shepherd (John 10:11) to lead them, care for them, and *teach them.* Luke records that Jesus taught them "about the kingdom of God, and healed those who needed healing" (Luke 9:11 NIV).

While Jesus had hoped to be alone with the disciples for a time of rest, he did not send away this needy crowd. He had compassion for the people and took it upon himself to meet their needs. He did not ask his weary disciples to teach or heal. Jesus knew that his time on earth was short, so he took advantage of every opportunity to teach the good news of the kingdom to those willing to listen.

JUST SAY "WELCOME"
Jesus had tried to slip quietly away from the crowds, but they found out where he was going and followed him. Instead of showing impatience at this interruption, Jesus welcomed the people with compassion and ministered to their needs. Jesus had not found time to eat (3:20); it was happening again. Instead of being able to tend to his own needs and to those of the disciples, he was ministering to others. How easy it is to regard those who interrupt our schedules as nuisances. With Christ's help we can love them as the very reason for our life and ministry.

6:35-36 By this time it was late in the day, so his disciples came to him. "This is a remote place," they said, "and it's already very late. Send the people away so they can go to the surrounding countryside and villages and buy themselves some-

thing to eat."^{NIV} Jesus had been teaching the people until *late in the day* (after 3:00 P.M.). Sunset was approaching, and the disciples wondered what Jesus planned to do with this crowd that had come far from their homes to be with them. The place where Jesus had been teaching was *remote,* far from any town or village. The disciples thought Jesus would be wise to let the people go before it got dark in order for them to find food and lodging for the night. So they brought their suggestion to Jesus: *"Send the people away."* No doubt, the disciples also hoped to soon get the rest they had anticipated when they had set out on this journey (6:31).

THAT'S IMPOSSIBLE
In this chapter, many different people have examined Jesus' life and ministry: his neighbors and family, Herod the king, and the disciples. Yet none of these appreciated Jesus for who he was. The disciples were still pondering, still confused, still unbelieving. They did not realize that Jesus could provide for them. They were so preoccupied with the immensity of the task that they could not see what was possible with God. Do you let what seems impossible about Christianity keep you from believing? Nothing is beyond his ability.

6:37 But he answered them, "You give them something to eat."^{NRSV} The disciples were being very compassionate regarding the people's needs when they suggested that Jesus send them away. After all, they would need to reach the town before sunset if they were going to obtain food. Jesus' answer both astounded and exasperated them: *"You give them something to eat."* They probably thought, *Wait a minute, we came here to rest! Now you want us to feed over five thousand people?* What could Jesus possibly be thinking? The disciples' doubt is reminiscent of Moses' plea to God, "Where am I to get meat to give to all this people?" (Numbers 11:13 NRSV).

They said to him, "That would take eight months of a man's wages! Are we to go and spend that much on bread and give it to them to eat?"^{NIV} A quick calculation (or a consideration of the entire amount of money they had) figured that to feed all these people *would take eight months of a man's wages.* Some translations say "two hundred denarii." A denarius was Roman currency—a silver coin that was the average daily wage of a laborer in Palestine. The disciples summed up the situation and found it hopeless. If they had that much money in their possession, were they supposed to walk from the remote place to several villages in order to track down enough bread, *spend that much on bread,* then somehow carry it all back to this remote

---

CAN YOU HANDLE IT?
When the disciples expressed concern about where the crowd of thousands would eat, Jesus offered a surprising solution—"You give them something to eat." The disciples protested, focusing their attention on what they didn't have (food and money). Do you think God would ask you to do something that you and he together couldn't handle? Don't let your lack of resources blind you to seeing God's power. Often your meager resources are the starting point for what God wants to do.

---

place, and then *give it to them to eat?* No matter how they looked at it, the disciples saw Jesus' request to be impossible. So what did he mean, and why would he ask them to do something so obviously impossible?

6:38 But He said to them, "How many loaves do you have? Go and see." And when they found out they said, "Five, and two fish."^{NKJV} In reply to their question about going and spending an extravagant amount of money on bread, Jesus told them first to check out their resources. *"Go and see* how many loaves you have." John records that the five loaves (round barley cakes) and two dried fish they found were from the lunch of a young boy (John 6:9). Apparently, in their hurry, no one else in the crowd had thought to bring along food to eat, or they were unwilling to share it. The young boy offered his lunch to the disciples (specifically to Andrew, see John 6:8), but again the disciples could see only the impossibility of the situation. Andrew, while answering Jesus' question regarding the resources, added pessimistically, "But how far will they go among so many?" (John 6:9 NIV). The normal answer: It will feed one hungry young boy. But Jesus had an entirely different answer.

6:39-40 Then Jesus directed them to have all the people sit down in groups on the green grass. So they sat down in groups of hundreds and fifties.^{NIV} Jesus did not answer the disciples, nor explain what he would do. Instead, he gave them the task of organizing the people to sit *on the green grass* (a detail specific to Mark's Gospel) in groups of hundreds and fifties. We don't know why Jesus organized the people this way—it may have been to make food distribution more efficient, or it may have been to emulate what Moses did (see Exodus 18:21). The men were probably separated from the women and children for the

meal according to Jewish custom. The words "in groups" in
6:40 could literally be translated, "garden plot by garden plot."
The eyewitness account (probably of Peter) recalled the green
of the grass and the colorful clothing of the people grouped on
the hillsides. They probably looked like colorful flower gar-
dens. Mark's inclusion of the words "green grass" may refer to
the prophet Ezekiel's hope that the wilderness will be restored
and renewed by God (Ezekiel 34:23-31), and to David's concept of the Lord as his shepherd, restoring his people in green
pastures (Psalm 23:1-2).

CONSIDER THE NEED
Why did Jesus bother to feed these people? He could just as
easily have sent them on their way. But Jesus does not ignore
needs. He is concerned with every aspect of our lives—the
physical as well as the spiritual.
   We might well ask why the church has taken so lightly the
command "You give them something to eat," when other words
of Christ are emphasized so strongly. Jesus' compassion for
these hungry people is recorded in all four Gospels. If over the
last fifty years even one percent of our total giving had been
designated to feed the hungry, perhaps the gospel would have
reached farther around the world. For people who are desperately hungry, there is no better way for us to show God's love to
them than to give them food.
   As we work to bring wholeness to people's lives, we must
never ignore the fact that all of us have both physical and spiritual needs. It is impossible to minister effectively to one type of
need without considering the other.

The disciples did not know what Jesus would do, but they
knew enough to stop talking about the impossibility of the task
and obey his directions. So they did as Jesus said, directing the
people to sit as if at tables and await their evening meal to be
served to them—somehow—by Jesus. In this wilderness, the
Good Shepherd was about to feed his sheep (6:34).

**6:41 Taking the five loaves and the two fish and looking up to
heaven, he gave thanks and broke the loaves.**NIV Jesus, acting
as the host of the soon-to-be banquet, took *the five loaves and the
two fish,* looked up to heaven, thanked God beforehand for the
provision he was about to give, and then *broke the loaves.* As
Jesus broke the loaves, the miracle occurred.
   Some commentators see a parallel to the Lord's Supper in the

CONTRASTING FEASTS

	Herod, the official ruler (6:14)	The people, who were without a leader (6:34)	Jesus, the Shepherd supreme (6:39-40)
Who's in charge			
Occasion	All-male birthday party and sumptuous feast for rich and influential people (6:21)	Following Jesus into the wilderness (6:35-36)	Provides a simple "poor man's" meal of bread and fish (6:41)
Result	Ends in murder, grief, and guilt (6:26-28)	Wondering where to get food (6:37)	This meal points to the heavenly banquet and rest promised to all believers (6:42)

words of this verse (see 14:22). However, most reject this view because there were no fish at the Last Supper, nor was there mention of two loaves, only one. There is no indication that the disciples ate anything in this instance, only that they served the people. Presumably they were to eat later. Also, in the Last Supper, there was no miraculous multiplication of the bread. The differences are so many as to indicate that this was not a Eucharist meal.

Then he gave them to his disciples to set before the people. He also divided the two fish among them all.^{NIV} The verbs in this verse are in different tenses in the Greek. The word "broke" is in the aorist, implying an instantaneous act. The word "gave" is in the imperfect, implying a continuous act. Thus the miracle occurred in Jesus' hands. He broke the bread and then kept on giving it to his disciples to then *set before the people.* The same thing happened with the fish. The disciples acted as waiters to the groups of hungry people seated on the grass, taking bread and fish, distributing it, and then returning to Jesus to get more. They continued to serve the crowd until everyone had had enough to eat (6:42).

The God who multiplied the bread was authenticating Jesus as his Son and portraying the kingdom. Just as God provided manna to the Hebrews in the desert (Exodus 16), multiplied oil and meal for Elijah and the widow at Zarephath (1 Kings 17:7-16) and for Elisha (2 Kings 4:1-7), he was providing bread for the people on this day. It points to the feast that the Messiah will provide for people in the wilderness (Isaiah 25:6).

6:42-43 They all ate and were satisfied, and the disciples picked up twelve basketfuls of broken pieces of bread and fish.^{NIV} The five loaves and two fish multiplied so that every person ate as much as he or she could. Even the leftovers were more than they had begun with. The disciples picked up twelve basketfuls of the broken pieces of food. The number "twelve" could simply indicate that there was one basket for each of the twelve disciples, or it could also signify fullness and completeness. In any event, there would be no waste at this banquet. The disciples may have taken the food to feed themselves for a few days. While Jesus could have, he did not make a habit of supplying food out of nothing for himself and the disciples.

 DO WHAT YOU CAN, ASK GOD FOR THE REST
When Jesus asked the disciples to provide food for over five thousand people, they asked in astonishment if they should go and spend eight months' wages on bread. How do you react when you are given an impossible task? A situation that seems impossible with human resources is simply an opportunity for God. The disciples did everything they could by gathering the available food and organizing the people into groups. Then, in answer to prayer, God did the impossible. When facing a seemingly impossible task, do what you can and ask God to do the rest. He may see fit to do the impossible.

6:44 Those who had eaten the loaves numbered five thousand men.^{NRSV} As if to cap off the record of this miracle, Mark added, "By the way, there were *five thousand* men who ate the loaves and fish." If the readers weren't impressed already, now they should be astounded. The Greek word for men is *andres,* meaning not "people," but "male individuals." Therefore, there were five thousand men in addition to the women and children. The total number of people Jesus fed could have been over ten thousand. The number of men is listed separately because in the Jewish culture of the day, men and women usually ate separately when in public. The children ate with the women. We don't know if this was the case at this particular meal.

Jesus did what the disciples thought was impossible. He multiplied five loaves and two fish to feed over five thousand people. What he was originally given seemed insufficient, but in his hands it became more than enough. While we may feel that our contribution to Jesus is meager, he can use and multiply whatever we give him, whether it is talent, time, or treasure. When we give our resources to Jesus, they are multiplied.

MIRACLE, OR NOT?
Skeptics who believe in normal natural process cannot imagine five thousand hungry people fed on so little food. But most of the people on the hillside that day didn't see the miracle, either. They were simply put in a group and given supper. Then they cleaned up. Only the disciples knew what was happening.

Scientific materialism removes the miraculous from the miracles. It would explain this miracle meal by suggesting that the boy's generosity set in motion a wave of giving so that all the people brought out the food they had and shared it with each other. Such a view makes the "miracle" easier to swallow, but it downplays Jesus' miraculous power. His miracles, however, demonstrated the same power that raised Jesus from the dead. Those who find it difficult to accept these miracles usually find it difficult to believe in the Resurrection. When we accept the Resurrection, miracles like the multiplying of fish and loaves do not seem impossible.

JESUS WALKS ON WATER / 6:45-52 / 97

The series of miracles beginning with Jesus' calming the storm in 4:35-41 concludes with a double demonstration of Jesus' power. He walked on the water and calmed the wind.

A long and stressful day was coming to a close. Jesus insisted that his disciples go on ahead in a boat while he dismissed the crowd. As people dispersed, Jesus went alone to pray. His time of silence and fellowship with his Father did not prevent his noticing the disciples struggling to make headway against the wind out on the lake. So Jesus ended his day (and began the next) by meeting the needs of his disciples as they floundered in the waves.

The presence of trouble does not mean that we are working against God's purposes. Nor does it mean that God does not notice. We can be certain of his help. In desperate moments, we may feel as if Christ is passing us by. When we recognize our helplessness, we are ready to receive his help. Even when our trust is inadequate, Christ comes to our aid because he is trustworthy. We must guard against having hardened hearts. Stubborn refusal to believe in Christ's presence and power leaves us fearful and floundering.

6:45 Immediately he made his disciples get into the boat and go on ahead to the other side, to Bethsaida, while he dismissed the crowd.[NRSV] As soon as the crowd had been fed and the disciples had picked up the scraps, Jesus *immediately* got his disciples and the crowd moving. His sudden desire to dismiss the crowd and send the disciples off in their boat is explained in John's Gospel.

Upon seeing (and participating in) the miracle of multiplied loaves
and fish, the people "intended to come and make [Jesus] king by
force," so Jesus "withdrew again to a mountain by himself" (John
6:15 NIV). Jesus' kingdom would not be an earthly one, and he
didn't want the enthusiasm of the crowd to deter him or his disciples from fulfilling their true mission. Before the crowd could
become an unruly mob, Jesus *made his disciples get into the boat
and go on ahead to the other side, to Bethsaida."* It was getting late
in the day, so Jesus *dismissed the crowd* with a few final words
before going up to the mountainside by himself (6:46).

Exactly *where* the disciples were going causes some confusion
if one compares the Gospel accounts. Mark records that Jesus
told the disciples to go "to the other side, to Bethsaida. According
to Matthew 14:22, Jesus told the disciples to get into a boat and
go on ahead to "the other side." According to Luke 9:10, Jesus
and the disciples were in Bethsaida for the feeding of the five
thousand. According to John 6:17, the disciples "set off across
the lake for Capernaum" (NIV). One solution is that two commu-
nities were named Bethsaida. Luke 9:10 identifies Bethsaida
(near Julias) on the northeast side of the Sea of Galilee. The reference in Mark 6:45 identifies Bethsaida as a village (near Capernaum) on the western shore.

WHEN IT'S TIME TO LEAVE
Jesus instructed his disciples to leave quickly. He, too, said
good-bye to the crowd and sought privacy to pray. Suddenly
after the meal, he abandoned the crowd. Why such a fast get-
away?

Jesus recognized the rising tide of emotion in the crowd.
They were looking for a warrior-Messiah. Perhaps Jesus could
sense Satan's temptation that he had faced once before in the
wilderness: the prospect of power on earth here and now (Mark
1:13).

When you sense temptation coming, do you linger or leave?
When you know a compromising situation is ahead, do you presume on your own fortitude or hurry to pray? When you think
that everything is warming up just right, are your eyes clear
enough to see the problem catching fire? Don't debate the situation in your mind, just leave. Seek God's presence.

6:46 After leaving them, he went up on a mountainside to pray.[NIV]
Jesus "dismissed" the crowd, but then also decided to "leave"
them—apparently it wasn't easy for Jesus to get away. The disciples had been instructed to meet him in Bethsaida. So Jesus went
alone *up on a mountainside to pray.* Jesus wanted time to pray
and communicate with his Father. During his ministry on earth,

Jesus was in constant prayer with the
Father—he may often have gone off
alone to pray, so his desire to do so may
not have surprised the disciples, who
left in the boat as instructed. Mark
recorded three specific times when
Jesus went off alone to pray: (1) after

> He came treading the
> waves, and so he puts the
> swelling tumults of life
> under his feet. Christians,
> why afraid? *Augustine*

the successful ministry in Capernaum where he healed many sick
and demon-possessed people (1:35); (2) here, after he fed more
than five thousand people; (3) in Gethsemane, just prior to his
arrest, trial, and crucifixion (14:32-42).

Jesus had just left a crowd that wanted to make him their king.
Popularity was a temptation in itself, for it could threaten to turn
Jesus away from his mission—death on the cross to accomplish
salvation. His prayer on the lonely mountainside may have
focused on fulfilling the mission of suffering when it seemed (at
least humanly) more credible to accept their offer of kingship.
Jesus, in his humanity, may have continued to face the temptation
to turn away from the difficult path and take the easier one. He
constantly sought strength from God. Going into the wilderness,
alone with the Father, helped Jesus focus on his task and gain
strength for what he had to do.

TOO BUSY FOR GOD?
Seeking solitude was an important priority for Jesus (see also
1:35). He made room in his busy schedule to be alone with the
Father. Spending time with God in prayer nurtures a vital relationship and equips us to meet life's challenges and struggles.
We need to follow Jesus' example by praying more frequently,
making available the time, place, and opportunity to pray
before and after we fulfill our responsibilities. Develop the discipline of spending time alone in God's presence because it will
help you grow spiritually and become more and more like
Christ.

**6:47 Now when evening came, the boat was in the middle of the
sea; and He was alone on the land.**[NKJV] The disciples had left
sometime before sunset, so by the time evening came, they were
well out in the lake (the words *in the middle* do not refer to the
geographical middle). The disciples often fished during the night,
so sailing out into the night was not unusual. However, John
records that "the sea became rough because a strong wind was
blowing" (John 6:18 NRSV), and Matthew adds that "the boat, bat-
tered by the waves, was far from the land, for the wind was
against them" (Matthew 14:24 NRSV). The disciples were being

blown off course, fighting the sea in their boat. Once again (as in 4:35-39), Jesus had sent them out to sea, when they were already bone tired, right into a storm. At least previously Jesus had been in the boat with them (although they had to awaken him to get his help). This time, *he was alone on the land,* and the disciples were left to fend for themselves (or so they thought) against another raging storm.

6:48-50 **He saw the disciples straining at the oars, because the wind was against them.**NIV The disciples took down the sails and tried to keep control of the boat by strenuous rowing. For the entire night they fought the storm, able to row only about three or four miles (John 6:19).

As Jesus prayed on the mountainside, he *saw the disciples straining at the oars.* Jesus' concern for the disciples reminds us that our Lord sees us straining at the oars of our work and responsibilities. He does not desert us; he comes to meet our needs.

About the fourth watch of the night he went out to them, walking on the lake.NIV From evening until *the fourth watch of the night*
(between 3:00 and 6:00 A.M.), the disciples had been out on the sea, much of that time "straining at the oars," fighting a strong head wind and rough seas. Jesus, seeing their plight, *went out to them, walking on the lake.* While some might try to explain away this miracle by saying Jesus was simply on the shore, Mark clearly states that Jesus walked *on* the lake. Not only that, but he had walked a great distance. John records that the disciples had gone three or four miles by the time Jesus came to them (John 6:19).

The Old Testament often describes God's control over the seas. Jesus walking on the sea was an unmistakable picture of his identity and power (see Job 9:8; 38:16; Psalm 77:19; Isaiah 43:16).

He was about to pass by them, but when they saw him walk-

Jesus Walks on the Water
After feeding the people who had followed to hear him at Beth-saida, Jesus sent the people home, sent his disciples by boat toward Bethsaida, and went to pray. The disciples encountered a storm and Jesus walked to them on the water. They landed at Gennesaret.

ing on the lake, they thought he was a ghost. They cried out, because they all saw him and were terrified.^{NIV} Much confusion surrounds the phrase *he was about to pass by them.* While the text sounds like Jesus meant to walk on by and leave the disciples to their fate, obviously that was not the case because he did help them. Theories on the meaning of this phrase include:

- Jesus "meant to pass beside" them to reassure them with his presence. This was meant to be a display of his divine glory, such as is recorded in Exodus 33:19, 22; 1 Kings 19:11.

- Jesus "was about to pass by" as he waited for the disciples to see him and call out to him for help. He wanted them to confess their need. This is compared to Luke 24:28-29 when, on the Emmaus Road, Jesus made as if to go on, and the two disciples urged him to remain with them.

- The phrase was written from the disciples' standpoint (from Peter's eyewitness account) that, when they saw Jesus, it appeared to them that his intention was to "pass by them."

- Most likely, the phrase simply means Jesus "intended to pass their way," that is, to go to them, which is exactly what he did.

In any case, Mark once again focused on the human perspective. When *they* all *saw* Jesus walking on the water, the disciples thought he was a ghost; so they screamed in terror. They thought they had left Jesus back on the mountainside. The Greek word for "ghost" used here is *phantasma,* meaning an apparition or specter. The word was associated with magic and charms. The word differs from *pneuma,* also sometimes translated "ghost"; *pneuma* meant a disembodied spirit of someone who had died (Luke 24:37). Jesus was (as far as they knew) alive and well, so they were terrified by what they saw. Once again, Jesus was doing the unexpected, the impossible, and they were terrified.

DEEP WATER
The disciples were surprised to see Jesus walking beside them on the water. But they should have realized that Jesus would help them when they were in trouble. Though they had lost sight of Jesus, he had not lost sight of them. His concern for them overcame their lack of faith. Why are we so surprised when God helps us and when Christ feels compassion? The next time you are in "deep water," remember that Christ knows your struggle and cares for you.

Immediately he spoke to them and said, "Take courage! It is I. Don't be afraid."[NIV] Jesus called out to the disciples over the storm, telling them to take courage. He identified himself and told them not to be afraid any longer. The literal reading for *"It is I"* is "I am" (Greek, *ego eimi*); it is the same as saying "the I AM is here" or "I, Yahweh, am here" (see Exodus 3:14; Isaiah 41:4; 43:10; 52:6). Jesus, the "I AM," came with unexpected help and encouragement during the disciples' time of desperate need.

CALMING PRESENCE
The disciples were afraid, but Jesus' presence calmed their fears. Surprises happen. Calm evenings turn stormy. Stress interrupts repose. Fear overruns faith. Jesus offered three short sentences to his boatload of frightened, tired disciples: "Take courage. It is I. Don't be afraid." The middle sentence is the key: "It is I."
Courage is never easy, and fear is a formidable emotion. If we hear gunshots, see a fire, watch two cars collide, fear will strike. If a doctor announces cancer, courage may not be our first response. In times of fear and uncertainty, it is calming to know that Christ is always with us (Matthew 28:20). Recognizing Christ's presence is the antidote for fear.
Jesus says, "I am here," taking charge, saving us, keeping us forever. That's why fear gives way to courage: God is with us.

6:51-52 **Then he climbed into the boat with them, and the wind died down.**[NIV] Jesus then *climbed into the boat* with the disciples. They must have been speechless as they helped Jesus into the boat. Then, as had occurred once before when the disciples had been tossed about by a storm at sea, *the wind died down* and the sea once again became calm (see also 4:39). Jesus had revealed to them his complete mastery over nature. (See Isaiah 51:9-16 for a dramatic description of God's power over the sea.)

They were completely amazed, for they had not understood about the loaves; their hearts were hardened.[NIV] The disciples had seen Jesus perform numerous healings, calm a raging sea, multiply food to feed over five thousand people, and walk to them on the water. Their responses to the last miracle had been fear and then amazement. While they had seen the miracles, *they had not understood* them. They had seen the loaves multiplied, but they didn't realize who Jesus was and what he could do. Even after watching Jesus miraculously feed five thousand people, they still could not take the final step of faith and believe that he was God's Son. If they had understood about the loaves (in other words, if they had learned what the miracle was meant to teach them), they would not have been amazed that Jesus could walk on water.

Mark explained that *their hearts were hardened.* Peter, Mark's source for the story, probably felt a little sheepish as he recounted his and the disciples' continued lack of belief. This was not merely misunderstanding; instead, it meant a hard-hearted refusal to believe (the word is used elsewhere only when describing unbelievers, see 3:5; 10:5). But why wouldn't the disciples believe? Perhaps they simply couldn't bring themselves to consider that this human being was actually God's Son. Or maybe they thought that if and when the Messiah really did come, he wouldn't choose *them* for followers. The disciples needed a good healthy dose of faith in order to be able to see and understand what their Master, the Messiah, so beautifully and amazingly continued to teach them.

HARD HEARTS SINK SHIPS
Are our hearts hardened against Jesus? Even Christians can be hard-hearted to Jesus' word. We can be informed about what his Word says, and we can be amazed at how he has worked in other people's lives, but we can refuse to believe he will come to our aid in time of trouble. Such a reaction is not unbelief, but willful, hard-hearted rejection of Christ's help. Trust that he will help you when you need it.

JESUS HEALS ALL WHO TOUCH HIM / 6:53-56 / *98*

Jesus had achieved celebrity status. Wherever he and his disciples showed up, crowds gathered to watch. The sick flocked for healing. Mark's earlier comment that the people were like "sheep without a shepherd" (6:34) fits this new scene. The places and faces had changed, but the cries for help were the same.

Jesus healed all those who were brought to him. Some who benefitted from Jesus' healing touch went unchanged in other ways (Luke 17:11-19), but many were changed forever. Do you regard Jesus as an important, essential resource, yet still retain final control of your own decisions? Do you desire Jesus' help and friendship, but still want to be lord of your own life?

6:53 When they had crossed over, they came to land at Gennesaret and moored the boat.NRSV The storm had blown the disciples off course, and they did not land at Bethsaida as planned (6:45). They were to meet Jesus in Bethsaida, but Jesus had come to them on the water; so after the storm ceased, *they came to land at*

Gennesaret and moored the boat. Gennesaret was a small fertile plain located on the west side of the Sea of Galilee as well as the name of a small town there. Capernaum (from where they had sailed that morning, 6:32) sat at the northern edge of this plain.

6:54 As soon as they got out of the boat, people recognized Jesus.NIV Jesus was well known in the region of Galilee, and his presence always created great excitement. Immediately upon getting out of the boat, people recognized Jesus, and a flurry of activity began. There still would be no rest for the weary.

6:55 They ran throughout that whole region and carried the sick on mats to wherever they heard he was.NIV The news of Jesus' arrival spread like wildfire through the area. As Jesus moved through the region, people brought *the sick on mats* to him so that he might heal them.

The disciples had seen great miracles, but their hearts remained hardened. The people recognized Jesus as a great healer, but few understood who he truly was. Miracles do not produce faith, only temporary excitement. The sick people were brought to Jesus for physical healing, but few came for spiritual healing. They prolonged their lives on earth, but did they secure eternal life? Jesus, facing the disciples' unbelief and the crowds' empty excitement, still compassionately taught, loved, and healed the people. Perhaps he continued to see them as "sheep without a shepherd" (6:34).

EAGER BELIEVERS
Finally at Gennesaret, people started to get the picture. They came not out of curiosity, nor did they agitate for rebellion against Rome. The people came to touch Jesus and be healed.
Did they all fully understand? Probably not. Did their faith have mountain-moving missionary fervor? Not likely. But neither did they hesitate to approach Jesus and accept his gifts. In fact, they came eagerly, as young believers anxious for his company, his power.
Christians of all ages should feel this expectancy, this happiness. We all need the enthusiasm that comes from recognizing Jesus. Each morning we should meet Jesus at the boat, give him our hurts, and go throughout the whole countryside to bring others to him.

People may seek Jesus to learn valuable lessons from his life or to find relief from pain. But we miss Jesus' whole message if we seek him only to heal our body but not our soul, if we look to him for help only in this life, rather than for his eternal plan for us. Only when we understand the real Jesus Christ can we appreciate how he can truly change our lives.

6:56 **And wherever he went, into villages or cities or farms, they laid the sick in the marketplaces, and begged him that they might touch even the fringe of his cloak; and all who touched it were healed.**^{NRSV} Jesus had gained widespread reputation as a healer; so the people came in droves for healing. Their attitude was different than those in 6:6 whose lack of faith kept Jesus' work to a minimum. In a day when medicines and medical help were few and limited, sickness was rampant and constant. As Jesus walked through Galilee, people *laid the sick in the marketplaces*. Perhaps the story had spread of the woman in Capernaum who had been healed by touching Jesus' cloak. For now the people *begged him that they might touch even the fringe of his cloak*. Jewish men wore tassels on the hem of their robes, according to God's command (Deuteronomy 22:12). By Jesus' day, these tassels were seen as signs of holiness (Matthew 23:5). It was natural that people seeking healing should reach out and touch these. No one missed out on Jesus' loving compassion, even if they could only touch the fringe of his cloak. Mark records that *all who touched it were healed.* But as the woman in Capernaum learned, healing came from faith in Jesus' ability to heal, not from Jesus' garment (Matthew 9:20-22).

Mark 7

After the eye-opening demonstrations of Jesus' power in chapter 6, Mark provided a pause in the action by telling of another confrontation between Jesus and the Pharisees. Similar confrontations had already occurred: 2:6-12; 2:15-17; 2:18-20; 2:23-28; 3:1-6; 3:22-30. Jesus' dramatic actions were met by determined resistance from groups that Mark identified as "Pharisees and teachers of the law." Unable to overcome Jesus directly, their tactics shifted to the disciples. They were sure that the disciples were the weak point in Jesus' defenses.

This could be called a "conflict of interest." Both the religious leaders and Jesus were questioning each other's application of the law. The religious authorities had long-established interpretations of the law that tended to confirm and expand the power of the religious ruling class while making a mockery of God's standards. In Matthew 23:24, Jesus characterized their error as fruitlessly straining out gnats while allowing camel-sized disobedience of the law to go unchallenged. He charged them with demanding that others carry heavy loads of obligations while excusing themselves. The freedom to obey God that the disciples learned from Jesus threatened the status and control wielded by the religious leaders. Their reaction against Jesus paved the way to Calvary.

Let us examine our own efforts to apply God's Word. We must not give our own rules, policies, and applications of Scripture the same authority as God's Word.

7:1-2 Now when the Pharisees and some of the scribes who had come from Jerusalem gathered around him, they noticed that some of his disciples were eating with defiled hands, that is, without washing them.NRSV Another delegation came from Jerusalem to investigate this new rabbi who was causing such a stir throughout the country. In 2:18, the Pharisees attacked Jesus through his disciples by claiming that the disciples were wrong not to fast (breaking the religious leaders' additions to God's law); then in 2:24, they claimed that the disciples were wrong to pluck heads of grain and eat them on the Sabbath (again, only breaking one of their additions to God's law); in 3:22, such a delegation had incorrectly concluded that Jesus was casting out demons because he himself was demon possessed.

In this chapter another delegation arrived, ready to debate Jesus about his disciples' disregard of the oral traditions and rituals. During the centuries since the Jews' return from Babylonian captivity, Jewish religious leaders had added hundreds of religious traditions to God's laws. These laws regulated every part of Jewish life. The Pharisees and scribes considered these religious traditions to be as binding and unbreakable as God's law itself. In this assumption they were wrong, as Jesus would point out.

The common people did not follow all the strict extra rules and rituals of the Pharisees; thus, these religious leaders looked down on them as ignorant. The fact that Jesus' disciples did not follow all of the laws of the Pharisees' oral tradition led this Jerusalem delegation to resent Jesus' teaching and try to discredit him. If Jesus were truly a rabbi, he and his disciples would be following all the traditions. The Pharisees had religious blinders on their eyes, seeing only their own rituals and traditions. Jesus flouted their authority, criticized some of their rules and regulations, and had become dangerously popular.

THE PHARISEES

We must be careful not to gloss over the Pharisees and teachers of the law as out-of-touch religionists or nitpicky legalists. To do so would be to miss the dynamic message to our times today.

Undoubtedly there were many authoritarian religious leaders who wanted to keep their place in the power structure at any cost. There were also many who were genuine religious conservatives, enraged by the challenge of the new teacher who cast long-established traditions aside. There were many religious people who thought they were rightly defending the honor of Yahweh. Some were profoundly self-serving, but many were sincere.

Many Bible-believing Christians also struggle with change and tradition. The Pharisees had established codes of conduct that they made equal with Scripture. Don't we still do the same? In trying to maintain our faith against competitors and challenges, don't we resent those who don't conform and who disregard the history of why we do what we do? What human-made rules, policies, and doctrines have we given the same authority as God's Word? Do we reject someone's thought because we don't like his or her background, training, or personal style? Pharisees exist today. Ask God for insight so as not to be one of them.

The delegation was *from Jerusalem,* the center of Jewish authority, and was made up of *Pharisees* (who advocated minute obedience to the Jewish law and traditions) and *scribes* (also called teachers of the law—professional interpreters of the law who especially emphasized the traditions). As these religious leaders scrutinized Jesus and his disciples, *they noticed that some of his disciples were eating with defiled hands.* For his Roman readers, unfamiliar with Jewish customs, Mark explained that "defiled hands" meant that they were eating without first washing their hands. This referred not to washing for cleanliness, but to a particular kind of washing that made a person "ceremonially clean" before eating.

7:3 (The Pharisees and all the Jews do not eat unless they give their hands a ceremonial washing, holding to the tradition of the elders.)[NIV] Mark explained for his Roman readers why the disciples eating with "defiled" hands was such a point of contention with the Pharisees. This *ceremonial washing* cleansed a person from any defilement he or she might have contacted without knowing it. *The Pharisees* did not want to eat with defiled hands, for they believed that they then would become defiled. They scrupulously followed this law, thinking that this ceremony would cleanse them from any contact they might have had with anything considered unclean.

The origin of this ceremonial washing is seen in the laver of the tabernacle, where the priests washed their hands and feet prior to performing their sacred duties (Exodus 30:17-21). That *was* part of God's law. But oral tradition extended this law ("they shall wash with water so that they will not die" Exodus 30:20 NIV) to all Jews to be performed before formal prayers and then before eating. Thus, before each meal, devout Jews performed a short ceremony, washing their hands and arms in a specific way. But this was tradition, not a requirement of God's law.

Jesus discerned that the Pharisees' purpose was not to get clean, but to keep up appearances, to demonstrate that they were not Gentiles, and to outdo the common people in priestlike devotion. Are we like the Pharisees? Do we reduce spiritual Christianity to legalism or to empty patterns, adhere to them rigidly, but give our willful thought life full reign?

Mark's statement that *all the Jews* followed this practice is a generalization of Jewish custom. As mentioned in 7:1-2 above, the common people did not follow all the minutiae of the *tradition of the elders.* This ceremonial washing was not part of God's law, but was instead part of the rules and regulations added later. The "tradition of the elders" refers to the oral interpretation of

God's laws, interpretations that affected every aspect of Jewish daily life. The elders of earlier generations (members chosen from the older people to be part of the Sanhedrin, the most powerful religious and political body of the Jewish nation) passed along this oral tradition until, in the third century B.C., it was collected and written down, eventually forming the foundation of the Jewish Talmud. As such, the tradition of the elders was made up of oral laws originated by Jewish religious leaders. Jesus came into direct conflict with these traditions, explaining to these self-righteous religious leaders that "you nullify the word of God for the sake of your tradition" (Matthew 15:6 NIV). By their scrupulous observance of minute traditions and rituals, they had completely lost their perspective on the reason the law of God had been given: to bring God's kingdom to earth, to provide reconciliation between God and his people, and to bring peace *(shalom)*.

SERIOUS RELIGION
Whenever people take religion seriously, they try to simplify its mystery and conquer its unknowns by building rituals designed to appease or even control the gods. The Pharisees thought that if they could only live perfectly, even God would have to respect them.

How futile to try to control God. Jesus knew that these rituals actually obscured God and misled people about their basic spiritual needs. How many add-on rules and rituals do you impose on young people or new converts who want to know God? How many formulas have you added to the Bible and made them law? The Pharisees' problems can be as current as last night's church board meeting . . . if we don't watch out!

7:4 (When they come from the marketplace they do not eat unless they wash. And they observe many other traditions, such as the washing of cups, pitchers and kettles.)[NIV] Mark explained this Jewish ceremonial cleansing ritual a bit further for his Roman audience. The religious leaders were aware that in daily business they might unknowingly come into contact with a Gentile or an unclean Jew and thereby become defiled. If they were defiled, they would be unable to perform their religious duties. This would be inevitable in the *marketplace* with all its busy jostling of people. Thus, upon return from the market, they would not eat until they washed—that is, performed the ceremonial cleansing. This washing was not to clean dirty hands; it was a ceremonial washing to cleanse them from their contact with defiled "sinners" or Gentiles.

Mark encapsulated the rest of the convoluted rituals regarding cleansing by briefly explaining that the devout leaders observed *many other traditions,* including laws about how to wash their dishes. There were laws for everything; no wonder the common people didn't bother themselves with strictly following them. But the religious leaders kept all these laws because they believed their "cleanliness" equaled "godliness." In their minds, keeping these laws showed their devotion and service to God. But Jesus could not have disagreed more.

TO MARKET?
Christians become like Pharisees when they worry that contact with unbelievers may leave them tainted—avoiding "worldly" places where sinners hang out, shortening conversations that challenge their ideas (again, to avoid taint), and rejecting books or speakers whose ideas do not conform to theirs.

Some Christians and some Pharisees have a lot in common: Both would try to stop Jesus from working the back alleys of a poor urban neighborhood because it's too dirty for religious people. Jesus wants us to go out into the world, the marketplace (see Paul's example in Acts 17:17) and make contact. Jesus didn't intend for us to withdraw, purify ourselves, and never reach out.

7:5 So the Pharisees and the scribes asked him, "Why do your disciples not live according to the tradition of the elders, but eat with defiled hands?"[NRSV] Picking up from 7:2, Mark continued the narrative. The Pharisees and scribes, having "noticed that some of his disciples were eating with defiled hands," asked Jesus why they were doing this. Notice that the Pharisees themselves realized that this was a *tradition of the elders,* but they believed that this tradition had the same authority as God's law. Their underlying question was, "If you are really a rabbi, as holy and righteous and versed in the law as we are, then you should know that we don't eat without first ceremonially washing our hands. We won't attack you personally, but since your disciples aren't washing, you obviously haven't taught them what's important. Maybe you don't even know this law. That makes you no better than a common sinner, certainly not a rabbi whom all these people should be following!"

7:6-7 He answered and said to them, "Well did Isaiah prophesy of you hypocrites."[NKJV] Jesus answered not their spoken question, but their underlying one, by quoting the Scripture that they claimed to know so well. The Greek word translated *well* means "beautifully, excellently." The great prophet Isaiah had written beautifully correct words describing these religious leaders.

GREAT TRADITIONS
People who strongly oppose all tradition are misguided. Good traditions give us a sense of time and place, a home base. Religious tradition helps us understand who we are.

Great traditions shine a spotlight on God's Word, move us to obedient service, and help our hearts sing the joy of freedom in Christ. They should explain and reinforce the teachings of God, not be screens that block out the light. God's Word should always be the focus, and tradition a means of making that Word lively.

Celebrate your traditions with the prayer that Christ would be exalted. Change your tradition when it becomes king or when it amplifies a substitute for God's Word.

Jesus blasted these self-righteous leaders with one word; he called them *hypocrites.* They must have been enraged to be addressed that way by such a person. The Greek word *hupocrites* is made up of *hupo,* meaning "under," and *krino,* meaning "to judge." Thus a hypocrite is one who makes judgment from under a cover. The Pharisees pretended to be holy and close to God, thus judging all other people as sinners. But what they pretended on the outside was not true on the inside.

IT'S TRADITIONAL
Many traditions are good. Some religious traditions can add richness and meaning to life. But we must not assume that certain traditions are sacred because they have been practiced for years. God's principles never change, and his law doesn't need additions. Traditions should help us understand God's laws better, not become laws themselves. If your tradition no longer serves a valid purpose, don't be afraid to drop it.

"As it is written: 'This people honors Me with their lips, but their heart is far from Me. And in vain they worship Me, teaching as doctrines the commandments of men.'"[NKJV] The Pharisees and scribes also knew this Scripture by memory, but evidently they never had applied it to themselves. The prophet Isaiah criticized hypocrites (Isaiah 29:13), and Jesus applied Isaiah's words to these religious leaders. *This people* begins the quotation from Isaiah 29:13. Mark's version resembles more closely the ancient Greek translation of the Old Testament known as the Septuagint and is not exactly the same as the Hebrew text of Isaiah, though the substance is the same. The religious leaders might say all the right words and give lip-service to God, but their hearts were far from God.

While the scribes and Pharisees may have been well-intentioned in their observance of Jewish rituals and traditions and in their attempts to honor God, Jesus attacked their true heart condition. They had lip-worship but sadly lacked in heart-worship. Instead of the godliness they attempted to portray, they were actually far away from God. The problem: The authority for their teaching was human *(the commandments of men)*, and they taught their human-made rules as though they were given by God. Their focus on minute laws and rules of everyday life caused them to forget the scope of God's law and what it meant for the people. As leaders, they were especially culpable, for they should have been teaching the people about God. Instead, they looked down on the people as ignorant sinners and spent their time busily staying pure. Isaiah explained that their worship was *in vain.* They worshiped for appearances, not out of love for God. When people claim to honor God while their hearts are far from him, their worship means nothing. It is not enough to *act* religious. A person's actions and attitudes must be sincere.

THE GREAT PRETENDERS
Hypocrisy is pretending to be something you are not and have no intention of being. Jesus called the Pharisees hypocrites because they worshiped God for the wrong reasons. Their worship was not motivated by love but by a desire to attain profit, to appear holy, and to increase their status. We become hypocrites when we (1) pay more attention to appearance or reputation than to character, (2) carefully follow certain religious practices while allowing our heart to remain far away from God, and (3) emphasize *our* virtues and others' sins.

7:8 "You abandon the commandment of God and hold to human tradition."[NRSV] The religious leaders had done the very thing they had tried not to do. Jesus charged that they had abandoned God's law (the word for "abandon" could also be translated "disregard, send away from oneself"). They had supposedly devoted their lives to protecting the law; in reality, they had left *the commandment of God* behind in order to *hold to human tradition.* They may have been able to keep both their traditions and God's law, but they had become so zealous for the traditions that they had lost their perspective and had altered and missed the point of God's law entirely. Jesus also charged that they were doing this on purpose (7:9), for they had tried to win praise from people for their displays of piety as they kept all the rituals.

7:9 Then he said to them, "You have a fine way of rejecting the commandment of God in order to keep your tradition!"^{NRSV}
Jesus restated his indictment of the scribes and Pharisees. Not only had they abandoned God's commandments while holding tightly to their traditions (7:8), they had rejected God's commandments outright for the same reason. The Greek word translated "rejecting" is *atheteo,* meaning something that had been laid down or prescribed was being done away with or made void. God had laid down his law, and the Pharisees had made that law void in order to keep their tradition. They had completely lost sight of the merciful and loving intent of God's law as they placed upon themselves and the people minute regulations that were burdensome to keep. They didn't even bother to teach the law; instead, they focused on all their rules and their own piety in keeping their traditions and rules. Nowhere is this better illustrated than in 14:1: "The chief priests and the scribes were looking for a way to arrest Jesus by stealth and kill him" (NRSV). Despite all their strict adherence to the rituals, they had completely forgotten about God's command not to murder. Jesus accused these religious leaders of rejecting God's commands even as they kept their own traditions. Next, Jesus gave an example to illustrate how the tradition could be (and was being) used to negate God's law.

THE LAST WORD
The Pharisees added hundreds of their own petty rules and regulations to God's holy laws; then they tried to force people to follow these rules as the "tradition of the elders." These men claimed to know God's will in every detail of life. Some religious leaders today still add rules and regulations to God's Word, causing much confusion among believers. It is idolatry to claim that your interpretation of God's Word is as important as God's Word itself. It is especially dangerous to set up extrabiblical standards for *others* to follow and give those standards equal authority with the Bible. Instead, look to Christ for guidance about your own behavior, and let him lead others in the details of their lives.

7:10 "For Moses said, 'Honor your father and your mother'; and, 'He who curses father or mother, let him be put to death.'"^{NKJV} Jesus first quoted Moses, an especially relevant choice because the scribes traced the oral law back to him (see Deuteronomy 4:14). Jesus chose an example about people's duty toward their parents. One of the Ten Commandments, *Honor your father and your mother* (Exodus 20:12; Deuteronomy 5:16) states that people are to respect their parents in honor of who they are and what they have done. The commandment did not apply just to young children, but to anyone whose parents were living. Honor includes speaking respectfully and showing care and consideration.

The same law is written negatively in Exodus 21:17, *He who curses father or mother, let him be put to death* (see also Leviticus 20:9). "Cursing" one's parents is the opposite of honoring them. It means to speak ill of, to ridicule, to abuse verbally. The natural result of such behavior is that the person will not honor his parents for who they are, will not speak respectfully, and will certainly show no care or consideration to them. Such action carried a severe penalty—a person who cursed his parents could be put to death.

The scribes and Pharisees knew Moses' words backward and forward. They knew these laws. But they found a way to break them while still looking pious.

7:11-12 **"But you say that if a man says to his father or mother: 'Whatever help you might otherwise have received from me is Corban' (that is, a gift devoted to God), then you no longer let him do anything for his father or mother."**[NIV] Jesus then went on to explain how the Pharisees had found a way to completely sidestep God's command to honor parents. The words *but you say* demonstrated their complete opposition to what Moses had written (7:10).

The practice of *Corban* (literally, "offering") meant that a person could dedicate something to God for his exclusive use. Thus, it was reserved for sacred use and withdrawn from profane or ordinary use by anyone else. Some people had done this, but in such a way that they didn't give it to the temple. Instead, they only legally excluded their parents from using it. They could dedicate money to God's temple that otherwise would have gone to support their parents (based on Deuteronomy 23:21-23 and Numbers 30:1-16). Thus, a man could simply take the vow of Corban, saying that all his money was dedicated to God. He could still use his money any way he chose, but could use his Corban vow as an excuse not to give any money to help his needy parents. Corban had become a religiously acceptable way to neglect one's parents, circumventing responsibility to them. Although the action—dedicating money to God—seemed worthy and no doubt conferred prestige on the giver, these religious leaders were ignoring God's clear command to honor parents. Even worse, this was an irrevocable vow. If a son later decided that he needed to help his parents, the Pharisees would not permit it—*you no longer let him do anything for his father or mother.* The money was "dedi-cated," and nothing could change that. No Pharisee would surren-der the purse. These actions were extremely selfish. Jesus rightly described the Pharisees as going to great pains to set aside God's law.

FAMILY MATTERS
The Pharisees' selfish reasons had made rigid a law that twisted God's higher purpose. They had used one law to play against another with the motive of making it easier on them-selves. Some Christians still do this. They rationalize using up all their finances and let aging family members go on welfare. While we should give money and time to God, we must never use God as an excuse to neglect our family responsibilities. Helping a family member in need is one of the most important ways to honor God (see 1 Timothy 5:8).

7:13 **"Thus you nullify the word of God by your tradition that you have handed down. And you do many things like that."**NIV The Corban vow effectively put tradition above God's Word. To be able to exempt oneself from one of God's commandments by tak-ing a human vow meant that the Pharisees had attempted to *nul-lify* or make void *the word of God.* The Pharisees took advantage of this law themselves and taught it to the young men in their schools, handing it down to the next generation.

Jesus added that the Pharisees did *many things like that.* This was only one example of the premeditated selfishness of these religious leaders who set themselves above all the people and, in effect, destroyed the laws that they attempted to keep (we have already read about their ridiculous commands regarding the Sab-bath, 3:1-6). In his example, Jesus clarified to these hypocritical religious leaders that God's law, not oral tradition, was the true authority over people's lives.

THE NULL PRINCIPLE
Making add-on rules that serve special interests and thwart God's purposes does more damage than just creating inconve-nience or aggravation. In effect, making extra rules calls God's law null and void. What a serious charge! What a scary indict-ment!
Be careful about imposing rules on people. Avoid rules that are not clear biblical mandates. Don't require inflexible alle-giance. You may be getting into more trouble than you think. Be very careful about joining groups that impose secretive rules. Invariably, those rules work to nullify God's work in your life.

7:14-15 **Then he called the crowd again and said to them, "Listen to me, all of you, and understand: There is nothing outside a person that by going in can defile, but the things that come out are what defile."**^{NRSV} After explaining the true value of "the tradition of the elders" (7:5) in 7:6-13, Jesus addressed the crowd and the disciples regarding the true nature of "defilement." The people had listened to Jesus' stinging accusation of the religious leaders; here Jesus called the crowd to *listen . . . and understand,* for he would make his final point and have the final say in this debate. The Pharisees thought that to eat with defiled hands meant to be defiled (7:5). Jesus explained that the Pharisees were wrong in thinking they were acceptable to God just because they were "clean" on the outside. He explained that defilement is not an external matter (keeping food laws, washing ceremonially, keeping Sabbath requirements), but an internal one.

There is nothing outside a person that by going in can defile refers directly to the Pharisees' question about the disciples eating with "defiled" hands. A person does *not* become morally defiled by eating with hands that have not been ceremonially washed. Instead, the opposite is true: *The things that come out are what defile* a person. The condition of a person's heart will be revealed by his or her words and actions—thus, those actions, "the things that come out," are what defile (or reveal true defilement). Sin begins in the heart, just as the prophet Jeremiah had said hundreds of years before: "The heart is devious above all else; it is perverse—who can understand it? I the LORD test the mind and search the heart, to give to all according to their ways, according to the fruit of their doings" (Jeremiah 17:9-10 NRSV).

The Pharisees should have known this. Many times in the Old Testament God had told his people that he valued mercy and obedience based on love above merely observing rules and rituals (see 1 Samuel 15:22-23; Psalms 40:6-8; 51:16-19; Jeremiah 7:21-23; Hosea 6:6; Amos 5:21-24; Micah 6:6-8). Jesus explained his words more fully to his disciples in 7:17-23.

7:16 **"If anyone has ears to hear, let him hear!"**^{NKJV} This verse is not included in the earliest manuscripts and therefore is not printed in the text of most modern English versions. Scribes added it, borrowing directly from 4:23, to provide a conclusion to Jesus' discourse.

7:17 **When He had entered a house away from the crowd, His disciples asked Him concerning the parable.**^{NKJV} Jesus and the disciples left the religious leaders and the crowd and *entered a house.* They were probably in Capernaum, and this may have been the same house that had become their residence while in that city (see 2:1-2; 3:20). There, in private, the *disciples asked Him* to explain the parable. Matthew records that it was Peter who asked (Matthew 15:15). Peter often acted as spokesman for the disciples, so he brought their question to Jesus.

7:18-19 He said to them, "Then do you also fail to understand?"^{NRSV} Jesus knew the crowd didn't understand, but he may have been saddened again that his disciples had failed to understand as well (see also 4:13, 40; 6:51-52). Jesus may have been calling the Twelve to evaluate their own residue of respect for the oral tradition. He may have been chiding them for their own failure to believe that he offered the true interpretation of Old Testament rules and regulations in contrast to traditional authority.

"Do you not see that whatever goes into a person from outside cannot defile, since it enters, not the heart but the stomach, and goes out into the sewer?"^{NRSV} According to the Pharisees, the disciples had been guilty of eating with "defiled" hands, for they had not performed the ceremonial washing prior to eating. Jesus exonerated the disciples before the Pharisees and the crowd, but the disciples still did not follow Jesus' logic. Jesus explained that what goes into a person cannot make that person unclean. Thus, to eat food with hands that may have touched a "defiled" person or article did not mean that a person was ingesting defilement. Logically, as Jesus explained, food goes in the mouth, down into the stomach, and then out into the latrine. It has no effect whatever on the moral condition of the heart. Moral defilement has nothing to do with food. Sin in a person's heart is what defiles (see 7:14-15), not the lack of ceremonial cleansing or the type of food eaten.

(Thus he declared all foods clean.)^{NRSV} The Roman Christians, the primary audience of Mark's Gospel, may have been confused about the Jewish food laws and whether they had to follow them. These words clarified this issue for them (although it took the early church several years to fully understand; see Acts 10 and 15).

Leviticus 11 records many of the Jewish dietary laws, including foods considered "clean" and "unclean." The Jews had a restricted diet for three main reasons: (1) To ensure the health of the nation. The forbidden foods were usually scavenger animals that fed on dead animals; thus, disease could be transmitted through them. (2) To visibly distinguish Israel from other nations. For example, the pig was a common sacrifice of pagan religions. (3) To avoid objectionable associations. The creatures that move about on the ground, for example, were reminiscent of serpents, a common symbol for sin.

Over the years, however, the laws had become more important than the meaning behind them. As the Jews interpreted the dietary laws recorded in Leviticus 11, they believed that they could be clean before God because of what they refused to eat. But Jesus *declared all foods clean* by pointing out that sin has nothing to do with food; sin begins in our attitudes and intentions. Jesus did not degrade the law—the law was meant to be obeyed. But sin and defilement did not come from eating the forbidden foods; it came to a person who chose to disobey the law by eating the forbidden foods. It is disobedience that defiles, and disobedience begins in the heart. Jesus' words paved the way for the change that was made clear when God removed the cultural restrictions regarding food (see Acts 10:9-29). Peter, when later faced with the issue of clean and unclean food, learned that Jewish ceremonial regulations should not be a barrier to proclaiming the gospel to the Gentiles (see also Acts 15:22-29).

The bottom line: People are not pure because of adherence to ceremonial laws and rituals. We become pure on the inside as Christ renews our minds and transforms us into his image.

WHAT WE TAKE IN

The Pharisees were very concerned about the kinds of foods they ate, how the food was prepared, and how well they observed laws of purity when they ate. But they were not as concerned about their thoughts, attitudes, and moral conduct. Today, many people, perhaps rightfully so, are concerned about what they eat. Some won't eat red meat, some refuse to eat any meat at all, and some eat only organically produced food. People read labels and count grams of fat or milligrams of salt. While being concerned about what we put into our bodies is a good, healthy practice, very few people are as stringent about what they put into their minds through reading or watching television. Jesus was more concerned about mind-set and thought processes than about food laws. Do you worry about what foods you eat, but neglect "health practices" for your mind?

7:20 And he said, "It is what comes out of a person that defiles."[NRSV] Defilement occurs because of sin. Sin begins in a person's heart, and what is in the heart comes out in words and actions. In Romans 6–8, Paul explained how this happens. Unless the Holy Spirit controls our sinful human nature, outbursts of the flesh will be prevalent.

Sinful words and actions defile both the one speaking or acting as well as the object of the act. There is a certain ambiguity in Jesus' words. While our first impulse is to believe that the *source* of the action is defiled, the text leaves wide open the possibility that the *target* of evil words and actions is also defiled. That is, we genuinely hurt people by words and actions that spring from evil motives or intentions.

7:21-22 **"For it is from within, from the human heart, that evil intentions come."**NRSV *Evil intentions* begin *within,* in a person's *heart.* Jesus made it clear why people sin—it's a matter of the heart. Our hearts have been inclined toward sin from the time we were born. While most people work hard to keep their outward appearance attractive, what is in their hearts is even more important. When people become Christians, God makes them different on the inside. He will continue the process of change inside them if they only ask. God wants us to seek healthy thoughts and motives, not just healthy food and exercise.

Then Jesus listed a catalog of twelve "evil intentions" that come from the heart. Six are evil individual actions; six are evil attitudes or principles. Notice that the evil attitudes, whether acted upon or not, are still considered sin. The following list is quoted from the NIV.

Sexual immorality—Various kinds of extramarital sexual activity
Theft—Taking something that belongs to another
Murder—Taking the God-given life of another person
Adultery—A married person having sex with someone other than his or her spouse
Greed—Relentless urge to get more for oneself
Malice—Doing evil despite the good that has been received
Deceit—To trick or mislead by lying
Lewdness—Immoral behavior that is neither restrained nor concealed
Envy—Desire for something possessed by another
Slander—To destroy another's good reputation
Arrogance—Making claims of superior intelligence or importance
Folly—Inability to discern between immorality and morality

7:23 **"All these evil things come from within, and they defile a person."**NRSV *All these evil* actions and attitudes begin in a person's heart. And it is those evil actions and attitudes that cause defilement. Many of the words Jesus used could have described the Pharisees.

The cure? The good news of the gospel offers the only cure for humanity's natural defilement. Cleansing can only come by the blood of Jesus Christ offered on our behalf. Only then can we become "pure" before God.

WHAT'S YOUR FOCUS?
An evil action begins with a single thought. Allowing our mind to dwell on lust, envy, hatred, or revenge will lead to sin. Don't defile yourself by focusing on evil. Instead, follow Paul's advice in Philippians 4:8, and think about what is true, noble, right, pure, lovely, and admirable.

JESUS SENDS A DEMON OUT OF A GIRL / 7:24-30 / **103**

Jesus' actions never yielded to simple explanations. Those who thought they had him "figured out" were usually about to be stunned. His opponents tended to see the hurting people who came to Jesus as cases to be solved or examples of those who broke the law. Jesus treated them as valuable human beings, worthy of his attention.

The presumption that Jesus was out to trample the Law might have led Jesus' opponents to expect him to quickly heal the daughter of this Gentile woman. But instead of adding this situation to his portfolio of unusual miracles performed, Jesus ignored the opportunity to make a statement; instead, he dealt with this woman as an individual whose own faith needed to be challenged and clarified.

Jesus did not belittle her by rejecting her. He did not overlook the fact that she was a woman or a Gentile. He gave his full attention to her faith!

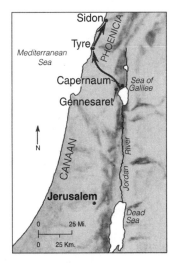

Ministry in Phoenicia
Jesus' ministry was to all people—first to Jews but also to Gentiles. Jesus took his disciples from Galilee to Tyre and Sidon, large cities in Phoenicia, where he healed a Gentile woman's daughter.

7:24 Jesus left that place and went to the vicinity of Tyre.[NIV] Jesus traveled about thirty miles to *the vicinity of Tyre* and then went to Sidon (7:31). These were port cities on the Mediterranean Sea north of Israel. Both cities had flourishing trade and were very wealthy. They were proud, historic Canaanite cities. In David's day, Tyre was on friendly terms with Israel (2 Samuel 5:11), but soon afterward the city became known for its wickedness. Its king even claimed to be a god (Ezekiel 28:1ff.). Tyre rejoiced when Jerusalem was destroyed in 586 B.C. because without Israel's competition, Tyre's trade and profits would increase. It is interesting that Jesus stressed the importance of inner purity just before visiting Tyre.

He entered a house and did not want anyone to know it; yet he could not keep his presence secret.NIV Jesus and the disciples probably went to this Gentile territory thinking that they would be less well known and thus could obtain privacy and rest time. They went to someone's house (probably the home of a Jew who lived in that area) and did not want anyone to know they were there. But even in this Gentile territory, *he could not keep his presence secret.*

7:25 In fact, as soon as she heard about him, a woman whose little daughter was possessed by an evil spirit came and fell at his feet.NIV The word of Jesus' arrival had spread from village to village. One woman in particular came to Jesus *as soon as she heard* that he was in the region. She had heard about Jesus' miracle-working power and how he cast out demons, so she humbly came and *fell at his feet* on behalf of her little girl who was *possessed by an evil spirit.*

PARENTS WHO PRAY
The afflicted girl did not pray; her mother did. The afflicted girl's faith was not measured; her mother's was. Yet the healing was for the girl. The mother recognized the lordship of Christ; she cried, "Lord, help me" (Matthew 15:25). She confessed her need, and she trusted Jesus to meet it.

Parents praying for children can expect God to act. Children who are rebellious, wayward, worldly-wise, far from God—sick of soul—yet covered by a parent's faithful prayer, are in for surprises as God moves in response to faith. Never give up, parents; keep praying for that child's heart, body, and spirit. God will answer.

7:26 Now the woman was a Gentile, of Syrophoenician origin.NRSV Mark described this woman as a Gentile, a Syrophoenician; Matthew calls her a woman of Canaan. These are both correct descriptions. Mark's designation referred to her political background. His Roman audience would easily identify her by the part of the empire that was her home. Matthew's description was designed for his Jewish audience, who remembered the Canaanites as bitter enemies when Israel was settling the Promised Land. Some Bible translations identify her as a Greek. This is also correct because she was a Greek-speaking native of the Phoenician area, an area converted to Greek language and culture after the conquest of Alexander the Great in the fourth century B.C.

She begged him to cast the demon out of her daughter.NRSV The woman wasted no time. As she fell at Jesus' feet, she gave her request—that Jesus would cast the demon out of her little daughter.

7:27 He said to her, "Let the children be fed first, for it is not fair to take the children's food and throw it to the dogs."NRSV Jesus answered her in the language of a parable. Jesus probably spoke Greek to this woman, for she would not have known Aramaic. Jesus used the word *kunarion,* referring to a little dog, a household pet. The simple parable meant that the children at the table are fed before the pets; it would not be right to take the children's food and give it to the dogs. While it is true that in Jewish tradition Gentiles at times were referred to derogatorily as "dogs," that probably does not apply here. The Greek word used as a derogatory nickname applied to wild dogs or scavenger dogs, not household pets.

By these words, Jesus may have meant that his first priority was to spend time feeding his *children* (teaching his disciples), not to take food away from them and throw it to the pets. This woman was interrupting Jesus' purpose in being in Tyre. He had come to spend time teaching his disciples, not to be interrupted to do miracles for a woman who was not even a Jew. Jesus was not insulting the woman; instead, he was saying that she should wait until God's appointed time when the Gentiles would receive the good news of the gospel.

Jesus' words could also be taken to mean that his ministry was to the Jews first (the children of Israel) and that he would not take away from them to perform miracles for a Gentile. If that was what Jesus meant, we should realize that his words do not contradict the truth that God's message is for all types of people (Psalm 22:27; Isaiah 56:7; Matthew 28:19; Romans 15:9-12). Jesus was simply telling the woman that the Jews were to have the first opportunity to accept him as the Messiah because God wanted them to present the message of salvation to the rest of the world (see Genesis 12:3). Jesus was not rejecting the Syrophoenician woman. He may have wanted to test her faith, or he may have wanted to use the situation as another opportunity to teach that faith is available to all races and nationalities.

7:28 But she answered him, "Sir, even the dogs under the table eat the children's crumbs."NRSV Unlike many of Jesus' Jewish listeners, this woman understood his parable.

Her answer was wise, for she explained to Jesus, by extending his parable, that the children who love the pets often drop morsels of food to them. Not all the Jews accepted Jesus, while some Gentiles chose to follow him. Why

> And Satan trembles when he sees
> The weakest saint upon his knees. *William Cowper*

couldn't she have some of those "leftovers" that the Jews didn't "eat"? She adroitly pointed out that such "dogs" ate with (not after) the children. She did not ask for the entire meal, just for a few crumbs—or one crumb in particular—one miracle of healing for her daughter.

A PET PROJECT

On the surface, Jesus' words in 7:27 may have seemed harsh and unsympathetic. But the woman recognized them as a wide-open door to God's throne. Quickly, she stepped in, taking a cue from Jesus' "pet" terms and adding to his analogy of a family dining table. Jesus did not use the negative term for "dog" that referred to a scavenger dog (the word sometimes used by Jews to refer to Gentiles); instead, he used the term for a household pet. Her attitude was expectant and hopeful, not prickly or hypersensitive. The woman knew what she wanted; she believed Jesus could provide; she persevered; she seized the opportunity.

We could learn from this woman's singular purpose and optimistic resilience. Jesus really does want to answer. When we pray, we're talking to a friend.

Ironically, many Jews would lose God's spiritual healing because they rejected Jesus, while many Gentiles, whom the Jews rejected, would find salvation because they recognized Jesus.

7:29 Then he told her, "For such a reply, you may go; the demon has left your daughter."NIV Jesus was delighted by the faith of the woman. He granted her request because of her humility and persistence. Her faith and understanding were in contrast to the misunderstanding of the disciples (6:52; 8:14-21). Her request had been made in faith that Jesus could perform the healing. His words had been meant to test her, and she had passed the test. She understood Christ's lordship and that, as a Gentile, she had no right to request mercy from Jesus. She also willingly accepted his conditions. On that basis, Jesus healed the woman's daughter.

GOSPEL ACCOUNTS FOUND ONLY IN MARK

Section	Topic	Significance
4:26-29	Story of the growing seed	We must share the Good News of Jesus with other people, but only God makes it grow in their lives.
7:32-35	Jesus healed a deaf man who could hardly talk.	Jesus cares about our physical as well as spiritual needs.
8:22-26	Jesus healed the blind man at Bethsaida.	Jesus is considerate because he made sure this man's sight was fully restored.

With his words, the demon left the little girl. This miracle showed that Jesus' power over demons is so great that he doesn't need to be present physically, or even to speak any word to the demon, in order to free someone. His power transcends any distance.

7:30 So she went home, found the child lying on the bed, and the demon gone.NRSV The woman knew that her request had been granted. She did not beg Jesus to come with her; she took him at his word that her child was healed. Sure enough, when she arrived at her home, the child was resting quietly on the bed. The demon had left; the cure was complete and permanent.

In Jesus there is hope for all of us. The woman was a Gentile, yet Jesus crossed the barrier to reach out to her. He actually crossed many barriers: nationality, religion, and tradition. No barrier can keep Jesus from reaching us.

THE CROWD MARVELS AT JESUS' HEALINGS / 7:31-37 / **104**

The healing of the Syrophoenician woman's daughter occurred during Jesus' northernmost travels. He concluded that mission by taking a long route back to Galilee. Then Jesus healed a deaf-mute who depended on others to speak for him.

Mark selected instances from Jesus' life to illustrate the many ways the Lord shows compassion for others. Mark seems to have made a connection between the deaf-mute here and the blind man in 8:22-26 with the deafness and blindness of the disciples described in 8:18. Jesus wants to open the ears and eyes of all who are deaf and blind so that they may receive the light of life.

7:31 Then Jesus left the vicinity of Tyre and went through Sidon, down to the Sea of Galilee and into the region of the Decapolis.^{NIV} *The Decapolis* (or Ten Cities) was a Gentile area, so this continues the emphasis of the previous miracle. Jesus had been in a part of this region before, when he had healed a demon-possessed man and then sent him on to tell others about his healing (5:19-20).

7:32 There some people brought to him a man who was deaf and could hardly talk, and they begged him to place his hand on the man.^{NIV} Mark alone recorded the miracle of the healing of this deaf and mute man. Apparently several of this man's friends brought him to Jesus; they knew he couldn't ask for help himself, so they would intercede for their friend. They had faith that Jesus could heal the man, so they brought him.

The key to Mark's recording of this miracle may be found in the Greek word *mogilalon,* translated "could hardly talk." That word is found only here and in the Greek Septuagint version of the Old Testament in Isaiah 35:6, where Isaiah wrote that one day "the mute tongue [will] shout for joy" (NIV). Mark saw the fulfillment of Isaiah's words in the healing ministry of Jesus.

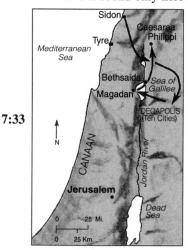

7:33

He took him aside in private, away from the crowd, and put his fingers into his ears, and he spat and touched his tongue.^{NRSV} Jesus wanted to heal this man, but again he wasn't looking for crowd acclaim in his healings. Thus, he took the man aside in private so they could be away from the crowd (see also 8:23). Jesus intended to deal with the man on a personal level—not use him as an advertisement of healing power.

Mark described this miracle in detail—apparently the disciples were with Jesus and the man. In this instance, Jesus *put*

Continued Ministry
After taking a roundabout way back to Galilee through Decapolis (the Ten Cities), Jesus returned to Dalmanutha where Jewish leaders questioned his authority. From there he want to Bethsaida and on to Caesarea Philippi. Here he talked with his disciples about his authority and about coming events.

his fingers into [the man's] ears and then *spat and touched [the man's] tongue.* Jesus communicated to the deaf man through these actions and encouraged his faith. Jesus often used touch in his healings. In addition, spittle was commonly recognized in the ancient world as having healing properties. The man responded in faith and desire for healing.

WINDOWS TO THE SOUL
Jesus used language that this deaf man would understand. The healing message was personal and unique. Whoever thought spittle might be the conduit of a miracle?
　　If there's only one holy means of witness in your church (sermons, for instance), many people likely will not hear. Churches need lots of different methods to meet diverse needs. Let musicians play, singers sing, actors act, and writers write. Let each creative Christian tell the story. Jesus used spit and mud; surely we can find windows to the minds and hearts of people as well.

7:34 Then looking up to heaven, he sighed and said to him, "Ephphatha," that is, "Be opened."^{NRSV} Jesus looked upward to God (the source of his power) and *sighed.* The sigh was probably in sympathy for the suffering man. Whether Mark recorded these details to describe what always happened in healings or whether this was unusual, is uncertain. In any case, the healing took place. Jesus spoke the word *Ephphatha.* The word may have been either Hebrew or Aramaic (the two languages are closely related, and both were used by Jews in ancient Palestine), but most scholars believe it was Aramaic. Ancient magicians and exorcists would use incantations made up of nonsense words or syllables to perform their tricks or healings. However, Mark showed that Jesus used one simple and easy-to-understand Aramaic word, which might mean the man was a Jew and not a Gentile. He probably lip-read that word in great excitement, for Jesus was opening his ears and loosening his tongue! Mark then translated the Aramaic word for his Roman audience.

> Silence is the soil of the Word; only when we are alone with the Word do we gain the depth of insight that enables us to preach with power and clarity. Yet silence is only a means to a higher end. Silence that does not give rise to speech is dumbness. Speech that does not grow out of silence is chatter. *Donald Bloesch*

7:35 And immediately his ears were opened, his tongue was

released, and he spoke plainly.NRSV Immediately upon Jesus' speaking the word, the deaf man's *ears were opened* and *his tongue was released.* The man could hear, and he could speak plainly and clearly.

OPEN UP
We need this miracle today in a spiritual opening up of each of us.
- We need to be opened up to wholeness of life: to allow our salvation to affect every area of our lives.
- We need to be opened up to be able to witness: to hear and to speak clearly to those around us about what happened when Jesus saved us.
- We need to be opened up so we can act: to have more than a conceptual conversion, but to have the real touch of Jesus. Let Jesus open up your life.

7:36 Then He commanded them that they should tell no one; but the more He commanded them, the more widely they proclaimed it.NKJV Even though the miracle had been done in private (7:33), its results were obvious to the waiting crowd. The man, formerly deaf and barely able to talk, suddenly could hear and speak. Jesus asked the people not to talk about this healing because he didn't want to be seen simply as a miracle worker. He didn't want the people to miss his real message. But the people simply could not keep quiet, and *they proclaimed* the miracle widely.

7:37 They were astounded beyond measure, saying, "He has done everything well; he even makes the deaf to hear and the mute to speak."NRSV As Mark recorded many times, the people's response was astonishment (see also 1:22; 2:12; 4:41; 10:26; 11:18). The Jews in the crowd, responding that *he even makes the deaf to hear and the mute to speak,* certainly recalled Isaiah's prophecy of the Messiah's day: "Then will the eyes of the blind be opened and the ears of the deaf unstopped. Then will the lame leap like a deer, and the mute tongue shout for joy" (Isaiah 35:5-6 NIV). They knew this man *has done everything well.* If only they could have gone a step farther and realized who he was, "the Christ" (8:29 NIV), the Son of God, their promised Messiah, the fulfillment of Isaiah's prophecies.

Mark 8:1–9:1

Differences in detail distinguish this miracle from the feeding of the five thousand described in chapter 6. At that time, those fed were mostly Jews. At this second feeding, Jesus ministered to a mixed crowd of Jews and Gentiles in the predominantly Gentile region of the Decapolis. Jesus also began with different quantities of bread and fish, and he did not require his disciples to admit their own inability to solve the problem.

Even in Israel, Jesus took the gospel to a mixed audience. Jesus' actions and message had a significant impact on large numbers of Gentiles right from the start. Mark had his readers in mind when he recorded these facts. Examples of Jesus' compassionate ministry to non-Jews would be very reassuring to Mark's primarily Roman audience. We ought to be thankful for Jesus' compassion toward us as well.

8:1-2 In those days when there was again a great crowd without anything to eat, he called his disciples and said to them, "I have compassion for the crowd, because they have been with me now for three days and have nothing to eat."NRSV The phrase *in those days* picks up the narrative from the end of chapter 7. Jesus was ministering in the region of the Decapolis (7:31), where he had healed a deaf man, causing his popularity to spread throughout the area.

It comes as no surprise, then, that *there was again a great crowd* surrounding Jesus and the disciples. The story sounds very much like the feeding of the five thousand recorded in 6:30-44 but is a separate event. Both Matthew and Mark include both miracles. Jesus himself referred back to each incident separately when he asked the disciples, "When I broke the five loaves for the five thousand, how many baskets full of fragments did you take up? . . . Also, when I broke the seven for the four thousand . . ." (8:19-20 NKJV).

In the previous recorded episode, Jesus had been in Galilee, ministering among the Jews; here he was in a Gentile region. (The crowd was probably made up of both Jews and Gentiles.

This was the beginning of Jesus' expanded ministry to the Gentiles.) In the previous episode, Jesus and the disciples had desired rest, but the crowd had interrupted that rest. Out of compassion, Jesus had taught them (6:34). The disciples had to come to Jesus suggesting that the crowd would be getting hungry and that he should send them away to get their own food. In this episode, the crowd had been following Jesus for three days, listening to his teaching, and observing his miracles. Jesus took the initiative in his concern for their need for food, and he shared his concern with the disciples. The wording probably does not mean that the people hadn't eaten for three days. Instead, whatever supplies they had brought along were depleted, so most of them had nothing left to eat. Thus, Jesus was concerned about sending them away hungry. Finally, after the feeding of the five thousand, the people wanted to make him a king. There was no such movement by the people in this episode.

BASIC LOVE
Moved with compassion, Jesus fed another great crowd. Many times, a meal or some other "human" incentive is attached to a loftier spiritual goal. We cook a church dinner in order to get more people to listen to a sermon, a Bible lesson, a musical, or anything with a message. But Jesus simply loved these people and thought they needed food.

Should we love others simply and without condition? Should we delight in meeting basic human needs? Should we continue to reach out to the unsaved? Jesus blessed the loaves and fishes, and he wants us to help to pass them around.

Mark often recorded parallel episodes to expand on his theme that the disciples continued to be blind to the true person of their Master and that Jesus did indeed act with God's power. Parallel episodes between 6:31–7:37 and 8:1-30 include:

- Jesus feeding a crowd of people with little food (6:31-44 and 8:1-9)

- Jesus crossing the sea (6:45-56 and 8:10)

- Jesus debating the Pharisees (7:1-23 and 8:11-13)

- Jesus giving a discourse about bread (7:24-30 and 8:14-21)

- Jesus healing people (7:31-36 and 8:22-26)

- Jesus hearing confessions of faith (7:37 and 8:27-30)

■ the disciples' misunderstanding contrasting with the
Syrophoenician woman's understanding (7:24-30 and 8:14-21)

Although the disciples had seen Jesus feed five thousand people,
they had no idea what Jesus would do in this situation (thus
revealing their spiritual blindness). This miracle again revealed
Jesus' divine power.

**8:3 "If I send them home hungry, they will collapse on the way,
because some of them have come a long distance."**[NIV] Jesus'
words to the disciples came as a test of their understanding of his
power. He had called the disciples and presented his concern for
the people (much as the disciples had done in 6:35-36, except
they had more selfish motives at that time). Jesus always had
compassion for the crowds and was always willing to meet a
need when he saw it. The people had run out of food in order to
listen to Jesus teach. They did not expect a miracle, but Jesus, not
wanting to send them on their way without food, would perform
one. Some of the people had come *a long distance*. While the
location of this feeding of four thousand is unknown, many scholars put it in the region of the Decapolis on the southeastern shore
of the Sea of Galilee, near where the preceding miracle took
place (7:31-37).

In addition, Jesus may have been testing what the disciples
would say in response to the need (see also John 6:6). Would they
say, "Well, let's see how many resources we can gather, and we'll
trust God to provide as he did before"? Or would they again
doubt?

WHAT, ME WORRY?
Do you ever feel as though God is so busy with important concerns that he couldn't possibly be aware of your needs? Just as
Jesus was concerned about these people's need for food, he is
concerned about our daily needs. At another time Jesus said,
"Therefore do not worry, saying, 'What shall we eat?' or 'What
shall we drink?' or 'What shall we wear?' . . . Your heavenly
Father knows that you need all these things" (Matthew 6:31-32
NKJV). Jesus knows that you have come a long way or that you
may be at the point of collapse. Do you have concerns that you
think would not interest God? There is nothing too large for him
to handle and no need too small to escape his interest.

**8:4 His disciples answered, "But where in this remote place can
anyone get enough bread to feed them?"**[NIV] Once again the
disciples focused on the impossible. As before, the crowd was
in a *remote place* (6:35), and the disciples asked the obvious

question: *Where . . . can anyone get enough bread to feed them?* A "remote place" (called a "desert" in some versions) refers not to any specific location, but merely to an uninhabited area. Mark used the term to remind his readers of when God had supplied food for Israel in the desert (Exodus 16) and to point to God's promises for the future when the desert would become abundant (Isaiah 49:8-12).

Jesus had already found the resources in a previous remote place for an even larger crowd (6:35), yet the disciples were completely perplexed as to how they should be expected to feed them. People often give up when faced with difficult situations. Like the disciples, we often forget God's provision for us in the past. When facing a difficult situation, remember how God cared for you and trust him to work faithfully again.

REMEMBERING
How could the disciples experience so many of Jesus' miracles and yet be so slow to comprehend who he was? They had already seen Jesus feed over five thousand people with five loaves and two fish (6:35-44), yet they doubted whether he could feed another large group. Sometimes we are also slow to catch on. Although Christ has brought us through trials and temptations in the past, we don't believe that he will do it in the future. Is your heart too closed to take in all that God can do for you? Don't be like the disciples. Remember what Christ has done, and have faith that he will do it again. With Christ, nothing is impossible.

8:5 He asked them, "How many loaves do you have?" And they said, "Seven."NKJV Some scholars have pointed out the symbolism of seven loaves. In the Bible, the number seven often signifies perfection or completeness, as in the seven days of creation (Genesis 1) and forgiving seven times (Matthew 18:21). Yet the numbers seven and seventy were also associated with Gentiles. In Jewish tradition, Gentile nations numbered seventy (from Genesis 10:1-32), and Gentiles were sometimes said to be bound, not by the Israelite covenant, but by God's covenant with Noah that is said to have seven commandments (Genesis 9:1-17). In Acts 6:1-7, seven leaders were chosen for the Greek-speaking Christians. Thus, in this passage the number seven may have symbolic significance. It may hint at the worldwide scope of Jesus' message. Probably the connection is coincidental, but the church used that connection to enlarge the Gentile mission. (See also note on 6:44.)

NOT ENOUGH
Jesus' question penetrates our self-sufficiency: "How many
loaves do you have?" The disciples' answer really meant, "Not
enough." His question accomplished several purposes:
- It helped them analyze their situation.
- It made them realize the inadequacy of their resources.
- It reminded them of previous miracles.
- It opened them up to relying on God.
  Do you trust in your own wisdom or your own resources?
Have you become self-satisfied with your organization or plan-
ning? Remember not to trust in your own strength, but in God.

8:6 **Then he ordered the crowd to sit down on the ground; and he**
took the seven loaves, and after giving thanks he broke them
and gave them to his disciples to distribute; and they distrib-
uted them to the crowd.NRSV In the previous miracle, Jesus had
told the disciples to order the people to sit in groups on the
ground; here Jesus himself gave the order for everyone to sit
down. Perhaps he took over, realizing that the disciples just
hadn't understood. In any case, he then *took the seven loaves* and
gave thanks to God for the provision he was about to give. In
Greek, the term for giving thanks is connected with the Christian
Eucharist (or Lord's Supper) as in 1 Corinthians 11:24. Later, in
14:22-25, Mark used the term meaning "to bless" to describe
Jesus' prayer over the bread, and the term "to give thanks" (the
same word as used here) to describe his prayer over the cup.

Next Jesus broke apart the loaves, then he allowed the disciples to pass them out as before (6:41). Perhaps the "hands-on"
experience by the disciples would jog their memories. The verbs
for Jesus giving the bread and the disciples distributing it could
read, "Jesus kept on giving bread to the disciples, and they kept
on distributing it" to the crowd.

TABLE GRACE
Jesus gave thanks for the food, and he serves as a model for
us. Life is a gift, and the nourishment life requires, while it
comes from the work of many hands, conveys God's material
blessing. Mealtime provides an opportunity to thank God for
daily needs met, for taste and beauty, and for human company
and divine companionship. Giving thanks keeps us from regarding a plate of food as a trough, our stomachs as bottomless
pits, and our gathering to eat as a bothersome interruption.
  Keep up this good tradition, and let your gratefulness to God
be genuine.

8:7 They had also a few small fish; and after blessing them, he ordered that these too should be distributed.^{NRSV} The people would receive not just bread, but fish as well, forming a fairly complete meal in ancient days. Such a meal certainly would provide enough energy for the people's trips back home. Like the bread, the fish was blessed and distributed until everyone had enough to eat.

8:8 The people ate and were satisfied. Afterward the disciples picked up seven basketfuls of broken pieces that were left over.^{NIV} As had happened before, each person in the crowd ate and was filled—no one went away hungry from this banquet. The seven loaves and few fish multiplied so that, again, even the leftovers were more than they had begun with.

In the previous feeding episode, Jesus had asked the disciples to divide the crowd into a specific arrangement; this time, he did not do so. The Greek word for "baskets" carries an interesting twist on this story. In the feeding of the five thousand, there were twelve baskets of leftovers, and the "baskets" were *kophinos,* large baskets. After the feeding of the four thousand, there were seven baskets of leftovers, and the "baskets" were different; these were *spuris,* baskets that were large enough to hold a person. (Paul was let down over the Damascus wall in a *spuris*—Acts 9:25). The abundance of leftovers in these seven baskets may have been more than the leftovers from the twelve baskets in the previous incident. If the disciples took some of the leftovers as their own food supply for the coming days (as alluded to in 6:42-43 notes), then the abundance of the supply for them was a reminder over several days of their lack of faith in what Jesus could accomplish.

STINGY SAINTS
They were satisfied. Jesus had provided enough to fill everyone up. Not just a taste, not merely a helping, but more than required. Because Christ has abundant compassion, his work on our behalf satisfied our needs superabundantly. Because Christ has given so much to us, we should have compassion toward others that reflects God's gracious provision. When we have the means, we should err on the side of generosity. Those under our care should say, "I have had plenty!" Let Jesus' generosity encourage you to give big portions to needy people.

8:9-10 About four thousand men were present.^{NIV} As before, the Greek word used here for "men" is *andres,* meaning not "people," but "male individuals." Therefore, there were four thousand men in addition to the women and children.

And having sent them away, he got into the boat with his disciples and went to the region of Dalmanutha.[NIV] Once Jesus knew the people had eaten their fill and would not faint from hunger on their journey home (8:3), he sent them on their way. Jesus and the disciples once again got into the boat and sailed to *the region of Dalmanutha.* While there is no site identified as "Dalmanutha," it may have been another name for Magdala or Magadan (Matthew 15:39), a town located on the western shore of the Sea of Galilee. This was Mary Magdalene's hometown (Luke 8:2-3).

RELIGIOUS LEADERS ASK FOR A SIGN IN THE SKY / 8:11-13 / **106**

The frustrated Pharisees tried a tactical maneuver with Jesus called "control by demanding proof." They had labeled his miraculous acts of compassion as evidence of Satan at work (3:22-30). Their objective was not to believe in Jesus but to destroy him. If they could raise doubts and thus get Jesus to do miracles at their command, then he would literally be under their control. But Jesus bluntly refused.

We can anticipate similar tactics in our own efforts to communicate the gospel. We may be asked to "prove" the existence of God. Such approaches are rarely honest; they are attempts to derail our message. These demands for proof, like the ones Jesus heard, are usually smoke screens covering up a refusal to believe. Unbelief can be a mind-set against God, a willful rebellion of the intellect such that no amount of evidence will overcome it. Resistance, however, should not make us insensitive to honest questions. Though he was constantly under attack, Jesus always received those who were genuine seekers.

Note that this brief paragraph summarizes what must have been a curtailed mission. Mark 8:10 describes the destination of the apostolic band, but they departed from Dalmanutha immediately after the confrontation.

8:11 The Pharisees came and began to question Jesus. To test him, they asked him for a sign from heaven.[NIV] Jesus had been able to escape the probing Pharisees for a while as he visited in Gentile areas (7:24–8:10). His last dealing with them had involved the issues of the law and ceremonial defilement, and Jesus had called the Pharisees hypocrites (7:6). But the Pharisees weren't going to give up in their relentless attempts to discredit Jesus before the crowds. So, upon Jesus' return to Jewish territory, *the Pharisees came and began to question Jesus.*

Mark pointed out that this was a *test,* just as Satan had previously tempted Jesus to perform feats that would have revealed his power (see Matthew 4:1-11). From their standpoint, it was a test for a false prophet. From Mark's standpoint, it was an evil test. The Pharisees had tried to explain away Jesus' previous miracles by claiming that they had been done by luck, coincidence, or evil power (see 3:22). Here they demanded *a sign from heaven*— something beyond a mere miracle. What exactly did they want? They may have wanted something so spectacular that there could be no doubt that Jesus had come from God. They reasoned that God alone had cosmic power.

> Do we know anything of likeness to Christ, and fellow-feeling with him? Do we feel hurt, pained and sorrowful when we see people continuing in sin and unbelief? Do we feel grieved and concerned about the state of the unconverted? These are heart-searching questions, and demand serious consideration. There are few surer marks of an unconverted heart than carelessness and indifference about the souls of other people.
> *J. C. Ryle*

Mark 13:21-23 records Jesus warning the disciples about imposters who would use signs to deceive people and lead them astray. A sign was used by God and his prophets to accomplish two purposes: (1) A sign showed trustworthiness or reliability— if a prophet said something would happen and it came to pass, it demonstrated that in all his prophecies he was telling the truth from God. (2) A sign showed power—if a message was accompanied by a sign, it authenticated the power and authority of the prophet.

The Pharisees were asking for a sign to back up Jesus' claims and miracles. Perhaps they regarded his other miracles merely as random occurences. Using the principle from Deuteronomy 13:1-3 and 18:18-22, the Pharisees were trying to draw Jesus into a trap. If he could not produce a sign, they could accuse him of being a false prophet. If Jesus claimed to be God, then he'd better back it up with proof. This, they were sure, would be beyond Jesus' power. More likely, they may have wanted, not a spectacular show, but some word or vision from heaven that would unmistakably show that Jesus did indeed act with God's authority. In either case, they expected Jesus to work by their demands on their timetable. They had already seen and heard about many miracles, but that was not enough for them. They wanted Jesus to answer to them.

8:12 And he sighed deeply in his spirit and said, "Why does this generation ask for a sign? Truly I tell you, no sign will be given to this generation."NRSV Jesus' sigh was a groan from the depths of his heart. In 7:34, Jesus had sighed over a disease; here, in 8:12, he was sighing over moral failure. The obstinate rejection by those who should have been most able and eager to recognize him deeply distressed Jesus. His rhetorical question reveals his amazement that *this generation* (represented by these stubborn religious leaders) would ask for a sign—they had already seen many miracles and heard incredible, life-changing teaching. But they chose to reject Jesus. And Jesus knew their heart. He knew that no matter what he might do—and he could have

> We cannot expect the world to believe that the Father sent the Son, that Jesus' claims are true, and that Christianity is true, unless the world sees . . . the oneness of true Christians. *Francis Schaeffer*

done *any* type of spectacular cosmic miracle—they would not believe in him, or they would believe in him for the wrong reasons. They would explain it away as they had all the others, for they had already chosen *not* to believe in him.

PROOF POSITIVE
In the previous story, Jesus had been generous to the hungry crowd caught in a remote place without food. Here he gave a flat no to a request for food for thought. The Pharisees asked for irrefutable proof; Jesus gave them nothing except (as Matthew records) an indirect invitation to watch the coming drama at Golgotha.

Should Christians be stingy when skeptics want proof? Not exactly. We should just keep on pointing to signs already given: Jesus, crucified and risen; Jesus, Lord of the heart, leader of the church; Jesus, coming again soon in spectacular power. Our faithful witness should always portray Jesus. Amazing signs of God's love have been generously given. Point to them.

The words "truly I tell you" are a formula for making a solemn oath or a vow. With those powerful words Jesus promised that *no sign will be given to this generation.* While Jesus had done and would continue to do miracles *(dunamis)* in response to people's faith and to reveal God's presence and power within him, he would never give a sign *(semeion)* in answer to the demands of religious hypocrites who would not believe it anyway.

Matthew's Gospel records that Jesus added that no sign would be given "except the sign of Jonah" (Matthew 16:4 NIV). By using the sign of the prophet Jonah, who was inside a great fish for three days, Jesus was predicting his death and resurrection (see also Matthew 12:38-42). The Resurrection, of course, was the most spectacular sign of all. That sign would come, not in Jesus' timing or in answer to the Pharisees' demands, but in God's plan. And when it occurred, even that sign would be dismissed by the religious leaders. Mark's

Gospel, however, says that no sign (at all) would be given because of their unbelief. Jesus was rejecting these leaders.

PROVE IT

Many people, like these Jewish leaders, say they want to see a miracle so that they can believe. But Jesus knew that miracles usually won't convince hard-hearted people. Jesus had been healing the sick, raising people from the dead, and feeding thousands, and still people wanted him to prove himself. Do you doubt Christ because you haven't *seen* a miracle? Do you expect God to prove himself to you personally before you believe? Jesus says, "Blessed are those who have not seen and yet have believed" (John 20:29 NKJV). We have all the miracles recorded in the Old and New Testaments, two thousand years of church history, and the witness of thousands. With all this evidence, those who won't believe may be too proud or too stubborn. Don't harden your heart.

8:13 And He left them, and getting into the boat again, departed to the other side.[NKJV] Jesus did not come to earth to convince people to come to him by performing wonders; he came inviting people to come to him in faith, and as a response to their faith, he performed great miracles. But for these self-righteous religious leaders there was little hope. After this encounter, Jesus left abruptly, got into the boat, and departed back toward the northeastern shore of the Sea of Galilee. This event marked the end of his public ministry in the region of Galilee.

MOVING TOWARD FAITH

Honest skeptics want to solve their riddles and find answers to their questions. Such seekers may be slow to change, but change they must as truth becomes clearer. Phony skeptics erect their questions as barriers against God, lest the truth force their stubborn lives to change. They use the rhetoric of inquiry like cement blocks. Eventually the walls get so high that light and heat no longer penetrate.

Moving toward faith engages head and heart and hand. Honest skeptics want a gospel that makes sense, a gospel that meets real human needs, and a gospel that makes a difference in practical living. Many skeptics resist big leaps toward truth (though the arch skeptic Paul converted rather quickly), preferring small steps, paced and measured.

So, honest skeptic, take a step, make a move. The hand extended to you from just beyond the next rocky ledge, that strong hand—the one scarred in its palm—that hand is for you. Step toward it, reach for it, grasp it, and know that you've found a friend.

JESUS WARNS AGAINST WRONG TEACHING /
8:14-21 / **107**

Up to this point, Mark has conveyed the rejection of Jesus by his family and the religious leaders. At the same time, Mark has shown the inability of Jesus' closest followers to grasp his identity. With the two feeding miracles still fresh in their minds, the disciples failed to reach a conclusion about Jesus. While demons attested his identity and those who had benefited from his healing recognized his lordship, those with the best vantage point remained ignorant. The question Jesus asked the original disciples applies to us: "Do you still not understand?"

8:14 Now the disciples had forgotten to take bread, and they did not have more than one loaf with them in the boat.^{NKJV} Jesus had left his confrontation with the Pharisees abruptly, and the disciples went along with him. Apparently, at some point out on the sea, they realized that they *had forgotten to take bread.* Perhaps the disciples were feeling guilty for not having planned ahead well enough to have ample supplies on the boat.

There may also be a symbolic meaning in the "one loaf." Jesus himself was the "one loaf" sufficient to meet all their needs. As the "bread of life" (John 6:35-40), Jesus was the source of life. With him along, the disciples lacked nothing.

POOR PLANNING
Did the disciples expect Jesus to feed them at every meal, even with so much left over from the last one? Were they just poor travel agents, neglecting the details, perhaps thinking that God would provide whatever they forgot?

Christians should never lazily assume that God will fill the gaps. Sloppy planning and lazy living stunt the growth of Christian stewards. If we have the health, opportunity, and ability to do so, we must show the will to work hard and the discipline to do our best for God.

8:15 And he cautioned them, saying, "Watch out—beware of the yeast of the Pharisees and the yeast of Herod."^{NRSV} As the disciples were worrying about bread, Jesus used the opportunity to teach of the danger of the *yeast* of the Pharisees and Herod. Yeast is a key ingredient in bread, for it causes the dough to rise. Mark mentioned the yeast (also called "leaven") of the Pharisees and of Herod, while Matthew wrote about the leaven of the Pharisees and Sadducees (Matthew 16:6, 12). Mark's audience, mostly non-Jews, would have known about Herod, but not necessarily about the Jewish religious sect of the Sadducees. Thus Mark quoted the part of Jesus' statement that his readers would understand. This reference to Herod may mean the Herodians, a group of Jews who supported the king. Many Herodians were also Sadducees. The Herodians were known for their skepticism, materialism, and political opportunism. The Pharisees were self-righteous, maintaining a form of religiousness without inner strength and spiritual insight.

"Yeast" in this passage symbolizes evil. The Jews were required to celebrate an annual period beginning with Passover during which no yeast was to be found in their homes; all bread eaten had to be made without yeast ("unleavened," see Exodus 12:14-20). Just as only a small amount of yeast is needed to make a batch of bread rise, so the evil teachings and hypocrisy of the religious and political leaders could permeate and contaminate the entire society. Jesus used yeast as an example of how a small amount of evil can affect a large group of people. The wrong teachings of the Pharisees were leading many people astray. Jesus warned his disciples to constantly *watch out* for the contaminating evil of the religious leaders (see also Galatians 5:9).

8:16 They said to one another, "It is because we have no bread."NRSV Jesus issued a warning, and the disciples quietly talked among themselves. They didn't understand the warning and interpreted Jesus' words in an odd manner, perhaps out of self-induced guilt that they had forgotten to bring ample supplies for the journey. The phrase might also be translated, "But we have no bread at all." In other words, "How can we be in danger of their yeast if we don't even have any bread?" Their literal understanding missed Jesus' point entirely.

8:17-18 Aware of their discussion, Jesus asked them: "Why are you talking about having no bread? Do you still not see or understand? Are your hearts hardened?"NIV Nothing got past Jesus. He heard them talking about having no bread. Jesus was saddened that the Jewish religious leaders, the people who should have rejoiced at Jesus' arrival, had completely rejected him. And it angered him that these religious leaders had the power to spread their hard-heartedness and unbelief throughout the nation. Jesus' disciples had not escaped the contamination, for even they consistently failed to realize who Jesus was. Jesus' rebuke in these verses is a series of questions focusing on the disciples' hard-heartedness, blindness and deafness to the truth, and lack of memory regarding all that they had seen and experienced with Jesus. The disciple who shared this incident with Mark gave us an incredible account of the difficulty the disciples had in believing. These men, closest to Jesus, would carry a huge responsibility after he was gone. Jesus wanted to be sure that they were getting the message.

The questions came one after another: Why did they talk about bread, something merely temporal, when their spiritual souls were at stake? Did the disciples still not perceive who Jesus was and what he had come to do? Was the "soil" of their heart so hard that his deep truths could never penetrate (see 4:10-20)? Each question was a stinging rebuke to the disciples.

Jesus continued, **"Do you have eyes but fail to see, and ears but fail to hear?"**[NIV] These words recalled the Old Testament prophets' injunctions against faithless Israel. As Jesus had already said in 4:12 (NIV), Isaiah had written about Israel, "They may be ever seeing but never perceiving, and ever hearing but never understanding" (Isaiah 6:9). Jeremiah had written, "Hear this, O foolish and senseless people, who have eyes, but do not see, who have ears, but do not hear" (Jeremiah 5:21 NRSV). Ezekiel also had described the people of Israel, saying they "have eyes to see but do not see, who have ears to hear but do not hear" (Ezekiel 12:2 NRSV). Finally his words, **"And don't you remember?"**[NIV] vividly describe the disciples' short memories. They couldn't even remember the meaning of his miracles.

THE HARDHEART CLUB
Today the Hardhearts believe
(1) that poverty is caused by laziness; helping poor people only reinforces their failures;
(2) that youth are vicious and spoiled and should be taught from early age to respect their elders (be seen and not heard) as their first duty;
(3) that worship is best conducted in one way—our way—which has worked very well for forty years, thank you, and need not be changed;
(4) that evangelism doesn't apply; people will never change anyway, so we don't need to do it.
Many churches have chapters of this distinguished club. The stronger the club, the more money is saved from frivolous expense (like a youth program), and the more time is saved from silliness like innovative programming and special ministries to needy populations. Joining the Hardheart Club requires only one pledge: You must refuse to listen to Jesus' questions. Don't be a hardheart. Be open to Christ's truth. Let him change your heart.

8:19 **"When I broke the five loaves for the five thousand, how many baskets full of fragments did you take up?" They said**

to him, **"Twelve."**^{NKJV} Jesus quizzed the disciples again over
their lack of perception. These were his trainees—those to whom
his mission would be entrusted once he was gone. Would they
ever understand? Jesus, for all his incredible power, did not and
would not force understanding and belief upon his disciples.
They had to understand and come to him on their own, in faith.

Did they even remember the feeding of the five thousand?
Jesus asked a question to see. When he had broken only five
loaves and fed more than five thousand, how many baskets full of
leftovers did they collect? They remembered that there were
twelve baskets full. They had taken up considerably more leftovers than the food they had at the beginning.

**8:20 "Also, when I broke the seven for the four thousand, how
many large baskets full of fragments did you take up?" And
they said, "Seven."**^{NKJV} Then Jesus reminded them of an almost
exact duplicate of the feeding of the five thousand. When he had
broken only seven loaves and fed more than four thousand, what
was the amount in leftovers? Again, the disciples remembered
that there were seven large baskets full. For a second time, they
had collected more leftovers than food that they had at the beginning.

REBUKE FOR ALL SEASONS
When Jesus questioned his disciples about the recent miracles,
he was dealing with unbelief and lack of sensitivity, not giving a
quiz on numbers of breadbaskets full of leftovers.

We must not become self-righteous or proud of our own religious knowledge or spiritual progress. There is always more for
us to understand (1 Corinthians 8:1-3). Also, we must be gracious to new believers and slow learners. There are sincere
Christians among us who don't read as they should or think
through all the issues (see John 10:16; 14:9).

For our part, we need to soften our hearts so we can
- remember the compassion of Jesus for the needy and his
  mercy to us;
- avoid the materialism, hypocrisy, and empty forms of the Pharisees and Herodians, and the dullness and insensitivity of the
  disciples;
- recall Jesus' ability to save the lost and help his disciples; and
- ask the Holy Spirit to keep us sensitive to his leading.

8:21 He said to them, "Do you still not understand?"^{NIV} The disciples correctly answered Jesus' questions (8:19-20). In doing so,
the conclusion should have been obvious. His question, *"Do
you still not understand?"* was more of an appeal, asked over
and over as he considered the issues at stake. The disciples

needed to understand, and after all they had seen and heard, they should have reached the obvious conclusion. Jesus had shown incredible compassion for people and had performed miracles to meet their needs. The disciples should have thereby understood that Jesus would meet their needs as well—whether for bread or for spiritual insight regarding the religious leaders. Jesus wanted the disciples to think about what they had seen, especially in the two feeding miracles. If they considered what had happened, they would conclude that Jesus was their Messiah, the Son of God.

JESUS RESTORES SIGHT TO A BLIND MAN / 8:22-26 / **108**

Before revealing the central concept of his Gospel, Mark recorded one last incident from Jesus' ministry. His miraculous healing of the blind man from Bethsaida served at least two purposes. It showed how Jesus responded with compassion to an obvious need. It also gave a vivid "acted-out parable" to demonstrate that insight seldom comes instantly.

This miracle seems to connect with Peter's declaration that follows. Mark's first words (1:1) portrayed that the gospel reveals Jesus as God's Son. But Mark patiently developed his theme. The disciples' struggle to grasp the meaning of the Cross parallels the blind man's experience of receiving his sight. Both follow an all-too-real pattern in our own lives. We don't understand Christ's purpose for us all at once. God has provided a clear enough record upon which to base our faith. Unfortunately, having a wonderful picture of Jesus' life will not do us any good if we insist on keeping our eyes closed to him.

8:22 **They came to Bethsaida, and some people brought a blind man and begged Jesus to touch him.**[NIV] Jesus and the disciples went back across the sea to Bethsaida. The miracle recorded in this section was recorded only by Mark and is a fitting story following the account of the disciples' persistent spiritual blindness in 8:14-21. We learn from John 1:44 that Bethsaida was Peter's hometown. Bethsaida Julias was in the territory of Herod Philip (6:45) on the northeastern shore of the Sea of Galilee. It was the size of a city but had the structure of an agricultural village, probably with a population of about fifteen thousand.

The healing of this blind man in Bethsaida and the healing of the deaf-mute (7:31-37) are recorded only in Mark's Gospel. These two miracles have several things in common: In both, Jesus took the man away from the crowd before performing the miracle, he used saliva, he touched him, and he did not publicize the event. This healing of the blind man is unique because it is the only record of Jesus healing in stages.

Once again, upon Jesus' arrival, people brought the sick to him. This time some people brought a blind man (obviously he needed to be brought because he would never find Jesus on his own), and they *begged Jesus to touch him.* They had faith that Jesus' touch would make their friend see again.

Don't miss the bridge from the story of the disciples' spiritual blindness to the story of the blind man being healed. Sight is a metaphor for understanding. Though they had different kinds of blindness, the disciples and the blind man could be given sight if they would have faith.

8:23 He took the blind man by the hand and led him out of the village; and when he had put saliva on his eyes and laid his hands on him, he asked him, "Can you see anything?"NRSV The miracles recorded in Mark are more often public than not; however, Mark recorded three more or less private miracles: raising the little girl from the dead (5:40-43), healing the deaf man with the speech impediment (7:32-35), and healing the *blind man,* recorded here. In this instance, Jesus *led him out of the village* by the hand. The people who had brought the blind man and some of the disciples probably went along. At times Jesus chose to avoid publicity and the crowds; in this case he may have wanted to give a lesson in "spiritual sight" to the disciples.

Some have placed a great deal of symbolic significance on Jesus' special handling of this miracle. They see the two-part healing as a type of parable, teaching that insight into salvation or one's spiritual life may be progressive for many converts. We may first discover Jesus as our Savior, then slowly grasp his lordship over our life. Others see this two-part healing as a dramatization of the disciples' understanding of Jesus. First they believed him to be the promised Messiah; then, after the Crucifixion and Resurrection, they more fully understood his work as the Son of God. The Bible text simply does not tell us about Jesus' intentions beyond healing the man. So we are left with several questions.

- We don't know why Jesus took the man by the hand personally. Another disciple could have done it. The blind man couldn't follow on his own, so Jesus led him. This teaches us servanthood because Jesus wasn't too proud to do it himself.

- We don't know why Jesus took the man out of the village. It may have been to establish a more personal one-to-one relation-ship with him or to overcome any passivity the man may have had to his ailment.

- We don't know why Jesus put saliva, or spit, on the man's eyes. We do know that spittle was commonly recognized in these times as having healing properties.

- We don't know why Jesus did the healing in two stages. It may have been because of the man's lack of faith or to show that spiritual sight may be incomplete but can be restored gradually and fully by faith. We do know that Jesus was not faltering in his power or daunted by the man's blindness. He healed the man fully. God is sovereign even if people and the church are slow to perceive it.

As in the miracle of healing the deaf man (7:32-35), Jesus com-municated with the blind man by his actions. Touch would be especially meaningful to a blind person. The blind man knew Jesus was doing something as he felt Jesus touch his eyes with the spittle. Jesus removed his hands and asked what the man could see.

8:24 And the man looked up and said, "I can see people, but they look like trees, walking."NRSV In answer to Jesus' question, the man replied that he saw people (probably the disciples and the people who brought him), but they were blurry, like trees. If the man had been blind from birth, he had never seen trees, but he knew the shapes from having touched them. This may suggest that all the technical apparatus for sight was in place by this stage, but the man's mental categories—cognitive and interpre-tive—were lacking.

The incomplete healing was not an indication of Jesus' inabil-ity to heal thoroughly the first time. Instead, it was a vivid teach-ing for the disciples. Sight was there, but it was not complete. The disciples too had spiritual sight, but it was far from com-plete. Jesus had rebuked the disciples for their lack of sight, but there was hope for them, just as there would be complete healing for this man.

8:25 Once more Jesus put his hands on the man's eyes. Then his eyes were opened, his sight was restored, and he saw every-thing clearly.NIV After Jesus touched the man a second time, the man's sight was perfectly restored. Perhaps Jesus healed the man gradually to build his faith so that he would believe Jesus for perfect vision. Jesus' question, "Can you see anything?" (8:23) indicates that Jesus sensed that something was wrong.

Jesus' words also may have been an encouragement for the man to believe with his whole heart in order to receive complete healing.

Scholars may ponder why Jesus did this miracle in two stages, but we would do well to consider this miracle from another angle. Mark gave a matter-of-fact record of this unusual healing, sharing the honesty and reliability of his account. We are not left to doubt that Jesus could heal; rather, we know that Jesus heals completely all the time.

8:26 **Jesus sent him home, saying, "Don't go into the village."**^{NIV} Jesus told the blind man to return home, but not to go into town or tell anyone about what had happened. Obviously people were going to find out, but Jesus did not want an immediate outpouring of sick people coming to him for healing. This gave Jesus time to move away from the area before the miracle was discovered. Jesus always had compassion on people in need, but he never lost sight of the fact that his mission was first and foremost the healing of people's souls. He did not want to be known as merely a healer or miracle worker. Jesus had asked others to be silent about their healings as well (see 1:44; 5:43; 7:36).

PUBLICIZING YOUR MINISTRY
Christians who do great things for God should follow Jesus' example. In effect, he said to the healed man, "Let's keep this one between us!"

Be cautious of Christian leaders who prance and strut over every moment of success that comes their way. Jesus' low-key style has the advantage of keeping pride and ego under control and of focusing instead on the heart of the matter, which is an intimate relationship between you and God, a relationship "just between us."

PETER SAYS JESUS IS THE MESSIAH / 8:27-30 / **109**

Mark made no secret of the purpose of his Gospel. He stated his central theme in the first sentence of his book: "The good news of Jesus Christ" (1:1 NRSV). In the first eight chapters, Mark built up the tension caused by lack of understanding of Jesus' identity. Jesus' family, the crowd, the religious leaders, and his own disciples did not really know who he was. Peter's exclamation, "You are the Messiah" (8:29 NRSV), and Jesus' confirmation of his true identity come at the middle—or apex—of the Gospel.

The previous eight chapters recorded enough evidence to make

Peter's confession reasonable. Further evidence in the Gospel reveals that Peter was saying more than he knew for sure. Matthew's parallel account of this incident includes Jesus' statement that Peter had made this declaration with the Holy Spirit's help. But Mark, presumably recalling Peter's own recollections, simply highlighted Peter's statement.

The final eight chapters of Mark's Gospel point to Jesus' death. From this point on, the journey leads to Jerusalem and to Jesus' crucifixion and resurrection. The full impact of Peter's declaration would not be reached until Jesus' resurrection. With that event, the central spotlight of history came to rest on the person of Christ.

8:27 Jesus went on with his disciples to the villages of Caesarea Philippi.NRSV A beautiful site on the northern shore of the Sea of Galilee, *Caesarea Philippi* was located about twenty-five miles north of Bethsaida. The city lay in the territory ruled by Philip (Herod Antipas's brother, mentioned in 6:17). The influence of Greek and Roman culture was everywhere. The city was primarily non-Jewish, known for its worship of Greek gods and its temples devoted to the ancient god Pan. When Philip became ruler, he rebuilt and renamed the city after Caesar Tiberius and himself. The city was originally called Caesarea, the same name as the capital city of Philip's brother Herod's territory. Jesus probably avoided the city itself but visited the *villages* surrounding it.

On the way he asked his disciples, "Who do people say that I am?"NRSV As Jesus and the disciples walked toward Caesarea Philippi, Jesus asked his disciples what they had heard from the people regarding his identity. This would be a springboard into his question recorded in 8:29.

8:28 They replied, "Some say John the Baptist; others say Elijah; and still others, one of the prophets."NIV The disciples answered Jesus' question with the common view that Jesus was one of the great prophets come back to life. This concurred with the record of the people's beliefs in 6:14-16. This belief may have stemmed from Deuteronomy 18:18, where God said he would raise up a prophet from among the people. (For the story of John the Baptist, see 1:1-11 and 6:14-29. For the story of Elijah, see 1 Kings 17–21 and 2 Kings 1–2.)

All of these responses were incorrect, revealing that Jesus' true identify was still unrecognized by the people. They didn't see that Jesus was the Messiah, the Son of God.

WHO DO YOU SAY JESUS IS?
Jesus asked the disciples who other people thought he was; then he asked them the same question. We must each answer this question for ourselves. T. S. Elliot criticized modern thinking when he said, "Jesus, now there was a man; we need more like him. Take Abraham Lincoln, for example."
     Was Jesus just a man with some good ideas, one of many spiritual leaders? Or was he the true God, the one mediator, our only source of life and peace with the Father? It is not enough to know what others say about Jesus: You must know, understand, and accept for yourself that he is the Messiah. You must move from curiosity to commitment, from admiration to adoration. If Jesus were to ask you this question, how would you answer? Is he your Lord and Messiah?

8:29 **He asked them, "But who do you say that I am?" Peter answered him, "You are the Messiah."**[NRSV] Mark's Gospel thus far has built up to this very question. Jesus had just recently asked the disciples, "Do you still not understand?" (8:21). Here they have their "final exam," their opportunity to show their understanding of Jesus, apart from what the crowds and religious leaders thought. The pointed question *"But who do you say that I am?"* was undoubtedly meant to hit Mark's readers between the eyes. Just as the disciples had to come to a personal understanding, acknowledgment, and acceptance of Jesus, so each person must do the same.

Peter, often the one to speak up when the others might be silent, declared what he had come to understand, *"You are the Messiah."* Other translations say, "You are the Christ." "Christ" is from the Greek; and "Messiah" is based on Hebrew—both mean "the Anointed One." Psalm 2:2 mentions "the Lord and his anointed," referring to the Messiah—the king whom God would provide to Israel, the king who would sit on David's throne forever. In his declaration, Peter revealed his belief in Jesus as the promised King and Deliverer. The problem now was to help these disciples understand the *kind* of king Jesus would be. Peter, and indeed all Israel, expected the Messiah to be a conqueror-liberator who would free the nation from Rome. Jesus would be a totally different kind of conqueror-liberator. He would conquer sin and free people from its grasp.

From this point on, Jesus spoke plainly and directly to his disciples about his death and resurrection. He began to prepare them for what was going to happen to him by telling them three times that he would soon suffer and die and then be raised back to life (8:31; 9:31; 10:33-34).

A HEARTFELT CONFESSION
In Matthew 16:17-19, Jesus congratulated Peter for having God's illumination in making his confession. For Peter, this confession was heartfelt and sincere. Jesus was poor, lacked honor or political clout, and was held in contempt by the religious authorities. Yet Peter affirmed Christ's deity without hesitation. Peter had zeal and good intentions, but in the next section (8:32-33) he would be rebuked. Peter did not understand why Jesus had to die on the cross.

We can learn from Peter to beware of pride over having the right words or the right beliefs. We may have partial insight and lack full substance. We can learn to be gracious to others who lack full understanding.

8:30 Jesus warned them not to tell anyone about him.NIV Jesus told his disciples *not to tell anyone* that he was the Messiah because at this point they didn't fully understand the significance of Peter's confession—nor would anyone else. Everyone still expected the Messiah to come as a conquering king. But even though Jesus was the Messiah, he still had to suffer, be rejected by the leaders, be killed, and rise from the dead. When the disciples saw all this happen to Jesus, they would understand what the Messiah had come to do. Only then would they be equipped to share the gospel around the world.

JESUS PREDICTS HIS DEATH THE FIRST TIME / 8:31–9:1 / **110**

Matthew, Mark, and Luke connect Peter's declaration that Jesus was the Messiah with the Lord's teaching about his crucifixion. This comes as no surprise. After all, messianic expectations were in the air. There was no shortage of people claiming to be the "Awaited One." A strong consensus had developed about the political role the Messiah would play once he made himself known. The idea that the Messiah would "save people from their sins" had gotten lost among the list of social and political evils that the Christ would correct. Ultimately, the people wanted a Messiah who would crush the Roman occupation and raise Israel to prominence among the nations.

Instead, Jesus explained that the Son of Man must die. Peter's response to Jesus clearly indicates how difficult it was for people to accept the idea of a suffering, dying Savior.

The Lord went on to give both the crowd and the disciples another glimpse of the "big picture." At some point, following Jesus would become costly. Only those whose allegiance to him exceeded their own love for life would discover the way to real living.

8:31 And He began to teach them that the Son of Man must suffer many things, and be rejected by the elders and chief priests and scribes, and be killed, and after three days rise again.[NKJV] This was the turning point in Jesus' instruction to his disciples. From then on he began teaching clearly and specifically what they could expect, so that they would not be surprised when it happened. Contrary to what they thought, Jesus did not come to set up an earthly kingdom *yet.* He would not be the conquering Messiah because he first had to *suffer, be rejected, be killed,* and *rise again.* But one day he would return in great glory to set up his eternal kingdom.

Son of Man was Jesus' preferred designation for himself (see also 2:10, 28) and the name most often used other than "Jesus" in the New Testament. He used it most often after Peter's confession of faith recorded in 8:29, and then usually when speaking to his disciples (see 8:38; 9:9, 12, 31; 10:33, 45; 13:26; 14:21, 41, 62). The Son of Man was the figure prophesied by Daniel to come as God's agent to gather his people and to judge. . . . In Mark, Son of Man brings out

- Jesus' authority—to forgive sin (2:10) and as Lord of the Sabbath (2:28);

- Jesus' suffering and resurrection (8:31; 9:9; 10:33);

- Jesus' future coming in power and glory to judge all human beings (8:38; 13:26; 14:62).

The title "Son of Man" emphasized Jesus as the vindicated, authoritative, and powerful agent of God.

Jesus' teaching that the Son of Man must suffer corresponds to Daniel's prophecies that God was in complete control of the plan for redemption: The Messiah would be cut off (Daniel 9:26); there would be a period of trouble (Daniel 9:27); and the king would come in glory (Daniel 7:13-14). The suffering also recalls Isaiah's prophecy of the suffering Servant in Isaiah 53. The fact of his being rejected looks back to the rejected "stone" in Psalm 118:22.

Jesus knew exactly from what quarter the rejection would come: the elders and chief priests and scribes. The *elders* were the leaders of the Jews who decided issues of religious and civil law. Each community had elders, and a group of them was included in the Council (or Sanhedrin) that met in Jerusalem. "Chief priests" refers not only to the present chief priest, but also to all those who formerly held the title and some of their family members. *Scribes* were the teachers of the law. These three groups made up the Sanhedrin, the Jewish supreme court that ultimately sentenced Jesus to be killed (14:53, 64). Despite all this, a light shone through Jesus' words, for he also mentioned that he would be raised from the dead. Yes, Jesus would die, but that would not be the end. For he would come back to life and then return as the conquering King.

The disciples were not ready for this. Despite the Old Testament prophecies, they were surprised that this popular man whom they now realized to be the true Messiah would first have to suffer many things. Jesus already had submitted to his mission as planned, and he understood exactly what that mission entailed. Mark made the point that following Jesus meant taking part in both his suffering and his glory. The disciples would endure the same suffering as their King and, like him, would be rewarded in the end.

8:32 He spoke plainly about this, and Peter took him aside and began to rebuke him.[NIV] Jesus *spoke plainly* about his coming suffering, death, and resurrection; that is, he did not speak in parables. The meaning of Jesus' words was unmistakable.

> Natural man never objects to the concept of a Messiah, provided it be a Messiah who commends himself to natural man. *Alan Cole*

This was too much for Peter. Jesus had spoken "plainly," but his news was most unwelcome. It sounded defeatist. If Jesus was going to die, what did this mean for the disciples? If he was truly the Messiah, then what was all this talk about being killed? So Peter took Jesus aside and *began to rebuke him.* The word for "rebuke" was used earlier of Jesus rebuking the demons (1:25; 3:12). It is a strong term meaning that Peter was rejecting Jesus' interpretation of the Messiah as a suffering figure.

AN UNCOMFORTABLE PART OF THE PLAN
Peter, Jesus' friend and devoted follower who had just eloquently proclaimed Jesus' true identity, sought to protect Jesus from the suffering he prophesied. But if Jesus hadn't suffered and died, Peter, and we, would have died in our sins. Great temptations can come from those who love us and seek to protect us. Be cautious of advice from a friend who says, "Surely God doesn't want you to face this." Sometimes suffering is the very means God is using to help us develop (Romans 5:3-5; James 1:2-4). Often our most difficult temptations come from those who want to protect us from suffering.

**8:33 But turning and looking at his disciples, he rebuked Peter
and said, "Get behind me, Satan! For you are setting your
mind not on divine things but on human things."**^{NRSV} Peter
often spoke for all the disciples. In singling Peter out for rebuke,
Jesus may have been addressing all of them indirectly. In his wilderness temptations, Jesus had been told that he could achieve
greatness without dying (Matthew 4:8-9). Peter, in his rebuke of
Jesus' words about dying, was saying the same thing. Peter had
just recognized Jesus as Messiah; here, however, he forsook
God's perspective and evaluated the situation from a human one.
Peter was speaking Satan's words, thus Jesus rebuked Peter with
the words *"Get behind me, Satan!"* Satan is always trying to get
us to leave God out of the picture and to focus on human concerns. God's plan included suffering and death for the Messiah.
This didn't make sense to Peter. Jesus had already dealt with the
temptation to bypass the Cross; he would fulfill his mission
exactly as planned.

Unknowingly, the disciples were trying to prevent Jesus from
going to the cross and thus fulfilling his mission on earth. The disciples were motivated by love and admiration for Jesus; nevertheless, their job was not to guide and protect Jesus, but to follow
him. Only after Jesus' death and resurrection would they fully understand why he had to die.

GOD'S PURPOSE
In this moment, Peter was not considering God's purposes, but
only his own natural human desires and feelings. Peter's previously recorded confession (8:29) contrasts with his self-
centered reaction. Peter wanted Christ to be king, but not the
suffering Servant prophesied in Isaiah 53. He was ready to
receive the glory of following the Messiah, but not the persecution. The Christian life is not a paved road to wealth and ease.
It often involves hard work, persecution, deprivation, and deep
suffering. Peter saw only part of the picture. Don't repeat
Peter's mistake. Satan wants to deter us from sacrifice and service by telling us that our difficulties are meaningless, our pain
is futile, and that evil will win anyway. Instead, focus on the
good that God can bring out of suffering and on the resurrection that follows crucifixion.

**8:34 When He had called the people to Himself, with His disciples
also, He said to them, "Whoever desires to come after Me, let
him deny himself, and take up his cross, and follow Me."**^{NKJV}
These words were addressed to *the people* in general, as well as
to the disciples. Jesus began to speak publicly of his identity as

the Messiah, but it was only the suffering aspect that was public; the final disclosure awaited the cross.

The words applied to the disciples and to all who want to *come after* Jesus—that is, to become a disciple and enter his fellowship. Those words include us. This statement offered special comfort to the Christians in Rome to whom Mark was writing, for they often faced persecution for their faith. Jesus invites every person to follow, but one who desires to follow him must have two attitudes: (1) a willingness to deny self and (2) a willingness to take up his or her cross.

To *deny* oneself means to surrender immediate material gratification in order to discover and secure one's true self and God's interests. It is a willingness to let go of selfish desires and earthly security. This attitude turns self-centeredness to God-centeredness.

To *take up [the] cross* was a vivid illustration of the humility and submission Jesus asked of his followers. When Jesus used this picture of his followers taking up their crosses to follow him, the disciples, the people, and the Romans (Mark's original audience) knew what taking up the cross meant. Death on a cross was a form of execution used by Rome for dangerous criminals. A prisoner carried his own cross to the place of execution, signifying submission to Rome's power. Following Jesus, therefore, meant identifying with Jesus and his followers, facing social and political oppression and ostracism, and no turning back. For some, taking up the cross might indeed mean death. But Jesus' words meant that his followers had to be prepared to obey God's Word and follow his will no matter what the consequences for the sake of the gospel (8:35). Soon after this, Jesus would take up his own cross. Jesus is speaking prophetically here as well.

COSTLY COMMITMENT
Christians follow their Lord by imitating his life and obeying his commands. To take up the cross meant to carry your own cross to the place where you would be killed. Many Galileans had been killed that way by the Romans. Applied to the disciples, to take up the cross meant to identify completely with Christ's message, even if death were to result. We must deny our selfish desires to use our time and money our own way and to choose our own direction in life without regard to Christ. Following Christ is costly now, but we are promised true victory and eternal rewards.

The initial decision to "come after" Christ and be his disciple is a once-for-all act. From then on the believer is no longer his or her own; that person belongs to Christ. To *follow* Christ is also a moment-by-moment decision, requiring denial of self and taking up one's cross. Following Jesus doesn't mean walking behind him, but taking the same road of sacrifice and service that he took. The blessing for us is that we can fellowship with him along the way.

8:35 **"For whoever desires to save his life will lose it, but whoever loses his life for My sake and the gospel's will save it."**NKJV The Christian life is a paradox: to attempt to *save* your life means only to *lose* it. The Greek word for "life" is *psuche* referring to the soul, the part of the person that includes the personality with all its dreams, hopes, and goals. A person who "saves" his or her life in order to satisfy desires and goals apart from God ultimately "loses" life. Not only does that person lose the eternal life offered only to those who believe and accept Christ as Savior, but he or she loses the fullness of life promised to those who believe.

By contrast, those who willingly "lose" their lives for the sake of Christ and of the gospel (that is, God's kingdom) actually "save" them. To lose one's life for Christ's sake refers to a person refusing to renounce Christ, even if the punishment were death. To lose one's life for the gospel's sake implies that the person is on trial for preaching and circulating the Christian message.

To be willing to put personal desires and life itself into God's hands means to understand that nothing that we can gain on our own in our earthly lives can compare to what we gain with Christ. Jesus wants us to *choose* to follow him rather than to lead a life of sin and self-satisfaction. He wants us to stop trying to control our own destiny and to let him direct us. This makes good sense because, as the Creator, Christ knows better than we do what real life is about. He asks for submission, not self-hatred; he asks us only to lose our self-centered determination to be in charge.

REAL VICTORY, REAL PROGRESS
Jesus would lose his physical life; the possibility of death was very real for the disciples as well. We may not be called to die for our faith, but real discipleship implies real commitment—pledging our whole existence to his service. If we try to save our physical life from death, pain, or discomfort, we may risk losing our true eternal life. If we protect ourselves from pain, we begin to die spiritually and emotionally. Our lives turn inward, and we lose our intended purpose. When we give our lives in service to Christ, however, we discover the real purpose of living.

8:36 "For what will it profit a man if he gains the whole world, and loses his own soul?"NKJV To reinforce his words in 8:35, Jesus asked his listeners a rhetorical question. What good would it be for a person to gain *the whole world* (that is, to have power or financial control over the entire world system of which Satan is the head) but to lose his or her soul

> He is no fool who gives what he cannot keep to gain what he cannot lose.
> *Jim Elliott*

(that is, to lose eternal life with God)? Every person will die, even those most powerful or most wealthy. If they have not taken care to "save" their lives for eternity with God, then they have gained nothing and have lost everything.

Jesus had faced this exact temptation in the wilderness: "The devil took him to a very high mountain and showed him all the kingdoms of the world and their splendor. 'All this I will give you,' he said, 'if you will bow down and worship me.' Jesus said to him, 'Away from me, Satan! For it is written: "Worship the Lord your God, and serve him only"'" (Matthew 4:8-10 NIV).

TRUE WEALTH
True wealth is, above all else, having eternal life. People will die in their sins if they reject Christ, because they are rejecting the only way to be rescued from sin. Sadly, many are so taken up with the values of this world that they are blind to the price-less gift Christ offers. Where are you looking? Don't focus on this world's values and miss what is most valuable—eternal life with God.

8:37 "Or what will a man give in exchange for his soul?"NKJV Many people spend all their energy seeking pleasure. Jesus said, however, that a world of pleasure centered on possessions, position, or power is ultimately worthless. Whatever a person has on earth is only temporary; it cannot be exchanged for his or her soul. If you work hard at getting what you want, you might eventually have a "pleasurable" life, but in the end you will find it hollow and empty. The answer to the question, then, is that nothing is of enough value that it can be exchanged for one's soul. Even if a person gained the world, that person would lose his or her soul—and the soul counts for eternity. No amount of money, power, or status can buy back a lost soul. Believers must be willing to make the pursuit of God more important than the selfish pursuit of pleasure. If we follow Jesus, we will know what it means to live abundantly now and to have eternal life as well.

8:38 **"Those who are ashamed of me and of my words in this adul-**
terous and sinful generation, of them the Son of Man will also
be ashamed when he comes in the glory of his Father with the
holy angels."[NRSV] Jesus constantly turned the world's perspective
upside down with talk of first and last, saving and losing. Here he
offered his listeners a choice. If they chose to be *ashamed* of
Jesus, Jesus would in turn be ashamed of them at his second coming (they would be rejected from eternal life with him). In the
Bible, "ashamed" means more than embarrassment. It refers to
the judgment of God: "[Idolmakers] will be put to shame" (Isaiah
44:11 NIV). It stands for deep and contrite repentance: "That they
may be ashamed of their sins" (Ezekiel 43:10 NIV). It can mean
submission before God: "Nations will see and be ashamed"
(Micah 7:16 NIV). When God judges unbelieving people, his
"being ashamed of them" means he will reject them.

By extension, those who were not ashamed of Jesus and his
words, in spite of the *adulterous and sinful generation* that
believed otherwise, would be accepted by Christ *when he comes*
in . . . glory. Many are fearless in business, battle, or sports but
cower at potential ridicule. Speak up for your faith, for your convictions, and for Christ.

LOSERS AND WINNERS
Peter was not happy to learn that Jesus would be humiliated
and crucified. That was not Peter's plan for the Messiah. We
can understand his feelings. Few people today want to identify
with a "loser." Like Peter, we fail to see the whole story, which
will conclude with a grand and spectacular climax of amazing
power and triumph—Jesus' return in glory.
  Have you been ashamed to identify with a "loser"? When
Jesus returns, who will be the loser? Take your stand for Jesus
now. On that day when he returns, you'll greet him as Savior,
friend, and Lord, as happy as a tired traveler rounding the bend
toward home.

Jesus was speaking in the third person, but was referring to
himself as the *Son of Man* who will judge when *he comes* with
his Father and the angels. Jesus Christ has been given the authority to judge all the earth (Romans 14:9-11; Philippians 2:9-11).
Although his judgment is already working in our lives, there is a
future final judgment when Christ returns (see Matthew 25:31-
46) to review and evaluate everyone's life. (See 1 Thessalonians
5:4-11 on how we are to live until Jesus returns and 2 Thessalonians 1:5-10 on how God will judge those who trouble us.) This
judgment will not be confined to unbelievers; Christians too will

be judged. Their eternal destiny is secure, but Jesus will review how they handled gifts, opportunities, and responsibilities in order to determine their heavenly rewards. At the time of judgment, God will deliver the righteous and condemn the wicked. Rejecting Christ may help us escape shame for the time being, but it will guarantee an eternity of shame later.

9:1 And he said to them, "I tell you the truth, some who are standing here will not taste death before they see the kingdom of God come with power."[NIV] When Jesus said some would not *taste death* (die) before seeing the coming of the kingdom, he may have been referring

- to Peter, James, and John, who would witness the Transfiguration a few days later;

- to all who would witness the Resurrection and Ascension; and

- to all who would take part in the spread of the church after Pentecost.

Many people reading this passage have been troubled because they think Jesus was promising the disciples would not die before Jesus came back to set up his glorious kingdom. But since history tells us that the disciples did die before his second coming, this passage has to be interpreted differently. Jesus' transfiguration, which immediately follows (9:2-8), was a preview of that coming glory.

In the Transfiguration, Peter, James, and John saw Jesus' glory, identity, and power as the Son of God. In 2 Peter 1:16-18, Peter definitely says, "We told you about the power and coming of our Lord Jesus Christ . . . we were eyewitnesses of his majesty" (NIV). Thus, certain disciples *were* eyewitnesses to the power and glory of Christ's kingdom. Jesus' point was that his listeners would not have to wait for another, future Messiah because the kingdom was among them, and it would soon come in power.

Mark 9:2-50

Jesus revealed some of his most unusual demonstrations of power and divinity to his disciples alone. He stood up in their partly swamped boat and took command of the wind and the waves. Later, they saw him walk on water. On this occasion, he took three of them to an isolated spot and allowed them to witness his appearance without some of the limitations of his humanity. After teaching them the rigors of self-denial, he gave them a reassuring glimpse of his glory.

The disciples struggled to completely understand Jesus' identity. Eventually they relied upon their experiences as eyewitnesses. Note, for instance, Peter's train of thought in his sermon in Acts 2: "Jesus of Nazareth, a man attested to you by God with deeds of power, wonders, and signs that God did through him among you, as you yourselves know" (Acts 2:22 NRSV); "This Jesus God raised up, and of that all of us are witnesses" (Acts 2:32 NRSV). The disciples certainly were not easily convinced that Jesus was God's Son. Attempts by modern critics to view them as simpleminded men who were easily duped contradict the Gospel reports. Those accounts reflect the disciples' amazement over Jesus' power and their reluctance to jump to conclusions. It would be arrogant to claim that we would have been more easily convinced by Jesus if we had been in their place.

God relates to men and women today as he did in Mark's Gospel. Those who actually walked with Jesus were never forced to believe in him, but were invited to do so from the moment he called them. After the Resurrection, they really "saw" Christ, and they looked back at everything else they had seen and heard in a very different light. If you have trusted in Jesus Christ, how has that decision changed the way you look at your past? How can you share your story with others?

9:2-3 Six days later, Jesus took with him Peter and James and John, and led them up a high mountain apart, by them-

selves.NRSV Rarely did Mark give exact times in his narrative, so his definite *six days later* is significant. This reference probably recalls Exodus 24:16, where it is recorded that Moses waited for six days before meeting the Lord on Mount Sinai. The words also tie into 9:1, where Jesus had told the people that "some who are standing here will not taste death before they see the kingdom of God come with power" (NIV). If Jesus had been referring to his coming transfiguration, then three of those with Jesus at the time (Peter, James, and John) *did* get a glimpse of the kingdom during this significant event. While Luke says "about eight days" had passed (Luke 9:28), his was a more general reckoning, measuring partial days as whole days. Matthew also wrote that this event occurred six days after Jesus' previous conversation (see Matthew 17:1).

Jesus singled out *Peter and James and John* for this special revelation of his glory and purity. Perhaps they were the ones most ready to understand and accept this great truth. These three disciples comprised the inner circle of the group of Twelve. They were among the first to hear Jesus' call (1:16-19), they headed the list of disciples (3:16), they were present at certain healings where others were excluded (5:37), and they were with Jesus as he prayed in Gethsemane (14:33). Seeing Jesus transfigured was an unforgettable experience for Peter (see 2 Peter 1:16).

Jesus took the disciples *up a high mountain*—either Mount Hermon or Mount Tabor. Mount Hermon is about twelve miles northeast of Caesarea Philippi (where Jesus had been in 8:27); Mount Tabor is in Galilee. A mountain was often associated with closeness to God and readiness to receive his words. God had appeared to both Moses (Exodus 24:12-18) and Elijah (1 Kings 19:8-18) on mountains.

And he was transfigured before them, and his clothes became dazzling white, such as no one on earth could bleach them.NRSV The Transfiguration was a brief glimpse of Jesus' true glory, a special revelation of his divinity to Peter, James, and John. This was God's divine affirmation of everything Jesus had done and was about to do. It reminds us of the glory Moses experienced on Mount Sinai when for six days the glory of the Lord appeared to him in a cloud. Jesus had spoken to the disciples about his impending death, and they had not understood (8:31). He had assured them that "whoever desires to save his life will lose it, but whoever loses his life for My sake and the gospel's will save it" (8:35 NKJV). The disciples wondered how this could be true in light of Jesus' death. The Transfiguration clearly revealed not only that they were correct in believing Jesus to be the Messiah (8:29), but that their commitment was well placed and their eternity was secure. Jesus was truly the Messiah, the divine Son of God.

The Greek word translated "transfigured" is *metamorphothe,* from which we get our word "metamorphosis." The verb refers to an outward change that comes from within. It was not a change merely in appearance, but it was a complete change into another form. On earth Jesus appeared as a man, a poor carpenter from Nazareth turned itinerant preacher. But at the Transfiguration, Jesus' body was transformed into the glorious radiance that he had before coming to earth (John 17:5; Philippians 2:6) and which he will have when he returns in glory to establish his kingdom (Revelation 1:14-15). The glory of Jesus' deity came from within; it was inherent within him because he was and is divine, God's only Son. The glory shone out from him and his homespun clothes *became dazzling white, such as no one on earth could bleach them.* The white was not of this earth; it was a white that no human had seen. The words, unique to Mark's Gospel, reflect an eyewitness report (probably Peter's). These were the radiant robes of God, clothing "white as snow" (Daniel 7:9). The expression "dazzling white" suggests supreme glory, purity, and holiness. Matthew and Luke also described Jesus' radiant face (Matthew 17:2; Luke 9:29). Peter, James, and John saw what Jesus will look like when he returns to bring his kingdom. See Revelation 1:9-18 for John's description of the glory of Christ.

A GLIMPSE OF HIS GLORY
Through art, stories, and motion pictures, people try to portray what they imagine heaven will be like. Here Jesus gives a glimpse to three special disciples. They were amazed!
    What did they learn? First, that heaven operates at an energy level unknown to earth. It dazzles, and we need a welder's eyeshade to glimpse at it. Second, Jesus is the center of it. This humble, suffering servant is the source of heaven's all-surpassing glory and light. Third, people are invited to share it: people who follow God (like Moses), people who witness about God's message (like Elijah), and people just like you, transformed by this amazing power, gladdened by this light. To face your duties and trials, you need a glimpse of his glory. Imagine what awaits you!

9:4 And there appeared to them Elijah with Moses, who were talking with Jesus.^{NRSV} Jesus took Peter, James, and John to the top of a mountain to show them who he really was—not just a great prophet, but God's own Son. Moses and Elijah were considered the two greatest prophets in the Old Testament. They were the two primary figures associated with the Messiah (Moses was his predictor and Elijah was his precursor), and they were the only two people to see theophanies—i.e., special appearances of God (Exodus 24; 1 Kings 19). *Moses* represented the Law, or the Old Covenant. He had written the Pentateuch and had predicted the coming of a great prophet (Deuteronomy 18:15-19). *Elijah* represented the prophets who had foretold the coming of the Messiah (Malachi 4:5-6). Moses' and Elijah's presence with Jesus confirmed Jesus' messianic mission to fulfill God's law and the words of God's prophets (Matthew 5:17). Their appearance also removed any thought that Jesus was a reincarnation of Elijah or Moses. He was not merely one of the prophets. As God's only Son, he far surpassed them in authority and power. Also, their ability to talk to Jesus supports the promise of the resurrection of all believers. Colossians 3:4 says, "When Christ, who is your life, appears, then you also will appear with him in glory" (NIV).

9:5 Peter said to Jesus, "Rabbi, it is good for us to be here. Let us put up three shelters—one for you, one for Moses and one for Elijah."NIV Elijah and Moses were talking with Jesus (9:4), and there is no indication that Peter was addressed. But Peter impetuously interrupted to suggest making *three shelters,* one for each of them. He may have had in mind the Feast of Tabernacles, where shelters were set up to commemorate the Exodus, God's deliverance from slavery in Egypt when the Israelites lived in temporary lean-tos or shelters as they traveled (Leviticus 23:42-43). Peter may have thought that God's kingdom had come when he saw Jesus' glory. Peter had forgotten (or was hoping to put aside) Jesus' words that suffering and death would come before glory. Peter saw the fulfillment of Christ's glory for a moment. He wanted the experience to continue, so he tried to capture it without going through Christ's suffering. Also, Peter mistakenly made all three men equal. He had missed Jesus' true identity as God himself.

Peter called Jesus *Rabbi* (Master, Teacher), obviously missing what Jesus was showing them by his revealed glory. His words *it is good for us to be here* revealed a further lack of understanding. He desired to prolong the experience, to keep Moses and Elijah there with them. But that was not the point of the experience nor the lesson to be learned by it.

9:6 (He did not know what to say, they were so frightened.)NIV This parenthetical comment, perhaps added by Peter himself, describes what Peter felt. Having awakened from sleep (Luke

9:32) to a dazzling display of Jesus' glory and the visitation of
two ancient prophets, the three disciples were *frightened*. Impetu-
ous Peter should have only observed and learned. Instead, he
spoke inappropriately because *he did not know what to say.*

LET US HELP . . . WE CAN BUILD
Poor Peter takes a lot of heat for blurting out words which, in
retrospect, show how far out in left field he still was. It began
with his startled fear. He may have reacted with his instinct to
do something or his desire to help, or perhaps with his hope
that a great messianic era would begin that night, the kind
Israel had always dreamed of.
  The better part of wisdom, for Peter and for us, is to wait for
understanding before getting all worked up about offering one's
impressive plans and ambitions. Christ has more to teach us.
  Jesus is God's Son, the Messiah, our Savior. In the face of
his glory, our first response should be to listen and learn. In
churches and in families, that's a good idea, too. In our urge to
help, we speak too quickly. In our tendency to direct the show,
we nominate ourselves as program director before we've understood the program. Jesus wants our worship now; the time for
action will come later.

**9:7 Then a cloud appeared and enveloped them, and a voice
came from the cloud: "This is my Son, whom I love. Listen to
him!"**[NIV] A cloud suddenly appeared and enveloped this group on
the mountain. This was not a vapor cloud, but was, in fact, the
glory of God. This was the cloud that had guided Israel out of
Egypt (Exodus 13:21), that had appeared to the people in the desert (Exodus 16:10; 24:15-18; 34:5; 40:34-38), that had appeared
to Moses (Exodus 19:9), and that had filled the temple with the
glory of the Lord (1 Kings 8:10).

God's voice came from the cloud, singling out Jesus from
Moses and Elijah as the long-awaited Messiah who possessed
divine authority. In the same way that God's voice in the cloud
over Mount Sinai had given authority to his law (Exodus 19:9),
God's voice at the Transfiguration gave singular authority to
Jesus' words.

As he had done at Jesus' baptism, God was giving verbal
approval of his Son (see 1:11). At that time, the message had
been addressed to Jesus ("You are my beloved Son") and had benefited John the Baptist; here, the voice spoke to Peter and the
other two disciples ("This is my Son"). God was identifying
Jesus as his dearly loved Son and the promised Messiah.

The voice then commanded Peter and the others to *listen* to
Jesus and not to their own ideas and desires about what lay

ahead. The command recalled the prophecy of Deuteronomy 18:15: "The LORD your God will raise up for you a prophet like me from among your own brothers. You must listen to him" (NIV), and it identified Jesus as the Messiah, the fulfillment of that prophecy. The Greek verb *akouete,* translated "listen," means not merely hearing, but the hearing that leads to obeying what is heard.

LISTENING, SPEAKING
God the Father puts love at the center of his relationship to Jesus. He said, "This is my Son, whom I love" (9:7). That's good news for us, for the love from their relationship reaches out to us today. God also gave the command to "listen to him!" God gave all Jesus' disciples the same profound love, as well as an important message to hear. God intended for all people to listen to Jesus.

We cannot regard Jesus as merely one rabbi among equals, but as God's only unique beloved Son. What religious leader and authority has accomplished more in organization, government, law, and miraculous events than Moses? Yet Moses deferred to Jesus. What prophet or reformer has done more miracles or shown more zeal than Elijah? Yet Elijah deferred to Jesus. Don't overlook what Jesus says—listen to him.

9:8 Suddenly, when they looked around, they no longer saw anyone with them except Jesus.[NIV] Peter may have wanted to keep Jesus and Elijah and Moses there in glory on the mountainside, but his desire was wrong. The event was merely a glimpse of what was to come—no more. Thus *suddenly* the glory and the prophets were gone. Jesus alone would accomplish the mission. We still have the words of Moses and the acts of Elijah recorded in Scripture, but the men are gone. Yet Jesus is still with us. May God give us vision to see only him. Jesus had been revealed as God's glorious divine Son, but his mission on earth still had to be completed.

9:9 As they were coming down the mountain, he ordered them to tell no one about what they had seen, until after the Son of Man had risen from the dead.[NRSV] Jesus told Peter, James, and John *to tell no one about what they had seen,* presumably not even the other disciples because they would not fully understand it, *until after the Son of Man had risen from the dead.* This is the only injunction to silence with a time limit. It does suggest that once the temporary time limit had expired, they would not need to keep Jesus' identity secret anymore. Furthermore, after the Resurrection, these three disciples would understand the Transfiguration and be able to correctly interpret and proclaim it. They would then realize that only through dying could Jesus show his power over death and his authority to be King of all. The disciples could not be powerful witnesses for God until they had grasped this truth. It was natural for the disciples to be confused because they could not see into the future. They knew that Jesus was the Messiah, but they had much more to learn about the significance of his death and resurrection.

DESPERATE REALITY
Descending from their mountaintop high, the three disciples come back to startling reality. They could not tell what they had seen (yet), and they could not presume that anything had altered the suffering Jesus must undergo. In a word, God's way of introducing the Messiah differed radically from all their expectations: He must suffer and die, then be resurrected.
   Mark's Roman readers could take a lot of comfort from this verse. During the new era of God's "last days," they would suffer too. Around the world today, Christians do not become disciples without the call to bear the cross and to respond to the world's anger with love, not hostility. Your scar of suffering will be your badge of discipleship that leads, by promise, to a wonderful future.

9:10 **They kept the matter to themselves, discussing what "rising from the dead" meant.**[NIV] Jesus had said to keep quiet about the Transfiguration until he "had risen from the dead" (9:9). They did so, for Mark records that the three disciples *kept the matter to themselves.* These men knew the termination date for their silence—when Jesus rose from the dead. But they didn't understand what "rising from the dead" meant. They certainly believed in a future resurrection, but Jesus clearly was speaking of some other event, something that would happen to only him. The necessity of Jesus' suffering and death was beyond their grasp. They understood it for the end of the world, but not for the Son of Man. They dared not think about Jesus dying, so they could not comprehend "rising again." Even when Peter and John saw the empty tomb, "they did not understand . . . that he must rise from the dead" (John 20:9 NRSV).

9:11 **Then they asked him, "Why do the scribes say that Elijah must come first?"**[NRSV] The appearance of Elijah on the mountain caused a question in the disciples' minds. Based on Malachi 4:5-6, the Jewish scribes believed that Elijah had to appear before the Messiah to usher in the messianic age. Elijah had appeared on the mountain, but he had not come in person to prepare the people

for the Messiah's arrival (especially in the area of repentance).
The disciples fully believed that Jesus was the Messiah, but they
wondered where Elijah was, for he *must come first.* These disciples may have hoped that if Elijah were to come and restore all
things (9:12), then perhaps Jesus' suffering and death would not
be required.

It was difficult for the disciples to grasp the idea that their Messiah would have to suffer. The Jews who studied the Old Testament prophecies expected the Messiah to be a great king, like
David, who would overthrow the enemy, Rome. Their vision was
limited to their own time and experience. They could not understand that the values of God's eternal kingdom were different
from the values of the world. They wanted relief from their present problems. But deliverance from sin is far more important than
deliverance from physical suffering or political oppression. Our
understanding of and appreciation for Jesus must go beyond what
he can do for us here and now.

THAT IS THE QUESTION
This question posed a real problem for the disciples. Elijah had
to appear to set things right before the Messiah came. If all is
set right, why this talk about suffering, death, and resurrection?
The incongruity baffled them. Yet Jesus discussed their questions with them.

Is it permissible to question the Bible? to talk about incongrui-
ties? to ask for answers?

Jesus apparently thought so because he answered the question with another of his own, an even more direct approach to
the riddle of the Messiah's suffering. Then he gave an astounding declaration that forced the disciples to acknowledge his
divine authority.

Before those seeking Christ are fully persuaded, they may
have many questions. Many people need time to process and
absorb all the new realizations about Jesus. Allow them time for
discussion and regard each question as significant as you lead
them to faith.

**9:12 Jesus replied, "To be sure, Elijah does come first, and restores
all things. Why then is it written that the Son of Man must
suffer much and be rejected?"**[NIV] Jesus explained to the disciples that the scribes were correct in their interpretation that Elijah
would come before the Messiah and restore all things by bringing
spiritual renewal (see Malachi 4:5-6). But Jesus answered the
implicit question regarding his own suffering. The fact that Elijah
would come and restore all things would not change the plan of
salvation that would require the suffering and rejection of the Son

of Man. That the Messiah would *suffer much and be rejected* was *written* in Scripture (for example, Psalm 22:14, 16-17; Isaiah 53:1-12). The prophecies would not have been written if they were not going to come true. Jesus was showing them the close connection between the Cross, the Transfiguration, and the messianic passages in the Bible. He was also reminding them of what he said in 8:33. If they rejected the reality of his suffering, they would not have in mind the things of God.

> Trust wholly in Christ. Rely altogether on His sufferings. *John Wycliffe*

9:13 **"But I tell you that Elijah has come, and they did to him whatever they pleased, as it is written about him."**NRSV Elijah was supposed to come first; Jesus explained that, in fact, Elijah had already come. Mark didn't say it, but Matthew explained that "the disciples understood that he was speaking to them about John the Baptist" (Matthew 17:13 NRSV).

Jesus was referring to John the Baptist, not to the Old Testament prophet Elijah. John the Baptist took on Elijah's prophetic role—boldly confronting sin and pointing people to God. Malachi had prophesied that a prophet like Elijah would come (Malachi 4:5). John the Baptist had come and had "restored all things" just as Malachi had foretold. He had come like Elijah to prepare the way for the Messiah's first coming (1:1-4); Elijah himself will reappear before Jesus' second coming (see Revelation 11).

As "Elijah" then, John the Baptist's work of restoration also involved suffering. Elijah was severely persecuted by King Ahab and Queen Jezebel and fled for his life (1 Kings 19). John the Baptist also suffered when Herod and Herodias *did to him whatever they pleased,* ultimately leading to his death (6:14-29). All of this occurred in God's plan; rejection never surprises him, for it happened *as it is written.* The religious leaders rejected John the Baptist (Luke 7:30), the Messiah's herald; thus, they would ultimately reject the Messiah himself. This further supports Jesus' words to the disciples that suffering is the necessary prelude to glory. There would be no easy road for true followers of Jesus.

JESUS HEALS A DEMON-POSSESSED BOY / 9:14-29 / **112**

When they descended from the mountaintop of transfiguration to the flatland of common experience, the three disciples and Jesus found a scene of confusion. The other disciples had felt Christ's absence in a humiliating way. They had been asked to perform a miracle in his name but had failed.

Modern attempts to diagnose the boy's condition as epilepsy do not alleviate the need for a miracle; nor do they eliminate the possibility that demonic possession may have taken the form of this disease. Interestingly, the demon kept its cover of muteness and deafness until it was ejected, at which time it "shrieked" (9:26 NIV).

In any case, this instance became a testing of faith, both for the child's father as well as for the disciples. When the father expressed to Jesus, "I do believe; help me overcome my unbelief!" (9:24 NIV), he represented the deepest trust of a human. An honest self-examination of our faith may reveal more lack than substance. But Christ regards even our weak faith. After all, it is not the quantity of our faith that makes the greatest difference, but the quality of him in whom our faith rests.

9:14 When they came to the disciples, they saw a great crowd around them, and some scribes arguing with them.NRSV Jesus, Peter, James, and John came down from the mountain and returned to the other nine disciples (Luke 9:37 says this occurred "the next day"). They came upon a crowd that surrounded the disciples and the scribes in a heated argument. The nature of the argument is not stated, but we can assume that the scribes were arguing with the disciples about their power and authority, or the power and authority of their Master, because the disciples had tried and failed to cast out a demon (9:17-18).

DOWN IN THE VALLEY
Jesus did not stay on the mountaintop. On the mountain, Jesus shone with divine glory; in the city he confronted doubt, bewilderment, sickness, and powerlessness. Why not stay on the mountain? Because he responded in compassion to us. He obeyed God the Father's will; thus, he returned to our world to deal with our sinful condition by his death and resurrection.

Jesus was all God and all man; therefore, he lived both on the mountain of transcendent glory and also in the city of great need. Christians today need to worship and pray, but they must also go out into the needy world to serve, work, confront, and intercept Satan just as Jesus did. We must not neglect prayer or service. Both are required of all who follow Jesus.

Religious leaders, including scribes and Pharisees, had been following Jesus for some time (for the last encounter, see 8:11-12). They apparently arrived on this scene in Jesus' absence and were quite delighted at the disciples' inability to perform the miracle (6:7).

**9:15 When the whole crowd saw him, they were immediately over-
come with awe, and they ran forward to greet him.**^{NRSV} Jesus'
popularity with the people had not waned. When he unexpectedly
arrived on the scene, the people ran to greet him. Their "wonder"
(NIV) at his very presence is a new twist and may indicate a glim-
mer of understanding on the part of the people. Usually they
were in awe of his teaching and miracles; here they were in awe
at his very presence with them (see also 1:27; 5:20). It is unlikely
that the awe would be caused by his radiant face, such as Moses
had when he returned from receiving the law from God (Exodus
34:29). If Jesus' appearance had been spectacular, it would have
contradicted his instructions to his disciples in 9:9 not to tell anyone about what had occurred until after his resurrection.

**9:16 He asked them, "What are you arguing about with
them?"**^{NRSV} We cannot be sure who *them* refers to. It may have
been the scribes. The word for "arguing" means "disputing," a
word often used with the scribes. Jesus may have asked the question of the crowd that had run forward to greet him, assuming
that everyone was involved in the fracas. Besides, a man in the
crowd answered (9:17).

**9:17 A man in the crowd answered, "Teacher, I brought you my
son, who is possessed by a spirit that has robbed him of
speech."**^{NIV} The answer regarding the nature of the argument
came from *a man in the crowd,* the father of the demon-
possessed boy. Respectfully calling Jesus *Teacher,* he explained
that he had come looking for Jesus to heal his son who was possessed by an evil spirit, making him unable to utter any sound
(and he could not hear, see 9:25). This was not just a case of deafness and muteness; it was the work of an evil spirit, as the man
explained.

TRAPPED
Without the ability to speak or hear, this sick son could not connect with the outside world. His desperate father could not
know him. The boy's life had been reduced to tenuous survival.
    How typical of Satan to isolate a person, to trap this child in a
body and deprive him of human connection. Satan robbed his
speech and sought to totally destroy him. This boy had no
future, no possibility of even learning to pray, apart from a
miracle. Satan would even attempt to ruin the family with the
burden of caring for their son.
    We must be on guard for Satan's attacks. His is not merely
an alternate way of life, an option of free choice. His desire is
always to destroy.

9:18 **"Whenever it seizes him, it throws him to the ground. He foams at the mouth, gnashes his teeth and becomes rigid. I asked your disciples to drive out the spirit, but they could not."**NIV The symptoms described by the father sound much like an epileptic convulsion, but the destructive intent of the demon described in 9:22 reveals that this was more than mere epilepsy. Mark stressed the dramatic effects of the demon possession four times (9:18, 20, 22, 26) and showed the great conflict between Jesus and the demons. Although they aggressively displayed their power, Jesus' supernatural power is far greater. Of the thirteen healing stories in Mark's Gospel, four have to do with exorcism of demons.

Having heard of Jesus' power to cast out demons, the father had come to Jesus, hoping for a cure for his son. Not being able to find Jesus, he had asked the disciples *to drive out the spirit,* an appropriate request since the disciples had been given this power and had recently returned from a preaching tour where they had demonstrated that power (6:7, 13).

The disciples could not drive out the demon, however. This perplexed and upset them (Jesus explained why in 9:28-29). Mark recorded this story to show that the battle with Satan is a difficult, ongoing struggle. Victory over sin and temptation comes through faith in Jesus Christ, never through our own efforts (see John 15:5).

The disciples' powerlessness to drive out the demon had apparently caused a commotion with the crowd and an argument with the prevalent and nosy scribes (9:14) who were seeking to discredit Jesus in any way possible.

THE CONTRAST
As the disciples came down from the mountain with Jesus, they passed from a reassuring experience of God's presence to a frightening experience of evil. The beauty they had just seen must have made the ugliness seem even uglier. As our spiritual vision improves and allows us to see and understand God better, we will also be able to see and understand evil better. We would be overcome by its horror if we did not have Jesus with us to take us through it safely. Don't be afraid to confront evil and suffering, no matter how ugly or horrible. Jesus goes with you.

9:19 **He answered him and said, "O faithless generation, how long shall I be with you? How long shall I bear with you? Bring him to Me."**NKJV Jesus cried out in exasperation (see 3:5; 8:12). He was fed up with unbelief. His unusual words carry a biting rebuke. They parallel Moses' frustration as intercessor for God's people (Deuteronomy 32:5, 20) and portray God's frustration with his people (Numbers 14:11; Isaiah 63:8-10). The disciples had been given the authority to do the healing, but they had not yet learned how to appropriate God's power. Jesus' frustration was with the unbelieving and unresponsive generation, including the crowd, the teachers of the law (scribes), the man, and the nine disciples. His disciples merely reflected that attitude of unbelief so prevalent in the society. The disciples were not singled out for criticism because Jesus did not rebuke them (9:28-29), but merely answered their question. Jesus would not leave the young boy in the power of the demon so he told the father to bring the boy.

> It is time that the Christian recover the consciousness of belonging to a minority and of often being in opposition to what is obvious, plausible, and natural for "the world." It is time to find again the courage of nonconformism, the capacity to oppose many of the trends of the surrounding culture.
> *Cardinal Ratzinger*

9:20 So they brought him. When the spirit saw Jesus, it immediately threw the boy into a convulsion. He fell to the ground and rolled around, foaming at the mouth.[NIV] The young boy was brought to Jesus. When the evil spirit saw Jesus, it knew that its rule over the boy would soon end. The demon responded with one last attack, throwing the boy to the ground, showing its contempt for and rebellion against Jesus.

PITIFUL POSTURING
Watch this demon demonstrate. It's as if the demon wants one more round of child's play before the end—an exercise in futility, one final shudder of pitiful posturing.

When Satan snarls, we need not fear. Behind every cynical threat is God's sure victory, coming soon. Satan may throw us in a whirl, but it's only a last gasp before the word of Jesus brings relief and wholeness. Trust in that word. You are safe in Jesus' care.

9:21-22 Jesus asked the father, "How long has this been happening to him?"[NRSV] While it may seem odd that Jesus would ask this question, Jesus asked it not for his own sake, but for the father's sake. By answering the question, the father was indicating just what a difficult and seemingly hopeless case this was. Jesus was truly the man's only hope.

And he said, "From childhood. It has often cast him into the fire and into the water, to destroy him; but if you are able to do anything, have pity on us and help us."^{NRSV} The boy had been possessed by the demon for some time. That this was not merely epilepsy is revealed in the demon's destructive intent as it *often cast him into the fire and into the water* (compare this incident with the demons described in 5:5). The poor father had probably saved his son's life numerous times, constantly having to watch the boy in order to protect him. Beyond that he had been unable to do anything.

The father had brought the son to the disciples, only to be disappointed in their inability to cast out the demon. Perhaps the demon was too strong or had been in possession of the boy for too long, or the disciples really didn't have the power, he may have thought. In any case, the failure of the disciples had cast a shadow of doubt on the ability of their Master. Thus, the father pled that if Jesus was *able to do anything,* would he please have pity on them both. The father used the word "us," showing that he identified with his son's suffering and would also benefit from Jesus' help.

9:23 Jesus said to him, "If you are able!—All things can be done for the one who believes."^{NRSV} The father's words in 9:22 revealed his own doubt regarding Jesus' ability to heal his son. But Jesus repeated the father's words and turned them around to put doubt in the right place. In a sense, Jesus was saying, "If *I am* able to do *anything?* I can do *all things*—but it depends on whether *you* believe that I can." Spiritual power comes only when a person turns from self to God in faith. Then the possibilities are limitless: *All things can be done.* This father had placed limits on God's power.

Jesus' words do not mean that we can automatically obtain anything we want if we just think positively. Jesus meant that anything is *possible* if we believe because nothing is too difficult for God, even when our experience seems to indicate otherwise. We cannot have everything for which we pray as if by magic; but with faith, we can have everything we need to serve Christ. We are free to ask whatever we want, as long as we realize that God will answer according to his will (1 John 3:21-22; 5:14). When we will what he wills, then we truly will have the mind of Christ and can ask anything, being assured of God's answers (see also John 14:13-14; 15:7).

9:24 Immediately the father of the child cried out and said with tears, "Lord, I believe; help my unbelief!"^{NKJV} Contrary to the

patterns of confusion and unbelief the disciples had displayed, this
father modeled the faith required of true discipleship. The father immediately understood Jesus' meaning. From calling Jesus
"Teacher" at first (9:17), the man here called him "Lord." He had
not meant to doubt the Master. With
Jesus' words to the man about his need to | When man is bereft of
believe, the man *immediately* answered | every security, the reality
"I believe," declaring his faith in Jesus | of hope opens wide
power. Then he added honestly and hum- | before him. *Jacques Ellul*
bly, *"Help my unbelief!"* Like the Syro-
phoenician woman who came to Jesus humbly asking for help
(7:25-30), this man realized that he had nothing in himself to make
him worthy of having Jesus answer his request; yet he had come.
He acknowledged that his faith was as weak as his exhausted and
distressed body. At the feet of the Master, the man cried out with
tears, confessing both his faith and its weakness.

The man came to the right place. The attitude of trust and confidence that the Bible calls "belief" or "faith" (Hebrews 11:1, 6)
is not something we can obtain without help. Faith is a gift from
God (Ephesians 2:8-9). No matter how much faith we have, we
never reach the point of perfection. Faith is not stored away like
money in the bank. Growing in faith is a constant process of
daily renewing our trust in Jesus.

A LITTLE FAITH, A LITTLE HELP
This father was an honest man. He knew that he needed help
to cross the last bridge before his son would be healed: faith.
The father asked Jesus for the help that all of us need.
   Jesus did not require a huge stockpile of faith from this man.
In Matthew's version of the story, Jesus said that even faith the
size of a mustard seed would suffice. Jesus simply wanted the
man to realize what this miracle involved, and what its impact
should be in his family: growing faith.
   Faith and unbelief lie mixed in our hearts. We must foster
faith and resist unbelief. To do so, focus on Christ's ability, recognize your own inability, and call on the faith and prayers of
others. Ask Jesus daily for stronger faith.

**9:25 When Jesus saw that a crowd was running to the scene, he
rebuked the evil spirit. "You deaf and mute spirit," he said, "I
command you, come out of him and never enter him
again."**[NIV] It seems from the text that Jesus must have withdrawn,
away from the crowd, with the father and the boy (and probably
the disciples), as he had done with other healings (as in 7:33;
8:23). Jesus tried to keep the miracle from becoming a circus; so

when he saw people coming, he quickly rebuked the spirit, commanding it to come out and never return.

9:26 After crying out and convulsing him terribly, it came out, and the boy was like a corpse, so that most of them said, "He is dead."NRSV The demon came out of the boy, but in its rage it convulsed the boy terribly one last time (see also 1:26). The demon's shriek also showed Jesus' power over the mute spirit. It could no longer rob this boy of his speech (9:17). Demons are never pleased to be told to leave their human dwellings, but they have no choice but to submit to the higher authority.

After the terrible convulsion, probably prolonged by the angered demon, the child's exhausted body went limp as the demon left him. In fact, he was so still and quiet that most of the people in the crowd thought he was dead.

9:27 But Jesus took him by the hand and lifted him up, and he was able to stand.NRSV Jesus did not free the child from the demon and then leave him to die. He took the child by the hand and drew him to his feet. That he was *able to stand* indicates not only that the demon had left, but that Jesus had given strength back to the child's body. As always, the cure was complete.

THE FINAL STEP
We can imagine the demon saying, "Ha, I left this kid like a corpse. He's dead, for all practical purposes. Your move, Jesus!"

And as the crowd watched and the father winced at his son's stillness, Jesus took the boy's hand and brought him to his feet—a wonderful picture of Jesus' resurrection power that stops demons cold.

This is our promise. Though hit with evil's mighty force, a greater power will prevail. When you counsel the ill, or face your own approaching death, remember the hand that raises to life, extended to you.

9:28-29 After Jesus had gone indoors, his disciples asked him privately, "Why couldn't we drive it out?" He replied, "This kind can come out only by prayer."NIV Jesus left behind the excited crowd and returned to a lodging for privacy with his disciples. After dealing with the distressed man and his son, Jesus knew he needed to discuss the situation with the nine disciples who had been unable to drive out the demon.

They must have been very perplexed. They had cast out demons before (6:7, 13); why hadn't this demon responded? Jesus pointed to their lack of faith. Perhaps the disciples had tried to drive out the

demon with their own ability rather than God's. If so, their hearts
and minds were not in tune with God, so their words had no power.
Their question revealed their error; they centered on themselves
("we"), not on Christ. Jesus explained that *this kind can come out
only by prayer,* and the disciples had not depended on God's power
through prayer. God's power must be requested and relied upon in
each instance. This presents a strong message to our present-day
church: Arguing among ourselves disables (9:14); prayer enables.
The disciples had been debating and not praying.

Prayer is the key that unlocks and reveals faith. Effective
prayer needs both an attitude of complete dependence and the
action of asking. Prayer demonstrates complete reliance on God.
Thus, there is no substitute for prayer, especially in situations that
seem impossible. Often the disciples would face difficult situations that could be resolved only through prayer. Their humiliation made this a painful lesson to learn.

Several manuscripts add the words "and fasting" at the end of
this verse. The words may have been added by some scribes to
support the strong practice of fasting in the early church. The purpose of fasting would be the same as the purpose of prayer—to
take the mind off oneself and focus totally on God and thereby
become prepared to deal with a difficult situation.

WHY PRAY?
When Jesus faced a particularly tenacious demon, he talked to
God the Father all the more. We can pray, too, and should
every day

- that doubts about God's power be wiped away. God can and
  will put down all demons and raise us to life.
- that doubts about Jesus vanish. He is the true Messiah, sent
  by God, our Savior and Lord.
- that fears evaporate. In a showdown of power, God will have
  the final word.
- that greater reliance on Jesus will make our service more
  effective.

When we feel like arguing, retreating, or resigning, it's time to
pray. If the demon has frustrated you, let Jesus give you new
confidence. Pray often. That's your source of power.

JESUS PREDICTS HIS DEATH THE SECOND TIME / 9:30-32 / **113**

Jesus clearly warned his disciples that he would eventually die in
his role as Son of Man. His assurance that death would only hold
him three days did not allay the disciples' confusion. Since they

failed to understand what would be accomplished by his death, the disciples concluded that having to rise from the dead could best be avoided by not dying in the first place. In any case, they were afraid to ask for details.

9:30-31 **They left that place and passed through Galilee. Jesus did not want anyone to know where they were, because he was teaching his disciples.**[NIV] Jesus and the disciples left *that place,* perhaps somewhere near Caesarea Philippi (see 8:27), and headed southwestward, passing *through Galilee* and going toward Capernaum (9:33). Jesus had ended his public ministry and thus began his final journey toward Jerusalem. Jesus *did not want anyone to know where* he and the disciples were, desiring to keep his presence and whereabouts a secret. This was time for him to focus on teaching the disciples. He needed to equip them to carry on the ministry when he returned to heaven and to prepare them for coming events so they would not be taken by surprise.

He said to them, "The Son of Man is going to be betrayed into the hands of men. They will kill him, and after three days he will rise."[NIV] The disciples had persisted in their resistance to Jesus' predictions of his suffering and death. He had already told them that he would die (8:31), so this was the second time he clearly told the disciples that he *(the Son of Man)* would suffer. Whereas Jesus had spoken before about being rejected, this time he added the element of betrayal. Yet Jesus understood, and he wanted the disciples to understand, that all this would happen according to God's plan and in his sovereign will (see Romans 4:25; 8:32). He again said that he would be killed and that *after three days he will rise.* There was always the assurance of victory, although the disciples seemed to miss this point in their concern over Jesus' talk of death.

9:32 **But they did not understand what he was saying and were afraid to ask him.**[NRSV] The disciples' misunderstanding continued; they didn't understand why Jesus would keep talking about dying because they expected him to set up a political kingdom. His death, they thought, would dash their hopes. They didn't know that Jesus' death and resurrection would make his spiritual kingdom possible. They may have been afraid to ask Jesus about his prediction because the last time they reacted to Jesus' sobering words, they were scolded (8:32-33). In their minds, Jesus seemed morbidly preoccupied with death. Actually it was the disciples who were wrongly preoccupied—constantly thinking about the kingdom they hoped Jesus would bring and their possible positions in it (9:34). If Jesus died, the kingdom as they imagined it could not come. Consequently, they preferred not to ask him about his predictions.

SLOW LEARNERS
Once again Jesus predicted his death but also told of his resurrection. Unfortunately, the disciples heard only the first part of Jesus' words and became discouraged. They couldn't understand why Jesus wanted to go back to Jerusalem where he would walk right into trouble. The disciples didn't fully comprehend the purpose of Jesus' death and resurrection until Pentecost (Acts 2). We shouldn't get upset at ourselves for being slow to understand everything about Jesus. After all, the disciples were with him, saw his miracles, heard his words, and still had difficulty understanding. Despite their questions and doubts, however, they believed. We should do no less.

THE DISCIPLES ARGUE ABOUT WHO WOULD BE THE GREATEST / 9:33-37 / 115

This and the next episode provide examples of prestige issues within the band of disciples. Verse 33 begins with the disciples arguing; verse 50 ends with "Be at peace." The disciples were jostling for position among themselves as well as trying to preserve their special status with outsiders. Though this incident is included in the first three Gospels, each one recorded the exchange from a slightly different perspective. Mark captured the immediacy of the original argument as they walked along the way: They were debating their present pecking order. Although they were silent about admitting that argument, they eventually asked the question noted by Matthew, "Who is the greatest in the kingdom of heaven?" (Matthew 18:1 NIV). Luke summarized the argument as having forward-looking aspects, but he moved quickly to Jesus' response. Though Mark does not record Jesus' comments about the humility of a little child, Jesus' use of the child as an example provided a

> Pride is one of the commonest sins which beset human nature . . . . It is a subtle sin. It rules and reigns in many a heart without being detected, and can even wear the clothing of humility. It is a most soul-ruining sin. It prevents repentance, keeps people back from Christ, checks brotherly love and nips spiritual concern in the bud. Let us watch against it and be on our guard. Of all clothing, none is so graceful, none wears so well and none is so rare as true humility. *J. C. Ryle*

clear rebuke to the petty arguments about status among his followers.

9:33 Then they came to Capernaum; and when he was in the house he asked them, "What were you arguing about on the way?"^{NRSV} Jesus and the disciples arrived in Capernaum; the house to which they returned was probably Peter's home, where they usually stayed when in that city (1:21, 29). Apparently the disciples had kept somewhat to themselves as they followed Jesus along the road, but Jesus knew they were having a heated discussion.

The disciples didn't understand Jesus' words about his death. They still thought of Jesus as just an earthly king, and they were concerned about their place in the kingdom he would set up. So they had ignored Jesus' words about his death and had begun arguing about who would be the greatest in the kingdom. Mark made a conscious contrast between the Son of Man who voluntarily submitted to martyrdom and the disciples who cared for their status.

Apparently Jesus already knew what the disciples had been discussing; for even though he asked the question, he didn't receive an answer (9:34). But he then gave them an unforgettable lesson in true greatness.

SAFE AMBITION
The disciples, caught up in their desire for personal success, were embarrassed to answer Jesus' question. It is always painful to compare our motives with Christ's. It is not wrong for believers to be industrious or ambitious. But when ambition pushes aside obedience and service, it becomes sin. We are all like the disciples and even like the Pharisees in this regard. Pride or insecurity can cause us to overvalue position and prestige. In God's kingdom, such motives are destructive. The only safe ambition is directed toward Christ's kingdom, not our own advancement. We must renounce pride and status seeking. They are Satan's tools, not Christ's.

9:34 But they were silent, for on the way they had argued with one another who was the greatest.^{NRSV} Jesus' pointed question gave way to embarrassed silence. No one wanted to admit that *they had argued with one another who was the greatest.* In Jewish culture, a person's rank was of considerable importance (see Luke 14:7-11 for an example); thus, the disciples were naturally curious about their rank in the coming kingdom. The argument may have been fueled by the special privileges given to Peter, James, and John at various times, most recently their going with Jesus on the mountain and then not even being able to tell the others what had happened there (9:2, 9). Matthew 18:1 says that one of the disciples asked Jesus to settle the argument; Luke 9:47 says that since Jesus knew their thoughts, he was aware of the content of their argument without having to ask.

9:35 He sat down, called the twelve, and said to them, "Whoever wants to be first must be last of all and servant of all."[NRSV]
Clearly Jesus had his work cut out for him in teaching these disciples who would be responsible to carry on his mission. So he *sat down* in the house (as a Jewish teacher would) and called the disciples to sit at his feet. In a sentence, he taught the essence of true greatness, *"Whoever wants to be first must be last of all and servant of all"* (see 10:45). Greatness is determined by servanthood. The true leader places his or her self and needs last, as Jesus exemplified in his life and in his death. Being a "servant" did not mean occupying a servile position; rather it meant having an attitude of life that freely attended to others' needs without expecting or demanding anything in return. Jesus expounded on this concept in his call to self-denial (8:34) and in his emphasis on loving your neighbor as yourself (12:31). Seeking honor, respect, and the attention of others runs contrary to Jesus' requirements for his servants. An attitude of service brings true greatness in God's kingdom.

> Instead of telling others what to do, disciples should do it for others.
> *Gilbert Bilezikian*

IT'S YOUR SERVE
Serving others is real leadership. Jesus described leadership from a new perspective. Instead of *using* people, we are to *serve* them. Jesus' mission was to serve others and to give his life away. A real leader has a servant's heart. Servant leaders appreciate others' worth and realize that they're not above any job. If you see something that needs to be done, don't wait to be asked. Take the initiative and do it like a faithful servant. Don't approach life expecting high positions, honors, and special privileges. Look instead for ways to help others.

9:36-37 Then He took a little child and set him in the midst of them. And when He had taken him in His arms, He said to them, "Whoever receives one of these little children in My name receives Me; and whoever receives Me, receives not Me but Him who sent Me."[NKJV] Jesus' action in these verses clarified his words in 9:35. The Aramaic language has the same word for "child" and "servant." Thus when Jesus took a little child into his arms (probably one of the host's children, maybe one of Peter's children), the explanation of greatness was made even more distinct. Only Mark mentions Jesus taking the child in his arms.

When we receive Jesus, we actually "enter" or are "received into" his kingdom. The way into this kingdom is to turn to God from sin in the same spirit of humility that a child exhibits when he shows simple trust in someone he loves. A child comes to a trusted adult without achievements or personal greatness; instead, the child comes simply trusting that he will be received and loved. Thus, when the disciples argued about greatness, they were way off base. Jesus explained that such an attitude alone was enough to keep one from ever finding and entering his kingdom. We must humbly recognize that Jesus already paid the price for our entrance into his kingdom. Any greatness we might have comes only from humble service to our Savior and Lord.

Jesus' statement can be better understood when compared with the parallel passage in Matthew 18:1-5. Matthew recorded more of Jesus' words: "Truly I tell you, unless you change and become like children, you will never enter the kingdom of heaven. Whoever becomes humble like this child is the greatest in the kingdom of heaven. Whoever welcomes one such child in my name welcomes me" (Matthew 18:3-5 NRSV). The disciples had become so preoccupied with the organization of Jesus' earthly kingdom that they had lost sight of its divine purpose. Instead of seeking a place of service, they were seeking positions of advantage. Jesus used a child to help his self-centered disciples get the point. They were to have servant attitudes, being not "childish" (arguing over petty issues), but "childlike," with humble and sincere hearts.

KNOWING GOD

Jesus said, "Whoever receives me, receives . . . him who sent me." Of all the things that are mysterious to us, God heads the list. The question of how to know God has occupied people since the first day of human life, and still the question remains.

But Jesus unlocks the mystery for us. To know Jesus, to embrace him and trust confidently in his Word, is to know God. We do not know all about God, but we know enough to be saved. We do not know him face-to-face, but we do know him through Jesus as our mediator. We do not have every question answered, but we gain growing sensitivity and compassion, like a child attaching to a parent.

Jesus warmly invites us to know God. No one else can make that introduction. No one else knows both this time-bound life and worlds beyond. Accept the invitation today because there's no reason for delay.

In addition, Jesus taught the disciples to welcome children. This was a new approach in a society where children were usually treated as second-class citizens. Jesus equated the attitude of receiving children with a willingness to receive him. Hidden in this statement is a profound truth of Jesus' identity. Jesus added that to receive him is to receive the one who sent him, God the Father. Jesus and God the Father are one.

THE DISCIPLES FORBID ANOTHER TO USE JESUS' NAME / 9:38-41 / 116

Minor conflicts over leadership positions among the disciples also had their public aspect. In this case, the disciples displayed the tendency to become a closed group. They challenged the "credentials" of an outsider. But Jesus rebuked their attempt to be exclusive. We must welcome and encourage all who serve in the name of Christ. Having the same Lord covers a multitude of differences.

9:38 **"Teacher," said John, "we saw a man driving out demons in your name and we told him to stop, because he was not one of us."**NIV John, brother of James the son of Zebedee, one of the inner circle of three among the disciples, told Jesus of a recent event. Perhaps he either hoped that Jesus would congratulate them, or he felt concerned that they had done wrong. In any case, John told Jesus that they had seen a man driving out demons by using Jesus' name. The disciples had told the man to stop because he was not one of the group, that is, not one of the chosen Twelve. The incident has special irony considering that this unknown man apparently had success driving out demons while the disciples, who had been given special power to do so, had recently failed (9:18).

Throughout his ministry, John was sensitive to the issue of those teaching in Jesus' name. Not all were acceptable, as this man turned out to be. In Ephesus, John warned against antichrist teachers (1 John 2:18-27; 4:1-6; 2 John 1:7-11). Some of these false teachers taught alternative forms of Christianity.

Mark pointed out that even the disciples in the inner circle did not completely understand Jesus' mission. After each of the three predictions that Jesus gave concerning his death, one or more of these three men failed Jesus in completely misunderstanding his true mission and were corrected by Jesus: Peter in 8:31-33; John here (see 9:30-32); James and John in 10:32-37.

9:39 **But Jesus said, "Do not stop him; for no one who does a deed**

of power in my name will be able soon afterward to speak evil of me."NRSV The disciples had been incorrect to stop the man from exorcising demons in Jesus' name; and incidentally, they were also incorrect in their supposition that they alone should have a monopoly on Jesus' power. Jesus explained that no one would do such a miracle as exorcising a demon in Jesus' name and then turn around and publicly speak against Jesus. The man, whatever his motivation, had at least done a deed of mercy for a possessed person and had stood against Satan in so doing. (See Numbers 11:24-29 where Moses permitted two elders to prophesy in the Spirit, even though they were not part of the meeting.) When Jesus had been accused of casting out demons because he was in league with Satan, he had said that Satan would not work against himself (3:22-29). The man, therefore, was on Jesus' side.

NO EXCUSES

The disciples were jealous of a man who healed in Jesus' name because they were more concerned about their own group's position than in helping to free those troubled by demons. We do the same today when we refuse to participate in worthy causes because (1) other people or groups are not affiliated with our denomination, (2) these projects do not involve the kind of people with whom we feel most comfortable, (3) others don't operate the way we are used to, or (4) our efforts won't receive enough recognition. Correct theology is important but should never be an excuse to avoid helping people in need.

9:40 "Whoever is not against us is for us."NRSV Matthew 12:30 records the same statement in the opposite, "He who is not with Me is against Me" (NKJV). Jesus was not saying that being indifferent or neutral toward him was as good as being committed; instead, he was pointing out that neutrality toward him is *not* possible. Nevertheless, his followers would not all resemble each other or belong to the same groups. People who are on Jesus' side have the common goal of building up the kingdom of God, and they should not let their differences interfere with this goal. Those who share a common faith in Christ should cooperate. As the man did not have to belong to the select group of disciples to be God's servant, so people don't have to be just like us to be following Jesus with us.

9:41 "For truly I tell you, whoever gives you a cup of water to drink because you bear the name of Christ will by no means lose the reward."NRSV Not only did the man who exorcised demons serve

Christ's kingdom in his stand against Satan, but even someone who offered a cup of water to a person who bears *the name of Christ* was also serving the kingdom. Good treatment of Christ's representatives is important to God (9:37). The Twelve did indeed have a special calling, but God willingly uses all people and all gifts for furthering his kingdom. There are no "trivial" or unimportant services to God. Jesus explained that giving a cup of cold water to a person in need is the same as giving an offering to God. In the hot dry climate of Palestine, a cup of cold water (that had to be brought from the well) was an important act of hospitality. Likewise, we should be hospitable to God's workers.

NOT BAD . . . JUST DIFFERENT
Jesus has many friends and workers. Some have different styles of worship, follow different preferences, and use different methods, but they focus on the common goal of telling people that God's kingdom has come in Jesus Christ.

We must not confuse loyalty to Christ with loyalty to our approach. We must not be jealous of others whose methods prove more effective. Our common goal to share the gospel and serve others should lift us above rivalry, jealousy, petty loyalties, and bickering. We must be committed to the truth of God's Word, but we do not have exclusive rights to certain teaching and ministry methods. Enjoy and appreciate the variety of people who follow the Lord—our brothers and sisters in faith. Encourage someone from another church or ministry.

When Jesus said the hospitable person *will by no means lose the reward,* he was not teaching that righteousness is attained by works. Our reward will be a place in God's kingdom (see 9:47; 10:29-30; Matthew 25:34-40), not on the basis of merit (a good deed), but because of God's gracious promise to people of faith (Luke 12:31-32). In the Bible, God rewards his people for good works according to his justice. In the Old Testament, obedience often was rewarded in this life (Deuteronomy 28), but obedience and immediate reward are not always linked. If they were, good people would always be rich, and suffering would always be a sign of sin. The believer's true reward is God's presence and power through the Holy Spirit. Later, in eternity, we will be rewarded for our faith and service. If material rewards in this life were to come to us for every faithful deed, we would be tempted to boast about our achievements and act out of wrong motivations. No act of mercy is forgotten; no true believer is abandoned. (For more on rewards, see Matthew 16:27; 19:27-30; Luke 6:23, 35; 1 Corinthians 3:8, 13-15; 9:25; James 1:12.)

▬▬▬▬ *JESUS WARNS AGAINST TEMPTATION / 9:42-50 / **117***

This teaching ties closely to the two preceding ones. In 9:33-37, Jesus held up a child as an example of servanthood and a standard for judging our openness. How do we treat one another, and how do we welcome strangers? In 9:38-41, we find Jesus confronting exclusions. Are we experts at finding theological faults, or are we eager to fellowship with others who name Christ as Lord? Failure in any of the cases above puts believers in danger of creating "a stumbling block before one of these little ones who believe in me" (9:42 NRSV).

Jesus emphasized the need for continual self-appraisal. His illustrations were vivid and painful: The loss of a hand, foot, or eye could hardly pass unnoticed. But self-righteousness creates a more terrible hazard. Self-evaluation and self-denial keep us prepared for ministry.

9:42 **"And if anyone causes one of these little ones who believe in me to sin, it would be better for him to be thrown into the sea with a large millstone tied around his neck."**NIV While even small acts of kindness to believers carry great rewards, so acts of misguidance toward believers carry great penalties. *Little ones* could mean children or anyone considered to be insignificant or weak in faith. Children are trusting by nature. They trust adults; and because of that trust, their capacity to trust in God grows. God holds parents and other adults who influence young children accountable for how they affect these little ones' ability to trust God.

To cause a child or someone weak in the faith to sin means to purposely put a stumbling block in the way to make him or her trip and fall. Jesus warned that anyone who turns little children away from him will receive severe punishment. If our ambition or rivalry causes young people or new Christians to doubt or fall back into sin, this is a grievous sin with terrible consequences. A *millstone* was a heavy, flat stone used to grind grain. There were two common kinds of millstones in use at this time. One was smaller and operated by a person. The larger one was connected to an ox or donkey, which would walk in a circle, causing the stone to roll and crush the grain. Mark used the word for the huge animal-operated millstone in his description. To have a millstone tied around one's neck and then be dumped into the sea meant certain death by drowning. Even the horror of such a death was minor compared to what this person would face in eternity.

LITTLE ONES
This caution against harming little ones in the faith applies both to what we do individually as teachers and examples and to what we do collectively in our Christian fellowships. Our thoughts and actions must be motivated by love (1 Corinthians 13), and we must be careful about judging others (Matthew 7:1-5; Romans 14:1–15:4). However, we also have a responsibility to confront flagrant sin within the church (1 Corinthians 5:12-13). Those who lead others astray should be removed from their place of influence and in some cases be put out of the church (see Matthew 18:6-9).

9:43, 45, 47 **"If your hand causes you to sin, cut it off. It is better for you to enter into life maimed, rather than having two hands, to go to hell, into the fire that shall never be quenched."**NKJV The Greek word for "to sin" is the same one used in 9:42. In this verse, it seems as though Jesus was adding even more condemnation to the disciples' incessant ambition. This needed to be dealt with because their ambition could be a stumbling block for others who might want to follow Jesus (Matthew 5:29-30). While prideful ambition is bad, Jesus' statement here includes *anything* that might cause another person to stumble. Those older and more mature in the faith have a responsibility not to let *themselves* be led astray or to place stumbling blocks in their own way by inviting temptation. With strong language (not meant to promote self-mutilation), Jesus described how the disciples should renounce anything that would cause them to sin or turn away from the faith. The action of surgically cutting sin out of their lives should be prompt and complete in order to keep them from sin. The same metaphor is used in Matthew 18 and definitely applies to pulling people out of the church who cause such trouble.

Temptation to sin can come from various sources. Thus Jesus adds further instructions that **"if your foot causes you to sin, cut it off. It is better for you to enter life lame, rather than having two feet, to be cast into hell, into the fire that shall never be quenched."**NKJV and **"if your eye causes you to sin, pluck it out. It is better for you to enter the kingdom of God with one eye, rather than having two eyes, to be cast into hell fire."**NKJV In the Bible, feet are often associated with traveling to do evil, hands with accomplishments, and eyes with vision or desires of the heart, aspirations, or ambitions.

All who desire to follow Jesus must remove any stumbling blocks that cause sin. Jesus did not mean to literally cut off a part of the body; he meant that any relationship, practice, or activity that leads to sin should be stopped. As a person would submit to losing a diseased appendage (hand or foot) or a sense (sight) in order to save his or her life, so believers should be just as willing to "cut off" any temptation, habit, or part of their nature that could lead them to hold onto this world and turn away from Christ and into sin. Just cutting off a limb that committed sin or gouging out an eye that looked lustfully would still not get rid of sin, for that begins in the heart and mind. Jesus was saying that people need to take drastic action to keep from stumbling.

The reason? Jesus explained that it would be better to have lost some worldly possession, attitude, or action than to keep it and *to go to hell* because of it. This is true, radical discipleship. While none of us will ever be completely sin-free until we get to heaven, what God wants is an attitude that renounces sin instead of one that holds on to sin.

The word translated "hell" is *Gehenna;* it is derived from the Valley of Hinnom, south of Jerusalem, where children had been sacrificed by fire to the pagan god Moloch (see 2 Kings 23:10; 2 Chronicles 28:3; Jeremiah 7:31; 32:35). Later, during the reign of good king Josiah, the valley had become the city's garbage dump where fire burned constantly to destroy the garbage and the worms infesting it. Thus "Gehenna" accurately described the place of *fire that shall never be quenched* (Matthew 5:22; 10:28; Luke 12:5; James 3:6; Revelation 19:20) prepared for the devil, his angels, and all those who do not know Christ (Matthew 25:46; Revelation 20:9-10). This is the final and eternal state of the wicked after the resurrection and the Last Judgment.

IT HURTS
Jesus used startling language to stress the importance of cutting sin out of our lives. He requires painful discipline from his true followers. Giving up a relationship, job, or habit that is against God's will may seem just as painful as cutting off a hand. Our high goal, however, is worth any sacrifice; loyalty to Christ is worth any possible loss. Nothing should stand in the way of faith. We must be ruthless in removing sins from our lives now in order to avoid being stuck with them for eternity. Make your choices from an eternal perspective.

9:44, 46 **"Where 'Their worm does not die and the fire is not quenched.'"**[NKJV] These verses are not included in the best manuscripts. The phrase occurs only once, in 9:48.

9:48 **"Where 'Their worm does not die and the fire is not quenched.'"**[NKJV] Still describing "hell" *(Gehenna),* Jesus spoke of a place, like the garbage dump in the valley outside of Jerusalem, where worms infested the garbage and fires burned constantly. With these strange words, picked up from Isaiah 66:24, Jesus pictured the serious and eternal consequences of sin and the absolute destruction of God's enemies (see also Matthew 3:12; 5:30). Worms and fire represented both internal and external pain. Hell will be a place of unbearable and unending torment reserved for those who refuse to believe in Jesus Christ and the salvation and eternal life he offers.

9:49 "Everyone will be salted with fire."NIV This verse, exclusive to Mark, has received dozens of interpretations. The most probable are included here. Some have suggested that "everyone" refers to every person. Thus, the meaning would be that every person will be *salted* somehow—either with the unquenchable fire of hell or with the painful but life-giving power of self-discipline for the sake of the kingdom. Everyone will be "salted," but each person will have a choice as to which "salting" will be received.

The "everyone" could refer back to 9:44, 46 in that everyone who refuses to believe will be salted with the fire of eternal punishment, the fire described in 9:48.

Another view is that "everyone" refers to believers who will be salted with the fire of trials in order to purify them. This view gains credence from Leviticus 2:13 and the possible translation of this verse as, "Every sacrifice will be salted with salt." Grain offerings given as sacrifices in the temple had to be accompanied by salt, which symbolized a pure sacrifice, acceptable to God (salt was considered to be a purifying agent). These offerings were then burned as "an offering made to the LORD by fire" (Leviticus 2:16 NIV). Thus Jesus was looking upon the disciples as sacrifices to God and at discipleship as a purifying process. The "fire" that purified them probably referred to trials and persecutions that made them fit for service (see Matthew 5:10-12; 1 Corinthians 3:13; 1 Peter 1:7; 4:12). This third view is most probable in light of the following verse.

9:50 "Salt is good, but if it loses its saltiness, how can you make it salty again? Have salt in yourselves, and be at peace with each other."NIV Jesus carried on his metaphor from 9:49. In that verse the salt purified the disciples; here the salt symbolized the disciples and the work they were called to do.

Salt is good, Jesus said, for in the ancient world "salt" was both a condiment and a preservative for food. Jesus had said to the disciples, "You are the salt of the earth" (Matthew 5:13 NIV).

They were to be life-producing agents in a dying world; they were to be preservatives in a world spoiled by sin.

CHARRED CHRISTIANS
Countless times in God's Word, the writers tell us that persecution makes us fit for service. Peter later wrote, "In this you rejoice, even if now for a little while you have had to suffer various trials, so that the genuineness of your faith—being more precious than gold that, though perishable, is tested by fire—may be found to result in praise and glory and honor when Jesus Christ is revealed" (1 Peter 1:6-7 NRSV).

When Peter wrote of trials, he was not talking about natural disasters or the experience of God's punishments, but the response of an unbelieving world to people of faith. All believers face such trials when they let their light shine into the darkness. We must accept trials as part of the refining process that burns away impurities and prepares us to meet Christ. Trials teach us patience (Romans 5:3-4; James 1:2-3) and help us grow to be the kind of people God wants.

Jesus said to rejoice when we're persecuted. Persecution can be good because (1) it takes our eyes off earthly rewards, (2) it strips away superficial belief, (3) it strengthens the faith of those who endure, and (4) it provides an opportunity for us to serve as good examples to others who follow. We can be comforted to know that God's greatest prophets were persecuted (Elijah, Jeremiah, Daniel). The fact that we are being persecuted proves that we have been faithful; faithless people would be unnoticed. In the future, God will reward the faithful by receiving them into his eternal kingdom where there is no more persecution.

Most of the salt came from the area southwest of the Dead Sea (a sea so salty that nothing can live in it). Salt had commercial value, but the impure salt taken from the sea and its environs was susceptible to deterioration that left only flavorless crystals. Once salt *loses its saltiness,* the flavor cannot be returned. Thus, it is of no value to anyone. Jesus stressed the responsibility of each disciple toward God. The disciples would be held accountable by God to maintain their "saltiness" (that is, their usefulness) by maintaining a close relationship with him.

Finally, the disciples were told to *have salt in yourselves*—good, useful salt. The "salt" that believers have in themselves refers to true discipleship: obedience, denial of self, humility, and willing suffering for the sake of the kingdom. The disciples were to allow God's purifying work to be done in them. They, in turn, would be purifying agents in the community and in the world. The result, then, would be *peace with each other.*

If the disciples had the "salt" in themselves, then they would

not be arguing about who would be the greatest in Christ's kingdom (9:34). They must not allow the salt within them to be made
useless by their wrangling over position and concerns of this
world. Instead, they must serve Christ; then they would be doing
their duty in the world and be at peace with each other. This
peace among the disciples would be of vital importance after
Christ's return to heaven (see 1 Thessalonians 5:13). The future
of the gospel and of Christianity would be left in their hands.

Mark 10

Mark 10 notes the geographic shift in Jesus' ministry from Galilee to Judea. The occasional travels to Jerusalem became a single-minded movement toward the Cross. As Mark recorded the divine nature of Jesus, he also reported Jesus' warnings about his fate. The trip to Jerusalem had dangerous implications for the disciples.

The geography may have changed, but several customary actions remained unchanged: (1) Wherever Jesus went, crowds gathered and he taught them. (2) Within his audiences there were always some whose purpose was to destroy Jesus. (3) Jesus had confrontations with teachers of the law usually involving an Old Testament teaching that they had twisted to hurt rather than help people. (4) Jesus used God's Word to show his opponents their own error. (5) Later, Jesus provided for his disciples a correct application of God's principle that they had been discussing.

The religious leaders defined their theological issues in all-male terms. Mark alone added the note that Jesus applied God's rules both to men and women. Jesus held men to a standard of conduct; he gave women dignity. He saw women not as property for keeping or disposal, but as full partners.

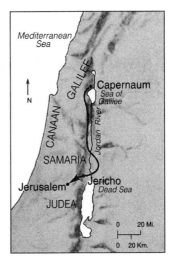

Final Trip to Judea
Jesus quietly left Capernaum, heading toward the borders of Judea before crossing the Jordan River. He preached there before going to Jericho. This trip from Galilee was his last; he would not return before his death.

10:1 Jesus then left that place and went into the region of Judea and across the Jordan. Again crowds of people came to him, and as was his custom, he taught them.^{NIV} After a quiet time of teaching his disciples, Jesus *left that place* (Galilee, probably Capernaum, see 9:33 and Matthew 19:1) and continued his journey southward toward Jerusalem. As he traveled south on the western side of the Jordan River, he went through Samaria and then *into the region of Judea.* Mark records that Jesus then crossed the Jordan, arriving in the region of Perea. John the Baptist had ministered there, and crowds had come to Jesus from the region earlier (see 3:8). Jesus was already well known, and on his arrival there, *crowds of people came to him,* and Jesus *taught them.*

WHY BOTHER?
Wherever Jesus went, he continued to teach the people. It was his custom. He taught them even when there were no results, no fruit. We have much to learn from our Lord's patience and perseverance as a teacher when hearts seemed hardened and indifferent. Every pastor, Sunday school teacher, club leader, or parent in charge of children must follow Christ by seizing every opportunity and not giving up. You may acknowledge that success rests in God's hands, but can you be faithful even when you see no immediate response?

10:2 Some Pharisees came, and to test him they asked, "Is it lawful for a man to divorce his wife?"^{NRSV} John the Baptist was put in prison and killed, at least in part, for his public opinions on marriage and divorce. The *Pharisees* hoped to trap Jesus, as well, by getting him to choose sides in a theological controversy and incriminate himself in the process.

Moses' words about divorce as recorded in Deuteronomy 24:1-4 begin, "If a man marries a woman who becomes displeasing to him because he finds something indecent about her, and he writes her a certificate of divorce, gives it to her and sends her from his house . . ." (Deuteronomy 24:1 NIV). The religious leaders' controversy focused around the interpretation of the words "something indecent." There arose two schools of thought representing two opposing views. One group (who were the followers of Rabbi Hillel) said a man could give his wife a "certificate of divorce" for almost any reason, even finding another woman more attractive than his wife; "something indecent" could refer to anything that "displeased" him. The other group (who were followers of Rabbi Shammai) believed that a man could divorce his wife only if she was unfaithful to him; that is, "something indecent" referred to adultery.

But there was also another issue. In ancient Jewish marriages, when a woman got married, her father gave her a dowry that reflected her father's wealth. The dowry—that could consist of money, slaves, or other property—remained the woman's throughout her marriage. If she was divorced, her husband had to return the dowry to her, unless she was guilty of sexual misconduct. To divorce his wife, a man merely had to write a document stating that the wife was free from him and could remarry. No court action was necessary; it was a very simple process. As a result, some Jewish men were divorcing their wives and using this interpretation of the divorce law to avoid returning a wife's dowry.

The Pharisees asked the question *to test* Jesus. They perhaps hoped that he might have very lax views about divorce (considering his apparent lack of concern for their laws about the Sabbath and fasting) and would show himself to be an impostor. If Jesus supported divorce, he would be upholding the Pharisees' procedures; they doubted that Jesus would do that. If Jesus chose sides in the controversy, some members of the crowd would dislike his position, for some may have used the law to their advantage to divorce their wives. Or, if he spoke against divorce altogether, he would appear to be speaking against Moses' law (which allowed divorce). The Pharisees wanted to test or trap Jesus. They were serving their own desires, not seeking to know his view of God's will based on God's Word. Our motives in examining the divorce issue must be to do God's will, not to serve our own desires.

AVOIDING TRAPS
Jesus avoided the trap set for him. When Christians today are asked about nuclear war, fetal life, or any number of social problems, any answer tends to polarize the discussion. The key to Jesus' response to the Pharisees is that he reinterpreted and prioritized Deuteronomy and Genesis, and so taught the Bible's meaning while he avoided being hung on the Pharisees' dilemma.

When we get caught in discussions where the Bible has no clear answer or where we simply don't know what to say, we need guidance. We don't have the knowledge of Scripture or the wisdom that Christ had. But we can come back to the central message of the love of Christ and God's mercy to all who believe.

10:3 He answered them, "What did Moses command you?"[NRSV]
With these words, Jesus removed any possible condemnation of

laxity about divorce or ignorance of God's law. Jesus turned the Pharisees from their wrangling about his possible answers and sent them directly to the Pentateuch (the books of Genesis through Deuteronomy). He asked, *"What did Moses command you?"* From their answer in 10:4, the Pharisees thought Jesus was referring to Moses' writing in Deuteronomy 24:1-4; but Jesus' response reveals that he was referring to Moses' words in Genesis about the ideal state of creation and particularly of marriage.

10:4 They said, "Moses permitted a man to write a certificate of divorce and send her away."^{NIV} In their answer, the Pharisees summarized the law recorded in Deuteronomy 24:1-4. Notice that Jesus had asked what Moses "commanded" and the Pharisees answered with what Moses *permitted.* Moses did not command divorce; instead, he recognized its presence, permitted it, and gave instructions on how it should be carried out. What Moses "commanded" was what God commanded about marriage in Genesis 1–2; Jesus would elaborate on this in the following verses.

Because sinful human nature made divorce inevitable, Moses instituted laws to help its victims. Under Jewish law, only a husband could initiate and carry out a divorce. The civil laws protected the women who, in that culture, were quite vulnerable when living alone. Because of Moses' law, a man could no longer just throw his wife out—he had to write a formal letter of dismissal, a *certificate of divorce,* so she could remarry and reclaim her dowry. This was a radical step toward civil rights, for it made a man think twice before sending his wife away. Moses' words gave protection to the wife and limited abuses of divorce.

WHAT ABOUT DIVORCE?
We know that divorce is sometimes necessary (for physical survival, for well-being of children, etc.), but is it ever biblically legitimate? Jesus clearly gave God's ideal for marriage in Genesis priority over Moses' permission for divorce. But Jesus did not cancel the teaching of Deuteronomy. For possible exceptions, see Matthew 5:32 and 19:9, where Jesus permitted divorce when the spouse had been unfaithful; and 1 Corinthians 7:15, where Paul recognized divorce when the unbelieving partner leaves the marriage.

Divorce is wrong; it severs a holy union. But divorce is permitted. Jesus did not elaborate on the permissible reasons, but his high view of marriage surely requires that divorce be a last resort to avoid greater disaster.

10:5 "It was because your hearts were hard that Moses wrote you this law," Jesus replied.[NIV] In Moses' day, as well as in Jesus' day, the practice of marriage fell far short of God's intention. Jesus said that Moses gave this law only because the people's *hearts were hard;* in other words, they were completely insensitive to God's will for marriage. "Hard-heartedness" refers to a stubborn, willful attitude (for example, see Deuteronomy 10:16). This is not the same wording in Greek that describes the spiritual dullness of the disciples (Mark 8:17), but the words may be synonymous. Many refused to follow through with their marriages as God had intended, so God allowed divorce as a concession to their sinfulness. Divorce was not approved, but it was preferred to open adultery. The Ten Commandments includes two statements relative to this situation: "You shall not commit adultery. . . . You shall not covet your neighbor's wife" (Exodus 20:14, 17 NIV). Jesus explained that divorce was never God's intent; instead, God wants married people to consider marriage to be permanent.

Jesus turned the Pharisees' "test" question back on them by using it as an opportunity to review God's intended purpose for marriage and to expose the Pharisees' selfish motives. They were not thinking about what God intended for marriage, but had settled for marriages of convenience. In addition, they were quoting Moses unfairly and out of context. Jesus showed these legal experts how superficial their knowledge really was.

HARD HEARTS AND WEDDING BELLS
We must not enter marriage with the option of getting out. Your marriage is more likely to be happy if, from the outset, you are committed to permanence. Don't be hard-hearted like these Pharisees, but be hardheaded in your determination, with God's help, to stay together.

10:6-8 "But at the beginning of creation God 'made them male and female.' 'For this reason a man will leave his father and mother and be united to his wife, and the two will become one flesh.' So they are no longer two, but one."[NIV] The Pharisees quoted Moses' writings in Deuteronomy; Jesus also quoted from Moses' writings (Genesis 1:27; 2:24), but he went back to Genesis, *the beginning of creation,* to God's ideal in creating *male and female.* The Hebrew words for "male" and "female" reveal that the two were made complementary to each other. God's plan was that in marriage the husband and wife *become one flesh,* an intimate closeness that cannot be separated. The wife is not property to be disposed of, but an equally created person. (Evidently the law required the husband to only return the original dowry, so these women were abandoned with no support.) The law of God is higher than Moses' authority or human law.

Jesus drew a distinction: God's creation of marriage and his absolute command that it be a permanent union versus the human injunction written hundreds of years later tolerating divorce because of people's utter sinfulness (their "hard hearts," 10:5). God permitted divorce as a result of sin, but his command was that husband and wife be *no longer two, but one,* describing an indissoluble union.

HOMOSEXUAL MARRIAGE?
Today, many homosexuals want to commit to "marry" with the blessing of the church. Reasons for homosexual feelings and desires are complex and serious. Christians should not trivialize the situation or flippantly condemn the homosexual person. But Jesus made God's ideal very plain: At creation he approved one kind of marriage bond, man to woman. These become one flesh—one before God. See Romans 1:24-27 for further discussion.
  Where does that leave homosexual marriage? At best, it is a human invention without any biblical precedent. God created man and woman. Heterosexual monogamy is God's plan for marriage—the best plan, the only one.

10:9 "Therefore what God has joined together, let no one separate."NRSV In his answer, Jesus focused on marriage rather than divorce. He pointed out that God intended marriage to be a covenant, a permanent promise of love and faithfulness. The Pharisees used Deuteronomy 24:1 as a proof text for divorce. They saw divorce as a legal issue rather than a spiritual one, regarding marriage and divorce as transactions similar to buying and selling land (with women being treated as property). But Jesus condemned this attitude, clarifying God's original intention—that marriage bring oneness that *no one* should separate, especially not the husband by simply writing a "certificate."

Jesus recognized Moses' law, but held up God's ideal for marriage and told his followers to live by that ideal. Jesus also was saying to the self-righteous Pharisees who had hoped to trick him with the question, "True followers of God will hold his ideals above any laws—and especially those laws written as a concession to hard-heartedness and sin."

Jesus basically said that John the Baptist had been right when he had proclaimed it unlawful for Herod to be married to his

WHAT THE BIBLE SAYS ABOUT MARRIAGE

Genesis 2:18-24	Marriage is God's idea.
Genesis 24:58-60	Commitment is essential to a successful marriage.
Genesis 29:10-11	Romance is important.
Jeremiah 7:34	Marriage holds times of great joy.
Malachi 2:14-15	Marriage creates the best environment for raising children.
Matthew 5:32	Unfaithfulness breaks the bond of trust, the foundation of all relationships.
Matthew 19:6	Marriage is permanent.
Romans 7:2-3	Ideally, only death should dissolve marriage.
Ephesians 5:21-33	Marriage is based on the principled practice of love, not on feelings.
Ephesians 5:23-32	Marriage is a living symbol of Christ and the church.
Hebrews 13:4	Marriage is good and honorable.

brother's wife (6:18). The Pharisees could not accuse Jesus of a lax view of divorce or of going against Moses' law. And Jesus didn't bother to take sides in the Pharisees' theological debate (described in 10:2 above), so he hadn't divided the people as the leaders had hoped. Thus, the Pharisees left with no evidence against Jesus.

10:10 Then in the house the disciples asked him again about this matter.NRSV Mark continued his theme of the disciples' misunderstanding of Jesus' teaching. Once they were again in privacy (probably the home of some believer in Perea who offered hospitality), the disciples asked Jesus what he had meant in his answer to the Pharisees' question (see also 4:10; 7:17). Matthew records their words: "If this is the situation between a husband and wife, it is better not to marry" (Matthew 19:10 NIV). They believed that the standard Jesus upheld was so impossible that it would be better for people not to get married than to get into the unbreakable covenant of marriage. It seemed better not to make the vow than to make the vow and not be able to keep it.

10:11-12 He said to them, "Whoever divorces his wife and marries another commits adultery against her."NRSV Jesus had clearly explained that divorce dissolved a divinely formed union. These people were divorcing in order to get remarried. Here he explained that marriage after divorce is adultery. To say that a man could commit adultery *against* his wife went beyond Jewish teaching and elevated the status of the wife to a position of equality. Women were never meant to be mere property in a marriage relationship; God's plan had always been partnership and the two becoming "one flesh" (10:8).

The rabbis' interpretation of Moses' law permitted remarriage after divorce, but Jesus said that was committing adultery. Matthew recorded the same words of Jesus but added that he gave one exception: "I tell you that anyone who divorces his wife, except for marital unfaithfulness, and marries another woman commits adultery" (Matthew 19:9 NIV, see also Matthew 5:32). The Greek word translated "marital unfaithfulness" is *porneia*. It has a broad range of definitions; it refers to (1) committing adultery (one offense); (2) unfaithfulness during the betrothal (or "engagement") period; (3) an illegitimate or incestuous marriage (the man and wife were later discovered to be near relatives); or (4) continued and unrepented unfaithfulness. Scholars agree that Jesus' words refer to both husband and wife; that is, the unfaithfulness of one could be grounds for divorce by the other, because Jesus then added, **"And if she divorces her husband and marries another man, she commits adultery."**NIV These were earth-shaking words to Jewish ears. In Jewish society, only men had the right to divorce. Jesus' words *if she divorces her husband* were a departure from the normal Jewish understanding. Mark alone recorded these words, probably with his Roman audience in mind. They would not have been shocked, for in Roman society a woman could initiate a divorce.

MAY A DIVORCED PERSON REMARRY?

It appears that Jesus was forbidding divorced persons from remarrying, forcing them to live either in celibacy or sin. His main point was to teach that the divorce laws should not be used to dispose of a partner in order to get another one.

The nagging question for Christians remains: May a divorced person, who truly repents of a sinful past and commits his or her life to God, remarry?

We long for a simple, direct reply to that question, but we have only biblical context as an answer. We have Jesus' high view of marriage and low view of divorce recorded in the Gospels. Jesus proclaimed new life—full forgiveness and restoration—to all who would come to God in repentance and faith. Spiritual discernment is essential here, but the gospel—God's promise of wholeness and full healing—includes the sacred bond of marriage. Churches should be reluctant to deny a repentant, formerly married person the opportunity to marry another believer.

While the exact meaning of Jesus' words is in question, one truth is inescapable: God created marriage to be a sacred, permanent union and partnership between husband and wife. When both husband and wife enter this union with that understanding and commitment, they can provide security for each other, a stable home for their children, and strength to weather any of life's storms or stresses.

JESUS BLESSES LITTLE CHILDREN / 10:13-16 / **174**

There is a natural progression from Jesus' teaching on the permanence of marriage to his insistence on bringing children to him for blessing. Jesus declared the value of children and his love for them by his actions. And he used their receptivity as a guideline for the kind of response required of anyone who would want to enter the kingdom of God.

Jesus' words forcefully confront parents and all those in contact with children: Are we helping or hindering children from coming to Christ? Are we, ourselves, receiving the kingdom of God with childlike trust?

10:13 People were bringing little children to Jesus to have him touch them, but the disciples rebuked them.[NIV] It was customary for people to bring their children (the Greek word *paidia* could refer to children ranging in age from babies to preteens) to a rabbi for a blessing. Thus people were bringing children to Jesus so that he could *touch them* and bless them. The disciples, however, thought the children were unworthy of the Master's time—less important than whatever else he had to do. In the first century, Jewish households were patriarchal—men came first, women and children next. Adults were the key members of society; children were to be seen but not heard, and their needs were secondary.

Considering their inability to have any quiet time together, the disciples may have viewed these parents and children as another intrusion and drain of time and energy. So they *rebuked* the people. Once again Mark emphasized that the disciples misunderstood both Jesus' compassion and his mission. Their rebuke was incorrect and went unheeded. The Greek verb tenses indicate that the disciples kept on rebuking while the people kept on bringing their children.

10:14 When Jesus saw this, he was indignant. He said to them, "Let the little children come to me, and do not hinder them, for the kingdom of God belongs to such as these."[NIV] When Jesus saw his disciples rebuking the people for bringing their children, *he was indignant.* The Greek word *(aganakteo)* suggests strong emo-

tion. This is the only place in the Gospels where Jesus directed
such strong anger at his disciples. Elsewhere in Mark, Jesus'
anger was directed at unbelief (3:5) and, in a lesser way, at illness
(1:41, 43 see NRSV comment). Here it was leveled at the disciples
for their prejudice against this age group. They thought children
were a waste of time, but Jesus welcomed them. He, in turn,
rebuked the disciples, telling them in a double command to *let
the little children come* and *do not hinder them*. Jesus explained
that little children have the kind of faith and trust needed to enter
God's kingdom. Anyone of any age who exhibits such faith and
trust is promised access to Jesus and to the kingdom. The kingdom of God is God's universal, dynamic rule over his people,
and children represent the essence of discipleship. They came to
Jesus in humility and received his blessing as a gift. They had no
authority or rights, but they came to him in trust and love.

CHILD CARE?
Most church people would never intentionally keep children
away from services or do anything to thwart them. In this story,
another important group of people was unintentionally slighted.
The disciples had rebuked the ones bringing the children. Parents and relatives brought children to receive Jesus' touch of
blessing. It was customary to have a rabbi bless your child, and
Jesus had extraordinary power and authority. These people
had needs based on their love for their children. But the disciples had another agenda.
    We must be careful not to rebuke the "child-bringers." Par-
ents have needs and concerns. They may want to talk and
receive prayer for what others may think are inconsequential
issues. Sermons, Sunday school classes, and small groups
should encourage people to bring their children. Also, we
should listen carefully to those who represent children's ministries in our churches so we will do nothing to hinder young ones
from coming to Christ.

10:15 **"I tell you the truth, anyone who will not receive the kingdom
of God like a little child will never enter it."**NIV The disciples
must have forgotten what Jesus had said about children (9:36-37).
Jesus wanted little children to come because he loved them and
because children have the kind of attitude needed to approach God.
Jesus didn't mean that heaven is only for those who believe when
they are children, but that people need childlike attitudes of trust in
God. To feel secure, children need only a loving look and gentle
touch from someone who cares. Complete intellectual understanding is not one of their requirements. They believe us if they
trust us. Jesus said that people should believe in him with this kind

of childlike faith. We should not have to understand all the mysteries of the universe; it should be enough to know that God loves us and has provided forgiveness for our sin. This doesn't mean that we should be childish, immature, selfish, or spoiled, but that we should *receive the kingdom* with a child's simplicity and trust. Unless we can completely trust in God, we *will never enter* the kingdom.

CHANGE YOUR MIND
Adults considering Christian faith for the first time will know some things kids do not know, will have felt pain kids have not felt, know passions kids do not know, and carry griefs kids do not carry.
   Jesus does not ask us to put aside our mind and passions. But he does require a change of attitude: adult self-sufficiency must recognize its need for the sovereign God; adult moral defensiveness must humble itself before the holy God; and adult skeptical toughness must soften before the loving God. Children do not feel supremely powerful, perfectly righteous, or totally autonomous. These are adult fantasies. Coming to Jesus means that we accept his goodness on our behalf, confess our need, and commit our lives to God's tender guidance.

10:16 And he took the children in his arms, put his hands on them and blessed them.[NIV] One by one, Jesus took each child in his arms, laid his hands on them (rather than just "touching" them as he had been asked, 10:13), and *blessed them.* The Greek verb *(kateuloei)* is intensive in force, suggesting that his blessing was fervent. The verb is also in the imperfect tense, meaning that he kept on blessing. Jesus took time with each child, blessing each as he or she was brought to him. This certainly took time, but Jesus did not rush through the process or pass it off as unimportant. It probably brought him great joy to spend time with little children whose faith and trust was so pure and simple.

The receptiveness of these children was a great contrast to the stubbornness of the religious leaders, who let their education and sophistication stand in the way of the simple faith needed to believe in Jesus; and the dullness of the disciples, whose self-centeredness continued to blind them to Jesus' true mission. No wonder Jesus used children as an example for hard-hearted adults.

JESUS SPEAKS TO THE RICH YOUNG MAN / 10:17-31 / **175**

Jesus stopped in an unnamed town for several days. He was questioned about divorce and made a point to bless little children. But it was time to move on because he had an appointment with the Cross. Jesus was on his way out of town when a young person flagged him down with a question: "What must I do to inherit eternal life?" (10:17). This question by the rich young ruler gains significance as the only wealthy person's direct query to Jesus recorded in Mark's Gospel.

Apparently, this young man was trying his best but knew it wasn't enough. He lacked something and wanted Jesus to tell him what he had missed. Jesus told the young man what he needed to hear, not what he wanted to hear. He wanted to have another possession in his collection—an inheritance called eternal life. He wanted to have the kingdom, but as it turned out, he wasn't ready for the kingdom to have him.

This episode with the rich young man contrasts sharply with the previous episode of Jesus blessing the children. The children are an example of faith and trust; they do nothing to gain eternal life, but they receive it because of their simple faith. The rich young man thought he could gain eternal life by what he did, only to find that he could not have it.

This rich young man made an impression on the disciples—three Gospels have this story. This rich man represents a circle of people that thus far had gone untouched by the gospel—the wealthy. His response to Jesus' instructions may indicate why.

GET TO THE POINT
This young man knew what he wanted and did not fiddle with secondary matters. He had thought about it. He sought out Jesus. He came right to the point: He wanted eternal life.

Do we as quickly get to the main point of our faith? When we select a church, or even consider attending one, does our checklist include facility preferences, convenience needs, and social compatibility? Do we come to Jesus today only if the nursery is supplied with toys our kids enjoy? In the process, do we forget to seek out Jesus?

Credit this young man with eagerly coming to the heart of the matter. He ran to Jesus and fell on his knees. In our own spiritual journey, we could use his focus, his attention to the big question, and his concern with the state of his soul.

10:17 As Jesus started on his way, a man ran up to him and fell on his knees before him. "Good teacher," he asked, "what must I do to inherit eternal life?"[NIV] Jesus *started on his way* from Perea, continuing his journey toward Jerusalem. On his way, a man ran up to him (Matthew called him a young man in 19:22; Luke referred to him as a ruler in 18:18). This was a relatively

young man who was both wealthy (Mark 10:22; Luke 18:23) and
of prominent social standing. Considering his own position, his
falling on his knees before Jesus reveals his respect for Jesus. He
called Jesus *"Good teacher"* (not the more common "rabbi") and
eagerly asked a pressing question. This rich young ruler wanted
to be sure he would receive *eternal life,* so he asked what he
could *do to inherit* it. He viewed eternal life as something that
one achieves. While he had kept the commandments (or so he
thought, 10:20), he still had some concern about his eternal destiny. He thought Jesus would have the answer.

**10:18 Jesus said to him, "Why do you call me good? No one is good
but God alone."**[NRSV] On the surface, it seems that Jesus was dis-
tancing himself from God by implying that only God was good,
not he. Actually, Jesus was uniting himself with God by recognizing that to be called good is to be called God. Jesus did not at
first address the man's question, but instead challenged him to
think about God. Goodness is not measured by one's works; in
fact, *no one is good but God alone.* Jesus wanted the man to turn
his attention from himself and from Jesus (who he thought was
merely a "good teacher") and think about God's absolute goodness. If he truly did so, he would conclude that he could *do* nothing to inherit eternal life.

In addition, by asking this question, Jesus was saying, "Do you
really know the one to whom you are talking?" Jesus did not deny
his deity, but instead confirmed it by these words. Because only God
is truly good, the man, without knowing it, was calling Jesus "God."
He was correct in so doing, but Jesus preferred that people use such
words only when they meant and understood them.

 ARROGANCE
The young man had eagerness and dash, but behind his words
and his kneeling posture lay the crux of his problem. Jesus, no
less direct than the man himself, came right to the heart of it.
The young man was trusting in himself and his wealth; sadly,
he was self-reliant and arrogant.

We are arrogant when we believe that our unusual capability
sets us apart morally from the common herd. Then our moral
superiority looks for some sort of payoff. Jesus sensed that this
young man wanted a big payoff. He wanted Jesus' declaration
that the young man's own moral achievements were payment
for an eternal life insurance policy. Don't come to Jesus
proudly; your achievements cannot earn your salvation.

The good news we need is that Jesus alone saves us. Arrogance blinds us to that need.

10:19 **"You know the commandments: 'Do not commit adultery,'**
'Do not murder,' 'Do not steal,' 'Do not bear false witness,'
'Do not defraud,' 'Honor your father and your mother.'"NKJV
Having established the nature of true goodness (and recognizing
that the man did not have a real understanding of God and how
he gives eternal life), Jesus rehearsed six of the Ten Commandments—those dealing with people's relationships with one
another. (Jesus did not yet mention the other four commandments
that deal with a person's relationship to God.) Interestingly, Jesus
was not strict in rehearsing the commandments. He put the fifth
commandment last and used the word "defraud" either for the
tenth commandment or to expand on the eighth and ninth commandments. That the man kept these laws was the easily verifi-
able outward proof of an "upward" response to God—an answer
to what the man could *do.* Jesus' list showed that he was focusing
on the man's actual lifestyle and not just his knowledge of these
commandments. But Jesus would show the man that the law had
far deeper meaning than just a list of rules to be kept.

10:20 **He said to him, "Teacher, I have kept all these since my**
youth."NRSV The young man replied that he had kept all the commandments since his *youth* (from age twelve when a boy entered
manhood and became responsible to keep the commandments).
The man sincerely believed that he had not broken any commandments; now he wanted Jesus to guarantee his eternal life. Such is
the condition of one who tries to attain eternal life or a relationship with God by his or her own merit. Even if it seems that the
person has kept all the laws perfectly, he or she still needs assurance. Jesus would reveal to this man what he lacked.

BUYING ETERNAL LIFE
The young man had worked so hard at moral piety that he was
not bashful about boasting to a rabbi. He may have kept fastidi-
ous records of all his moral achievements. He felt secure knowing he had done everything right.
   Life for the Christian is dynamic and risky. Life for the young
man was a self-absorbing facade of achievements. The Christian ventures forward in faith, confident that sins are forgiven
through Jesus. The young man was worried about falling from
perfection, yet he couldn't venture a small bit of self-sacrifice.
   Instead of trying to secure eternal life and peace by personal
achievement, come to Jesus. He offers you freedom from trying
to earn salvation and releases you from moral pride. Following
Jesus requires a relationship based on love for God and love
for our neighbors. We must renounce our personal moral
achievements and surrender to him.

10:21 Jesus looked at him and loved him. "One thing you lack," he said. "Go, sell everything you have and give to the poor, and you will have treasure in heaven. Then come, follow me."^{NIV} Jesus had great compassion and love for this eager young man. Sincere in both his desire for eternal life and his willingness to do anything to obtain it, the man did not understand that an inheritance need not be earned, only accepted.

Jesus showed genuine love for this man, even though he knew that the man might not follow him. Jesus was not put off by the man's youth or his wealth. We must remember to love all those whom Jesus died to save. Love is able to give tough advice; it doesn't hedge around the truth. Christ loved us enough to die for us, and he also loves us enough to talk straight to us. If his love were superficial, he would give us only his approval; but because his love is complete, he gives us life-changing challenges.

The young man said he had never once broken any of the laws Jesus mentioned (10:19-20), and perhaps he had even kept the Pharisees' loophole-filled version of them. But Jesus lovingly broke through the young man's pride with a challenge that answered his own question: *Sell everything you have and give to the poor.* This challenge exposed the barrier that could keep this young man out of the kingdom: his love of money. Money represented his pride of accomplishment and self-effort. Ironically, his attitude made him unable to keep the *first* commandment, one that Jesus did not quote in 10:19: "You shall have no other gods before me" (Exodus 20:3 NRSV; see also Matthew 22:36-40). The young man did not love God with his whole heart as he had presumed. In reality, the man's wealth was his god, his idol. If he could not give it up, he would be violating the first and greatest commandment.

The task of selling all his possessions would not, of itself, give the man eternal life. But such radical obedience would be the first step for this man to become a follower of Jesus. The emphasis is not so much on "selling" as on "following." Jesus' words to this rich young man were a test of his faith and his willingness to obey. The man thought he needed to do more; Jesus explained that there was plenty more he could do, but not in order to obtain eternal life. Instead, he needed an attitude adjustment toward his wealth. Only then could he submit humbly to the lordship of Christ. By putting his treasure in heaven and "following" Jesus along the road of selflessness and service to others, the man could be assured of his eternal destiny.

In this story, we see clearly the essence of the gospel—repent and believe. Jesus told the rich young man to turn his back on his past (repent) and to begin following him (believe). The young man may have wanted to believe, but he was unwilling to repent.

SELL OUT

What does your money mean to you? Although Jesus wanted this man to sell everything and give his money to the poor, this does not mean that all believers should sell all their possessions. Most of Jesus' followers did not sell everything, although they used their possessions to serve others. Sometimes being a good manager and steward of our money requires more effort and proves to be more difficult than giving to the needy. But it is easy to rationalize. We are responsible to care for our own needs and the needs of our family so as not to be a burden on others, but we are also responsible to care for the poor. We should be willing to give up anything God asks us to. God may require us to give up our money as well if money becomes our idol. When God blesses us with economic prosperity, he is giving us a ministry opportunity. If we use the money selfishly, we miss God's opportunity and become like the rich young ruler.

But if we are willing to share and to give, we allow nothing to come between us and God. That kind of attitude keeps us from using our God-given wealth selfishly. This story shows us that we must not let anything we have or desire keep us from following Jesus. If Jesus asked, could you give up your house? your car? your investments? your level of income? your position on the ladder of promotion? Your reaction may show your attitude toward money—whether it is your servant or your master.

10:22 At this, the man's face fell. He went away sad, because he had great wealth.NIV This man's wealth made his life comfortable and gave him power and prestige. When Jesus told him to sell everything he owned, Jesus was touching the very basis of the man's security and identity. The man did not understand that he would be even more secure if he followed Jesus than he was with all his wealth. He could not meet the one requirement Jesus gave—to turn his whole heart and life over to God. The one thing he wanted, eternal life, was unattainable because he deemed the price too high. The man came to Jesus wondering what he could do; he left seeing what he was unable to do. No wonder he *went away sad.* How tragic—to be possessed by possessions and miss the opportunity to be with Jesus.

> But do not let it trouble your mind that we see the unrighteous possessing wealth while the servants of God experience hardships. Let us have faith, brothers and sisters! We are competing in the contest of a living God, and are being trained by the present life in order that we may be crowned in the life to come. *Second Clement*

GET RID OF IT
Jesus does not ask all believers to sell everything they have,
although this may be his will for some, but it is his will for all of
us to care for the needy (1 Timothy 6:17-19; Hebrew 13:16).
And he does ask us all to get rid of anything that has become
more important than God. If your basis for security has shifted
from God to what you own, get rid of those possessions. What
keeps you from turning your life over to Christ? What does your
wealth mean to you? Is there anything you would be unwilling
to relinquish in order to make Christ your Lord above all lords?

**10:23 Then Jesus looked around and said to His disciples, "How
hard it is for those who have riches to enter the kingdom of
God!"**NKJV Jesus looked at his disciples and taught them a lesson
from this incident with the rich young man. Jesus explained that
it was very difficult for the rich to enter the kingdom of God (not
impossible, but difficult). This is true because the rich, with most
of their basic physical needs met, often become self-reliant.
When they feel empty, they can buy something new to dull the
pain that was meant to drive them toward God. Their abundance
and self-sufficiency become their deficiency. People who have
everything on earth can still lack what is most important—eternal
life. They have riches, but they don't have God's kingdom.

This young man may have been very wealthy, but any of us
who own anything could also be considered wealthy by someone
else's standards. Whatever you own could become a barrier to
entering the kingdom if it comes between you and God.

MONEY STRUGGLES
Everyone struggles to get money. Few people have enough,
and getting more requires very hard work. Most people believe
that happiness is tied to wealth. Certainly some forms of happiness are.
    Christians live in tension with money. We need it for survival
and to realize our dreams, but we also need to break its hold
on us lest it become our ultimate purpose, the big reason for
our work.
    Jesus alone provides the Christian's security; God's kingdom
alone provides our true purpose. The more money we have,
the more potential it has to take God's place. We need to rid
ourselves of the love of wealth as if cleaning grit from eye-
glasses, so we can keep Jesus in sharp focus.

**10:24 The disciples were amazed at his words. But Jesus said again,
"Children, how hard it is to enter the kingdom of God!"**NIV Jesus'

words *amazed* the disciples, and so he repeated them. As Jews, these disciples regarded wealth as a sign of God's blessing (see, for example, Job 1:10; 42:10; Psalm 128:18; Isaiah 3:10). Thus, they thought wealth came from God and would bring a person closer to God; it certainly did not pose an obstacle. The rich young man, with all his advantages, probably seemed like perfect "kingdom material." Yet he went away empty-handed. What kind of kingdom was this if those most blessed and advantaged would have difficulty entering? What did that mean for the disciples? It seemed to them that if the rich had a hard time, the disciples would *never* make it.

Jesus repeated his statement. Some manuscripts add that he also repeated the words "for those who have riches" (to match 10:23), while other manuscripts leave it as above. According to the longer reading, Jesus was simply restating what he had already said to make sure they heard it right. As translated in the NIV in the verse quoted above, Jesus was generalizing his statement to reveal that the demands of the kingdom are rigorous for everyone. Each person, rich or poor, will have something to give up (for example, favorite sins, attitudes, or possessions). All people are on equal ground before God; no one comes with any prior advantage. It is difficult for the rich to enter, yet it is difficult for all. Ironically, however, it is we who make it difficult. God asks for simple acceptance of him, but we attempt to hold on to temporal things as if they will never fade away.

THE ULTIMATE GOAL
What does Jesus want from us? He desires total dedication, not halfhearted commitment. We can't follow Jesus selectively; we have to accept the cross along with the crown, judgment as well as mercy. We must count the cost and be willing to abandon everything else that has given us security. With our focus on Jesus, we should allow nothing to distract us from the ultimate goal of eternal life with him.

10:25 **"It is easier for a camel to go through the eye of a needle than for a rich man to enter the kingdom of God."**[NKJV] Jesus used a common Jewish proverb describing something impossible and absurd. With all their advantages and influence, rich people may find it difficult to have the attitude of humility, submission, and service required by Jesus. Because money represents power, authority, and success, wealthy people often have difficulty realizing their need and their powerlessness to save themselves. Those rich in talent or intelligence suffer the same difficulty. It is difficult for a self-sufficient person to realize his or her need and come to Jesus. It's hard to give away the control over life that money provides. Thus Jesus explained that it would be easier to get a camel (the largest animal in Palestine) through the eye of a sewing needle than for a person who trusts in riches to get into the kingdom of God.

Some commentators have said that "needle" refers to a certain gate in the wall of Jerusalem. However, the Greek word refers to a needle that is used with thread, and the Needle's Eye Gate didn't exist in Jesus' day. It was put in later when the city was rebuilt. Thus, Jesus' image was purposely hyperbolic.

10:26 **They were greatly astounded and said to one another, "Then who can be saved?"**^{NRSV} The disciples were *greatly astounded* almost to the point of exasperation. Again, they wondered what Jesus meant. It seemed that they would never understand him. Was not wealth a blessing from God, a reward for being good? If the rich—those who from the disciples' vantage point seemed to be first in line for salvation—cannot be saved, then who *can* be saved?

ASKING GOOD QUESTIONS
The disciples were extrapolating from Jesus' teaching, teasing out the implications and testing his words against worldly realities. In the process, they raised a very good question, the answer to which is "no one by his or her own effort."

Finally the disciples may have been getting the picture. There's no point in trying to be saved because no one can be saved . . . unless God does the saving.

Without realizing it perhaps, the bewildered disciples achieved a breakthrough with their good question. Now they must listen attentively to Jesus' answer. Disciples today should be as eager to probe and to wonder.

10:27 **But Jesus looked at them and said, "With men it is impossible, but not with God; for with God all things are possible."**^{NKJV} The answer to the disciples' question, "Who can be saved?" turns out to be quite simple. In reality, it is not just the rich who have difficulty, for salvation is not possible for anyone from a human standpoint. No one can be saved by his or her wealth or achievements or talents: *With men it is impossible.* But the situation is not hopeless, for God had an entirely different plan: *With God all things are possible.* Salvation cannot be earned; God gives it to us as a gift. No one needs money, talent, or advantage to obtain it. Instead, it is offered to all people equally. *No one* is saved on merit; but *all* are saved who humbly come to God to receive salvation. As Paul wrote to the Ephesians, "For by grace you have been saved through faith, and this is not your own doing; it is the gift of God—not the result of works, so that no one may boast" (Ephesians 2:8-9 NRSV).

10:28 Peter said to him, "We have left everything to follow you!"ᴺᴵⱽ Peter, once again acting as spokesman for the Twelve, contrasted the disciples with the rich young man. He refused to give up what he had, but the disciples had *left everything* to follow Jesus. The Greek word *(aphekamen)* is in the aorist tense, implying a once-for-all act. They had done what the rich young man had been unwilling to do. They had abandoned their former lives. Matthew recorded Peter's question to emphasize this fact: "What then will we have?" (Matthew 19:27 NRSV). They had done the ultimate in self-denial and had followed Jesus' call. Wouldn't they then receive some great reward for having done so?

10:29-30 "I tell you the truth," Jesus replied, "no one who has left home or brothers or sisters or mother or father or children or fields for me and the gospel will fail to receive a hundred times as much in this present age (homes, brothers, sisters, mothers, children and fields—and with them, persecutions) and in the age to come, eternal life."ᴺᴵⱽ Peter and the other disciples had paid a high price—leaving their homes and jobs and secure futures—to follow Jesus. But Jesus reminded them that following him has its benefits as well as its sacrifices. Although they had to leave everything (10:28) to follow Christ, they would be paid back in *this present age* (the time period between Jesus' first and second comings) as well as *in the age to come* (after Jesus' second coming). Jesus assured the disciples that anyone who gave up something valuable for his sake would be repaid a hundred times over, although not necessarily in the same form. It is difficult to say whether Jesus had in mind material as well as spiritual blessings; although in light of 10:17-31 it probably means that God will give spiritual blessings for material sacrifices. For example, someone may be rejected by his or her family for accepting Christ, but he or she will gain the larger family of believers with all the love it has to offer.

Along with these rewards, however, *persecutions* must be expected because the world hates God. Jesus emphasized persecution to point out to the disciples that they must not selfishly follow him only for the rewards. This fact was also important for Mark's Roman readers who may have been facing persecution, or would soon be. The pressure of persecution did not mean that God wasn't keeping his promises or that the disciples had been wrong in putting faith in him. Rather, during persecution, God still blesses all those who believe in him.

Here was the answer to the rich young ruler's question about how to obtain eternal life (10:17). Jesus explained that by submitting to his authority and rule, making him top priority over all else, and giving up anything that hinders following him, each person can have *eternal life*. For the rich young man, that meant giving up money as his idol. For each person the sacrifice may be different, though no less difficult. We may have little or much, but are we willing to give it all up in order to have eternal life?

GIVE AND GAIN
If you must give up a secure job, you will find that God offers a secure relationship with himself now and forever. If you must give up your family's approval, you will gain the love of the family of God. The disciples had begun to pay the price of following Jesus, and Jesus said they would be rewarded. Don't dwell on what you have given up; think about what you have gained, and give thanks for it. You can never outgive God.

10:31 "But many who are first will be last, and the last first."NKJV Jesus explained that in the world to come, the values of this world will be reversed. Those who believe but who still seek status and importance here on earth will have none in heaven. Jesus may have been speaking to the disciples' mixed-up motives. They had given up everything and hoped for rewards, for status in God's kingdom (whatever that would be). Jesus was saying, "Yes, there will be restoration, but watch your attitude." Other servants may come who will get more honor or bear more fruit. Jesus explained that yearning for position would cause them to lose any position they might have. Those who have desired to be Christ's disciples and have humbly served others are most qualified to be great in heaven. Rewards in heaven are given not on the basis of merit or "time served" or other earthly standards. What matters in heaven is one's commitment to Christ.

CHANGING THE SYSTEM
Jesus seems to defy logic in this exchange about winners and losers. He seems to be saying: The reasons why people achieve power and wealth are exactly wrong for my kingdom, where the poor and hungry who come to faith are models of citizenship, and those who serve are the true leaders.
     Jesus, so unimpressed with worldly prestige, holds places of honor in reserve for faithful disciples who see beyond trophies and blue ribbons to what the Bible elsewhere calls a "crown of glory." Have you set your eyes above earth's rewards?

JESUS PREDICTS HIS DEATH THE THIRD TIME / 10:32-34 / **177**

As if to underscore his destination, Jesus once again spoke to the disciples about his impending death. He included the Resurrection in his prediction. Located as we are on the other side of the "grand proof," we can hardly appreciate the difficulty of the disciples in understanding Jesus' words. This prediction was the most graphic, which made it memorable when it was finally understood weeks later after the Resurrection.

10:32 **They were on their way up to Jerusalem, with Jesus leading the way, and the disciples were astonished, while those who followed were afraid.**^{NIV} Jesus and the disciples continued toward Jerusalem. This is the first mention in Mark of their destination. Jesus led the way, setting his face toward the city where he knew death awaited him (see also Luke 9:51). Going *up to Jerusalem* refers to the ascent of the land toward the city that sat on the highest point around. Anyone walking toward Jerusalem went "up" in elevation.

Jesus had just spoken to them about facing persecution and had told them of his impending death twice before. Thus, the disciples *were astonished* that he so steadfastly headed toward Jerusalem. The impending danger weighed on Jesus as well as on the disciples, and the crowds following behind sensed a change and reacted with fear.

 PICTURE OF LIFE
If our life seems like a scary journey, this group of travelers presents a perfect picture: Jesus leading, disciples amazed at what he says and does, followers fearful. Most people could fit into this group very well.

If you feel frightened by what lies ahead, you're not alone. Even people who traveled with the Lord felt fear. If you're astonished and cannot explain all that's happening in your life, join the crowd. The disciples walked abreast of Jesus with those same feelings.

For every traveler that day and today, a leader is guiding the journey. He knows your heart and your worries; he knows the way home. Follow close, and your faith will be strengthened.

Again he took the Twelve aside and told them what was going to happen to him.^{NIV} The crowds did not know the information Jesus was giving his disciples regarding his coming death. Jesus once again *took the Twelve aside* so that he might speak to them privately about *what was going to happen to him.* This was the third time Jesus told the disciples about his impending death (see also 8:31; 9:30-31). This time he gave much more detail about what was coming.

10:33-34 **"We are going up to Jerusalem," he said, "and the Son of Man will be betrayed to the chief priests and teachers of the law."**^{NIV} Jesus' death and resurrection should have come as no surprise to the disciples. Here Jesus clearly explained to them what would happen to him. Unfortunately, they didn't really hear what he was saying. Jesus said he was the Messiah, but they thought the Messiah would be a conquering king. Instead, Jesus clearly explained that he, the *Son of Man,* the human being who was also the Messiah, God's Son, would be *betrayed* (someone who had loved him would turn on him) to the Jewish leaders *(the chief priests and teachers of the law).*

"They will condemn him to death and will hand him over to the Gentiles, who will mock him and spit on him, flog him and kill him."^{NIV} The Sanhedrin (or Jewish supreme court comprised of the Jewish leaders) would condemn Jesus to die. But because Israel was occupied territory, they had to submit to Rome's authority in cases of capital punishment. The right of capital punishment had been taken from them. They could punish lesser crimes, but only Rome could execute an offender. Thus, the Jewish leaders could condemn Jesus, but they had to *hand him over to the Gentiles* in order to achieve his death.

In Mark's Gospel, this is the first time we discover that others besides the Jewish leaders would be involved in Jesus' death. "The Gentiles" refers to Pilate, the Roman governor, who represented Rome in Palestine. The Gentile Romans would show great contempt for their prisoner, mocking and beating him before killing him.

"Three days later he will rise."^{NIV} Jesus spoke to them of resurrection, but they heard only his words about death. Because Jesus often spoke in parables, the disciples may have thought that his words on death and resurrection were another parable they weren't astute enough to understand. The Gospels include Jesus' predictions of his death and resurrection to show that these events were God's plan from the beginning and not accidents. What would happen to Jesus had been predicted by the prophets (see, for example, Psalm 22:6-8; Isaiah 50:6; 52:13–53:12).

JESUS TEACHES ABOUT SERVING OTHERS / 10:35-45 / **178**

Jesus devoted much of his final time on earth to two objectives: to prepare the disciples for his own death and resurrection, and to prepare the disciples for life together without his physical presence. James and John's special request provides another view of the disciples' overall state of mind. They didn't understand what Jesus was saying, but they were convinced that great events were about to occur. They were jostling for position. In 9:33-37, Jesus had already confronted one argument among the Twelve about their relative status with each other. Here he drew a larger picture of what life would be like in the kingdom of God. Greatness, as defined and illustrated by Jesus' words and life, finds its clearest expression in service. In what ways are you living out the kingdom by serving others?

10:35 Then James and John, the sons of Zebedee, came to Him, saying, "Teacher, we want You to do for us whatever we ask."NKJV
Two of Jesus' disciples, *James and John* (brothers who along with Peter made up the inner circle of disciples, 9:2) came to Jesus. They requested that Jesus promise to fulfill their request before they even asked it. They may have misconstrued Jesus' promise that the twelve disciples would "sit on twelve thrones, judging the twelve tribes of Israel" (Matthew 19:28 NIV). Mark records that James and John went to Jesus with their request; in Matthew, their mother, Salome, made the request. There is no contradiction in the accounts—mother and sons were in agreement in requesting honored places in Christ's kingdom. Their mother may have been in the crowd that continued to follow Jesus—one of those who believed in him but was not one of the Twelve. According to Matthew 27:56, she was at the cross when Jesus was crucified. Some have suggested that she was the sister of Mary, the mother of Jesus. Thus James and John may have hoped that, as Jesus' cousins, their close family relationship would lend weight to their request.

SANTA CLAUS GOD
One of our greatest temptations is to treat God like a magic genie. We want to get our way and have him make life good, so we pray our wish list until the goodies start falling around us. We want golden eggs; producing them should be well within God's powers.

But God is not a cosmic Santa Claus. God does not write us a blank check, and God's promises are not a grab bag. Disciples carry no magic wands.

By prayer, we talk to God about our needs and wants. God hears and answers according to his holy will. By his Spirit, he aligns our prayers and desires to conform to his interests. We must remember that he, like any good parent, has the right to say no. Only the false and phony gods of religious fiction pretend to be magic genies. We must not treat God so foolishly.

The disciples' request highlighted the problem with most of our prayers. We also want Jesus to do whatever we ask. According to John 14:13-14, we offer true prayer when we pray in Jesus' name; but these disciples wanted to pray in their own names. Jesus does promise to answer our prayers when we pray according to his will and according to his interest. He does not give us blanket coverage for whatever we want.

10:36 And He said to them, "What do you want Me to do for you?"^{NKJV} Jesus was thinking about what he would face in Jerusalem and the death he knew awaited him there. Yet he showed remarkable patience with these two beloved disciples who came with a request. Jesus made no promises, but simply asked what they wanted him to do.

We should pause frequently to ask ourselves the same question before we make requests of God. Just what do we really want him to do? If Christ were to give us anything we ask, would we really ask for prestige and position over all his gifts?

RIVALRY
Rivalries, arguments, and disagreements among believers can be destructive in three ways: (1) They damage goodwill, trust, and peace—the foundations of good human relations. (2) They hamper progress toward important goals. (3) They make us self-centered rather than love-centered. Jesus understood how destructive arguments among brothers could be. In his final prayer before being betrayed and arrested, Jesus asked God that his followers be "one" (John 17:21).

10:37 They replied, "Let one of us sit at your right and the other at your left in your glory."^{NIV} The disciples, like most Jews of that day, had the wrong idea of the Messiah's kingdom as predicted by the Old Testament prophets. They thought Jesus would establish an earthly kingdom that would free Israel from Rome's oppression. As the disciples followed Jesus toward Jerusalem, they realized that something was about to happen; they certainly hoped Jesus would be inaugurating his kingdom. James and John wanted to sit beside Christ in his glory—these were the most honored places in the kingdom. In ancient royal courts, the persons chosen to sit at the right and left hands of the king were the most powerful people in the kingdom. James and John were asking for the equivalent of those positions in Jesus' court. They understood that Jesus would have a kingdom; they understood that Jesus would be glorified (they had seen the Transfiguration); and they approached him as loyal subjects to their king. However, they did not understand that Jesus' kingdom is not of this world; it is not centered in palaces and thrones, but in the hearts and lives of his followers. None of the disciples understood this truth until after Jesus' resurrection.

10:38 But Jesus said to them, "You do not know what you are asking. Are you able to drink the cup that I drink, or be baptized with the baptism that I am baptized with?"[NRSV] It must have been difficult for Jesus, steadfastly heading toward his death, to deal with these ambitious and blind disciples. It must have been frustrating to realize that soon his time on earth would end with the disciples seeming to have no inkling of who he was or what he had come to do.

But Jesus responded to James and John that in making such a self-centered request, they did not know what they were asking. To request positions of highest honor meant also to request deep suffering, for they could not have one without the other. Thus, he asked first if they were able to *drink the cup* that he would drink. The verb tense in Greek indicates an event that has not yet occurred but is so certain that it can be spoken of as already having happened. The "cup" to which Jesus referred was the same "cup" mentioned in his prayer in Gethsemane, "Take this cup from me. Yet not what I will, but what you will" (14:36 NIV). It was the cup of suffering that he would have to drink in order to accomplish salvation for sinners. Jesus would not only endure horrible physical pain, but he would also bear the wrath of God's punishment for sin, causing him to be abandoned by God for a time (Matthew 27:46).

Then Jesus asked if they were able to *be baptized* with the baptism he would face. The reference to "baptism" picks up an Old Testament metaphor for a person being overwhelmed by suffering. In the Old Testament, "deep waters" often described calamity, suffering, and the divine judgment of God (see, for example, Job 22:11; Psalm 18:16; 42:7; Isaiah 43:2). The "cup" and the "baptism" refer to what Jesus would face on the cross.

Mark alone recorded references to both the "cup" and "baptism." These words would be familiar to the early church because of the rites of Eucharist and baptism. Mark may have intended to show his readers the true importance of these rites. To drink Jesus' cup and to be baptized with his baptism meant more than just taking part in a ritual; it also meant taking up his mission and his sufferings. The two disciples misunderstood the implications of Jesus' questions and answered glibly. Mark may have been concerned that his readers in Rome would understand what being a Christian truly meant.

Jesus' cup of suffering was unique, for it had a unique purpose. But in both questions, Jesus was asking James and John if they were ready to suffer for the sake of the kingdom.

10:39-40 **They replied, "We are able."**^{NRSV} James and John replied confidently to Jesus' question. They answered that they were able to drink the cup and be baptized with Jesus. Their answer may not have revealed bravado or pride as much as it showed their willingness to follow Jesus whatever the cost, to fight the battle that was before them. As loyal followers, they hoped to receive their request of honor along with Jesus.

Then Jesus said to them, "The cup that I drink you will drink; and with the baptism with which I am baptized, you will be baptized."^{NRSV} James and John said they were willing to face any trial for Christ. Jesus replied that they would be called upon to do so: James died as a martyr, put to death by the sword (Acts 12:2); John lived through many years of persecution before being forced to live the last years of his life in exile on the island of Patmos (Revelation 1:9).

MAJORING IN THE MINOR
It is easy to say we will endure anything for Christ, yet most of us complain over the most minor problems. If we say we are willing to suffer on a large scale for Christ, we must also be willing to suffer the irritations and humiliations that come with serving others.

"But to sit at my right hand or at my left is not mine to grant, but it is for those for whom it has been prepared."^{NRSV} Although these two disciples would face great suffering, this still would not mean that Jesus would grant their request for great honor. Suffering is the price of greatness, but it is the price required to follow Christ at all. They would follow and they would suffer, but they would not thereby sit at his right and left in the kingdom. Jesus would not make that decision; instead, those places were reserved *for those for whom it has been prepared.* God's omniscience is revealed in the statement that he already knew who would gain those places of great honor.

Jesus' words reveal that, while he will distribute eternal rewards (2 Timothy 4:8), he will do so according to God's decisions. Jesus showed by this statement that he was under the authority of the Father, who alone makes the decisions about leadership in heaven. Such rewards are not granted as favors. They are reserved for those who have maintained their commitment to Jesus despite severe trials.

Jesus didn't ridicule James and John for asking, but he denied their request. We can feel free to ask God for anything, but our request may be denied. God wants to give us what is best for us, not merely what we want.

10:41 When the ten heard about this, they became indignant with James and John.[NIV] The other disciples were *indignant* that James and John had tried to use their relationship with Jesus to grab the top positions. Why such anger? Probably because *all* the disciples desired honor in the kingdom. Perhaps Peter, his temper getting the best of him, led the indignant ten disciples, for he had been the third with James and John in the group closest to Jesus. This probably seemed like a real slight to him. The disciples' attitudes degenerated into pure jealousy and rivalry. Before we react harshly to the disciples' behavior, we should recall how easy it is for us to be irritated at the honors others seek or receive. Jesus immediately corrected their attitudes, for they would never accomplish the mission to which he had called them if they did not love and serve one another, working together for the sake of the kingdom.

10:42 Jesus called them together and said, "You know that those who are regarded as rulers of the Gentiles lord it over them, and their high officials exercise authority over them."[NIV] Jesus once again patiently called his disciples around him. They were angry with one another, upset about James and John's private attempt to gain preferential status in Jesus' kingdom. So Jesus explained to them the difference between the kingdoms they saw in the world and God's kingdom, which they had not yet experienced.

The kingdoms of the world (an obvious example being the Roman Empire) have rulers and high officials who *lord it over* people, exercising authority and demanding submission (see 1 Peter 5:1-3). These Jews knew how very unpleasant it was to live under Rome's oppression. Jesus was delicately saying that they were no better than the despised Gentiles and their rulers. In this Gentile kingdom, people's greatness depended on their social standing or family name. But Jesus explained that his kingdom would be like nothing they had ever experienced.

10:43-44 "But it is not so among you; but whoever wishes to become great among you must be your servant, and whoever wishes to be first among you must be slave of all."[NRSV] Jesus' kingdom had already begun right there in that group of twelve disciples.

But the kingdom was not set up with some who could lord it over others. Instead, the greatest person would be the servant of all. Jesus used the imagery of both a household *servant* and a *slave* to demonstrate what a servant attitude looked like. While the Old Testament often spoke of submission and service, it usually referred to a person's relationship with God. Jesus applied the concept of the servant attitude to a person's relationship to other people. In doing so, he transformed the ethics of the ancient world. The Greeks considered humility to be the lowest virture; Jesus made it the highest.

Peter heard this message and remembered it well, for later he would write in one of his letters about leaders being servants (see 1 Peter 5:1-4). James and John wanted the highest positions in Jesus' kingdom. But Jesus told them that true greatness would come in serving others.

What did this mean for the disciples? A real leader has a servant's heart, willingly helping out others as needed. Servant leaders appreciate others' worth and realize that they're not above any job. They work together, not trying to gain positions of status or authority. They don't keep count of who did what or why. They aren't jealous about someone else's gifts, but gladly fulfill their duties. The disciples could not mistake Jesus' explanation that they were to serve sacrificially. Only with such an attitude would the disciples be able to carry out the mission of sharing the gospel across the world. Jesus was their perfect example of a servant leader.

SERVANT LEADERSHIP
By saying that the first will be last and the last first, Jesus changed the terms of winning and losing, as well as terms of leadership. In Jesus' kingdom, leaders are those who work toward the best interests of others, not parading their authority or lording it over others.

Servant leadership in Jesus' kingdom has a lot of the "can do" spirit in it, a big portion of "follow me to the hard work," and a huge helping of "your pile looks bigger than mine, let me help you." In your role as a leader, how can you look out for the best interests of others?

10:45 "For even the Son of Man did not come to be served, but to serve, and to give His life a ransom for many."[NKJV] Many scholars think that these words of Jesus are the main focus in all of Mark. Why would the disciples have to be willing to serve? Because that was the example set by their Master. Jesus explained that he *did not come to be served, but to serve, and to* *give.* Again Jesus referred to himself as *the Son of Man.* In Mark, the Son of Man is shown as receiving glory through serving and conquering evil through suffering. While Jesus is the Son of God, his glory was hidden in the form of a servant who paid the ultimate price to serve others: He gave his life. Paul later wrote:

■ *Your attitude should be the same as that of Christ Jesus: Who, being in very nature God, did not consider equality with God something to be grasped, but made himself nothing, taking the very nature of a servant, being made in human likeness. And being found in appearance as a man, he humbled himself and became obedient to death—even death on a cross! (Philippians 2:5-8* NIV)

Jesus' mission was to serve—ultimately by giving his life in order to save sinful humanity. His life wasn't "taken"; he "gave" it, offered it up as a sacrifice for people's sins. A *ransom* was the price paid to release a slave from bondage. Jesus paid a ransom for us, and the demanded price was his life. The Greek word translated "for" *(anti)* includes the idea of substitution. Some scholars think that the concept of substitutionary atonement did not begin with Jesus, but with Paul's writings. However, here and in the words of institution in the Last Supper, Jesus showed awareness of his death as substitution.

Jesus took our place; he died the death we deserved. Peter later wrote that the payment was not in silver or gold, but "the precious blood of Christ" (1 Peter 1:18-19 NIV). That payment freed us from our slavery to sin. The disciples thought that Jesus' life and power would save them from Rome; Jesus said his death would save them from sin, an even greater slavery than Rome's. Jesus often told his disciples that he must die, but here he told them why—to redeem all (the word *many* does not mean "quite a few," but "all") people from the bondage of sin and death (see also 14:24). "Many" is a term used in the Old Testament (Isaiah 53:11-12) and in the Qumran writings to refer to the covenant community, the elect who will inherit the kingdom of God. Jesus' words that he would give his "one" life for "all" people may allude to Isaiah 53:11-12 (see also Romans 5:19). Because Jesus willingly took the lowest place, he has the right to the highest seat in God's kingdom. All who repent and believe can come to him.

JESUS HEALS A BLIND BEGGAR / 10:46-52 / **179**

The healing of Bartimaeus was the final event before the Passion Week. Mark described Jesus' time in Jericho with a single sentence. Perhaps Jesus arrived late at night and departed the next morning. The distance to Jerusalem was about eighteen miles, a walk culminating in the Triumphal Entry.

Matthew's version of this healing mentions two beggars but no names. Mark's version does not preclude the possibility of another beggar or that Jesus performed other miracles on the way to Jerusalem that day. But it does raise the question of why Mark chose to include this particular miracle. Perhaps it was to demonstrate the need for boldness in coming to Jesus.

Chapter 9 focused on wrong perceptions of Jesus by the disciples and the crowds. Some still misunderstood Jesus, but many were rejecting him. People tried to prevent Bartimaeus from contacting Jesus. Jesus responded, not to Bartimaeus's understanding of Jesus' lordship, but to the boldness of his faith. Bartimaeus believed, not because of the clarity of his sight, but as a response to what he heard. Blind Bartimaeus asked for mercy and received his sight.

10:46 They came to Jericho.^{NRSV} Jesus and the disciples arrived in the city of Jericho. The Old Testament city of Jericho had been destroyed by the Israelites (Joshua 6:20). But during Herod the Great's rule over Palestine, he had rebuilt the city (about a mile south of the original city) as a site for his winter palace. Jericho was a popular and wealthy resort city, not far from the Jordan River, about eighteen miles northeast of Jerusalem. Jesus was on his way to Jerusalem (10:32), and after crossing over from Perea, he would naturally enter Jericho.

> Incarnational communication is aimed at meeting needs. . . . The attempt to divorce the physical from the spiritual . . . finds no support in the life and ministry of Jesus. *Robert Webber*

As Jesus and his disciples, together with a large crowd, were leaving the city, a blind man, Bartimaeus (that is, the Son of Timaeus), was sitting by the roadside begging.^{NIV} Jesus passed through the city, accompanied by his disciples and a large crowd (probably made up of Jews also on their way to Jerusalem for the Passover). They came upon a blind beggar sitting by the roadside. Beggars often waited along the roads near cities, because that was where they were able to contact the most people. Jericho, with its fairly wealthy inhabitants, was a popular location for beggars. Usually disabled in some way, beggars were unable to earn a living. Medical help was not available for their problems, and people tended to ignore their obligation to care for the needy (Leviticus 25:35-38). Thus, beggars had little hope of escaping their degrading way of life.

Matthew records that there were two blind men, while Mark and Luke mention only one. This is probably the same event, but Mark and Luke singled out the more vocal of the two men. *Bartimaeus* is an Aramaic name meaning *Son of Timaeus.*

10:47 And when he heard that it was Jesus of Nazareth, he began to cry out and say, "Jesus, Son of David, have mercy on me!"NKJV The blind man could not see, but he *heard* that Jesus of Nazareth was at the head of the approaching crowd. In order to be heard above the din, he shamelessly *began to cry out* for Jesus' attention. He had undoubtedly heard that Jesus had healed many (including blind people, 8:22-25 for example), and he took hope that Jesus would *have mercy* on him and heal his eyes. There were no healings of the blind in the Old Testament; the Jews believed that such a miracle would be a sign that the messianic age had begun (Isaiah 29:18; 35:5).

Bartimaeus called Jesus *Son of David* because he, along with all Jews, knew that the Messiah would be a descendant of King David (see Isaiah 9:6-7; 11:1; Jeremiah 23:5-6). The fact that Bartimaeus called Jesus the Son of David shows that he recognized Jesus as the Messiah. This blind beggar could *see* that Jesus was the long-awaited Messiah, while so many who witnessed Jesus' miracles were blind to his identity, refusing to open their eyes to the truth. Seeing with one's eyes doesn't guarantee seeing with the heart.

THE EYES OF FAITH
We do not know how long Bartimaeus had been blind, but it only took a moment to decide to call on Jesus for help. Jesus met many spiritually blind people—religious leaders, family members, people in the crowd. Though their eyes were fine, they could not see the truth about Jesus. But Bartimaeus heard the report that Jesus was coming and boldly cried out.

In coming to Jesus, we need Bartimaeus's boldness. We must overcome our reticence and doubts and take the step to call on him. Bartimaeus had not seen Jesus' miracles, but he responded in faith to what he had heard. We have heard Jesus described in the Gospels. May we be like those of whom Peter wrote, "Though you have not seen him, you love him; and even though you do not see him now, you believe in him" (1 Peter 1:8 NIV).

10:48 Many sternly ordered him to be quiet, but he cried out even more loudly, "Son of David, have mercy on me!"NRSV The crowd tried to get the man to be quiet. It was most natural for the people, even Jesus' disciples, to attempt to shield Jesus from being harassed by beggars. But this only caused Bartimaeus to cry louder. His blindness meant he could not find his way through the crowd to touch Jesus' cloak, as the sick woman had done (5:27-28). Thus, he kept on crying out in an attempt to gain Jesus' attention. And it worked.

10:49 Jesus stopped and said, "Call him." So they called to the blind man, "Cheer up! On your feet! He's calling you."^{NIV} Although Jesus was concerned about the coming events in Jerusalem, he demonstrated what he had just told the disciples about service (10:45) by stopping to care for the blind man. Blindness was considered a curse from God for sin (John 9:2), but Jesus refuted this idea when he told the people to call the man to him. At first the crowd had sternly rebuked the blind man (10:48), but after Jesus called him, their tone changed to friendly encouragement.

10:50 Throwing his cloak aside, he jumped to his feet and came to Jesus.^{NIV} Bartimaeus had incredible faith. He knew Jesus could heal him, and he would not miss the opportunity, even at the risk of being a very loud pest. So when the people told him that Jesus had called him, he tossed off his outer cloak (a large heavy garment used as a coat as well as a sleeping mat) despite the chilly spring air. Bartimaeus's attitude of joy came out in his jumping to his feet. The absence of any reference to help is deliberate and gives the impression that he would allow no barrier, even blindness, to keep him from his goal, Jesus.

NO BARRIERS
Bartimaeus demonstrated both perseverance and obedience. He persistently overcame the barriers to his healing and becoming a disciple of Jesus. He was blind and could not get to Jesus; he was rebuked when he called out for mercy. Yet he ignored the reaction of the crowd and came to Jesus. He obeyed immediately by jumping to his feet, leaving behind his only comfort and possession. He knew his desperate condition. Perhaps that is our final barrier. Many do not come to Jesus because they don't feel they need him. Do you recognize your spiritual blindness? Are you willing to leave everything behind and quickly respond to Christ?

10:51 "What do you want me to do for you?" Jesus asked him. The blind man said, "Rabbi, I want to see."^{NIV} Obviously Jesus already knew what Bartimaeus wanted. Jesus' question was not to gain information, but to allow Bartimaeus to specify his need and, in the process, to declare his faith that Jesus could meet that need. He addressed Jesus as *Rabboni,* meaning "my dear master," showing his respect for Jesus. *I want to see* is literally "I want to recover my sight." The blind man had at one time been able to see.

10:52 **Jesus said to him, "Go; your faith has made you well." Immediately he regained his sight and followed him on the way.**NRSV The result of Bartimaeus's request was that *he regained his sight.* His faith (evidenced in his persistence) had made him well. Unlike Matthew and Luke, Mark mentioned no healing touch or word of Jesus. The stress is not so much on the miracle, but on the faith that led to it.

The restoring of sight led to discipleship, for Bartimaeus then *followed* Jesus. The man had been made physically well (with restored sight) and spiritually well (with the assumed acceptance of salvation because of his faith). He followed Jesus *on the way;* that is, he remained with the crowd that followed Jesus to Jerusalem. It could also mean that he followed Jesus as a disciple.

Mark 11

As in the other Gospels, the story slows now, from Jesus' entry
into Jerusalem until his resurrection a week later. Up to this
point, the Gospels have presented a sampler of Jesus' life and
ministry. But the closing chapters of each account present powerful details.

Mark's account relates that Jesus went directly from Jericho to
Jerusalem, while John's Gospel supplies the added stop in Bethany. The crowd that accompanied the Lord into David's city was
made up of Jesus' followers and pilgrims on their way to Passover. Jesus raised Lazarus from the dead. The crowd joyfully
escorted Jesus into Jerusalem, perhaps hoping that this would be
the time when he would declare his political intentions and expel
the Romans.

**11:1-2 Now when they drew near Jerusalem, to Bethphage and Beth-
any, at the Mount of Olives.**^{NKJV} Mark continued to give his
readers Jesus' itinerary as Jesus and the disciples headed toward
Jerusalem. After passing through Jericho and healing the blind
man (10:46), they *drew near Jerusalem* and came to the villages
of Bethphage and Bethany. These two villages were about one
mile apart, one and two miles respectively from the eastern wall
of Jerusalem, and sat on the eastern slope of the Mount of Olives.
Bethany was the home of Jesus' dear friends Mary, Martha, and
Lazarus; he often stayed there with his disciples (see John 11:1).
He may have returned to their home each night after his visits to
Jerusalem during the days of this final week.

The Mount of Olives is a ridge about two and a half miles long
on the other side of the Kidron Valley east of Jerusalem. The
view from the top of this twenty-nine-hundred-foot ridge is spectacular—one can see the whole city. From this site, Jesus discussed the coming destruction of the city and temple (13:1-4).
The mention of the Mount of Olives is probably intentional by
Mark, pointing to the messianic fulfillment by Jesus. This moun-

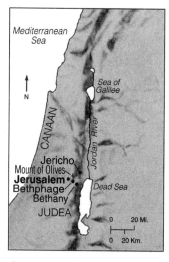

Jesus nears Jerusalem
Leaving Jericho, Jesus headed toward acclaim, then crucifixion, in Jerusalem. During his last week, he stayed outside the city in Bethany, a village on the Mount of Olives, entering Jerusalem to teach, eat the Passover, and finally be crucified.

tain is important in the Old Testament as the place of God's final revelation and judgment (see Ezekiel 43:2-9; Zechariah 14:1-19).

Jesus sent two of his disciples, saying to them, "Go to the village ahead of you, and just as you enter it, you will find a colt tied there, which no one has ever ridden. Untie it and bring it here."NIV When Jesus spoke these words, they were probably in Bethphage. He sent two disciples to Bethany to get the colt and bring it back. Once again Jesus sent not one, but two disciples (as on the preaching mission, 6:7). This was a mission of faith, for the disciples simply had to go on Jesus' words. The specification that this be a colt *which no one has ever ridden* is significant in light of the ancient rule that only animals that had not been used for ordinary purposes were appropriate for sacred purposes (Numbers 19:2; Deuteronomy 21:3; 1 Samuel 6:7).

Matthew mentions a donkey and a colt (Matthew 21:2), while the other Gospels mention only the colt. This was the same event, but Matthew focused on the prophecy in Zechariah 9:9, where a donkey and a colt are mentioned, thus affirming Jesus' royalty. He showed how Jesus' actions fulfilled the prophet's words, thus giving another indication that Jesus was indeed the Messiah. When Jesus entered Jerusalem on a donkey's colt, he affirmed his messianic royalty as well as his humility. When Jesus came to Jerusalem, he did not fulfill the people's hopes as the conquering deliverer to drive out the Gentiles, but he nonetheless gave all the signs of a royal person making entrance into the city. Mark emphasized Jesus' humility and his sovereign control of the situation. The divine Son of God was coming to sacrifice his life. The disciples did indeed find everything just as Jesus said.

This was Sunday of the week that Jesus would be crucified, and the great Passover festival was about to begin. Jews came to Jerusalem from all over the Roman world during this week-long celebration to remember the great Exodus from Egypt (see Exodus 12:37-51). Many in the crowds had heard of or seen Jesus and were hoping he would come to the temple (John 11:55-57).

Jesus did come to the temple, not as a warring king on a horse or in a chariot, but as a gentle and peaceable king on a donkey's colt, just as Zechariah 9:9 had predicted. Jesus knew that those who would hear him teach at the temple would return to their homes throughout the world and announce the coming of the Messiah.

BUDDY SYSTEM
Jesus sent two disciples for mutual support, since faith is stronger when two "go out" with prayer and determination.

Is your church's Sunday school dull and tedious, your outreach program flat, your youth ministry a burnout? Make sure no one works alone. Teamwork helps in most other areas, too, like family, business, and athletics. By prayer, support, and encouragement, good partners help move mountains.

11:3 "If anyone asks you, 'Why are you doing this?' tell him, 'The Lord needs it and will send it back here shortly.'"[NIV] Mark emphasized Jesus' supernatural knowledge and control in this incident. He knew the disciples would be asked why they were taking the colt. Donkeys and their colts were valuable; this could be compared to borrowing someone's car. So Jesus, sensitive to this fact, told them to explain that the colt would be returned. By this time Jesus was extremely well known. Everyone coming to Jerusalem for the Passover feast had heard of him, and Jesus had been a frequent visitor in Bethany. *The Lord needs it* was all the two disciples would have to say, and the colt's owners (Luke 19:33) would gladly let them take the animal.

JESUS NEEDS IT
Two simple lessons come from this verse. First, Jesus has needs. Amazing! Jesus did not create a donkey; he sent disciples to find one. Today, Jesus needs workers too. The Son of God needs you!

Second, while Jesus does not hold legal title to all the world's property, he is owner of all by virtue of his work in creation and redemption. When Jesus needs something, the appropriate response is to surrender the title and let the Lord use it. Today, we call that stewardship or giving.

If the Lord needs something today, give generously with love and gratitude. Apart from Jesus, you wouldn't have your life, so don't hold back anything. Do you recognize his prior claim on all you own? Are you in touch with what Jesus needs from you?

11:4-6 They went away and found a colt tied near a door, outside in the street. As they were untying it, some of the bystanders said to them, "What are you doing, untying the colt?" They told them what Jesus had said; and they allowed them to take it.^{NRSV} The disciples went and found everything just exactly as Jesus had said. Some commentators suggest that those who owned the colt may have been spoken to ahead of time by Jesus; thus, they expected this incident. However, that seems unlikely because Luke records that these *bystanders* who asked this question were actually the colt's owners (Luke 19:33). These owners surely knew Jesus and probably recognized the disciples; for they were frequent visitors in Bethany, and Jesus had just recently raised one of their neighbors from the dead (see John 11). Yet the disciples only had to quote the words Jesus had told them to say, and the owners allowed them to take the animal.

11:7 Then they brought the colt to Jesus and threw their cloaks on it; and he sat on it.^{NRSV} The two disciples walked the colt back to Bethphage. The colt, having never been ridden (11:2), did not have a saddle, so the disciples threw their cloaks on its back so that Jesus could sit on it. The action of placing the cloaks on the donkey and Jesus riding it connotes majesty (see 2 Kings 9:13 where cloaks were spread out for King Jehu).

POOR CHOICE
The Lone Ranger's calling cards were a silver bullet, a black mask, and a mighty horse named Silver. Give the Ranger a donkey and you'd ruin the show.

But a simple donkey was just right for the Son of God. Jesus shunned earthly power (and its symbols) in order to demonstrate a kingdom of love and peace. The Messiah entered Jerusalem on the back of a borrowed burro. In that picture, there is poverty, humility, and majesty: "Yet for your sakes he became poor" (2 Corinthians 8:9 NIV). There is no shame in being poor.

Today, when Christians flaunt symbols of financial success, remember the donkey. If your own dreams include rising above the brutish pack to a place of wealth and comfort, remember Jesus' limousine: a seat of sweaty overcoats on a one-gear beast of burden. We must fulfill our responsibility to serve him with whatever financial resources he has chosen for us.

11:8 Many people spread their cloaks on the road, and others spread leafy branches that they had cut in the fields.^{NRSV} Crowds of people had already gathered on this stretch of road a mile outside of Jerusalem, going to the city for the Feast of Unleavened Bread and Passover. When Jesus mounted the colt

and headed toward the city, they recognized that he was fulfilling
the prophecy in Zechariah 9:9, "Rejoice greatly, O Daughter of
Zion! Shout, Daughter of Jerusalem! See, your king comes to
you, righteous and having salvation, gentle and riding on a donkey, on a colt, the foal of a donkey" (NIV). All pilgrims walked
the final ascent to Jerusalem; Jesus' riding was a clear sign. The
crowd's spontaneous celebration honored Jesus; it was demonstrated when they spread their cloaks on the road for him to ride
over (compare with 2 Kings 9:12-13).

In addition, they took leafy branches from the fields. These
branches were used as part of the pilgrimage into Jerusalem. Matthew says branches were cut from the trees (Matthew 21:8). Probably they came from both places; some were also spread along
Jesus' path, others were probably waved in the air (see Psalm
118:27). Christians celebrate this event on Palm Sunday.

11:9-10 **Then those who went before and those who followed cried**
out, saying: "Hosanna! 'Blessed is He who comes in the name
of the LORD!' Blessed is the kingdom of our father David that
comes in the name of the Lord! Hosanna in the highest!"^{NKJV}
The crowd was chanting words from Psalm 118:25-26. Those in
front and those behind Jesus exclaimed, *"Hosanna."* Although
the word technically means "save now," the people were probably not asking God to do so. They were using a phrase like
"Praise the Lord" or "Hallelujah," not really thinking about the
meaning. The expression *He who comes in the name of the LORD*
may have been recited as part of the Passover tradition—as a
blessing given by the people in Jerusalem to the visiting pilgrims.
Thus, not all the people saying this would have realized its
messianic significance. Of course, others did. They spoke of *the*
kingdom of our father David because of God's words to David in

DON'T BE BASHFUL
Two observations grip most readers of this story. First, Jesus
came humbly into the big city (11:7). There were no official delegations, no pomp, no displays of power. It was a low-key arrival
for the long-awaited Messiah.

Second, the crowds burst with joyful praise. This band of
people was *very* happy. Something wonderful was happening,
a breakthrough, an evening to remember. Once in a lifetime . . .
once in all time!

That's Jesus' coming: no spotlights, amplifiers, or press, but
much happiness bursting all around, vivid songs of praise filling
the air. Get ready to sing, shout, and dance. Don't be bashful in
expressing your love and praise for Christ.

2 Samuel 7:12-16. The people lined the road, praising God, waving palm branches, and throwing their cloaks in front of the colt as it passed before them. "Long live the King" was the meaning behind their joyful shouts because they knew that Jesus was intentionally fulfilling prophecy.

This was Jesus' announcement that he was indeed the long-awaited Messiah. He chose a *time* when all Israel would be gathered at Jerusalem, a *place* where huge crowds could see him, and a *way* of proclaiming his mission that was unmistakable. The people went wild. They were sure their liberation from Rome was at hand. While the crowd correctly saw Jesus as the fulfillment of these prophecies, they did not understand where Jesus' kingship would lead him. The people who were praising God for giving them a king had the wrong idea about Jesus. They expected him to be a national leader who would restore their nation to its former glory; thus, they were deaf to the words of their prophets and blind to Jesus' real mission. When it became apparent that Jesus was not going to fulfill their hopes, many people would turn against him. A similar crowd would cry out, "Crucify him!" when Jesus stood on trial only a few days later. It takes more than participation at a praise gathering to be a true friend and follower of Jesus.

EXPECTATIONS
Like those who witnessed Jesus' victory parade into Jerusalem, we have expectations for what we think God should do to make life better, safer, and more enjoyable. Like excited spectators, we can't wait to see suffering stopped, injustice corrected, and prosperity begun. Like the people on the road to Jerusalem that day, we have much to learn about Jesus' death and resurrection. We must not let our personal desires catch us up in the celebration and shouting lest we miss the meaning of true discipleship. In our excitement and celebration, we must remember that following Christ involves hardships. It may include suffering, even death.

11:11 Jesus entered Jerusalem and went to the temple. He looked around at everything, but since it was already late, he went out to Bethany with the Twelve.^{NIV} Jesus entered the great city and went to the temple, entering its outer courts as did many in the crowd. The temple in Jerusalem was already rich with history. There had been three successive temples on the same site. The first, Solomon's glorious temple, was built in the tenth century B.C. and was destroyed in 586 B.C. when the Babylonians captured Jerusalem. The second was Zerubbabel's temple, much smaller than Solomon's temple, but built on the same site by the exiles who returned from captivity in the sixth century B.C. The third temple, the one Jesus entered, was built by Herod the Great.

The magnificent structure, much larger and more elaborate, was begun in 20 B.C. and may not have been completely finished before it was destroyed by the Romans in A.D. 70 in response to a Jewish revolt.

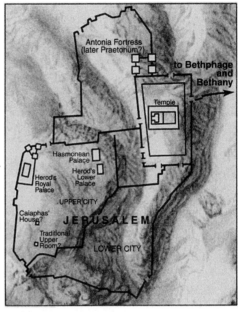

The Jewish sacrifices were to be offered only in the temple. The temple was run by the high priest and his associates. All adult male Jews were required to go to Jerusalem for three annual celebrations: Passover (in late spring), the Feast of Tabernacles (or Booths) in the fall, and the Feast of Weeks in early summer.

From Jerusalem to Bethany
During his last week, Jesus ministered in Jerusalem, where he faced heavy opposition from the religious leaders. He would then retreat to Bethany to be with his friends Mary, Martha, and Lazarus.

Mark notes that Jesus *looked around at everything.* This seems somewhat pointless until we read of Jesus' actions in the temple the next day (11:15-17) and understand that Jesus had already cleared the temple of these racketeers on an earlier Passover week (John 2:12-25), only to find here that they had returned. He probably would have acted right then except that *it was already late.* So he and the disciples returned to Bethany for the night, perhaps to the home of Mary, Martha, and Lazarus. It was not safe for Jesus to stay in the city. His only night in the city was the night of his arrest. Jesus' dear friends must have been a great comfort to him during this final week.

The disciples were probably a bit confused by this. They most likely thought, with the prophecy-fulfilling arrival of Jesus and the celebration parade, that the kingdom was coming and that Jesus had been all wrong about predicting his death. Yet, as far as they could see, no kingdom had been inaugurated. Instead, the crowds dispersed and they went home. They must have had quite a discussion into the night.

JESUS CLEARS THE TEMPLE AGAIN / 11:12-19 / *184*

Jesus was patient with ignorance, but he confronted arrogance. He was in constant conflict with those who knew better but did wrong. Jesus once again faced the desecration of the temple by opportunists and profiteers. The peddlers and parasites he had expelled during a previous visit had returned (see John 2:12-25). When a cleansed temple isn't filled up with goodness, it is soon restocked with evil.

Mark bracketed this account of the temple cleansing with the cursing of a fig tree. Matthew told the incident in a single narrative, but Mark, who had used this device in several places, told the story in two parts, probably as it occurred (see 3:20-21 and 31-34; 5:22-24 and 35ff.). Jesus' cleansing of the temple and cursing of the fig tree both demonstrate divine judgment on the apostasy of Israel.

11:12 The next day as they were leaving Bethany, Jesus was hungry.NIV This *next day* was Monday. Jesus and the disciples got up and headed back into Jerusalem. They spent the nights in Bethany and went into Jerusalem during the day. Bethany was about two miles outside of Jerusalem, making it a suburb of the city.

Somewhere along the way, Jesus mentioned that he was hungry. His hunger portrays his humanity. Jesus can sympathize with our human experience and daily needs. When we pray to him, expressing our weaknesses and troubles, we can be confident that he knows what we are facing. He has faced it too (Hebrews 4:15).

11:13 Seeing in the distance a fig tree in leaf, he went to see whether perhaps he would find anything on it. When he came to it, he found nothing but leaves, for it was not the season for figs.NRSV Fig trees were a popular source of inexpensive food in Israel. In March, the fig trees had small edible buds; in April came the large green leaves. Then in May the buds would fall off, replaced by the normal crop of figs. This incident occurred in April, and the green leaves should have indicated the presence of the edible buds which Jesus expected to find on the tree, because *it was not* *the season for figs.* However, this tree, though full of leaves, had no buds. Fig trees require three years from the time they are planted until they can bear fruit. The absence of buds indicated that the tree would not produce figs that year. The tree looked promising but offered no fruit.

11:14 He said to it, "May no one ever eat fruit from you again." And his disciples heard it.^NRSV Jesus did not curse this fig tree because he was angry at not getting any food from it. Instead this was an acted-out parable intended to teach the disciples. They didn't know that Jesus was on his way to once again cleanse the temple of the people who were desecrating it. By cursing the fig tree, Jesus was showing his anger at religion without substance. Jesus' curse did not make the tree barren of figs; instead, it sealed the way the tree had always been (see Matthew 13:13-15). Mark deliberately placed this story within the story of the cleansing of the temple. Jesus' harsh words to the fig tree could be applied to the nation of Israel and its beautiful temple. Fruitful in appearance only, Israel was spiritually barren. Just as the fig tree looked good from a distance but was fruitless on close examination, so the temple looked impressive at first glance, but its sacrifices and other activities were hollow because they were not done to worship God sincerely (see Jeremiah 8:13; Hosea 9:10, 16; Micah 7:1). If our churches spend large amounts on their physical buildings and ignore missions, evangelism, and care for the poor, they will likewise come under God's judgment.

THE SHELL GAME
Religious faith has a thousand veneers. Temples of impressive beauty, generosity of unusual proportion, eloquent prayers, robes, ornamental crosses, and incantations are only a few. All of religious show misses the point and amounts to nothing—an empty shell—without humble worship of the true and living God.
Real faith begins in the heart. Jesus asks us to repent and trust in him. Strong, vibrant, living faith requires a personal relationship with the risen Christ. Jesus is Lord; we are his disciples. Move beyond the veneer and trappings of Christianity to genuine faith in Christ. Faith puts fruit on your tree; it fills life's shell with love forever.

11:15-16 On reaching Jerusalem, Jesus entered the temple area and began driving out those who were buying and selling there.^NIV Jesus and the disciples arrived in Jerusalem and went straight to the temple. He had some "cleansing" to do, and he began by *driving out those who were buying and selling there.*

What were people *buying and selling?* People came to the temple in Jerusalem to offer sacrifices. God had originally instructed the people to bring sacrifices from their own flocks (Deuteronomy 12:5-7). However, the religious leadership had established four markets on the Mount of Olives where such animals could be purchased. Some people did not bring their own animals and planned to buy one at the market. Others brought their own animals, but when the priests managed to find the animal unacceptable in some way (it was supposed to be an animal without defect, Leviticus 1:2-3), worshipers were forced to buy another.

> Anger is the necessary handmaiden of sympathy and fairness, and we are wrong to try to make everyone sweet and reasonable. *James Q. Wilson*

Next, in an economic move that surely lined many pockets and enriched the temple coffers, the high priest had authorized a market to be set up right in the Court of the Gentiles, the huge outer court of the temple (see the map of "The Temple in Jesus' Day"). This was the only place Gentile converts to Judaism could worship. They could not go any farther into the temple because they were not "pure" Jews. But the market filled their worship space with merchants so that these foreigners, who had traveled long distances, found it impossible to worship. The chaos in that court must have been tremendous.

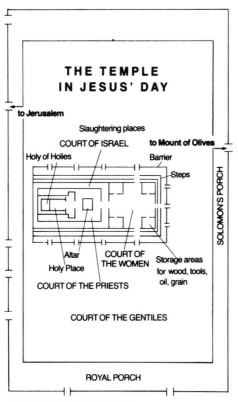

THE TEMPLE IN JESUS' DAY

to Jerusalem

Slaughtering places

COURT OF ISRAEL

to Mount of Olives

Holy of Holies

Barrier

Steps

SOLOMON'S PORCH

Altar

COURT OF THE WOMEN

Holy Place

Storage areas for wood, tools, oil, grain

COURT OF THE PRIESTS

COURT OF THE GENTILES

ROYAL PORCH

The Temple in Jesus' Day

Josephus, an ancient Jewish historian, wrote that 255,600 lambs were sacrificed at the Passover in A.D. 66. But lack of worship atmosphere didn't seem to bother the religious establishment who saw lots of money to be made in conveniently offering animals, grain, oil, and salt for the various sacrifices. Because both those who bought and those who sold were going against God's commands regarding the sacrifices, Jesus drove them all out.

NO SUBSTANCE
This passage contains two unusual incidents: the cursing of the fig tree and the clearing of the temple. The temple was supposed to be a place of worship, but true worship had disappeared. The fig tree showed promise of fruit, but it produced none. Jesus was showing his anger at religious life without substance. If you claim to have faith without putting it to work in your life, you are like the barren fig tree. Genuine faith has great potential; ask God to help you bear fruit for his kingdom.

He overturned the tables of the money changers and the benches of those selling doves, and would not allow anyone to carry merchandise through the temple courts.NIV The *money changers* did big business during Passover. Those who came from foreign countries had to have their money changed into Jewish currency because this was the only money the merchants accepted and the only money accepted for payment of the temple tax. The inflated exchange rate often enriched the money changers, and the exorbitant prices of animals made the merchants wealthy. The money changers exchanged Hebrew shekels for Roman drachmas for the temple tax. Because the drachmas had the stamped image of Caesar (who was an idol worshiper) on them, they were considered blasphemous by the Jews.

The mention of *doves* referred to an alternate sacrifice for those too poor to purchase larger animals. Doves were also sacrificed for the cleansing of women and lepers (Leviticus 12:6; 14:22). Imagine money boxes spilling and clattering across the floor as doves escaped from their overturned cages and scattered above the crowd. Jesus became angry because God's house of worship had become a place of extortion and a barrier to Gentiles who wanted to worship.

Mark alone recorded that Jesus *would not allow anyone to carry merchandise through the temple courts.* Jesus was so zealous for the sanctity of God's temple and the need for the Gentiles to have a place of worship that he enforced one of the Talmudic rules that forbade anyone to use the Court of the Gentiles as a thoroughfare or shortcut between the city and the Mount of Olives.

WHEN TO GET ANGRY
Jesus became angry, but he did not sin. There is a place for righteous indignation. Christians are right to be upset about sin and injustice and should take a stand against them. Unfortunately, believers are often passive about these important issues and instead get angry over personal insults and petty irritations. Make sure your anger is directed toward the right issues.

11:17 Then He taught, saying to them, "Is it not written, 'My house shall be called a house of prayer for all nations'? But you have made it a 'den of thieves.'"NKJV Obviously Jesus' actions stunned the many people crowded into the temple area, and probably drew spectators from both inside and outside. Jesus recognized an opportunity to teach and didn't waste it. He asked a rhetorical question, quoting from Isaiah 56:7, and used it to explain God's purpose for the temple. God's *house* was meant to be a house of prayer, but they were using it for other purposes. Mark added that Jesus said that this was a house of prayer *for all nations.* These were important words in light of Jesus' concern for the Gentiles who had come to worship, and considering the Gentile audience to whom Mark was writing. God welcomed the Gentiles into his temple to worship, but they were unable to do so because of the thousands of animals bellowing and merchants haggling.

Not only that, but all these merchants were no more honest than *thieves* (the word would be more correctly rendered "robbers," those in organized bands who worked on large-scale robberies). Jesus had just come from Jericho a few days before, along a road known for its dangerous bands of robbers that preyed on travelers. (In the story of the Good Samaritan, the man was robbed on the road between Jerusalem and Jericho—Luke 10:30.) No organized band of robbers along that treacherous stretch of road could possibly match the thievery going on in the temple. The merchants had turned the temple into their *den.* This was a horrible desecration. No wonder Jesus was so angry.

In this instance, Jesus set himself in authority above the religious leaders—the high priest (Caiaphas) and all those on the Sanhedrin. They were in charge of the temple, and they would soon have words with Jesus about this episode (11:27-28).

NO MORE BAKE SALES?
Jesus would probably not drive out most bake sales to fund youth ministries, book tables, or sign-ups for camp from your church foyer. He stood against lack of faith and altering the purpose for worship. Those who use the church people or the worship gathering for social, political, or financial advantage are clearly wrong. God opposes those who attempt to leverage power or status or to meet their need for self-importance in his house of prayer. Don't throw bake sales out of your church; instead, throw hypocrisy out of your life.

11:18 And when the chief priests and the scribes heard it, they kept looking for a way to kill him; for they were afraid of him, because the whole crowd was spellbound by his teaching.NRSV
It didn't take long for news of Jesus' rampage through the temple to reach the ears of the chief priests and scribes. The chief priests were mostly Sadducees (the wealthy, upper class, priestly party among the Jewish political groups); the scribes were usually Pharisees (experts and teachers of the law). These two parties had great contempt for each other (see, for example, Acts 23:6-10). That these two groups could agree on anything was highly out of the ordinary. But Jesus was becoming a real problem: undermining their authority in the temple, performing great miracles of healing, refusing to answer their trick questions, showing them up in his answers, and teaching the people in such an exciting and refreshing manner that they were *spellbound.* Again Mark used the Greek word *ekplesso* to describe a state of being out of one's mind with amazement. These religious leaders agreed that Jesus needed to die, so they began to plot how to *kill him.* But Jesus was so popular with the crowds that they dared not make a move immediately. In short, *they were afraid of him.* If he were to incite the crowds, they might end up the targets.

NO MIDDLE GROUND
After this episode, people could not ignore Jesus or be indifferent to him. They had to take sides. Either Jesus was a subversive radical who must be restrained (death is an effective restraint), or he was someone to be listened to, believed, and followed.
    Today, indifference is common because people are not listening to Jesus' words. When Christians tell the real story, there is no middle ground. Either Jesus is God's Son, the world's Savior, or he is a befuddled, perhaps demented, imposter.
    Today listen, believe, and follow—while there's time—before Jesus comes to clean the area of false religion one last time.

11:19 And when evening came, Jesus and his disciples went out of the city.^{NRSV} With the religious leaders plotting to kill him, Jerusalem would hardly be a safe place for Jesus to spend the night. Safely outside the city, Jesus could not be surprised and arrested by the temple priesthood. So when evening came on that Monday night, Jesus and the disciples left the city and most likely returned to Bethany as before (because they passed the same fig tree the next morning, 11:13, 20).

JESUS SAYS THE DISCIPLES CAN PRAY FOR ANYTHING / 11:20-26 / **188**

Mark split his account of Jesus' cursing the fig tree into two parts: the curse itself as an acted-out parable about God's judgment of fruitless Israel, and the disciples' response. Our perspective tends to be different from that of the disciples. They accepted the cursing of the fig tree, but wondered how Jesus had caused the plant to wither. We take Jesus' power for granted but want to know why Jesus did it. The parallel between Jesus' cursing the tree and cleansing the temple reveals his motive. The power of faith and prayer can make us effective. For our prayers to be effective, we must have faith and we must forgive others.

> When I wrote my Confessions, I was already old and disillusioned with the vain pleasures of life, all of which I had tasted and felt their emptiness in my heart. *Jean Jacques Rousseau*

11:20 Now in the morning, as they passed by, they saw the fig tree dried up from the roots.^{NKJV} The next morning, Tuesday, Jesus and disciples passed by the same fig tree they had passed the day before (11:13-14). Jesus had cursed the tree, saying that no one would ever eat from it. By the next day, in the morning light, they could see that the tree had *dried up from the roots.* Jesus had done more than condemn the tree, he had killed it.

11:21 Peter remembered and said to Jesus, "Rabbi, look! The fig tree you cursed has withered!"^{NIV} Peter remembered what Jesus had said the day before, and expressed surprise that the tree not only would never bear fruit, but that it had completely *withered.* This parable of spiritually dead Israel revealed a severe judgment. The early church later applied this parable to the total destruction of Jerusalem in A.D. 70.

11:22-23 "Have faith in God," Jesus answered. "I tell you the truth, if anyone says to this mountain, 'Go, throw yourself into the sea,'

**and does not doubt in his heart but
believes that what he says will happen,
it will be done for him.**"[NIV] Jesus did not
explain why he cursed the fig tree, and
we don't know whether the disciples
understood Jesus' meaning. Yet his
words to them could mean that despite
the coming judgment on spiritual laxity
in Israel, they would be safe if they had
faith in God. Their faith should not rest
in a kingdom they hoped Jesus would set
up, in obeying the Jewish laws, or in
their position as Jesus' disciples. Their
faith should rest in God alone.

Jesus then taught them a lesson about
answers to prayer. Jesus had cursed the
fig tree; the fig tree had died; the disciples had expressed surprise. Then Jesus
explained that they could ask anything
of God and receive an answer. Jesus
again used the words *I tell you the truth* to introduce this important message. They should not have been surprised that a fig tree
could be withered at Jesus' words. Jesus was using a figure of
speech to show that God could help in any situation: *This mountain* (referring to the Mount of Olives on which they stood) could
be sent into *the sea* (the Dead Sea, that could be seen from the
Mount). Jesus' point was that in their petitions to God they must
believe without doubting (that is, without wavering in their confi-

> Prayers are not always
> granted—in the crude
> factual sense of the
> word—"granted." This is
> not because prayer is a
> weaker kind of causality,
> but because it is a
> stronger kind. When it
> "works" at all, it works
> unlimited by space and
> time. That is why God
> has retained a
> discretionary power of
> granting or refusing it;
> except on that condition
> prayer would destroy us.
> *C. S. Lewis*

PRAYING THE IMPOSSIBLE
The kind of prayer that moves mountains is prayer for the effec-
tiveness of God's kingdom. It would seem impossible to move a
mountain into the sea, so Jesus used that picture to say that
God can do anything (see Paul's use of it in 1 Corinthians
13:2). God will answer your prayers, but not as a result of your
positive mental attitude. Other conditions must be met:
- You must be a believer.
- You must not be holding a grudge against another person.
- You must not pray with selfish motives.
- Your request must be for the good of God's kingdom.
- Your request must be in line with God's will and accepting of
  whatever that will might be.
   To pray effectively, you need faith in God, not faith in the
object of your request. If you focus only on your request, you
will be left with nothing if your request is refused.

dence in God). The kind of prayer Jesus meant was not the arbitrary wish to move a mountain; instead, he was referring to prayers that the disciples would need to endlessly pray as they faced mountains of opposition to their gospel message in the years to come. Their prayers for the advancement of God's kingdom would always be answered positively—in God's timing.

11:24 **"Therefore I tell you, whatever you ask for in prayer, believe that you have received it, and it will be yours."**[NIV] This verse was not a guarantee that the disciples could get anything they wanted simply by asking Jesus and believing. God does not grant requests that will hurt people or that will violate his own nature or will. Jesus' statement was not a blank check. To be fulfilled, requests made to God in prayer must be in harmony with the principles of God's kingdom. They must be made in Jesus' name (John 14:13-14). The stronger our faith, the more likely our prayers will be in union with Christ and in line with God's will; then God would be happy to grant them. God can accomplish anything, even if it seems humanly impossible.

> A further crisis of all [false] morality [occurs when] man does not give himself. Instead he lets himself be represented by his sacrifices, his merits. Instead of being reconciled with his brother, he omits this self-giving and takes a gift to the altar. *Helmut Thielicke*

WHOSE INTERESTS?
Jesus, our example for prayer, prayed, "Everything is possible for you. Take this cup from me. Yet not what I will, but what you will" (14:36 NIV). Our prayers are often motivated by our own interests and desires. We like to hear that we can have anything. But Jesus prayed with *God's* interests in mind. When we pray, we should express our desires, but we should want his will above ours. Check to see if your prayers truly focus on God's interests, not yours.

11:25 **"And when you stand praying, if you hold anything against anyone, forgive him, so that your Father in heaven may forgive you your sins."**[NIV] Jesus gave another condition for answered prayer, this one referring to believers' relationships with others. He told the disciples that when they stood praying, if one of them held a grudge against someone, he ought to first forgive that person before praying. Standing was the common position for the Jews in prayer. If a person becomes bitter and angry over a wrong done, prayer is impossible. God wants us to deal with our "horizontal" relationships in order to have a clear "vertical" relationship (see also Matthew 5:23-24).

Why would this matter? Because all people are sinners before God. Those who have access to him have it only because of his mercy in forgiving their sins. Believers should not come to God asking for forgiveness or making requests, all the while refusing to forgive others. To do so would be to reveal that they have no appreciation for the mercy they have received. God will not listen to a person with such an attitude. God wants those who are forgiven to forgive others.

ANYTHING BUT
Forgiving others is tough work—so much so that many people would rather do something totally distasteful, like run a mile uphill, shovel gravel all day, wash greasy pots, or clean diapers . . . anything but forgive that rotten, no-good scoundrel.

For a person to pray while bearing a grudge is like a tree sprouting leaves and bearing no fruit (11:13). True faith changes the heart. Real prayer dismantles pride and vengeance, filling the holes with love. Real faith seeks peace. For our churches to have prayer power, there must be harmony and forgiveness evident in the body of believers. Let go of hurts, abandon grudges, and forgive others.

11:26 **"But if you do not forgive, neither will your Father in heaven forgive your trespasses."**^{NKJV} This verse is not included here in some Bible versions. It was probably not originally included in Mark's text, but was added later on the basis of Matthew 6:15 and Luke 11:4. Yet the principle is true: If we don't forgive others, God will not forgive us.

RELIGIOUS LEADERS CHALLENGE JESUS' AUTHORITY / 11:27-33 / *189*

At this point Mark began an extended section (11:27–12:34) showing Jesus under constant attack yet emerging victorious over his opponents. With the one exception of the teacher who asked Jesus about the greatest commandment (12:28), Jesus' opponents tried desperately to catch him in a wrong answer. In each case, Jesus turned their question around with a question of his own. He proved that their motives were evil and their premises were wrong.

In this first clash in the temple, Jesus forced those seeking his death to reveal their unwillingness to believe him. Jesus responded to their evasive "We don't know" by refusing to answer their question. But in doing so, he also was pointing out that they had answered their own question.

11:27 They arrived again in Jerusalem, and while Jesus was walking in the temple courts, the chief priests, the teachers of the law and the elders came to him.^{NIV} The teaching recorded in 11:22-26 transpired on Tuesday morning as Jesus and the disciples were on their way back into Jerusalem. They returned to the temple, where Jesus had thrown out the merchants and money changers the day before. The religious leaders were afraid to act on their plot to kill Jesus in the public surroundings of the temple. He was safe in the temple courts among the people with whom he was so popular.

But a delegation of *the chief priests, the teachers of the law and the elders* stopped Jesus. These were representatives of the three groups that made up the seventy-one-member Sanhedrin, the Jewish ruling council. These three groups were mentioned when Jesus predicted his execution (8:31; 9:31; 10:33). This was an angry official group sent on an official mission to question Jesus regarding his actions.

11:28 "By what authority are you doing these things?" they asked. "And who gave you authority to do this?"^{NIV} This group of leaders was already plotting to kill Jesus (11:18), but they couldn't figure out how to do it. His popularity was far too widespread and his miracle-working powers too well known. The Sanhedrin probably met on Monday night in a hastily called session to decide how to handle this man who was flouting their authority. So they brought him a question that they hoped would trap him into saying something for which he could be arrested. They asked for his credentials and demanded that he tell them who gave him the authority to cast the money changers and merchants out of the temple. That this delegation would even ask these questions indicates that Jesus had not yet openly declared himself to be the Messiah.

POWER STRUGGLE
These religious leaders were concerned about authority. They wanted to keep theirs, and they knew Jesus' teaching was challenging their power structure. Their actions illustrate the potential for spiritual blindness of those in power in the church. Although bishops, pastors, and deacons hold important positions, wrong motives can render them ineffective. These Pharisees had the power to renew Jewish faith, but they would neither change the religion nor let anyone else do it. They challenged Jesus' authority, but they had no real spiritual insight or power of their own. If you hold a position of leadership in the church, base that authority on a heart for God and a desire for service.

If Jesus were to answer that his authority came from God, which would be tantamount to saying he was the Messiah and the Son of God, they would accuse him of blasphemy and bring him to trial (blasphemy carried the death penalty, Leviticus 24:10-23). If Jesus were to say that his authority was his own, they could dismiss him as a fanatic and could trust that the crowds would soon return to those with true authority (themselves). But Jesus would not let himself be caught. Turning the question on them, he exposed their motives and avoided their trap.

11:29 Jesus said to them, "I will ask you one question; answer me, and I will tell you by what authority I do these things."^{NRSV} To expose the leaders' real motives, Jesus countered their question with a question. This was a common debating technique among rabbis. But he explained that his answer would depend on their answer. The questions the religious leaders asked were perfectly valid questions to check for a false prophet or false teacher, but their sinister motives made it an evil test.

11:30 "Did the baptism of John come from heaven, or was it of human origin? Answer me."^{NRSV} The question seems totally unrelated to the situation at hand, but Jesus knew that the leaders' attitude about John the Baptist would reveal their true attitude toward him. In this question, Jesus implied that his authority came from the same source as John the Baptist's. So Jesus asked these religious leaders what they thought: Did John's authority to baptize come from heaven, or was it merely human authority?

CROWDED OUT
These religious leaders were afraid of the crowd's reaction. They had not loved the people or led them properly. All they wanted was to stay on top. Proverbs 29:25 says, "The fear of others lays a snare" (NRSV). Christian leaders must not give in to public opinion and pressure. They must stay faithful to God whether people praise or condemn. Don't use people to gain support. Don't let circumstances or people's expectations sway you. Stand true to God, and you will have no need to fear the crowd.

11:31 They discussed it among themselves and said, "If we say, 'From heaven,' he will ask, 'Then why didn't you believe him?'"^{NIV} The interchange recorded among these factions of the religious leaders revealed their true motives. They weren't interested in the truth; they didn't want an answer to their question so they could finally understand Jesus—they simply hoped to trap him. But they found themselves in a position of looking foolish in front of the crowd. If they answered that John's baptism had come from divine authority, then they would incriminate themselves for not listening to John and believing his words. The people knew that the religious leaders had been silent about Herod's murder of John. If they accepted John's authority, they would be accepting John's criticism of them as a brood of vipers who refused to repent (see Matthew 3:7-10). They would then have to admit that Jesus also had divine authority.

11:32 "But shall we say, 'Of human origin'?"—they were afraid of the crowd, for all regarded John as truly a prophet.^{NRSV} If they rejected John as having any divine authority, then they also were rejecting Jesus' authority and would be in danger of the crowd (see 12:12). Luke recorded that they were afraid the crowd would stone them for such an answer (Luke 20:6), *for all regarded John as truly a prophet.* They would have preferred this answer, but they could not give it because of the crowd.

THE BIG LIE
The religious leaders were lying through their teeth, but they covered their lying with official and scholarly respectability. They were saving face, cloaking their deceit and envy. They were guilty for the murder of John the Baptist because they neither tried to get him released nor spoke up against his murder. They knew the answer to their own question but refused to acknowledge Jesus as an authority. In John 3:19, Jesus summed up this attitude: "but men loved darkness instead of light because their deeds were evil" (NIV). People who reject Jesus' claims have a greater problem than intellectual doubt. They are rebelling against Christ's control of their lives. Are you trying to cover up your rebellion, or have you made Christ your authority?

11:33 So they answered and said to Jesus, "We do not know." And Jesus answered and said to them, "Neither will I tell you by what authority I do these things."^{NKJV} The Pharisees couldn't win, so they hoped to save face by refusing to take either alternative. Thus, Jesus was not obligated to answer their question. In reality, he had already answered it. His question about John the Baptist implied that they both received their authority from the same source. The crowds believed that John was a prophet; Jesus' words should have made them realize that he was victorious over the Pharisees and that his authority was from God. While some in the crowd might understand and believe, the religious leaders had already decided against Jesus, and nothing would stand in the way of their plan to kill him. They had already rejected both Jesus and John as God's messengers, carrying on a long tradition of the leaders of Israel rejecting God's prophets. This is the point Jesus makes in the following parable (12:1-12).

Mark 12

Jesus immediately followed up his first clash with the religious leaders by telling parables. Matthew included three (Matthew 21:28–22:14), but Mark included only one. Apparently, all the parables Jesus told on this occasion were linked by a common theme of acceptance/rejection. Jesus confronted the religious leaders with their hard-heartedness.

In the parable of the wicked farmers, Jesus used a strong image of judgment from the Old Testament (Isaiah 5:1-7). Isaiah's ancient poem incriminated Jerusalem by name. The religious leaders immediately heard the charges leveled against them.

The tenant farmers thought they could take the land into their own hands, when all the while they were betraying themselves into someone else's hands. We must not think that we can take some of God's truth and all of his blessings without regarding him as the rightful owner.

12:1 He then began to speak to them in parables.^{NIV} Jesus was presumably still in the temple, where the representatives of the Sanhedrin (the Jewish supreme court) had come to question him. They had failed in their first attempt at tricking Jesus into an answer that would condemn him (11:27-33).

Here Mark recorded that Jesus *began to speak to them in parables.* Parables are story illustrations that use something familiar to help us understand something new. This method of teaching compels listeners to discover truth for themselves. Jesus wants us to understand God's truth for ourselves, applying it personally and obeying it. Merely knowing information is not enough. This particular parable pointedly described the religious leaders who stood before Jesus, showed that Jesus knew their intention to kill him, and warned them of their ultimate punishment for their actions.

"A man planted a vineyard. He put a wall around it, dug a pit for the winepress and built a watchtower. Then he

rented the vineyard to some farmers and went away on a journey."^{NIV} The moment Jesus spoke of a *vineyard,* the well-versed religious leaders would have recognized the correlation with the words of Isaiah 5:1-7, where Isaiah described Israel as a vineyard. Thus, they immediately understood that Jesus was speaking of the nation of Israel in his parable. Isaiah's parable described judgment on Israel; Jesus' parable described judgment too. The vineyard also portrays God's grace. God bypassed Egypt and Assyria and chose Israel as his special people (Psalm 80:7-11; Jeremiah 2:14-21). But Israel turned away from God and rejected his grace.

The situation pictured in this parable was by no means unusual. Galilee had many such estates with absentee owners who had hired tenant farmers to care for the fields and crops. Much land was dedicated to grape vineyards, with wine being one of the major exports of Galilee. The tenant farmers paid their "rent" by giving a portion of the crop to the landowner, who would send servants at harvesttime to collect it. Tensions often arose; records exist of bitter disputes between landowners and their tenants. The angry tenants in Jesus' parable reflected the social upheaval in Palestine at the time.

This was a choice vineyard that required protection. A stone *wall* protected it from thieving people or animals; a *pit* collected the juice of the grapes as they were crushed; and a *watchtower* was a lookout and a shelter for the grape gatherers. These details provide local color but have no particular allegorical significance. The characters, however, provide the allegory.

The main elements in this parable are (1) the man who planted the vineyard—God, (2) the vineyard—Israel, (3) the tenant farmers—the Jewish religious leaders, (4) the landowner's servants (12:2)—the prophets and priests who remained faithful to God and preached to Israel, (5) the son—Jesus (12:6), and (6) the others to whom the vineyard was given (12:9)—the Gentiles.

Israel, pictured as a vineyard, was the nation that God had cultivated to bring salvation to the world. The religious leaders not only frustrated their nation's purpose; they also killed those who were trying to fulfill it. They were so jealous and possessive that they ignored the welfare of the very people they were supposed to be bringing to God. By telling this story, Jesus exposed the religious leaders' plot to kill him, and he warned them that their sins would be punished.

12:2 **"At harvest time he sent a servant to the tenants to collect from them some of the fruit of the vineyard."**^{NIV} When the grape harvest came, the absentee landowner *sent a servant* to col-

PERSECUTED PROPHETS

The Persecuted	The Persecutors	Reason	Result	Reference
Prophets	Jezebel	Jezebel didn't like to have her evil ways pointed out.	Many prophets were killed.	1 Kings 18:3-4
Elijah	Ahab and Jezebel	Elijah confronted their sins.	Elijah had to flee for his life.	1 Kings 18:16–19:2
Elisha	A king of Israel	The king thought Elisha had caused the famine.	Elisha ignored the threatened persecution and prophesied the famine's end.	2 Kings 6:31
Hanani	Asa	Hanani criticized Asa for trusting in Syria's help more than in God's help.	Hanani was thrown in jail.	2 Chronicles 16:7-10
Micaiah	Ahab	Ahab thought Micaiah was stirring up trouble rather than prophesying from God.	Micaiah was thrown into prison.	2 Chronicles 18:12-26
Zechariah	Joash	Zechariah confronted the people of Judah for disregarding God's Word.	Zechariah was executed.	2 Chronicles 24:20-22
Uriah (Urijah)	Jehoiakim	Uriah confronted Jehoiakim about his evil ways.	Uriah was killed.	Jeremiah 26:20-23
Jeremiah	Zedekiah	Zedekiah thought Jeremiah was a traitor for prophesying Jerusalem's fall.	Jeremiah was thrown in prison, then into a muddy cistern.	Jeremiah 37:1–38:13
John the Baptist	Herod and Herodias	John confronted their adultery.	John was beheaded.	Mark 6:14-29

lect the "rent"—namely *some of the fruit of the vineyard.* Generally this amounted to a quarter to a half of the crop, probably in the form of wine, not grapes. In Jesus' parable, the "servants" that were sent to the tenants refer to the prophets and priests whom God had sent over the years to the nation of Israel.

TELLING STORIES

Telling stories is one of our most effective ways of teaching values, of making a lesson palatable. Would you rather hear a lecture on trust or be engaged by a story with a plot as tempting as chocolate, a climax as soothing as hot cinnamon rolls?

Parents raising children should seize bedtime moments to read stories or just tell them. Pastors should encourage churches with stories that spice up a sermon's teaching. Jesus told stories when he could have given lectures. Try it yourself, and watch those audiences—young and older—perk up with interest.

12:3 "And they took him and beat him and sent him away empty-handed."ᴺᴷᴶⱽ The picture of angry tenants beating the landowner's slave and sending him on his way without any "rent" did not shock Jesus' audience. The rapidly deteriorating situation in Palestine, with guerrillas fighting for freedom from Rome and bandits rampaging the land, made this an especially poignant parable. The tenants who were entrusted with the care of the vineyard represented the religious leaders who were entrusted with the spiritual care of Israel. But instead of listening to the prophets, God's "servants," the religious leadership had mistreated them and had stubbornly refused to listen.

12:4 "Then he sent another servant to them; they struck this man on the head and treated him shamefully."ᴺᴵⱽ The first servant returned empty-handed to the landowner. Determined to collect his due, the landowner sent a second servant. This one was treated even more harshly; a wound to the head was a serious injury.

RAW TREATMENT

So maybe these servants represented a wealthy landowner. Maybe the tenants thought these servants were uppity or insensitive to their situation as workers. Yet we cannot excuse the tenants' behavior. They were not owners; they were permitted to live on and work the land, keeping 75 percent of the produce.

The parable indicts Israel for hurting God's prophets. It applies to us each time we reject a messenger from God. Have you spurned a friend or spouse who came with a caring word? Have you rejected a minister who had words from God for you?

12:5 "Then he sent another, and that one they killed. And so it was with many others; some they beat, and others they killed."ᴺᴿˢⱽ The landowner sent still another servant; that servant was murdered. Not to be put off, the landowner continued to send servants, but every servant met harsh treatment. While some were beaten; others were killed.

Jesus could hardly have made his point more clear. Throughout Israel's history, the leadership constantly rejected the prophets God sent to them, refusing to turn away from idols or to follow God's guidance. Many of God's prophets were beaten; others were killed (see the chart, "Persecuted Prophets"). The fact that he sent so many portrays God's patience, mercy, and loving-kindness.

12:6 **"He had one left to send, a son, whom he loved. He sent him last of all, saying, 'They will respect my son.'"**NIV With all the servants having been mistreated or killed, the landowner had only one messenger left—his beloved son. This son was sent to the tenant farmers to collect the fruit of the vineyard in hopes that the farmers would give the son due honor and respect. This "beloved son" refers to Jesus. This is the same description God used at Jesus' baptism (1:11) and at the Transfiguration (9:7). The son was sent *last of all* to the stubborn and rebellious nation of Israel to win them back to God and away from the self-serving religious leadership.

IS GOD NAIVE?
A landowner who loses several servants, then sends his only son, may be accused of closing his eyes to the dangers of the mission. The son, after all, is a land-grabber's prime target. Getting rid of him clears title for greedy tenants. The landowner should know this.

Why would God send Jesus if the prophets had already been badly treated? Because the mission required it, and love required that the mission be completed.

Next time you feel depressed and sullen, gray and cloudy, as though there's not much to live for, remember that divine love looked for you. God's Son came for you.

12:7-8 **"But the tenants said to one another, 'This is the heir. Come, let's kill him, and the inheritance will be ours.' So they took him and killed him, and threw him out of the vineyard."**NIV The tenants probably thought that the arrival of the son meant that his father (the landowner) had died. In Palestine at that time, "ownerless" or unclaimed land could be owned by whoever claimed it first. Thus they reasoned that if they killed the son, they could claim the property *(the inheritance)* as their own. So they killed the son and threw his body over the wall without burial—a horrible indignity in Israel.

Jesus came to call Israel back to God. But the religious leaders, caught up in their positions, wanted to hold on to their power and prestige with the people. Jesus threatened to take that away; they couldn't match his teaching, his miracles, or his popularity. They thought that killing Jesus was the only way to gain back the respect of the people that seemed to be slipping from their grasp. Notice that Mark made the point that the body was thrown *out of the vineyard;* therefore, the son was killed *in* the vineyard. Jesus would be killed *in* Israel yet *outside* the walls of Jerusalem as the result of a plot formed by Israel's religious leaders.

VIOLENCE
The inheritance will be ours. We are shocked that these renters killed the owner's son with such disregard, ungratefulness, and violence. Yet we do violence to Jesus and his messengers when we think they disrupt our security, leisure plans, or pleasure. How are we "killing" God's claim on our time and treasure?

- Are we possessive and murderously resentful when our leisure or pleasure gets bumped for Christian responsibilities?
- Would his return be unwelcome because of the plans that we have made?

12:9 "What then will the owner of the vineyard do? He will come and kill those tenants and give the vineyard to others."NIV
Jesus then asked his listeners to consider what the landowner would do once he heard of his son's murder. In Greek, "owner" is *kurios,* meaning "master"; it was also a title for God (the Lord). In using this word, Jesus was giving a deliberate hint about who the "owner" represented.

Jesus then answered his own question. All agreed that the landowner would come, kill the tenants, and give the vineyard to others who would care for it and pay the rent on time. The answer also reflects Isaiah 5:4-13, in which God spoke of Israel as a vineyard that yielded only wild grapes and thus would be destroyed. But Jesus made a departure from Isaiah's prophecy. In Isaiah, the vineyard itself (the people of Israel) was at fault; in Jesus' parable, it was the tenants who angered God—that is, Israel's religious leadership was at fault.

Over hundreds of years, Israel's kings and religious leaders had rejected God's prophets—beating, humiliating, and killing them. Most recently, John the Baptist had been rejected as a prophet by Israel's leaders (11:30-33). Next Jesus, the beloved Son of God, already rejected by the religious leaders, would be killed. Jesus explained that the Jewish leaders would be accountable for his death because in rejecting the messengers and the Son, they had rejected God himself.

God's judgment would be spiritual death and the transfer of the privileges of ownership *to others,* namely, the Gentiles. In Romans 11:25-32, the apostle Paul explained that "a hardening has come upon part of Israel, until the full number of the Gentiles has come in" (Romans 11:25 NRSV). In this parable Jesus spoke of the beginning of the Christian church among the Gentiles. God would not totally reject Israel; in ancient times he always preserved a remnant of true believers (see, for example, 1 Kings 19:18). Yet the religious leaders—who should have recognized the Messiah, rejoiced at his arrival, and led the people to him—instead would put him to death.

LOSING THE EDGE
Along with the Bible's assurances of God's long-suffering love come warnings that love turns to judgment when we reject God's message. This is such a warning.

Bible warnings aim straight at us. For the Christian, failure to follow Christ leads to loss of spiritual gifts and a loss of a sense of God's presence and power. Will God give our responsibilities to others who will use them appropriately? To the person who is not yet a Christian, putting God off leads to spiritual deafness or hardening. Soon that person can't hear God's Word at all.

At all times, we must embrace God's truth eagerly, follow his lead faithfully, and respect the importance of his message daily.

12:10-11 **"Have you not even read this Scripture: 'The stone which the builders rejected has become the chief cornerstone. This was the LORD's doing, and it is marvelous in our eyes'?"**^{NKJV} Not only was Jesus making the religious leaders the "bad guys" in his parable, he was adding insult to injury by asking them if they had ever read this particular Scripture. Jesus was quoting from Psalm 118:22-23. Psalm 118 was a key part of the Passover service, and all the pilgrims coming to Passover would recite 118:25-26 as they came to Jerusalem. They had been reciting it for years without understanding or applying it (see John 5:39-40). In his quotation, the "son" of the parable became the "stone" of this prophecy; the "tenant farmers" of the parable became the "builders."

Like the son who was rejected and murdered by the tenant farmers, Jesus referred to himself as *the stone which the builders rejected.* The *cornerstone* was the most important stone in a building, used as the standard to make sure the other stones of the building were straight and level. Israel's leadership, like the builders looking for an appropriate cornerstone, would toss Jesus aside because he didn't seem to have the right qualifications. They wanted a political king, not a spiritual one. Yet

God's plans will not be thwarted. One day that rejected stone will indeed become the "cornerstone" with all the right qualifications—for Jesus *will* come as King to inaugurate an unending kingdom. And he had already begun a spiritual kingdom as the cornerstone of a brand-new "building," the Christian church (Acts 4:11-12; 1 Peter 2:7). Jesus' life and teaching would be the church's foundation.

Among all the Gospel writers, only Mark quoted the words, *This was the LORD's doing, and it is marvelous in our eyes.* Mark stressed divine intervention and its meaning for God's people. By quoting from Psalm 118, a passage the Jews took to be messianic, Jesus was, in fact, applying it to himself and claiming to be the Messiah. The religious leaders missed the point, but many of the people accepted Jesus as their promised Messiah and accepted his offer of salvation.

12:12 When they realized that he had told this parable against them, they wanted to arrest him, but they feared the crowd. So they left him and went away.NRSV We don't know exactly when during Jesus' story the truth dawned on the leaders, but *when they* (the religious leaders, representatives from all the groups of the Sanhedrin, 11:27) realized that they were the wicked people in Jesus' parable, *they wanted to arrest him.* Thus far in Jesus' ministry, the parables had held veiled truths that only believers could understand (4:11-12). The fact that these religious leaders understood the parable and its meaning brings a new tension to Mark's Gospel, for it appears that Jesus would soon reveal his true identity to everyone.

PRESSURE
Peer pressure influences our behavior, from the foods we eat to the clothes we wear to church. We make a thousand fewer decisions a day because conforming is easier than creating.

Because we feel peer pressure so strongly, choosing our group becomes very important. The crowd we follow will influence how we live.

In this case, religious leaders were influenced by two pressure groups, negatively by their own peers and positively by the crowd they feared. But how many of these leaders rose above their group's pressure and began to follow Jesus? It is tough to run alone against the wind. Yet we must stand for our faith against indifference, hostility, and rejection.

The crowd in the temple once again protected Jesus from arrest (as in 11:18). The mere presence of all those people, hanging on Jesus' every word, caused these religious leaders to fear a riot if they were to forcibly take Jesus away. They'd had enough humiliation for one day. A riot would also make them look bad in

the eyes of the Roman government to whom they were accountable for keeping the peace. There was nothing to do but go away
somewhere to gather new ideas and think of new questions to try
to trap Jesus.

RELIGIOUS LEADERS QUESTION JESUS ABOUT PAYING TAXES / 12:13-17 / **193**

The retreat mentioned in 12:12 was only temporary. Soon the
attacks against Jesus resumed. The religious leaders sent a delegation with the purpose of trapping Jesus with the same kind of
question he used on them earlier (11:29-33). They thought they
could catch him on one of the horns of a dilemma: to pay or not
to pay taxes to Caesar. Jesus showed them that their "horns" were
actually attached to two different animals. They had set up a false
conflict between the honor due God and the honor due human
authorities. By living under the authority and monetary system of
the Romans, the people were obligated to follow through on their
responsibilities under that human structure while still being accountable to God. Where they saw an impossible conflict, Jesus
described parallel duties. They presented Jesus with a question
that they were sure would trap him, no matter how he answered.
But he snared them with their own trap.

**12:13 Later they sent some of the Pharisees and Herodians to Jesus
to catch him in his words.**NIV The Jewish leaders would not be
put off because they were so intent on killing Jesus. The Pharisees were a religious group opposed to the Roman occupation of
Palestine. The Herodians were a political party that supported the
Herods and the policies instituted by Rome. These groups with
diametrically opposed beliefs usually had nothing to do with each
other. It may seem strange that any group of Jews would support
Rome and Herod's dynasty, but the Herodians' real hope was to
keep the nation together so that one day they might again be free.
After Herod the Great's death in 4 B.C., Palestine had been
divided among his sons. Although the nation had been split apart,
the rulers were still of one family. The Herodians' love was more
for country than for Herod; they realized that the only way to preserve their land and national identity was to keep Herod's family
together in the ruling positions.

But these two groups found a common enemy in Jesus. The Pharisees did not like Jesus because he exposed their hypocrisy. The Herodians also saw Jesus as a threat. They had lost political control when,
as a result of reported unrest, Rome had deposed Archelaus (Herod's
son with authority over Judea) and replaced him with a Roman gov-

ernor. The Herodians feared that Jesus would cause still more insta-
bility in Judea and that Rome might react by never replacing the
Roman leaders with a descendant of Herod.

Despite Jesus' solemn warning to the Jewish leaders in his previous parable, they didn't let up. More delegates arrived whose intentions were simply to *catch* Jesus in his words. Matthew 22:16 shows
that those sent were disciples of the Pharisees. The word translated
"catch" is found only here in the New Testament and was used for
catching a wild animal in a trap. These two groups, on different
sides of religious and political issues, hoped to get an answer from
Jesus that one of them would be able to use against him.

12:14 **And they came and said to him, "Teacher, we know that you
are sincere, and show deference to no one; for you do not
regard people with partiality, but teach the way of God in accordance with truth."**NRSV The men in this delegation, pretending to be honest men, flattered Jesus before asking him their trick
question, hoping to catch him off guard. Their flattering words
focused on Jesus' sincerity, his refusal to show deference or partiality toward those in authority, and his truthfulness. These
words reeked with irony, for these men hoped that through their
question, these very qualities would become Jesus' downfall.

FLATTERY
People appreciate heartfelt praise, but flattery always manipu-
lates. The men in the delegation thought that flattery would trap
Jesus. Many people whose egos are out of control or who have
low self-esteem fall prey to flattery. Jesus did not.
   If you're the target of flattery, a straight reply can cut through
another's phoniness. Using flattery against flattery would be
like Jesus answering these fellows: "O great leaders of faithful
Israel." Jesus did not play such games, and neither should we.
Double-sided words are like hidden weapons; Christians should
always be straightforward and bold.

"Is it right to pay taxes to Caesar or not?"NIV Thinking they had a
foolproof plan to corner him, the representatives of the Pharisees
and Herodians asked Jesus about paying Roman taxes. Judea had
been a Roman province since 63 B.C. But the Jews had fairly
recently been forced to pay taxes or tribute to Caesar—in A.D. 6, the
Sanhedrin (Jewish Council) was made responsible to collect taxes.

There were three basic types: (1) a land or produce tax took one-
tenth of all grain and one-fifth of all fruit (or wine), (2) everyone
aged fourteen to sixty-five paid a head or poll tax collected when a
census was taken—one day's wages, and (3) a custom tax was col-

lected at ports and city gates as tolls for goods transported—rates were 2 to 5 percent of the value of the goods. This question may have been focusing on the poll tax or on taxes in general.

This was a hot topic in Palestine. The Jews hated to pay taxes to Rome because the money supported their oppressors and symbolized their subjection. Much of the tax money also went to maintain the heathen temples and luxurious lifestyle of Rome's upper class. The Jews also hated the system that allowed tax collectors to charge exorbitant rates and keep the extra for themselves. The Roman government allowed tax collectors to contract for tax collection by paying the Romans a flat fee for a district. Then the tax collectors could profit from collecting all they could get. Anyone who avoided paying taxes faced harsh penalties. This was a valid (and loaded) question, and the crowd around Jesus certainly waited expectantly for his answer.

The leaders, however, did not really want an answer; their motives were only to put Jesus in a dilemma between the religious and political implications of their question. The Pharisees were against these taxes on religious grounds; the Herodians supported taxation on political grounds. Thus, either a yes or a no could lead Jesus into trouble. If Jesus agreed that it was right to pay taxes to Caesar, the Pharisees would say he was opposed to God, and the people would turn against him. If Jesus said the taxes should not be paid, the Herodians could hand him over to Herod on the charge of rebellion.

Jesus' questioners thought they had him this time, but Jesus outwitted them again.

12:15 **"Should we pay or shouldn't we?"**NIV The first question (12:14) reflects a legal standpoint ("Is it lawful for a Jew to pay these taxes?"). This seemingly repeated question here stems more from a practical standpoint—forcing Jesus to give a yes or no answer. The religious leaders weren't going to let Jesus out of any loophole in his answer.

But Jesus knew their hypocrisy. "Why are you trying to trap me?" he asked. "Bring me a denarius and let me look at it."NIV These crafty religious leaders were not able to deceive Jesus. He immediately saw through their flattering words and their pretense to the underlying hypocrisy. He knew this was a trap, and without hesitation he asked them why they were testing him with their question. Of course, Jesus knew why, but his question exposed their motives and revealed the motives to those listening.

Jesus then asked them to produce *a denarius* for him so he could look at it. A denarius was the usual day's wage for a laborer. It was a silver coin with Caesar's portrait on it. The tax paid to Rome was paid in these coins.

Someone had to go get this coin. It would not have been readily available because they were in the temple area, and most of the people would have already exchanged their Roman coins for Jewish or temple money. The crowds and the religious leaders must have been breathless as they waited for this coin to be brought to Jesus.

12:16 So they brought it. And He said to them, "Whose image and inscription is this?" They said to Him, "Caesar's."^{NKJV} The coin was brought to Jesus. They did not need to see it to answer his question, for they all well knew what the coin looked like and what it said. The denarius had a portrait *(image)* of Caesar, probably Tiberius Caesar who reigned A.D. 14–37, the ruling Caesar at that time. The *inscription* referred to Caesar as divine and as "chief priest." The Caesars were worshiped as gods by the pagans, so the claim to divinity on the coin itself repulsed the Jews. In addition, Caesar's image on the coins was a constant reminder of Israel's subjection to Rome.

THE SECULAR IMAGE
Some people in the past gained great reputations for holiness by refusing to even look at a secular image. Their "otherworldliness" seemed pious and disciplined.

But Jesus showed a different face to the world. He called for a worldly object, a coin, and recognized the title and power of a secular ruler. He cared enough about the practical world to know whose image local coinage carried, and he didn't believe that handling the world's artifacts would taint his character.

Jesus illustrates what it takes to be a great evangelist today. We should be aware of our world and use examples from everyday life. By understanding and respecting your audience, and by moving from the known to the unknown, you can introduce the world to Jesus' redemptive power.

12:17 And Jesus answered and said to them, "Render to Caesar the things that are Caesar's, and to God the things that are God's."^{NKJV} The Pharisees and Herodians thought they had the perfect question to trap Jesus. But Jesus answered wisely, again exposing their self-interest and wrong motives. Jesus said, *"Render to Caesar the things that are Caesar's"*—that is, the coin bearing the emperor's image should be given to the emperor. In their question, the religious leaders used the word *didomi,* meaning "to give." Jesus responded with the word *apodidomi,* meaning "to pay a debt." In other words, having a coin meant being part of that country, so citizens should acknowledge the authority of Caesar and pay for the benefits accorded to them by his empire (not the least of which were peace and an efficient road system). The Jews may not have been happy about the situation, but God had placed Caesar on the throne and Judea under his rule. The Pharisees and Herodians tried to make it appear that it was incompatible to be a Jew and pay taxes to a pagan emperor who claimed to be divine. But Jesus explained that no such incompatibility existed because God was ultimately in control. They would lose much and gain little if they refused to pay Caesar's taxes (see Romans 13:1-7; 1 Timothy 2:1-6; 1 Peter 2:13-17).

However, paying the taxes did not have to mean submission to the divinity claimed by the emperor. The words on the coins were incorrect. Caesar had the right to claim their tax money, but he had no claim on their souls. The Jews had a responsibility to render *to God the things that are God's.* While they lived in the Roman world, the Jews had to face the dual reality of subjection to Rome and responsibility to God. Jesus explained that they could do both if they kept their priorities straight. The tax would be paid as long as Rome held sway over Judea, but God had rights on eternity. To Jesus, this was the crucial issue. Were they giving to God their lives? Were they loving God with all their heart, soul, mind, and strength (12:30)? These Jews (and especially the self-righteous Pharisees) claimed to be God's chosen people. But were they even "rendering" to God what truly belonged to him—themselves?

GOOD CITIZENS
Jesus avoided the Pharisees' and Herodians' trap by showing that believers have dual citizenship (1 Peter 2:17). Our citizenship in the nation requires that we pay money for the services and benefits we receive. Our citizenship in the kingdom of heaven requires that we pledge to God our primary obedience and commitment. (See Acts 4:18-19 and 5:29 for discussions on obeying God rather than people.) As God's followers, we have legitimate obligations to both God and the government. But it is important to keep our priorities straight. When the two authorities conflict, our duty to God always must come before our duty to the government.

And they were utterly amazed at him.[NRSV] Everyone was once again *utterly amazed.* The Pharisees and Herodians probably stood with their mouths open, unable to believe that somehow Jesus had answered the question, and yet not answered it. True to their flattering words, he was sincere, showed no deference or partiality, and truthfully taught God's way even when asked about a hot emotional topic. For the Pharisees to be "amazed" is very unusual in Mark's Gospel; normally it was the crowds that were "amazed." This attests to Jesus' complete victory over his opponents.

RELIGIOUS LEADERS QUESTION JESUS ABOUT THE RESURRECTION / 12:18-27 / **194**

No sooner had one delegation withdrawn from Jesus in amazement than another appeared to take up the cause. One way or another, the religious leaders were determined to eliminate Jesus. This time, they would use an unfair religious question.

The Sadducees, handicapped by their unbelief in the resurrection, thought they had a thorny problem from God's Word that would make the very idea of life beyond death ludicrous. This was probably a standard challenge posed by the Sadducees to those who believed in the resurrection, such as the Pharisees.

This challenge by the Sadducees reveals that Jesus' opponents were running out of weapons. Had he failed their test, he probably would have been shamed and discredited. This result would not have been satisfactory to those who wanted Jesus permanently out of the picture, but perhaps they were desperate enough to settle for a small victory against Jesus. They would not even get that.

12:18 Then the Sadducees, who say there is no resurrection, came to him with a question.[NIV] The combined group of religious leaders from the Sanhedrin had failed with their first question (11:27-33); the paired antagonists of Pharisees and Herodians had failed with a political question (12:13-17); here the *Sadducees,* a group of conservative religious leaders, smugly stepped in to try to trap Jesus with a theological question. The Sadducees were at odds theologically with the Pharisees (the other major group of Jewish leaders) because they honored only the Pentateuch—Genesis through Deuteronomy—as Scripture, and because they rejected most of the Pharisees' traditions, rules, and regulations. The Pharisees expected a cataclysmic restoration by the Messiah, while the Sadducees were pro-Herod and favored cooperation with political powers and pursuit of earthly prosperity. Little more is known about the Sadducees. We have no writings from them; the only descriptions come from Christian or Jewish sources, both of which put them in a negative light. The group may have originated in the second century B.C.

The Sadducees said *there is no resurrection* of the dead

WHAT WE KNOW ABOUT HEAVEN

Much of what we know about heaven is found in Revelation's description of the New Jerusalem. This city will be the eternal dwelling place of God and his people, who will enjoy the everlasting blessings of a new heaven and new earth.

Heaven is being prepared by Christ himself.	John 14:3
Heaven is only for those who have been born again.	John 3:3
Heaven is described as a glorious city.	Revelation 21:11, 18
Heaven will shine with and be lighted by God's glory.	Revelation 21:11, 23; 22:5
Heaven's gates wili never be shut.	Revelation 21:25
Heaven has the river of the Water of Life to insure everlasting life.	Revelation 22:1
Heaven has the Tree of Life to insure abundant life.	Revelation 2:7; 22:19
Heaven has the throne of God at its center.	Revelation 4:2; 22:1-2
Heaven is a place of holiness.	Revelation 21:27
Heaven is beautiful.	Psalm 50:2
Heaven is a place of unity.	Ephesians 1:10
Heaven is a place of perfection.	1 Corinthians 13:10
Heaven is joyful.	Psalm 16:11
Heaven is a place for all eternity.	John 3:15; Psalm 23:6
Heaven has no night.	Revelation 21:25; 22:5
Heaven has singing.	Isaiah 44:23; Revelation 14:3; 15:1-3
Heaven has serving.	Revelation 7:15; 22:3

because they could find no mention of it in the Pentateuch. Apparently, the Pharisees had never been able to come up with a convincing argument from the Pentateuch for the resurrection, and the Sadducees thought they had trapped Jesus for sure. But Jesus was about to show them otherwise.

12:19 "Teacher," they said, "Moses wrote for us that if a man's brother dies and leaves a wife but no children, the man must marry the widow and have children for his brother."[NIV] Obviously, since the Sadducees recognized only the books attributed to Moses (Genesis through Deuteronomy), their question came from Moses' writings. In the Law, Moses had written that when a man died without a son, his unmarried brother (or nearest male relative) was to marry the widow and produce children. The first son of this marriage was considered the heir of the dead man (Deuteronomy 25:5-6). The main purpose of the instruction was to produce an heir and guarantee that the family would not lose their land. The book of Ruth gives us an example of this law in operation (Ruth 3:1–4:12; see also Genesis 38:1-26). This law, called levirate marriage, protected the widow (in that culture widows usually had no means to support themselves) and allowed the family line to continue.

ACTIVE UNBELIEF
The Sadducees knew more about what they didn't believe than what they believed. This kind of active unbelief is widespread today. For example:

- Moral truth. In many circles, to speak moral opinion based on consensus or to defend a special interest group is acceptable, but to claim to speak Christian moral absolutes is said to be arrogant.
- Immortality. Like the Sadducees, who saw no evidence for a life after death in their limited Scriptures, many people today see a corpse in a casket and assume that is the end. They refuse to believe in hell and so also must reject heaven and the resurrection.
- God. As psychologists define "God" as merely our need for an authority figure and physicists regard creation as merely the by-product of atomic forces, God as a divine, sovereign, and loving being seems to be a human invention sparked by the religious imagination.

Where active unbelief is strong, Christians need to concentrate strong intellect, persuasive witness, and steady prayer. Remember to pray for professors, educators, student workers, and missionaries who present Christ in atmospheres of aggressive and hostile unbelief.

12:20-22 "**Now there were seven brothers. The first one married and died without leaving any children. The second one married the widow, but he also died, leaving no child. It was the same with the third. In fact, none of the seven left any children. Last of all, the woman died too.**"NIV The Sadducees took their hypothetical situation to a rather ridiculous length as they tried to show the absurdity of believing in the resurrection.

The book of Tobit (an apocryphal book not accepted by Protestants as part of the Old Testament canon but highly regarded by Jewish scholars at that time) includes the story of a woman who was married to seven men successively without ever having children. In Tobit the men are not brothers.

UNFAIR QUESTIONS
The Sadducees' unfair question was not really about a woman or her hypothetical situation, because the Sadducees did not even believe in the concept of a resurrection. Their question had made the Pharisees look ridiculous in previous debates, so they asked it in hopes that it would do the same with Jesus. But they were misusing Scripture, reading into it their own purposes and politics.

As Christians, we will face unfair theological questions from religious leaders who do not believe in Christ as Lord or in his Word as divine. We also will face unfair questions from unbelievers who have no knowledge. To stand our ground, we must discern the thoughts and feelings that lie beneath their questions.

- Do their own consciences suffer, so they are reacting against Christianity as the source of their conviction?
- Do they resent the assurance of faith that Christians hold?
- Have they been severely hurt or disappointed by so-called religious people?
- Do they wish to proudly flaunt their own freedom and power of intellect?
- Are they reacting on partial knowledge, misconceptions of God, or poor interpretations of Scripture?
- Have they confused the love and compassion of Jesus Christ with the sometimes improper actions of professing Christians?
  Many who attack the Bible have never truly studied it or considered Christ's claims. Turn the discussion to the love of Christ.

12:23 **"In the resurrection whose wife will she be? For the seven had married her."**NRSV The law of levirate marriage, written by Moses in Deuteronomy 25:5-10, would cause a real problem for the woman in the situation they described, for she had been married seven times to seven different men, all according to the law. The Sadducees reasoned that since this was in the law, there could not be a resurrection. When all eight of them were resurrected (the seven brothers and the woman), *"Whose wife will she be?"* The Sadducees erroneously assumed that *if* people were resurrected, it would be back to a continuation of life on earth—and that would be too confusing to be possible. They were incapable of understanding that God could both raise the dead and make new lives for his people, lives that would be different from what they had known on earth. The Sadducees had brought God down to their level. Because they could not conceive of a resurrection life, they decided that God couldn't raise the dead. And Moses hadn't written about it, so they considered the "case closed."

12:24 Jesus said to them, "Is not this the reason you are wrong, that you know neither the scriptures nor the power of God?"NRSV Jesus wasted no time dealing with their hypothetical situation, but went directly to their underlying assumption that resurrection of the dead was impossible. Jesus clearly stated that they were wrong about the resurrection for two reasons: (1) They didn't know the Scriptures (if they did, they would believe in the resurrection because it is taught in Scripture), and (2) they didn't know the power of God (if they did, they would believe in the resurrection because God's power makes it possible, even necessary). Ignorance on these two counts was inexcusable for these religious leaders.

LIFE IN THE KINGDOM
What life will be like after the resurrection is far beyond our ability to understand or imagine (Isaiah 64:4; 1 Corinthians 2:9). However, we need not dread eternal life because of the unknowns. God is good. We know he loves us and wants the best for us. Instead of wondering what God's coming kingdom will be like, we should concentrate on our relationship with Christ right now because in the new kingdom we will be with him. If we learn to love and trust Christ *now,* we will welcome what he has in store for us then.

12:25 "When the dead rise, they will neither marry nor be given in marriage; they will be like the angels in heaven."NIV Furthermore, Jesus said, *when the dead rise* (spoken with certainty—it will happen, so the Sadducees were wrong at the very foundation of their beliefs), they will not rise to an extension of their earthly lives. Instead, life in heaven will be different. Believers *will be like the angels in heaven* regarding marriage. Believers do not become angels, for angels were created by God for a special purpose. Angels do not marry or propagate; neither will glorified human beings. On earth where death reigns, marriage and childbearing are important in order to "fill the earth and subdue it" (Genesis 1:28 NKJV); but bearing children will not be necessary in the resurrection life because people will be raised up to glorify God forever—there will be no more death. Those in heaven will no longer be governed by physical laws but will be "like the angels"; that is, believers will share the immortal nature of angels.

Jesus' statement did not mean that people will not recognize their partners in heaven. Jesus was not dissolving the eternal aspect of marriage, doing away with sexual differences, or teaching that we will be asexual beings after death. We cannot tell very much about sex and marriage in heaven from this one statement

WHAT WE KNOW ABOUT OUR BODIES IN HEAVEN

They will be recognizable.	1 Corinthians 13:12
They will be like Christ's body.	1 John 3:2
They will be bodies in which the spirit predominates.	1 Corinthians 15:44, 49
They will be unlimited by space.	Luke 24:31; John 20:19, 26
They will be eternal.	2 Corinthians 5:1-5
They will be glorious.	Romans 8:18; 1 Corinthians 15:43
They will not have pain.	Revelation 21:4
They will not die.	1 Corinthians 15:26; Revelation 21:4
They will not hunger or thirst.	Revelation 7:16
They will not sin.	Revelation 21:27

by Jesus. He simply meant that we must not think of heaven as an extension of life as we now know it. Our relationships in this life are limited by time, death, and sin. We don't know everything about our resurrection life, but Jesus affirmed that relationships will be different from what we are used to here and now. The same physical and natural rules won't apply.

Jesus' comment in this verse was not intended to be the final word on marriage in heaven. Instead, this response was Jesus' refusal to answer the Sadducees' riddle and fall into their trap. The Sadducees did not believe in angels either (Acts 23:8), so Jesus' point was not to extend the argument into another realm. Instead, he was showing that because there will be no levirate marriage in the resurrection or new marriage contracts, the Sadducees' question was completely irrelevant. But their assumption about the resurrection needed a definitive answer, and Jesus was just the one to give it.

12:26 "And as for the dead being raised, have you not read in the book of Moses, in the story about the bush, how God said to him, 'I am the God of Abraham, the God of Isaac, and the God of Jacob'?"NRSV Because the Sadducees accepted only the Pentateuch as God's divine Word, Jesus answered them from the book of Exodus (3:6). God would not have said, *"I am the God of Abraham, the God of Isaac, and the God of Jacob"* if he thought of Abraham, Isaac, and Jacob as dead (he would have said, "I *was* their God"). Thus, from God's perspective, they are alive. This evidence would have been acceptable in any rabbinic debate because it applied a grammatical argument: God's use of the present tense in speaking of his relationship to the great patriarchs who had been long dead by the time God spoke these words to Moses. God had a continuing relationship with these men because of the truth of the resurrection.

SEX IN HEAVEN?
Many people are jolted at the prospect of eternal life without sex, because it is one of earth's greatest pleasures. At first reading, Jesus seems to imply as much here.

At its very best, sexual activity creates a great sense of oneness between lovers, a superb moment of intense intimacy, and wonderful physical feelings. Lovers wish their excitement would last and last, but too quickly life returns to normal.

People who ponder eternity (and who doesn't?) are right to hope that the freedom, intensity, and intimacy they experience now will be transformed, expanded, and made utterly glorious in new life with God in heaven, where joys last and last, and never grow old.

We don't know what God has planned for us, but we trust in his love. We believe that the beauty and excitement we feel now is not a trick, but a foretaste of an even better experience.

In heaven, our relationship with all our brothers and sisters will be so intense, so filled with love, that earthly marital bliss will seem shallow by comparison. Heaven will be a wonderful place for you. Trust Jesus fully to lead you there.

12:27 **"He is God not of the dead, but of the living; you are quite wrong."**NRSV God had spoken of dead men as though they were still alive; thus, Jesus reasoned, the men were not dead but living. God would not have a relationship with dead beings. Although men and women have died on earth, God continues his relationship with them because they are resurrected to life with him in heaven.

Some might argue that this shows only the immortality of the soul, not necessarily the resurrection of the body. But Jesus' answer affirmed both. The Jews understood that soul and body had inseparable unity—thus the immortality of the soul necessarily included a resurrection of the body. Therefore, the Sadducees were *quite wrong* in their mistaken assumption about the resurrection. Case closed.

RELIGIOUS LEADERS QUESTION JESUS ABOUT THE GREATEST COMMANDMENT / 12:28-34 / **195**

Several defined groups had taken their best shot at Jesus. As each antagonist engaged the Lord, the others apparently looked on

with mixed emotions. On one hand, they had a common purpose
in destroying Jesus. On the other, each group wanted to claim
supremacy by being the one who eliminated the troublemaker.
Matthew hints at the background tension (Matthew 22:34).

Matthew provides a brief account of this exchange between
Jesus and the lawyer. He reported only the original question and
Jesus' response. Mark's version fills in the picture and adds a positive note to the conflict. Jesus' responses did not always antago-
nize his opponents. Often they expressed amazement (12:17) and
even agreement (12:32).

Mark's account makes perfectly clear that Jesus was looking
for greater commitment from people, not that they merely knew
the right answers. Jesus told this lawyer that he had the truth but
had not yet expressed his trust. Knowing God's requirement of
wholehearted faith and surrendering ourselves to him are separate steps of entering into the kingdom. We may know the requirements for citizenship without ever deciding to become a citizen
of the kingdom of God.

**12:28 One of the teachers of the law came and heard them debat-
ing. Noticing that Jesus had given them a good answer, he
asked him, "Of all the commandments, which is the most
important?"**[NIV] This discussion continued within the temple
courts. Jesus and the disciples were surrounded by a crowd of
people, while various groups of religious leaders came and went
with their questions.

One of these leaders actually came with a sincere question. He
wasn't trying to trick Jesus; he really wanted to learn from him.
Note that Jesus was not prejudiced against the Pharisees. He
treated each one who was sincere differently from the group. He
showed particular interest in a Pharisee named Nicodemus (see
John 3:1-21). This man was a teacher of the law (also called a
"scribe"); Matthew explained that he was of the party of Pharisees (Matthew 22:34-35). He probably was delighted to hear
Jesus' definitive answer about the resurrection that finally
silenced the Sadducees. So he brought his question: *"Of all the
commandments, which is the most important?"*

"All the commandments" the man referred to focused on a popular debate about the more important and less important of the
hundreds of laws the Jews had accumulated. The Pharisees had
classified over six hundred laws and spent much time discussing
which laws were weightier than others. Some religious leaders
tried to distinguish between major and minor laws; some taught
that all laws were equally binding and that it was dangerous to
make any distinctions. The question was not asking Jesus to set

up one law as the most important, but to point out which types of commandments should have priority. As a Pharisee himself, the man had in mind the debates over the relative importance of ritual, ethical, moral, and ceremonial laws, as well as the positive versus negative laws. Jesus' definitive answer about the resurrection caused this man to hope he might also have the final answer about all these laws. He wouldn't be disappointed.

12:29 **"The most important one," answered Jesus, "is this: 'Hear, O Israel, the Lord our God, the Lord is one.'"**^{NIV} Among all the Gospel writers, only Mark recorded Jesus' quote from Deuteronomy 6:4, which is the first part of what the Jews know as the Shema (referring to the opening word of the sentence in Hebrew). The Shema is made up from Deuteronomy 6:4-9; 11:13-21; Numbers 15:37-41 and is the major creed of Judaism that was recited twice daily (morning and evening) by devout Jews. The teachers of the law could debate all they wanted, but Jesus brought them back to the basics by giving new life to the oft-repeated words *The Lord our God, the Lord is one.* What mattered were not laws and their relative importance; what mattered was a relationship with the one true God.

12:30 **"'Love the Lord your God with all your heart and with all your soul and with all your mind and with all your strength.'"**^{NIV} Jesus recited words of the Shema (12:29), then answered the man's question by explaining what those words should mean in the daily lives of the Jews. Because they believed that there was one God (as opposed to other religions, such as the Romans with their pantheon of gods), they ought to love the one true God with every part of their being. Jesus quoted from Deuteronomy 6:5, "Love the LORD your God with all your heart and with all your soul and with all your strength" (NIV). Matthew, Mark, and Luke add "with all your mind." Jesus' purpose was to show that a person's total being must be involved in loving God. Nothing must be held back because God holds nothing back. The rest of the New Testament follows Jesus' addition to Deuteronomy 6:5 by strongly emphasizing the place of much spiritual growth as in the renewing of the mind (Romans 12:2; Ephesians 4:23). We need Jesus' emphases every bit as much as this scribe who came to Jesus. Much of modern-day spirituality attempts to bypass the mind and replace it with "spirit" in spiritual growth. We need to take every thought captive for Christ (2 Corinthians 10:5).

The word for "love" is *agapao,* totally unselfish love, a love human beings are capable of only with the help of the Holy

Spirit. God's Spirit helps us love him as we ought. God wants our warmhearted love and devotion, not just our obedience. The *mind* was considered to be the center of a person's intellect, the *soul* was the person's "being" and uniqueness, the *heart* was the center of desires and affections, and the *strength* referred to physical capabilities.

> Every man must be thought of as a neighbor, for evil must be committed toward no one.
> *St. Augustine*

To love God in this way is to fulfill completely all the commandments regarding one's "vertical" relationship.

ALL OF ME
Jesus taught that love for God involves every aspect of our being. As you consider your devotion to God, does he have all of you?

Your heart
- Is he the focus of your affections?
- Is your love for him warm and real?
- Do you take pleasure in his ultimate worth?

Your soul
- Are you willing to give him your life itself?
- Does your worship genuinely reflect your inner desires and intentions?
- Do you love him with your total being?

Your mind
- Does your commitment fully involve your intellectual capabilities?
- Is your faith fully informed or based on blind trust?
- Is your mind trained to think of his moral perfection?

Your strength
- Do you strive to love and serve him energetically?
- Have you devoted all your physical and material capabilities to him?
- Can you sustain intense love for him even under pressure or when doubts arise?

12:31 **"The second is this: 'Love your neighbor as yourself.' There is no commandment greater than these."**[NIV] In addition to the law quoted in 12:30, there is a second and equally important law. This law focuses on "horizontal" relationships—our dealings with fellow human beings. A person cannot maintain a good "vertical" relationship with God (loving God) without also caring for his or her neighbor. For this second law, Jesus quoted Leviticus 19:18: "Love your neighbor as yourself." The word "neighbor" refers to fellow human beings in general. The love a person has

WHAT JESUS SAID ABOUT LOVE

In Mark 12:28 a teacher of the law asked Jesus which of all the commandments was the most important to follow. Jesus mentioned two commandments, one from Deuteronomy 6:5, the other from Leviticus 19:18. Both had to do with love. Why is love so important? Jesus said that all of the commandments were given for two simple reasons—to help us love God and love others as we should.

What else did Jesus say about love?	Reference
God loves us.	John 3:16
We are to love God.	Matthew 22:37
Because God loves us, he cares for us.	Matthew 6:25-34
God wants everyone to know how much he loves them.	John 17:23
God loves even those who hate him; we are to do the same.	Matthew 5:43-47; Luke 6:35
God seeks out even those most alienated from him.	Luke 15
God must be your first love.	Matthew 6:24; 10:37
You love God when you obey him.	John 14:21; 15:10
God loves Jesus, his Son.	John 5:20; 10:17
Jesus loves God.	John 14:31
Those who refuse Jesus don't have God's love.	John 5:41-44
Jesus loves us just as God loves Jesus.	John 15:9
Jesus proved his love for us by dying on the cross so that we could live eternally with him.	John 3:14-15; 15:13-14
The love between God and Jesus is the perfect example of how we are to love others.	John 17:21-26
We are to love one another and demonstrate that love.	Matthew 5:40-42; 10:42; John 13:34-35
Jesus' love extends to each individual.	John 10:11-15; Mark 10:21
Jesus wants our love to be genuine.	John 21:15-17

for himself or herself (in the sense of looking out for oneself, caring about best interests, etc.) should be continued, but it should also be directed toward others.

In answer to the man's question, Jesus explained that *there is no commandment greater than these*—loving God and loving others. The Ten Commandments and all the other Old Testament laws are summarized in these two laws. By fulfilling these two commands to love God totally and love others as oneself, a person will keep all the other commands.

TWO SIMPLE PRINCIPLES
God's laws are not burdensome. They can be reduced to two simple principles: Love God and love others. These commands are from the Old Testament (Deuteronomy 6:5; Leviticus 19:18). When you love God completely and care for others as you care for yourself, then you have fulfilled the intent of the Ten Commandments and the other Old Testament laws. According to Jesus, these two commandments summarize all God's laws. Let them rule your thoughts, decisions, and actions. When you are uncertain about what to do, ask yourself which course of action best demonstrates love for God and love for others.

12:32 **Then the scribe said to him, "You are right, Teacher; you have truly said that 'he is one, and besides him there is no other.'"**^{NRSV} The man had received his answer (12:28), and he commended Jesus for his true and insightful answer. The man realized that after all the Pharisees' wrangling about the laws, the answer had been amazingly simple. The man reaffirmed the Shema (12:29) quoted from Deuteronomy, saying *he is one* (rather than "God is one") because Jews characteristically omitted speaking the divine name unnecessarily out of great respect for it. He then added *besides him there is no other,* echoing Deuteronomy 4:35 (see also Exodus 8:10; Isaiah 45:21). Jesus' victory was complete; even his opponents recognized that he was right.

12:33 **"And to love Him with all the heart, with all the understanding, with all the soul, and with all the strength, and to love one's neighbor as oneself, is more than all the whole burnt offerings and sacrifices."**^{NKJV} This man understood that the laws of love for God and love for neighbor were more important than *the whole burnt offerings and sacrifices.* In other words, love was more important than all the ritual and ceremonial laws. This man understood what the entire nation had been unable to understand from the time of the judges. God had told them many times, "To obey is better than sacrifice" (1 Samuel 15:22 NRSV). The prophets Isaiah and Hosea repeated it (Isaiah 1:11; Hosea 6:6). But still the religious leaders loved their rituals and their ceremonies, all the while missing God and looking down with loathing on the common people. In so doing, they had missed the

SACRIFICES OF THE HEART

God says many times that he doesn't want our gifts and sacrifices when we give them out of ritual or hypocrisy. God wants us first to love and obey him.

1 Samuel 15:22-23	Obedience is far better than sacrifice.
Psalm 40:6-8	God doesn't want burnt animals; he wants our lifelong service.
Psalm 51:16-17	God isn't interested in penance; he wants a broken and contrite heart.
Jeremiah 7:21-23	It isn't offerings God wants; he desires our obedience and promises that he will be our God and we shall be his people.
Hosea 6:6	God doesn't want sacrifices, he wants love; he doesn't want offerings, he wants us to know him.
Amos 5:21-24	God hates pretense and hypocrisy; he wants to see a flood of justice.
Micah 6:6-8	God is not satisfied with sacrifices; he wants us to be fair and just and merciful, and to walk humbly with him.
Matthew 9:13	God doesn't want gifts; he wants us to be merciful.

point completely—they didn't love God *or* their neighbor. This man, one of the few among the Pharisees, was able to see that loving God with all one's heart, understanding (substituted for "mind"), soul, and strength, and to love one's neighbor revealed a level of love and obedience that went far beyond the offering of sacrifices. God doesn't want just our work for him (preaching, teaching, giving), he wants our heart.

EASY TO FORGET
This Pharisee reminds us to love God; how easily we forget to do so. We obey God, fear him, and ask him for help and forgiveness, but do we stop all our activities just to love him? Remember to love God for his absolute goodness and perfect holiness. Pause to thank him for his loving care for you. Praise him for the wonderful gifts he provides for you to use serving him and others. Appreciate his unsurpassed grace and long-lasting mercy toward you.

12:34 Now when Jesus saw that he answered wisely, He said to him, "You are not far from the kingdom of God."NKJV Jesus was pleased by the man's response and told him that he was *not far* *from the kingdom of God.* This man had caught the intent of God's law as it is so often stressed in the Old Testament—that true obedience comes from the heart. Because the Old Testament commands lead to Christ, the man's next step toward obtaining God's kingdom was faith in Jesus himself. This, however, was the most difficult step to take.

But after that no one dared question Him.[NKJV] Delegations of each group of Jewish leadership had come to Jesus with questions, and each had received a tough lesson from him. The last question, sincere in intent, taught the man, the crowd, and the other leaders that even those who got past the rituals and ceremonies to an understanding of obedience to God still did not have the kingdom; they were "not far" from it, but they did not have it. The final truth to be grasped was that God's kingdom is obtained through faith in Jesus Christ as God's Son. Perhaps after Jesus' death and resurrection, this understanding Pharisee also became a believer.

In any case, this was unconditional surrender; the religious leaders gave up trying to catch Jesus in his words (12:34). Obviously their efforts had been fruitless, and it was *they* who had ended up looking foolish. They would have to resort to other plans in order to kill Jesus.

SO CLOSE AND SO FAR
We do not know if this Pharisee ever became a true believer. But we must remember that being "close" to being a Christian is infinitely far if a person never commits to Christ. Our salvation cannot rest on intellectual knowledge alone. We must repent, follow Christ, and be made new creatures by his Holy Spirit. Don't be content with being close; take the step, make the commitment.

RELIGIOUS LEADERS CANNOT ANSWER JESUS' QUESTION / 12:35-37 / **196**

Jesus did not settle for a silent, seething truce with the religious leaders. He continued to teach. He demonstrated that God's Word had not been fully examined regarding the identity of the Messiah. His provocative questions brought delight to the crowds, thoughtfulness to the attentive, and continued anger to his enemies.

The Lord's approach to Bible study ought to always be part of our own thinking. In whatever part of the Scriptures we may be searching, we can always ask at least one question: How might this passage help me understand Jesus Christ better?

12:35 While Jesus was teaching in the temple, he said, "How can the scribes say that the Messiah is the son of David?"^{NRSV} This was still Passion week, presumably still Tuesday of that week, and *Jesus was teaching in the temple.* The Pharisees, Herodians, and Sadducees had asked their questions. Then Jesus turned the tables and asked them a question that went right to the heart of the matter—what they thought about the Messiah's identity. The central issue of life—for these ancient religious leaders as well as for us today—is what we believe about Jesus. Other spiritual questions are irrelevant unless we first decide to believe that Jesus is who he said he was.

The Pharisees expected a Messiah (the Christ, the Anointed One), but they erroneously thought he would be only a human ruler who would reign on King David's throne, deliver them from Gentile domination by establishing God's rule on earth, and restore Israel's greatness as in the days of David and Solomon. They knew that the Messiah would be a *son* (descendant) of David, but they did not understand that he would be more than a human descendant—he would be God in the flesh. They were correct, but only halfway.

Jesus' question was designed to force them to take the extra step that would explain the truth of the Messiah's identity. This first question was rhetorical—the scribes said that the Messiah would be the son of David because the Old Testament Scriptures clearly state this (see chart "King David's Famous Descendant").

12:36 "David himself, by the Holy Spirit, declared, 'The Lord said to my Lord, "Sit at my right hand, until I put your enemies under your feet."'"^{NRSV} The Jews and early Christians knew the Old Testament was inspired by God, bearing his authority in its teachings. Jesus quoted Psalm 110:1 to show that David, speaking under the influence of the Holy Spirit, understood the Messiah to be his Lord (that is, one who had authority over him), not just his descendant. The Messiah would be a human descendant of David, but he would also be God's divine Son. The religious leaders did not understand that the Messiah would be far more than a human descendant of David; he would be God himself in human form, much greater than David. (Hebrews 1:13 uses the same text as proof of Christ's deity.)

Using the same type of rabbinic debate technique that he had used before (12:26), Jesus took the specific words of this verse in David's psalm and explained their implications.

KING DAVID'S FAMOUS DESCENDANT

David's descendant will be on the throne forever.	2 Samuel 7:8-16
David was promised that his line would last forever.	Psalm 89:3-4
David's descendant will be called Wonderful Counselor, Mighty God, Everlasting Father, Prince of Peace. His reign on David's throne will last forever.	Isaiah 9:2-7
David's descendant will have the Spirit of the Lord upon him, and his rule will bring lasting peace.	Isaiah 11:1-9
David's descendant will reign wisely, do what is just and right, and be called the Lord Our Righteousness.	Jeremiah 23:5-6
David's descendant will be raised up by the Lord and will restore Israel.	Jeremiah 30:8-9
David's descendant will be a righteous "Branch" who will restore Judah and Jerusalem.	Jeremiah 33:15-17
David's descendant will rule over God's people and be a prince among them.	Ezekiel 34:23-24
David's descendant will be the people's king and shepherd.	Ezekiel 37:24
The Israelites will turn back to God and to David's great descendant.	Hosea 3:5 ·

- David said, *"The Lord."* This first word, "Lord," is *Yahweh,* the Hebrew name for God the Father.

- The second word, "Lord," in Hebrew is *Adonai* (in Greek, *Kurios*) and refers to David speaking of the coming Messiah as his "Lord."

- *Sit at my right hand* means the Messiah would sit at the right side of God's throne, the place of highest honor and authority in God's coming kingdom. In ancient royal courts, the right side of the king's throne was reserved for the person who could act in the king's place.

- *Until I put your enemies under your feet* describes the final conquering of sin and evil. In ancient Oriental battles, the conquered ruler was forced to put his neck under the foot of the triumphant ruler, showing defeat and subjection.

12:37 "David himself calls him Lord; so how can he be his son?"^{NRSV} If the great King David himself called the coming Messiah his *Lord* in Psalm 110:1, then how could the scribes say that the Messiah would be merely David's *son* (meaning "descendant")? David himself didn't think the Messiah would be just a descendant; instead, David, under the inspiration of the Holy Spirit, realized that the Messiah would be God in human form and would deserve due respect and honor.

The answer to Jesus' question is that David was clearly saying the Messiah was his Lord. Without clearly stating it, Jesus was lifting the veil of his divine identity. The divine Messiah would indeed come in human form, and he was standing among them.

And the large crowd was listening to him with delight.^{NRSV} Again Mark contrasted the common people with the religious leaders. They listened to Jesus *with delight.* The crowd was on Jesus' side. They may not have completely understood Jesus' words, but they obviously enjoyed seeing the self-righteous religious leaders put in their place.

JESUS WARNS AGAINST THE RELIGIOUS LEADERS / 12:38-40 / **197**

This section offers a preview and provides a transition to the Olivet discourse in chapter 13. Here Jesus explained why such judgment will occur. As we read and think about Jesus' scathing evaluation of the teachers of the law, we ought to keep our own behavior in mind. Some of the religious leaders liked the show. They were doing nothing more than playacting, pretending to be religious and righteous. Jesus confronted their lack of heartfelt obedience. What would he say about ours? Insincerity and showmanship plague the church today. Don't be a leader who depends on appearances and applause. And don't hold in high regard those people who seek nothing more than earthly praise. As Jesus explained, that is all the reward they will ever get.

12:38-39 As he taught, he said, "Beware of the scribes, who like to walk around in long robes, and to be greeted with respect in the marketplaces, and to have the best seats in the synagogues and places of honor at banquets!"^{NRSV} This denunciation of the religious leaders (specifically the scribes) probably occurred right in the temple and was spoken to the surrounding crowd that had been "listening to him with delight" (12:37). Matthew has an entire chapter of such denunciations—seven "woes" to the scribes and Pharisees whom Jesus unhesitatingly called "hypocrites" (Matthew 23). Mark recorded a shortened version, signaling Jesus' final break with the religious leaders.

Having silenced the questioning of the religious leaders, Jesus turned to the crowd and told them to *beware* (or watch out) for the scribes. While the scribes had a lot of education and a certain amount of authority because of their position, Jesus denounced their conduct. They liked *to walk around in long robes.* The robes of the intellectuals and aristocrats were long, reaching to the feet. The religious leaders wore white linen robes, with white symbolizing religious purity. These robes were supposed to be worn mainly for religious duties. However, the religious leaders had taken to wearing them into public, such as to the *marketplaces,* for attention. The white robes singled them out and thus caused the people to recognize them as authorities and greet them respectfully. The leaders had no reason for these actions except vanity. *The best seats in the synagogues* referred to the seats reserved for the most important people; these were situated in front of the box containing the scrolls and faced the general congregation. The *places of honor at banquets* were generally the seats closest to the host. Those seated there received special treatment during the meal.

In short, the scribes had lost sight of their priority as teachers of the law and were enjoying their position merely because of the "perks" it offered. Jesus condemned this attitude.

PRAISE LOVERS
Jesus warned against trying to make a good impression. These scribes were religious hypocrites who, though they appeared godly, had no love for God. John recorded that these leaders loved praise from men more than praise from God (John 12:43). True followers of Christ are not distinguished by showy spirituality. Reading the Bible, praying in public, or following church rituals can be phony if the motive for doing them is to be noticed or honored. Resist the temptation to put on a spiritual front or to do good deeds for the sake of appearances. Let your actions be consistent with your beliefs. Live for Christ, even when no one is looking.

12:40 "They devour widows' houses and for the sake of appearance say long prayers. They will receive the greater condemnation."[NRSV] Not only did the scribes walk around expecting perks and honor from everyone, they also actively abused their position. Their behavior strongly contrasts with the widow in 12:42. Because they received no pay for their services, they depended on the hospitality of devout Jews. It was considered an act of

piety for people to help the scribes. That they *devour widows'
houses* was a vivid picture of these religious men using their position to defraud the gullible. Some people would even go so far as
to place all their finances in the scribe's control (especially widows who trusted them). As the nation's lawyers, scribes were
often employed in handling the money a widow received from
her father's dowry. Some abused their trusted positions by unethi-
cally obtaining the dowry for the temple and then keeping it
themselves. They were in a position to exploit people, cheating
the poor out of everything they had and taking advantage of the
rich. How could they deserve anything but condemnation!

Even their prayers were merely *for the sake of appearance.*
Their long prayers were not conversations with the Lord they
loved, but were merely ploys to make people think they were
especially holy. Through their pious actions they hoped to gain
status, recognition, and respect.

The punishment for these scribes would be especially severe
because as teachers they were responsible for shaping the faith of
the people. But they saddled people with petty rules while they
lived greedily and deceitfully. Their behavior gave a pretense of
piety, while they oppressed and misled the very people they were
supposed to lead. Jesus solemnly announced, *"They will receive
the greater condemnation."* These words certainly affected the
disciple James, for he later wrote, "Not many of you should
become teachers . . . for you know that we who teach will be
judged with greater strictness" (James 3:1 NRSV).

A POOR WIDOW GIVES ALL SHE HAS / 12:41-44 / **200**

Almost unheard in the clash of ideas and the noisy crowd, the
ring of the widow's small coins became an eloquent example of
truth. Her act sharply contrasted with the much more obvious giving of others, and with the scribes who "devoured widows'
houses" (12:40). But it also represented an alternative to business
as usual in the temple. All around her were large examples of
meaningless worship, shallow honor given to God, frivolous giving, and downright evil. But this woman's unnoticed act of sacrifice spoke volumes about herself and her faith.

Do we depend on immediate response or gratification as the
primary motive for our faithfulness?

**12:41 Jesus sat down opposite the place where the offerings were
put and watched the crowd putting their money into the
temple treasury. Many rich people threw in large amounts.**[NIV]
Jesus completed his teaching (which might have taken place in

the Court of the Gentiles, where he had thrown out the merchants) and *sat down* in the area of the temple called the Court of Women (see the map of "The Temple in Jesus' Day" on page 320). The treasury was located there or in an adjoining walkway. In this area were seven boxes in which worshipers could deposit their temple tax and six boxes for freewill offerings. From his vantage point, Jesus *watched the crowd putting their money into the temple treasury.* A lot of money came into the temple treasury during Passover; the increased crowds meant increased money amounts in the coffers. Whether or not they made a show of how much they tossed into the offering boxes, Jesus knew that the rich people came and *threw in large amounts* of money. Perhaps the coins clattered loudly.

12:42 But a poor widow came and put in two very small copper coins, worth only a fraction of a penny.NIV In contrast to the loud clattering of the rich people's offerings, a poor widow came with a freewill offering for the temple (that is, she was not paying a required tax, but rather giving a gift). As a widow, she had few resources for making money. If a widow in New Testament times had no sons, no protector, and remained unmarried, she was often destitute. Since there was no social security or public aid for widows, a widow would often be without financial support. Widows were often oppressed and helpless with no legal recourse (Luke 18:1-5). When Jesus raised the only son of the widow of Nain (Luke 7:11-15), he was restoring her only protector and perhaps her only source of income.

This widow's offering totaled only *two very small copper coins,* the smallest Jewish coin in circulation in Palestine. Each coin was called a *lepton* (plural was *lepta*). Two *lepta* amounted to one-sixty-fourth of a denarius, the coin worth a day's wage for a laborer (see 12:15). These were Jewish coins, but Mark translated their amounts for his Roman audience ("two mites, which make a quadrans" NKJV). The NIV translates them for us as amounting to merely *a fraction of a penny.* Her small gift was a sacrifice, but she gave it willingly.

> Do not pray for tasks equal to your powers, pray for powers equal to your tasks. Then the doing of your work shall be no miracle, but you shall be a miracle. Every day you shall wonder at yourself, at the richness of life which has come to you by the grace of God.
> *Phillips Brooks*

We don't know how Jesus knew that this woman was a widow. Perhaps her dress revealed it. Perhaps she discussed her contribution and situation with a priest. Or Jesus may have known because of his divine knowledge. As a poor person, she was only

required to give one of the coins. Because she gave them both,
Jesus used her as an example.

**12:43 Then he called his disciples and said to them, "Truly I tell you,
this poor widow has put in more than all those who are contributing to the treasury."**ᴺᴿˢⱽ Jesus seized the opportunity to teach
his disciples an important lesson in giving. His words *Truly I tell
you* once again introduced a statement of solemn importance. In
Jesus' eyes, the poor widow had *put in more* than all the others,
even the rich people who had contributed large amounts to the treasury. Though her gift was by far the smallest in monetary value, it
was the greatest in sacrifice. The value of a gift is not determined
by its amount, but by the spirit in which it is given. A gift given
grudgingly or for recognition loses its value. When you give,
remember that gifts of any size are pleasing to God when they are
given out of gratitude and a spirit of generosity.

WHERE IS YOUR HEART?
Jesus noticed the self-denying liberality of this vulnerable
widow. Her gift and sacrifice stand as an example of the true
commitment required of all Jesus' followers. We may not be
asked to give all we have; Jesus was not making that point in
this example. But we must have the generous heart attitude of
this widow and not the deceitful heart attitude of the Pharisees.
Our Lord notices every act of service coming from a sincere
heart. "With such sacrifices God is pleased" (Hebrews 13:16
ɴɪⱽ). Where is *your* heart?

**12:44 "For they all put in out of their abundance, but she out of her
poverty put in all that she had, her whole livelihood."**ᴺᴷᴶⱽ The
widow's gift was proportionally greater and more sacrificial than
the gifts of all the rich people. They were giving *out of their
abundance,* while she had given *her whole livelihood.* The
widow could have kept back one coin, but she willingly gave
both coins. She gave everything and trusted God to care for her.
Jesus wanted the disciples to see this lesson in total surrender of
self, commitment to God, and willing-
ness to trust in his provision.

There is a parallel to the situation
that Paul observed where the poorer
Macedonians had made a contribution
to the famine-stricken believers in Jerusalem. Paul wanted to spur on the
wealthy Corinthian church that had not
yet contributed to the collection for the

> Most of us would like to
> think that from time to
> time we please God by
> giving until it really hurts.
> How many of us would
> even consider giving
> until it is gone?
> *Anonymous*

poor in Jerusalem. He said, "Out of the most severe trial, their overflowing joy and their extreme poverty welled up in rich generosity" (2 Corinthians 8:2 NIV). How sad that in this country, giving goes down as the bank account goes up.

GIVING OUT OF OUR ABUNDANCE
This widow gave all she had to live on, in contrast to the way most people handle their money. When we consider giving a certain percentage of our income a great accomplishment, we resemble those who gave "out of their abundance." Here, Jesus was admiring generous and sacrificial giving. As believers, we should consider increasing our giving—whether of money, time, or talents—to a point beyond convenience or safety.

Mark 13

Chapter 13 of Mark has a conversation between Jesus and his disciples as they left the temple and Jerusalem, walking back to Bethany where they spent their nights. Jesus took advantage of this "teachable moment." A casual remark about the magnificent temple by a disciple led Jesus to make a startling prophetic statement about the fate of the temple. The group paused on the Mount of Olives, where they could glance back across the valley toward Jerusalem. Perhaps they watched the sun set behind the ancient city.

Several disciples chose that moment to ask two curious questions: When will these things happen? What will be the sign? With his answers, Jesus prepared his disciples for the difficult years ahead. He warned them about false messiahs, natural disasters, and persecutions. But he also assured them that he would be with them to protect them and make his kingdom known through them. Jesus promised that, in the end, he would return in power and glory to save them. Jesus' warnings and promises to his disciples also apply to us as we look forward to his return:

- We must be ready.

- We must continue to proclaim the gospel.

- We must endure great trials.

- We must wait patiently.

13:1 As he was leaving the temple, one of his disciples said to him, "Look, Teacher! What massive stones! What magnificent buildings!"NIV Jesus and the disciples were leaving the temple (this may have been either Tuesday or Wednesday evening of the week before the Crucifixion). This was Jesus' last visit to the temple area. He would do no more preaching or public teaching. One of the disciples remarked on the incredible beauty of the temple. Although no one knows exactly what this temple looked like, it must have been magnificent, for in its time it was considered one of the architectural wonders of the world. This was not

Solomon's temple—it had been destroyed by the Babylonians in the seventh century B.C. (2 Kings 25:8-10). This temple had been built by Ezra after the return from exile in the sixth century B.C. (Ezra 6:14-15), desecrated by the Seleucids in the second century B.C., reconsecrated by the Maccabees soon afterward, and enormously expanded by Herod the Great.

About fifteen years before Jesus was born (around 20 B.C.), Herod the Great began a massive reconstruction project to help the Jews remodel and beautify their temple. Herod had no interest in the Jews' God, but he wanted to stay on friendly terms with his subjects, as well as build what he thought would be a lasting monument to his dynasty. Though the Jews disliked Herod, they were very proud of the temple. At this time, the construction project was still going on, for Herod's reconstruction of the temple would not be finished until about A.D. 64 (just a few years before it was destroyed by Rome).

The temple was impressive, covering about one-sixth of the land area of the ancient city of Jerusalem. It was not one building, but a majestic mixture of porches, colonnades, separate small edifices, and courts surrounding the temple proper (see the map of "The Temple in Jesus' Day" on page 320). Next to the inner temple, where the sacred objects were kept and the sacrifices offered, there was a large area called the Court of the Gentiles (this was where the money changers and merchants had their booths). Outside these courts were long porches. Solomon's porch was 1,562 feet long; the royal porch was decorated with 160 columns stretching along its 921-foot

> The eyes of our Lord Jesus Christ could find no pleasure in looking at the very temple which contained the holy of holies and the golden candlestick and the altar of burnt offering. Much less, we may suppose, can he find pleasure in the most splendid place of worship among professing Christians, if his Word and his Spirit are not honored in it.
> *J. C. Ryle*

length. The disciples gazed in wonder at marble pillars forty feet high, carved from a single solid stone. The temple's foundation was so solid that it is believed that some of the original footings remain to this day. The Jews were convinced of the permanence of this magnificent structure, not only because of the stability of construction, but also because it represented God's presence among them. The *massive stones* the disciple mentioned were huge white stones, some of them measuring twenty-five by eight by twelve feet and weighing more than one hundred tons.

13:2 Then Jesus asked him, "Do you see these great buildings? Not one stone will be left here upon another; all will be thrown

down."^NRSV Jesus acknowledged the *great buildings* but then
made a startling statement: This wonder of the world would be
completely destroyed. As in the days of the prophet Jeremiah, the
destruction of the Jews' beloved temple would be God's judgment against them for turning away from him. Jeremiah had spoken God's words to the rebellious nation, "I will make Jerusalem
a heap of ruins, a haunt of jackals" (Jeremiah 9:11 NIV). Jerusalem had been attacked and leveled before. Here Jesus prophesied
that Jerusalem and the beautiful temple would again be completely destroyed. This happened only a few decades later when
the Romans sacked Jerusalem in A.D. 70.

Gazing at the massive stones, the disciples surely found it difficult to believe that not one of the stones would be left on top of
another. Because the temple symbolized God's presence among
them, the Jews would be horrified to see it destroyed.

Today, are we proud of our large churches, our high attendance
numbers, and our great Christian institutions? What are our symbols of power and victory? our best-selling authors? our Christian
magazines? We must watch out for pride. All that truly matters is
each person's relationship with Jesus Christ.

TOPSY-TURVY
While the disciples admired the incredible temple, Jesus fore-
saw its destruction. When the disciples asked for honor and
glory in his kingdom, Jesus told them that the last would be
first. Truly, Jesus sees a reality behind and beyond what we
see.
What is your relationship with God? All the show of religious
observance won't cover emptiness at the center of your life. Is
your life given to Jesus? People can resemble buildings that
are outwardly impressive but inwardly crumbling and bound for
destruction.
Jesus wants to build your life to last forever, strong and true.
Let him be your architect.

13:3-4 Now as He sat on the Mount of Olives opposite the temple.^NKJV
The Mount of Olives rises above Jerusalem to the east. As Jesus
left the city to return to Bethany for the night, he would have
crossed the Kidron Valley and then headed up the slopes of the
Mount of Olives. From this slope, he and the disciples could look
down into the city and see the temple, with the sun setting behind
it to the west. The prophet Zechariah predicted that the Messiah
would stand on that very mountain when he would return to set
up his eternal kingdom (Zechariah 14:1-4). This was a fitting
place for the four disciples to ask Jesus when he would come in

power and what they could expect at that time. It is natural for us to want to know also.

Peter, James, John, and Andrew asked Him privately.^{NKJV} The inner circle of disciples (this time with Andrew added—Andrew was Peter's brother; James and John were brothers) came to Jesus privately because they wanted to understand what Jesus meant and when this terrible destruction would happen. These were the first four disciples whom Jesus had called (1:16-20).

"Tell us, when will these things happen? And what will be the sign that they are all about to be fulfilled?"^{NIV} The disciples' question had two parts: (1) They wanted to know when *these things* would happen (especially the destruction of the temple), and (2) they wanted to know what *sign* would show that *they are all about to be fulfilled.* The second part of their question referred to the end of the age. In the disciples' minds, one event would occur immediately after the other. They expected the Messiah to inaugurate his kingdom soon, and they wanted to know the sign that it was about to arrive.

Jesus gave them a prophetic picture of that time, including events leading up to it. He also talked about far future events connected with the last days and his second coming when he would return to earth to judge all people. Like much of Old Testament prophecy, Jesus predicted both near and distant events without putting them in chronological order. The coming destruction of Jerusalem and the temple only foreshadowed a future destruction that would ultimately usher in God's kingdom.

In order to understand the prophecy, picture yourself standing on a mountaintop looking across a distant mountain range. The mountain peaks appear to be next to each other, while in reality they are miles apart because of the valleys in between. Jesus' prophecy pictured "mountain peaks" (significant future events) as though they would occur together, when in reality they may be thousands of years apart. Some of the disciples lived to see the destruction of Jerusalem in A.D. 70, while some of the events Jesus spoke of have not yet—to this day—occurred. But the truth of Jesus' prediction regarding Jerusalem assured the disciples (and assures us) that everything else Jesus predicted will also happen.

There are three primary views on the Olivet discourse:

(1) that all of chapter 13 is describing *both* the destruction of Jerusalem and the last days before Christ's return;

(2) that the first part of the prophecy (13:2-23) deals only with the destruction of Jerusalem, and then the last part (13:24-27) switches to the return of Christ;

(3) that all of chapter 13 gives a prediction only of the destruction of Jerusalem; it says nothing about the return of Christ.

It is reasonable to interpret this, as with most Old Testament prophecies, as having a double fulfillment. Jesus was predicting the destruction of Jerusalem *and* the end times. However, in the first part of the prophecy, the destruction of Jerusalem is more prominent; in the second part, the last days before Christ's return are more prominent.

READY AND WAITING
Jesus warned his followers about the future so that they could learn how to live in the present. Jesus did not make these predictions so that we would guess when they might be fulfilled, but to help us remain spiritually alert and prepared at all times as we wait for his return. We must live each day close to Christ, always mindful that he is in charge of the timetable.

13:5-6 **Then Jesus began to say to them, "Beware that no one leads you astray. Many will come in my name and say, 'I am he!' and they will lead many astray."**[NRSV] Jesus first answered the disciples' second question about the end of the age and the coming kingdom. The disciples wondered what sign would reveal these things, but Jesus warned them against seeking signs: *"Beware that no one leads you astray."* Jesus knew that if the disciples looked for signs, they would be susceptible to being deceived. There would be many "false prophets" (13:22) with counterfeit signs of spiritual power and authority. Jesus predicted that before his return, many believers would be misled by false teachers coming "in Jesus' name," that is, claiming to be Christ. Even more confusing, these people would falsely use the words *I am,* long known as words claiming deity (see Exodus 3:13-14). Many scholars believe that 2 Thessalonians 2:3-10, which talks about a man of lawlessness who will lead people astray, is built upon this passage. Throughout the first century, there were many such deceivers (see Acts 5:36-37; 8:9-11; 2 Timothy 3; 2 Peter 2; 1 John 2:18; 4:1-3).

In every generation since Christ's resurrection, individuals have claimed to be the Christ or to know exactly when Jesus would return (remember Sun Myung Moon and David Koresh?). Obviously, no one else has been Christ, and no one has been right about the timing of the Second Coming. According to Scripture, the one clear sign of Christ's return will be his unmistakable appearance in the clouds, which will be seen by all people (13:26; Revelation 1:7). In other words, believers never have to wonder whether a certain person is the Messiah. When Jesus returns, believers will know beyond a doubt because he will be evident to all.

DON'T BE SIDETRACKED
Beware of groups who claim special knowledge of the last days because no one knows when Christ will return (13:32). In fact, it's not important to know. Jesus tells us that the best way to prepare for the future is to stay faithful to him and away from imposters. We must not be sidetracked by promises for social, economic, military, or political reform. The only sure way for the disciples (and all believers) to keep from being deceived is to focus on Christ and his words.

13:7 **"When you hear of wars and rumors of wars, do not be alarmed; this must take place, but the end is still to come."**[NRSV] The key phrase in this verse comforts all believers, *do not be alarmed.* As political situations worsen, as wars and rumors of wars ravage the world, Jesus instructed his disciples and all his followers not to be afraid that somehow God had lost control of his creation or that his promises would not come true. Just as false messiahs and religious frauds come and go, so do worldly crises. Even when the world's situation gets worse, God is in control. *This must take place* as part of God's divine plan. However, the wars and rumors of wars do *not* signal "the end" (the end of the world). The disciples probably assumed that the temple would only be destroyed at the end of the world as part of God establishing his new kingdom. Jesus taught that horrible events would happen, *but the end is still to come.*

WAR
War always hurts people, even when people fight for just causes. War's suffering prompts us to want the world to end and Christ to return. For many war victims, the world does end.
   Hold on, Jesus says to his followers. Through the pain of war, hold on. Don't let even war discourage your hope. God is in control; Jesus is coming. The violence that rips your world today will pass. Worldly empires will rise and fall. God promises peace of heart no matter what happens, and complete peace in the new heaven and earth.
   Many Christians speculate on when and how Jesus will return. Charts and signs abound. Some churches predict the future with scientific zeal. But Jesus wants us to stay faithful to him even when imposters and violence seem to rule. He gives no charts, only a promise and a pledge. Don't guess about the future; instead, give your days to him until he comes.

JESUS' PROPHECIES IN THE OLIVET DISCOURSE

In Mark 13, often called the Olivet Discourse, Jesus talked a lot about two future events: the end times and his second coming. By sharing these prophecies with his disciples, Jesus was not trying to encourage them to speculate about exactly when he would return. Instead, he was urging all his followers to be watchful and prepared for his second coming. Serve Jesus faithfully now and you will be ready for his return.

Type of Prophecy	Old Testament References	Other New Testament References
The Last Days		
Mark 13:1-23	Daniel 9:26-27	John 15:21
Matthew 24:1-28	Daniel 11:31	Revelation 11:2
Luke 21:5-24	Joel 2:2	1 Timothy 4:1-2
The Second Coming		
Mark 13:24-27	Isaiah 13:6-10	Revelation 6:12
Matthew 24:29-31	Daniel 7:13-14	1 Thessalonians 4:16
Luke 21:25-28	Ezekiel 32:7	Mark 14:62

13:8 **"For nation will rise against nation, and kingdom against kingdom; there will be earthquakes in various places; there will be famines. This is but the beginning of the birthpangs."**[NRSV] The "wars and rumors of wars" (13:7), the nations at odds, and the earth's turmoil revealed in increased earthquakes and famines would *not* signal the end. Instead, this is *but the beginning of the birthpangs;* in other words, these would be preliminary sufferings. Jesus' words subtly explained to the eager disciples that there would be a span of time before the end of the age and the coming kingdom—it would not happen this week, or immediately upon Jesus' resurrection, or even right after the destruction of Jerusalem. Instead, much suffering would occur as a part of life on earth, while history is moving toward a single, final, God-planned goal—the creation of a new earth and a new kingdom (Revelation 21:1-3). The description of sufferings as "birthpangs" is a typical biblical metaphor for the beginning of prekingdom travail and suffering (see Isaiah 13:6-8; 26:16-18; Jeremiah 4:31; 22:20-23; Hosea 13:9-13).

But all these troubles must not make Christians alarmed. Because Jesus has warned us about them, we know that these are a necessary step on the way to the coming of God's glorious kingdom. Preachers on prophecy who count up the number of earthquakes as signs of the end have not read Jesus' words carefully. Everything will happen according to God's divine plan. Our responsibility is to be prepared, to endure, and to continue to preach the Good News to all nations (13:10).

13:9 "You must be on your guard. You will be handed over to the local councils and flogged in the synagogues. On account of me you will stand before governors and kings as witnesses to them."^{NIV} Jesus personalized his prophecy by explaining that the disciples themselves would face severe persecution; thus, they must be on their guard in order to stay true to the faith. Being "on guard" means to be cautious and careful. We should not be shocked or surprised that the world hates us (see John 15:18-21). On the other hand, we shouldn't be overly suspicious or totally withdraw from the world (see 1 Corinthians 5:9-11). As the early church began to grow, most of the disciples experienced the kind of persecution that Jesus was discussing. Luke recorded many of these persecutions in the book of Acts. Being *handed over to the local councils* referred to the local Jewish courts *(sunedria)* held in the synagogues (smaller versions of the Sanhedrin in Jerusalem). Jesus didn't say it, but the disciples would find out that loyalty to Christ meant separation from Judaism. Two of the disciples listening to Jesus (Peter and John, 13:3) faced the Sanhedrin not long after Jesus' resurrection (Acts 4:1-12). At that time, they certainly remembered these words of Jesus. *On account of* the disciples' belief in Jesus, the Jews would brand them as traitors or heretics, pass down the sentence right in their synagogue, and have them *flogged.* Flogging was the punishment given to Jews who were found guilty of serious offenses. A flogging consisted of thirty-nine lashes across the back with a leather whip. This was based on Deuteronomy 25:1-3, which calls for forty lashes; thirty-nine were given in order to avoid accidentally giving too many. The apostle Paul wrote that he had received such floggings five different times (2 Corinthians 11:24). This punishment could only be given to Jews who would submit to it in order to remain in the Jewish community.

It is important to know of pain. It destroys our self-pride, our arrogance, our indifference toward others. It makes us aware of how frail and tiny we are and of how much we must depend upon the Master of the Universe.
Chaim Potok

Not only would Jesus' followers be in trouble with Jews, they would also find themselves standing trial before Gentile *governors and kings.* But such trials would have a purpose—the disciples were to be *witnesses* to these leaders. It would be through such trials that Gentile rulers would be able to hear the gospel (perhaps their only opportunity). The apostle Paul spoke to the Sanhedrin (Acts 22:30), Governor Felix (Acts 24:10), Governor Festus (Acts 25:1-6), and King Agrippa (Acts 26:1) and had hoped to speak to the emperor himself (Acts 26:32).

Peter later wrote this advice to persecuted believers: "Conduct yourselves honorably among the Gentiles, so that, though they malign you as evildoers, they may see your honorable deeds and glorify God" (1 Peter 2:12 NRSV). He also urged them to remember the suffering and abuse that Jesus had borne for their sakes (1 Peter 2:21-25). The apostle Paul also endured an incredible amount of persecution and suffering. Paul wrote from prison that he suffered gladly because it helped him know Christ better and do Christ's work for the church (Philippians 3:10; Colossians 1:24). The early church thrived despite intense persecution. In fact, late in the second century, the church father Tertullian wrote, "The blood of Christians is seed" because opposition helped spread Christianity.

PERSECUTED BELIEVERS
Since the time of Christ, Christians have been persecuted in their own lands and on foreign mission fields. Though you may be safe from persecution now, your vision of God's kingdom must not be limited by what happens only to you. A glance at a newspaper will reveal that many Christians in other parts of the world face hardships and persecution. Persecutions are an opportunity for Christians to witness for Christ to those opposed to him. These persecutions serve God's desire to have the gospel proclaimed to everyone.

13:10 **"And the gospel must first be preached to all the nations."**[NKJV] Jesus said that before his return, the gospel of the kingdom (the message of salvation) would be preached throughout the world. This was the disciples' mission—and it is ours. Jesus talked about the end times and final judgment to emphasize to his followers the urgency of spreading the good news of salvation to everyone. Although they would face persecution, Jesus' followers must never give up in their mission of actively preaching the Good News to *all the nations* and getting the Word of God to every language group.

By the time Mark's readers would hear these words, Jesus' prediction had already begun to happen. It occurred at Pentecost (Acts 2:5-11) and was spreading to all the world (Romans 1:5, 8; 15:19; Colossians 1:6, 23; 1 Timothy 3:16). It will also happen at the worldwide revelation of Jesus' power and glory at his second coming (13:26-27).

PREACHING SKILLS

How are your preaching skills? You're a plumber, you say, and not much of a public speaker. You're a waitress, or you're a computer programmer, not a speaker?

Preachers aren't the only ones who preach, at least as Jesus used the term. By using your skills, your mind, and your tongue (even in conversation), you "preach" the Good News and witness to Jesus' love and power.

It's wrong for Christians to expect professional clergy to do all the preaching. This mission belongs to every believer. Use your many talents to share Jesus' message until every part of God's world has heard.

13:11 **"When they bring you to trial and hand you over, do not worry beforehand about what you are to say; but say whatever is given you at that time, for it is not you who speak, but the Holy Spirit."**NRSV Not *if* the disciples would go on trial, but *when* they would go on trial, they were not to worry about defending themselves, but instead they were to concentrate on proclaiming the gospel. Standing before the Jewish leadership or Roman proconsuls or governors would be intimidating, but Jesus dealt with that fear ahead of time, explaining that the Holy Spirit would give them God's peace and the words to say. These words would help the disciples be bold witnesses as they made their defense before the rulers (13:9). Notice that Jesus did not guarantee acquittal. James, one of the disciples here listening to Jesus, would be killed because of his faith (Acts 12:1-2).

TAKING THE STAND

Jesus did not imply that studying the Bible and gaining knowledge is useless or wrong. Neither was he saying that a preacher should not prepare his message. Every Christian is responsible to study Scripture, and those who teach must know Scripture well. Jesus was teaching the kind of attitude to have when we must take an unexpected stand for the gospel, when we are forced to make a defense without any preparation. We don't have to be fearful or defensive about our faith because the Holy Spirit will be with us, giving us the right words to say.

We must be prepared spiritually: "Always be prepared to give an answer to everyone who asks you to give the reason for the hope that you have" (1 Peter 3:15 NIV). But most often we will not be able to prepare the words ahead of time when defending our faith. So we must trust the Holy Spirit to give us immediate guidance for each present situation. (For example, see the defenses Paul made in Acts 22 and 26.)

13:12 "Brother will betray brother to death, and a father his child. Children will rebel against their parents and have them put to death."NIV Jesus warned that in the coming persecutions his followers would be betrayed by their family members and friends as well as by religious and civil authorities. Certainly this was a reality for the Roman believers to whom Mark was writing. The fear of being *put to death* for one's Christian faith would pit family members against one another.

> Not all that the world hates is good Christianity, but it does hate good Christianity and always will. *William Temple*

Christians in every age have had to face this possibility. Sometimes hatred of the gospel has caused betrayal. More often, it has been the desire to get approval from oppressors by betraying Christian parents. Betrayal of Jews during the Holocaust, revealed how desperate people can get. It is reassuring to know that even when we feel completely abandoned, the Holy Spirit will stay with us. He will comfort us, protect us, and give us the words we need. This assurance can give us the courage and hope to stand firm for Christ no matter how difficult the situation.

HOME ALONE
Everyone dreads isolation. To be imprisoned alone for long periods is a form of punishment called solitary confinement. When we are shunned or betrayed, we feel unable to trust and unable to have a friend.

God created us to experience life together, connected to others. But Jesus warned us that we may face solitary confinement as part of the world's reaction to our faith in God. Two promises will keep us steady: (1) The Holy Spirit is our constant comfort and companion, here and now, no matter what. (2) In heaven we will have a wonderful crowd of friends, dearer than any we've yet known. A day or two of loneliness here cannot compare. As you face persecution and ostracism, remember God's promise to be near and your future in heaven, and take hope (see Romans 8:28-39).

13:13 "And you will be hated by all because of my name. But the one who endures to the end will be saved."NRSV Not only would the disciples face hatred from religious and civil leaders as well as their own families, they would be *hated by all*. For a Jew to convert to Christianity would soon become very dangerous, because it would lead to hatred and ostracism. And Jesus' words looked forward to the time of the end when hatred of Christians would again occur. To believe in Jesus and endure to the end will

ENDURE TO THE END
(Verses taken from NRSV.)

"The one who endures to the end will be saved."	Matthew 10:22
"By steadfastness . . . we might have hope."	Romans 15:4
"When reviled, we bless; when persecuted, we endure."	1 Corinthians 4:12
"Patiently endure the same sufferings that we are also suffering."	2 Corinthians 1:6
"As servants of God we have commended ourselves in every way: through great endurance, in afflictions, hardships, calamities, beatings, imprisonments, riots, labors, sleepless nights, hunger."	2 Corinthians 6:4-5
"May you be prepared to endure everything with patience."	Colossians 1:11
"Remembering before our God and Father your work of faith and labor of love and steadfastness of hope in our Lord Jesus Christ."	1 Thessalonians 1:3
"Pursue righteousness, godliness, faith, love, endurance, gentleness."	1 Timothy 6:11
"Share in suffering like a good soldier of Christ Jesus."	2 Timothy 2:3
"Therefore I [Paul] endure everything for the sake of the elect."	2 Timothy 2:10
"If we endure, we will also reign with him."	2 Timothy 2:12
"You have observed . . . my steadfastness."	2 Timothy 3:10
"Always be sober, endure suffering . . . carry out your ministry fully."	2 Timothy 4:5
"Tell the older men to be . . . sound in faith, in love, and in endurance."	Titus 2:2
"Endure trials for the sake of discipline."	Hebrews 12:7
"Because Christ also suffered for you, leaving you an example, so that you should follow in his steps . . . When he was abused, he did not return abuse; when he suffered, he did not threaten; but he entrusted himself to the one who judges justly."	1 Peter 2:21, 23
"I, John, your brother who share with you in Jesus the persecution and the kingdom and the patient endurance."	Revelation 1:9
"I also know that you are enduring patiently and bearing up for the sake of my name, and that you have not grown weary."	Revelation 2:3
"Here is a call for the endurance and faith of the saints."	Revelation 13:10 (14:12)

take perseverance because our faith will be challenged and
opposed. Severe trials will sift true Christians from fair-weather
believers. Enduring to the end does not earn salvation for us; it
marks us as already saved. The assurance of our salvation will
keep us going through the times of persecution. While some will
suffer and some will die, none of Jesus' followers will suffer spiritual or eternal loss. On earth, everyone will die, but believers in
Jesus will be saved for eternal life.

13:14-16 **"But when you see the desolating sacrilege set up where it
ought not to be (let the reader understand)."**[NRSV] Jesus warned
against seeking signs, but as a final part of his answer to the disciples' second question (13:4), he gave them the ultimate event that
would signal coming destruction. The *desolating sacrilege* (also
translated "abomination of desolation") refers to the desecration
of the temple by God's enemies. Mark's phrase, *let the reader understand,* was a sort of code for his Roman readers. A more precise explanation might have been dangerous for them if the letter
fell into the wrong hands, so Mark urged them to understand
Jesus' words in light of the prophecy from the Old Testament
prophet Daniel (see Daniel 9:27; 11:31; 12:11). The "desolating
sacrilege" refers to pagan idolatry and sacrifice (see Deuteronomy 29:16-18; 2 Kings 16:3-4; 23:12-14). The "sacrilege" or
"abomination" (pagan idolatry) that would occur in the temple
itself would cause the temple to be abandoned (left desolate).

The first fulfillment of Daniel's prophecy occurred in 168 B.C.
by Antiochus Epiphanes. He sacrificed a pig to Zeus on the
sacred temple altar. This act incited the Maccabean wars.

The second fulfillment occurred when Jesus' prediction of the
destruction of the temple (13:2) came true. In just a few years
(A.D. 70), the Roman army would destroy Jerusalem and dese-
crate the temple. Mark's Roman audience understood the sacrilege that would occur, for the Roman army was notorious for its
disregard for the religious life and freedom of the peoples it conquered.

Some scholars say that the third fulfillment is yet to come.
Jesus' words may also look far forward to the end times and to
the Antichrist (the Greek reads, "the desolating sacrilege set up
where *he* should not be"). In the end times, the Antichrist will
commit the ultimate sacrilege by setting up an image of himself
in the temple and ordering everyone to worship it (2 Thessalonians 2:4; Revelation 13:14-15).

**"Then those in Judea must flee to the mountains; the one on
the housetop must not go down or enter the house to take any-**

thing away; the one in the field must not turn back to get a coat."NRSV Many of Jesus' followers (including Mark's readers) would live during the time of the destruction of Jerusalem and the temple in A.D. 70. Jesus warned his followers to get out of Jerusalem and Judea and *flee to the mountains* across the Jordan River when they saw the temple being profaned. The Jewish historian Josephus wrote that from A.D. 66, Jewish Zealots clashed with the Romans. Many people realized that rebellion would bring the wrath of the Empire, so they fled to Pella, a town located in the mountains across the Jordan River. As Jesus had said, this proved to be their protection, for when the Roman army swept in, the nation and its capital city were destroyed. The reference to *the housetop* points to the construction of homes where a flat roof was used like a family room. People used the housetop to work and converse; in the evening, they enjoyed the cooler air on the roof.

The people were to leave immediately, without trying to pack bags to take along or even to return from the field to the city to get a coat (a most basic necessity). They should leave everything behind as they fled from the coming crisis.

WHEN TO RUN
By constraint of their conscience, some Christians have faced death rather than flee from murderous oppressors. Their deaths have served as witnesses for Christ in their countries. Some missionaries have chosen to stand with national citizens who could not flee rather than abandon them. But these words of Christ show that he permits us to provide for our own safety in times of calamity. Fleeing from certain death does not diminish our Christian character. While it is true that God sometimes gives special help, we should not neglect whatever preparations we can make. The apostle Paul often fled from one city to another to protect his life so he could live on to present the gospel. We should ask God to tell us when to stay or when to run. We need both courage and wisdom.

13:17 **"How dreadful it will be in those days for pregnant women and nursing mothers!"**NIV Here Jesus expressed sympathy and concern for those who would have difficulty fleeing because they were pregnant or had small children.

13:18-19 **"Pray that this will not take place in winter, because those will be days of distress unequaled from the beginning, when God created the world, until now—and never to be equaled again."**NIV Jesus told the disciples to pray that the crisis would not break *in winter* because that would make it difficult for everyone to get away. Winter means swollen rivers, which would make passage difficult across the usually small streams, as well as across the Jordan River, as they made their way out of Judea.

NO KIDS?
Some Christian couples who are contemplating pregnancy have been discouraged by this verse. They wonder if kids should be brought into a world like this. Since the end is near and the world is decadent and dangerous, should they risk pregnancy and child rearing?

The decision to have children is personal and private. Many couples feel strongly that they want to add more Christians to the world. The church needs strong and faithful young men and women to continue to carry out its mission.

At times, however, risking a pregnancy may be unwise. Even today, there are situations so desperate and dangerous that adding the further burden of a pregnancy would cause harm to both the mother and the child.

Jesus was not making a general warning against pregnancy. All periods of history have risks and drawbacks; no place or time is perfect. At all times, Christian couples have the support of the church in their child-raising task, which is, after all, one of life's greatest joys and responsibilities. Above all, we must remember that God will look out for the welfare of our children as he has looked out for us.

Jesus gave this warning to get out quickly *because those will be days of distress unequaled from the beginning.* The time would be evil and filled with suffering. This language, while sounding like an exaggeration, is not unusual in Scripture when describing an impending disaster. The Jewish historian Josephus recorded that when the Romans sacked Jerusalem and devastated Judea, one hundred thousand Jews were taken prisoner and another 1.1 million died by slaughter and starvation. So many Jews were crucified that the hills were emptied of trees in order to build enough crosses.

While Jesus' words could be taken as referring to the coming destruction of Jerusalem by the Romans in A.D. 70, they are so emphatic and clear that they must point ultimately to the final period of tribulation at the end of the age, because, as he stated, nothing like it had ever been seen nor would ever be seen again.

13:20 "If the Lord had not cut short those days, no one would survive. But for the sake of the elect, whom he has chosen, he has shortened them."[NIV] Many interpreters conclude that Jesus, talking about the end times, was telescoping near future and far future events, as the Old Testament prophets had done. Many of these persecutions have already occurred; more are yet to come. While a certain amount of persecution happened in the destruction of Jerusalem, Jesus may also have envisioned the persecution of believers throughout history. The persecution will be so severe that *if the Lord had not cut short those days,* that is, if they had not had a specific ending time, *no one would survive.* This refers to physical survival (as opposed to 13:13, which speaks of spiritual survival). The time would be cut short *for the sake of the elect,* God's chosen people. The shortening of the time will limit their duration so that the destruction will not wipe out God's people and thus their mission. God is ultimately in charge of history and will not allow evil to exceed the bounds he has set. Jesus had predicted the Cross for himself; here he was predicting persecution, death, and resurrection for his disciples.

Those who believe that Jesus will return in the middle of the Tribulation (mid-Tribulation rapture) center on this verse, linking it with Revelation 11:7-14, where the Tribulation is interrupted after "three and a half days" or halfway through the tribulation period. The main thrust of Jesus' teaching, however, is to show God's mercy toward the faithful and to show that God is in ultimate control.

Who are the "elect"? In the Old Testament, "elect" referred to Israel, particularly those faithful to God (see 1 Chronicles 16:13; Psalm 105:43; Isaiah 65:9, 15). In the New Testament, "elect" refers to the church (Romans 8:33; Colossians 3:12; 2 Timothy 2:10; 1 Peter 1:1-2). In this verse, the words "elect" and "chosen" refer, not to Old Testament Jews, but to all faithful believers, whether Jews or Gentiles. Paul wrote, "For those whom he foreknew he also predestined to be conformed to the image of his Son. . . . Those whom he predestined he also called; and those whom he called he also justified; and those whom he justified he also glorified" (Romans 8:29-30 NRSV). Some believe these verses mean that before the beginning of the world, God chose certain people to receive his gift of salvation. Others believe that God foreknew those who would respond to him and upon those he set his mark (predestined). What is clear is that God's purpose for people was not an afterthought; it was settled before the foundation of the world. People are to serve and honor God.

When the time of suffering comes, the important point for the disciples and all believers to remember is that God is in control. Persecution will occur, but God knows about it and controls how long it will take place. He will not forget his people.

13:21 "Then if anyone says to you, 'Look, here is the Christ!' or, 'Look, He is there!' do not believe it."NKJV In times of persecution even strong believers will find it difficult to be loyal. They will so much *want* the Messiah to come that they will grasp any hope that he has arrived. To keep us from being deceived by false messiahs, Jesus explained that his return will be unmistakable (13:26); no one will doubt that it is he. If they had to be told that the Messiah has come, then he hasn't (Matthew 24:27). Christ's coming will be obvious to everyone.

Most false messiahs like Jim Jones and David Koresh build their following from faithful church attenders who have been led astray. So often the leader's appeal is based on "I am the true way," "I will fulfill the expectations you have," or "I will be the power you need." Church leaders must be alert and prevent weak Christians from becoming sucked into such cults.

 TRULY FALSE TEACHING
To penetrate the disguises of false leaders and teachers, we can ask

- Have their predictions come true, or do they have to revise them to fit what's already happened?
- Does their teaching utilize a small section of the Bible to the neglect of the whole?
- Does the teaching contradict what the Bible says about God or about known Christian morality?
- Are the practices meant to glorify the leader or Christ?
- Do the teachings promote isolation from or hostility toward other Christians rather than love for them?

Jesus' warnings about false teachers still hold true. Upon close examination it becomes clear that many nice-sounding messages don't agree with God's message in the Bible. Only a solid foundation in God's Word can equip us to perceive the errors and distortions in false teaching.

13:22 **"False Christs and false prophets will appear and perform signs and miracles to deceive the elect—if that were possible."**[NIV] The Old Testament frequently mentions *false prophets* (see 2 Kings 3:13; Isaiah 44:25; Jeremiah 23:16; Ezekiel 13:2-3; Micah 3:5; Zechariah 13:2). False prophets claimed to receive messages from God, but they preached what the people wanted to hear, even when the nation was not following God as it should. There were false prophets in Jesus' day, and we have them today. They are the popular leaders who tell people what they want to hear—such as "God wants you to be rich," "Do whatever your desires tell you," or "There is no such thing as sin or hell." Jesus also said that *false Christs* would come, and he warned his disciples, as he warns us, not to be swayed by whatever *signs and miracles* they might produce. They will be able to perform miracles designed to convince people that their claims are true. But their "power" will be by trickery or from Satan, not from God. Both false and true prophets can work miracles (see Deuteronomy 13:1-5; 2 Thessalonians 2:1-12; 1 John 4:1-3; Revelation 13:11-18).

Yet will they be so convincing that they might even lead the elect astray? Is it possible for Christians to be deceived? Yes, and Jesus pointed out the danger (see also Galatians 3:1). The arguments and proofs from deceivers in the end times will be so convincing that it will be difficult to be faithful. If we are prepared, Jesus says, we can remain faithful. With the Holy Spirit's help, the elect will not give in and will be able to discern what the deceivers say as false.

13:23 **"So be on your guard; I have told you everything ahead of time."**[NIV] The disciples had been given special knowledge about the coming kingdom, as well as the coming crises and deceptions preceding it. This gave them all the more reason to *be on guard* or alert so as to be aware of the deceptions. While they might not be taken in, they would be responsible to help keep others from being deceived. Spiritual vigilance is a major theme of the Olivet Discourse. Spiritual alertness and moral preparation are taught by Jesus and portrayed by Mark throughout chapters 13 and 14: Beware that no one leads you astray (13:5); be on your guard (13:9, 23, 33); keep awake (13:35); do not be found asleep (13:36); keep watch (14:34); watch and pray (14:38).

ALWAYS VIGILANT
"Don't let your guard down" is good advice to anyone facing an enemy. Jesus warns that our spiritual enemies are never on vacation, that we must be vigilant every day (1 Peter 5:8-9).

Keeping our guard up is smart defense. It's our side of the two-way arrangement that will see us through troubles to come. God has promised to protect and save; but we must also be alert and ready.

We stay "on guard" through regular prayer and Bible study by ourselves and with others, worship, cultivating loyal Christian friends, and learning to discern between right and wrong, true and false. We must keep these projects going, always in progress. These disciplines make or break a Christian's preparedness for whatever the enemy throws at us.

JESUS TELLS ABOUT HIS RETURN / 13:24-31 / *202*

This section provides Jesus' true answer to the questions his disciples asked in 13:4. But Jesus went well beyond what he had been asked. The original questions focused on the destruction of the temple and the devastation of the nation. In his answer, Jesus predicted the destruction of Jerusalem and his return in full glory without any of the limitations he took on by becoming human. He was not speaking of his immediate resurrection, but his eventual, glorious return.

In the previous paragraphs, Jesus painted a picture of hardship, confusion, and waiting. But when it seems as though things can't possibly get any worse, they will. Heaven and earth will be irreversibly changed. There will be a sunset, but no sunup. That completely dark stage will make the arrival of the Son of Man visible to all.

13:24-25 **"But in those days, following that distress, 'the sun will be darkened, and the moon will not give its light; the stars will fall from the sky, and the heavenly bodies will be shaken.'"**[NIV] The little word *but* reveals a huge contrast between the false prophets and messiahs and the return of the true Messiah. The phrase *in those days* signaled that Jesus was talking specifically about the end times (see similar wording in the Prophets: Isaiah 34:4; Joel 2:30-31; Zechariah 8:23). After the time of tribulation, nature itself would experience change. As taught in Romans 8 and 2 Peter 3, the entire universe became involved in humanity's sin predicament; thus, the entire universe will be changed when humanity is changed.

The changes in the heavens will be an intended contrast to the pseudo "signs and omens" (13:22) of the false messiahs. There will be a variety of changes—the sun going dark, the moon not being seen, stars falling, heavenly bodies being shaken (perhaps planets going out of their normal orbits in the solar system). These words also recall the words of the prophets (Isaiah 13:10; Joel 2:10-11). What Jesus here described, John saw in his vision of the end times recorded in Revelation: "I watched as he opened the sixth seal. There was a great earthquake. The sun turned black . . . the whole moon turned blood red, and the stars in the sky fell to earth. . . . The sky receded like a scroll, rolling up" (Revelation 6:12-14 NIV).

Mark 13:24-26 and Matthew 24:29-31 form the heart of the teaching that Jesus' coming will not occur until after the Tribulation (post-Tribulation rapture). Those who hold this view feel that Christ will not come until the ultimate destruction has occurred. But the connection of these verses to their Old Testament roots in the prophets seems to connect them more with judgment on the nations and the political powers than on the destruction of the world.

The coming persecutions and natural disasters will cause great sorrow in the world. But when believers see these events happening, they will know that the return of their Messiah is near, and they can look forward to his reign of justice and peace. Rather than being terrified by what is happening in our world, we should confidently await Christ's return to bring justice and restoration to his people.

THE LONGED-FOR LEADER
God's promise of a future kingdom where Christ rules in great power and glory gives us reason for hope.
   Today, leaders are shortsighted, prone to bend principle for political gain, and sometimes corrupt. Yet we ask them to be for us what only Christ can be. When Christ returns to rule, his leadership will be just, strong, and wise. He will bring the world for which we have hoped and longed, led by the leader we needed and for whom we have waited.
   When injustice ruins your plans today, spoils your program, or angers your soul, take hope. God calls us to work and live for the next administration, led by the one whose program brings justice and love.

13:26 **"Then they will see 'the Son of Man coming in clouds' with great power and glory."**NRSV After the cosmic events recorded in 13:25, all the people on earth *will see 'the Son of Man coming in clouds.'* Jesus' return will be unmistakable; no one will wonder about his identity. The "clouds" are pictured as the Son of Man's royal chariot, bringing him from heaven to earth in the Second Coming (to the Jews, clouds signified divine presence; see, for example, Exodus 13:21; 19:9; Psalm 97:1-2; Daniel 7:13). Jesus' second coming will not be as a humble, human carpenter, but as the powerful, glorious, and divine Son of Man. He will arrive to defeat Satan, judge all people, and set up his kingdom (8:38).

13:27 **"And then He will send His angels, and gather together His elect from the four winds, from the farthest part of earth to the farthest part of heaven."**NKJV Upon his return to earth, Jesus will send his angels out to *gather together His elect from the four winds* (that is, from all across the world, see also Psalm 50:3-5; Isaiah 43:6; 66:18; Jeremiah 32:37; Ezekiel 34:13; 36:24; 37:9; Daniel 7:2; 8:8; 11:4; Zechariah 2:6). The angels' gathering of the elect signifies the triumphant enthronement of the Son of Man, who will be revealed in all his power and glory. The manifestation of the angels and the gathering of the people will gloriously mark the end of Jesus' keeping secret his divine power and authority. Jesus' second coming marks the core of the Christian hope. When he comes, the whole world will know that Jesus is Lord, and Christians' hope and faith will be vindicated.

Mark's wording, *from the farthest part of earth to the farthest part of heaven,* combines a couple of Old Testament expressions—from Deuteronomy 13:7 and Deuteronomy 30:4. The wording gives special stress to the concept that none of the elect will be overlooked or forgotten. God won't lose track of anyone.

Some have interpreted *He will send His angels* to mean that Christ will not touch the earth, that the angels will gather up the elect. But Jesus refers to the gathering together of the saints from everywhere, not to lifting them up from earth to heaven.

13:28 **"Now learn this lesson from the fig tree: As soon as its twigs get tender and its leaves come out, you know that summer is near."**[NIV] In the form of a parable, Jesus answered the disciples' question regarding when the events he spoke about would happen (13:4). So far in this lengthy discourse, Jesus has traced two key themes: (1) the disciples' suffering and (2) their need to be watchful. The Greek word *engus* means "close" or "nearby"; it does not mean "soon" or "immediately."

The disciples, like anyone living in Palestine, knew how to interpret the coming of summer from the twigs and leaves of the fig trees. Fig trees lose their leaves in winter and bloom in late spring. The dry, brittle twigs getting tender with rising sap and the leaves coming out were certain signs that summer was near.

SUMMER BREEZE
"Pay attention," Jesus urged. "Summer follows spring. My return is as certain as these signs," he said. "Don't worry, I'm coming."

Of seasonal change we feel confident. We plan on it and never worry about mix-ups in nature's timetable. With the same confidence we should hope for Jesus' return.

But what about today? Are you deep in a personal winter? Do you need more warmth right now? more light? God's sunshine comes to you today by faith in the living Christ. God's warming winds bring out the new leaves on your life's tree and promise you a long and gentle season ahead—the summer of Jesus' return.

13:29 **"So also, when you see these things taking place, you know that he is near, at the very gates."**[NRSV] In the same way that they could interpret the season by the leaves on trees, so the disciples could know *when* these significant events would occur. When they saw *these things* (referring to the events described in 13:5-23), they would know that the destruction of Jerusalem would soon follow. Some scholars feel that the phrase *he is near* refers back to 13:14 and the coming desecration of the temple. But this interpretation makes too abrupt an interjection in Jesus' thought. Since Jesus was reassuring the disciples, it makes more sense to interpret "he" as referring to the Son. Thus, this verse means that the second coming of Jesus is near. The fulfillment of Jesus' prophecy would assure the disciples that the other prophecies he had given regarding the end times would also come true.

13:30 **"Truly I tell you, this generation will not pass away until all these things have taken place."**NRSV The solemn phrase *Truly I tell you* introduces an important truth, an assurance like an oath. There are three views of the meaning of this verse: (1) It refers only to those alive at this time who would be alive also at the destruction of Jerusalem; (2) it refers to the end times only; (3) it refers both to the destruction of Jerusalem and the end times.

Jesus singled out *this generation,* using the Greek word *genea,* which can refer both to those living at a given time as well as to race or lineage (therefore, he was speaking of the Jewish race). That makes the third view above most likely. Jesus used "generation" here to mean that the events of 13:5-23 would occur initially within the lifetime of Jesus' contemporaries. Jesus explained that many of those alive at that time would witness the destruction of Jerusalem. In addition, the Jewish nation would be preserved and remain on earth, so Jews also would witness the end-time events.

13:31 **"Heaven and earth will pass away, but My words will by no means pass away."**NKJV There could be no doubt in these disciples' minds about the certainty of these prophecies. While heaven and earth as we know them would eventually come to an end, Jesus' words (including all his teachings during his time on earth) would never pass away into oblivion. They were true and would remain for all eternity.

TRUTH NEVER CHANGES
In Jesus' day the world seemed tangible, dependable, and permanent. These days many people fear its destruction by nuclear war or environmental disaster. Jesus tells us, however, that even if the earth should pass away, the truth of his words will never be changed or abolished (see also 2 Timothy 2:9). God and his Word provide the only stability in our unstable world. People who spend their time only learning about this temporary world and accumulating its possessions, while neglecting the Bible and its eternal truths, are very shortsighted! Focus on God's "world," not this one.

JESUS TELLS ABOUT REMAINING
WATCHFUL / 13:32-37 / **203**

Probably because Jesus knew that the question about when he
would return would be asked most often, he saved his answer to
the disciples' question, "When will all this happen?" for last. His
answer was blunt: "No one knows; not even me." He then
pointed out that the mark of a disciple was not having inside
information, but serving Christ faithfully. Spiritual vigilance,
"not sleeping," becomes the essential theme of the entire chapter.
Jesus' servants must be so busy that they have no time to speculate about his schedule.

13:32 **"No one knows about that day or hour, not even the angels in
heaven, nor the Son, but only the Father."**NIV While Jesus had

given general "signs" to observe regarding the coming of the end, he clearly
explained to the disciples that the exact
day or hour was not known by the
angels or the Son (Jesus himself). When
Jesus said that even he did not know the
time of the end, he was affirming his
humanity (see Philippians 2:5-8). Of

> The desire of power in
> excess caused angels to
> fall; the desire of
> knowledge in excess
> caused man to fall.
> *Francis Bacon*

course, God the Father knows the time, and Jesus and the Father
are one. But when Jesus became a man, he voluntarily gave up
the unlimited use of his divine attributes. On earth, Jesus laid
aside his divine prerogatives and submitted to the Father's will.
Thus, *only the Father* knows the exact time of Jesus' return.

The emphasis of this verse is not on Jesus' lack of knowledge,
but rather on the fact that *no one knows*. It is God the Father's
secret to be revealed when he wills. No one can predict by Scripture or science the exact day of Jesus' return. Jesus was teaching
that preparation, not calculation, was needed.

13:33 **"Be on guard! Be alert! You do not know when that time will
come."**NIV Because no one except the Father knows when Christ
will return (*you do not know* points to every one of us), Jesus
explained that believers must be on guard and alert, ready for his
return to happen at any moment. Christ's second coming will be
swift and sudden. There will be no opportunity for last-minute
repentance or bargaining. The choice that people have already
made will determine their eternal destiny.

13:34 **"It is like a man going on a journey, when he leaves home and
puts his slaves in charge, each with his work, and commands
the doorkeeper to be on the watch."**NRSV In this parable of

JESUS AND THE FATHER ARE ONE

During his earthly life, Jesus subordinated himself to the will of his Father. He perfectly obeyed what his Father willed (see John 4:34; 5:30; 6:38; 7:28; 8:29). The cult called Jehovah's Witnesses has used these verses to attack Jesus' divinity. Others have used similar arguments to undermine faith in Jesus. (References are quoted from NIV.)

Incorrect Conclusions	*The Complete Truth*
Jesus is a creature. Those who believe this use Acts 2:36, "God has made this Jesus . . . both Lord and Christ" and Colossians 1:15, "He is . . . the firstborn over all creation."	**BUT** in context, these verses apply to Jesus' office and function, not his origin. In Colossians, "firstborn" means first in rank.
Jesus is not God. Those who believe this use John 17:3, "Now this is eternal life: that they may know you, the only true God, and Jesus Christ, whom you have sent."	**BUT** in context, Jesus' prayer was contrasting the Father with false gods and spiritual rivals— not with himself, the Son.
Jesus is inferior to the Father. Those who believe this use John 14:28 where Jesus said, "The Father is greater than I."	**BUT** in context, in his earthly ministry, Jesus took upon himself a functional subordination of his will and divine powers. During his incarnation, he was dependent upon God for his divine attributes.
Jesus didn't have divine knowledge, so he couldn't be divine. Those who believe this use Mark 13:32, where Jesus said, "No one knows about that day or hour, not . . . the Son, but only the Father."	**BUT** in context, Jesus voluntarily took on limitations to accommodate his humanity. These are not limitations of his essential divinity, but only of his physical humanity.

Jesus and the Bible affirm the Trinity and Jesus' essential oneness, equality, and interchangeability with God the Father. See Matthew 28:19; John 10:30; 17:21-22; 2 Corinthians 13:14.

---

watchfulness, Jesus described himself as *a man going on a journey* (literally, to another country or abroad; Jesus would be returning to heaven). The disciples are those left behind to carry on their work. The doorkeeper, another of the slaves, is commanded to keep watch for the master's return. The slaves understand that they are in charge of themselves, had their own work to do, and would not want the master to return suddenly and find them being lazy.

Each of us has enough assigned work to do that we shouldn't be neutralized or paralyzed by fear or doubt. We do not need to worry about how other servants compare to us; instead, we should devote ourselves to doing what God has given us to do.

POSTPONED PREPARATIONS
Months of planning go into a wedding, the birth of a baby, a career change, a speaking engagement, the purchase of a home. Do you place the same importance on preparing for Christ's return, the most important event in your life? Its results will last for eternity. You dare not postpone your preparations because you do not know when his return will occur. The way to prepare is to study God's Word and live by its instructions each day; remain morally alert and avoid the spiritual lethargy Paul warned about in 1 Thessalonians 5:6; and refuse to be distracted from doing the work or fulfilling the role that God has assigned to you.

13:35 "Therefore, keep awake—for you do not know when the master of the house will come, in the evening, or at midnight, or at cockcrow, or at dawn."NRSV Not just the doorkeeper, but all the slaves want to *keep awake.* In the context of the parable, this meant that the slaves were doing their various work conscientiously. Jesus meant that none of his followers would want to be found spiritually lax, but instead conscientiously going about the work given by God for them to do.

Mark's depiction of the four watches of the night (evening, midnight, cockcrow, and dawn) is another evidence of his writing for the Roman audience. This was the Roman format; Jews had only three watches of the night. The doorkeepers or guards, those on duty during their particular watches of the night, were never to be found asleep on duty. All believers must be ready and alert for Jesus' return, working for the kingdom, both because they know of the certainty of Christ's return and because they don't know *when* that return will happen.

It is good that we believers don't know exactly when Christ will return. If we knew the precise date, we might be tempted to be lazy in our work for Christ. Worse yet, we might plan to keep sinning and then turn to God right at the end. Heaven is not our only goal; we have work to do here. And we must keep on doing it until death or until the return of our Savior.

13:36 "If he comes suddenly, do not let him find you sleeping."NIV Jesus told the disciples to keep a constant watch for his return. Although nearly two thousand years have passed since Jesus spoke these words, their truth remains: Christ is coming again, and when he returns, his followers must not be *sleeping.* We need to watch and be spiritually fit. This means working faithfully at the tasks God has given us. Don't let your mind and spirit be dulled by careless living or the foolish pursuit of pleasure. Don't let life's anxieties overburden you. Instead, be ready to move at God's command. Jesus' followers should be less concerned with knowing the exact date and more concerned with being prepared—living God's way consistently—so that no matter when Jesus comes in glory, he will claim us as his own.

ONE EYE OPEN
Must we never sleep? We're meant to have regular periods of real sleep, of course. We need sleep to stay alert. "Sleep" here refers to spiritual sluggishness, the kind we experience when sports consumes a Sunday, when frenzy pushes prayer aside, when books and magazines replace the Bible—and we hardly notice. In this sleep we doze away wondering, *Who is God, anyhow? How does he fit in?*

In all your varied interests, keep one eye peeled for Christ. Be like a smoke detector, always charged. Be like a fire station, always ready.

13:37 "And what I say to you, I say to all: Watch!"[NKJV] Jesus had spoken this discourse to only four of his disciples (13:3). Here he instructed them to carry these words to the rest of the disciples, for their truth was of vital importance. By extension, the words were meant for all believers. Even today, we do well to be on the alert, watching out for false teaching and watching expectantly for Christ's return as we do his work in the world.

SO NOW WHAT?
The entire thirteenth chapter of Mark tells us how to live while we wait for Christ's return:
- We are not to be misled by confusing claims or speculative interpretations of what will happen (13:5-6).
- We should not be afraid to tell people about Christ, despite what they might say or do to us (13:9-11).
- We must stand firm by faith and not be surprised by persecution (13:13).
- We must be morally alert, obedient to the commands for living found in God's Word.

This chapter was not given to promote discussions on prophetic timetables, but to stimulate right living for God in a world where he is largely ignored. Jesus' purpose was to warn us to be prepared. Will you be ready? The only safe choice is to obey him *today.*

Mark 14

Mark's account of the final acts in Jesus' ministry begins with a simple summary of the scene. It was almost Passover. Jesus' enemies were looking for a way to kill him. Their concern about timing had to do with keeping control of the people. They wanted to kill Jesus without anyone noticing. But God had a different purpose in the timing of events.

14:1 Now the Passover and the Feast of Unleavened Bread were only two days away, and the chief priests and the teachers of the law were looking for some sly way to arrest Jesus and kill him.NIV The *Passover* commemorated the night the Israelites were freed from Egypt (Exodus 12), when God "passed over" homes marked by the blood of a lamb. This was the last great plague on Egypt; in the unmarked homes the firstborn sons died. After this horrible disaster, Pharaoh let the Israelites go.

The day of Passover was followed by a seven-day festival called the *Feast of Unleavened Bread.* This, too, recalled the Israelites' quick escape from Egypt when, because they wouldn't have time to let their bread rise, they baked it without leaven (yeast). This holiday found people gathering for a special meal that included lamb, wine, bitter herbs, and unleavened bread. Eventually the eight days (the day of Passover and the week of the Feast of Unleavened Bread) came to be called the Passover Feast. Passover was celebrated on the fourteenth day of the Jewish month of Nisan (by our calendar, the last part of March and the first part of April).

All Jewish males over the age of twelve were required to go to Jerusalem for Passover and the Feast of Unleavened Bread (Deuteronomy 16:5-6). For these feasts, Jews from all over the Roman Empire would converge on Jerusalem to celebrate a very important event in their history. For this holiday, Jerusalem, a town of about 50,000, swelled to 250,000 people.

The Jewish leaders *(chief priests and the teachers of the law)* plotted secretly to kill Jesus. They had already decided that Jesus must die (see John 11:47-53); they just needed the opportunity.

14:2 "But not during the Feast," they said, "or the people may riot."[NIV] The leaders were afraid of Jesus' popularity, so they needed "some sly way" (14:1) to arrest Jesus and convict him with the death penalty. They did not want to attempt to arrest Jesus during the Passover because they feared that the crowd would riot on his behalf. They feared that such an uprising might bring the wrath of Rome. While Roman reprisals for riots in its territories were not as automatic as some have thought (politics in Rome at this time favored a moderating position), it was a possibility. The religious leaders did not want to take that chance. They probably planned to arrest him after the festival when the vast crowds were gone. However, Judas's unexpected offer (14:10-11) moved up their timetable.

WHO'S IN CONTROL?
Most Jews in Jerusalem were preparing to observe Passover, a time of solemn remembrance, but also a time for families to celebrate. But some of the religious leaders had more important things to accomplish. Jesus had disrupted their security, revealed their sham, and opposed their authority. Now they would put him away. But the world is controlled by our all-wise God, not puny politicians. God would turn the religious leaders' murder plot into the greatest blessing that mankind would ever know. When grief or disaster seem to be dominating, remember that your life is in God's hands and remember what Jesus did for you.

A WOMAN ANOINTS JESUS WITH EXPENSIVE PERFUME / 14:3-9 / **182**

Matthew and Mark put this event just before the Last Supper, while John included it just before the Triumphal Entry. Of the three, John placed this event in the most likely chronological position. Mark sandwiched this beautiful event between two sections dealing with the plot to eliminate Jesus. This act of devotion by Mary, who is a true heroine in this narrative, is contrasted with the treachery of the villains—the religious leaders and Judas.

We must remember that the main purpose of the Gospel writers was to give an accurate record of Jesus' message, not to present an exact chronological account of his life. When Gospel writers placed events out of order, they were following (1) the inspiration of the Holy Spirit and (2) the acceptable practice for historians in the ancient world to place events out of chronological order so each could develop his particular thematic presentation. Matthew and Mark's accounts make thematic use of this event without claiming that it occurred at a certain time in the week. They may have simply placed this event here to contrast the complete devotion of Mary with the betrayal of Judas, the next event they recorded in their Gospels.

This incident represents another way in which Jesus recognized the unique perspectives, gifts, and actions of women. He previously pointed out the costly discipleship of the widow who gave all she had (12:41-44); now he presents a woman's extravagant display of love for her Lord. The home where they were staying and dining on this occasion belonged to Simon, but Martha was probably the hostess at the meals. The woman here may well have been Mary, Martha and Lazarus's sister.

14:3 While he was in Bethany, reclining at the table in the home of a man known as Simon the Leper.[NIV] Bethany was located on the eastern slope of the Mount of Olives (Jerusalem is on the western side). This town was the home of Jesus' friends Lazarus, Mary, and Martha (who were also present at this dinner, John 11:2). Jesus had been returning to Bethany from Jerusalem each night during this final week, probably staying with his dear friends (11:11).

One night, a dinner had been prepared and Jesus was an honored guest (thus his position of *reclining at the table*). The host, *Simon the Leper,* did not have leprosy at this time, for lepers had to live separately from people because of the extreme contagiousness of the disease. Jesus may have healed Simon of his leprosy, but this name (or nickname) had stuck.

WHAT'S IN A NAME?
Who knows where Simon got his name? For certain, he did not have leprosy at this point. Perhaps Mark used it to distinguish him from Simon Peter or Simon the Zealot (3:18). If he once had leprosy ("leprosy" in ancient times covered a range of diseases), he was now clean; but he couldn't shake the past.

No one would choose such a name, the ancient equivalent of Joe Psychotic or HIV George. We shun people with certain diseases, and Simon's name was like a strobe-lit sign telling everyone: Keep Your Distance.

Apparently Jesus ignored such signs, as should we. His love and acceptance gave dignity to all men and women who followed him. Our attitude should be like his, even if that means we must love the unlovely.

MAJOR EVENTS OF PASSION WEEK
Sunday through Wednesday Jesus spent each night in Bethany, just two miles east of Jerusalem on the opposite slope of the Mount of Olives. He probably stayed at the home of Mary, Martha, and Lazarus. Jesus spent Thursday night praying in the Garden of Gethsemane. During Friday and Saturday nights, Jesus' body lay in the garden tomb.

Day	Event	References
Sunday	Triumphal Entry into Jerusalem	Matthew 21:1-11 Mark 11:1-10 Luke 19:29-40 John 12:12-19
Monday	Jesus clears the temple	Matthew 21:12-13 Mark 11:15-17 Luke 19:45-46
Tuesday	Greeks ask to see Jesus	John 12:20-26
	Jesus' authority is challenged in the temple	Matthew 21:23-27 Mark 11:27-33 Luke 20:1-8
	Jesus teaches in stories and confronts the Jewish leaders	Matthew 21:28–23:36 Mark 12:1-40 Luke 20:9-47
	Jesus gives the Olivet Discourse	Matthew 24 Mark 13 Luke 21:5-38
	Judas agrees to betray Jesus	Matthew 26:14-16 Mark 14:10-11 Luke 22:3-6

A woman came with an alabaster jar of very costly ointment of nard, and she broke open the jar and poured the ointment on his head.NRSV This woman was probably Mary, the sister of Martha and Lazarus, who lived in Bethany (John 12:1-3). An *alabaster jar* was a beautiful and expensive vase with a long, slender neck carved from translucent gypsum. *Ointment of nard* was a fragrant ointment imported from the mountains of India. This was pure and genuine ointment, thus very costly. The beautiful jar was broken, and the costly ointment was poured on Jesus' head. (John records that the oil was poured on Jesus' feet—Mary probably did both, for Jesus was reclining with his legs stretched out behind the table.) It was a common custom at some Jewish meals for the honored guests to be anointed with oil (see Luke 7:44-46), but it would not be expensive nard. Such an anointing, with expensive oil and pouring it on the head as well as the feet, pictured a royal (messianic)

Day	Event	References
Wednesday	Bible doesn't say what Jesus did. But he probably remained in Bethany with his disciples	
Thursday	Jesus and the disciples celebrate the Last Supper	Matthew 26:26-29 Mark 14:22-25 Luke 22:14-20
	Jesus speaks to the disciples in the upper room	John 13–17
	Jesus struggles in Gethsemane	Matthew 26:36-46 Mark 14:32-42 Luke 22:39-46 John 18:1
	Jesus is betrayed and arrested	Matthew 26:47-56 Mark 14:43-52 Luke 22:47-53 John 18:2-12
Friday	Jesus is tried by Jewish and Roman authorities and denied by Peter	Matthew 26:57–27:2, 11-31 Mark 14:53–15:20 Luke 22:54–23:25 John 18:13–19:16
	Jesus is crucified	Matthew 27:31-56 Mark 15:20-41 Luke 23:26-49 John 19:17-30
Sunday	Jesus rises from the dead	Matthew 28:1-10 Mark 16:1-11 Luke 24:1-12 John 20:1-18

anointing. Mary's gift to Jesus (a pint of this costly perfume, according to John 12:3-5) was worth a year's wages. Three hundred denarii (see NIV margin) was the yearly wage paid for an average worker at the rate of one denarius a day.

14:4 But some were there who said to one another in anger, "Why was the ointment wasted in this way?"NRSV Where Mark says *some . . . said,* John specifically mentions Judas (John 12:4-5). Mark probably was referring to all the disciples. This is the first of many times in this chapter that the disciples will fail Jesus: Judas will betray Jesus (14:10); the disciples will deny that they would ever desert Jesus (14:19, 31); the disciples will fall asleep three times when they should be watching (14:37-41); all the disciples will desert Jesus (14:48-50); Peter will deny three times that he knows Jesus (14:66-72).

Judas's indignation over Mary's act of worship would not have been based on concern for the poor (14:5), but on greed. Because Judas was the treasurer of Jesus' ministry and had embezzled funds (John 12:6), he no doubt wanted the perfume sold so that the proceeds could be put into his care. This event probably pushed Judas over the edge in his determination to betray Jesus.

14:5 "It could have been sold for more than a year's wages and the money given to the poor." And they rebuked her harshly.^{NIV} The disciples used a pious phrase to hide their true motives. They concluded that the expensive ointment had been wasted on Jesus, so they rebuked Mary for such an act because the ointment *could have been sold* and *the money given to the poor.* John attributes this statement to Judas; Matthew and Mark record that all the disciples were indignant over the wasting of the ointment. They certainly resented this gesture as apparent waste. Besides, Passover was the time of special giving to the poor (see John 13:27-29), and the sale of this ointment would certainly have provided a generous amount to give. The disciples felt moral outrage at the loss of resources for the poor. But Jesus knew what was in Judas's heart. Judas wasn't interested in helping the poor; he was interested in getting his hands on the money.

CALCULATING GOODNESS
In one sense, the disciples were right. Lots of hungry people could be fed from the sale of that nard, now spilled and spent. An accountant bearing down on the economics of the encounter would have to consider such cost-benefit calculations.
As we must today. Should your church refurbish its sanctuary or give to a mission project? Should your daughter get a new bike or give a hungry foreign orphan a meal? Should you work harder to earn more to give more, or work less and become a deacon or missionary volunteer?
In a world of limited resources, such calculations are always with us. Yet Jesus' approval of this woman's solitary, costly, and love-inspired act breaks the calculation and frees us to be radically his, at any price.

14:6 But Jesus said, "Let her alone; why do you trouble her? She has performed a good service for me."^{NRSV} Jesus reprimanded the disciples for their lack of insight. They had missed the intention of this rare moment of adoration by using conventional criteria to judge it. Their words obviously criticized Mary's actions; she may have wondered if she had been wrong after all in her devotion to Jesus. But Jesus' words comforted her. The expensive ointment poured on

Jesus had been *a good service* to him—a beautiful, acceptable, appealing act of love and sacrifice—and Jesus declared it to be so.

We must not discount the good intentions and good works of other believers. Some efforts of worship don't have value according to our reckoning. But a heart of worship is still valuable to Christ.

14:7 **"For you always have the poor with you, and you can show kindness to them whenever you wish; but you will not always have me."**[NRSV] This was a unique act for a specific occasion—an anointing that anticipated Jesus' burial and a public declaration of faith in him as Messiah. Jesus was not saying that we should neglect the poor, nor was he justifying indifference to them. (For Jesus' teaching about the poor, see Matthew 6:2-4; Luke 6:20-21; 14:13, 21; 18:22.) Jesus was affirming Mary's unselfish act of worship. The essence of worshiping Christ is to regard him with utmost love, respect, and devotion, as well as to be willing to sacrifice to him what is most precious.

Jesus' purpose in these words was to explain that the opportunity to show him such devotion and to anoint him with oil (in preparation for burial) would soon be past. The phrase *you will not always have me* meant that Jesus would soon be gone from them physically. However, they could and should show kindness to the poor, and opportunities to do so would continue until the end of time. There would always be poor people who needed help. Jesus brought to mind Deuteronomy 15:11: "The poor will never cease from the land" (NKJV). This statement does not justify ignoring the needs of the poor. Scripture continually calls us to care for the needy. The passage in Deuteronomy continues: "Therefore I command you, saying, 'You shall open your hand wide to your brother, to your poor and your needy, in your land'" (NKJV). By saying this, Jesus was highlighting the special sacrifice Mary had made for him.

PRIORITY OF WORSHIP
Christians have significant social responsibilities to the poor. But in all our efforts to feed hungry people or assist sick populations, we must not dismiss or ignore the priority of worship.

- A hundred bowls of rice given to refugees do not cover for a heart empty of God.
- A thousand inoculations against disease do not provide peace to a soul resisting God.
- A multidigit check written to charity does not ransom a person who regards God as irrelevant or nonessential.

Worship of God precedes all acts of love and gives them meaning and purpose. Open your heart to God, and God will make your acts of charity pure joy.

Jesus' words should have taught Judas and the disciples the valuable lesson that devotion to Christ is worth more than money. Unfortunately, Judas did not take heed; soon he would sell his Master's life for thirty pieces of silver.

14:8 "She has done what she could. She has come beforehand to anoint My body for burial."^{NKJV} Mary may not have set out to anoint Jesus for burial; she was merely showing great respect for the Teacher she so loved and respected. She probably did not understand Jesus' approaching death any more than the disciples, although she was known for truly listening to Jesus (Luke 10:39). She might have realized something was going to happen to Jesus, and thus she sympathized with him and did *what she could* by honoring him with the greatest gift she could give.

In this culture, fragrant ointments were used for anointing dead bodies to prepare them for burial. Jesus said that Mary had prepared his body *for burial.* Jesus would die just before the Sabbath, preventing the women who came with ointments from putting the ointments on his body before he was buried. That's why they came early Sunday morning to do so. But at that point Jesus had already been resurrected.

MARY'S EXAMPLE
All four Gospels record Mary's example of devotion. Three important lessons remind us how we should love the Lord and not repress those who do good works:

1. *Let her alone.* We must not disregard or depreciate someone else's loving act of service just because it's not our style of serving. Sometimes envy, ignorance, or hardness of heart keep us from seeing the value of showing honor and praise to Christ.
2. *She has performed a good service.* Mary's act was courageous and sacrificial. Christ welcomed her and regarded her efforts. We must not be so practical in our stewardship of resources that we criticize the genuine and beautiful ways others express their love for Christ.
3. *She has done what she could.* Mary took the initiative. She did an act of devotion when no one else would. She gave of her resources in a way only she could. Some people only talk about what they can do or wish they would have done, but Mary did what she felt led to do.

14:9 "Truly I tell you, wherever the good news is proclaimed in the whole world, what she has done will be told in remembrance of her."^{NRSV} Mary's unselfish act would be remembered forever. This has come true because we read about it today. While the disciples misunderstood Jesus' mission and constantly fought about places in the kingdom, and while the religious leaders stubbornly refused to believe in Jesus and plotted his death, this one quiet woman so loved Jesus and was so devoted to him that she considered no sacrifice too great for her beloved Master. She is an example to us all of unselfish devotion to our Savior.

SMALL UNFORGETTABLES
Headlines are written about presidents and prodigies. Movies are made about world-class heroes. Yet we remember small acts of kindness and compassion. They fill our personal memories and iron out the creases of our lives. Small acts of love fuel our days.

God's memory is greater. He notices everything we do to serve and honor him. Never think of your seemingly insignificant gesture as just a blip on the screen. God is pleased with your kindness, and he will remember. God regards heartfelt devotion to him as heroic and noteworthy.

JUDAS AGREES TO BETRAY JESUS / 14:10-11 / *208*

Each of the Gospel writers reported Judas's treachery with remarkable restraint. Their treatment of Peter's denial actually seems harsher than their references to the betrayer. Mark, the shortest account, conveys the simple facts. The enemies of Jesus were delighted. We're not told how Judas felt at this point. Since Mark was reflecting Peter's account, the reticence about Judas may indicate Peter's shame in recalling his own treatment of Jesus. We are much more likely to present a fair picture of the flaws and faults of others if we keep our own clearly in sight.

14:10 Then Judas Iscariot, one of the Twelve, went to the chief priests to betray Jesus to them.[NIV] Why would *Judas Iscariot* want to betray Jesus? Very likely, Judas expected Jesus to start a political rebellion and overthrow Rome. As treasurer, Judas certainly assumed (as did the other disciples—see 10:35-37) that he would be given an important position in Jesus' new government. But when Jesus praised Mary for pouring out the perfume, thought to be worth a year's salary, Judas finally began to realize that Jesus' kingdom was not physical or political. Judas knew the religious leaders had it in for Jesus, and he knew they would have the power to arrest Jesus. So that was where he went. Judas's greedy desire for money and status could not be fulfilled if he followed Jesus, so he betrayed him in exchange for money and favor from the religious leaders. (See 3:19 on the meaning of Judas's name.)

MARK CONTRASTS MARY AND JUDAS
When Mark placed the response of Mary prior to the response of Judas in his Gospel account, he was deliberately telling us to be like Mary, not like Judas. We need Mary's heart.

Mary	Judas
Had a loving heart	Had a loveless heart
Gave generously	Bartered greedily
Praised Jesus by her actions	Plotted against Jesus
Attributed worth to Christ	Doubted and despaired
Pursued heavenly values	Sought earthly solutions
Is remembered for her unselfishness	Is remembered as a traitor

14:11 **When they heard it, they were greatly pleased, and promised to give him money. So he began to look for an opportunity to betray him.**^{NRSV} Obviously the chief priests were *greatly pleased* to have discovered a traitor among Jesus' followers. They had been having difficulty figuring out how to arrest Jesus (14:1-2); so when an offer of help came from this unexpected corner, they took advantage of it. Matthew records that Judas hoped for a monetary reward: "What will you give me if I betray him to you?" (Matthew 26:15 NRSV). So the religious leaders *promised to give him money.* Matthew alone records the exact amount of money Judas accepted to betray Jesus—thirty silver coins, the price of a slave (Exodus 21:32). The religious leaders had planned to wait until after the Passover to take Jesus, but with Judas's unexpected offer, they accelerated their plans. Judas, in turn, *began to look for an opportunity to betray him* when there would be no Passover crowds to prevent Jesus' capture and no possibility of a riot (14:2). Judas knew where they could find Jesus alone on Passover night and could positively identify him.

BETRAYAL
Few persons in history rank as low in public opinion polls as Judas. Most people despise the treachery of traitors and opportunists, no matter what the turncoat's reason. Not many parents name their children Judas.

Judas we hate, but too often we wear his mask. We condemn Judas but complacently rationalize other ways to betray our Lord. It's popular in some theological circles to "turn in" the Master by denouncing his deity or by clucking about Jesus the good teacher who never assumed to be a Savior. Church members "turn in" the Lord, too, when we betray each other or use Christian status to line our pockets. We must all answer for our treatment of Christ. Don't be one who betrays our Lord.

DISCIPLES PREPARE FOR THE PASSOVER / 14:12-16 / **209**

Jesus and his disciples had been together long enough to celebrate Passover several times. Apparently, despite the gloominess
of Jesus' predictions and the tension of constant scrutiny by the
religious leaders, the disciples tried to keep a semblance of nor-
mality. They asked Jesus for instructions about Passover. His
response indicates that he had planned their itinerary in advance.

**14:12 On the first day of the Feast of Unleavened Bread, when it was
customary to sacrifice the Passover lamb.**[NIV] The Passover took
place on one night and at one meal, but the Feast of Unleavened
Bread, which was celebrated with it, continued for a week. The first
day of the feast was technically the day after Passover, but the two
were often equated. Thus, this was either Wednesday night (the day
before Passover) or Thursday of Jesus' last week (the night of the
Passover meal). The highlight of the festival was the Passover
meal, a family feast with the main course of lamb. The sacrifice of
a lamb and the spilling of its blood commemorated Israel's escape
from Egypt when the blood of a lamb painted on their doorposts
had saved their firstborn sons from death. They then were to prepare the meat for food and eat it in their traveling clothes.

This event foreshadowed Jesus' work on the cross. As the spotless Lamb of God, his blood would be spilled in order to save his
people from the penalty of death brought by sin.

Scholars are puzzled over whether this Last Supper was a Passover meal. Most likely it was. In John, Jesus seems to have this
meal on the evening before Passover. But Mark and Luke both
identify this meal that Jesus had with his disciples as a Passover
meal (14:12-16; Luke 22:7-16). Certain descriptions in the Gospels indicate that this was a Jewish seder:

- Everyone ate in a reclining position (Matthew 26:20; Mark
  14:18; Luke 22:14; John 13:23). Jews reclined only at Passover. The rest of the time they sat up, thus differentiating themselves from other cultures like the Egyptians and the Romans.

- A traditional Passover contains a hand-washing ceremony that
  could have been the opportunity for the foot washing (John
  13:1-11).

- The use of bread and wine in the seder provided a natural way
  for Jesus to present the new covenant.

- The dipping of the unleavened bread into the preparation of bitter herbs comes from Passover (Mark 14:20; John 13:26).

- Though eating lamb was not mentioned by any of the Gospel writers, it was not an exact requirement to complete the celebration. A Passover could be celebrated without eating lamb. Those Jews traveling or living away from Jerusalem could not eat the officially slain Passover lambs either. Also, it would be possible to have lamb, but not one of the officially sacrificed ones.

Another question concerns whether this meal took place on Wednesday or Thursday. Traditionally, the Passover went from sundown (6:00 P.M.) on Thursday to sundown on Friday, the fifteenth day of the month of Nisan. Matthew, Mark, and Luke seem to indicate that Jesus and the disciples celebrated the Last Supper on Thursday evening. However, several verses in John suggest that the Last Supper occurred on a Wednesday (see John 13:1, 29; 18:28; 19:14, 31, 42).

The following three attempts have been made to solve this apparent problem:

1. There were two calendars being used to determine the day of Passover. The official calendar that the Pharisees and Sadducees followed was lunar. Jesus and the disciples followed a solar calendar, possibly used at Qumran (a monastic Dead Sea community). The two calendars differed by one day, so that Jesus ate the Passover meal one full day before the Jerusalem Passover. There have been no conclusive historic arguments to support this theory.

2. Jesus and his disciples had the Passover meal one day early in anticipation of Passover. This view does explain John 18:28 and allows Jesus to be the Passover Lamb—crucified at the same time as the Passover lambs were slaughtered. If Jesus can heal on the Sabbath because he is the Lord of the Sabbath, he could certainly authorize eating the Passover meal one day early.

This view harmonizes the chronology of all the Gospel writers and preserves their authority and reliability. Furthermore, it allows for a full three-day period when Jesus was in the grave—not just part of Friday, all of Saturday, and part of Sunday—but from Thursday evening to Sunday morning.

3. Jesus and the disciples did eat the meal on the official day of Passover. In A.D. 30 (the year of Jesus' crucifixion), the Passover was celebrated on Thursday evening (the fourteenth of Nisan) and was immediately followed by the Feast of Unleavened Bread, which lasted from the fifteenth of Nisan (Friday)

to the twenty-first of Nisan. During each day of this celebration, special meals *(chaggigah)* were eaten. According to this view, the other references in John are to the Feast of Unleavened Bread, not the Passover meal (John 13:29; 18:28; 19:14). In John 13:29, after the Passover meal, Judas went out—actually to betray Jesus—but the disciples thought he went out to buy provisions for the upcoming feast. In John 18:28 the Pharisees did not want to make themselves unclean by entering Pilate's palace and thereby be unable to partake of the feast. In John 19:14 "the preparation for the Passover" was not for the Passover meal but for the whole week that followed, which in New Testament times was called both the Passover and Feast of Unleavened Bread.

Therefore the chronology was:
Thursday—Lambs slain in the afternoon, Passover begins at 6:00 P.M., Last Supper, Gethsemane, arrest
Friday—Official trial, crucifixion, burial by sundown, Feast of Unleavened Bread and Sabbath begin at 6:00 P.M.
Saturday—Jesus' body was in the tomb
Sunday—Early morning resurrection

Jesus' disciples asked him, "Where do you want us to go and make preparations for you to eat the Passover?"[NIV] Jesus' disciples assumed that they would eat the Passover meal together with Jesus. However, the meal had to be eaten in Jerusalem, so the disciples asked Jesus where they should go in order to make preparations. Peter and John, the two disciples Jesus sent on this errand (Luke 22:8), had to buy and prepare the unleavened bread, herbs, wine, and other ceremonial food.

SEVEN FAITHFUL WORDS
Now at the last, the faithful eleven were becoming real disciples. The first words of their question, "Where do you want us to go" show that they were willing to venture out and were waiting only for directions. It's a pattern they would follow many times in the early missionary activity of the church: willing, waiting, directed, gone!
   We need that same faith. Rushing to a mission without instructions from God is foolhardy. Getting instructions but then staying put is weak-willed. We must be disciples who move out by God's authority, at God's time, eager for the opportunity.

14:13 So he sent two of his disciples, saying to them, "Go into the city, and a man carrying a jar of water will meet you; follow him."[NRSV] The two disciples Jesus sent were Peter and John

(Luke 22:8). Whether Jesus had supernatural knowledge in this instance or if he had made arrangements in advance is unclear (as in the incident with his Triumphal Entry, see 11:1-6). It seems that in this instance this room had been reserved previously and kept secret—none of the disciples knew where they would eat this meal. Jesus already knew that Judas would be looking for an opportunity to betray him without crowds around, so Jesus may have made these arrangements and kept them secret.

The two disciples were dispatched in the morning from Bethany to Jerusalem to prepare the Passover meal. Jesus told them that as they entered the city, they would meet a man carrying a jar of water. Ordinarily women, not men, went to the well and brought home the water. So this man would have stood out in the crowd. This may have been a prearranged signal, or Jesus may have supernaturally known that this man (most likely a servant) would be there and would lead them to the right house. This kept the plans secret and security tight. Tradition says that this may have been Mark's home (the writer of this Gospel). If this speculation is true, the owner of the house would then have been Mark's father. Mark may have kept his anonymity here for safety's sake; it may have been dangerous to divulge this information at the time of Mark's writing.

14:14 "Say to the owner of the house he enters, 'The Teacher asks: Where is my guest room, where I may eat the Passover with my disciples?'"[NIV] Jesus' wording here indicates that Jesus had arranged for this room. He told the disciples to ask the owner, "Where is *my* guest room?" The owner was probably one of Jesus' followers. He knew exactly who the Teacher was and probably knew the disciples by sight. As mentioned in 14:13, this may have been Mark's home, so this would have been Mark's father.

14:15 "He will show you a large room upstairs, furnished and ready. Make preparations for us there."[NRSV] Many homes had large upstairs rooms, sometimes with stairways both inside and outside the house. This room was large enough to accommodate Jesus and his twelve disciples for a banquet at a large table with reclining couches. It seems that Jesus had prearranged this because he already knew what the room looked like—it was large, furnished, and ready. Again this indicates a prearrangement on Jesus' part to have security and privacy during this last supper with his disciples.

14:16 So the disciples set out and went to the city, and found everything as he had told them; and they prepared the Passover meal.[NRSV] As before, when two disciples went to get the donkey for Jesus to ride into Jerusalem (11:1-6), these two disciples *found everything as he had told them.* The preparations for the Passover would have included setting the table, buying and roasting the Passover lamb, and making the unleavened bread, sauces, and other ceremonial food and drink that were a traditional part of every Passover meal.

THE DISCOVERERS
The disciples found everything as Jesus had told them. These faithful men could not know what each day would bring, but they were learning that each step was guided by God's sovereign will. And they were coming to understand the partnership of their calling: They go, God provides; they work, God blesses. The Passover meal did not miraculously appear; someone had to prepare it! The disciples were discovering that this kind of personal, daily walk with God had some very exciting dimensions to it. No job could be too difficult; no place too far.
 Disciples today have the same Lord. We must trust God with the future, realizing that whatever it is, he will be with us. For our part, we must be flexible, responsive, and ready to follow.

JESUS AND THE DISCIPLES HAVE THE LAST SUPPER / 14:17-25 / **211**

We know from John's Gospel that a great deal was said during the Passover meal. But Mark mentioned only two central events that occurred during the supper itself. First, Jesus disclosed that there was a betrayer among them. Then he instituted the sacrament of the Lord's Supper. Mark's description recaptures how a participant might have remembered the event. John reflected the details of Jesus' words.

14:17 In the evening He came with the twelve.[NKJV] On that evening (Wednesday or Thursday), Jesus arrived in Jerusalem *with the Twelve.* Perhaps Peter and John returned to Bethany after all was prepared to tell the others that the meal was ready. Then, just after sunset, Jesus and the Twelve went back into Jerusalem to the upper room. The meal was not to be eaten until after sunset and was supposed to be finished by midnight.

14:18 Now as they sat and ate, Jesus said, "Assuredly, I say to you, one of you who eats with Me will betray Me."[NKJV] The disciples and Jesus took their places on the reclining couches around the table. During such an important meal as the Passover, everyone would recline at the table, symbolizing the freedom the people gained after the very first Passover and their subsequent release from slavery in Egypt. The meal was organized around drinking four cups of red wine, symbolizing the four-part promise of redemption found in Exodus 6:6-7. (1) "I will bring you out"; (2) "I will rid you of bondage"; (3) "I will redeem you"; and (4) "I will take you for my people, and I will be your God."

There was a traditional program for the meal. First would come a blessing of the festival and the wine, followed by drinking the first cup of wine (this also made this meal special, for usually water was served with meals). Then the food would be brought out. The youngest son would then ask why this night was distinguished from others; the father (certainly Jesus in this instance) would answer with the story of the Exodus and would point to each item on the table as he explained its symbolic significance (for example, bitter herbs symbolized the bitter bondage of slavery in Egypt). This would be followed by praise to God for the past and future redemption (taken from the first part of the Hallel in Psalms 113–115). Then the second cup of wine would be drunk. After the second cup, the bread would be blessed, broken, and distributed, and then eaten with bitter herbs and a fruit-paste dish.

This would be followed by eating the meal, which was not to last beyond midnight. The Passover meal included roasted lamb sacrificed in the temple. At the end of the meal, the father would bless a third cup of wine, which would be followed by singing the second part of the Hallel (from Psalms 116–118). A fourth cup of wine would conclude the meal (see 14:25).

Jesus and the disciples were at the point of eating the bread with the sauce of herbs and fruit (14:18) when Jesus spoke the stunning words *"One of you who eats with Me will betray Me."* Jesus knew who would betray him. The betrayer was one of his own chosen twelve disciples, one with whom the meal was at that moment being shared. Jesus alluded to Psalm 41:9, "Even my close friend, whom I trusted, he who shared my bread, has lifted up his heel against me" (NIV).

COLD-BLOODED
Judas, the very man who would betray Jesus, was at the table with the others. Judas had already determined to betray Jesus, but in cold-blooded hypocrisy he shared the fellowship of this meal. It is easy to become enraged or shocked by what Judas did; yet professing commitment to Christ and then denying him with one's life is also betraying him. It is denying Christ's love to disobey him; it is denying his truth to distrust him; it is denying his deity to reject his authority. Do your words and actions match? If not, consider a change of mind and heart that will protect you from making a terrible mistake.

**14:19 They were saddened, and one by one they said to him,
"Surely not I?"**NIV Jesus' words caused quite a stir among the disciples. They had heard Jesus tell them three different times that
he would soon die, but that one of them would actually betray
Jesus saddened them greatly. From the accounts of Mark and
John we know that the betrayer was Judas Iscariot. Although the
other disciples were confused by Jesus' words, Judas knew what
he meant. Apparently Judas was not the obvious betrayer. After
all, he was the one the disciples trusted to keep the money (John
12:4-6). So the disciples asked Jesus who the betrayer was;
"Surely not I?" each one asked in turn. The Greek form of the
question would be rendered, "It is not I, is it?" and implied a negative answer. Each disciple hoped to clear himself and wondered
if he would have the courage to remain faithful. Matthew records
that even Judas asked this question: "Then Judas, the one who
would betray him, said, 'Surely not I, Rabbi?'" Jesus answered
Judas, "You yourself have said it" (Matthew 26:25 NIV margin).
This answer was ambiguous enough so that only Judas would
know that Jesus had identified him as the betrayer.

"ME? IS IT ME?"
Eleven of the twelve men could ask this question with clean
hearts—they did not intend to do wrong, but would they? Only
one was hiding, deceiving, wrecking his own conscience, trad-
ing loyalty for money.
　　Eleven came forward. Not one assumed his own virtue. Each
disciple wanted to know if the Master Surgeon could see a cancer in his soul.
　　Only one did not need to be told, for he already knew.
　　To renounce our sin, we need the loyal and responsive
attitude of the eleven. And if our consciences have already
declared us guilty, we need to learn from Judas the high cost of
denying the truth.

**14:20 He said to them, "It is one of the twelve, one who is dipping
bread into the bowl with me."**NRSV Jesus answered that the
betrayer was indeed *one of the twelve.* Then he added that this
betrayer was dipping his bread into the bowl with Jesus. In Jesus'
time, some food was eaten from a common dish into which everyone dipped their hand. Meat or bread was dipped into a dish
filled with sauce often made from fruit. Jesus' words emphasized
the treachery of the betrayer. To eat with a friend and then turn
around and betray him was treachery at its worst.

**14:21 "For the Son of Man goes as it is written of him, but woe to
that one by whom the Son of Man is betrayed! It would have**

been better for that one not to have been born."ᴺᴿˢⱽ Jesus would indeed be betrayed and would indeed die as he had already told his disciples. His death would not occur merely because of the betrayer, for the *Son of Man* had to die to complete God's plan and fulfill Scripture (for example, Psalm 41:9-13; Isaiah 53:1-6). All would happen *as it is written of him.*

But (and this small word makes all the difference) *woe to that one* who betrayed Jesus. Again Jesus' words were reminiscent of Psalm 41, this time verses 10-12, where the sufferer was vindicated by God and his enemies punished. Jesus felt true pity for this one who would betray him because he was acting as Satan's agent. His fate would be so awful that Jesus expressed his pity by saying that it would have been better for that person not to have been born. Jesus knew that Judas was going to betray him, and he also knew that Judas would not repent. Jesus next predicted Peter's denial. The words were not so full of doom, however, for Peter repented and was forgiven of his sin.

STERN WARNING
A moment before, Jesus had warned Judas indirectly. Here he lowered the boom. Judas knew that the big "Woe!" was for him. And what a judgment! Judas would have been better off to never have been born.

Denying Jesus, refusing his claim on our lives, and scoffing at his words bear serious consequences. Soon Judas would know in his heart that Jesus was right.

Don't let your life break down so tragically. Seeing the truth, don't deny it. Hearing the truth, don't refuse it. Knowing the truth, don't betray it.

Luke wrote that "Satan entered Judas, called Iscariot" before he went to the religious leaders (Luke 22:3 NIV). However, Satan's part in the betrayal of Jesus does not remove any of the responsibility from Judas. In God's sovereign will and according to his timetable, he uses sinful men. But that doesn't excuse their sin. All people will be held accountable for their choices and actions. Disillusioned because Jesus was talking about dying rather than about setting up his kingdom, Judas may have been trying to force Jesus' hand and make him use his power to prove that he was the Messiah. Or perhaps Judas, not understanding Jesus' mission, no longer believed that Jesus was God's chosen one. Whatever Judas thought, Satan assumed that Jesus' death would end Jesus' mission and thwart God's plan. Like Judas, Satan did not know that Jesus' death and resurrection were the most important parts of God's plan all along.

John records that upon this pronouncement, Jesus told Judas to "do quickly what you are going to do" (John 13:27 NRSV). Then Judas went out into the night.

14:22 And as they were eating, Jesus took bread, blessed and broke it, and gave it to them and said, "Take, eat; this is My body."NKJV Jesus and the disciples were eating the bread, and Jesus took the loaf of unleavened bread, blessed, and broke it. The "blessing" of the bread refers to the Jewish practice of giving thanks for bread at a meal by saying, "Blessed are you, Lord, our God, who brings forth bread from the earth." Bread was considered a gift from God. It was irreverent to cut it with a knife, so it was torn (or broken) with the hands. Jesus gave the bread to the disciples to eat with the sauce. As he did so, he gave this Passover practice an entirely new meaning.

The book of Mark explains the origin of the Lord's Supper, also called Communion, table of the Lord, the breaking of the bread, or Eucharist (thanksgiving), which is still celebrated in worship services today. Jesus and his disciples ate a meal, sang psalms, read Scripture, and prayed. Then Jesus took two traditional parts of the Passover meal, the passing of bread and the drinking of wine, and gave them new meaning as representations of his body and blood. He used the bread and wine to explain the significance of what he was about to do on the cross. For more on the significance of the Last Supper, see 1 Corinthians 11:23-29.

Jesus told the disciples to *"Take, eat; this is My body."* Jesus used literal terms to describe a figurative truth. Just as he had so many times said, "I am" the door, the bread, the light, the vine, so the bread symbolized Jesus' work of salvation on behalf of humanity. His words "this is my body" symbolize the spiritual nourishment believers obtain from a personal relationship with the Savior. The phrase would more clearly be translated, "This is my self." It was Jesus' pledge of his personal presence with all his disciples whenever they would partake of this meal.

BY ANY OTHER NAME
Each name believers today use for this sacrament brings out a different dimension to it. It is the "Lord's Supper" because it commemorates the Passover meal that Jesus ate with his disciples; it is the "Eucharist" (thanksgiving) because in it we thank God for Christ's work for us; it is "Communion" because through it we commune with God and with other believers. As we eat the bread and drink the wine, we should be quietly reflective as we recall Jesus' death and his promise to come again, grateful for God's wonderful gift to us, and joyful as we meet with Christ and the body of believers.

Christians differ in their interpretation of the meaning of the commemoration of the Lord's Supper. There are three main views: (1) The bread and wine actually become Christ's body and blood; (2) the bread and wine remain unchanged, yet Christ is spiritually present by faith in and through them; and (3) the bread and wine, which remain unchanged, are lasting memorials of Christ's sacrifice. No matter which view they favor, all Christians agree that the Lord's Supper commemorates Christ's death on the cross for our sins and points to the coming of his kingdom in glory. When we partake of it, we show our deep gratitude for Christ's work on our behalf, and our faith is strengthened.

Just as the Passover celebrated deliverance from slavery in Egypt, so the Lord's Supper celebrates deliverance from sin by Christ's death.

14:23 Then He took the cup, and when He had given thanks He gave it to them, and they all drank from it.[NKJV] Luke mentions two cups of wine, while Matthew and Mark mention only one. In the traditional Passover meal, wine is served four times. Most likely the cup mentioned in this verse was the third cup; verse 25 refers to the fourth cup that Jesus did not drink, vowing first to complete his mission before drinking again of wine. Christ spoke the words about his body and his blood when he offered the fourth and last cup. He gave thanks and gave it to them. Matthew includes the command, "Drink from it, all of you" (Matthew 26:27 NIV).

PRAYER OF THANKS
This wine cup was to picture a painful death just ahead. It would represent Jesus' blood for the rest of time. Yet Jesus treated it with the same reverent gratitude as all other cups of wine when he paused to thank God the Father for it.

Table grace is not an empty ritual, a moment to let food cool off. It's our giving thanks, however briefly, for provision and protection and heavenly mercies. Prayer brings the awareness of God's presence to the table. It reminds us of the source.

Jesus blessed the food, thanking God for it, even at his last meal before his death. So should we express thanks to God for all his provision.

The celebrations in the Christian church (Communion, Eucharist, the Lord's Supper) have first a sharing of bread (including a repetition of Jesus' words, "This is my body"), and then a sharing of wine (including a repetition of Jesus' words, "This is my blood," 14:24). Thus, the Christian celebration incorporates the initial and ending portions of this last supper of Jesus.

Jesus gave thanks for the cup of wine. The Greek word translated "had given thanks" is *eucharisteo,* from which we get the
English term "Eucharist." It shows the joyous nature of the early
celebrations of the Lord's Supper.

THEY ALL DRANK
That they all drank from the cup reflects our common experience at Communion. We experience the presence of Christ; we
remember his life and death for us; we acknowledge again his
lordship in our life.

- Communion humbles us before God. We all come; we all eat
  and drink together. We confess our sin and restate our need
  for him to lead our lives. This ritual gets rid of our pride.
- Communion reminds us that we are forgiven. It reaffirms for
  us that sins confessed are sins forgiven because of Christ's
  death. Communion cleanses our guilt.
- Communion expresses our oneness in Christ. We participate
  as a body of believers in one communion; thus, we are unified
  in our faith and in our experience of Christ.
- Communion encourages us to recommit. As we recall the sacrifice of Christ, we are reminded to pledge ourselves to service like his.

**14:24 He said to them, "This is my blood of the covenant, which is
poured out for many."**^{NRSV} As with the bread, Jesus spoke words
in figurative language. *"This is my blood"* means "This wine represents my blood." Jesus' blood, shed on behalf of many (that is,
all the elect community), began a *covenant* between God and
people. In later manuscripts, the word "new" has been inserted
before "covenant." This insertion is based on Luke 22:20 and
1 Corinthians 11:25, where the word "new" appears in all Greek
manuscripts. The *many* are those who will become part of the
covenant that his death created (10:45). According to Isaiah
53:11-12, the Qumran usage of the term, and rabbinic teaching,
"many" is a key word that refers to the chosen people, the elect
community of salvation who will inherit the kingdom of God.

The word "covenant" refers to an arrangement established by
one party that cannot be altered by the other party. In other
words, God established the covenant, and humans can only
accept or reject it; they cannot alter it in any way. Jesus was saying these words at the drinking of the third cup at the Last Supper, the cup that stands for "I will redeem" (see the note on
14:18). Jesus' words recall Exodus 24:6-8, where Moses poured
half of the blood of the covenant on the altar and sprinkled the
people with the other half to seal the covenant. Jesus understood

his death as sacrificial, inaugurating and sealing the new covenant.

What did Jesus mean by a "new covenant"? In Old Testament times, God had agreed to forgive people's sins if they would bring animals for the priests to sacrifice. When this sacrificial system was inaugurated, the agreement between God and human beings was sealed with the blood of animals (Exodus 24:8). But animal blood did not in itself remove sin (only God can forgive sin), and animal sacrifices had to be repeated day by day and year after year.

Jesus instituted a "new covenant," or agreement, between humans and God. This concept is key to all New Testament theology and forms the basis for the name of the New Testament portion of the Bible. Under this new covenant, Jesus would die in the place of sinners. Unlike the blood of animals, his blood (because he is God) would truly remove the sins of all who would put their faith in him. And Jesus' sacrifice would never have to be repeated; it would be good for all eternity (Hebrews 9:23-28). The prophets looked forward to this new covenant that would fulfill the old sacrificial agreement (Jeremiah 31:31-34), and John the Baptist called Jesus "the Lamb of God who takes away the sin of the world" (John 1:29 NKJV).

The old covenant was a shadow of the new, pointing forward to the day when Jesus himself would be the final and ultimate sacrifice for sin. Rather than an unblemished lamb slain on the altar, the perfect Lamb of God was slain on the cross, a sinless sacrifice so that our sins could be forgiven once and for all. Jesus explained that his blood would be *shed* (or "poured out"), referring to a violent death. Once again Jesus was teaching his disciples that he would soon face a violent death, dying on behalf of others.

Those who accept Christ's sacrifice and believe in him receive forgiveness. Now all people can come directly to God through faith because Jesus' death has made us acceptable in God's eyes (Romans 3:21-24).

SEALED AGREEMENT
Jesus' death for us on the cross sealed a new covenant between God and people. The old covenant involved forgiveness of sins through the blood of an animal sacrifice (Exodus 24:6-8). But instead of a spotless lamb on the altar, Jesus offered himself, the spotless Lamb of God, as a sacrifice that would forgive sin once and for all. Jesus was the final sacrifice for sins, and his blood sealed the new agreement between God and us. Come boldly to God through Jesus, in full confidence that God will hear you and save you from your sins.

14:25 **"Assuredly, I say to you, I will no longer drink of the fruit of the vine until that day when I drink it new in the kingdom of God."**[NKJV] Again Jesus assured his disciples of his victory over his imminent death and of a future in *the kingdom of God.* The next few hours would bring apparent defeat, but soon they would experience the power of the Holy Spirit and witness the great spread of the gospel message.

Jesus' vow to abstain from wine was made before the fourth cup, which was drunk with the words, "I will take you as my people, and I will be your God" (Exodus 6:7 NRSV). Jesus reserved the drinking of this cup for the future restoration. This powerful scene is accented by Jesus' taking the third cup, saying "I will redeem you," sharing it with the disciples, and then pledging that he would finish this celebration in the kingdom of God (see also Luke 14:15; Revelation 3:20; 19:6-9). See Isaiah 25:6-8 for the Old Testament purpose of the messianic feast. Matthew 26:29 adds the words of Jesus "with you," giving real assurance to his disciples and to all of us. Because Jesus would be raised, so his followers will be raised. One day we will all be together again in God's new kingdom. The *fruit of the vine* in the kingdom will be *new* in quality—joyous, complete, fully realized.

INVITATION TO DINNER
What the disciples could not see, but Jesus did, was all the trouble just ahead—all the clamor, pain, and public humiliation. Here Jesus determined to see it through (no more eating until . . .); he also turned his gaze to the future and the promise.

How would Jesus endure the pain? He knew a big banquet was coming. There he would celebrate and break the fast with all his loved ones gathered around.

When you face imminent trouble and need courage, do as Jesus did. Remember the promise and look to the future. Trust Christ even in circumstances you don't understand and when they seem overwhelming. Thank God for the victory that wipes away all tears.

By the way, have you sent your R.S.V.P.? This banquet is for you, and the price has been already paid. Look forward to joining him at the heavenly feast.

JESUS AGAIN PREDICTS PETER'S DENIAL / 14:26-31 / **222**

Both Luke and John reported that Jesus predicted both the disciples' abandonment and Peter's denial while they were still having supper. Mark and Matthew placed Jesus' comments in the break be-

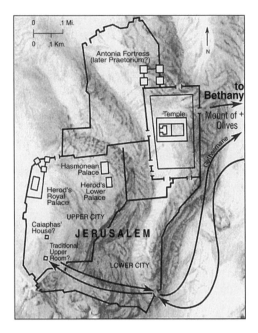

Upper Room and Gethsemane
Jesus and the disciples ate the traditional Passover meal in an upper room in the city and then went to the Mount of Olives into a garden called Gethsemane. In the cool of the evening, Jesus prayed for strength to face the trial and suffering ahead.

tween the meal and their arrival in Gethsemane. Since there are no time or location indicators for Jesus' prediction in either Mark or Matthew, the event may refer to a separate incident. There are enough differences in detail to support the idea that Jesus warned Peter on two occasions that he would deny the Lord (see also John 13:31-38). For instance, Luke's and John's accounts involve Peter directly, while Mark and Matthew introduce the announcement with Jesus' statement that all of them will "fall away" (Mark 14:27 NIV).

True to form, Peter reacted to Jesus' prediction. He could not imagine the disciples abandoning Jesus. Least of all himself. He said so: "Even though all become deserters, I will not" (Mark 14:29 NRSV). If Jesus warned Peter twice, as well as included him in the general warning that all of them would fall away, then Peter actually received a threefold prediction of his denial. But before we criticize Peter, we should first see ourselves in him. Peter reminds us how easy it is to profess our faith and how difficult it is to remain loyal under pressure.

14:26 And when they had sung a hymn, they went out to the Mount of Olives.NKJV The hymn they sang was most likely taken from Psalms 116–118, the second part of the Hallel that was traditionally sung after eating the Passover meal. John included a lengthy discourse that Jesus had with his disciples

(John 13:31–17:26) before he and the eleven remaining disciples left the upper room and *went out to the Mount of Olives,* located just to the east of Jerusalem. Leaving the room did not surprise the disciples, for they had not been staying in Jerusalem at night and had left the city every evening to return to Bethany. This time, however, Jesus went only as far as the southwestern slope, to an olive grove called Gethsemane, which means "oil press."

14:27 And Jesus said to them, "You will all become deserters; for it is written, 'I will strike the shepherd, and the sheep will be scattered.'"NRSV This was the second time in the same evening that Jesus predicted the disciples' denial and desertion, which probably explains their strong reaction (14:31). (For Jesus' earlier prediction, see Luke 22:31-34 and John 13:36-38.) That the disciples would become *deserters* means that they would take offense at him and turn away. Fearing what would befall Jesus, they would not want to experience the same treatment. So Jesus explained that they would desert him, deny association with him, and distance themselves from him. Jesus would go to the cross totally alone.

It's easy to think that Satan temporarily had gained the upper hand in this drama about Jesus' death. But we see later that God was in control, even in the death of his Son. Satan gained no victory—everything occurred as God had planned. Jesus himself explained that the disciples' desertion would also occur just as it had been predicted in Scripture, specifically Zechariah 13:7.

STRAIGHT TALK
Jesus warned the disciples that they would desert him. He spoke with devastating honesty. He didn't rationalize their mistake or ease their guilt. He confronted head-on the sorry behavior of his disciples.

There's nothing quite so helpful as straight talk from someone totally dedicated to your well-being and growth. Hear it from Jesus; practice it with Jesus' care. Straight talk such as Jesus gave could help untangle a lot of emotional knots in families, at work, and among friends. We can speak honestly when we say: "I know you are weak, vulnerable, and mistaken—it's not OK, and you ought to worry about it—but I love you, and I'm willing to forgive you."

In Zechariah, God commanded that the shepherd be struck down. As a result, the sheep would be scattered. Without a shepherd and on their own, the sheep would go through a period of

great trial and be refined. The refining process would strengthen
them and create a new, faithful people for God. The disciples
would be staggered by what would happen to Jesus, but Jesus'
death ("striking the shepherd") would ultimately produce their
salvation and regather the sheep. Zechariah 13 ends on a note of
hope, "They will call on my name and I will answer them; I will
say, 'They are my people,' and they will say, 'The LORD is our
God'" (Zechariah 13:9 NIV).

14:28 "But after I have risen, I will go ahead of you into Galilee."[NIV]
After his prediction of their desertion, Jesus then predicted their
reunion after his resurrection. Jesus promised that he would go
ahead of them into Galilee and meet them all there. Galilee is
important in Mark's Gospel as the place of restoration. That is
where their relationship would be renewed, their failures forgiven, and their pattern of ignorance and rejection broken. Indeed
the angel at the tomb would reassure the women, "He has risen!
He is not here. . . . But go, tell his disciples and Peter, 'He is
going ahead of you into Galilee. There you will see him, just as
he told you'" (16:6-7 NIV). Jesus made resurrection appearances
in Galilee (Matthew 28:16; John 21:1-23) and in Jerusalem and
the surrounding area (Luke 24:13-52; John 20:11-29; 1 Corinthians 15:5-8).

THE LORD'S SOLUTION
After the experience on the Mount of Transfiguration (9:2-9),
Jesus told Peter, James, and John not to tell anyone of his
glory until after the Resurrection. Here Jesus gives them the
solution to all problems of misunderstanding and failure they
had experienced all along—to be reunited with their risen Lord
in Galilee. Yet Peter immediately protested, and even after the
Resurrection, the angel had to remind them of Jesus' words:
"But go, tell his disciples and Peter that he is going ahead of
you to Galilee; there you will see him, just as he told you" (16:7
NRSV). No matter how confused we may feel, no matter how
many times we have failed, the solution is to be reunited with
our Lord. As we trust in him, we are forgiven, restored, and
empowered to be his disciples in our world.

**14:29 Peter said to him, "Even though all become deserters, I will
not."**[NRSV] Peter, always ready to speak up at inopportune
moments, declared that his allegiance to Jesus would prove to be
much stronger than all the other disciples'. He seemed to ignore
what Jesus had said in 14:28, but he was not rejecting the reality
of Christ's suffering as he had in 8:32.

SPEAK UP AND SPEAK OUT
In a culture so dominated by passive activity (watching television, watching athletics, watching politicians), rarely does a person speak up and declare his or her mind. Peter had the gift of speaking up.

Although Peter's ambitions did not match his performance, we should not fault his motives—he wanted to declare his loyalty to Jesus. Peter spoke up when, too often, Jesus' disciples retreated to silence. Peter's words would return to sting him, but through him the world would hear the gospel preached.

Peter would be brought pretty low before he realized how fully he must trust Jesus. But we would not have expected Peter to respond passively, "OK, Jesus, if you say we'll desert you, then sure, we'll desert you." From Peter we must learn to be bold enough to speak up but humble enough to obey Christ's teaching.

14:30 Jesus said to him, "Assuredly, I say to you that today, even this night, before the rooster crows twice, you will deny Me three times."NKJV Jesus' words to Peter were solemn, begun with the formula *"Assuredly, I say."* Instead of being the only loyal disciple, Peter would in fact prove himself the least so. Not only would he desert Jesus, he would also deny him—not once, but three times. And this would happen in the space of the next few hours. Before the night was over, that is before the rooster crowed a second time, Peter would deny the Master to whom he claimed such loyalty. Only Mark recorded a second crowing of the rooster (see also 14:72). If Peter was, in fact, Mark's source for this Gospel, he certainly remembered this minor detail.

TALK IS CHEAP
Peter was so emphatic. It is easy to say we are devoted to Christ, but our claims are meaningful only when they are tested in the crucible of persecution. How strong is your faith? Is it strong enough to stand up under intense trial? We need the Holy Spirit, not boastfulness and human resolve. We must never discount our vulnerability to pride, greed, or even indifference.

14:31 But Peter insisted emphatically, "Even if I have to die with you, I will never disown you." And all the others said the same.NIV Peter did not think it possible for him to actually deny any relationship with Jesus. Perhaps he was worried that *he* was the betrayer Jesus had mentioned during their meal (14:18). Not only Peter, but all the disciples declared that they would die before disowning Jesus. A few hours later, however, they all scattered.

"MY MOST EMBARRASSING MOMENT"
Peter remembered this moment for the rest of his life. How stupidly he had promised what he so miserably failed to do. Yet his most embarrassing moment afforded the greatest lesson of his life. He learned the gospel here, that "God so loved" even disciples who fail.

Your life includes some real blunders, too. Do you hear God's loving assurance? Do you feel God picking up the pieces? Do you sense the grace?

It's easy to imagine that Peter told many people about the gospel by using this story, his own most embarrassing moment. Perhaps you should tell others of God's patience with you. Your mistake plus God's grace equals the wonderful story of salvation.

JESUS AGONIZES IN THE GARDEN / 14:32-42 / **223**

Apart from the Cross itself, the moments in Gethsemane were the most intense in Jesus' life. He experienced the crushing weight of the task he was about to undertake. He witnessed the weakness that his disciples demonstrated by falling asleep. He saw the betrayer coming. And he sensed with anguish that the cup would not pass. He would drink it alone.

This section also portrays the varied purposes of prayer. For Jesus, prayer was not escape, but respite; not a way to avoid difficulty, but a way to endure it. We miss the opportunity of communion and fellowship with God if we treat prayer as merely telling God what we want him to know.

The Cross did not catch Jesus by surprise. His self-sacrifice was deliberate, calculated, and undertaken with a great flow of human emotions that we can see in the garden. A noble and loving purpose doesn't necessarily make the work easy. "Let us fix our eyes on Jesus, the author and perfecter of our faith, who for the joy set before him endured the cross, scorning its shame, and sat down at the right hand of the throne of God" (Hebrews 12:2 NIV).

14:32 **Then they came to a place which was named Gethsemane; and He said to His disciples, "Sit here while I pray."**NKJV After eating the meal, the disciples left Jerusalem and went out to a favorite meeting place, the gardenlike enclosure called *Gethsemane* (see John 18:1-2). *Gethsemane* means "olive press"; the garden was probably an orchard of olive trees with a press for extracting oil. The garden was in the Kidron Valley just outside the eastern wall of Jerusalem and just below the Mount of Olives. Jesus told eight of the disciples to sit down, probably near the garden's entrance, while he went farther in to pray.

Plenty of drama surrounds Mark's terse account. The elders of Jerusalem were plotting to kill Jesus and had already issued a warrant for his arrest. Jesus left Jerusalem under cover of darkness in order to pray. The disciples must also have been physically and emotionally exhausted from trying to comprehend what would transpire. Instead of watching, they gave in to their exhaustion and fell asleep.

14:33 **And He took Peter, James, and John with Him, and He began to be troubled and deeply distressed.**^{NKJV} Jesus then took the other three disciples, his inner circle, farther into the garden with him. To these closest friends, Jesus revealed his inner turmoil over the event he was about to face. Jesus was *troubled and deeply distressed* over his approaching death because he would have to be separated from the Father and would have to bear the sins of the world. The divine course was set, but Jesus, in his human nature, still struggled (Hebrews 5:7-9). His coming death was no surprise; he knew about it and had even told the disciples about it so they would be prepared. Jesus knew what his death would accomplish. He also knew that the means to that end would mean taking upon himself the sin of the world, thus, for a time, alienated from his Father who would be unable to look upon sin: "God made him who had no sin to be sin for us, so that in him we might become the righteousness of God" (2 Corinthians 5:21 NIV). Jesus bore our guilt by "becoming a curse for us" (Galatians 3:13 NIV). As the time of this event neared, it became even more horrifying. Jesus naturally recoiled from the prospect.

JESUS KNOWS
Sometimes we forget how fully human Jesus, Son of God, Savior, really was. Here we see it. His agony fills the garden.
    Agonies consume us, too. To face the imminent death of a loved one or the accidental death of a child or our own approaching demise—these agonies can tear at our souls.
    Do we have a Savior who knows how heavily we tremble, how deeply we groan? Yes, we do. Can we come to this Savior in prayer and find a friend? Yes, we can. Jesus is with you; he's been there; he knows the feeling. He will help you come through.

14:34 **"My soul is overwhelmed with sorrow to the point of death,"** **he said to them. "Stay here and keep watch."**NIV To these three disciples Jesus revealed his inner agony. He was shuddering in horror at the prospect before him. Early in Jesus' ministry Satan had tempted him to take the easy way out (Matthew 4:1-11); later Peter had suggested that Jesus did not have to die (Mark 8:32-33). In both cases, Jesus had dealt with the temptation soundly. Now, as his horrible death and separation from the Father loomed before him, he was *overwhelmed with sorrow to the point of death.* Jesus did not attempt to run from it, nor did he doubt that God would raise him from the dead and return him to glory. Jesus, in his humanity, agonized over the inevitable horror that would soon come, yet he faced it courageously (Hebrews 12:2-3). Some see in Jesus' words an allusion to Psalm 42:6.

Jesus asked Peter, James, and John (14:33) to stay with him. James and John had professed that they could drink the cup of Jesus' suffering (10:38-39). Jesus wanted these men to *keep watch;* Jesus knew Judas would soon arrive, and Jesus wanted to devote himself to prayer until that time came. Jesus also wanted them to stay awake and participate with him in his suffering. This is a vital part of discipleship. Jesus wanted these disciples to understand his suffering and to be strengthened by his example when they would face persecution and suffering.

PRAYER AND COURAGE
When the road you're on is irreversible and you're unsure about what's ahead, pray for courage to take another step forward. We all need courage to face tough reality.
When grim injustice and devilish hatred are robbing you of life's treasure, pray for the courage to trust God completely through the pain and for the eventual victory of love.
At the worst moment of his life, Jesus prayed. Now he is our advocate in heaven—and he knows the courage we need.

14:35 **And going a little farther, he threw himself on the ground and prayed that, if it were possible, the hour might pass from him.**NRSV Jesus went still farther into the garden to be alone with God. His agony was such that he threw himself on the ground before God in deep spiritual anguish, praying that if possible *the hour might pass from him*—that his mission might be accomplished some other way. Here and in 14:41, "the hour" figuratively refers to the entire event Jesus was facing. The "hour" and the "cup" were used synonymously. Yet Jesus humbly submitted to the Father's will. Luke tells us that Jesus' sweat resembled drops of blood. His prayer was filled with extreme emotion. Jesus was in terrible agony, but he did not give up or give in. He went ahead with the mission for which he had come.

14:36 **And He said, "Abba, Father, all things are possible for You. Take this cup away from Me; nevertheless, not what I will, but what You will."**ᴺᴷᴶⱽ *Abba* was Aramaic for "father" and implied familiarity and closeness. Only Jesus could have used the word *Abba* in a prayer to God, because Jesus had a special Father/Son relationship with him. Jesus' using it showed his surrender to and faith in the Father's will. Children addressed their fathers as "Abba," but the term was far too familiar for adult Jews to use in speaking to God. Paul used the term in Romans 8:15 and Galatians 4:6, showing that the early church picked up the term from this prayer of Jesus.

The words *all things are possible for You* indicate God's omnipotence. He could accomplish anything. Jesus was affirming God's sovereign control over the coming suffering (see 10:27).

With the words *take this cup away from Me,* Jesus was referring to the suffering, isolation from God, and death he would have to endure in order to atone for the sins of the world. Jesus, as God's Son, recoiled from sin, yet part of his task would be to take the sins of the whole world upon himself. This was a cup he truly hated to drink. In addition, Jesus, as God's Son, knew constant fellowship with the Father. Yet for a time on the cross he would have to be deprived of that fellowship. This too was a cup he hated to drink. The physical suffering would be horrible enough, but what God's Son feared most was the cup of spiritual suffering—taking on sin and being separated from God (Hebrews 5:7-9).

Yet Jesus was not trying to get out of his mission. Jesus expressed his true feelings as a human being, but he did not deny or rebel against God's will. (Some scholars think Jesus was referring to Isaiah 51:22, where God lifted the cup of judgment for the righteous in Jerusalem.) Jesus' human will was distinct from God's will, but it did not oppose God's will. He reaffirmed his desire to do what God wanted by saying, *"Nevertheless, not what I will, but what You will."* His prayer reveals to us his terrible suffering. Jesus paid for all sin by being separated from God. The sinless Son of God took our sins upon himself to save us from suffering and separation.

God did not take away the "cup," for the cup (to judge the sins of the world) was his will. Yet he did take away Jesus' extreme fear and agitation. Jesus moved serenely through the next several hours, at peace with God, knowing that he was doing God's will.

COSTLY COMMITMENT
In times of suffering people sometimes wish they knew the future, or they wish they could understand the reason for their anguish. Jesus knew what lay ahead of him, and he knew the reason. Even so, his struggle was intense—more wrenching than any struggle we will ever have to face. What does it take to be able to say "as God wills"? It takes firm trust in God's plans; it takes prayer and obedience each step of the way. Trust God that his way is best, even when it doesn't seem like it.

14:37 Then he returned to his disciples and found them sleeping. "Simon," he said to Peter, "are you asleep? Could you not keep watch for one hour?"^{NIV} Jesus got up from his prayer to return to the three disciples. He had told them to stay and keep watch (14:34), but instead of showing support for Jesus by remaining awake with him and praying themselves for strength in the coming hours, they had fallen asleep, "exhausted from sorrow" (Luke 22:45 NIV). Also, the hour was very late, perhaps after midnight.

Jesus spoke to Peter, calling him *Simon,* his name before he had met Jesus. Apparently Peter's recent boasting (14:31), present sleepiness, and coming denial rendered him less than "Peter, the rock" (see John 1:42). Peter had said he would never leave Jesus; yet when Jesus needed prayer and support, Peter wasn't even there for him. He had fallen asleep. Thus, Jesus rebuked him for his failure to keep watch for even one hour. Only Mark mentions the Lord's words to Peter. Perhaps Peter wanted Mark to tell this part of the story.

WAKE UP!
Peter wasn't the only sleeper. James and John were sleeping, too. Should Peter feel singled out for blame? Yes, he was. Peter was supposed to be the leader of his group. He professed his loyalty, and he knew that leadership required extra responsibility. Peter should have kept the others awake, along with himself.
   Yet aren't we like Peter? How difficult is it for us to pray for one hour when we're worried and exhausted, when our energy and motivation are at low levels?
   We must be leaders who are watchful, who remain prepared for the Lord's work. We must learn leadership skills from teachers who see our potential and work hard to build our character. When Jesus singles you out for a special responsibility, he wants you to grow into a leader. Stay awake; step up; follow Christ.

14:38 **"Watch and pray, lest you enter into temptation. The spirit
indeed is willing, but the flesh is weak."**[NKJV] Jesus told the disciples that this was the time to *watch and pray,* for soon difficult
temptations would come. Jesus was not asking that they pray for
him; rather, that they pray for themselves. Jesus knew that these
men would need extra strength to face the temptations ahead—
temptations to run away or to deny their relationship with him. For
this they needed the three-pronged strategy of vigilance, prayer,
and resisting temptation. Jesus warned the disciples about vigilance
throughout chapters 13 and 14. "Enter into" could also be translated "fall into." Jesus wanted them to pray that their faith would
not collapse. The word "temptation" can mean testing or trial. Jesus
wanted his disciples to pray for strength to go through the coming
ordeal. The disciples were about to see Jesus die. Would they still
think he was the Messiah? The disciples' strongest temptation
would undoubtedly be to think they had been deceived.

Many have interpreted "spirit" to mean "human spirit" because
"spirit" is not capitalized. Thus it would mean that while their *spirit*
might be willing, their *flesh* would be weak. Their inner desires and
intentions would be, as they had previously boasted, to never deny
Jesus and to die with him. Their relationships with Jesus had made
them eager enough to serve him in any way possible. Yet their
human inadequacies, with all their fears and failures, would have difficulty carrying out those good intentions. A willing spirit (see Psalm
51:12) needs the Holy Spirit to empower it and help it do God's will.

RESISTERS
We may not face execution for our faith, but we face many
problems that wear us down. We deal with irritating people
whom we must love and serve; we face the burden of unfin-
ished tasks or lack of obvious results; we cope with helpers
who let us down or fail to comprehend. We must remember
that in times of great stress, we are vulnerable to temptation,
even if we have a willing spirit. Jesus told us how to resist:
- *Keep watch* (14:34)—we must stay awake and be morally vigilant.
- *Pray to God* (14:35)—this is how we maintain our vigilance.
- *Seek support of friends and loved ones* (14:33, 37, 40-41)—
  this is how we build up our resistance and help one another;
  when one is weak, others are strong.
- *Focus on the purpose God has given us* (14:36)—this is how
  we do God's will and not our own.

14:39 **And again he went away and prayed, saying the same
words.**[NRSV] Jesus went away from the three disciples and went
back to his previous conversation with the Father (14:35-36).

NO PRAYER, NO SHARE
Perhaps disgusted, at least disappointed, Jesus left the slumbering disciples who could not stay awake. This pictures what happens when Christians and their churches fail to pray.
    Where no one prays, Jesus, as it were, walks away. The church without prayer functions as little more than a vacant structure. The person without prayer is going it alone, in a stupor, in a slumber, not really alive.
    To have a share of the Savior's life and power, we must do what links our hearts to his: pray.

14:40 And when He returned, He found them asleep again, for their eyes were heavy; and they did not know what to answer Him.NKJV Jesus came back once again to the three disciples, and once again they were asleep. Despite his warning that they should be awake, alert, and praying not to fall into the coming temptations, *their eyes were heavy,* and all three went back to sleep. Apparently Jesus again awakened them, and in their embarrassment *they did not know what to answer Him.* The three of them had reacted the same way at Jesus' transfiguration. During Jesus' time of prayer beforehand, they also had fallen asleep (Luke 9:32) and had been unable to express themselves appropriately to Jesus (Mark 9:6). At that time they had been filled with fear; here in the garden, they were filled with grief.

14:41 He came a third time and said to them, "Are you still sleeping and taking your rest? Enough! The hour has come; the Son of Man is betrayed into the hands of sinners."NRSV Jesus went away to pray a third time, only to come back and find the disciples still asleep. Jesus, after much time in prayer, was ready to face his *hour.* The disciples had missed great opportunity to talk to the Father, and there would be no more time to do so, for Jesus' hour had come. Thus Jesus did not again tell them to pray. Jesus had spent the last few hours dealing with the Father, wrestling with him, and humbly submitting to him. Now he was prepared to face his betrayer and the sinners who were coming to arrest him.

This began the fulfillment of 14:27, "You will all become deserters," and characterized the isolation that Jesus had to face during his last hours. From here on, Jesus had to go it alone. *The Son of Man is betrayed* ties into the three predictions of his death (see 8:31; 9:31; 10:33-34).

"Sinners" was the term used for Jews who did not live according to God's will and for Gentiles, who were viewed collectively as sinners because they didn't live by God's law. Jesus probably used the term to refer to the priestly authorities who were being disobedient in their actions against Jesus, and to the Romans who were participating in the arrest, mockery, and death of Jesus.

14:42 **"Rise! Let us go! Here comes my betrayer!"**^{NIV} Jesus roused the three sleeping disciples (and perhaps the other eight as well) and called them together. His words *"Let us go!"* did not mean that Jesus was contemplating running. Instead, he was calling the disciples to go with him to meet the traitor disciple, Judas, and the coming crowd. Jesus went forth of his own will, advancing to meet his accusers rather than waiting for them to come to him. Jesus' *betrayer,* Judas, had arrived. Judas knew where to find Jesus and the disciples because Gethsemane had been a favorite meeting spot (John 18:1-2). It was to this quiet garden in the very early hours of the morning that Judas brought a crowd to arrest Jesus.

SEMPER PARATUS
"Always Prepared." The motto of the U.S. Coast Guard rings true about spiritual life, and this scene illustrates the difference between prayer and preparation on the one hand and no prayer and disoriented bewilderment on the other. As Jesus moved forward to meet his adversaries, the disciples, alarmed into wakefulness, disintegrated before the posse.

Do you want that *semper paratus* attitude? Pray, live close to Jesus your Savior, and there find the courage to meet your life standing up, awake and alert.

JESUS IS BETRAYED AND ARRESTED / 14:43-52 / **224**

All four Gospels describe the moment of betrayal, but Mark's version is the shortest. He began by using his favorite storytelling device, the phrase "and immediately." He then moved rapidly through the sequence of events: Judas's arrival with the crowd, the ironic kiss, the feeble defense by the unnamed disciple who cut off the servant's ear, Jesus' confrontation of his captors, and the disciples' terrified retreat. Mark alone added the description of a young man wrapped in a sheet who left his only covering behind in his hurry to escape. Many think this was Mark's own, somewhat humorous, signature to the Gospel.

In spite of all they had seen and heard with Jesus, when the moment of truth arrived, the disciples all fled. When we feel safe in our surroundings or we take life lightly, it is easy to consider ourselves prepared for anything. The disciples trusted in Jesus all right, but their trust came and went with what they saw and felt.

As long as the Lord was in control, everything was fine. But when external circumstances changed, the weakness of their faith was revealed. Hardships open our eyes and enable us to deal with our true character.

14:43 **Just as he was speaking, Judas, one of the Twelve, appeared. With him was a crowd armed with swords and clubs, sent from the chief priests, the teachers of the law, and the elders.**[NIV] Even as Jesus spoke to his disciples to rouse them from their sleep, *Judas, one of the Twelve,* appeared. Judas, who had left the Last Supper at Jesus' request (John 13:27), had apparently gone to the religious leaders to whom he had spoken earlier (14:10-11). They had given him a contingent of police and soldiers (John 18:3) in order to seize Jesus and bring him before the religious court for trial. The religious leaders had issued the warrant for Jesus' arrest, and Judas was acting as Jesus' official accuser. Judas led the group to one of Jesus' retreats where no onlookers would interfere with them. While to the leaders this was an official detachment of the temple police, to Mark they were a *crowd* or mob. He refused to dignify them.

The armed crowd was probably made up of members of the temple guard, Jews given authority by the religious leaders to make arrests for minor infractions. The detachment of soldiers mentioned in John 18:3 may have been a small group of Roman soldiers who did not participate in the arrest, but accompanied the temple guard to make sure that matters stayed under control. The armed men came in the middle of the night when most of the people were asleep and they could arrest Jesus without commotion. Although there were no crowds to worry about, Jesus was surrounded by eleven loyal followers who the temple guards feared might put up a fight. So they came armed with *swords and clubs* in addition to lanterns and torches to light their way (John 18:3).

Mark mentions that these men had been sent from the chief priests, the teachers of the law, and the elders. These were the three groups that made up the Sanhedrin, the Jewish supreme court. Jesus mentioned these three groups in his predictions of his death (see 8:31; 10:33). The entire religious leadership issued the warrant for Jesus' arrest and was together in the attempt to condemn Jesus to death.

14:44 **Now the betrayer had given them a sign, saying, "The one I will kiss is the man; arrest him and lead him away under guard."**[NRSV] Judas *(the betrayer)* had told the crowd to arrest the man that he would kiss. This was not an arrest by Roman soldiers under Roman law, but an arrest by the religious leaders. Judas pointed Jesus out, not because Jesus was hard to recognize, but because Judas had agreed to be the formal accuser in case a trial was called. A kiss on the cheek or hand was a common form of greeting in the Middle East, so this was not unusual. Judas would affectionately greet the man the guards were to arrest and lead away.

14:45 Going at once to Jesus, Judas said, "Rabbi!" and kissed him.^{NIV} Judas had expected to find Jesus and the disciples in Gethsemane, and he was correct. He entered the garden followed by the armed band and went directly to Jesus. In a friendly gesture of greeting and affection, Judas called Jesus "Rabbi" and then gave him a kiss (on the cheek or on the hand), a sign of respect from a student to his teacher. While a rabbi did not have an official office like pastor today (the office of rabbi did not begin for another century), the title was an unofficial sign of respect. Once again Judas showed himself to be the ultimate traitor. Not only had he eaten with Jesus only hours before, here he used a sign of friendship and affection in his betrayal.

TWO-FACED
No words convey their normal meaning if we hide our intentions. A greeting, a handshake, a promise, a kiss—each means whatever the heart means. And sometimes the heart deceives.
　　Masking a deceitful heart behind common everyday "happy talk" is both draining and destructive. Eventually it catches up to you. It is better for you to be "up front," tell the truth, and take the consequences. Judas turned against the Lord, then hid his evil intentions behind a common greeting. Inside, his heart cracked, and his life was ruined.

14:46 The men seized Jesus and arrested him.^{NIV} The religious leaders had not arrested Jesus in the temple for fear of a riot. Instead, they had come secretly at night, under the influence of the prince of darkness, Satan himself. Jesus offered no resistance and was duly arrested. Although it looked as if Satan were getting the upper hand, everything was proceeding according to God's plan. It was time for Jesus to die.

　　Mark omitted Jesus' response to Judas (included in Matthew and Luke) in order to center on the stark portrayal of Jesus at the mercy of his enemies.

14:47 But one of those who stood near drew his sword and struck the slave of the high priest, cutting off his ear.^{NRSV} According to John 18:10, the person who pulled the sword was Peter, who

cut off the right ear of a servant named Malchus. Peter was trying
to prevent what he saw as defeat. He wasn't going to let this
crowd arrest Jesus without putting up a fight. Luke 22:51 records
that Jesus immediately healed the man's ear and prevented any
further bloodshed. Jesus then told Peter to put away his sword
and allow God's plan to unfold. Peter didn't realize that Jesus had
to die in order to gain victory. But Jesus demonstrated perfect
commitment to his Father's will. His kingdom would not be
advanced with swords, but with faith and obedience.

RESISTING AND SURRENDERING
Jews at Hitler's Auschwitz, Christians at Nero's Colosseum,
Bonhoeffer at the scaffold—all of them submitted. Should they
have fought back instead?

On the other hand, black Americans in Montgomery, Wilber-
force in England, Mennonites facing conscription—all of them
resisted. Should they have submitted instead?

Christians are called to resist evil and submit to God, but
knowing when, how, and where becomes a hard lesson in discipleship.

Jesus' peaceful surrender shows his supreme confidence in
God's sovereign mercy, his concern to avoid harm to the disciples, and his mature recognition that some losses (even his
own life) are necessary for ultimate victory.

We live under the flag of that heavenly victory, no matter
what happens today. We must resist the temptation to compul-
sively strike out. Our righteous indignation does not justify
doing evil.

14:48 **"Am I leading a rebellion," said Jesus, "that you have come
out with swords and clubs to capture me?"**[NIV] Jesus protested,
not his arrest, but the *way* he was arrested. They did not need to
come against him with weapons, for he was voluntarily surrendering himself. Jesus was not a revolutionary leading a rebellion; he
was a religious teacher who had been teaching in the temple daily
during the past week. Jesus also mocked their show of worldly
power. He who could summon angels was not afraid of swords.
Did the guards imagine that swords would intimidate Jesus?
They didn't understand who he was.

14:49 **"Day after day I was with you in the temple teaching, and you
did not arrest me. But let the scriptures be fulfilled."**[NRSV] Jesus
had been in the temple on three consecutive days during that week
(as summarized in 11:1–12:44). On one of them, he had emptied
the temple of merchants and money changers (11:15-18). Yet no
one had arrested him. The religious leaders had Jesus arrested at
night because they were afraid of the crowds that were following

him each day (14:2). While Jesus mentioned this to reveal the religious leaders' evil motives and cowardice, he knew why the events were unfolding as they were—that *the scriptures be fulfilled.* Judas's treachery, the coming mockery of a trial against Jesus, and its ultimate outcome had all been prophesied (see, for example, Psalms 22:7-8, 14, 16-17; 41:9; Isaiah 50:6; 53:7-8).

IN CONTROL
Even when faced with swords, civil warrants, and a traitor, Jesus affirmed, "Let the scriptures be fulfilled." He may have had in mind Isaiah 53:12, that Jesus would be "numbered with the transgressors" (NRSV), or Zechariah 13:7, "Strike the shepherd, that the sheep may be scattered" (NRSV), predicting that the disciples would soon scatter and leave Jesus to face the cross alone (see Mark 14:27). Jesus believed that all these events were no accident but were happening according to God's Word and sovereign control. Psalm 22 and Isaiah 53 were being fulfilled according to God's design. We may be distressed by hostility against Christians, concerned about the church's internal struggles, and frantic about the decline of moral integrity, but we must take heart that God is in control. Jesus declares this solid truth; we must believe it.

14:50 Then everyone deserted him and fled.[NIV]
Just hours earlier, these disciples had vowed never to desert Jesus (14:31). The "all" who promised total allegiance was now the "everyone" who fled. Judas's kiss marked a turning point for the disciples. With Jesus' arrest, each one's life would be radically different. For the first time, Judas openly betrayed Jesus before the other disciples. For the first time, Jesus' loyal disciples *deserted him and fled,* fulfilling his earlier prophecy that "You will all become deserters" (14:27). Their world was crumbling. The teacher who had held forth in the temple was now under arrest. The treasurer had become a traitor. The garden sanctuary that had always been "safe" was turned into the place of confrontation. What confusion! The disciples' primary loyalty to Jesus should have kept them from running. But fear took its toll.

> The Scriptures are being fulfilled year by year. Not one detail in them will ever fail to be accomplished. The kings of the earth may take their stand, and the rulers may gather together agianst Christ (Psalm 2:2), but the resurrection morning will prove that, even at the darkest time, everything was being done according to the will of God. *J. C. Ryle*

This culminates Mark's theme of the constant misunderstanding and failure of the disciples. Only the Resurrection would turn them around. The band of disciples would undergo severe testing before they were transformed from hesitant followers into dynamic leaders.

14:51-52 **A young man, wearing nothing but a linen garment, was following Jesus. When they seized him, he fled naked, leaving his garment behind.**[NIV] Only Mark records the incident of this young man (a man between twenty-four and forty years old) who also fled the scene. Tradition says that this young man may have been John Mark, the writer of this Gospel, in whose home the Last Supper may have taken place (see the explanation on 14:13). If that is true, at some point Mark had awakened from sleep (he had probably been sleeping in a linen garment or had a sheet wrapped around him) and had followed the disciples to the garden. Perhaps soldiers had come to the house looking for Jesus and this young man had attempted to warn Jesus before the soldiers reached him. He had left the house quickly, with only a linen garment or sheet wrapped around him.

But in Gethsemane, the crowd had already arrested Jesus and the disciples had fled. Someone grabbed this young man, perhaps hoping to use him as a witness. At that, the young man fled, *leaving his garment behind.*

COURAGE TO STAND
If Mark was the young man who fled, then he did not want to appear "holier-than-thou" in this writing. He identified with the frightened disciples; he participated in their flight. We need to be charitable and forgiving toward other Christians who fail. If those closest to Jesus got confused and ran, what confidence do we have that our courage and loyalty would have been stronger? Like Mark and the disciples, we need the Resurrection to give us the courage to stand.

CAIAPHAS QUESTIONS JESUS / 14:53-65 / **226**

Only John has the events immediately following Jesus' capture. The other Gospels go right to the preliminary hearing at Annas's house. All of the accounts convey that the religious leaders had already decided Jesus' fate. Jesus' opponents merely wanted to solidify their case against him.

Mark included Jesus' unambiguous claim about his identity (14:62). Mark contrasted Peter's agitation with Jesus' calmness.

Peter crouched outside, warming himself by the fire while his Lord stood inside, caught in the crucible of rejection and condemnation. The parade of false witnesses highlighted the murderous intent of the religious leaders. They eagerly acted out their hatred for Jesus with spitting, striking, and taunting. Injustice turned to brutality.

The vehemence with which the world rejects Jesus ought not shock or surprise us. When proud people feel threatened, they counterattack in force.

14:53 They took Jesus to the high priest; and all the chief priests, the elders, and the scribes were assembled.NRSV By now it was very early Friday morning, before daybreak. Jesus was taken under guard from the garden back into Jerusalem. First he was questioned by Annas, the former high priest and father-in-law of Caiaphas. Annas had been Israel's high priest from A.D. 6 to 15, when he had been deposed by Roman rulers. Then Caiaphas had been appointed high priest. He held that position from A.D. 18 to 36/37. According to Jewish law, the office of high priest was held for life, but the Roman government had taken over the process of appointing all political and religious leaders. Caiaphas served for eighteen years, longer than most high priests, suggesting that he was gifted at cooperating with the Romans. Caiaphas was the first to recommend Jesus' death in order to

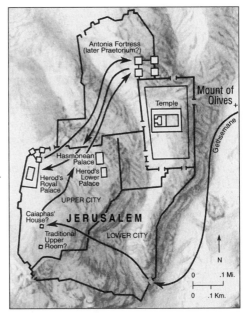

Jesus' Trial
From Gethsemane, Jesus' trial began at the home of Caiaphas, the high priest. Jesus was then taken to Pilate, the Roman governor. Luke records that Pilate sent him to Herod, who was in Jerusalem—presumably in one of his two palaces (Luke 23:5-12). Herod sent him back to Pilate, who handed Jesus over to be crucified.

"save" the nation (John 11:49-50). However, many Jews still considered Annas to be the high priest. Annas may have asked to question Jesus after his arrest and was given first rights to do so. This hearing is described in John 18:12-24.

After that preliminary hearing, Jesus was taken to the home of Caiaphas, the ruling high priest. That *all the chief priests, the elders, and the scribes* were speedily assembled shows that this was a trial by the Sanhedrin (the Jewish council of religious leaders consisting of seventy members plus the high priest). Because of their haste to complete the trial and see Jesus die before the Sabbath, less than twenty-four hours later, the religious leaders first met in Caiaphas's home at night to accomplish the preliminaries before their more formal meeting in the temple at daylight. They finally had Jesus where they wanted him, and they were determined to accomplish their plans as quickly as possible.

The trial by the Sanhedrin had two phases. This first phase occurred during the night (recorded here in 14:53-65); then another meeting was held "as soon as it was morning" (15:1 NRSV) to satisfy a law that allowed trials only during the daytime. That meeting was a mere formality held at daybreak, during which the verdict was given and Jesus was led off to the Roman procurator for sentencing. The Sanhedrin was the most powerful religious and political body of the Jewish people. Although the Romans controlled Israel's government, they gave the people power to handle religious disputes and some civil disputes; so the Council made many of the local decisions affecting daily life. But a death sentence had to be authorized by the Romans (John 18:31).

14:54 Peter had followed him at a distance, right into the courtyard of the high priest; and he was sitting with the guards, warming himself at the fire.NRSV Jesus had been taken immediately to the high priest's house, even though this was the middle of the night. The Jewish leaders were in a hurry—they wanted to complete the execution before the Sabbath and get on with the Passover celebration. The high priest's residence was a palace with outer walls enclosing a courtyard. Here a charcoal fire was burning, around which the servants and soldiers were warming themselves against the early morning chill.

Although all the disciples had fled when the soldiers arrested Jesus, two of them, Peter and another disciple (perhaps John), returned to where Jesus was taken (John 18:15). After securing permission to enter the courtyard, Peter joined the others as they warmed themselves around the fire.

Peter's experiences in the next few hours would revolutionize his life. He would change from a halfhearted follower to a repentant disciple, and finally to the kind of person Christ could use to build his church. Peter's story continues at 14:66.

PLAYING WITH FIRE
Scripture does not tell us what Peter's motives were for entering the high priest's courtyard. Perhaps he thought he could still rescue Jesus. But we learn from his encounter that he foolishly put himself into temptation. He had already deserted and fled, so he knew his own weakness and vulnerability. But he tried to hide his identity, and this would lead him to deny his master. When we struggle with failure or guilt or find ourselves surrounded by those hostile to Christ, we must recognize our vulnerability and resist the temptation to compromise our faith, values, or morals.

14:55 The chief priests and the whole Sanhedrin were looking for evidence against Jesus so that they could put him to death, but they did not find any.^{NIV} Here Mark described the scene going on upstairs in the high priest's palace. *The chief priests and the whole Sanhedrin* (meaning the group of seventy-one leaders of the Jews—priests and respected men) assembled in the middle of the night to get this trial under way, but they had a dilemma on their hands. They wanted evidence to convict Jesus of a crime deserving death, but *they did not find any.* The obvious conclusion should have been that Jesus was innocent of any crime. But this was not a trial for justice; it was a trial to accomplish an evil purpose. These leaders held a trial, in keeping with all the trappings of their law, while their whole purpose was to kill Jesus.

14:56 For many gave false testimony against him, and their testimony did not agree.^{NRSV} There was no shortage of witnesses; the problem was in finding two testimonies that agreed. During a trial, each witness was called upon separately to give his testimony. But the stories these witnesses gave did not agree in the details. According to Moses' law, no one was to be put to death on the testimony of only one witness (Numbers 35:30); there had to be two or three agreeing witnesses (Deuteronomy 19:15). This must have been exasperating for the desperate religious leaders. They weren't going to let Jesus get away on a technicality!

These witnesses who *gave false testimony* had been hired by the Sanhedrin; but Mark knew that any testimony against Jesus would have to be false, and he knew that, in essence, false testimony was exactly what the Sanhedrin needed. Otherwise, they had no grounds to convict Jesus (14:55). Ironically, these religious guardians of the law were breaking one of the Ten Commandments, "You shall not give false testimony" (Exodus 20:16 NIV). We should not expect any better treatment from those today who hate Christianity. If they slandered Jesus, we should not be surprised when they slander us.

RATIONALIZATIONS
The religious leaders knew in their hearts that they wanted Jesus out of the way. Then they could go back to their practice of appeasing Rome to keep peace and to keep their own power. Their envy of Jesus' popularity and fear of losing control caused them to hate Jesus. The next steps they took required them to rationalize away their own law. Plots, hiring a traitor, and finding so-called witnesses all made sense to their hate-filled minds.

We must not rationalize sin and guilt. We must guard against the cascading effect of covering up evil desires. Do you find yourself suppressing your conscience? Have you ignored clear scriptural truths? Are you finding reason to support what you want even though you know you are wrong? Such behavior means you're lying to yourself and despising Jesus' authority in your life.

14:57-58 **Then some stood up and gave this false testimony against him: "We heard him say, 'I will destroy this man-made temple and in three days will build another, not made by man.'"**NIV Finally they found a couple of witnesses who testified regarding Jesus' words about the temple. Mark labeled their testimony as *false* because they twisted Jesus' words and because their testimony even on this same point did not agree (14:59).

The witnesses claimed that Jesus had said he could destroy the temple in Jerusalem—a blasphemous boast. Such a claim would bring wrath from even the Romans because destroying temples was considered a capital offense throughout the Roman Empire. However Jesus had not spoken in the first person (*"I will destroy"*); nor had he said anything linking his words with the temple building. (The witnesses added the words, "this man-made temple" and thus showed how they had misunderstood Jesus' words.) Instead, Jesus had spoken in the second person plural, issuing a command, "Destroy this temple, and in three days I will raise it up" (John 2:19 NKJV). Jesus, of course, was talking about his body, not the building. Ironically, the religious leaders were about to destroy Jesus' body just as he had said, and three days later he would rise from the dead.

14:59 **But even on this point their testimony did not agree.**NRSV The witnesses had given testimony on the same topic, but still there

were unspecified discrepancies, thus rendering them worthless
for the purpose of sentencing Jesus to death.

**14:60 Then the high priest stood up before them and asked Jesus,
"Have you no answer? What is it that they testify against
you?"**^{NRSV} Caiaphas was getting frustrated. Now his only hope
was to get Jesus to say something that would give them evidence
to convict him. The religious leaders had tried and failed on prior
occasions to trap Jesus with trick questions (12:13-34); here the
high priest simply *stood up* in this revered group and spoke
directly to Jesus. He may have been hoping that Jesus was ignorant enough to not realize that the witnesses had invalidated themselves. Caiaphas tried to make up in intimidation what was
lacking in evidence. He asked Jesus to answer his accusers and
then to explain the accusations against him.

14:61 But Jesus remained silent and gave no answer.^{NIV} Jesus refused
to say anything. He had nothing to say to the group of liars who
had spoken against him, and he had no reason to explain a bunch
of false accusations. So he *remained silent and gave no answer.*
This had been prophesied in Scripture: "He was oppressed and
afflicted, yet he did not open his mouth; he was led like a lamb to
the slaughter, and as a sheep before her shearers is silent, so he
did not open his mouth" (Isaiah 53:7 NIV). With Jesus' silence,
the court proceedings ground to a halt.

STRATEGY FOR STRESS
Jesus' first response to the use of intimidation and fear used by
the religious leaders was to remain silent. They wanted Jesus
to make a self-incriminating statement; Jesus maintained his
composure. Peter later wrote, "When they hurled their insults at
him, he did not retaliate. . . . Instead, he entrusted himself to
[God] who judges justly" (1 Peter 2:23 NIV). Jesus is an example for us. We may find ourselves confronted by people hostile
to Christ in the classroom, in the workplace, on the athletic
field, or in the neighborhood, and we must have a way to deal
with their attacks. Our goal should be to face attacks as Jesus
did—with patience, calmness, and confidence that God is in
complete control.

**Again the high priest asked him, "Are you the Christ, the Son
of the Blessed One?"**^{NIV} But Caiaphas had another tactic up the
sleeve of his priestly robe. He decided to ask Jesus point blank,
"Are you the Christ?" The Sanhedrin must have held their collec-
tive breath in anticipation. Here was the question that could make
or break the entire plot. Would Jesus outright claim to be the Mes-

siah, *the Son of the Blessed One* (meaning, the Son of God)? We may wonder why Jesus refused to answer the first question and then chose to answer this one. Matthew's account points out that Caiaphas put Jesus under oath (Matthew 26:63) so that Jesus would be forced to answer by law (Leviticus 5:1); thus he would be forced to incriminate himself. Caiaphas's action was unlawful in trial proceedings, but no one voiced that fact to him. As mentioned above, this trial had nothing to do with justice; it was merely a ploy to get rid of Jesus.

14:62 **"I am," said Jesus. "And you will see the Son of Man sitting at the right hand of the Mighty One and coming on the clouds of heaven."**[NIV] To the first questions (14:60), Jesus made no reply because the questions were based on confusing and erroneous evidence. Not answering was wiser than trying to clarify the fabricated accusations. But if Jesus had refused to answer the second question (14:61), it would have been tantamount to denying his deity and his mission. So Jesus answered without hesitation, *"I am."* The pronoun emphasized that Jesus himself, distinct from all others, was indeed "the Christ, the Son of the Blessed One." This is the first time, recorded in this Gospel, that Jesus openly declared himself to be the Messiah. The two words, "I am," both answered the high priest's question and alluded to Jesus divinity ("I AM" being God's self-designation, see Exodus 3:14). Mark was specifically pointing out Jesus' divinity through this answer. (See the records of Jesus' answer in Matthew 26:64 and Luke 22:67-70.)

ASSURANCE!
Mark did not mean that Christ would return in glory during the lifetime of these religious leaders. Jesus' words assured these self-righteous religious leaders that judgment would come and they would be accountable to God. Their foolish and spiteful actions would be revealed as sinful. But these words also give confident assurance to all true disciples that the King is coming and will bring justice. No matter how terrible our suffering or how cruel the injustice brought against us, let us remember that God is the "Mighty One." Nothing anyone can do to us will lessen his power.

Then Jesus gave a startling prophecy. The words *the Son of Man sitting at the right hand of the Mighty One* refer back to Psalm 110:1, and *coming on the clouds of heaven* recall Daniel 7:13-14. The clouds represented the power and glory of God (see the note on 9:7). Both verses were considered to be prophecies of the coming Messiah, and Jesus applied them to himself. "The Son of Man" stood for Jesus' role as the divine agent appointed by God to carry out judgment (see the note on 8:31). In Psalm 110:1, the Son is given the seat of authority at the right hand of God. In Daniel 7:13-14, the Son was given "authority, glory and sovereign power" (NIV). Jesus used these verses to predict a powerful role reversal. Sitting on the right hand of power, one day he would come to judge his accusers, and they would have to answer *his* questions (Revelation 20:11-13). This represented the highest view of Jesus' deity possible. Jesus used the highest titles for God's deity and then applied them to himself.

14:63-64 Then the high priest tore his clothes and said, "Why do we still need witnesses? You have heard his blasphemy! What is your decision?" All of them condemned him as deserving death.NRSV Tearing one's clothing was an ancient expression of deep sorrow (see Genesis 44:13). The law forbade a priest from tearing his garments over personal grief (Leviticus 10:6; 21:10), but it was appropriate in an instance when blasphemy had been spoken in his presence. Blasphemy was the sin of claiming to be God or of attacking God's authority and majesty in any way. Caiaphas tore his clothes to signify his outrage at the audacity of the claims of this mere teacher from Nazareth. Jesus had identified himself with God by using a familiar title for God found in the Old Testament, "I AM" (Exodus 3:14) and by applying two messianic prophecies to himself. The high priest recognized Jesus' claim and exclaimed to the Sanhedrin, *"You have heard his blasphemy!"*

While claiming to be God was blasphemy, there is no evidence that claiming to be the Messiah was blasphemy. So why did the high priest accuse Jesus of blasphemy? A combination of Jesus' words and actions may give the answer. Jesus had prophesied a future exaltation of the Son of Man (14:62), a position next to God himself. Thus, part of Jesus' offense was this portrayal of his status next to God (on the "right hand" referred to the ability to act on behalf of God). In addition, Jesus' ministry had included teachings and actions that the religious leaders had found to be unlawful (such as his teachings about the Sabbath). Thus, according to them, Jesus claimed divinity, yet taught lawbreaking. These religious leaders thought that Jesus was leading the people astray and bringing dishonor to God's holy name. For any other human being, this claim would have been blasphemy; in this case, the claim was true.

Blasphemy was punishable by death (Leviticus 24:15-16). *"Why do we still need witnesses?"* asked Caiaphas without expecting any answer. They needed no more false witnesses (Caiaphas probably was relieved, since the witnesses had been worthless). Jesus had incriminated himself. Caiaphas asked for their decision. The Jewish leaders had the evidence they wanted, so *all of them condemned him as deserving death.* The "all" refers to those present, or at least to the majority. Nicodemus would not have agreed (John 3:1-21; 19:38-40), nor would Joseph of Arimathea "who, though a member of the council, had not agreed to their plan and action" (Luke 23:50-51 NRSV).

Of all people, the high priest and members of the Sanhedrin should have recognized the Messiah because they knew the Scriptures thoroughly. Their job was to point people to God, but they were more concerned about preserving their reputations and holding on to their authority. They valued human security more than eternal security.

CULTURE SHOCK
Given the mind-set of the religious leaders, Jesus' claims were blasphemous. How could this man have the authority of God? Popular culture and modern thought still view Christ's claims as blasphemous, and if we express our faith, people will view us as bigoted and intolerant. They will be outraged by our claims to know the truth. Our belief that God controls our life violates their desire to have a human-centered life. Our view of moral law offends their belief that all values are relative to each person and situation. Our conviction about controlling our desires radically disagrees with their pleasure- and experience-oriented outlook. Be ready for the world to be morally outraged at your single-minded belief in Christ and his truth.

14:65 Then some began to spit at him; they blindfolded him, struck him with their fists, and said, "Prophesy!" And the guards took him and beat him.NIV Then some of the members of the Sanhedrin acted in a most brutish way. After all their finagling with false witnesses, lack of evidence, and trying to force Jesus to incriminate himself, finally they simply beat up on him. To spit in someone's face was the worst insult possible (see Numbers 12:14), but they weren't content to stop at that. Jesus was blindfolded, and they took turns hitting him and then asking him to tell who it was that hit him. Some scholars think that this was a traditional test applied to anyone who claimed to be the Messiah. Based on Isaiah 11:2-4, the Messiah was supposed to be able to sense what would happen without sight. But Jesus continued to keep silent, refusing to play their game, knowing that to speak would be of no value. He was already sentenced (though not formally), so he refused to submit to their childish test.

When the Sanhedrin was finished with Jesus, the guards came and took him. Following the example of their esteemed superiors, these guards also beat Jesus. Yet even this had been prophesied in Scripture: "His appearance was so disfigured beyond that of any man and his form marred beyond human likeness" (Isaiah 52:14 NIV). Jesus suffered great pain, humiliation, and brutality to take away our sin.

PETER DENIES KNOWING JESUS / 14:66-72 / 227

As soon as Peter opened his mouth he gave himself away. His accent was Galilean. He was an out-of-towner who couldn't explain his presence in the high priest's courtyard. The disciple's earlier brash confidence wilted under pressure. Each denial distanced Peter farther from Jesus: First, he denied being with Jesus in any way; second, he denied being one of Jesus' followers; third, he strenuously denied even knowing Jesus.

Few of us get repeated opportunities, as Peter did, to profess or reject our allegiance to Christ. More often, our first denial of Jesus would keep away any further inquiries. But it is not our identification with Peter's weakness that helps us most. Rather, what happened later becomes our source of hope. Peter's repentance and the Lord's restoration of him give us confidence that God can handle our failures.

14:66 While Peter was below in the courtyard, one of the servant-girls of the high priest came by.[NRSV] This servant-girl was actually guarding the gate to the inner courtyard (John 18:16). She had seen Peter enter. Jesus' trial had been held in an upper story of the high priest's palace; thus, Peter was *below in the courtyard.*

14:67 And when she saw Peter warming himself, she looked at him and said, "You also were with Jesus of Nazareth."[NKJV] When the girl saw Peter's face more clearly in the light of the fire, she *looked at him* intently and recognized him as one who had been with Jesus (that is, one of Jesus' disciples). This put Peter in a difficult position. Standing among the soldiers and servants right there in enemy territory, Peter did not necessarily want to be identified with the man in an upstairs room on trial for his life. So Peter made a natural and impulsive response—he lied.

Temptation came when Peter least expected it, and this serves to warn us to be prepared. Peter had been ready to fight with a sword but not to face the accusations of a servant.

14:68 But he denied it. "I don't know or understand what you're talking about," he said, and went out into the entryway.[NIV]

Peter gave the answer Jesus had predicted: He denied knowing Jesus, although his answer here is less committal. He simply got out of this sticky situation by saying he didn't understand what the girl was talking about; then he scooted out into the entryway, away from the fire.

Matthew, Mark, and Luke say that Peter's three denials happened near a fire in the courtyard outside Caiaphas's palace. John places the first denial outside Annas's home and the other two denials outside Caiaphas's home. This was the same courtyard. The high priest's residence was large, and Annas and Caiaphas undoubtedly lived near each other.

> Hidden and unknown temptations are the most dangerous. . . . Signs of such temptations are that we can no longer pray, take refuge in grace and forgiveness, or have anything conclusive in which to believe. The whole Christian terminology is known and even respected; it rolls out of our mouths without a hitch, but it has no grip on our hearts.
> *Dietrich Bonhoeffer*

14:69 And the servant-girl, on seeing him, began again to say to the bystanders, "This man is one of them."[NRSV] Once again Peter was put to the test. Another servant-girl (Matthew 26:71) saw him. She didn't question him; she just told those standing around that Peter was indeed *one of them,* meaning one of Jesus' disciples.

What exactly would have transpired had Peter admitted the fact is unknown. In any case, the accusation scared him and once again he lied, this time more vehemently. This was Peter's second denial.

TAKE A STAND
Peter was afraid to identify himself as a follower of Christ. What kept him from doing so? Was it the hostility of the crowd, the strange situation he was in, or confusion about his own role? Peter knew running away was wrong; yet he had fought, and Jesus had rebuked him. So what should he do?

We fall into Peter's temptation when we fail to identify ourselves as Christians. Do we fear the rejection of friends and coworkers? Are we confused about what to do when we are in strange or potentially hostile circumstances? Even worse, are we indifferent to the eternal destiny of others? Before we condemn Peter for his failure, we should look at our own heart and determine to stand for Christ.

14:70 But again he denied it. Then after a little while the bystanders again said to Peter, "Certainly you are one of them; for you are a Galilean."NRSV About an hour passed (Luke 22:59), and another bystander also recognized Peter. John wrote that this last person to question Peter was "one of the servants of the high priest, a relative of him whose ear Peter cut off" (John 18:26 NKJV). He noticed Peter's Galilean accent (Matthew 26:73). Peter's dialect was closer to Syrian speech than to that of the Judean servants in that Jerusalem courtyard. While Peter may have hoped to seem a natural part of the group by joining in the conversation, instead he revealed, by his speech, that he did not belong there. Peter's dialect and his action against the high priest's servant (now confirmed by that servant's relative) brought the group to the conclusion that Peter must have been with the Galilean who was on trial inside the palace.

DON'T DENY IT
It is easy to get angry at the Sanhedrin and the Roman governor for their injustice in condemning Jesus, but Peter and the rest of the disciples also contributed to Jesus' pain by deserting him (14:50). While most of us may not be like the Jewish and Roman leaders, we are like the disciples because all of us have been guilty of denying Christ as Lord in vital areas of our lives. We may pride ourselves that we have not committed certain sins, but we are all guilty of sin. Don't try to excuse yourself by pointing at others whose sins seem worse than yours.

14:71 He began to call down curses on himself, and he swore to them, "I don't know this man you're talking about."NIV This was too much for Peter. They wouldn't leave him alone! So Peter decided to make the strongest denial he could think of by denying with an oath, *I don't know this man you're talking about* (he was careful not even to use Jesus' name). Peter's curse was more than just a common swear word. He was saying, in effect, "May God strike me dead if I am lying." This was the third denial (14:30).

Peter's denial progressed in intensity. At first he pretended not to understand the question; then he denied being one of the disciples; finally he sealed his denial with an oath so there could be no doubt about it.

14:72 Immediately the rooster crowed the second time. Then Peter remembered the word Jesus had spoken to him: "Before the rooster crows twice you will disown me three times." And he broke down and wept.NIV Immediately upon Peter's final words, *the rooster crowed the second time.* The period of the night from midnight to about 3:00 A.M. was known as "cockcrowing." A rooster would crow first at about 12:30 A.M., then again at about 1:30 A.M. Peter's denials fulfilled Jesus' words to him after he promised never to deny Jesus (14:31). When Peter heard the rooster crowing and then saw Jesus look down at him from the upper story where the trial was being held (Luke 22:61), Peter was reminded of what Jesus had said to him earlier. Peter had indeed disowned Jesus three times before the rooster crowed.

VERBAL HOSTILITY

After three confrontations, Peter began to curse himself. His failure, sin, and guilt had gotten the best of him, so he used a more aggressive response to cover what was in his heart. Many people who swear, use abusive speech, or are verbally hostile are covering up deep needs in their lives. Perhaps, like Peter, they are dealing with guilt, or facing deep disappointment and anger with themselves. When not dealt with, this hostility can come out. When dealing with verbally hostile people, look to the deeper cause and attempt to bring Christ's forgiveness and healing to meet that problem.

Peter *broke down and wept* bitterly, not only because he realized that he had denied his Lord, the Messiah, but also because he had turned away from a very dear friend, a person who had loved and taught him for three years. Peter had said that he would *never* deny Christ, despite Jesus' prediction. But when frightened, he went against all he had boldly promised. Unable to stand up for his Lord for even twelve hours, he had failed as a disciple and as a friend.

Fortunately, the story does not end there. Peter's tears were of true sorrow and repentance. Peter reaffirmed his love for Jesus, and Jesus forgave him (see 16:7; John 21:15-19). From this humiliating experience, Peter learned much that would help him later when he became leader of the young church.

BE CAREFUL LEST YOU FALL

Peter's example served to warn both the first Christians in Rome and us as well. No matter how courageous we profess we will be, we must stand firm under trial. We need to be aware of our own breaking points and not become overconfident or self-sufficient. In 1 Corinthians 10:12 Paul wrote, "So, if you think you are standing firm, be careful that you don't fall!" (NIV). But Peter's example also encourages us. If we fail Jesus, we must remember that Christ can use those who recognize their failure and return to him for forgiveness.

Mark 15

Mark's writing took on an added urgency as he neared the climax of his story. He stated the verdict of the Sanhedrin as an inevitable decision. The next steps the Council took were not so much another phase of justice as an administrative necessity. Because a death sentence required Roman approval, Pilate awakened one morning to the sounds of an angry mob outside his window.

Where the other Gospels offer details of the conversation between Pilate and Jesus, Mark focused on the central question: "Are you the king of the Jews?" (15:2). Jesus answered yes. The cascade of accusations from the religious leaders and Jesus' persistent silence left the Roman ruler "amazed."

15:1 **Very early in the morning, the chief priests, with the elders, the teachers of the law and the whole Sanhedrin, reached a decision. They bound Jesus, led him away and handed him over to Pilate.**^{NIV} At daybreak, the entire Sanhedrin (which included the chief priests, the elders, and the teachers of the law) reached a decision. They had actually reached it before daybreak (14:64), but they had to make the decision at a meeting during the daytime in accordance with their law. Thus *very early in the morning* they made it official that Jesus was worthy of death. So Jesus was bound like a common criminal and sent off to Pilate.

The Sanhedrin had to get permission from Pilate, the Roman governor of the region, in order to carry out the death penalty. The Romans had taken away the Jews' right to inflict capital punishment; so in order for Jesus to be condemned to death, he had to be sentenced by a Roman leader. The Jewish leaders wanted Jesus executed on a cross, a method of death that they believed brought a curse from God (see Deuteronomy 21:23). They wanted the death to appear Roman-sponsored so that the crowds wouldn't blame them. The Jewish leaders had arrested Jesus on theological grounds—blasphemy; but because this charge would be thrown out of a Roman court, they had to come up with a political reason for Jesus' death. Their strategy was to show Jesus as a rebel who claimed to be a king and thus a threat to Caesar. The charge against Jesus in the Roman court was treason.

Pontius Pilate was the Roman governor for the regions of Samaria and Judea from A.D. 26–36. Jerusalem was located in Judea. Pilate's normal residence was in Caesarea on the Mediterranean Sea, but he happened to be in Jerusalem because of the Passover festival. With the large crowds that flocked to the city for that celebration, Pilate and his soldiers came to help keep the peace. He stayed in his headquarters, called the Praetorium. Pilate was a harsh governor who felt nothing but contempt for the Jews; they, in turn, felt the same about him. He seemed to take special pleasure in demonstrating his authority over the Jews; for example, he had impounded money from the temple treasuries to build an aqueduct and had insulted the Jewish religion by bringing imperial images into the city.

Pilate was not popular, but the religious leaders had no other way to get rid of Jesus than to go to him. So they interrupted his breakfast on this early Friday morning, bringing a man whom they accused (of all things) of treason against the hated Romans! Ironically, when Jesus, a Jew, came before him for trial, Pilate found him innocent. He could not find a single fault in Jesus, nor could he contrive one.

The Jewish Council thought that *they* had reached a decision; Pilate thought that *he* had jurisdiction and final authority. Little did they know that everything was happening according to *God's* plan.

GROUP THINK
Years ago, sociologists concluded that intelligent, capable people would fail to see the fault in their group decisions as each person dismissed evidence that might thwart consensus. They called it "group think."

The people who condemned Jesus were not stupid, just afraid, confused, and desperate. Alone they would never perpetrate this crime—setting up a man for crucifixion by perjured testimony and concocted allegation. Together they pulled it off without dissent. They were wrong, but no one raised a voice once momentum built.

Be careful about group think. It can lead companies down Red-Ink Road, families down Turmoil Lane, and churches down Bitter Avenue. Against bad decisions based on fear, prejudice, and greed, you may need to speak the word that clarifies, the alternative that saves the day.

15:2 Then Pilate asked Him, "Are You the King of the Jews?" He answered and said to him, "It is as you say."[NKJV] The charge

was treason, so Pilate asked Jesus directly if he claimed to be a
king. Jesus' answer was basically yes but with a qualification
attached. Jesus did claim to be a king—to remain silent would be
like denying it (see also 14:62). But he wasn't claiming kingship
in any way that would threaten Pilate, Caesar, or the Empire.
Jesus' kingship was spiritual; a charge of treason required it to be
political. The religious leaders were attempting to build a case on
this political twist—their only and best chance of winning
Pilate's approval for a crucifixion. But something in Jesus' reply
alerted Pilate to the discrepancy between indictment and reality.
Pilate wasn't stupid. He could sense that the Sanhedrin's case
was embarrassingly weak. Pilate could sense that the solemn
rabbi standing before him was unlikely to lead a revolt against
Rome. In Jesus' eyes, Pilate did not see the hardened glare of a
zealot. Jesus was no revolutionary.

Jesus' answer was not enough for Pilate to convict him, so
Pilate turned back to the accusers, perhaps to test how far into
ludicrous fiction they were willing to press their case. The Sanhedrin did not disappoint him; they gladly bolstered their case with
more ridiculous accusations.

15:3 Then the chief priests accused him of many things.^NRSV Luke
records the essence of these charges in Luke 23:1-2. The Jewish
leaders had to fabricate new accusations against Jesus when they
brought him before Pilate. The charge of blasphemy would mean
nothing to the Roman governor, so they accused Jesus of three
other crimes: (1) encouraging the people not to pay their taxes to
Rome; (2) claiming he was a king—"the King of the Jews"; and
(3) causing riots all over the countryside. Tax evasion, treason,
and terrorism—all these would be cause for Pilate's concern.
These accusations were false, but the religious leaders were determined to have Jesus killed.

DISCIPLESHIP
So many twisted statements, exaggerated allegations, hate-
filled accusations. No matter how silly the charges, how
transparent the evidence, how deceitful the prosecution—they
will condemn the Christ. The world will not tolerate God among
us. It cannot imagine love incarnate. If five charges are not
enough for Pilate to condemn, they'll find another fifty. But they
will be rid of this Jesus.
    People who follow Jesus must be prepared for insane and
hate-filled days like this. The prejudice falls on Jesus' disciples,
too. It's the cross Jesus' people carry. In the face of trials, our
only task is to follow the Lord's example.

15:4 Pilate asked him again, "Have you no answer? See how many charges they bring against you."^{NRSV} Pilate then turned back to the condemned man—so quiet and serene, not at all the revolutionary to fit the crimes of which he was accused. But someone had to speak up to call this charade what it was. Pilate's low regard for the Jewish leadership sank even lower as their frenzied testimony continued. Pilate knew the charges were preposterous, and he obviously expected Jesus to defend himself against the false accusations.

15:5 But Jesus still made no reply, and Pilate was amazed.^{NIV} Jesus' silence had been prophesied in Scripture (Isaiah 53:7). Why didn't Jesus answer Pilate's questions? It would have been futile to answer, and the time had come to give his life to save the world. Jesus had no reason to try to prolong the trial or save himself. His was the ultimate example of self-assurance and peace, which no ordinary criminal could imitate. Nothing would stop Jesus from completing the work he had come to earth to do.

Pilate was amazed that Jesus, facing the death penalty, didn't try to defend himself. Pilate's amazement was similar to the amazement of many of the people in the crowds that had followed Jesus (see 1:27; 5:20; 10:24, 32; 15:44); however, amazement is not the same as belief and faith. Recognizing the obvious plot against Jesus, Pilate wanted to let him go, but he was already under pressure from Rome to keep peace in his territory. The last thing Pilate needed was a rebellion over this quiet and seemingly insignificant man. Mark wrote Jesus' answers as very brief, while John recorded, in detail, Jesus' final answer to Pilate regarding the nature of his messiahship (John 18:33-38). These words made Pilate realize that Jesus was innocent of any crime against Roman law.

Luke recorded a middle phase in all of this action. When Pilate found that Jesus was from Galilee, he sent him off to Herod Antipas, who was also in town for the Passover. But Herod only mocked Jesus and returned him to Pilate (Luke 23:6-12). Peter later commented on how Jesus had handled these injustices (see 1 Peter 2:20-23).

PILATE HANDS JESUS OVER TO BE CRUCIFIED / 15:6-15 / **232**

In the custom of pardoning a criminal during Passover, Pilate saw an opportunity to avoid responsibility for the death of a man whom he perceived to be innocent. That Jesus died for Barabbas represents yet another example of the purpose of Jesus' death: to take the place, not just of one condemned man, but of all who stand condemned before God's perfect standard of justice.

The religious leaders were motivated by their desire for power and prestige with the crowd, while Pilate was driven by his fear of the crowd. He wanted to please them. Those who participated in Jesus' death did so for many different reasons, but they all had something in common with us—they all needed a Savior. Each person had personal objectives to accomplish, but God overruled their human plans with his divine plan.

15:6 Now at the feast he was accustomed to releasing one prisoner to them, whomever they requested.^{NKJV} Each year, during the Jews' Passover festival, Pilate had made it a custom to release any prisoner they requested. Pilate may have instituted this custom to be on good terms with the people as well as to help cover his many wrongful acts toward them. Nonetheless, it was a small act of mercy from the Roman overseer. Once a year the people had a say.

UNCONDITIONAL MERCY
In almost every circumstance, showing mercy depends on a person's guilt (we favor innocent people when we dole out mercy), a person's record (repeat offenders don't get a lot of mercy), and a person's character (hate-filled murderers and rapists go to the back of the line). What would you do if it were in your control to be merciful to others, no questions asked?

Ironically, we can perceive that Pilate's gesture of releasing a guilty prisoner was a powerful picture of the gospel to a people who were about to miss it completely. When God forgives you, it's not because your record or your character deserves it. God's mercy is totally free. Truly a gift. All yours. Life anew. God commutes your sentence and sets you free. Because of Jesus. Give thanks!

15:7 Now a man called Barabbas was in prison with the rebels who had committed murder during the insurrection.^{NRSV} Barabbas had taken part in a rebellion against the Roman government (an *insurrection*). Although he had been arrested with those who committed a murder, he may have been a hero among the Jews. The fiercely independent Jews hated to be ruled by the heathen Romans. They hated paying taxes to support the despised government and its gods. Most of the Roman authorities who had to settle Jewish disputes hated the Jews in return. Ironically, Barabbas was guilty of the crime for which Jesus was accused because the name *Barabbas* means "son of the father," which was actually Jesus' position with God. Barabbas had been convicted of murder and was in prison awaiting execution. He had no hope of acquittal, so he must have been surprised when the guards came to get him on that Friday morning.

15:8 The crowd came up and asked Pilate to do for them what he usually did.^{NIV} The proceedings of this hearing by Pilate were held in public, so a crowd was hearing all that transpired, and the crowd probably grew larger as news spread. Perhaps this was all part of the religious leaders' plan—to incite the crowd to ask that Pilate free a prisoner, but that it be someone other than Jesus. This crowd was most likely a group of people loyal to the Jewish leaders. But where were the disciples and the crowds who days earlier had shouted, "Hosanna in the highest" (11:10)? Jesus' sympathizers may have been afraid of the Jewish leaders and gone into hiding. Another possibility is that the multitude included many people who were in the Palm Sunday parade, but who turned against Jesus when they saw that he was not going to be an earthly conqueror nor their deliverer from Rome.

15:9 Then he answered them, "Do you want me to release for you the King of the Jews?"^{NRSV} Pilate knew Jesus was innocent of political sedition, which was Pilate's only interest, so he sought a way to be free of the guilt of killing an innocent man. His custom of releasing one prisoner at Passover seemed like an obvious way out.

So Pilate asked if they wanted *the King of the Jews* released. This is the second time Pilate used that title for Jesus (see 15:2), and he would use it again (see 15:12; see also 15:18 and 15:26). Pilate's words mocked the Jews—the meek and silent man standing on the platform beside Pilate was about as powerful as any Jew could be against the might and power of Rome. By contrast, the Jews later mocked Jesus with the term "King of Israel" (15:32).

15:10 For he realized that it was out of jealousy that the chief priests had handed him over.^{NRSV} The Jews hated Pilate, but they went to him for the favor of condemning Jesus to crucifixion. Pilate could see that this was a frame-up. Why else would these people, who hated him and the Roman Empire he represented, ask him to convict of treason and give the death penalty to one of their fellow Jews? Pilate *realized that it was out of jealousy* that the chief priests had handed Jesus over. Pilate realized that Jesus' only crime was his popularity. The religious leaders hated Jesus because of his popular ministry in Jerusalem as well as in Galilee. When Jesus had walked into the temple and had thrown out the money changers and merchants, he was directly opposing the religious leadership (11:15-18). This had been the last straw. Hatred and murder are the inevitable results for those desiring personal prominence at any cost.

Pilate was not concerned about allegations of blasphemy against Jesus, and he hoped to show his contempt for these religious leaders by suggesting that Jesus, "the King of the Jews," be set free. This would undo their obvious frame-up of Jesus. Pilate thought that the crowd certainly would also sympathize with Jesus, their popular teacher.

15:11 But the chief priests stirred up the crowd to have him release Barabbas for them instead.^{NRSV} But Pilate would not get off that easily. The power of the religious leaders took precedence with the Jewish crowd who would hardly side with the Roman governor. *The chief priests* went among the crowd, inciting the crowd to call for the release of Barabbas. Jesus may have been popular, but Barabbas's active role in the fight against the Romans made him a sort of hero. What great lengths the religious leaders went to in order to get rid of Jesus!

All the Gospels stress that it was actually the leaders more than the people who were guilty. Here we have the first time in Mark that the crowds turned against Jesus, and Mark stressed that they were incited to do so by the leaders.

MAKING A CHOICE
Faced with a clear choice, the people chose Barabbas, a revolutionary and a man convicted of murder, over the Son of God. Faced with the same choice today, people are still tempted to choose tangible political power over allegiance and submission to the sovereign God. But it is really not a choice at all. We need God first and foremost, and armed with his strength and loving concern, we can then start to work for public justice. First things first! Give God priority in your life.

15:12 "What shall I do, then, with the one you call the king of the Jews?" Pilate asked them.^{NIV} The crowd called for the release of Barabbas. This left Pilate wondering what to do with Jesus. His question was filled with irony, for he called Jesus *the one you call the king of the Jews.* It was almost as if Pilate was grating at the nerves of the religious leaders as much as possible. They had never called Jesus their king; they had accused him of saying so. But Pilate didn't bother with the difference. Perhaps Pilate hoped to let Jesus go as well, in an extra special offer at this Passover. Luke records that Pilate said, "He has done nothing to deserve death. Therefore, I will punish him and then release him" (Luke 23:15-16 NIV).

Josephus and Philo (two ancient Jewish historians) described Pilate as cruel and malicious toward the Jews; thus, the Jews hated him. (In fact, he was later removed from his post and sent to Rome, probably because of complaints from the Jews.) Pilate realized that he couldn't just set Jesus free. The huge crowd in the courtyard before him was on the verge of a riot. If the people were to lodge a formal complaint against his administration, Rome might remove him from his post. Pilate was already beginning to feel insecure in his position when the Jewish leaders brought Jesus to trial. Would he set free this innocent man at the risk of a major uproar in his region, or would he give in to their demands and condemn a man who, he was quite sure, was innocent? That was the question facing Pilate that springtime Friday morning nearly two thousand years ago.

WHAT WILL YOU DO?
"Believe him! Follow him!" Give up your political appointment if you must, Pilate; it's only temporary anyhow. For sure, don't let a Roman title in an outback province keep you from the source of life.
"Believe him! Follow him!" Forget the crowd and these priests. Do the right thing. Sure it's risky; all of life is risky. But you'll lose everything if you let this moment escape. Here is mercy—God before you. Don't miss your chance.
What would you do? What will you do? Against the howl of unbelieving crowds today, will you believe and follow the Savior?

15:13 They shouted back, "Crucify him!"[NRSV] The people made their choice, stated their preference, and confirmed their sin. This is just what the Jewish religious leaders wanted and the reason that they had whipped the mob into a frenzy. Crucifixion was the Roman penalty for rebellion. Only slaves or those who were not Roman citizens could be executed by crucifixion. If Jesus was crucified, he would die the death of a rebel and slave, not of the king he claimed to be. In addition, crucifixion would put the responsibility for killing Jesus on the Romans; thus, the crowds would not blame the religious leaders.

15:14 "Why? What crime has he committed?" asked Pilate. But they shouted all the louder, "Crucify him!"[NIV] The region of Judea where Pilate ruled as governor was little more than a hot and dusty outpost of the Roman Empire. Because Judea was so far from Rome, Pilate was given just a small army. The Roman government could not afford to put large numbers of troops in all the regions under their control, so one of Pilate's main duties was to do whatever was necessary to maintain peace. We know from historical records that Pilate had already been warned about other uprisings in his region. Although he may have seen no guilt in Jesus and no reason to condemn him to death, Pilate wavered when the Jews in the crowd threatened to report him to Caesar (John 19:12). Such a report, accompanied by a riot, could cost him his position and hopes for advancement. Pilate became afraid. His job was in jeopardy. The last thing Pilate needed was a riot in Jerusalem at Passover time, when the city was crowded with Jews from all over the Empire.

Pilate asked the people to specify some crime that would make Jesus worthy of death. The accusations they had made against him were flimsy in the face of Pilate's own questioning of Jesus. But the crowd had turned into a frenzied mob. They kept on shouting more wildly and loudly that they wanted Jesus crucified.

WHO'S GUILTY?
Who was guilty of mistreating Jesus? In reality, everyone was at fault. The disciples deserted him in terror. Peter denied that he ever knew Jesus. Judas betrayed him. The crowds who had followed him stood by and did nothing. Pilate tried to blame the crowds. The religious leaders actively promoted Jesus' death. The Roman soldiers tortured him. If you had been there, watching these trials, what would you have done? How do you treat Christ today?

15:15 So Pilate, wishing to satisfy the crowd, released Barabbas for them; and after flogging Jesus, he handed him over to be crucified.NRSV Matthew records that Pilate "took water and washed his hands in front of the crowd. 'I am innocent of this man's blood,' he said. 'It is your responsibility!'" (Matthew 27:24 NIV). Pilate decided to let the crowds crucify Jesus. Although Pilate washed his hands, the guilt remained.

Pilate desired only to satisfy the crowd, so he rationalized in order to settle his conscience. It is important to know that our conscience will tell us when we are going against our "moral code," but it can be quieted by self-deception and rationalization. For a leader who was supposed to administer justice, Pilate proved to be more concerned about political expediency than about doing what was right. He had several opportunities to make the right decision. His conscience told him Jesus was innocent; Roman law said an innocent man should not be put to death; and Pilate's wife had had a troubling dream about Jesus (Matthew 27:19). Pilate had no good excuse to condemn Jesus, but he was afraid of the crowd. So he decided to *satisfy the crowd.* He released Barabbas, then flogged Jesus before handing him over to the mob to do as they pleased.

The *flogging* Jesus received was a punishment that could have killed him. The usual procedure was to bare the upper half of the victim's body and tie his hands to a pillar before whipping him with a three-pronged whip. The whip was made of leather thongs that connected pieces of bone and metal like a chain. The continued lashing with these sharp instruments tore at the victim's skin, even baring the bones. The number of lashes was determined by the severity of the crime; up to forty were permitted under Jewish law, but Roman law had no regulations regarding the number of blows a prisoner could receive. The object of flogging was to cause as much pain and suffering as possible. This torture by flogging always would precede execution; thus, Jesus was flogged before he was sent to the cross. Flogging before crucifixion was not just an act of barbarity. The Romans did it to weaken the prisoner so he would die more quickly on the cross.

John records that Pilate hoped this flogging would cause the crowd to take pity on Jesus and allow him to be released. Pilate still hoped to clear himself of any blame in Jesus' death. "Look, I am bringing him out to you to let you know that I find no basis for a charge against him" (John 19:4 NIV). But even this ploy didn't work. The religious leaders still called for crucifixion. Pilate still tried to release Jesus until the religious leaders threatened to report Pilate to Caesar for allowing Jesus (with all the trumped-up accusations against him) to go free (see John 19:12). Pilate caved in to the pressure and *handed him over* to his soldiers *to be crucified.*

CAN'T PLEASE EVERYONE
Although Jesus was innocent according to Roman law, Pilate caved in to political pressure. He abandoned what he knew to be right. Trying to second-guess the Jewish leaders, Pilate gave a decision that he thought would please everyone while keeping himself safe. When we lay aside God's clear statements of right and wrong and make decisions based on the preferences of the unbelieving crowd, we fall into compromise and lawlessness. God promises to honor those who do right, not those who make everyone happy.

ROMAN SOLDIERS MOCK JESUS / 15:16-20 / 233

Jesus was placed in the hands of men who probably knew little or nothing about him other than the fact that he had just been condemned to die. In their eyes, Jesus represented the stiff-necked Jews who resented the power of Rome. Jesus had to endure their pent-up hatred. He was taunted, tortured, and killed by brutal and vulgar men, ignorant of his true identity and mission. All the more remarkable is the fact that one of them later confessed, "Surely this man was the Son of God!" (15:39 NIV).

15:16 The soldiers led Jesus away into the palace (that is, the Prae-torium) and called together the whole company of soldiers.NIV The Romans had to execute Jesus, so the Roman soldiers took him from the post where he had been flogged and led him, beaten and bleeding, back inside the Praetorium (Pilate's headquarters). The whole company of soldiers was called together. A company was a division of the Roman legion, containing the nearly two hundred men who had accompanied Pilate from Caesarea.

15:17 And they clothed him in a purple cloak; and after twisting some thorns into a crown, they put it on him.NRSV Someone found a purple cloak, probably one of the scarlet cloaks worn by Roman soldiers, and threw it around the shoulders of this sup-posed "king," pretending that it was a royal color. Someone else, with a brutal sense of humor, twisted some thorns into a crown that was then jammed onto Jesus head. The purpose of the crown was more for mockery than for pain. Matthew added that they put a staff in his hand, like a king's scepter (Matthew 27:29).

HE KNOWS, HE FEELS
The flogging helped weaken a condemned man, lowered his resistance, broke him down. Forty times the whip said, "You've got no future but pain." Then the sport of the soldiers added, "Dead men don't deserve human dignity." Jesus bore all of this horrible treatment so that he could die for you. God wants you to know the love that surpasses knowledge (Ephesians 3:19).
When you're having your worst day ever and the future appears bleak to hopeless, remember that the Savior knows the feeling and goes with you through the dark tunnel. Pain and contempt may break you down, but there's a hand ready to steady yours, an arm ready to pull you through. Trust him. He's been there.

15:18-19 And they began saluting him, "Hail, King of the Jews!" They struck his head with a reed, spat upon him, and knelt down in homage to him.NRSV Then they pretended to honor this "king" by saluting him over and over. Not only that, they continued beating him, striking him on the head. They insulted him by spitting on him and kneeling down in mock worship.

WHEN HE SHALL COME
The brutal guards, the power-hungry governor, and the conniving religious leaders had the upper hand. But they did not know the true power and authority of this man they were torturing and had condemned to death. Worldly powers and philosophies that mock Jesus' lordship will not be so arrogant when Jesus returns in judgment. Philippians 2:9-11 reminds us, "Therefore God exalted him to the highest place . . . that at the name of Jesus every knee should bow . . . and every tongue confess that Jesus Christ is Lord" (NIV). When you feel that unjust people who have control and viewpoints hostile to Christianity are carrying the day, rest assured that Jesus holds the highest place and will return in glory.

All of this had been prophesied. Isaiah had written, "I offered my back to those who beat me, my cheeks to those who pulled out my beard; I did not hide my face from mocking and spitting" (Isaiah 50:6 NIV; see also 52:14–53:6).

15:20 After mocking him, they stripped him of the purple cloak and put his own clothes on him. Then they led him out to crucify him.NRSV After having their fun, the soldiers took off the purple cloak and put Jesus' clothes back on him. Then he was taken out to be executed. Probably only four soldiers under the command of a centurion (15:39) actually went out to the site to perform the execution because John mentions that the soldiers at the cross divided his clothing into four piles, "one for each of them" (John 19:23 NIV).

THE LONELY WALK
Jabbering kids turn quiet along the narrow street as Jesus and the soldiers move slowly toward the city gates. Adults are watching, too, thinking, wondering, but not talking. The bloodied man shuffles under the weight of the wood and the pain of his open wounds. It's a pitiful sight, and there's nothing to do but watch.
So it is today. On Good Friday, set aside your work for a moment, your phone calls and your meetings, your frenzied errands, incessant chatter. Be silent and watch. Hold your bold exclamations, your grandiose sermons and solos. The Son of God passes by, in great pain, on his way to the spikes and splinters, the last sorry chapter of his last day.
He's going for you, but don't say anything now. Just watch. Just be quiet. Reflect on what this great Savior did for you.

In being led out to be crucified, condemned prisoners would carry the crossbeam of their own cross, which weighed about one hundred pounds. It was carried across the shoulders. Carrying the crossbeam was intended to break the prisoner's will to live. It said to the prisoner, "You are already dead." Like flogging, it caused the prisoner to die more quickly. The heavy crossbeam was placed on Jesus' already bleeding shoulders (John 19:17), and he began the long walk out of Jerusalem.

JESUS IS LED AWAY TO BE CRUCIFIED / 15:21-24 / **234**

Jesus bore our sins on the cross, but was unable to bear his cross to the crest of Golgotha. He had been flogged and abused repeatedly since his arrest the previous night. The soldiers were probably experienced in these matters. They knew how to read the crowd's reaction. They could read a bloodthirsty mob. A staggering criminal could be hated and humiliated by the crowd; but one completely unable to shoulder his cross might stir up the sympathy of the same people. So a stranger was drafted to carry the timber for Jesus.

The Gospels explain Jesus' suffering before the Crucifixion in greater detail than the execution itself. The original readers were quite familiar with the horrors of death on a cross and didn't require such a description. But they would have noted with interest that Jesus rejected the myrrh which would have numbed the pain.

Meanwhile, the soldiers who had just nailed three men to crosses now gathered to cast lots for the meager possessions they took from the condemned. Their gambling for the worthless benefits

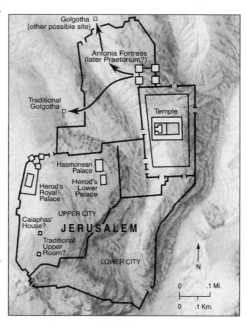

Jesus' Route to Golgotha
After being sentenced by Pilate, Jesus was taken from the Praetorium to a place outside the city, Golgotha, for crucifixion.

from their grisly work stands in stark contrast to the immeasurable benefits the Lord was making available to them as he hung dying above their heads.

15:21 A certain man from Cyrene, Simon, the father of Alexander and Rufus, was passing by on his way in from the country, and they forced him to carry the cross.[NIV] Colonies of Jews existed outside Judea. Simon was from Cyrene, in northern Africa (see Acts 2:10), and was either on a pilgrimage to Jerusalem for the Passover, or he was originally from Cyrene but resided in Palestine. His two sons, Alexander and Rufus, are mentioned as if Mark's readers in Rome knew them. Rufus may be the same man mentioned by Paul in Romans 16:13. If so, this could mean that Simon became a Christian through this incident.

Jesus started to carry his cross, but, weakened from the beatings he had received, he was physically unable to carry it all the way to the execution site. Roman soldiers had the right to enforce people to do tasks for them (see Matthew 5:41); so Simon, on his way into the city, was randomly picked out of the crowd by the soldiers to carry Jesus' cross.

THAT WOODEN BEAM
For Simon it was just a hunk of wood. He was strong and the Romans had swords. He would carry it.

For us it's a cross, a symbol rich in meaning, and the man Simon helped was the world's Savior. Who wouldn't do as much? If we were there, we would gladly have come forward to help Jesus.

We bear the cross, not because we love pain, but because Jesus loves us. It's the Christians' way of saying to everyone: I have died with Christ, this Savior has first place in my heart, and I will serve him as Lord.

Today the cross comes in different shapes. Christians must shoulder it when they suffer loss for Christ's sake—enduring a dread disease, losing a friend or a job, remaining chaste while unmarried, and a thousand more. Let us carry the cross courageously.

15:22 And they brought Him to the place Golgotha, which is translated, Place of a Skull.[NKJV] Some scholars say Golgotha (translated *Place of a Skull*) derived its name from its appearance, a hill with a stony top that might have been shaped like a skull. *Golgotha* is the Hebrew word for "skull." The familiar name "Calvary" is derived from the Latin *calvaria* (also meaning "skull"). Golgotha may have been a regular place of execution in a prominent public place outside the city along a main road. Executions held there served as examples to the people and as a deterrent to criminals.

15:23 Then they gave Him wine mingled with myrrh to drink, but He did not take it.[NKJV] *Wine mingled with myrrh* was offered to Jesus to help reduce his pain. Myrrh is generally understood to be a narcotic that was used to deaden pain. Tradition says women of Jerusalem prepared and offered this drink to condemned men. This also may allude to Psalm 69:21, "they . . . gave me vinegar for my thirst" (NIV). But Jesus refused to drink it. He would suffer fully conscious and with a clear mind.

15:24 And when they crucified Him, they divided His garments, casting lots for them to determine what every man should take.[NKJV] Mark's words are simple and direct, *they crucified Him.* Indeed, Mark's Roman readers needed no elaborate description; they knew it all too well. Crucifixion, instituted by the Romans, was a feared and shameful form of execution. The victim was forced to carry his cross along the longest possible route to the crucifixion site as a warning to bystanders. There were several shapes for crosses and several different methods of crucifixion. Jesus was nailed to the cross; condemned men were sometimes tied to their cross with ropes. In either case, death came by suffocation as the person lost strength and the weight of the body made breathing more and more difficult.

Contrary to the discreet paintings of the Crucifixion, Jesus was crucified naked. Roman soldiers had the right to take for themselves the clothing of those crucified, so they divided Jesus' clothes among themselves, *casting lots . . . to determine what every man should take.* John records that four soldiers divided the clothes (John 19:23). Casting lots was a way of making a decision by chance, like throwing dice or drawing straws. This act had also been prophesied: "They divide my garments among them and cast lots for my clothing" (Psalm 22:18 NIV).

JESUS IS PLACED ON THE CROSS / 15:25-32 / **235**

Crucifixion was a hellish method of killing. It caused the greatest possible amount of pain to the victim before his inevitable death. Such an execution could provide hours of grisly entertainment for spectators.

The Gospels describe various responses within the crowd as Jesus was dying. Some openly taunted him with the false accusations they had heard about him. His opponents gloated to one another about their victory over the troublemaker from Nazareth. Even the other two men crucified with Jesus recognized that he was different. Mark's description of both the criminals insulting Jesus probably records their early lashing out in pain. Luke added the detail of one of the criminal's touching conversion on the cross (Luke 23:39-43). Those who had the most information about Jesus rejected his claims, while one prisoner who had very little information placed his trust in him. Those who grow up in Christian circles and who are exposed to God's Word from earliest days may be prone to treat Jesus lightly or to reject his lordship.

15:25 It was nine o'clock in the morning when they crucified him.[NRSV] Some versions say this was the "third hour," which, in the Jewish method of counting time from sunrise to sunset, meant *nine o'clock in the morning.* At first, this seems to conflict with John's version that the trial before Pilate occurred at the "sixth hour" (John 19:14). However, John may have been using the Roman and modern method of counting time from midnight. Thus, the trial occurred about six o'clock in the morning, and the Crucifixion at nine o'clock. The interval was filled with the soldiers mocking Jesus and seeing to it that he got to the execution site.

NONSENSE

Pilate's sign was not meant to convey great honor. The Hebrew people were a sidetrack nation on a Roman spur—nothing to be king over. Yet the sign on that cross played its role in all the contradictions of that day: crucified Messiah, suffering Son of God, miracle worker dying as a criminal, king of the Jews. Who could make sense of this?

Even today lots of questions are far from crystal clear: Why does evil prosper? Why doesn't God heal my mom? Why did that car accident happen? Will Jesus really come again?

Those people confused at Golgotha should have remembered what Jesus said about conquering death. We now know the rest of the story. Jesus came back to life and now lives to give all our lives the proper meaning. Have faith in Christ. Soon his answers will come.

But Jesus, who turns the world's wisdom upside down, was just coming into his kingdom. His death and resurrection would strike the deathblow to Satan's rule and would establish Christ's eternal authority over the earth. Few people reading the sign that bleak day understood its real meaning, but the sign was absolutely true. All was not lost. Jesus is king of the Jews—and the Gentiles, and the whole universe.

15:26 The written notice of the charge against him read: THE KING OF THE JEWS.[NIV] A *written notice* or sign stating the condemned man's crime was placed on his cross as a warning. Pilate wrote this notice in three languages (Aramaic, Latin, and Greek, see John 19:20) so that anyone going to and from the city would be able to read it. Because Jesus was never found guilty, the only accusation placed on his sign was the "crime" of calling himself king of the Jews. This sign was meant to be ironic. A king, stripped and executed in public view, had obviously lost his kingdom forever. Surely Pilate hoped that this would be a warning to anyone attempting to rise up against Rome (John 19:21-22). The sign was probably also Pilate's way of showing how much he despised the Jewish religious leaders.

15:27 With Him they also crucified two robbers, one on His right and the other on His left.NKJV When James and John had asked Jesus for the places of honor next to him in his kingdom, Jesus had told them that they didn't know what they were asking (10:35-39). Here, as Jesus was preparing to inaugurate his kingdom through his death, the places on his right and on his left were taken by dying men—*robbers*. The robbers also may have been terrorists, like Barabbas. The ancient Jewish historian Josephus often referred to Jewish rebels or revolutionaries as robbers or bandits. Luke records that one of these robbers repented before his death, and Jesus promised this robber that he would be with him in paradise (Luke 23:39-43).

As Jesus explained to his two power-hungry disciples, a person who wants to be close to Jesus must be prepared to suffer and die as he himself was doing. The way to the kingdom is the way of the cross. If we want the glory of the kingdom, we must be willing to be united with the crucified Christ.

 IGNOBLE EPITAPH
We rightly wish to be remembered by our grandchildren as hard workers, loving caregivers, generous, and loyal. We'd like to think that our colleagues would remember us as successful and industrious.

Jesus, by all earthly estimates, would be remembered as a convict. The humility of it is numbing. There's nothing noble about this epitaph.

To follow Jesus all the way means joining this humble God-man in a death with only one guarantee: God is just and good. He will vindicate his people and raise them from the dust. That's all.

But that's quite enough—good news indeed!

15:28 So the Scripture was fulfilled which says, "And He was numbered with the transgressors."NKJV This verse is not included in some Bible versions. The present numbering of verses in the New Testament was made long ago using manuscripts that contained this statement. More modern versions translated from more ancient and superior manuscripts do not include this verse. When Pilate crucified two robbers on either side of Jesus, he unknowingly fulfilled the prophecy recorded in Isaiah 53:12.

15:29-30 Those who passed by hurled insults at him, shaking their heads and saying, "So! You who are going to destroy the temple and build it in three days, come down from the cross and save yourself!"NIV Insult was literally added to injury when it came to public crucifixion. People passing by insulted Jesus, *shaking their heads* (a gesture of derision). They once again used the twisted accusation that had been brought against Jesus at the Jewish Council (14:58), taunting him that if he could boast of building the temple in three days, surely he had the power to save himself from the fate of the cross. What Jesus had actually said was, "Destroy this temple, and in three days I will raise it up" (John 2:19 NKJV). Ironically, Jesus was in the very process of fulfilling his own prophecy. His body was being destroyed, but in three days he would rise again. Because Jesus is the Son of God who always obeys the will of the Father, he did not come down from the cross to save himself. If he had done so, he could not have saved us.

AMAZING LOVE
Jesus could have saved himself, but he endured this suffering because of his love for us. He could have chosen not to take the pain and humiliation; he could have killed those who mocked him. But he suffered through it all because he loved even his enemies. We had a significant part in the drama that afternoon because our sins were on the cross, too. Jesus died on that cross for us, and the penalty for our sins was paid by his death. The only adequate response we can make is to confess our sin and freely accept the fact that Jesus paid for it so we wouldn't have to. Don't insult God with indifference toward the greatest act of genuine love in history.

15:31 In the same way the chief priests, along with the scribes, were also mocking him among themselves and saying, "He saved others; he cannot save himself."NRSV Apparently the chief priests and scribes had followed the executioners out to Golgotha, eager to see their evil plot finally completed in Jesus' death. Not content to have brought him to an unjust death, they also mocked him as they talked among themselves. They gleefully dismissed his healings and miracles because even though he could save others, he couldn't save himself.

In another touch of irony, the religious leaders spoke the truth. If Jesus were going to save humanity from sin, then he could not save himself from the penalty sin deserved.

15:32 **"Let the Messiah, the King of Israel, come down from the cross now, so that we may see and believe." Those who were crucified with him also taunted him.**[NRSV] The irony of these leaders turns on them, for their words are an unconscious testimony to Jesus' power. All who read are thereby asked to see and believe. The religious leaders had once before asked Jesus to give them a miraculous sign so they would believe in him, but Jesus had refused (8:11-12). They did not believe that Jesus was the Messiah, nor the king of Israel, but they taunted him with these names. Obviously Jesus wasn't the Messiah, they thought, because he was dying just like the cursed robbers. One can almost see these religious leaders, with laughter under their breath, huddled in small groups saying, "Just try to get out of this one, 'Messiah'! Get off that cross. When we see it, we'll believe it!" But Jesus would not renounce his God-appointed path. The lesson for all believers is that faith cannot be based on visible demonstrations of power; instead, faith is belief in things not seen (Hebrews 11:1).

Mark recorded that the robbers also taunted Jesus; but Luke states that later one of these robbers repented.

THE POWER OF LOVE
The religious leaders ridiculed Jesus. They could not accept a Messiah so devoid of power and authority. Their view of a king was one who would drive out the pagans and rule with power on earth. Yet later, after Jesus had risen from the dead, many would still be hostile and unbelieving. Often, convincing others to follow Christ is difficult because Christianity seems to be weak and powerless by worldly standards. But God showed his love rather than his power during the Crucifixion. "But God demonstrates his own love for us in this: While we were still sinners, Christ died for us" (Romans 5:8 NIV). When presenting the gospel to others, focus on this great gift of God's love.

JESUS DIES ON THE CROSS / 15:33-41 / **236**

Mark recorded the final scene of Jesus' earthly life with graphic imagery. The dark sky was pierced by an anguished cry of abandonment. Those watching were gripped with wonder. One person

OUR CONDITION WITHOUT SALVATION
In Scripture, darkness is a key concept. (Verses taken from NIV.)

Darkness represents the power of God's presence.	"The people remained at a distance, while Moses approached the thick darkness where God was" (Exodus 20:21).
Darkness stands for God's judgment.	"So Moses stretched out his hand toward the sky, and total darkness covered all Egypt for three days" (Exodus 10:22).
Darkness is controlled by God.	"I form the light and create darkness" (Isaiah 45:7).
Darkness represents people's sinful rebellion against God.	"The way of the wicked is like deep darkness" (Proverbs 4:19; see also John 3:19; Romans 1:21; Ephesians 5:8).
Darkness represents people's ignorance of God.	"The people living in darkness have seen a great light" (Matthew 4:16; see also John 1:5; Ephesians 4:18).
Darkness represents people's condition without hope in God.	"My God turns my darkness into light" (Psalm 18:28; see also 1 Peter 2:9).

responded to Jesus' pain by offering a wine-soaked sponge. The mood was one of anticipation: What amazing thing would happen next? But the spectators were disappointed. With a loud cry Jesus died. Luke added the detail of Jesus' final commitment of his spirit into God's hands (Luke 23:46). John recorded what was probably the final cry—"It is finished!" (John 19:30).

The screen on which we are watching this scene unfold now divides for a moment. On the left, the magnificent tapestry, which served as a curtain to keep people out of the holiest place in the temple, is split from top to bottom, torn by divine hands. On the right, the centurion standing guard at the cross concluded that the Son of God had just been crucified. The scene becomes larger as Mark describes, in the distance, the huddled group of women, faithful to the very end, mourning the death of Jesus.

15:33 When it was noon, darkness came over the whole land until three in the afternoon.^{NRSV} Jesus had been put on the cross at nine o'clock in the morning. Death by crucifixion was slow and excruciating, sometimes taking two or three days. Three hours passed while Jesus put up with abuse from bystanders. Then, at noon, darkness settled over the land for three hours. We do not know how this darkness occurred, but it is clear that God caused it. Nature testified to the gravity of Jesus' death, while Jesus' friends and enemies alike fell silent in the encircling gloom. The darkness on that Friday afternoon was both physical and spiritual. All nature seemed to mourn over the stark tragedy of the death of God's Son.

15:34 At three o'clock Jesus cried out with a loud voice, "Eloi, Eloi, lema sabachthani?" which means, "My God, my God, why have you forsaken me?"^{NRSV} Jesus did not ask this question in surprise or despair. He was quoting the first line of Psalm 22. Jesus' words were an Aramaic translation of the Hebrew words. The whole psalm is a prophecy expressing the deep agony of the Messiah's death for the world's sin. Jesus knew that he would be temporarily separated from God the moment he took upon himself the sins of the world because God cannot look on sin (Habakkuk 1:13). This separation was the "cup" Jesus dreaded as he prayed in Gethsemane (14:36). The physical agony was horrible, but the spiritual alienation from God was the ultimate torture. Jesus suffered this double death so that we would never have to experience eternal separation from God.

15:35 When some of the bystanders heard it, they said, "Listen, he is calling for Elijah."^{NRSV} The bystanders misinterpreted Jesus' words and thought he was calling for Elijah. Because Elijah had ascended into heaven without dying (2 Kings 2:11), there was the popular belief that Elijah would return to rescue those suffering from great trouble. He was associated with the final appearance of God's kingdom. At their annual Passover feast, each family would set an extra place for Elijah in expectation of his return.

15:36 One man ran, filled a sponge with wine vinegar, put it on a stick, and offered it to Jesus to drink. "Now leave him alone. Let's see if Elijah comes to take him down," he said.^{NIV} John records that Jesus said he was thirsty (John 19:28-29). In response, one man soaked a sponge with *wine vinegar* (this was not the same as the drugged wine offered to Jesus earlier). He put the sponge on a long stick and held it up so as to reach Jesus' lips. Whether this man spoke the words, or the bystanders said it to him just before he offered the drink (Matthew 27:49) is uncertain. In either case, the focus was probably on keeping Jesus alive a while longer so that the gaping onlookers could continue to taunt Jesus. Thinking Jesus had called for Elijah (15:35), they watched to see if Elijah would come to rescue Jesus.

15:37 And Jesus cried out with a loud voice, and breathed His last.^{NKJV} Jesus' loud cry may have been his last words, "It is finished!" (John 19:30). Jesus' loud cry climaxed the horror of this scene and showed his sudden death after over six hours on the

WHY DID JESUS HAVE TO DIE?

The Problem	We have all done things that are wrong, and we have failed to obey God's laws. Because of this, we have been separated from God our Creator. Separation from God is death; but, by ourselves, we can do nothing to become united with God.
Why Jesus Could Help	Jesus was not only a man; he was God's unique Son. Because Jesus never disobeyed God and never sinned, only he can bridge the gap between the sinless God and sinful mankind.
The Solution	Jesus freely offered his life for us, dying on the cross in our place, taking all our wrongdoing upon himself, and saving us from the consequences of sin—including God's judgment and death.
The Results	Jesus took our past, present, and future sins upon himself so that we could have new life. Because all our wrongdoing is forgiven, we are reconciled to God. Furthermore, Jesus' resurrection from the dead is the proof that his substitutionary sacrifice on the cross was acceptable to God, and his resurrection has become the source of new life for whoever believes that Jesus is the Son of God. All who believe in him may have this new life and live it in union with him.

cross. Jesus did not die the normal death of a crucified person who would merely breathe his last breath. Usually crucifixion caused a person to lapse into a coma from extreme exhaustion. Jesus, however, was completely conscious to the end. His cry exclaimed his victory.

15:38 And the curtain of the temple was torn in two, from top to bottom.NRSV This significant event symbolized what Christ's work on the cross had accomplished. The temple had three main parts—the courts, the holy place (where only the priests could enter), and the most holy place, a place reserved by God for himself. It was in the most holy place that the ark of the covenant, and God's presence with it, rested. The room was entered only once a year, on the Day of Atonement, by the high priest as he made a sacrifice to gain forgiveness for the sins of all the nation (Leviticus 16:1-34). The *curtain of the temple* could be the outer curtain hanging between the court with the altar for burnt offerings and the actual sanctuary (Exodus 26:37; 38:18), or it could be the curtain hanging between the two areas of the sanctuary— that is, between the holy place and the most holy place (also called the Holy of Holies, see Exodus 26:31-35; Leviticus 16:2,

12-15). Most likely, the curtain that was torn was between the
holy place and the most holy place. Symbolically, the curtain separated the holy God from sinful people. By tearing the curtain in
two, God showed that Christ had opened the way for sinful
people to reach a holy God.

Some scholars think the tearing of the curtain was merely a
foreshadowing of the destruction of Jerusalem and represented
the Son of Man's judgment on unbelieving Israel. However, the
New Testament stress is that the torn curtain represents our free
access to God and that barriers between God and people have
been broken (see Hebrews 10:19-22).

NOW WE HAVE ACCESS
The curtain that was torn was the curtain that closed off the
most holy place from the people. At Christ's death, the barrier
between God and sinful humanity was removed. His death for
our sins opened the way for us to approach our holy God. Now
people can approach God directly because of Christ's sacrifice
for sins (see Hebrews 9:1-14; 10:19-22). Spread the news!

Christ's death was accompanied by at least four miraculous
events: darkness (15:33), the tearing in two of the curtain in the
temple, an earthquake (Matthew 27:51), and dead people rising
from their tombs (Matthew 27:52). Jesus' death, therefore, could
not have gone unnoticed. Everyone knew something significant
had happened. The curtain splitting in two on its own must have
surprised the priests who were undoubtedly working in the
temple during this busy Passover week.

**15:39 And when the centurion, who stood there in front of Jesus,
heard his cry and saw how he died, he said, "Surely this man
was the Son of God!"**NIV A centurion (a person of rank in the
Roman guard) had accompanied the soldiers to the execution
site. Undoubtedly, he had done this many times. Yet this crucifixion was completely different—the unexplained darkness, the
earthquake, even the executed himself who had uttered the words
"Father, forgive them, for they do not know what they are doing"
(Luke 23:34 NIV). The centurion observed Jesus' relatively quick
and alert death. This Gentile Roman officer realized something
that most of the Jewish nation had missed: *"Surely this man was
the Son of God!"* Whether he understood what he was saying, we
cannot know. He may simply have admired Jesus' courage and
inner strength, perhaps thinking that Jesus was divine like one of
Rome's many gods. He certainly recognized Jesus' innocence.
While the Jewish religious leaders stood around celebrating

Jesus' death, a lone Roman soldier was the first to acclaim Jesus as the Son of God after his death. Mark used this centurion's words to highlight the central truth of all his Gospel.

15:40 There were also women looking on from a distance; among them were Mary Magdalene, and Mary the mother of James the younger and of Joses, and Salome.^{NRSV} There had been many people at the cross who had come only to mock and taunt Jesus or, like the religious leaders, to revel in their apparent victory. But some of Jesus' faithful followers were at the cross as well. Among the disciples, only John was there, and he recorded in his Gospel in graphic detail the horror he observed. Several women were also there *looking on from a distance.* John wrote that Jesus' mother, Mary, was present, and that Jesus spoke to John from the cross about taking care of Mary (John 19:25-27).

> Without the cross men are beguiled by what is good in human existence into a false optimism and by what is tragic into despair. The message of the Son of God who dies upon the cross, of a God who transcends history and is yet in history, who condemns and judges sin and yet suffers with and for the sinner, this message is the truth about life. *Reinhold Niebuhr*

This verse in Mark mentions that Mary Magdalene was there. She had been released from demon possession by Jesus (Luke 8:2). Another Mary is distinguished (from Mary Magdalene and Mary, Jesus' mother) by the names of her sons who may have been well known in the early church. Salome was the mother of the disciples James and John and was probably Jesus' mother's sister.

The male disciples had made great promises of loyalty to Jesus, but it was the women among Jesus' followers who waited at the cross and went to the tomb.

15:41 In Galilee these women had followed him and cared for his needs. Many other women who had come up with him to Jerusalem were also there.^{NIV} These women had come from Galilee with Jesus for the Passover. Mary Magdalene was from Magdala, a town near Capernaum in Galilee. They had been faithful to Jesus' ministry, following him and caring for his material needs (see Luke 8:1-3). The *other women* may or may not have been Jesus' followers, but they had come to Jerusalem and had witnessed the Crucifixion.

These women could do very little. They couldn't speak before the Sanhedrin in Jesus' defense; they couldn't appeal to Pilate;

they couldn't stand against the crowds; they couldn't overpower the Roman guards. But they did what they could. They stayed at the cross when the disciples had fled; they followed Jesus' body to the tomb; and they prepared spices for his body. Because these women used the opportunities they had, they were the first to witness the Resurrection. God blessed their devotion and diligence. As believers, we should take advantage of the opportunities we have and do what we *can* for Christ, instead of worrying about what we cannot do.

JESUS IS LAID IN THE TOMB / 15:42-47 / 237

Although Mark only mentioned Joseph of Arimathea, John mentioned both Joseph and Nicodemus, two secret disciples of Jesus who took action to ensure his burial (John 19:38-42). Their commitment to Jesus forced them out of hiding. Perhaps Mark's description of Joseph's "boldness" included a gentle irony regarding a man who may not have felt bold at all, but who carried out a bold plan of action anyway. Christians must often take action when they don't feel very bold or courageous.

The Gospels carefully note that Jesus was clearly dead. Pilate checked. One soldier made sure (John 19:34). So, two men who had followed Jesus from a distance undertook the compassionate task of removing Jesus' body from the cross and placing it in a tomb, while several women watched.

15:42-43 It was Preparation Day (that is, the day before the Sabbath).[NIV] The Sabbath began at sundown on Friday and ended at sundown on Saturday. Jesus died just a few hours before sundown on Friday (at about three o'clock, 15:34). Mark mentions the time frame and explains it to set up the next scene for his Roman readers. It was against Jewish law to do physical work or to travel on the Sabbath, so the day before was Preparation Day—preparing for the Sabbath. It was also against Jewish law to let a dead body remain exposed overnight (Deuteronomy 21:23).

Joseph came to bury Jesus' body before the Sabbath began. If Jesus had died on the Sabbath when Joseph was unavailable, his body would have been taken down by the Romans. An executed man lost all dignity—it was common to simply leave the body to rot away. Remains would be thrown into a common grave. Had the Romans taken Jesus' body, no Jews could have confirmed his death, and opponents could have disputed his resurrection.

So as evening approached, Joseph of Arimathea, a prominent member of the Council, who was himself waiting for the king-

**dom of God, went boldly to Pilate and asked for Jesus'
body.**NIV As evening and the Sabbath approached, Joseph of Arimathea (a town about twenty miles from Jerusalem) asked for
Jesus' body so he could give it a proper burial. Although an honored member of *the Council* (though not mentioned, this probably means the Sanhedrin), Joseph was a secret disciple of Jesus
(John 19:38). That he was *waiting for the kingdom of God* suggests that Joseph was a Pharisee, who hoped for God's deliverance.

Not all the Jewish leaders hated Jesus. In the past, Joseph had
been afraid to speak against the religious leaders who had
opposed Jesus; now he *went boldly to Pilate,* courageously asking to take Jesus' body from the cross and to bury it. Perhaps
Joseph, too, had been at the cross and had seen Jesus die. Obviously knowing the law that dead bodies should have a proper
burial, he went directly to Pilate who alone could give permission
to take down the body. He had to hurry; Sabbath was fast
approaching. Fortunately he had help. John wrote that Nicodemus, another member of the Sanhedrin, brought spices in which
to wrap Jesus' body. Probably along with the help of several servants, Jesus' body was carefully buried (John 19:38-42).

BOLD MOVE
The disciples who publicly followed Jesus had fled, but Joseph,
a Jewish leader who followed Jesus in secret, boldly came forward and did what was right. Joseph risked his safety and reputation to give a proper burial to his Lord. He could have been
identified as an insurrectionist. He went against propriety and
expectations.
It is frightening to risk one's reputation even for what is right.
If your Christian witness endangers your reputation or security,
think of Joseph. Today Joseph and Nicodemus are remembered with admiration in the Christian church. How many other
members of the Jewish Sanhedrin can you name?

15:44-45 **Pilate was surprised to hear that he was already dead. Sum-
moning the centurion, he asked him if Jesus had already died.
When he learned from the centurion that it was so, he gave
the body to Joseph.**NIV Pilate was surprised that Jesus had died
so quickly, so he asked an official to verify the report. He summoned the centurion who had been at the execution site (15:39).
Only Mark recorded Pilate's questioning of the centurion, perhaps to show his Roman readers that Jesus' death had been verified by a Roman military officer. No centurion so trained in
execution could make such a basic error.

That Pilate gave the body to Joseph was highly unusual. Mark described Joseph's action as "bold" (15:43) for several reasons. In doing this act, Joseph was expressing his love for Jesus; he would no longer be a secret disciple and would incur the wrath of his fellow Pharisees. Going to the Roman governor was not a Jew's favorite activity; Pilate hated the Jews and let his feelings be known. Joseph was not Jesus' relative—usually only relatives could take the body. Finally, Jesus had been executed for treason, so according to Rome he did not deserve a proper burial. But Pilate, probably still agitated about his latest dealings with the Jews, may have granted the request because he still believed that Jesus was innocent.

NO DENYING IT
Today, in an effort to deny the Resurrection, some say that Jesus didn't really die. They say that he only appeared to die. Muslims claim that Jesus only swooned on the cross, was revived in the tomb, then fled to Arabia, where he preached Islam for forty years. Jesus' death, however, was confirmed by the centurion, Pilate, Joseph of Arimathea, the religious leaders, John the apostle, and the women who witnessed his death and burial. Jesus suffered actual physical death on the cross.
Jesus *gave* his life. No one took it from him. God was in complete control of our salvation to the last detail. "He was delivered over to death for our sins" (Romans 4:25 NIV), and God "did not spare his own Son, but gave him up for us all" (Romans 8:32 NIV). Jesus' sacrifice was complete and effective. The facts remain the same: Jesus died and Jesus rose again. Jesus died and rose again *for you*. Praise God for his wonderful love for you.

15:46 Then Joseph bought a linen cloth, and taking down the body, wrapped it in the linen cloth, and laid it in a tomb that had been hewn out of the rock. He then rolled a stone against the door of the tomb.[NRSV] Joseph bought a linen cloth; Nicodemus "brought a mixture of myrrh and aloes, about seventy-five pounds" (John 19:39 NIV). The body was carefully taken down from the cross, wrapped in layers of cloth with the spices in between, and laid in a tomb. Jesus was given a burial fit for a king.

This tomb was probably a man-made cave cut out of one of the many limestone hills in the area around Jerusalem. It was large enough to walk into (John 20:6). Matthew records that this was Joseph's own previously unused tomb (Matthew 27:60). Joseph and Nicodemus wrapped Jesus' body, placed it in the tomb, and rolled a heavy stone across the entrance. The religious leaders also watched where Jesus was buried. They stationed guards by the tomb and sealed the stone to make sure that no one would steal Jesus' body and claim he had risen from the dead (Matthew 27:62-66). All of these actions give us verification that Jesus truly had died.

15:47 Mary Magdalene and Mary the mother of Joses saw where the body was laid.[NRSV] Two of the women who had been at the cross (15:40) followed these men as they carried Jesus' body to the tomb. They wanted to know where the body would be laid because they planned to return after the Sabbath with their own spices to anoint Jesus' body (16:1).

Mark 16

The resurrection of Jesus from the dead is the central fact of Christian history. On it, the church is built; without it, there would be no Christian church today. Jesus' resurrection is unique. Other religions have strong ethical systems, concepts about paradise and afterlife, and various holy scriptures. Only Christianity has a God who became human, literally died for his people, and was raised again in power and glory to rule his church forever.

Why is the Resurrection so important?

- Because Christ was raised from the dead, we know that the kingdom of heaven has broken into earth's history. Our world is now headed for redemption, not disaster. God's mighty power is at work destroying sin, creating new lives, and preparing us for Jesus' second coming.

- Because of the Resurrection, we know that death has been conquered and that we, too, will be raised from the dead to live forever with Christ.

- The Resurrection gives authority to the church's witness in the world. Look at the early evangelistic sermons in the book of Acts: The apostles' most important message was the proclamation that Jesus Christ had been raised from the dead!

- The Resurrection gives meaning to the church's regular feast, the Lord's Supper. Like the disciples on the road to Emmaus, we break bread with our risen Lord.

- The Resurrection helps us find meaning even in great tragedy. No matter what happens to us as we walk with the Lord, the Resurrection gives us hope for the future.

- The Resurrection assures us that Christ is alive and ruling his kingdom. He is not legend; he is alive and real.

- God's power that brought Jesus back from the dead is available to us so that we can live for him in an evil world.

- The power of God that brought Christ's body back from the

dead is available to us to bring our morally and spiritually dead selves back to life so that we can change and grow (1 Corinthians 15:12-19).

Christians can look very different from one another, and they can hold widely varying beliefs about politics, lifestyle, and even theology. But one central belief unites and inspires all true Christians—Jesus Christ rose from the dead!

16:1 When the Sabbath was over, Mary Magdalene, Mary the mother of James, and Salome bought spices so that they might go to anoint Jesus' body.[NIV] Mary Magdalene and Mary the mother of James and Joses had been at Jesus' cross and had followed Joseph, who took Jesus' body to the tomb, so that they would know where he had been laid (15:47). Salome had also been at the cross; she was probably the mother of the disciples James and John. The women went home and kept the Sabbath as the law required, from sundown Friday to sundown Saturday. So they bought and prepared their spices and perfumes before returning to the tomb early Sunday morning, for they could not do so on the Sabbath. Anointing a body was a sign of love, devotion, and respect. Bringing spices to the tomb would be like bringing flowers to a grave today. Since they did not embalm bodies in Israel, they would use perfumes as a normal practice. The women undoubtedly knew that Joseph and Nicodemus had already wrapped the body in linen and spices. They probably were going to do a simple external application of the fragrant spices.

JUST DO IT
These three women faced three overwhelming problems as they set out to honor Jesus' body. First, the soldier guard would prevent them; second, the rock in the tomb's doorway would be too heavy to move; and third, Jesus' body would have begun to decompose. Against such obstacles, what could these three women expect to accomplish? Yet urged on by love and gratitude, they were determined to do what they could.

The church's mission—to send the gospel to all the world—is fraught with overwhelming problems. Any one of them appears devastating. Against human stubbornness, disease, danger, loneliness, sin, greed, and even church strife and corruption, what can a few missionaries accomplish? Yet like these solitary women on that Sunday morning, we go out with love and gratitude for Jesus and leave the big obstacles with God.

Some scholars have argued that this could not be factual, for no one would have anointed a three-day-old corpse. Others had noted that the cool air of early spring in mountainous Jerusalem would have delayed deterioration of the body. But these women had experienced their Master's mercy and were full of gratitude for what he had done. Since Jesus' body was buried so rapidly after he was crucified, they had been unable to perform the anointing before Jesus' burial. All these women could think about was getting their spices and perfumes to the burial site.

16:2 Very early in the morning, on the first day of the week, they came to the tomb when the sun had risen.^{NKJV} Sabbath had ended at sundown on Saturday, so *very early* on Sunday morning while it was still dark (John 20:1), the women left their homes, arriving at the tomb just as the sun was rising. They wasted no time. This further illustrates their misunderstanding of Jesus. He had told them that he would rise from the dead, yet they expected nothing.

16:3 And they said among themselves, "Who will roll away the stone from the door of the tomb for us?"^{NKJV} Two of these women, Mary Magdalene and Mary the mother of Joses, had seen where the body had been placed and knew that a huge stone had been rolled across the entrance to the tomb (15:46). Apparently, they were unaware that the tomb had been sealed and a guard set outside it (Matthew 27:62-66). So as they approached the tomb, they remembered that the stone would be a problem. They wondered aloud who might be able to roll it aside so that they could get in. Yet their faith pushed them on; they believed that God would provide a way.

16:4 When they looked up, they saw that the stone, which was very large, had already been rolled back.^{NRSV} The women needn't have worried about the stone. Jesus had said he would rise again after three days. In the Jewish reckoning of time, a day included any part of a day; thus, Friday was the first day, Saturday was the second day, and Sunday was the third day. When the women arrived at daybreak, Jesus had already risen.

When they arrived at the tomb, *they looked up* (some tombs were carved into the hillside) and saw that the large stone had already been rolled aside. Matthew records that there had been an earthquake and an angel of the Lord had descended from heaven, had rolled back the stone, and had sat on it. The stone was not rolled away so that Jesus could get out, for he was already gone. It was rolled aside so others could get in and see for themselves that Jesus had indeed risen from the dead, just as he had said.

GOD IN FRONT
When problems appear too strong to handle and you feel like
quitting, remember that God is way out in front, already blazing
a trail for you. When you are so preoccupied by problems that
you don't even take time to pray, as perhaps happened to
these women, God still guides your way.

Does a stone block your way, a stone too heavy to budge?
Keep going and trusting. God moves big stones easily. Don't
balk at insurmountable problems; remember that God often prepares the way.

**16:5 And entering the tomb, they saw a young man clothed in a
long white robe sitting on the right side; and they were
alarmed.**^{NKJV} The women entered the tomb, as they had planned
to do. Once inside they were startled to see *a young man clothed
in a long white robe.* We learn from Matthew and John that this
young man in the shining white robe was an angel. When angels
appeared to people, they looked like humans. Mark described the
angel from the women's perspective.

Matthew and Mark wrote that one angel met the women at the
tomb, while Luke mentions two angels. Each Gospel writer chose
to highlight different details as he explained the same story, just
as eyewitnesses to a news story may each highlight a different
aspect of that event. Matthew and Mark probably emphasized
only the angel who spoke. The unique emphasis of each Gospel
shows that the four accounts were written independently. All four
are true and reliable.

**16:6 "Don't be alarmed," he said. "You are looking for Jesus the
Nazarene, who was crucified. He has risen! He is not here.
See the place where they laid him."**^{NIV} The angel spoke reassur-
ingly to the women. They were looking for Jesus the Nazarene,
the human being who had been crucified on the cross. But Jesus
was not there; he had risen. The angel said to the women,
"Remember how he told you, while he was still in Galilee, that
the Son of Man must be handed over to sinners, and be crucified,
and on the third day rise again." (Luke 24:6-7 NRSV). The words
He has risen are literally "He is raised." God raised Jesus from
the dead. The Resurrection was not an act of Jesus' power, but a
vindication of Jesus' divinity.

The angel invited the women to look into the inner burial cham-
ber and *see the place where they* (Joseph and Nicodemus, 15:46)
had *laid him.* John records that the linen cloths that had been
wrapped around Jesus' body were left as if Jesus had passed right
through them. The handkerchief was still rolled up in the shape of a

JESUS' APPEARANCES AFTER HIS RESURRECTION

1. Mary Magdalene	Mark 16:9-11; John 20:10-18
2. The other women at the tomb	Matthew 28:8-10
3. Peter in Jerusalem	Luke 24:34; 1 Corinthians 15:5
4. The two travelers on the road	Mark 16:12-13; Luke 24:13-35
5. Ten disciples behind closed doors	Luke 24:36-43; John 20:19-25
6. All eleven disciples (including Thomas)	Mark 16:14; John 20:26-31; 1 Corinthians 15:5
7. Seven disciples while fishing on the Sea of Galilee	John 21:1-14
8. Eleven disciples on a mountain in Galilee	Matthew 28:16-20; Mark 16:15-18
9. A crowd of 500	1 Corinthians 15:6
10. Jesus' brother James	1 Corinthians 15:7
11. Those who watched Jesus ascend into heaven	Mark 16:19-20; Luke 24:50-53; Acts 1:3-9

head, and it was at about the right distance from the wrappings that had enveloped Jesus' body (John 20:6-7). A grave robber couldn't possibly have made off with Jesus' body and left the linens as if they were still shaped around it. The best explanation was that Jesus had risen from the dead, just as he had said he would.

HE IS NOT HERE
No one could keep Jesus in the grave. The religious big shots who wanted him out of the way failed to do it; the power of the Roman army and justice system could not hold him; even the lack of faith on the part of the disciples couldn't keep him dead. They expected to find Jesus when he promised he would not be there. God's power to raise Jesus is greater than any power in the universe. Trust God's promises. He is greater than all our problems or infirmities. The Resurrection assures us that Christ is alive and real.

16:7 "But go, tell his disciples and Peter that he is going ahead of you to Galilee; there you will see him, just as he told you."NRSV The women who had come to anoint a dead body were given another task, that of proclaiming the Resurrection to the frightened disciples. According to Luke's account, several women ran to tell the disciples: "Now it was Mary Magdalene, Joanna, Mary the mother of James, and the other women with them who told this to the apostles. But these words seemed to them an idle tale, and they did not believe them. But Peter got up and ran to the tomb; stooping and looking in, he saw the linen cloths by themselves; then he went home, amazed at what had happened" (Luke 24:10-12 NRSV). John, in his personal account, added that he too dashed in amazement to the tomb (John 20:3-5). They saw, but they still did not understand (John 20:9).

The disciples had deserted Jesus in the hour of trial, but the angel's words held hope of renewal and forgiveness. The disciples had deserted, but they were invited to meet Jesus in Galilee—there was work to do. The angel made special mention of Peter to show that, in spite of Peter's denials, Jesus had not disowned and deserted him. Peter had wept bitterly after his denials (14:72). Jesus forgave Peter and still considered him to be one of his disciples. Besides, Jesus had great responsibilities for Peter to fulfill in the church that was not yet born.

The angel told the disciples to meet Jesus in Galilee *as he told you.* This was exactly what Jesus had told them during the Last Supper, that he would go ahead of them into Galilee after his resurrection (14:28). Galilee was where Jesus had called most of them and had said they would become "fishers of men" (Matthew 4:19 NIV), and it would be where this mission would be restated (John 21). But the disciples, filled with fear, remained behind locked doors in Jerusalem (John 20:19). Jesus met them first in Jerusalem (Luke 24:36) and later in Galilee (John 21). Then he returned to Jerusalem, where he ascended into heaven from the Mount of Olives (Acts 1:12).

BY FAITH
A Russian cosmonaut once claimed that he did not find God anywhere in space. But the cosmonaut traveled without faith. The disciples had been given evidence of Jesus' resurrection, but they still needed to appropriate the meaning of it by faith. They were told that Jesus would appear to them, but going to Galilee would take a lot of faith. Unfortunately, they lacked that faith and remained huddled in Jerusalem. Yet even there, in a locked room, Jesus came to them (see John 20:19).

Today we find Jesus not in ironclad certainties of logic, not by astronomical survey, nor by sitting still. Faith is a moment-by-moment commitment to act on what God says—acting, trusting, and expecting to find Christ when we arrive. We take a step of faith, and Jesus comes closer, another step and Jesus becomes clearer, another step and Jesus becomes dearer. Each time we seek in faith, we find. That's God's promise.

**16:8 So they went out and fled from the tomb, for terror and
amazement had seized them; and they said nothing to any-
one, for they were afraid.**^{NRSV} The women *fled from the tomb,*
realizing that they had seen the results of an awesome miracle in
the empty tomb and had been in the presence of an angel. This
revelation from God was too much for them, and they could not
deal with their awe and dread. They either went straight to the disciples with the news, not stopping to talk to anyone along the
way, or for a time they said nothing out of fear, perhaps expecting
the response of disbelief that they eventually did receive from the
disciples when they told the story (Luke 24:11).

JESUS APPEARS TO MARY MAGDALENE / 16:9-11 / *240*

While the material included in 16:1-8 is universally regarded as
being original to Mark's manuscript, the section of 16:9-20 is not
considered to have been original. Most scholars believe that
verses 9 to 20 were added sometime in the second century or
later. The earliest and best Greek manuscripts do not contain
these verses, and testimony of the early church fathers indicates
that these verses were not part of the original text of Mark's Gospel. The section seems to have been added to give this Gospel a
suitable ending (otherwise it would have ended rather abruptly)
and to parallel material from the other Gospels. Thus, most modern translations note that these verses are absent from our earliest
manuscripts but include them anyway. Whether Mark for some
reason did not complete his manuscript and stopped at 16:8, or
whether the real ending was somehow lost, is unknown.

Beginning in the second century, various scribes attempted to
complete the Gospel by adding an appropriate ending. The most
well-known ending is what appears in our English Bibles, as
printed in 16:9-20 (and is quoted below and commented on). In
some ancient versions, another shorter ending, placed after 16:8,
is as follows:

■ *And all that had been commanded them they told briefly to
those around Peter. And afterward Jesus himself sent out
through them, from east to west, the sacred and imperishable
proclamation of eternal salvation.*

In another ancient manuscript, there is an expansion after
16:14, which reads,

■ *And they excused themselves, saying, "This age of lawlessness
and unbelief is under Satan, who does not allow the truth and
power of God to prevail over the unclean things of the spirits.
Therefore reveal your righteousness now"—thus they spoke to
Christ. And Christ replied to them, "The term of years of
Satan's power has been fulfilled, but other terrible things draw
near. And for those who have sinned I was handed over to
death, that they may return to the truth and sin no more, that
they may inherit the spiritual and imperishable glory of righteousness that is in heaven" (from* NRSV *margin).*

There are other endings, some which combine both the longer
ending (16:9-20) and the shorter ending noted above. The reason
the longer ending became so popular is that it appears to be an
edition based on statements and events found in the other Gospels and the book of Acts.

**16:9 Now when He rose early on the first day of the week, He
appeared first to Mary Magdalene, out of whom He had cast
seven demons.**^NKJV After the women had told the disciples about
the Resurrection, and Peter and another disciple (presumably
John) had gone to see for themselves (John 20:3-9), Mary Magdalene apparently had returned to the tomb. Peter and John had
gone home amazed, but Mary "stood outside the tomb crying"
(John 20:11 NIV).

Although Mary Magdalene has been mentioned earlier in this
Gospel as one of the women at the cross and at the tomb (15:40,
47; 16:1), Mark reminded his readers of the reason for her devotion to Jesus: He had cast seven demons from her (see also Luke
8:2). The specifics of that particular healing are not recorded in
any of the Gospels, although several accounts of Jesus casting
out demons show the extreme horror of demon possession. It was
to this devoted and sorrowful woman that Jesus made his first
appearance after the Resurrection.

We don't know why Mary was chosen as the first, but that fact
should be very encouraging. She was a sinner, a woman with a
severely troubled past. Yet her simple faith, courage, and love
mark her as praiseworthy, not just for her quiet faith, but for her
love in action.

John recorded that Mary didn't recognize Jesus at first. Her
grief had blinded her; she couldn't see him because she didn't
expect to see him. Then he spoke her name, and immediately she
recognized him. Imagine the love that flooded her heart when she
heard her Savior saying her name (John 20:16). Jesus told Mary
to return and tell the disciples.

EVIDENCE THAT JESUS ACTUALLY DIED AND AROSE

This evidence demonstrates Jesus' uniqueness in history and proves that he is God's Son. No one else was able to predict his own resurrection and then accomplish it.

Proposed Explanations for the Empty Tomb	Evidence against These Explanations	References
Jesus was only unconscious and later revived.	A Roman soldier told Pilate that Jesus was dead.	Mark 15:44-45
	The Roman soldiers did not break Jesus' legs because he had already died, and one of them pierced Jesus' side with a spear.	John 19:32-34
	Joseph of Arimathea and Nicodemus wrapped Jesus' body and placed it in the tomb.	John 19:38-42
The women made a mistake and went to the wrong tomb.	Mary Magdalene and Mary the mother of Joses saw Jesus placed in the tomb.	Matthew 27:59-61; Mark 15:47; Luke 23:55
	On Sunday morning, Peter and John also went to the same tomb.	John 20:3-9
Unknown thieves stole Jesus' body.	The tomb was sealed and guarded by Roman soldiers.	Matthew 27:65-66
The disciples stole Jesus' body.	The disciples were ready to die for their faith. Stealing Jesus' body would have been admitting that their faith was meaningless.	Acts 12:2
	The tomb was guarded and sealed.	Matthew 27:66
The religious leaders stole Jesus' body to produce it later.	If the religious leaders had taken Jesus' body, they would have produced it to stop the rumors of his resurrection.	None

16:10 She went out and told those who had been with him, while they were mourning and weeping.NRSV The disciples did not

believe the women who came to them; Peter and John saw the
empty tomb and still did not understand what had happened.
They continued their *mourning and weeping.* Then Mary
returned to the disciples *(those who had been with him)* with the
news that she had actually seen and talked to the risen Jesus.

GOOD NEWS
What fun it is to be the one to tell good news, the kind of news
that turns people's tears into shouts of joy.
　　Imagine the joy of a doctor announcing a successful surgery,
a policeman telling that a lost child has been recovered, a pro-
fessor announcing the *summa cum laude* students, or a judge
declaring an innocent defendant not guilty. It's good news to
reward people or bring relief to those under pressure and fear.
　　Mary must have been the happiest person on earth as she
ran back to the disciples, eager to tell them about the risen
Lord. She had the best news of all.
　　Today this good news—Jesus risen—is just what people
need to hear. It turns lives around, from night to day, from
despair to joy. Eternal life, freedom from sin, death overcome!
This is wonderful news! Run and tell the world about it!

**16:11　When they heard that Jesus was alive and that she had seen
him, they did not believe it.**[NIV] Mary's news that *Jesus was alive
and that she had seen him* was too remarkable for the disciples.
They simply did not believe it. The disciples' stubbornness had
not abated; they would not even believe eyewitnesses (see 16:13-
14; Luke 24:22-27, 37-39).

　　Apparently a short time later, Mary Magdalene and Mary the
mother of James and Joses would return to the tomb, where Jesus
would appear to them both and once again urge them to bring the
news to the disciples (Matthew 28:8-10).

WHEN PEOPLE GO DEAF
It's not uncommon for people to refuse the truth. Even the disci-
ples had wax in their ears and cotton in their heads.
　　When listeners today turn a deaf ear, the right response is
love, care, and persistence. It's wrong to get angry or offended.
It's right to remember that even those closest to Jesus had a
tough time accepting the reality of a risen Lord.
　　Keep praying for the hard of heart. Keep sharing the Good
News in ways that connect with compassion. And like Mary,
return often to the presence of the Lord, there to find wonderful
assurance.
　　God wants those people—your friends and family—in his kingdom. You're the channel, but God makes the miracle happen.

JESUS APPEARS TO TWO BELIEVERS TRAVELING ON THE ROAD / 16:12-13 / **243**

Luke's description of Jesus' encounter with the two disciples on the road to Emmaus should be read when studying this brief paragraph—Luke 24:13-35.

16:12 Afterward Jesus appeared in a different form to two of them while they were walking in the country.[NIV] At another point, Jesus appeared *in a different form to two* of the disciples who had disbelieved Mary's report of seeing the resurrected Jesus. Luke records the story in Luke 24:13-35.

The two disciples were walking in the country returning to the small town of Emmaus (west of Jerusalem). These disciples knew that the tomb was empty but didn't understand that Jesus had risen. They were filled with sadness. Despite the women's witness and the biblical prophecies of this event, they still didn't believe. In their stubborn disbelief, they had missed the significance of history's greatest event. To compound the problem, they were walking in the wrong direction—away from the fellowship of believers in Jerusalem. They didn't recognize Jesus when he appeared beside them and walked with them—perhaps because his "different form" made him look different from the Jesus they had known.

16:13 These returned and reported it to the rest; but they did not believe them either.[NIV] After talking with these two disciples along the road and reprimanding them about their lack of knowledge of the Scriptures that described all that happened, Jesus revealed himself and then "vanished from their sight" (Luke 24:31 NRSV). When they realized what had happened, they immediately returned to Jerusalem and reported that they too had seen Jesus. Still the other disciples refused to believe. Perhaps they believed these people had seen *something,* an apparition perhaps. But Jesus truly alive again? It was too much to accept.

DO YOU KNOW JESUS?
When the two disciples finally realized who Jesus was, they rushed back to Jerusalem. It's not enough to read about Christ as a personality or to study his teachings. You must also believe he is God, trust him to save you, and accept him as Lord of your life. This is the difference between knowing Jesus and knowing about him. Only when you know Christ will you be motivated to share with others what he has done for you.

JESUS APPEARS TO THE DISCIPLES INCLUDING THOMAS / 16:14 / **245**

The disciples' reluctance to believe was resolved by Jesus' appearance to them all at one time. Jesus had already appeared to ten of them, but his visit with the entire remaining apostolic group was necessary. The common theme in Mark's list of appearances was the disciples' reluctance to believe. Jesus confronted his disciples, and he confronts us, about those times when lack of trust stems from willful disbelief rather than caution. This rebuke by Jesus serves as a warning to us to believe in the evidences for Christ and not to be like the disciples who showed weakness in their faith even though they were the best informed and closest to him.

16:14 **Later Jesus appeared to the Eleven as they were eating; he rebuked them for their lack of faith and their stubborn refusal to believe those who had seen him after he had risen.**NIV In another appearance, Jesus finally met with the disciples who had been refusing to believe, despite reports by their own that Jesus had risen from the dead. In fact, Jesus *rebuked them for their lack of faith and their stubborn refusal to believe those who had seen him.* Jesus had foretold his own resurrection. Every time he had told them he would die, he had also told them that he would rise again. The Old Testament prophesied all that had happened to Jesus and also spoke of his resurrection. The disciples had no excuse for the stubborn refusal to believe. They should have accepted the news with joy and gone on to Galilee where Jesus had said he would meet them (14:28). Instead, they stayed in Jerusalem, and Jesus had to meet them there.

JESUS GIVES THE GREAT COMMISSION/16:15-18 / **248**

This paragraph represents a change of scene. This was another post-Resurrection appearance, the last to the remaining eleven disciples and other followers. This paragraph outlines Jesus' final charge to his followers (see also Matthew 28:16-20). The phrase "And surely I am with you always" (Matthew 28:20 NIV) became, in this Gospel, a series of practical applications showing the disciples what Christ's ongoing presence would mean in their lives. We must also obey Jesus' final command, and we can also count on his presence as we go.

The Gospel of Mark is a record of the gospel (or Good News) from its beginning (1:1). As the book closes, the gospel does not end, but continues in the lives of Jesus' followers. Jesus' command is to go everywhere and preach the Good News.

16:15 And He said to them, "Go into all the world and preach the gospel to every creature."[NKJV] This is the Great Commission. The disciples had been trained well, and they had seen the risen Lord. God had given Jesus authority over heaven and earth. On the basis of that authority, Jesus told his disciples to make more disciples as they preached, baptized, and taught. With this same authority, Jesus still commands us to tell others the Good News and make them disciples for the kingdom.

TRUE DISCIPLES
Jesus told his disciples to go into all the world, telling everyone that he had paid the penalty for sin and that those who believe in him can be forgiven and live eternally with God. Christian disciples today in all parts of the world are preaching this gospel to people who haven't heard about Christ. The driving power that carries missionaries around the world and sets Christ's church in motion is the faith that comes from the Resurrection. Do you ever feel as though you don't have the skill or determination to be a witness for Christ? You must personally realize that Jesus rose from the dead and lives for you today. As you grow in your relationship with Christ, he will give you both the opportunities and the inner strength to tell his message. We are to go—whether it is next door or to another country—and make disciples. It is not an option, but a command to all who call Jesus "Lord." We are not all evangelists in the formal sense, but we have all received gifts that we can use to help fulfill the Great Commission. As we obey, we have comfort in the knowledge that Jesus is always with us.

16:16 "The one who believes and is baptized will be saved; but the one who does not believe will be condemned."[NRSV] The disciples were to baptize people because baptism unites a believer with Jesus Christ in his or her death to sin and resurrection to new life. It is not the water of baptism that saves, but God's grace accepted through faith in Christ. Because of Jesus' response to the criminal on the cross who died with him, we know it is possible to be saved without being baptized (Luke 23:43). Jesus did not say that those who were not baptized would be condemned, but that those who did *not believe* would be condemned. Baptism alone, without faith, does not automatically bring a person to heaven. Those who refuse to believe will be condemned, regardless of whether or not they have been bap-

> We shall do well always to fix in our minds that life is short, that [people] all around us are perishing, and that we incur a dreadful woe if we proclaim not the glad tidings of salvation.
> *William Carey*

tized. Baptism symbolizes submission to Christ, a willingness to live God's way, and identification with God's covenant people.

THE DOWNSIDE
We don't like to bring out Jesus' words of condemnation. John quoted Jesus as saying, "Whoever believes in the Son has eternal life, but whoever rejects the Son will not see life, for God's wrath remains on him" (John 3:36 NIV). Jesus made it clear that belief in him is not a matter of individual preference or personal choice; instead, belief in him is a matter of life or death, a decision with eternal consequences. In our smorgasbord culture where we pick and choose among brands and features, the tendency is to treat Christianity as a life-enhancer or an added feature rather than the source of life itself. Don't treat belief in Christ lightly.

16:17-18 **And these signs will accompany those who believe: In my name they will drive out demons; they will speak in new tongues; they will pick up snakes with their hands; and when they drink deadly poison, it will not hurt them at all; they will place their hands on sick people, and they will get well."**[NIV] These verses provide a summary of the miracles recorded in the book of Acts. As the disciples fulfilled their commission, and indeed as others believed and went on to spread the gospel, miraculous signs would accompany them. As with Jesus' miracles, these signs would authenticate the source of their power and draw people to belief. Driving out demons was a power already given to the disciples (3:14-15). This power proved that the believers were not from Satan, but from God. Speaking in tongues was a spiritual gift that enabled people to speak in foreign languages. This occurred at Pentecost when the disciples "began to speak in other languages" (Acts 2:4 NRSV). The disciples placed their hands on many sick people and healed them (Acts 3:7-8; 5:12-16).

> You see to what end he is seated—namely, that all creatures both in heaven and earth should reverence his majesty, be ruled by his hand, do him homage, and submit to his power. *John Calvin*

At times God would miraculously intervene on behalf of his followers. While some people have taken the "picking up snakes" literally, believing that one's faith is demonstrated by handling rattlesnakes, the writer seems to have in mind incidents like the one described in Acts 28:1-6 where Paul was bitten by a poisonous snake without being harmed. The same could happen for someone who accidentally drank deadly poison. This does not mean, however, that we should test God by putting ourselves in dangerous situations.

OFF THE DEEP END
Some sects practice handling poisonous snakes as a sign of faith. Such dramatic evidence tends to make some people more open to God's Word; however, others become more resistant.

Should Christians drink poison and make pets of rattlers as evidence of their faith?

No. God does not ask us to tempt the laws of nature. God is not a safety net for people who leap off of tall buildings. No one should build a religion on a portion of Scripture, not even in the New Testament canon. God calls us to live as new citizens in the eternal kingdom and to witness by word and service to God's love and power. Our witness should center on Jesus, not on superhero-type stunts.

JESUS ASCENDS INTO HEAVEN / 16:19-20 / **250**

Even though it is questioned as having been from Mark's pen, this ending provides an effective closure to the book. Jesus resumed his place and function at the "right hand of God." Meanwhile, those who were left behind carried the gospel everywhere, accompanied by the Lord's presence.

16:19 So then, after the Lord had spoken to them, He was received up into heaven, and sat down at the right hand of God.NKJV These final verses end where the book of Acts begins. Luke wrote in Acts that Jesus appeared to various people over a period of forty days before "he was taken up before their very eyes, and a cloud hid him from their sight" (Acts 1:9 NIV). As the disciples stood and watched, Jesus began rising into the air, and soon he disappeared into heaven. Jesus' physical presence left the disciples when he returned to heaven, but the Holy Spirit soon came to comfort them and empower them to spread the gospel of salvation (Acts 2:1-4). Jesus' work of salvation was completed, and he *sat down at the right hand of God,* where he has authority over heaven and earth (see also Romans 8:34; Hebrews 1:3; 8:1).

Seeing Jesus leave must have been frightening, but the disciples knew that Jesus would keep his promise to be with them through the Holy Spirit. This same Jesus, who lived with the disciples, who died and was buried, and who rose from the dead, loves us and promises to be with us always (Hebrews 7:25; 9:24).

We can get to know Jesus better through studying the Scriptures, praying, and allowing the Holy Spirit to make us more like Jesus.

16:20 And they went out and proclaimed the good news everywhere, while the Lord worked with them and confirmed the message by the signs that accompanied it.^{NRSV} While Jesus' work on earth was completed, the disciples' work was just beginning. This verse compacts the book of Acts. These doubting, stubborn disciples turned into powerful preachers who *went out and proclaimed the good news everywhere.* God was with them—giving them peace, strength through persecutions, and confirmation of their message with miraculous signs (16:17-18; Hebrews 2:4).

Mark's Gospel emphasizes Christ's power as well as his servanthood. Jesus' life and teaching turned the world upside down. The world sees power as a way to gain control over others. But Jesus, with all authority and power in heaven and earth, chose to serve others. He held children in his arms, healed the sick, acted patiently with his hardheaded disciples, and died for the sins of the world. Following Jesus means receiving this same power to serve. As believers, we are called to be servants of Christ. As Christ served, so we are to serve.

 STRONGER FAITH
Do you want fewer doubts and stronger faith? Jesus confirms the truth of God's Word as we live it and as we speak it. Living in faith means moving in orbit, not standing still. Jesus sets our compass, tracks our progress, and guides our mission, giving us faith enough to take the next step.

Want fewer doubts? Get off the shoulder and onto the highway. Want stronger faith? Pray for God to work through you, and watch what happens.

---

250 EVENTS IN THE LIFE OF CHRIST/ A HARMONY OF THE GOSPELS

All four books in the Bible that tell the story of Jesus Christ—Matthew, Mark, Luke, and John—stand alone, emphasizing a unique aspect of Jesus' life. But when these are blended into one complete account, or harmonized, we gain new insights about the life of Christ.

This harmony combines the four Gospels into a single chronological account of Christ's life on earth. It includes every chapter and verse of each Gospel, leaving nothing out.

The harmony is divided into 250 events. The title of each event is identical to the title found in the corresponding Gospel. Parallel passages found in more than one Gospel have identical titles, helping you to identify them quickly.

Each of the 250 events in the harmony is numbered. The number of the event corresponds to the number next to the title in the Bible text. When reading one of the Gospel accounts, you will notice, at times, that some numbers are missing or out of sequence. The easiest way to locate these events is to refer to the harmony.

In addition, if you are looking for a particular event in the life of Christ, the harmony can help you locate it more rapidly than paging through all four Gospels. Each of the 250 events has a distinctive title keyed to the main emphasis of the passage to help you locate and remember the events.

This harmony will help you to better visualize the travels of Jesus, study the four Gospels comparatively, and appreciate the unity of their message.

I. BIRTH AND PREPARATION OF JESUS CHRIST

	Matthew	Mark	Luke	John
1 Luke's purpose in writing			1:1–4	
2 God became a human being				1:1–18
3 The ancestors of Jesus	1:1–17		3:23–38	
4 An angel promises the birth of John to Zechariah			1:5–25	
5 An angel promises the birth of Jesus to Mary			1:26–38	
6 Mary visits Elizabeth			1:39–56	
7 John the Baptist is born			1:57–80	
8 An angel appears to Joseph	1:18–25			
9 Jesus is born in Bethlehem			2:1–7	
10 Shepherds visit Jesus			2:8–20	
11 Mary and Joseph bring Jesus to the temple			2:21–40	
12 Visitors arrive from eastern lands	2:1–12			
13 The escape to Egypt	2:13–18			
14 The return to Nazareth	2:19–23			
15 Jesus speaks with the religious teachers			2:41–52	
16 John the Baptist prepares the way for Jesus	3:1–12	1:1–8	3:1–18	
17 John baptizes Jesus	3:13–17	1:9–11	3:21, 22	
18 Satan tempts Jesus in the desert	4:1–11	1:12, 13	4:1–13	
19 John the Baptist declares his mission				1:19–28

	Matthew	Mark	Luke	John
20 John the Baptist proclaims Jesus as the Messiah				1:29–34
21 The first disciples follow Jesus				1:35–51
22 Jesus turns water into wine				2:1–12

II. MESSAGE AND MINISTRY OF JESUS CHRIST

	Matthew	Mark	Luke	John
23 Jesus clears the temple				2:12–25
24 Nicodemus visits Jesus at night				3:1–21
25 John the Baptist tells more about Jesus				3:22–36
26 Herod puts John in prison			3:19, 20	
27 Jesus talks to a woman at the well				4:1–26
28 Jesus tells about the spiritual harvest				4:27–38
29 Many Samaritans believe in Jesus				4:39–42
30 Jesus preaches in Galilee	4:12–17	1:14, 15	4:14, 15	4:43–45
31 Jesus heals a government official's son				4:46–54
32 Jesus is rejected at Nazareth			4:16–30	
33 Four fishermen follow Jesus	4:18–22	1:16–20		
34 Jesus teaches with great authority		1:21–28	4:31–37	
35 Jesus heals Peter's mother-in-law and many others	8:14–17	1:29–34	4:38–41	
36 Jesus preaches throughout Galilee	4:23–25	1:35–39	4:42–44	
37 Jesus provides a miraculous catch of fish			5:1–11	
38 Jesus heals a man with leprosy	8:1–4	1:40–45	5:12–16	
39 Jesus heals a paralyzed man	9:1–8	2:1–12	5:17–26	
40 Jesus eats with sinners at Matthew's house	9:9–13	2:13–17	5:27–32	
41 Religious leaders ask Jesus about fasting	9:14–17	2:18–22	5:33–39	
42 Jesus heals a lame man by the pool				5:1–18
43 Jesus claims to be God's Son				5:19–30
44 Jesus supports his claim				5:31–47
45 The disciples pick wheat on the Sabbath	12:1–8	2:23–28	6:1–5	
46 Jesus heals a man's hand on the Sabbath	12:9–14	3:1–6	6:6–11	
47 Large crowds follow Jesus	12:15–21	3:7–12		
48 Jesus selects the twelve disciples		3:13–19	6:12–16	
49 Jesus gives the Beatitudes	5:1–12		6:17–26	
50 Jesus teaches about salt and light	5:13–16			
51 Jesus teaches about the law	5:17–20			
52 Jesus teaches about anger	5:21–26			
53 Jesus teaches about lust	5:27–30			
54 Jesus teaches about divorce	5:31, 32			
55 Jesus teaches about vows	5:33–37			
56 Jesus teaches about retaliation	5:38–42			
57 Jesus teaches about loving enemies	5:43–48		6:27–36	
58 Jesus teaches about giving to the needy	6:1–4			
59 Jesus teaches about prayer	6:5–15			
60 Jesus teaches about fasting	6:16–18			
61 Jesus teaches about money	6:19–24			
62 Jesus teaches about worry	6:25–34			
63 Jesus teaches about criticizing others	7:1–6		6:37–42	
64 Jesus teaches about asking, seeking, knocking	7:7–12			
65 Jesus teaches about the way to heaven	7:13, 14			
66 Jesus teaches about fruit in people's lives	7:15–20		6:43–45	
67 Jesus teaches about those who build houses on rock and sand	7:21–29		6:46–49	
68 A Roman centurion demonstrates faith	8:5–13		7:1–10	
69 Jesus raises a widow's son from the dead			7:11–17	
70 Jesus eases John's doubt	11:1–19		7:18–35	
71 Jesus promises rest for the soul	11:20–30			
72 A sinful woman anoints Jesus' feet			7:36–50	
73 Women accompany Jesus and the disciples			8:1–3	
74 Religious leaders accuse Jesus of being under Satan's power	12:22–37	3:20–30		

	Matthew	Mark	Luke	John
75 Religious leaders ask Jesus for a miracle	12:38–45			
76 Jesus describes his true family	12:46–50	3:31–35	8:19–21	
77 Jesus tells the parable of the four soils	13:1–9	4:1–9	8:4–8	
78 Jesus explains the parable of the four soils	13:10–23	4:10–25	8:9–18	
79 Jesus tells the parable of the growing seed		4:26–29		
80 Jesus tells the parable of the weeds	13:24–30			
81 Jesus tells the parable of the mustard seed	13:31, 32	4:30–34		
82 Jesus tells the parable of the yeast	13:33–35			
83 Jesus explains the parable of the weeds	13:36–43			
84 Jesus tells the parable of hidden treasure	13:44			
85 Jesus tells the parable of the pearl merchant	13:45, 46			
86 Jesus tells the parable of the fishing net	13:47–52			
87 Jesus calms the storm	8:23–27	4:35–41	8:22–25	
88 Jesus sends the demons into a herd of pigs	8:28–34	5:1–20	8:26–39	
89 Jesus heals a bleeding woman and restores a girl to life	9:18–26	5:21–43	8:40–56	
90 Jesus heals the blind and mute	9:27–34			
91 The people of Nazareth refuse to believe	13:53–58	6:1–6		
92 Jesus urges the disciples to pray for workers	9:35–38			
93 Jesus sends out the twelve disciples	10:1–16	6:7–13	9:1–6	
94 Jesus prepares the disciples for persecution	10:17–42			
95 Herod kills John the Baptist	14:1–12	6:14–29	9:7–9	
96 Jesus feeds five thousand	14:13–21	6:30–44	9:10–17	6:1–15
97 Jesus walks on water	14:22–33	6:45–52		6:16–21
98 Jesus heals all who touch him	14:34–36	6:53–56		
99 Jesus is the true bread from heaven				6:22–40
100 The Jews disagree that Jesus is from heaven				6:41–59
101 Many disciples desert Jesus				6:60–71
102 Jesus teaches about inner purity	15:1–20	7:1–23		
103 Jesus sends a demon out of a girl	15:21–28	7:24–30		
104 The crowd marvels at Jesus' healings	15:29–31	7:31–37		
105 Jesus feeds four thousand	15:32–39	8:1–10		
106 Religious leaders ask for a sign in the sky	16:1–4	8:11–13		
107 Jesus warns against wrong teaching	16:5–12	8:14–21		
108 Jesus restores sight to a blind man		8:22–26		
109 Peter says Jesus is the Messiah	16:13–20	8:27–30	9:18–20	
110 Jesus predicts his death the first time	16:21–28	8:31–9:1	9:21–27	
111 Jesus is transfigured on the mountain	17:1–13	9:2–13	9:28–36	
112 Jesus heals a demon-possessed boy	17:14–21	9:14–29	9:37–43	
113 Jesus predicts his death the second time	17:22, 23	9:30–32	9:44, 45	
114 Peter finds the coin in the fish's mouth	17:24–27			
115 The disciples argue about who would be the greatest	18:1–6	9:33–37	9:46–48	
116 The disciples forbid another to use Jesus' name		9:38–41	9:49, 50	
117 Jesus warns against temptation	18:7–9	9:42–50		
118 Jesus warns against looking down on others	18:10–14			
119 Jesus teaches how to treat a believer who sins	18:15–20			
120 Jesus tells the parable of the unforgiving debtor	18:21–35			
121 Jesus' brothers ridicule him				7:1–9
122 Jesus teaches about the cost of following him	8:18–22		9:51–62	
123 Jesus teaches openly at the temple				7:10–31
124 Religious leaders attempt to arrest Jesus				7:32–52
125 Jesus forgives an adulterous woman				7:53–8:11
126 Jesus is the light of the world				8:12–20
127 Jesus warns of coming judgment				8:21–30
128 Jesus speaks about God's true children				8:31–47
129 Jesus states he is eternal				8:48–59
130 Jesus sends out seventy-two messengers			10:1–16	
131 The seventy-two messengers return			10:17–24	
132 Jesus tells the parable of the Good Samaritan			10:25–37	
133 Jesus visits Mary and Martha			10:38–42	
134 Jesus teaches his disciples about prayer			11:1–13	
135 Jesus answers hostile accusations			11:14–28	
136 Jesus warns against unbelief			11:29–32	

	Matthew	Mark	Luke	John
137 Jesus teaches about the light within			11:33–36	
138 Jesus criticizes the religious leaders			11:37–54	
139 Jesus speaks against hypocrisy			12:1–12	
140 Jesus tells the parable of the rich fool			12:13–21	
141 Jesus warns about worry			12:22–34	
142 Jesus warns about preparing for his coming			12:35–48	
143 Jesus warns about coming division			12:49–53	
144 Jesus warns about the future crisis			12:54–59	
145 Jesus calls the people to repent			13:1–9	
146 Jesus heals the crippled woman			13:10–17	
147 Jesus teaches about the kingdom of God			13:18–21	
148 Jesus heals the man who was born blind				9:1–12
149 Religious leaders question the blind man				9:13–34
150 Jesus teaches about spiritual blindness				9:35–41
151 Jesus is the Good Shepherd				10:1–21
152 Religious leaders surround Jesus at the temple				10:22–42
153 Jesus teaches about entering the kingdom			13:22–30	
154 Jesus grieves over Jerusalem			13:31–35	
155 Jesus heals a man with dropsy			14:1–6	
156 Jesus teaches about seeking honor			14:7–14	
157 Jesus tells the parable of the great feast			14:15–24	
158 Jesus teaches about the cost of being a disciple			14:25–35	
159 Jesus tells the parable of the lost sheep			15:1–7	
160 Jesus tells the parable of the lost coin			15:8–10	
161 Jesus tells the parable of the lost son			15:11–32	
162 Jesus tells the parable of the shrewd manager			16:1–18	
163 Jesus tells about the rich man and the beggar			16:19–31	
164 Jesus tells about forgiveness and faith			17:1–10	
165 Lazarus becomes ill and dies				11:1–16
166 Jesus comforts Mary and Martha				11:17–37
167 Jesus raises Lazarus from the dead				11:38–44
168 Religious leaders plot to kill Jesus				11:45–57
169 Jesus heals ten men with leprosy			17:11–19	
170 Jesus teaches about the coming of the kingdom of God			17:20–37	
171 Jesus tells the parable of the persistent widow			18:1–8	
172 Jesus tells the parable of two men who prayed			18:9–14	
173 Jesus teaches about marriage and divorce	19:1–12	10:1–12		
174 Jesus blesses little children	19:13–15	10:13–16	18:15–17	
175 Jesus speaks to the rich young man	19:16–30	10:17–31	18:18–30	
176 Jesus tells the parable of the workers paid equally	20:1–16			
177 Jesus predicts his death the third time	20:17–19	10:32–34	18:31–34	
178 Jesus teaches about serving others	20:20–28	10:35–45		
179 Jesus heals a blind beggar	20:29–34	10:46–52	18:35–43	
180 Jesus brings salvation to Zacchaeus's home			19:1–10	
181 Jesus tells the parable of the king's ten servants			19:11–27	
182 A woman anoints Jesus with perfume	26:6–13	14:3–9		12:1–11
183 Jesus rides into Jerusalem on a donkey	21:1–11	11:1–11	19:28–44	12:12–19
184 Jesus clears the temple again	21:12–17	11:12–19	19:45–48	
185 Jesus explains why he must die				12:20–36
186 Most of the people do not believe in Jesus				12:37–43
187 Jesus summarizes his message				12:44–50
188 Jesus says the disciples can pray for anything	21:18–22	11:20–26		
189 Religious leaders challenge Jesus' authority	21:23–27	11:27–33	20:1–8	
190 Jesus tells the parable of the two sons	21:28–32			
191 Jesus tells the parable of the wicked tenants	21:33–46	12:1–12	20:9–19	
192 Jesus tells the parable of the wedding feast	22:1–14			
193 Religious leaders question Jesus about paying taxes	22:15–22	12:13–17	20:20–26	
194 Religious leaders question Jesus about the resurrection	22:23–33	12:18–27	20:27–40	
195 Religious leaders question Jesus about the greatest commandment	22:34–40	12:28–34		
196 Religious leaders cannot answer Jesus' question	22:41–46	12:35–37	20:41–44	

	Matthew	Mark	Luke	John
197 Jesus warns against the religious leaders	23:1–12	12:38–40	20:45–47	
198 Jesus condemns the religious leaders	23:13–36			
199 Jesus grieves over Jerusalem again	23:37–39			
200 A poor widow gives all she has			12:41–44	21:1–4	
201 Jesus tells about the future	24:1–25	13:1–23	21:5–24	
202 Jesus tells about his return	24:26–35	13:24–31	21:25–33	
203 Jesus tells about remaining watchful	24:36–51	13:32–37	21:34–38	
204 Jesus tells the parable of the ten bridesmaids	25:1–13			
205 Jesus tells the parable of the loaned money	25:14–30			
206 Jesus tells about the final judgment	25:31–46			

III. DEATH AND RESURRECTION OF JESUS CHRIST

	Matthew	Mark	Luke	John
207 Religious leaders plot to kill Jesus	26:1–5	14:1, 2	22:1, 2	
208 Judas agrees to betray Jesus	26:14–16	14:10, 11	22:3–6	
209 Disciples prepare for the Passover	26:17–19	14:12–16	22:7–13	
210 Jesus washes the disciples' feet				13:1–20
211 Jesus and the disciples have the Last Supper	26:20–30	14:17–26	22:14–30	13:21–30
212 Jesus predicts Peter's denial			22:31–38	13:31–38
213 Jesus is the way to the Father				14:1–14
214 Jesus promises the Holy Spirit				14:15–31
215 Jesus teaches about the vine and the branches				15:1–17
216 Jesus warns about the world's hatred				15:18 – 16:4
217 Jesus teaches about the Holy Spirit				16:5–15 ·
218 Jesus teaches about using his name in prayer				16:16–33
219 Jesus prays for himself				17:1–5
220 Jesus prays for his disciples				17:6–19
221 Jesus prays for future believers				17:20–26
222 Jesus again predicts Peter's denial	26:31–35	14:27–31		
223 Jesus agonizes in the garden	26:36–46	14:32–42	22:39–46	
224 Jesus is betrayed and arrested	26:47–56	14:43–52	22:47–53	18:1–11
225 Annas questions Jesus				18:12–24
226 Caiaphas questions Jesus	26:57–68	14:53–65		
227 Peter denies knowing Jesus	26:69–75	14:66–72	22:54–65	18:25–27
228 The council of religious leaders condemns Jesus	27:1, 2	15:1	22:66–71	
229 Judas kills himself	27:3–10			
230 Jesus stands trial before Pilate	27:11–14	15:2–5	23:1–5	18:28–37
231 Jesus stands trial before Herod			23:6–12	
232 Pilate hands Jesus over to be crucified	27:15–26	15:6–15	23:13–25	18:38 – 19:16
233 Roman soldiers mock Jesus	27:27–31	15:16–20		
234 Jesus is led away to be crucified	27:32–34	15:21–24	23:26–31	19:17
235 Jesus is placed on the cross	27:35–44	15:25–32	23:32–43	19:18–27
236 Jesus dies on the cross	27:45–56	15:33–41	23:44–49	19:28–37
237 Jesus is laid in the tomb	27:57–61	15:42–47	23:50–56	19:38–42
238 Guards are posted at the tomb	27:62–66			
239 Jesus rises from the dead	28:1–7	16:1–8	24:1–12	20:1–9
240 Jesus appears to Mary Magdalene		16:9–11		20:10–18
241 Jesus appears to the women	28:8–10			
242 Religious leaders bribe the guards	28:11–15			
243 Jesus appears to two believers traveling on the road		16:12, 13	24:13–35	
244 Jesus appears to the disciples behind locked doors			24:36–43	20:19–23
245 Jesus appears to the disciples including Thomas		16:14		20:24–31
246 Jesus appears to the disciples while fishing				21:1–14
247 Jesus talks with Peter				21:15–25
248 Jesus gives the Great Commission	28:16–20	16:15–18		
249 Jesus appears to the disciples in Jerusalem			24:44–49	
250 Jesus ascends into heaven		16:19, 20	24:50–53	

BIBLIOGRAPHY

Bauer, Walter, William F. Arndt, and Wilbur F. Gingrich. *A Greek-English Lexicon of the New Testament and Other Early Christian Literature.* Chicago: University of Chicago Press, 1979.

Douglas, J. D., ed. *The Greek-English Interlinear New Testament.* Robert K. Brown and Philip W. Comfort, trans. Wheaton, Ill.: Tyndale House Publishers, 1990.

Christensen, Chuck, and Winnie Christensen. *God in Action: Mark's View of Jesus.* Wheaton, Ill.: Harold Shaw Publishers, 1972.

Cole, R. Alan. *The Gospel according to St. Mark: An Introduction and Commentary.* Tyndale New Testament Commentaries. Grand Rapids: William B. Eerdmans Publishing Company, 1988.

Douglas, J. D., and Philip W. Comfort, eds. *New Commentary on the Whole Bible:* New Testament. Wheaton, Ill.: Tyndale House Publishers, 1990.

English, Donald. "The Message of Mark, The Mystery of Faith." In *The Bible Speaks Today,* ed. John R. W. Stott. Downers Grove, Ill.: InterVarsity Press, 1992.

Guelich, Robert A. *Mark 1–8:26.* Word Biblical Commentary. Waco, Tex.: Word Publishers, 1989.

Hurtado, Larry W. *Mark.* New International Biblical Commentary. New Testament ed. W. Ward Gasque. Peabody, Mass.: Hendrickson Publishers, 1989.

Lane, William. *The Gospel according to Mark.* Grand Rapids: William B. Eerdmans Publishing Company, 1979.

Life Application Bible. New International Version. Wheaton, Ill.: Tyndale House Publishers, and Grand Rapids: Zondervan Publishing House, 1991.

Meyer, F. B. *Devotional Commentary.* Wheaton, Ill.: Tyndale House Publishers, 1989.

Morgan, G. Campbell. *The Gospel according to Mark.* New York: Fleming H. Revell Co., 1927.

Walvoord, John F., and Roy B. Zuck. *Bible Knowledge Commentary.* New Testament. Wheaton, Ill.: Victor Books, 1983.

Wuest, Kenneth S. *Mark in the Greek New Testament for the English Reader.* Grand Rapids: William B. Eerdmans Publishing Company, 1965.

INDEX